The Culture of the Copy

Striking Likenesses,
Unreasonable Facsimiles

Hillel Schwartz

ZONE BOOKS · NEW YORK

1996

© 1996 Hillel Schwartz
ZONE BOOKS
611 Broadway, Suite 608
New York, NY 10012

Printed in the United States of America.

Distributed by The MIT Press,
Cambridge, Massachusetts, and London, England

Library of Congress Cataloging-in-Publication Data

Schwartz, Hillel, 1948–
    The culture of the copy : striking likenesses, unreasonable facsimiles / Hillel Schwartz.
        p.   cm.
    Includes bibliographical references and index.
    ISBN 0-942299-35-3
    1. Doppelgängers. 2. Imposter phenomenon.
3. Copying – Psychological aspects. 4. Twins – Psychology. 5. Twins – Mythology. 6. Impersonation.
7. Copying – History. 8. Copying processes – History.
9. Authenticity (Philosophy) I. Title.
BF637.D65S38   1996
128–dc20   96-10162
                                                        CIP

In memoriam
Walter Grossmann

who knew about discernment

Recapitulation

Refrain

The Real McCoy was not.

I

Vanishing Twins

Identical twins are creatures of a terrible ambiguity, for they compromise the values we place upon the individual even as they promise what we so desperately want: faithful companionship, mutual understanding. The vanishing twin is our solution and absolution.

II

Doppelgängers

Siamesed twins are our horror stories, in bondage to likeness; they remind us of fateful Doppelgängers from whom we can never be separated till death do us part. We minister to these doubles by trying to restore singularity, the wholeness that is difference.

FIGURE R.1. Bin of mannequin hands, Van Calvin Manikin Restoration Studio, Portland, OR. Photo by Linda M. Strauss.

Refrain

...all the desperate variety
of which counterfeit is capable...
— William Gaddis, *The Recognitions* (1952)

To write an introduction is to prophesy post hoc: twins *will* vanish in Chapter I, parrots *will* speak in IV, stars *will* shine up from dusty blocks of resin in VI — when, in fact, the twins are already gone, the parrots have spoken, the stars have shone. All that's left is the posting of a card: Wish you had been here.

And I do. It has been some journey. If I write often in the first-person plural, this is not solely because a book about Siamesed sisters and Doppelgänger brothers begs for the trick-and-twin of the "we." It is also because a book about copying and camouflage, replication and reenactment must welcome a complicit company, readers intrigued with, or beset by, doubling, redoubling, and the One made Many.

Together, we will go at striking likenesses anew. The driving historical question is this: How has it come to be that the most perplexing moral dilemmas of this era are dilemmas posed by our skill at the creation of likenesses of ourselves, our world, our times? The more adroit we are at carbon copies, the more confused we are about the unique, the original, the Real McCoy.

We don't even know who the Real McCoy was. Some say it was Elijah McCoy, born in 1843 within a community of African-Americans who had escaped to Canada from slavery in the South. Taking ship to Scotland, McCoy apprenticed to a mechanical engineer. Upon his return across the Atlantic, the job he found with the Michigan Central Railroad was as a fireman, stoking the engine, but between 1872 and 1900 he was awarded patents on automatic engine-lubricating devices of such reliability that they were known to the industry as "The Real McCoy." He became a patent consultant to the railroads and moved to the Detroit area, where after a long life he died alone in an infirmary in 1929.[1]

Some say it was Bill McCoy, a sailor "with the heart of a mischievous, authority-scorning, rather gallant small boy." Six foot two, he was the Robin Hood of the Bahamas between 1919 and 1924, carrying

175,000 cases of rum across the Caribbean in the hold of his schooner, then selling the liquor on the high seas to rumrunners who smuggled it into Prohibition America, where it would be watered down four-to-one. "His erstwhile associates," wrote a friend in 1931, "have epitomized his square crookedness in a phrase that has become a part of the nation's slang: 'The Real McCoy' – signifying all that is best and most genuine."[2]

That friend had heard the phrase years before meeting Bill in 1923, and Elijah was rarely in the news. Either the Real McCoy was originally an Irishman, as in a song from the 1880s; or a Scot, "the real Mackay," as Robert Louis Stevenson wrote in a letter of 1883; or an American born in 1873 in Moscow, Indiana, and known as Kid McCoy, whose life and death would take in nearly every theme of this book.[3]

"Kid" was a moniker for gunslingers and boxers. Norman Selby, a boxer, won his first professional bout in Butte, Montana, at the age of seventeen. The next year, 1891, he became Charles McCoy, assuming a surname of renown in frontier Indiana. Throughout the 1890s, McCoy entered the ring about once a month, as a lightweight, a welterweight, then a middleweight, winning with footwork, guile, and a trademark left hook. He thought of himself, like Jim Corbett, as a "scientific fighter."[4]

Theatrical would be a better word. Corbett himself trod the boards in such melodramas as *Honest Hearts and Willing Hands*, simulating prize fights, and McCoy appeared in *The Pacific Mail*. As sparring partner to welterweight champion Tommy Ryan, the Kid was rumored to have conned Ryan into thinking that their match in March 1896 was just an exhibition, so the champ entered the ring unprepared for serious fisticuffs. Round after round saw Ryan running from McCoy until the Kid caught up with him in the fifteenth and knocked him out. Weeks later McCoy went down at the feet of Joe Choynski, but a timekeeper rang the bell forty seconds early; McCoy wound up victorious by throwing a punch *after* the bell of the last round, to cries of "Fraud! Fake! Robbery! Foul!" He divorced his first and obscure wife, an Ohio shop girl, to marry and shortly divorce a more obscure second wife, to court the suffrage lecturer and light-comic actress Julia Woodruff. Acting out a comedy of their own, Julia and the Kid would marry and divorce three times over the next seven years. Along the way, McCoy became as legendary for his wiles as for his "corkscrew" punch, fighting under pseudonyms in the United States, South Africa, and Europe. The Kid, wrote Damon Runyon, was "One of the cleverest, craftiest men who ever put on boxing gloves." With his winnings he bought the bar at Broadway's Casino Theatre, where men and women alike came to be seen at century's turn, and where McCoy became a gentleman. The *Broadway Magazine* suggested that "His manners might well be copied by other prominent men of the ring" – some of the lesser of whom had already been copping his name and reputation. When the Kid met Choynski again in San Francisco in 1899, he was knocked down sixteen times but KO'd Choynski in the twentieth. The headlines read, NOW YOU'VE SEEN THE REAL McCOY.[5]

Had they? Julia accused her on-again off-again husband of "faking" in the ring, of pretending to be on the verge of collapse so as to throw opponents off guard. On August 30th, 1900, at Madison Square Garden, gentleman Kid McCoy, "the shiftiest man in the ring, blocking or evading the fiercest blow in the fistic art," battled Gentleman Jim Corbett, recently accused of colluding with Tom Sharkey in a match "rehearsed blow for blow." The hype was hot — it was the Kid's shot at the heavyweight crown. The *New York World* showed McCoy filling out to 168 pounds, swimming and diving, "Bigger and Stronger Than Ever." During round five, however, the Kid dropped to the mat "and gave an excellent imitation of a man in distress." Nowhere in evidence had been his corkscrew punch, "an inward twisting of the fist for a distance of six inches or less that shatters bone where it lands and benumbs its victims." McCoy, it seemed, had taken a dive.[6]

Corbett's wife told a reporter, "The fight was a fake, and every sporting man in town knows. . . . McCoy did not train, knowing Corbett was to lie down. Half an hour before the fight Corbett refused to lie down and gave the 'Kid' the double cross. McCoy was so mad that he would not shake hands." It was true that McCoy had neglected the conventional bumping of gloves, but he denied the rest. "I fought a bad and a wrong kind of fight," he explained, "by smothering up and not being the aggressor." He was unhurt until he "received the hard punch in the stomach, a spot where it does not take a very hard punch to incapacitate one from being able to fight for the few seconds allowed to recover." Corbett's wife changed her story: the fight had not been fixed, but she was about to divorce Gentleman Jim and had wanted to get even with him for his infidelities.[7]

Julia, embarrassed by the scandal, sued the Kid for divorce then thought better of it. They went arm in arm to his health farm near Saratoga, where Julia met a Yale coxswain, with whom she rowed off to Japan. The Kid, a man of fortitude and rodomontade, got hitched in 1903 to actress Indianola Arnold, Dorothy in the stage hit *The Wizard of Oz*; the Kid also got hitched, as it were, to Lionel Barrymore, an admirer studying McCoy for the part of Kid Garvey in *The Pug and the Parson*, retitled for propriety's sake *The Other Girl*, that girl being an heiress Garvey aims to wed. The playwright, Augustus Thomas, could see the resemblance between Barrymore and McCoy from half a block away; it was easy to mistake the one for the other, he wrote, as they chummed the Broadway waters. Barrymore's success with the part was no less pronounced in 1903–04 than was McCoy's identification with the play, which he attended nightly to see himself reenacted.[8]

Bankrupt in 1904, the Kid in 1905 married an heiress. By 1906, as Norman Selby, he was head of a firm of diamond dealers and, possibly, smugglers. In 1907, he superintended the National Detective Agency. For this, he quickly admitted, he was ill suited: although he had read Arthur Conan Doyle and Edgar Allan Poe, he found that "Try as I will I cannot detect." He sold and raced automobiles, was caught speeding.

He "dug up a load of ancestors to fill out the bare branches of his family tree" and break into high society, or to make claims upon the two hundred million dollar estate of Lord Hume of London, to whom he was "closely related." He clumsily defeated a novice boxer in 1908, though "sans punch, sans 'corkscrew,' sans sneer, sans strength, sans speed, sans science, sans everything that goes to make a boxer." He invested in rathskellers, traded in jewelry, lost his shirt, and again declared bankruptcy; among his creditors was the Manhattan Press Clipping Bureau, which had kept track of every failure, for he was nothing if not a public man. He sailed to Europe, joked and sparred with Belgian poet Maurice Maeterlinck, then settled in London to run "a physical regeneration establishment" at a fashionable hotel. There too, wrote a reporter, "one feels that [McCoy] is constantly posing. At the present time a ten-minute talk with the ex-pugilist is sure to include a little 'new thought,' a mixed philosophy culled from a more-or-less complete reading of Hegel, Kant, and Nietzsche, and a sprinkling of his own unique personality." He was arrested as a jewel smuggler – mistaken identity, apologized the British police. "I am very pleased to be exonerated," said McCoy. "I never was dishonest in my life."[9]

Come 1913 he was back in the States, a car salesman running an "Auto Bluff" and advising the *Chicago News*, "Get your bluff in first. That's a rule of life that applies to motoring as well as to fighting." 1914 and he was in Los Angeles, tending a health farm, which failed despite his philosophy that "Nature's universal law is: GROW OR GO!" 1916 and he was roving New York again, staging fistfights for the National Guard and divorcing a fifth – or was it a sixth? – wife. "How can you promise to love a woman all your life?" he asked. "You change; the whole world changes." 1918 and Sergeant Selby of the 71st New York Infantry was discharged on account of his age, about which he had lied. He was forty-four and eager for a new career. In film.[10]

He had experience: he had collaborated with Corbett in a movie simulation of their infamous bout (they had to send for a newspaper to find out what each of them had done in the fight). Now he would simulate his own life on both sides of the law, playing a cool detective investigating a jewel heist in *The House of Glass*. In 1919, he appeared in D.W. Griffith's masterpiece, *Broken Blossoms: Or, The Yellow Man and the Girl*, with Richard Barthelmes and Lillian Gish, whose father is Battling Burrows, "a gorilla of the jungles of East London," a brutal prizefighter who KO's the Kid and beats Gish to death. By 1920 McCoy was living in Hollywood and running with Death, art dealer and gem smuggler Albert Mors. On screen the Kid seconded Buck Jones in a "daredevil picture," *To a Finish* (1921) and burlesqued a gumshoe in *Oathbound* (1922), an undistinguished film "for the cheaper daily change houses."[11]

His starring role came in 1924. While making his bucks as a gun-toting bodyguard to a shady promoter, he was making his bed as Mr. Shields to the Mrs. Shields of Theresa Mors, divorced from Albert, who called her "a curious mixture of saint and sinner." Selby called her suicidal; she'd been mopey since the Feds, going after Albert & Co., seized the ice in her safe deposit boxes as Austrian contraband. On the witness stand in December, before a capacity crowd, Selby sat very still, "like a manikin perched on a ventriloquist's knee." Then he began to rehearse, gesture by silent-screen gesture, the sad evening of August 12th past. He and Tess had been in their apartment, drinking scotch and soda out of a silver loving cup. He made sandwiches. Tess asked him to cut hers into morsels, which he did, with a kitchen knife that she abruptly took up, to plunge into her bosom. He struggled with her, wresting the knife away. Somehow she got hold of his pistol. Another struggle. (Here Selby wrestled himself, "stepping about with the agility of a younger Kid McCoy in the throes of a scene of shadow-boxing.") The gun went off. For a moment he did not know which of them had been shot. When that was obvious, he decided to end it all. He rested Tess on the floor, nestled a photograph of himself in her arms, and lay down beside her.

Why he didn't shoot himself, he couldn't say. He did rise, take a stiff drink, and drive around looking in vain for Albert. Thence to his sister Jennie's to tell her that Tess was dead and he had nothing more to live for. Next morning, to Mors's antique shop, intent on revenge. Mors was out, and Selby a little out of his mind (like Norman's sister Mary, who once had kicked and spat on her way to the hospital, and who tried a flipflop through the back of the car, saying "she was doing stunts for a motion picture"). He held at gunpoint the shop manager, the secretary, and several customers, shouting a silent-screen caption, "Nobody ever loved anyone like I loved Tess. I'd go to the electric chair for her." He asked lawyer Lewis Jones, caught browsing, to defend him once he bumped off Mors, telling Jones, "Stick around, kid. You'll see more fun here than you have ever seen in a courtroom in your life." He stuffed money into the suit of a customer who confessed to carrying no cash, had two other men strip to their shorts, and shot at a fourth who attempted an escape. He ordered the porter to "Strike up some music on the phonograph, George, so these people can pass out to slow music."[12]

Instead, Mors a no-show, Selby ran to his Ford, sped to the millinery shop owned by Mors's friends Sam and Anna Schapps (who had called Selby a "love pirate") and shot them both. Was he mad or remorseful enough to go finally to the nearest cop and hand him the gun – or, as the police swore, was he caught at the scene? The prosecution said that he was angry at having been excluded from the management of Tess's estate (worth $110,000) – and angry at Albert, who in a letter to Selby's brother-in-law had threatened Selby, calling him "a moral leper." The DA demonstrated that Theresa had been shot from behind, in cold blood, but he never had Albert testify, and the defense hinted that Mors had been seen running from the scene late that August night. The jury deliberated for seventy-eight hours before finding the most widely married man in America, "victor of a hundred prize-ring battles and breaker of a thousand hearts," guilty of (wo)manslaughter. In February there was

a second trial, this for assault with a deadly weapon in the three wound-
ings. Convicted, Selby was sentenced to 3–38 years at San Quentin.[13]

A model prisoner, he raised canaries and taught newcomers the ropes.
When he was paroled in 1933, Henry Ford appointed Selby director of
the guards for the twelve thousand company thrift gardens. Off work,
he spoke to church groups on the postural and dietary causes of juven-
ile delinquency and had occasion to save some children from drowning.
In 1937, with a full pardon for the murder of Theresa Mors, he pondered
a vaudeville tour, then married for a ninth (actually, a tenth) time and
lived with his new wife (her fourth marriage) in Detroit. There Norman grew agitated at the news from Europe and depressed about his
own efforts to uplift youngsters, which were not going well despite his
own use of health suspenders. In April 1940, Nazi troops racing across
Denmark, he "pulled a fast one" and said he had to go to Chicago on
business. He checked into a Detroit hotel, scribbled three suicide notes,
and swallowed sleeping pills. One note read, "For the past eight years
I have wanted to help humanity, especially the youngsters, who do not
know Nature's laws." A second, "To all my friends I wish you the best
of luck." The third, perhaps the Real McCoy: "I can no longer endure
this world's madness."[14]

"It had been a daffy world for McCoy," said *Variety* in its obit. "He
had been a convict, social lion, saloon porter, hero of a short story classic, dishwasher, owner of a New York jewelry store and night club, a
bankrupt, film actor, auto racer, confidante of Maurice Maeterlinck and,
in recent years, a Ford employee." It was paradigmatic of his life, and
of the fate of Real McCoys this century, that during his second trial,
being shuttled from court to county jail, Selby should meet a fan, throw
one arm around him, and shake hands warmly, although Charlie Chaplin
was in the halls of justice not to wish the Kid luck but to sue an impersonator who had stolen his costume and character. How determinedly
had Chaplin fashioned the costume and character? asked the Court. Very
determinedly, testified Chaplin, with regard to the costume, but as to
the character, "I'm unconscious while I'm acting. I live the role and I
am not myself."[15]

Norman Selby, who lived in the shadow of a Kid, perpetually failed
to be himself. That was the reason, he said, for his divorces: "All but one
of my wives married Kid McCoy. The other [the first, Lottie Piehler]
married Norman Selby." His pseudonym overtook the original and became eponymous, which is the way of things, and of people, in our
culture of the copy. We admire the unique, then we reproduce it: faithfully, fatuously, faithlessly, fortuitously. Who and which and where may
be the Real McCoy, those are uneasy questions. With fancy footwork
we may fight rearguard actions to hold the natural at arm's length from
the artificial and keep the one-of-a-kind out of the clinch of the facsimile, but the world we inhabit is close with multiples.[16]

Selby losing track of himself amidst his changing personae in and out
of the ring, on and off the silver screen, such is the motif of the first

two chapters, on twins and doubles. Selby placing a photograph of himself in the arms of Theresa Mors, that takes care of the third chapter, on self-portraits. Selby invoking Nature's laws is the nub of the fourth chapter, on parrots and monkeys. Selby bluffing and blustery takes us to the fifth, on camouflage and optical illusion. Selby bursting with cliché, his imitations transcending the original, that is what happens in the sixth, where copying machines become inspirited. Selby repeating himself, reenacting his life from marriage to marriage, career to career, trying to prove himself the Real McCoy, to his death at the age of sixty-six, that is the pattern of the seventh, on history, science, and documentary. The eighth and final chapter is a reprise of "this world's madness" at century's end.

Although I shall have recourse to historical narratives to make sense of what we have made of this world and of ourselves, the argument will be more often by similitude than chronological lockstep. And since I mean to show that the culture of the copy is pervasive, text and notes alike will jumble the lowbrow, the highbrow, and the middling – as did the Kid, who told his opponents their shoes were unlaced then threw them for a loop; who recited the lofty poetry of Maeterlinck; and whose funeral music was his friend Victor Herbert's "Ah, Sweet Mystery of Life!"[17]

The upshot is that we must reconstruct, not abandon, an ideal of authenticity in our lives.[18] Whatever we come up with, authenticity can no longer be rooted in singularity, in what the Greeks called the *idion*, or private person. That would be, in our culture of the copy, idiocy – as it was for the Greek geographer Pausanias of the second century. Coming across the myth of Narcissus, Pausanias thought it "utter stupidity to imagine that a man old enough to fall in love was incapable of distinguishing a man from a man's reflection." He preferred that version of the story in which Narcissus had a beloved twin sister; when she died, he went to the spring and gazed therein, knowing that it was his own image reflected back "but in spite of this knowledge finding some relief for his love in imagining that he saw, not his own reflection, but the likeness of his sister."[19] The impostors, "evil" twins, puppets, "apes," tricksters, fakes, and plagiarists who appear in this book may be agents provocateurs to a more coherent, less derelict sense of ourselves. They may call us away from the despair of uniqueness toward more companionate lives.

FIGURE 1.1. A turn-of-the-century advertisement from a reproduction in a 1963 *Newsletter* produced by the J. Walter Thompson Company advertising agency, in the collection of the John W. Hartman Center for Sales, Advertising, and Marketing History, Special Collections Library, Duke University.

CHAPTER ONE

Vanishing Twins

My twin, the nameless one, wild in the woods
— 255th Dream Song of John Berryman

We are conceived as twins and, most of us, born single. We conceive of ourselves, from the start, as twins, then one disappears. Together, the First Twins struggle with forces primeval, opening a space in this world for us to tame horses, plough the land, survive the lightning; then one devours the other. The vanished twin leaves behind a body as dry and thin as a fragment of papyrus.

Acts and images of doubling start here, at the root of our lives: our flesh, our blood, our coming to be. In an epoch proud of instant copiers but perturbed by errant copies, delighted with lightweight artificial limbs but disturbed by the likelihood of clones, biology itself is invested with the rich ambivalence of myth. The stories we tell about our bodies, under the sign of the double helix, are as generative as they are genetic; we are said to begin, literally and originally, by making copies of our cells. The stories we tell about fully twinned bodies, across a landscape of knockoffs and replicas, lead inevitably from science to social conscience, confronting us with uncomfortable parts of ourselves — emotional, cultural, historical. Those twins who burst out, early, squalling, need no longer be a grave surprise, but still they spring upon us compelling questions about our distinctness as individuals in a society of duplicates. From initial images on sonogram monitors, twins carry with them the age-old drama of a compound self and a modern legend of sisterhood sundered, brotherhood bereft.

Midwife to the modern legend was Dr. Arnold Gesell, meditating upon twins in 1922. If one fetal twin were stronger than the other, he wrote, its sibling might degenerate into a "vegetative mass of malformed or unformed tissue." Gesell, whose Clinic of Child Development at Yale shaped decades of childrearing manuals, came to believe that spontaneous abortion of a fetal twin was far from rare, given the frequency of papyrus-like residues (a *foetus compressus* or *foetus papyraceus*) found beside live newborns.[1]

Pillaging the books of psychologist René Zazzo, who had studied with Gesell in New Haven and then worked with pairs of French twins, Michel Tournier wrote a novel in which one of the set of identical twins Jean+Paul spins a yarn of universal twinship. "Every pregnant woman carries *two* children in her womb," claims Paul. "But the stronger will not tolerate the presence of a brother with whom he will have to share everything. He strangles him in his mother's belly and, having strangled him, he eats him, then comes into the world alone, stained with that original crime, doomed to solitariness and betrayed by the stigma of his monstrous size." These ogres live on, incomplete, seeking that perfect communion they sacrificed before birth.[2]

A twice-told tale. Two millennia ago, during Plato's *Symposium* on love, Aristophanes spoke of an originally double human being split by Zeus and searching always for the other half. Retold in 1975 by a French novelist obsessed with ogres, the tale became a parable of incommensurable love for a century of loneliness, imposture, and counterfeit. Twin and vanished twin stand in for what is most troublesome about the close of this millennium, where the more fluently we manage to reproduce ourselves and our world, the more fleeting seems our embrace.

Tournier knew it not, but that same year, 1975, Salvator Levi of the University Hospital in Brussels lifted the vanished twin out of fiction and philosophy into obstetric fact. Reporting the results of exams given to 6690 pregnant women, Levi found that "71 per cent of twin gestations diagnosed before 10 weeks were singletons when delivered." Such first-trimester disclosure of twins had been infeasible before fetoscopy and ultrasound. Levi did cite one textbook whose author in 1945 had suggested on evidence of *foetus papyraceus* that twin material might be resorbed in two-thirds of twin gestations "without leaving any trace." Thirty years later Levi had recovered such traces.[3]

By 1989, writing in the "First Person" column of *Psychology Today*, a twin could refer to "medical experts who believe that as many as a quarter of all those born as single children began life as twins." Drab statistics were quickly being adapted to a popular legend about an entire lost tribe of twins who might have kept true company with us among an overwhelming host of simulacra. As early as 1982, twin and synchronous swimmer Kay Cassill had speculated that "It may well prove to be the case, that for every one hundred singletons alive today, way over half of them may have begun life with a twin!" Unimpressed with the banal conjecture of uterine resorption, Cassill proposed that "the survivor may indeed be keeping his brother (or sister) alive *in some transformed state* within his own body." Who knew how many people with cysts were carrying around the "incomplete but living tissues of long-vanished brothers and sisters"? Reasoning that identical twins have identical blood types, so that an absorbed twin denizened within a singleton could be virtually invisible, Cassill claimed that "The potential exists that such an undiscoverable twin *might* be hidden away within *any* singleton."[4]

Each singleton a *vopiscus*, that is, as the Romans had it, someone born a sole surviving twin? Perhaps still bearing that vanished twin within? The notion seemed natural to Canadian writer Margaret Atwood in 1990 and her character Kat, from whom has been excavated a hairy ball of tissue, including brain tissue. "She'd asked the doctor if it could have started as a child, a fertilized egg that escaped somehow and got into the wrong place. No, said the doctor. Some people thought this kind of tumor was present in seedling form from birth, or before it. It might be the woman's undeveloped twin." It might well be, for "Hairball speaks to her, without words.... What it tells her is everything she's never wanted to hear about herself. This is new knowledge, dark and precious and necessary. It cuts."[5]

The emergent legend of the vanishing twin makes of our selves our own kin. Surrounded by forgeries and facsimiles, we look to that primitive twin for affidavits of faithfulness and apologies for faithlessness. In one body, at one and the same time, we may carry and confute our own nearest sister, closest brother. While vanished twinship assures us of a sempiternal human link, it affords us also the pathos of inexpressible loss.

How do we come by a legend in which, at the moment that we find ourselves shoulder to shadow with a fetal partner, we lose forever that bloodsister, bloodbrother? Were we already on the lookout for dark evanescent bodies, like astronomers bent on discerning dark twins circling sibling stars? Have we become so used to rescuing twins from the rapids of premature births that we mourn all the more deeply those fetal twins who elude us? Has the deferral of first maternity led to an upsurge in the percentage of twins conceived, with a consequently greater need to scout each pregnancy for signs of twins? Has finesse at laboratory insemination alerted us to expect multiple conceptions, beset by anxieties about an anomalous fetus for which we scan at earlier and earlier stages?[6]

Were the answers altogether affirmative, as I believe they are, these would constitute but a shallow underpinning for a legend of such depth. The legend ultimately has less to do with science or medicine than with the oracular powers of twins who, together, appear to tell us most of what we want to know about being uniquely human and, apart, more than we want to know about feeling alone. The legend of the vanishing twin articulates our profound uneasiness with postmodern confusions of identities and postindustrial contusions of the "real thing." It is not our immodest skill at detecting twins that warrants analysis so much as our singular inclination to make of the vanished twin a commanding figure within our culture of the copy.

Dual Spirits

Where twins are most frequent, there shall we find clues toward a convincing explanation for the appeal of the legend of the vanishing twin, which has waxed stronger as we have redeemed and borne more twins.

FIGURE 1.2. Ere Ibeji, Yoruba twin figures, fraternal. Western Nigeria, nineteenth–twentieth century. Reproduced courtesy of the Museum of Anthropology, University of British Columbia, Vancouver. Photo by Heidi Piltz Burton.

Identical twins (monozygotic or "one-egg") are biological rogues and everywhere equally rare, less than 4 per 1000 births. Fraternal (dizygotic or "two-egg") twinning rates are conditioned by the age of the mother, her health, her hormonal balance, the frequency with which she has sex, and her willingness to reveal a twin delivery to her community, which may adore or, as in premodern Japan, abhor twins.[7]

Among the Yoruba of western Nigeria, the twinning rate is triple that of Caucasian groups and, with a set of twins for every 16–22 births, by far the highest in the world. No one knows whether the Yoruba experienced a stark historical change in twinning rates, but not until the mid-eighteenth century did they begin to welcome twins. Before, they had shared their neighbors' antipathy for twins, practicing an infanticide customary among many African groups who saw that twins aggravated household economies and disturbed a natural order in which only animals should give birth to multiples. Newly born, one twin or both would be smothered and the parents quarantined until ritually cleansed. Women who had been delivered of twins might be exiled to "twin towns" to live among others possessed of so terrifying a fertility.[8]

With the opening of Porto Novo in 1730, Yoruba traders from that southwest (Nigerian) port brought forward a competing tradition, soon taken up by the King of Oyo in his contest with Dahomey for control of the Slave Coast. A new cult of twins, influenced also by Dahomeyan culture, arose among the coastal Yoruba and among Yoruba slaves transported to Brazil, such that twins were no longer a curse but a blessing:

> You are the ones who open doors on earth.
> You are the ones who open doors in heaven....
> You, who are dual spirits.[9]

When twins now arrived among the Yoruba, the two had already made a deal with the gods not to appear as colobus monkeys, who regularly give birth to twins and who, like Yoruba women, carry one infant in front, one on back. And already the two shared a soul. As each person has a guardian spirit in the sky, in cases of twin births the spirit must have gotten tangled up with its earthly counterpart. Since none could tell earth-walker from skydouble, both were sacred: *ejire*, "two who are one."

Should a twin die, an image would be carved for the parental home. These wooden figurines, first seen by foreigners in the 1830s, were carved six to ten inches high with the visage of the mask of the lineage. They were nonetheless specific to the twin who had died and were treated at bedroom altars as if alive, lest survivors be drawn into death with their twins. In a milieu of high infant mortality, parents tended these *ibeji* for years, laving them with oil even after both twins were gone and the two ibeji stood together, heads dyed indigo, bodies worn smooth by the devotions of many hands.[10]

Perhaps half a million ibeji are extant among the ten million Yoruba, strangers neither to the birth nor to the vanishing of twins, who "keep being reborn and dying again," says Ijebu, father of twins. These days, ibeji may be plastic dolls, or they may be photographs – not of the twin who has died but a copy of a picture of the twin who lives on, facing squarely front as do the wooden ibeji. A sister surviving her twin brother will pose in boys' clothing for his portrait. With triplets, she will pose twice, on each side replicating a dead brother.[11]

Recently, counselors in Europe and North America have begun to acknowledge the unique grief of surviving twins. Watching his identical twin dying, a man "felt that he was looking at a carbon copy of himself becoming shrunken, ill and vulnerable," and he experienced phantom pains like those pulling his twin into the next world. In memoriam, surviving twins may name their children after lost twins or take on the persona of the deceased whose familiar face they see daily in the mirror.[12]

It would seem that, like the Yoruba, we have begun to establish a cult around the vanished twin. Though we care little for wooden statuettes, we do have photograph albums, national twins associations, and a twin town, Twinsburg, Ohio. We presume, like the Yoruba, that attachments between twins must be transcendent: "My sister and I, you will recollect, were twins," Helen Stoner tells Sherlock Holmes in The

Case of the Speckled Band, "and you know how subtle are the links which bind two souls which are so closely allied." We presume that twins know instinctively that they have been twinned, as in the Italian story of a boy who creates for himself an imaginary twin only to find that he is truly "a poor survivor, a remaining soul, a mutilated life, a mere half which, by itself, is as sad as a ruin." We presume that identical twins, far apart, *will* live their lives alike. The legend of the vanished twin opens us to the notion that each of us may once have had a living copy.[13]

Ibeji are fulcrums between earthwalkers and skydoubles. The Yoruba twin cult shifts the moment of social action away from denial or infanticide toward investment. So long as they are two, twins herald not catastrophe but blessing; hence they must be affirmed as double even when one vanishes, returning to the sky (as do Nuer twins of the Sudan, whose one soul is the soul of a bird). Whether statuettes or Polaroids, ibeji are most ominous when ignored – that is, when the sky-bonded twoness of twins is not honored. Anthropologist Victor Turner has argued that, in societies where kinship is structurally significant, twins are a "source of classificatory embarrassment" because the two have but one social position to occupy. Infanticide would efface the problem/children; no longer would double beings need to be accommodated to a single societal slot. The Ndembu of Zambia, Turner's model, choose instead to work through the anomalies of twins in ceremonies that play up other coincidences of opposites. Their rituals express a "tensed unity."[14]

Within industrialized societies, by contrast, the vanishing twin is mute testimony to vanishing kin. Alarmed by fading networks of blood relations, we invoke scarcely visible traces of consanguinity to hold us together. The vanishing twin comes to the fore just as the ideal nurturant Family has been unnerved by barbed fears of child abuse and spousal violence. It makes its bow amidst biotechnologies that compensate for infertility and specious genealogies that repair Family Heritage under generic armorial crests. "Twins intimate a cosmic tenacity," writes one commentator who must have before him the image of a vanished twin, "the refusal of organic life to slip back into the nothingness of inorganic matter." Rather than expressing a tensed unity, our cult of the vanishing twin extends our selves through reconnected familial lines to a vital historical moment.[15]

From such extension may arise the oracular, as happens with the Lele of the Congo, whose parents-of-twins become diviners, and as happens with twins themselves among those peoples who know that paired infants arise from a woman's double intercourse, with a man and with a male deity. Western linguists and psychologists frown upon the belief, but singletons and multiples alike ascribe to twins extrasensory powers and magical languages. Seconded by a "miracle-working" biotechnology, twins assume a miracle-working presence. Vanishing twins themselves take on substance through our one icon of candid all-seeingness, the video monitor.[16]

Western twins inherit this mantic cloth across more ancient distances than those between clinic cots and sonogram screens. Our renewal of the legend of the vanishing twin draws its emblems and temperament from a long loop of myths in which primal twins bind thunder above to waters below, the land of the living to the land of the dead. At the font of Indo-European myth, Manu ("man") the first priest inaugurates this world by sacrificing his brother Yemo ("twin") the first king, who becomes Lord of the Dead. Each person's eventual encounter with Yemo is "a reunion with the totality of one's lineage. It is a meeting in which time turns backwards on itself."[17]

Enter the twin Aśvins, one conceived of the heavens, the other of a mortal woman. The Aśvins are celestial horsemen, drivers of chariots and cattle, healers of wounds and parched land. They gallop through the *Ṛg-Veda* four hundred times and are exalted in fifty Hindu hymns, yet the other gods scorn them for accepting the friendship of humans.

Sons of Dyaus the Sky, the Aśvins are related to the Greek Dioscuri ("Zeus's boys"), known best as mortal Castor and semidivine Pollux, son of Zeus through the woman Leda. Pollux renounces half his immortality to save his fatally wounded twin; thenceforth the two must pass half their time in the netherworld. Above, crowned by the morning/evening star, the Dioscuri ride the shore and countryside on white mounts, most popular of gods. Good earth, vigor, kind weather, clear sailing are their vouchsafe to worshippers, who swear by them as we still do, by jiminy. Soldiers catch glimpses of them at the height of battle; sailors descry them poised atop masts during thunderstorms. After a hurricanoed voyage from the eastern shore of the Mediterranean, apostles Paul and Luke arrive safely in Rome (Acts 28.11) aboard a ship whose prow bears the figureheads of Castor and Pollux. Glowing, the twins ascend into their own constellation, Gemini. At sea nineteen hundred years later, during WW II, the poet Karl Shapiro would contemplate those tutelary twins in the heavens:

> Likeness has made them animal and sky.
> See how they turn their full gaze left and right,
> Seeking the other, yet not moving close;
> Nothing in their relationship is gross,
> But soft, conspicuous, like giraffes. And why
> Do they not speak except by sudden sight?

Like the Aśvins, the Dioscuri as horseman and husbandman defend the land, make it fertile. They are oracular in that they work both sides of promises: oaths sworn before peaceful Pollux are, if forsworn, avenged by Castor. The twins themselves are rarely at odds, but gradually the husbandman fades away, like the forgotten dual king in much of Germanic mythology.[18]

Each is the other's soul and hears too much
The heartbeat of the other; each apprehends
The sad duality and the imperfect half.

Sometimes the disappearance must be violent. So Remus the shepherd is knocked off by Romulus the warrior. Versions of the legend are tricky, but as emperors demanded a truly imperial history, poets exalted earliest Rome in the person of a warrior-king. The martial Romulus became the founder; pastoral Remus, who violated Rome's sacred boundaries, had sadly to be killed.

Absent that ending, the story of Romulus and Remus follows the Greek pattern of dioscuric twins of mixed paternity, abandoned as infants, nourished by bitches or she-goats, maturing into strong men who rescue a mother or sister, dethrone tyrants, build solid new walls. Offspring of a vestal virgin raped by the god of war, Romulus and Remus are left to the elements and suckled by a she-wolf (totem of Mars). They grow up to lay out the city of Rome then quarrel over auguries. Romulus it is who populates the new town by repetition of the seminal rape: inviting neighboring Sabines to attend festive horse races, he and his men take by force their women. From fierce Romulus, not from Remus, proceeds the sovereignty of Rome.[19]

Is it not all-in-all of what they feared,
The single death, the obvious destiny
That maims the miracle their will designed?

Yet Romulus grieves for Remus no less than the apostle Thomas, called Didymos ("twin"), grieves for Jesus, his vanished other half, in the apocryphal *Acts of Thomas*, where he, like the Nazarene carpenter, builds masts for ships, works miracles, and (in gnostic sources) bears a secret gospel.[20]

For however much we are heir to ancient Zoroastrian[21] and Jewish dramas of twins pitted one against the other, darkness against light, few of our archetypes wrestle in the womb like Jacob and Esau. Our legend of the vanishing twin evokes instead a companionate sib, and what today we want of that sib, plagued as we are by furtive artifice and duplicity, is affirmation. To our eyes, the enmity of Jacob and Esau in Genesis 25–35 is overdetermined. Esau the firstborn, "a man of the open country," does not burst from Rebekah insisting upon his prerogatives. He is slow to anger against the wiles of Jacob, who has on his side a promise from Yahweh. Once and properly aroused, Esau refuses to vanish quietly into Seir; when finally he has become the nation of Edom, the entire thirty-sixth chapter of Genesis must be dedicated to listing his descendants. Jacob himself must wrestle with God, accept a new name (Israel, "strong against the Lord"), and undertake the brutal rape of a Canaanite town to demonstrate that he can outdo the nervy physical animal Esau has been from the beginning, held at the heel by Jacob.

Wasn't that love? asks Paul of Jean+Paul. Wasn't Jacob holding Esau one last time before a hurtful separation? Have we been presuming a struggle in the womb when, really, the split took place as Esau slipped out and away from the solidarity of a fetal brotherhood?[22]

Neither tragedy nor comedy but desperate romance, the tale of Jacob+Esau later served too well a desperately romantic reading of history: from the proud Jews, firstborn and beloved of blind patriarchs, their younger twins purchased the birthright with the red blood of Jesus; in the skins of hunted animals, as martyrs, the new Israelites, renamed Christians, received the blessing for the New Testament house of the Lord.[23]

Out of Genesis via Jacob+Esau and the Church Fathers came the folk motif of the Wandering Jew as the vanishing twin..the spiritual motif of the quest for the Ten Lost Tribes as a quest for vanished twins..the theological motif of the Jews as firstborn twins who must never quite vanish lest Christians lose sight of their antitype..the legal motif of Jews as precedent – how vanishingly insignificant are become those who turned their back upon the Christ!..and the literary motif of lurking evil, the Jews surviving as dark twins lying in wait for the naive.

Doubtless most familiar is this motif of the lurking evil twin. Dark twins are a staple of gothic fiction and journalistic exposés, of anti-Semitic tracts and war propaganda. Through Jacob+Esau it is slick passage from the intimidating twin to some pseudonymous enemy or conspiracy of ghosts.

But this book is not about paranoia except insofar as the paranoiac tends to be besieged by doubles, of which more in the next chapter. This is a book about what we are making of ourselves, in kind or in unkindness, as we so adeptly reproduce the world around us. The recurrent paradox of these pages is that the more pressing the ambiguities of our re-creations, the more we have looked toward binary pairs to determine how, one by one, each of us might make a stand. It should not startle, then, that we see twins where before we saw only singletons, nor that our legend of the vanishing twin should urge us to look toward twins for critical testimony about, and trial of, human nature.

Controls

In the Greek comedies of Menander, redone by the Roman playwright Plautus, adapted by Renaissance dramatists, a circus of meandering twins and mistaken identities causes people to doubt their senses. "Double-takes" pantomime hallucination; love misdirected hints at an unreliable heart; redoubled rendezvous (encounters with someone just seen off) reflect distortions of time. Such insecurities, multiplied from act to act as in Shakespeare's *Twelfth Night*, culminate in discovery of the true grounds of the self and the embrace of a life companion, a lost twin.[24]

Endlessly varied, these comedies of errors were slowly transformed into laboratory fictions. During the later 1700s, the companionable, often loving twins of the Renaissance were pulled apart neither for the

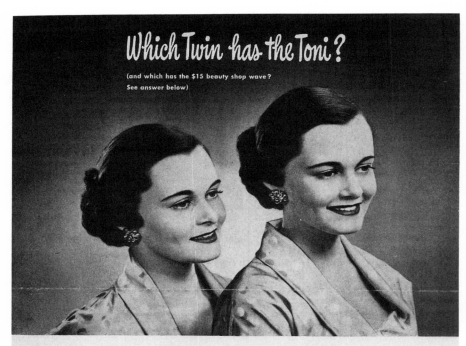

Which Twin has the Toni?

(and which has the $15 beauty shop wave?
See answer below)

Here's why more than 2 million women a month choose Toni Home Permanent!

A Toni wave looks more natural! The minute you see your Toni wave in the mirror you'll see why women like Toni better than any other cold wave. Those lovely deep Toni waves are so flattering, those lustrous Toni curls look so natural!

A Toni wave is softer, easier to manage! Because the famous Toni Waving Lotion isn't harsh like hurry-up salon type solutions. Toni is a creme cold wave made definitely milder and gentler. That's why it leaves your hair in such wonderful condition —so shiny soft and natural-looking!

A Toni wave is guaranteed to last for months! A Toni wave lasts till your hair grows out and is trimmed off. What's more, a Toni is guaranteed to look every bit as lovely as the most expensive beauty salon permanent—or your money back! No wonder more women use Toni than all other cold waves combined!

It's the world's most popular permanent! Toni has given millions of perfect permanents—including every type of hair that takes a permanent, even gray, dyed, bleached or baby-fine hair. Yet the Toni DeLuxe Kit with re-usable plastic curlers costs only $2 . . . the Toni Refill only $1.

Which twin has the Toni? Lovely lustrous hair is especially important to these pretty Leigh twins because they're New York fashion models! Janet, on the right, has the Toni! She says: "I've never before had a permanent that looked so soft and natural!" And Jane says: "Next time I'm going to have the wave with the natural look, too!"

The wave that gives that natural look . . . Toni

FIGURE 1.3. Twin as Control. A 1949 advertisement for a home permanent. Reproduced courtesy of the D'Arcy Collection of the Communications Library of the University of Illinois at Urbana-Champaign.

fun of bringing them back together nor for the pleasure of self-discovery. Instead, the lives of twins became object lessons in philosophical and then scientific debates over the tractability of human nature.

Young Wou'dbee, hump-backed rakehell, crows in 1702 at (premature) news of the death of his sober elder twin, for "'twas his crowding me that spoil'd my Shape, and his coming half an Hour before me that ruin'd my Fortune – My Father Expell'd me [from] his House some two years ago, because I would have persuaded him that my Twin-Brother was a Bastard." He must learn from a vanished then resurrected brother, opposite in mien as in fortune, the meaning of benevolence: farce and self-discovery. In 1792, however, Amelia, raised by the vain Lady Blomer to be a London heiress with every charm a finishing school can insinuate, must be met by her demure twin sister Mira, reared in the country by a foster mother who has followed Rousseau's pedagogy. "Amelia sung divinely, but though with fine expression, there seemed an effort in it that gave too much the appearance of design: while Mira's swelling notes and melting cadences flowed as if she felt the strains." Neither farcical nor self-revealing, such anharmonic twins displayed society's hegemony over human nature.[25]

Throughout the nineteenth century, popular fictions were brazenly plotted to show that no matter how similar twins may be at birth, a vicious upbringing eventuates in corrupt character. These were narratives not in the Old Testament mode of Jacob outmaneuvering Esau, not in the gothic mode of good seed haunted by bad, and certainly not in the German Sturm und Drang mode of a troubled man further troubled by the figure of a double. These were narratives in the experimental mode of the laboratory notebook: two subjects, as like as like can be, are treated oppositely until they prove to have diametrically different personalities and fortunes. For clearcut results, twins are orphaned early and farmed out. So, pampered by a wealthy aunt who believes that character "must be allowed to develop itself freely," Kitty grows up "thoughtless, exacting, self-indulgent, blasée," while twin Rosy, disciplined by an aunt of moderate but Christian means, becomes bright sun to Kitty's storm. So, "Their resemblance extend[ing] not only to their actual appearances, but enter[ing] into the very character of their minds," Herbert is sent to be reared by a scrupulous country Quaker and twin John by an unscrupulous city shopkeeper; it is John, of course, who gets into the murderous scrape for which Herbert is accused, and John who must redeem himself by clearing his brother.[26]

At the turn into this century, fictive twins testified on another side of the Nature-Nurture debate, proving that girls, given the same upbringing and social latitude as boys, had the same abilities. Mixed sets of energetic twins scurried through the Bobbsey Twins books by Laura Lee Hope and also through two dozen widely translated children's books written by Lucy Fitch Perkins between 1911 and 1934. Perkins, a New England artist and art teacher before marrying and moving to Chicago, illustrated all her books, from *The Dutch Twins* (1911) and *The Japanese*

Twins (1912) to *The Pickaninny Twins* (1931) and *The Spanish Twins* (1934), with nearly identical brother-sister pairs. In each, the girl is as smart and active as the boy and, in many cases, "You could tell at a glance that they were twins but it would have puzzled any one to tell whether they were both boys or both girls, or one of each kind."[27]

Those ideally conditioned identicals of the *Brave New World* must make their entrance here, as after 1932 (and the Dionne quintuplets of 1934) arose a succession of science fiction clones. Aldous Huxley's vision of assembly-line babies in the years After Ford was a wicked resolution to the Nature-Nurture debate: caste-ironic children were shaped from insemination to puberty's end by meddling humans (Nurture) so that their social-biological selves (Nature) were set from, exactly, scratch.[28]

Sociologists and biologists — parodied by Huxley, who knew them well, since they were all in the family — had long been keeping track of twins. With a patriotic eye, they had counted the Amelias and Miras, Johns and Herberts, upon the common belief that twins were infertile and too many could jeopardize the growth of an industrial working class. By the 1860s, suspecting a direct relationship between maternal age and twin births, political economists had begun to contrast national twinning rates with a European average (1 in every 90 births in 1859).[29]

Personal infertility may have prompted one well-connected Victorian to turn his capacious mind from meteorology and travel to a topic down to earth and closer to home: heredity. Ninth child of the cultivated Violetta Darwin and the banker Samuel T. Galton; husband for ten years and yet, like his married brothers, childless, Francis Galton in 1864 began to investigate "hereditary talent and character." Two years later he had a breakdown marked by obsessional thoughts which did not cease until his *Hereditary Genius* came out in 1869. He had no patience, he wrote, "with the hypothesis occasionally expressed, and often implied, especially in tales written to teach children to be good, that babies are born pretty much alike, and that the sole agencies in creating differences between boy and boy, and man and man, are steady application and moral effort." Objecting to "pretensions of natural equality," Galton imposed a normal statistical distribution upon human talent and mental ability, presuming to show that Nature held in her hands both ends of the curve; Nurturers at best might shape the lump in the middle.[30]

Partly in rebuttal to critiques, partly in defense of his constituency, Galton in 1874 published *English Men of Science: Their Nature and Nurture*, analyzing questionnaires he had circulated among friends, including his cousin Charles Darwin. This book too swarmed with data purporting to reveal the dominance of hereditary factors, but Galton conceded that "The effects of education and circumstance are so interwoven with those of natural character in determining a man's position among his contemporaries, that I find it impossible to treat them wholly apart."[31]

Whence, the next year, his essay on the "History of Twins, As a Criterion of the Relative Powers of" — he coined the phrase — "Nature and Nurture." Like-sex twins, twins so alike that as children "they have commonly to be distinguished by ribbons tied round their wrist," *very* similar twins must be the skeleton keys to truth. Their *very* similarity despite disparate upbringings could be proof positive of the perdurability of human Nature.[32]

Others, like Saint Augustine, had invoked twins to break the deadlock between Nature and Nurture. That coincidence of illnesses in two brothers which Hippocrates attributed to similar constitutions, Posidonius the astrologer had attributed to planetary alignments at the time of the brothers' conceptions and births. Augustine, devoted personally to the scrutiny of the inner life and dedicated professionally, as Bishop of Hippo, to Christ's power to effect soulful changes, sided with the doctors. Reared in the same house and climate, eating the same foods, the brothers must have developed the same physiques "and so they fall ill of the same diseases, at the same time, from the same causes." Augustine went on: Not all born under one celestial array are identical in character or in constitution. Consider the variant destinies of two children born simultaneously to neighboring mothers, one rich, one poor. Or consider twins, conceived simultaneously, yet rarely sharing the same fates.[33]

Born a millennium and a half later, Galton was almost as much in the dark about the actual propagation of human twins as were Greek physicians, Roman astrologers, and Christian Fathers. Discussing the legal conundrum of which twin was the elder and so entitled to the patrimony, an eighteenth-century encyclopedist had to admit that "what passes in the mother's womb between conception and childbirth is a secret so impenetrable to the eyes of men that not even the lights of Physiology can dispel our ignorance." The human ovum was first identified under the microscope of Karl Ernst von Baer decades later, in 1827. When Galton in 1870 began a series of transfusions between rabbits, hoping to filter out the organic essence of heredity, an Austrian obstetrician was just making clear the distinction between one-ovum and two-ova (identical and fraternal) twins. Galton in London soon learned of the paper by Joseph Späth in Vienna, but neither knew the work of a man born within months of them both, the Austrian monk Gregor Mendel, whose botanical studies of the twin scions of the sweet pea were obscurely published during the 1860s.[34]

Surveying what data he did have (the life histories of thirty-five presumably identical pairs of twins), Galton doubted that "nurture can do anything at all, beyond giving instruction and professional training." His cousin was of a like mind, as we read in *The Heavenly Twins* by Sarah Grand, whose novel of 1893 began with a quotation from Charles Darwin: "I am inclined to agree with Francis Galton in believing that education and environment produce only a small effect on the mind of anyone, and that most of our qualities are innate." Grand's book opened upon a dispute between Angelica and her twin Diavolo as to whether something on the table was water or a mirror; the plot hinged upon the degree to which the twins could escape their Nature.[35]

Had Galton read the oracles aright? Had he thought he was testing the waters when he was merely looking into a glass? What could anyone tell about the core of humanity from a few circulars filled out by genteel twins? Who was to say that Nature could not be significantly helped along by Nurture?

Critical questions, those, for educators and their new advisers, educational psychologists, as they began to administer intelligence tests. In 1905, while French psychologist Alfred Binet issued the first version of his potpourri of tests to assess the potential of students, Edward L. Thorndike at Columbia University's Teachers College published his studies of "mental likeness" in fifty sets of twins contrasted to pairs of common brothers or sisters. An avowed Galtonian, he came up with "well-nigh conclusive evidence that the mental likenesses found in the case of twins...are due, to at least nine-tenths of their amount, to original nature." Unwelcome news was this to fellow educators, and "Doubtless we all feel a repugnance to assigning so little efficacy to environmental forces," yet facts were facts: training could improve anyone, slightly; the effect of great teachers or high civilization was grossly overestimated.[36]

Binet himself was no hereditarian. His tests were meant to help teachers assist poor students. But once Binet had established "mental age" levels for the mastery of each task within his test set, a German psychologist could contrive and American psychologists could promote an Intelligence Quotient, dividing mental age by chronological age. Contrary to the spirit of Binet's own work, the IQ became a frontlet on the foreheads of children and then, from a reminder, it (d)evolved into what the reminder was thought to be about, the measurable Mind, i.e., Intelligence, a cranial entity and, if twinship could tell us anything of ourselves, probably inherited.[37]

Cyril Burt, who had helped Galton with the design of anthropometric surveys, was appointed educational psychologist to the London County Council in 1913. Immediately he asked permission to collect data on twins, for which project he was well situated. English working-class women early this century often felt economically constrained to send one of a set of twins to a foster home, for which the Council's social workers had the addresses. Burt mishandled statistics, magically multiplied his cases, masqueraded as many of the pseudonymous contributors to a journal he edited, invented field research and, perhaps, research assistants to go with it, but he did collect data on twins. Lifelong fraud or late dodderer, Burt believed that the twin data proved that inherited intelligence imposed an upper limit on achievement. His writings became crucial to the theory behind the British system of educational tracking and to American imbroglios over the supposedly inborn superiority of white IQ over black. The implicit truth-telling authority of twins (dizygotic or especially monozygotic, reared together or especially raised apart, fact or especially fiction) undergirded

Burt's personal hereditarianism, his public hereditarian stance, and his knighthood.[38]

Twins themselves seemed nobly eager to be used as scientific subjects. Six hundred twins responded when the American Genetic Association in 1918 announced a desire to communicate with twins anywhere. The association wanted to know "what changes, or failures to change, can be correctly traced to our very beginnings in that momentous meeting of the two parent cells which began our earthly lives." Were the lives of Assistant Attorney General Edwin Grosvenor and his brother Gilbert, founder of the National Geographic Society, determined by their identical twinness? Arnold Gesell's essay of 1922 had relied on data they and other twins provided, which by 1929 suggested to him that even the most identical of twins had inbred differences that could become more or less profound according to motor training and mental stimulation. His 1929 monograph on identical twins was subtitled, "An Experimental Study by the Method of Co-Twin Control."[39]

Notions of using one twin as a check to the other had been implicit in laboratory fiction, as they had been anciently explicit if figurative in the practice of accounting, where one register was verified by consulting a duplicate. An eighteenth-century play, *The Dispute*, was resolved by the purchase of white infants, two female, two male, each separately tended by black servants in a walled garden; matured, the four are allowed to meet so that their aristocratic keepers may observe the pristine grounds of love and gender. There had also been encounters with "wild children" presumably abandoned as infants and suckled by maternal animals. Lacking human language and upbringing, wild children were considered ideal specimens of unadulterated humanity and, like the Wild Boy of Aveyron in 1800, subjected to experiments intent upon determining the nub of human nature.[40]

Although a monolithic Human Nature was displaced by nineteenth-century models of a vibratory Average Man, statisticians played no mean role in the feud between heredity and environment, heated up by disputes over evolution. Again, Darwin's cousin Francis Galton was present at the creation, "in a *reddish recess* in the *rock*" along a path around a Cumberland castle in 1888. An idea flashed by — a way to mark the degree to which changes in variables are "due to common causes." Galton's friend Karl Pearson refined the mathematics of this Coefficient of Correlation, signified by r, and Charles Spearman in 1904 would spin out its complement, factor analysis, but Galton had once more mixed up data and destiny. Against the logic of the method itself, Galton believed that correlation coefficients, ranging in value from -1 to 0 (no correlation) to $+1$, could identify those similarities between parent and child that were due exclusively to heredity. As Stephen Jay Gould has demurred in *The Mismeasure of Man*, "The fact of correlation implies nothing about cause.... The inference of cause must come from somewhere else, not from the simple fact of correlation."[41]

And yet, the r's of correlation (and the vectors of factor analysis) seemed to work so well with the randomizing procedures of modern science, seemed so to enhance the claims of the social sciences to be hard sciences, that experimental results would thereafter seem naked without a cloak of coefficients.[42] The r's (and vectors) seemed especially tailored to the circumstance of twins, whose origins were the same and whose variations from each other could be clearly plotted. In 1923–24 Hermann Siemens, a German dermatologist, published the first full statement of the Twin Method: measure the agreement between identical twins for any given feature; contrast the degree of agreement between fraternal twins; if the "concordance" between twins produced from one egg is significantly greater than that between twins produced from two different eggs, said feature must be genetic. The biological power of the Coefficient of Correlation was wedded to the oracular powers of twins: a match arranged at birth.[43]

Whereupon twins became Controls, the ongoing life and body of one held as duplicate register against the other, or the lives and bodies of fraternals set against identicals. Previously, twins in science had been akin to sacrificial animals slit open by diviners who pronounce upon the world according to the condition of the entrails *at that moment*. During the 1920s, twins assumed a more active, continuous role as truth-tellers about human nature.

Single-egg twins, declared the chief surgeon at the Hôpital Bichat (Paris) in 1926, are two copies of the same person, not two truly individual beings. "It would be quite interesting, from the biological point of view," he mused, "to take two exactly similar twins and transplant them to different countries, giving them dissimilar educations." Shortly, one charitable institution did offer to the University of Chicago "a pair of identical-twin orphans a few weeks old, whom we could then separate and bring up in environments as different as we might wish." Horatio Newman et al. were tempted by the "fine opportunity, but the thought of having to wait twelve years for them to reach an age suitable for testing, and in the meantime acting as scientific parent to a pair of twins, would have been enough to dissuade us, even without the refusal of our better half to countenance any such wild scheme." Their better half rested content with offers of all-expenses-paid trips to Chicago's Century of Progress Exposition (1933) in return for participation in a study of adult twins reared apart. Arrived thereupon Ed and Fred, raised as only sons by foster parents a thousand miles apart, employed as telephone repairmen for two branches of the same company, married in the same year, owners of fox terriers named Trixie, and haunted since youth by the image of a dead brother.[44]

Hubris nor hassle prevented Arnold Gesell and Helen Thompson in 1927–28 from applying "the Method of Co-Twin Control" to twin infant girls, orphaned shortly after birth and placed in a public nursery, where at the age of six weeks they were segregated for study. Gesell and Thompson began their monograph with a feinting lament: "we should like to train or condition a child, and then later we should like to compare him with what he would have been if he had not received the training. Unfortunately, growth is not a reversible phenomenon...." Ah, "But one can study identical twins with just such problems in mind." Which they did with the two girls, from infancy to eighteen months, training one and watching both, for "It should be insisted that it would be difficult to devise a more comprehensive and, in some senses, a more delicate instrument of behavior measurement than one twin used in juxtaposition with an identical co-twin, who serves as a standard of reference." Gesell and Thompson's motor and visual training of the first twin barely affected (compared to the second, the Control) the onset of her developmental stages. Convincing evidence, it seemed, either for the age-fixedness of physiological turning points or for the prepotency of genetics in fixing physical ability. Students of Thompson and Gesell were still controlling the same pair when the girls were four.[45]

Use them, urged botanist and geneticist Albert F. Blakeslee in 1930. Blakeslee, soon president of the American Association for the Advancement of Science, was referring to "biological" controls (they were reliable) and to twins (there were plenty to go around). Used they would be, everywhere. By Kurt Gottschaldt of the Kaiser Wilhelm Institute for Anthropology, Berlin, 138 pairs of "Aryan" children at *Zwillenslager*, summer camps for the observation of twins, 1936–37, concluding that "hereditary influences far outweigh the environmental aspects in the entire area of intelligent action," followed up at Auschwitz by Dr. Josef Mengele, supervising the deaths of 250 pairs of Jewish and Gypsy twins. By S.G. Levit at the Maxim Gorky Medico-Biological Research Institute, Moscow, 800 pairs of twins, until banned in 1936 as conflicting with Marxist beliefs in a malleable human nature. By Franz J. Kallmann of the New York State Psychiatric Institute, 2536 twins over the age of sixty, studied 1945–56, concluding that "gene-specific intellectual differences persist into a well-advanced age." By Luigi Gedda at the Gregor Mendel Institute for Medical Genetics and Twin Research, Rome, 15,000 twins, since 1942, on the premise that identical twins "offer us, among other things, the possibility of demonstrating that, despite their psychophysical identicalness, resulting from their identical hereditary patrimony, they possess an *anemos*, that is a soul, an immaterial principle that differentiates the single individual and personalizes him." By René Zazzo of the Ecole Pratique des Hautes Etudes, Paris, 200 pairs of twins, some followed from birth to maturity during the 1950s, concluding that differences between twins result from their responses to being, willy-nilly, couples. By James Shields of the Institute of Psychiatry, Maudsley Hospital, London, 44 identical pairs reared apart, 44 reared together, and 32 fraternal pairs, interviewed 1954–56, concluding that differences between identical twins may be caused by the social pressure of being reared together. By Richard J. Rose and the Department of Public Health, Helsinki, 7626 twin sisters and 6662 twin brothers, concluding in 1988 – surprise, surprise – that shared

experiences have a substantial impact upon variation in the personalities of twins.[46]

Little of the research has been concerned with twins in and of themselves.[47] It has been concerned with what twins could reveal about
human beingness. About intelligence, criminality, sociability, sedation
thresholds, temperaments, obesity, homosexuality, depression, suicide,
emotionality, cynicism, compulsiveness, submissiveness, pessimism, sexual inhibition, narcissism, passivity, self-expressiveness.[48] About an illness that has seemed most twinlike and portentous: schizophrenia.[49]

Nonetheless, twins have enlisted in large numbers, stirred by the
paramountcy of their doubleness ("reared together") or lured by the
prospects of reunion with a vanished twin ("reared apart"). If, after lo
these many years, their oracular presence has not thoroughly unriddled
human nature, they are not to blame. Petitioners must always puzzle
out the oracles. Sociologists, political economists, and psychologists
turned to twins when biologists were unprepared to answer questions
about fertility and heredity; biologists and experimental psychologists
turned to twins when they had cell theory but found the microsciences
wanting; sociobiologists, geneticists, and neuropsychologists still turn
to them. Neither mathematics nor biotechnology has been able, quite,
to take the measure of twins. To this day we look toward them for the
measure of what is inalienably human.

Before and After

To this day, one cannot be certain that naturally conceived twins come
from the same egg. Rephrased: No study comparing supposedly monozygotic twins with each other or with dizygotic twins can be completely trusted. We are yet debating questions about how twins arise
in embryo. Judith C. Hall of the University of British Columbia proposed in 1992 that a genetically "discordant" cell will be expelled
immediately after a fertilized egg begins to divide, and that the expelled cell can become the focus of an embryo minutely different from
that of its otherwise identical sib – "a harsh notion," says a skeptical
Johns Hopkins University geneticist, "that one twin in every pair might
carry a genetic defect." And if we still are unsure what triggers the
formation of twins, then Nathaniel Hirsch's 1929 critique of earlier
twin studies remains apt: twins thought to be identical may not be.
Even the fact of two newborns issuing from a single placenta is inadequate guarantee of a single-egg origin, wrote Hirsch in *Twins: Heredity
and Environment*; the placental membranes may have fused. Vice versa,
multiple membranes may result from a single egg whose identicals
have separated.[50]

Horatio Newman in 1937 noted that the identical twins Johnny and
Jimmy studied by Gesell's pupil Myrtle McGraw were not, after all,
identical. Newman's own guide on "How to diagnose monozygotic
twins" listed such criteria as commonly mistaken identities, similar
dentition, similar friction ridges of the fingers and palms, and reversed

FIGURE 1.4. Twin as Control through Time. A 1952 advertisement for the Toni home permanent. Reproduced courtesy of the D'Arcy Collection of the Communications Library of the University of Illinois at Urbana-Champaign.

asymmetry, where "one hand of one twin must be more like one hand of the other than like his own other hand." The list has since expanded to red blood cells and genetic "fingerprints," but reservations have grown proportionately. Through DNA sampling techniques we learn that monozygotic twins are not precisely identical. Through reviews of research we learn that we may not have sound evidence for the two-egg origin of dizygotic twins, and that twins who make themselves available for study self-select for close similarity. Through recent observation we learn that mothers themselves are poor judges of the zygosity of their twins, and that a third of all parents of fraternal twins may be treating them as if they were identicals.[51]

Identical twins, toward whom modern novelists, scientists, and parents have gravitated, battle to intrauterine death more commonly than do sororal/fraternal twins, or thus our legend of the vanishing twin would have it. Competing furiously for a food supply arriving through a limited circulation system in (typically) one placenta, monozygotic twins are rarer not simply because they are genetic rogues but because, as the novelist Tournier might put it, a fetal ogre will often undo its placental partner by consuming a lion's share of the maternal provisions. The true vanishing twin of the legend is not just any twin. It is, or was, a vanquished identical twin.[52]

They could both be seen, vanquished and victor, in the before-and-after drawings of nineteenth-century medical books and temperance tracts. An unattractive, unclean, constipated, and/or bloated face on the left, the Before, vanishes beneath the glory of the beautiful, radiant, regular, or seductive After on the right. Structurally, the two are identical twins. The portrait to remember, the future, the saving grace, is on your right; the other is left behind. Victorian vanishing twins were sacrificed to the cause of abstinence by the grim visage of excess; our vanishing twins are sacrificed to the cause of consumerism by a millennial vision. Even the most familiar of before-and-afters, fronting one weight-loss miracle after another, promise a spicy menu as stimulant to a delicious new life.[53]

Advertisers this century first exploited twins for their exponential powers. If twins were double, could they not double the world? At century's turn the brunette beauties beneath the logo for Hall's Vegetable Sicilian Hair Renewer were captioned "DOUBLE. Why not double the beauty of your hair?" In 1932 circus audiences found in their programs two identical long-legged dancers saying, "Since we've been washing our stockings in Lux they give twice as many performances." The Wrigley Company summoned up twins around 1940, shortly after the singular Claudette Colbert was "made doubly lovely with healthful, delicious Double Mint gum." Voices on radio, photographs in magazines, and video footage of actual identical twins have since promised worldwide to "Double Your Pleasure." Floyd and Lloyd, grandfatherly twins with grandmotherly twin wives, can crunch Dorito corn chips twice as fast from the new-for-1992 twin-pack.[54]

Twin-packing was not enough. Gesell & Co.'s papers on co-twin controls had scarcely dried in print before the method was adapted to advertising. "**TWINS** report on **STOCKINGS**," read a Lux detergent ad in 1932. "TWIN SISTERS...given duplicate pairs of sheer hose...the only difference – one twin washed hers with a cake soap – the other washed hers the Lux way." And? "And the result showed *what* a difference the Lux way makes." Dorothy Brougham testified, "I used a cake soap and after the very first washing I noticed a decided fading, and after five washings I had a run." Betty, identical twin in identical clothes, testified, "I washed *my* pair in Lux. They're still lovely, though they've been washed more than twice as often as Dorothy's." Their twinship bore a specious relationship to the test they ran; they were rather doubling the visual impact of "The Lux Way to preserve ELASTICITY" than subjecting stockings to identical treatment – but the *revolutionary* new idea, as admen would say, was the idea of employing a twin "experiment" to validate products.[55]

Why should we today find twin experiments and twin-packing such common skeins in advertising's bag of wool? On the one side, posing identical twins hip to hip is a synecdoche of mass production. Like quality-controlled factory output, identical twins are ostensibly interchangeable replicas of each other. They have been used, indeed, to sell Genuine Ford Parts: "They **LOOK** alike...They **ARE** alike... They're **IDENTICAL TWINS!**" On the other side, pitting identical twins against each other is paradigmatic of mass marketing, whose task is to erect hedges of profit between apparently identical products. The co-twin experiment is paradigmatic of the process by which producers hope to gain and maintain advantage. If biologists have sought out identical twins for proof of what is genetic, makers of detergent have sought out identical twins for relief from the generic.[56]

Happened therefore an elegant bait and switch. Asking "Which Twin has the Toni?" and placing side by side identical twins with identical coiffures, admen reconceived the before-and-after tradition. One twin paid $20 for a salon permanent wave; the other gave herself a $2 Toni *creme* cold wave. Could you tell them apart? "This twin test shows you how beautiful a Toni Home Permanent really is – so soft, so smooth, so natural looking." Sometimes it was the twin on the left, Consuelo O'Connor, whose sister on the right, Gloria, had had a beauty shop permanent, "And none of our friends could tell which had which."[57]

Toni's campaign at midcentury, renewed in 1977, was simultaneously a twin-pack pitch and a twin experiment with Gloria as Control. Both women photographed well – the twin-pack's double whammy of two stunning women in matching outfits – but the Control, Gloria or Barbara or Roxie, would always wish she had been the one to get the Toni: "Next time I'm going to have the wave with the natural look, too!" Translation: Next time, after two hours at her mirror, the vanquished twin would achieve for herself, $18 to the good, an impermanently permanent wave, as natural-looking an unnatural curl as any achieved at costly salons. Two million women, identifying with the vanquished twin and what could well be a reprieve from the hell of the commercial hair dryer, were giving themselves Tonis each month as Toni's Twin Hunters fanned across the land "in search of America's loveliest twins!" Eleanor and Jeanne Fulstone of Nevada won the right in 1950 to model on national airwaves "a wave that *feels* and *behaves* like naturally curly hair."[58]

Lilt that year was promoted as "the *only* Home Permanent Wave that *looks...feels...behaves* so much like Naturally Curly Hair!" but the people of Toni, true to their faith in the power of the twin method to establish fine distinctions and the power of the twin-pack to assure brand loyalty, knew that *"Toni alone, of all home permanents — looks so natural, feels so soft!"* Toni's copywriters did, and I do, italicize the point that Nurture (the training of one's hair) had become one with Nature's chromosomatic curls — the dream of every hair stylist, monopoly capitalist, and genetic engineer.[59]

Whether as spokeswomen for German deodorant spray, British detergent, Japanese fax machines, or American soft drinks, or as adjuncts to a multinational promotion of Pond's Vanishing Cream, identical twins have met advertising's needs for the oracular. Framed in before-and-after pictures, they have prophesied new figures, new lives. Paraded in twin-packs, they have borne witness for each other, sworn oaths, and raised everything they touched to a higher power (as Dionne endorsements would quintuple sales, or so hoped the distributors of chest rubs, family cars, and cod-liver oil).[60] Exalted through twin experiments, they have revealed the natural curl, the real exponential you. What scientists took to be eminently oracular about identical twins, their "concordance," was at the heart of advertising copy. The sole difference between the identical twins of the Toni ads was a matter of money and time, not innate good looks or natural curl. Working girls or plain old housewives with less money and time could, through the two-dollar charm of Toni's twins, be mistaken for women of leisure.

Impolitic phrases — "working girls," "plain old housewives," "women of leisure" — but issues of gender should rear up at just this point, for the commercial display of twins has been predominantly of females. Demographic data offer no surplus of identical twin girls,[61] yet those who rode bicycles-built-for-two or dove off parallel boards in the merriment of 1980s Doublemint commercials were women, doubling our fun. Apart from advertising's swaggering sexism, against which critics have railed for decades, what may explain more specifically the engagement of twin women as prophets of human nature?

Their unique sexuality? Consider the common male fantasia about female twins, who carry out perfect multiple conjugations. "[I]magine how excitedly I looked forward to a session with Linda, one of the vivacious Thompson twins," writes a pornographer-cum-psychiatrist. "Double dipping, double fun, I thought with a grin." Linda has "perfectly symmetrical little breasts," a peaches 'n' cream complexion, and "another one exactly like her" back home. The shrink is aroused by a symmetrical and exponential sexuality, redoubled when Linda tells him: "You see, Doctor, twins are not like other people. We're deeply bonded, exactly alike and inseparable from birth. To have another human being – the mirror image of yourself – constantly around at the age when your sexual feelings begin to surface.... And all your erotic feelings are being felt at the same time...by another person who looks, talks, acts, eats and dresses like you! The possibilities are endless!" (Aristophanes had imagined some of the possibilities, in the *Symposium*: "After the division the two parts of man, each desiring his other half, came together, and threw their arms about one another eager to grow into one.") These are young women, barely seventeen; in the daydream Linda lays before the shrink, she and her sister come together under the sign of Castor and Pollux, "scared to death of thunderstorms!" Lucy dives into Linda's narrow bed, where the two huddle tightly together for security. ("...so ancient is the desire of one another which is implanted in us, reuniting our original nature, making one of two, and healing the state of man.") The young women become the lovers they were meant to be, probing "with fingers that were born with the knowledge of what turns each other on!" and on. This is mutual diddling, it is lesbianism, it is incest, it is companionate sex; the man imagines himself twin-packed between the sisters in a most reassuring and, ultimately, most Platonic love. ("For the intense yearning which each of them has towards the other does not appear to be the desire of intercourse, but of something else which the soul desires and cannot tell, and of which [the soul] has only a dark and doubtful presentiment.")[62]

Admen could hardly be oblivious to the thunderstruck fantasia or the dark presentiment. Photographs of and copy beneath Toni twins shimmered with overtones of sapphic completeness. The twins were sensuous twins, happy to be in each other's company, pleased – soon doubly pleased – with themselves. Dark hair immaculately waved, lips open, eyes downward, the identically styled Toni twins of *Life* (April 25, 1949) faced right but looked inward, bare breastbone of one pressed to silken shoulder blade of the other. "The minute you see your Toni wave in the mirror," began the narcissistic copy, "you'll see why women like Toni better."

Yes, yes, but these controlled images and contrived words were never directed at men. Unlike the bare-breasted Sia and Shane on the cover of *Playboy*, the milder Toni twins were meant to appeal exclusively to women, a target audience presumably insusceptible to male fantasias about twin-packing.[63]

This is not to say that sensual, sexy twins are absent from female fantasias. They may be found in anthologies of women's erotica – indirectly, through scenes of incest and lesbianism; proximately, through stories of sex with brothers who stick "close as two burrs" or with cousins one of whom is a "youthful replica" of the other; blatantly, through tales of lovemaking with Siamese twins. Male twins as objects of female desire (and experiment) may be found in Rosamond Smith's novel, *Lives of the Twins* (1987) in which Molly Marks, lover of Jonathan McEwan, goes undercover, dressed as she was when she met Jonathan, to meet his twin brother James. "For scientific, experimental purposes, Molly intends to duplicate her early experiences with Jonathan McEwan as closely as possible."[64]

Nor is it to say that women are unmoved by that urge toward primeval reunion common to androcentric epics and inherent in Toni advertisements. New Toni twins in 1952 were double sphinxes to the riddle, "Which Twin's Toni was set a week ago – *and which was set today?*" You couldn't tell; with Priceless Pink lotion the new Permafix method "'locks in' your Toni wave so it can't come out." Natural *and* permanent, the twins traveled through or were immune to time; either way they were original and still bonded, symbols of eternal sodality. Women recently have been seeking out their vanished birthmothers, rewriting family histories, reconstruing archaeology to uncover our origins in matriarchal societies, centered upon an all-enveloping goddess. The Great Mother, notes Barbara G. Walker in her *Woman's Encyclopedia of Myths and Secrets*, is she who, in culture after culture, gives blood and breath to celestial twins, as did Latona, primal mother of the Greek World Egg, who bore Castor and Pollux. There may once also have been female twins correlative to the Dioscuri; these have receded or lost their filiations, as has Sky-Daughter, incestuous sister-wife of the Indic Aśvins, and the "Shining" Helen, sister of Castor and Pollux, carried off from dioscuric legend toward the walls of Troy.[65]

I do mean to say that the sexual allure of twins is as inadequate an explanation for the prominence of twin women as is the allure of Aristophanic and Great Mother imagery or the rough handling of women by patriarchal societies. Unique sexuality, symbolic wholeness, historic sexism, and blithe scientism are necessary but insufficient answers to the question: Why, if advertisers resorted to identical twinship for its implicit oracular power, did the estimable gift of prophecy fall so overwhelmingly to identical twin women?

Because advertising has become our sibylline medium, deciphering our dreams, telling us who we are and what we should be doing. Because the intuitiveness, the communitarian sensitivity, the ecstasies of the oracular are qualities linked more tightly to women than to men ever since the Greeks found their Fates and sibyls. Because advertising is every which way twinning: a profession of repeating, of making the old seem new in a world of the Twice as Long and Twice as Much, Buy One Get One Free, Double Your Pleasure or Double Your Money Back. Because this twinning is sponsored by a commercial faith that consuming should be a passion, as it must have been in the womb; that the consumer must ever be unsatisfied, as is the singleton; that through hyperbole a commodity can leave behind its lookalike sisters to become a Brand; that, in other words, the Control will be forgotten as humanity is possessed in the name of the Other. Identical female twins appear

FIGURE 1.5. *Hawthorne's Twins*, by Karen Kovacik, 1987. A black-and-white photograph recorded directly onto computer disk through a video camera hooked up to a Commodore Amiga 2000 computer and manipulated using Deluxe Paint II software. First published in *The Gamut: A Journal of Ideas and Information* (Wint 1989). Reproduced by permission.

as oracles in advertisements not simply because they mirror a consuming culture but because they are templates to the process of advertising itself.[66]

Doubletrouble

One way or t'other, identical twins, male or female, have been walking advertisements, from the French *avertissement*, a warning, a prophecy, a call to attentiveness. They learn to live under the hard light of laboratory fictions, scientific reports, advertising copy. Like playing-card kings and queens of the nineteenth century – their faces suddenly doubled and inverted – identicals have been caught between images of fortune-telling and freakishness. Farces have had them on stage as tricksters deceiving suitors who "whisper vows to the wrong party" until "Every thing fast progresses to a happy state of confusion." When an actual Mrs. Kelley circa 1830 asked carpenter William Wiggin Smith for a plan of the chimneys to her house and then added, "They will be twins, you know, like yourself and your brother," her simile was, for all its innocence, a kind of imprisonment. Tucking in Sleeping Twins at midcentury, children must have thought that twins, like these dolls, slept and woke in concert. Late Victorian studio photographers set twin sisters as twin pillars to frame family portraits. D.W. Griffith's cinematic *Twin Brothers* ventured into the wide world of 1909 to make their separate ways; one found work inside a gorilla suit at a dime museum, playing across from the lion... his brother.[67]

Playing across from each other, twins have also had to inoculate themselves against *folie à deux*. Known since 1819 as *folie gémellaire*, twinly madness, the disorder was renamed and popularized in 1877 by two unrelated French physicians, Charles Lasègue and Jules Falret, studying cases of the "morbid interpsychology" of unrelated people. *Folie à deux* extended to delusions shared by husbands and wives, mothers and daughters, and pals in asylums, but psychologists took as their standard the possibly pathological likemindedness of twins. Observing that continual, repetitive contact could result in the "contagious" transfer of insane beliefs, Lasègue and Falret gave as the fifth of their examples the case of "old maid" twin sisters living together. It was not clear whether the two had contracted *folie à deux* merely because they were twins, but it was clear that because of their *folie à deux*, the doctors treated them as if they were *identical*. Rare in 1877, *folie à deux* is now a catchall in common parlance and prejudice; rare have been those identical twins not condemned to a species of *folie à deux* by singletons who ask, "How can you tell the difference between yourself and your sister?"[68]

Isabel Bolton could and could not. She remembered her twin sister Grace, who had drowned in her youth, as "the living image of myself.... Attuned to the same vibrations, with nerves that responded to the same dissonances and harmonies, we were one in body and in soul." Twins themselves have ever struggled to define themselves both as two and as one. Raphael Soyer would paint his identical twin Moses, a fellow artist, sometimes from his own image in the mirror, sometimes from life, even as the dying Moses wasted away. Artists Ivan and Malvin Albright came to Hollywood in 1943 to do two portraits for the film of Oscar Wilde's *The Picture of Dorian Gray*. Malvin, who had sat as a youthful model to his twin brother's painting, *Maker of Dreams*, painted the youthful Gray; Ivan, who would write, "We are shadows of the real but not the real; we live by half-truths and half facts," worked in the same studio at the portrait of a morbid, vitiated Gray. Contemplating the death of her twin sister, an identical twin at seventy tells me, "you can't be that stuck together and come completely unstuck." Could it have been coincidence that thanatology, the study of dying and bereavement, was brought to international attention largely through the efforts of Elisabeth Kübler-Ross, a surviving identical twin (of triplets), or that she would become preoccupied with life after death?[69]

Certainly, given the momentum of this chapter, it can be no coincidence that, behind their pseudonyms, the two most widely syndicated of North American oracles, Ann Landers and Abigail Van Buren, are identical twins. Née Esther Pauline and Pauline Esther Friedman of Sioux City, Iowa, "my sister and I were practically Siamese from the day we were born to the day we married (and naturally it was a double wedding)," writes Ann Landers. It was also almost a double divorce years later, but since 1955 millions have written to Dear Abby for advice and asked Ann Landers what oh what to do. About twins, says Landers, treat them as individuals and dress them differently. "God did not join these two at the hip," she tells parents of twins. "He gave them separate bodies, separate minds and separate nervous systems."[70]

Esther Pauline and Pauline Esther were born near the end of World War I, when the separateness of twins' nervous systems did not prevent parents from calling twins Sharon and Karen, Carol and Coral, Pete and Repeat, Nancy Jean and Norma Jane. During the 1920s an English father-to-be insured his wife for £1000 against the risk of bearing twins, and in 1946 Lloyds of London began issuing insurance against twin births. In those post–World War II years, however, childrearing theory shifted from an aweful regard for the consummate loyalty of twins to an emphasis upon their indivi/duality. Parents, pedagogues, and pediatricians, like copywriters for home permanents, adapted the twin experiment to environmentalist ends: what happened at home and at school could, like Toni, recreate the natural and make *that* permanent.[71]

Let them be individuals, wrote Dr. Benjamin Spock in boldface in the first edition of *Baby and Child Care*, completed at the end of World War II. His advice on twins, taken to heart by generations of parents in a world supposedly "made safe for democracy," was comparable to the U.N. charter: "Enjoy each one for what he is and he'll grow up at peace with himself, his twin, and the rest of the world."[72]

Thenceforward it would be gauche to raise or to speak of twins as companionate couples, especially when the former allies with twin nicknames, the U.S. and U.S.S.R., found themselves divided by an Iron Curtain. "Don't treat twins as a Unit!" urged Dr. Winifred de Kok in 1949. Those parents who "always hoped to have twins," wrote Marjorie Leonard for *Child Study* in 1953, were really wishing that they themselves, as lonely children, had had a twin, an ideal confidant, "one who understands everything even without being told." Telepathy, empathy were part of a "myth about twins" aligned by adults to their family romances – of a vanished or kidnapped twin.[73]

Shanghai, Australia, California, and the Walt Disney Studios were birthplace and training grounds for artist and copywriter Phyllis Graham, so when in 1955 she published the "first book written especially for the harassed parents of twins," she resisted any emphasis upon the individuality of twins, whose "amazing creative co-operation is often not noticed" and, in the West, less than welcome. True, twins should learn to appreciate healthy competition, but Graham wrote crossgrain that "Twins who develop the same tastes and interests do not always have special social problems, and all twins may realize a happiness available to no one else."[74]

Graham had not entered into the proper spirit of the Cold War. This multicultural mother of twins was behind, and ahead, of her times. The Canadian Department of National Health and Welfare in 1955 was au courant: "Even identical twins are *two* individuals who only happened to be born at the same time." The less that twins took leave of one another, the more likely that their likeness would become pathological, as with Bert and Bill, whom the English psychiatrist Dorothy Burlingham treated from 1955 to 1958. Born illegitimate and identical, Bill and Bert slept in the same positions as infants, crawled with the same motions, rocked with the same rhythms, and at fourteen months began "copying-games" in which Bill copied Bert clapping and Bert copied Bill banging until "it was impossible to tell who copied whom." They ignored other children, nurses, their mother, their "mother substitutes" (when at last the birthmother found them unbearable, since she also never could tell which baby she had in her arms). By age twelve they were in a Home for Maladjusted Children, locked in narcissistic rivalry and imitation, "Each boy's eyes, his whole attention...completely absorbed in the other twin." Anytime one developed a distinctive red nose or boil, the other gave himself the same. They had homosexual fantasies, fantasies of murdering each other, fantasies of being each two people, one good, one bad. "There is little doubt," wrote Burlingham, "that living in the presence of the twin was for them synonymous with living in the presence of their own reflection." They grew from brats to teenage brawlers "at the mercy of their instincts." Such was the dark scenario for parents who failed to nourish the individual talents of twins.[75]

"Doubletrouble" was the codeword. It meant that twins as distinct individuals were socially settled, but if they acted to remind you of doubleness, of anxieties over a lost twin, of antecedents of Cold War, they were antisocial, maybe inhuman:

"You have two heads!" [says their English teacher when the King Twins compose a collective autobiography.] "I would dare to hope, two brains. You are *two* individuals."

"Nothing ever happens to me," [says Enid King.] "It happens to *us*." [To her and Audrey, she means, in the 1964 teen romance, *Double Trouble*.]

"It's high time you quit being twins," [says boyfriend Hal, who won't take stupidity from girls of seventeen], "and began being people. Separate people."[76]

Stern and binary stuff: either twins or people. So great had grown the implicit oracular powers of twins-as-twins that they had either to be sliced into Control and Other, coerced into individuality, or euhemerized into the deities of advertising copy and sports (doubles partners, synchronous swimmers).

Only within the shadow cast by the year 2000, amidst the decline of a binary political world, have Bill and Bert and "doubletrouble" been succeeded by *The Joy of Twins*. (Bill, be it noted, became a bus driver tending his garden on weekends; Bert joined the air force, traveled, became a family man, and built model airplanes.) "Research" suddenly shows "that the vast majority of twins and their families are not only healthy, happy human beings, but many of them feel that being twins and having twins has given them an *advantage* in understanding them-selves and those around them." We have sore need of that advantage on our approach to the end of the century, when we come face to face to face with Janus, that triple-countenanced god of crossroads and cross-ings of the Rubicon. So we *Make Room for Twins*, who best embody our entwined emotions of anxiety and anticipation.[77]

Our return to the promise of companionate twinship is confluent with the public emergence of the legend of the vanishing twin, for at century's end each singleton may feel double in a doubled time of ends and beginnings. The vanished twin, the vanquished, the Control, stands proxy to our paradoxical sense of exhaustion and incompletion at this fin de siècle; the survivor, the Other, represents an exhilaration about a new calendrical world with its iconic 2 – another millennium, a sec-ond chance. The legend of the vanishing twin emerges just as we must breach an apocalyptic 1999 and send our children across as settlers to a foreign epoch already populated with fictive androids, cyborgs, lit-ters of clones. Small wonder that identical twins should have become our oracles, that vanishing twins should bind each singleton to a two-fold life.

Parasitic monster (after Paré).

Thoracopagus. Lazarus-Joannes Baptista Colloredo.

The Hungarian sisters.

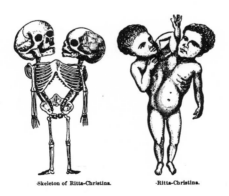

Skeleton of Ritta-Christina.

Ritta-Christina.

FIGURE 2.1. Conjoined twins. Top left, "parasitic monster" (b. 1516) after Ambroise Paré's *On Monsters and Marvels* (1573); top right, Lazarus and Joannes Baptista Colloredo, 1630s; middle, Judith and Helena Szony, ca. 1710; bottom, skeleton and sketch of Ritta-Christina, 1829. From George M. Gould and Walter Pyle, *Anomalies and Curiosities of Medicine* (1896).

CHAPTER TWO

Doppelgängers

How can I be merry, that have my true marrow as a dead
carrion upon my back....
— one of the Scottish brothers, ca. 1518

Twins there are who will not vanish, whose flesh is your flesh, whose
death is your death. Such intemperate affinity appears wherever a pair
seem to themselves "as nearly as possible, one being in two bodies."
Consider the lives of English twins Greta and Freda Chaplin, who at
fifty speak and move (and have been moved to love) in unison; consider
the deaths of twins Cyril and Stewart Marcus, Manhattan gynecologists
who committed double suicide in 1975, so addicted to each other that
a film about them could end most credibly in a scene spiked with monstrous instruments "for separating Siamese twins."[1]

Inseparable twins — *terata didyma*, *Doppelmissgeburten* — have a long
history as monsters, from the Latin *monstrum*, divine portent. Twofold
Peruvian skeletons have been dated to 7000 B.C.; glyphs of conjoined
figures were drawn throughout Copper Age Europe as images of natural abundance or as deities with the "power of two."[2] Crossing over from
the archaic world, however, double-bodied oracles have spoken less of
Nature than of the unnatural. Companionate, heavenly twins turn ugly
once they are bound together on earth. In our era, they have become
archetypes of the unreasonable facsimile: images of ourselves that arouse
consternation; omens of the peril of relentless copying.

Women giving birth to monsters, quoth 4 Esdras 5.8, would be a
sign of the End. That passage, from an apocalyptic text which was a
canonical part of the Roman Bible for fifteen hundred years, was mistranslated and miscopied: *menstrua* taken for *monstra*, the Latin read that
a woman who had sex during her period would bring forth a monster —
something excessive, or doubled. Children of these unseemly copula-
tions, wrote surgeon Ambroise Paré in 1573, suffer the wrath of God
against disorderly sexual appetites; they will be born disorderly of shape
and mass, a crazed and unkind fusion.[3]

Michel de Montaigne around that year went to see a live double monster. Dangling from an erect child fourteen months old was a second

child, shorter, thinner, headless. Montaigne "turned up the imperfect child" to see that the two were joined between nipples and navel, front to front, yearningly, "as if a smaller child were trying to throw its arms about the neck of a somewhat bigger one." Wrote the French wit: "This double body and these several limbs connected with a single head might supply the King with a favourable prognostic for maintaining those various parts and divisions of our state under the union of his laws." But political satire was perilous; the wit receded before the moralist: "What we call monsters are not so to God, who sees in the immensity of His work the infinity of forms that He has comprised within it." Summarily, Montaigne the skeptic: "Whatever falls out contrary to custom we call contrary to nature; but there is nothing that is contrary to nature, whatever it may be."[4]

As slowly as eschatology gave way to homily, so homily gave way to comparative anatomy. Montaigne rang the changes in perfect historical order, from monster as singularity, an ominous *event* no less celestial than terrestrial, through monster as marvel, an amazing *thing* under God's heaven, to monster as multiplicity, a polyform *being* nursed by extravagant Nature. Medieval preachers had stressed the births themselves, prodigious irruptions in the annals. Later commentators marveled at the bodiliness of the "concorporations," wondrous amalgams of limbs. Scientists of the eighteenth and early nineteenth centuries focused on process, the embryological problems posed by these human animals. As unexpected events, monsters had been unnatural and "frightening" and were put to death; as peculiar things, they were preternatural and "strange" and were displayed alive for a few sous, then sold at death to dissecting theaters; as novel beings, they were "anomalous" and were fitted to their own classes, orders, genera, then preserved in large glass jars.[5]

The "freak" (< freak of nature, *lusus naturae*) came into its own, the word and the "living curiosity," with nineteenth-century Odditoriums and circus sideshows, where conjoined twins were shown at profit as before they had been shown in childbed near Bruges (1682) for three stivers a stare. If educated elites now were instructed to look upon them as "sports" of Nature's inventiveness, nonetheless they scurried to shake hands with "Siamese" twins and engage them in games of chess, just as poorer folk flocked to their song-and-dance routines with a lively sense of them as puzzles, astonishing, possibly supernatural.[6]

Were they two or were they one? That was the question midwives and theologians had had to answer, for on it rested the spiritual status of the newborn(s). Thomas Aquinas in the thirteenth century delivered a Solomonic judgment: if there were two chests with separately beating hearts, or at least separate heads, then *they* had separate souls and should be baptized as two. His decision was codified in manuals for priests: if two chests and two heads, then two souls. In practice, some midwives up to 1800 smothered the monsters, theologians tested for two thought-centers, and priests remained perplexed. Was it two chests *and* two heads? *or* two heads? The first autopsy in the Americas was done on the corpse of conjoined girls at the request of a cleric of Santo Domingo, unsure whether he had baptized one soul or two.[7]

In contrast with the laboratory approach to identical twins, where concordance was crucial, what had to be attested in cases of conjoined twins was their innate discordance, which would establish that the two were individually ensouled. The Scottish brothers schooled at the court of James IV around 1500 were divided above the navel, with two trunks back to back, two necks, and two heads adept at singing parts, one treble, one tenor. "[S]ometimes the two Bodies," a chronicler had to write, "did discover several Appetites, disagreeing with one another, and so they would quarrel, one liking *this*, another *that*." Yet they could not abide a final separation, "for one of the Bodies died many days before the other; and that which survived, half putrified, pined away by degrees" at the age of twenty-eight. "How can I be merry," the relict was supposed to have said, "that have my true marrow as a dead carrion upon my back, which was wont to sing and play with me, to commune and talk in like manner. When I was sad he would give me comfort, and I would do likewise unto him; but now I have nothing but dolour of the bearing so heavy a burden, dead, cold, and decaying on my back, which takes all earthly pleasure from me in this present life."[8]

Some of this is apocryphal, but the story lingers, companion to accounts of Lazarus and Joannes Baptista Colloredo, joined at the navel and baptized as two souls in Geneva in 1617. John the Baptist was a parasite; he clung to the side of an erect Lazarus, and though his mouth was "ever open and gaping," he took no sustenance except through his brother. They toured Europe in the 1630s, revealing themselves to such as the Danish anatomist Thomas Bartholin, who had to write of John that "As he slept, sweated and stirred, when his greater brother was awake and not in motion and without perspiration, their vital and animal parts seem to be distinct from each other." A Londoner wondered about that, since Joannes, "though having sense and feeling, [is] yet destitute of reason and understanding: whence methinks a disputable question might arise, whether as they have distinct lives, so they are possessed by two souls; or but one imparted betwixt them both."[9]

Indivisibility yet individuality, that was the riddle. Even where double monsters shared between them one urinal passage and one anus, like the Szony twins of 1701, connected at the pelvic girdle, it was necessary to detail their discordance. "There seems to be no cheat in the thing," wrote a Fellow of London's Royal Society after inspecting the six-year-olds Judith-Helena at The Hague; "and the skin, where they are joined, is perfectly smooth, without any scar.... When one stoops to take up any thing, she carries the other quite from the ground; and that one of them often does, being stronger as well as more lively than the other. They have not their feeling common any where but in the place of their conjunction." A scholastic sort, asking how Judith-Helena might rise on Judgment Day, concluded that as they had been united by accident, so "we are indeed firmly persuaded that the sisters will rise again, and will appear with bodies separated or rent asunder." The sisters toured Europe, then withdrew to a convent. There, in 1723, Judith died of a disease of the brain and lungs, Helena shortly after.[10]

They had lived twenty-two years, a long life. Often, such twins succumbed in their first year from the stress of being carted around for exhibition — like Ritta-Christina, born in Sardinia on March 12, 1829, with two heads and two hearts, dead in Paris on November 23. France's premier anatomist dissected them. Etienne Serres was looking not for souls but for evidence supporting a law of embryological symmetry (organs that become single began double). Attached at pelvis and shoulder, with a leg and an arm apiece, Ritta-Christina had indeed begun as two, Serres decided, as had another creature he knew, a male with four legs and one head, for "it is evident that there are two *me*'s in this single head." Ominous event, astonishing thing, or polyform being, the double monster was in every era defined by polarities, discordances, distinctive selves. That it or he or she or they might be neither exactly one nor exactly two was too logically distressing and emotionally unsatisfying to be true.[11]

Thais So Strong

On the day that Ritta-Christina saw light in Sardinia, Luk-Chan and Luk-In were preparing to leave Siam. Their names (pronounced, in short, *Jun* and *In*) were mispronounced and misinterpreted by Westerners exaggerating the differences: "Chang" was (on the viewer's) "right" or "ripe yellow fruit" from the same tree as "Eng," who was "left" or "green fruit." They did stand with Jun's right shoulder to In's left, bound by an elastic band of flesh the size of a small hand reaching across above the waist, but at seventeen they were equally ripe for the picking. The two had been glimpsed five years before, swimming outside Bangkok, by Scottish sea captain and arms dealer Robert Hunter, whose gift of muskets to the embattled King Rama II had gained him access to a nation closed to Europeans. Hunter settled in the capital, married a Thai wife, and waited, not so much for permits to export the boys as for a chance at trading in other Thai resources. When Rama III ascended the throne in 1824, the new king was impressed with the conjoined twins and also with European weaponry. Hunter had his chance. He would help the Thais build a modern war fleet, alienate them by his arrogance, be caught smuggling opium from India; he would contract with the widowed mother of Jun-In for the services of her two sons, alienate them by his double dealing, and sell out his share of exhibition profits to a partner, New England sea captain Abel Coffin. Between the Hunter and the Coffin, the Cain and the Abel, Jun-In set sail as Chang-Eng on April 1, 1829, aboard the *Sachem*, the Narragansett Indian term for the chief of a confederation.[12]

On the day that Ritta-Christina died in a cold room in Paris, Chang-Eng were complaining of the chill of London. They had already been

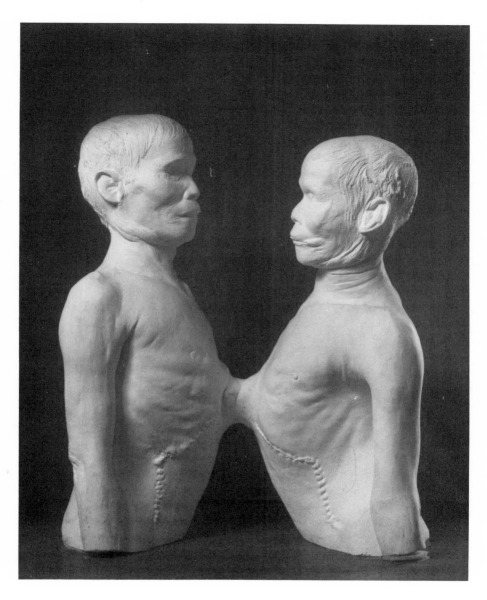

FIGURE 2.2. The Siamese Twins. Anatomical cast of Eng (left) and Chang (right) made after the partial autopsy, 1874. Reproduced courtesy of the Mütter Museum, College of Physicians of Philadelphia.

through Boston, New York, and Philadelphia as "The Siamese Double Boys," doing backflips and suffering the inspections of the best physicians, like John C. Warren, Professor of Anatomy at Harvard Medical School. Warren tied a cord to their cartilaginous band and pulled; Jun-In shifted fluidly together. But, as Warren had to write, this was "a habit, formed by necessity" to deal with disjunct volitions. "They much resemble each other; yet not so much but that upon little observation, various points of dissimilarity may be noticed." Now they were in London, "United Siamese Twins" catching a united catarrh and withstanding the scrutiny of anatomist Joshua Brookes, who declared them "totally devoid of deception."[13]

What was deceptive was their reception, for while Chang-Eng themselves and an enthusiastic public emphasized a companionate identity and the "perfect unanimity" of their "waltzing" motions, physicians and philosophers harped upon the medical possibilities of scission and the moral problematics of their twinship. Their young manager John W. Hale, ultimately less faithful to the investments of his employer, Abel Coffin, than to the interests of his charges, insisted that Chang-Eng "never disagree in the least on any point whatsoever." Phrenologists felt them up and found such an agreement in the size and shape of the two heads as "never before witnessed or heard of; and hence, the striking coincidence between the characters and dispositions of the two brothers, no longer remains a mystery." An admirer pleaded,

> Poor guileless boys; — let not the eye of pride
> That views its perfect self, your forms divide;
> Nor call those "monstrous" who a model prove
> Of hearts conjoined in harmony and love!

"After so long and so close a union," mused the *Boston Centinel* in 1829, "they would probably never be happy if separated."[14]

Nor did they then want to be separated, they who stood habitually with Chang's right arm around Eng's shoulders. Who dressed identically. Who signed themselves "Chang Eng." Who, zinc disc on one tongue, silver teaspoon on the other, completed a galvanic circuit. Who, to complete another circuit, went a-courting, playing flute duets, and in 1843 married two fat sisters, Adelaide and Sarah Yates, with whom they would sleep in one wide bed and produce twenty-two children. Was it humanity, as a New York newspaper suggested, that required that Chang-Eng be separated, if possible, into Chang and Eng?[15]

Yes and no. Enlightenment and romantic *constructs* of humanity demanded the separation, for the sake of personal liberty and the intelligent pursuit of happiness. Contemporaries were compulsively drawn to what a French journal called the "hyphen-mark between the two brothers." A Boston editor was upset that "these two pretty lads should be condemned all their lifetime to be as it were an eternal sticking plaster to one another." And what if one turned to Christ while the other remained a heathen? A naval surgeon examined their navels and the connecting band, then said that long before Judgment Day the t w o could be safely separated. They were – in 1834, by Captain Vivid at the finale of a farce: Dennis O'Glib and Simon Slow, accoutred in green tunics as "Ching" and "Wang," slaptalk their way across stage with Irish brogue and Cockney patois, one drinking brandy and the other getting drunk, so perfect in their act on behalf of Vivid that curiosity-monger Forceps offers his ward Marion to the man who will slash the twins apart and show "whether there is a real sympathy between the two bodies." That sympathy, so far as psychology went in 1836, proved more apparent than real: an experimenter had aides whisper the same questions separately to Chang and to Eng, from whom were received enough discrepant replies to conclude that Chang had the greater energy and will, Eng the greater powers of reflection. Elsewhere, Chang the slow, sagacious, and devout, addressed his hasty, clever, impious sib,

> I'm sure, dear Ching, you feel like me,
> How hard a thing it is to be
> Teased, worried, questioned, pulled about,
> Stared at, and quizzed by every lout....

They yearned therefore to be released from "This loathly and unnatural tie!" wrote the English novelist, poet, and politician Edward Bulwer-Lytton. If his long poem *The Siamese Twins* was *A Satirical Tale of the Times*, his later and last speech in Parliament would directly demand the immediate emancipation of West Indian Negroes. "All attempts to relax and mitigate slavery are hopeless and absurd," he spake. "There are no ways of patching up the everlasting distinction between slavery and freedom."[16]

Of the many tales about them, Chang-Eng took most offense at imputations of slavery. In 1832, catching wind of the rumor that their mother had sold them outright to Hunter and Coffin, "Chang-Eng's rage knew no bounds," and they felt "aggrieved in being made thus liable to be spoken of as 'Slaves' *bought* and *sold*." Their rage arose from deep fears that they might be forcibly detached from one another; from shame at "the idea of persons looking on them as children who had so hardhearted a mother"; and from remorse at having been away from her far longer than the twenty months originally contracted. In 1832, after forty-eight months of "servitude" (their word), they disengaged entirely, not from each other but from Coffin. Seven years down the road they retired handsomely from tours that had led them to all but two of the United States and twice to Europe. Married, they themselves would own thirty slaves, and their children would be raised by Grace Gates, a black woman given to them as a wedding present.[17]

Decades later, in San Francisco in 1860, they were planning at last to cross the Pacific to visit their mother. The Civil War intervened. Lukewarm Baptists (for "Blessed Be the Tie that Binds"), and legalized

Bunkers (a name adopted from New York friends), Chang-Eng returned to their homes in the Blue Ridge Mountains of North Carolina. Homes, for by this time they were supporting separate households between which they commuted every three days. The Civil War drove Chang-Eng further apart, not because one was Confederate and the other Union (both were loyal to the South), but because over the years Chang (always an inch shorter, his spine laterally curved) had became more burdensome upon the five-foot three-inch Eng, and their habits had diverged (Eng sat up all night playing poker, Chang read himself to sleep). Physically closer (their communal band of flesh had contracted and become less elastic, so they could no longer face away from each other), they were emotionally more distant, had dissolved their business partnerships, and seemed headed toward full Separation.[18]

Be two or not be two, that was the question. At least, that was the thrust of P.T. Barnum's promotion. In keeping with the spirit of a war fought "to preserve the Union" yet free the slaves, the famous Siamese Twins in 1868 were off to the prominent surgeons of Europe to see if any would sever their bond. For who would bear the scorns of time when they might have some quietus made with surgical steel? Chang-Eng had lost much of their wealth; they needed the funds an impresario could deliver, although the two thought Barnum shoddy and condescending, priding themselves on having appeared as sole attraction on dignified stages. Barnum himself detested their haughty independence but had experienced their appeal most intimately: his fast friend Rev. Edwin Chapin had for years referred to himself and Barnum as "Chang and Eng." Characters may have clashed, but both Chang-Eng and P.T. knew the draw of "the Tie that Binds."[19]

Advertised as "the living and breathing Siamese twins," now that youthful wax or plaster likenesses stood in many a museum, Chang in 1868 was visibly stooped, leaning against a wrinkled, greying Eng. Both were hard of hearing and, in photographs, grim of countenance. Would a bare bodkin relieve them of outrageous fortune or, nearing sixty, of life itself? Surgery to split conjoined twins usually ended with the death of one if not the pair. Ambidextrous Dr. Valentine Mott of Columbia University claimed he could undo the knot, but notable surgeons in England, Scotland, France, Germany, Austria, and Russia were dubious. Years ago it might have been possible, said some, but the twins were too old, Chang's blood vessels too weak. Publicity scheme or last-ditch effort, Chang-Eng cut short their European tour at the outbreak of the Franco-Prussian War in 1870 and took ship back to America, their band of flesh tragically intact.[20]

Seven days out from Liverpool, Chang had a stroke. He was paralyzed down the right side of his body. Over the next years, Eng became weakened by and short-tempered with this man he had to drag from place to place. Chang, whose favorite daughter had died in 1867, became despondent, vituperative, alcoholic. Eng, afraid that at Chang's demise he would find carrion on his back, begged local doctors to separate them immediately, which neither Joe Hollingsworth nor brother William would do; or to divide them instantly upon Chang's death, to which both physicians agreed.[21]

The scalpel would descend too late. Despite a bad bronchitis early in 1874, Chang refused to deviate from the rule of three-day stays at each household. On the frigid evening of January 15, Chang-Eng drove a mile and a half in an open buggy from Chang's home to Eng's. Friday night the 16th, Chang felt cold, had pains in his chest, was wheezy and restless, and could not sleep. Twice he roused Eng. They walked out onto the porch, drank some water, sat in the parlor before a fire. Eng, sleepy, grumbled about having to stay up. Chang said that "it would kill me to lie down," but around one they went back to bed. Eng slept, then woke at four feeling sick. He found Chang lifeless beside him and became alarmed. "I am dying," Eng said. In a cold sweat he twisted against the band and felt cramps in his arms. "The only notice he took of Chang was to move him nearer." He complained that he was choking. He fell into a stupor. His wife and children rubbed his limbs furiously, but before either Hollingsworth could reach him, Eng died.[22]

From horror. "Chang dying first from pulmonary pneumonia contracted by his intemperance and imprudent exposure... Eng his brother died in two hours after from fear and the sudden shock he received on awakening and finding his brother, instead of a breathing living soul, a cold and chilly corpse by his side. At least that is the explanation given by the distinguished and eminent physician of this place who attended them in their last illness," wrote a neighbor. To be exact, William Hollingsworth declared the cause of Eng's death "the great shock and terror inspired by such a union with death, added to which was the belief which prevailed between them that when one died the other would." Wrote a more distant neighbor, "The Siamese Twins are dead they died last month One died and the other one only lived 2 hours they say he was scared to death yes."[23]

"Nicely dressed in black with slippers," the two bodies were placed in a dry cellar. "We dare not bury their bodies," wrote Chang's daughter Nancy, "but have put them in a tin coffin lined with wood.... Dr. Joe says their bodies would not remain in the grave three nights if they were put there." Around the house it "was like a camp meeting so many people horses and carriages," wrote the tinsmith, and the Bunker families were right to fear the theft of Chang-Eng as valuable relics. A fortnight later, the widows gave permission for a partial autopsy, stipulating that Chang-Eng not be separated nor their band of flesh disfigured. Chang had died of a cerebral clot, not of pneumonia, concluded the Philadelphia pathologists, and "Eng probably died of fright, as the distended bladder seemed to point to a profound emotional disturbance of the nervous system." Reviewing the case in 1961, another clinician figured that Chang had died of atherosclerosis and heart failure, Eng of fright.[24]

You can see them yet, inside a glass case at the Mütter Museum of the College of Physicians of Philadelphia. Autopsy completed, Chang-Eng were embalmed and taken to be interred in White Plains, North Carolina, but casts of their bodies remain among bottles of tumors and the two heads of a bicephalic child who lived for thirteen months. As they had sheared their pigtails, traded tunics for frock coats, and converted from Buddhism to Baptism, so the white plaster makes them appear neither oriental nor occidental but, as they came to be, and are, generic.

Beside them, in a jar once filled with carbolic acid, rosemary flowers, and glycerine, float their livers, connected by a thin vascular string. Chang-Eng had been bound by more than tegument, after all; had the band been sundered, they would likely have died from bleeding or the cutting off of portal circulation. Omphelopagus Xiphodidymus, doublets united at navel and ensiform appendix, "They were not monsters," editorialized the *Lancet*, Britain's best medical journal, reporting the postmortem. "Chang and Eng were men. They were accidentally bound together in a living tie, it is true, but they were psychologically and, we may fairly say, physiologically distinct persons."[25]

Chang-Eng presented Western society with a finger puzzle. The more one tried to pull Chang from Eng, the more they tightened up. Mark Twain's "Personal Habits of the Siamese Twins" used finger puzzle humor: the more he exaggerated their differences, the more intricate seemed their bond. Eng fought on the side of the Union, Chang with the Rebels, grinned Twain; they captured each other at Seven Oaks then were forced to exchange prisoners. Where the modern definition of *humanity* was implicated, on one side, with the image of an independently rational *human being* and, on the other, with the *humane* sentiments of abolitionism and antivivisectionism, the Siamese Twins, rational but dependent, all-two-happily bound-for-life, were a horrible contradiction. "Chang is bitterly opposed to all forms of intemperance, on principle," Twain imagined; "but Eng is the reverse... every now and then, Eng gets drunk, and, of course, that makes Chang drunk too.... Yet all the while Chang's moral principles were unsullied, his conscience clear; and so all just men confessed that he was not morally, but only physically drunk." During an aggressive period of industrial capitalism, projected under the flags of national competition within an economic universe gusseted by telegraph cables and railroad ties, the Siamese Twins were at once a blatant anachronism (of village mutuality) and a close-fetched utopia (of union brotherhood, socialist cooperatives). They were indivisible but individual, and at the end, as they drew physically in upon one another, they grew emotionally apart. What happened to them was happening to the world beyond, which, as it shrank with quick news, seemed to be plagued with fits of (economic) depression, shortness of (political) temper, bursts of (military) anger. The Siamese Twins were no more monsters than other men and women of the nineteenth century who found themselves caught up in subtle, possibly fatal bonds.[26]

In which Ishmael found himself, in the seventy-second chapter of *Moby-Dick*. Queequeg, scrambling up a dead whale's back like a dancing ape on a cord, is secured by a "monkey-rope" attached between his waist and that of Ishmael his bowsman. "So that for better or for worse, we two, for the time, were wedded; and should poor Queequeg sink to rise no more, then both usage and honor demanded, that instead of cutting the cord, it should drag me down in his wake. So, then, an elongated Siamese ligature united us. Queequeg was my own inseparable twin brother; nor could I any way get rid of the dangerous liabilities which the hempen bond entailed." Thus far, a footnote, a fair analogy, and foreshadowing: Herman Melville's footnote, that only aboard the *Pequod* were monkey and holder tied together; fair analogy, to the ligature of Chang-Eng; foreshadowing, of the death of Ahab, lashed to the gashed white whale. But Ishmael is taken with the monkey-rope: "So strongly and metaphysically did I conceive of my situation then, that while earnestly watching his motions, I seemed distinctly to perceive that my own individuality was now merged in a joint stock company of two; that my free will had received a mortal wound; and that another's mistake or misfortune might plunge innocent me into unmerited disaster or death." He widens simile into synecdoche: "still further pondering, I say, I saw that this situation of mine was the precise situation of every mortal that breathes; only, in most cases, he, one way or other, has this Siamese connexion with a plurality of other mortals." A special case has become the general; Siamese twinship, no longer unique, is inescapable: "True, you may say that, by exceeding caution, you may possibly escape these and the multitudinous other evil chances of life. But handle Queequeg's monkey-rope heedfully as I would, sometimes he jerked it so, that I came very near sliding overboard. Nor could I possibly forget that do what I would, I only had the management of one end of it."[27]

Held at the other end is a tall black man, Queequeg the indecipherable, a top-hatted African whose bag of bones and gods can no more compass Ahab than the Calvinist Providence and scripture of Ishmael's New England ancestors. Queequeg and Ishmael are antipodal twins, one end of the earth bound to the other, black to white, pagan to Christian, as sternly opposed a pair as Twain had made of Chang-Eng, and loners both. The legend of the vanishing twin concerns a regretfully lost and companionate life, identical and reassuring; Siamese twins, configured by modern notions of the true self as independent and freely willed, evoke the terror of an antithetical, unshakeable double.

Opposing Ends
Lately, surgeons have become adept at dividing conjoined twins – much too adept, complained a carnival manager in 1980: "Odd and unusual freak attractions are literally dying out.... Siamese twins are separated. Extra fingers and toes are removed right after birth." Until recently, however, a succession of true and false ("gaffed") Siamese twins have

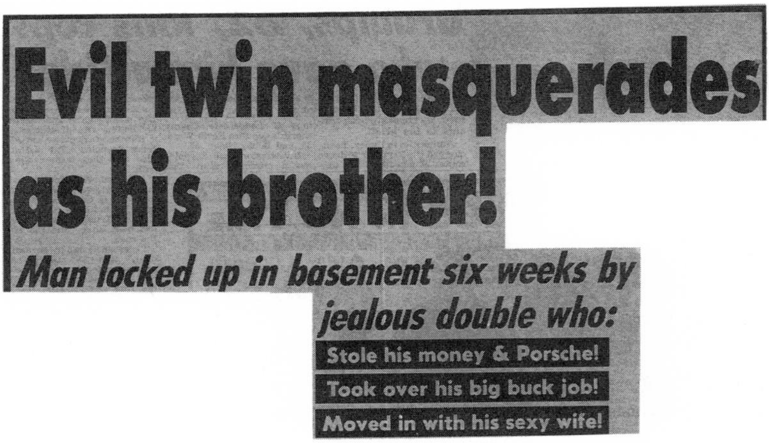

Evil twin masquerades as his brother!

Man locked up in basement six weeks by jealous double who:

Stole his money & Porsche!

Took over his big buck job!

Moved in with his sexy wife!

FIGURE 2.3. Headline from the *Weekly World News* (February 13, 1990). Reproduced by permission.

tested the limits and double meanings of *humanity*. Chang-Eng themselves toured with the teenage Carolina Nightingale, Millie-Christine, born back-to-back into slavery in 1851, two heads, four arms, four legs, and one torso on stage since the age of fifteen months, when she "began to talk with both her mouths," then singing sweet duets in soprano and contralto and, twisted toward each other, whirling in high spirits. "She is, or They are, certainly an anomaly," wrote Carolina State Senator Leander S. Gash, himself raising twin daughters in 1866. "The Siamese Twins are nowhere when compared to this double Negro," for Millie-Christine, though "two perfect persons from about the middle of the back up," could obviously never be separated. "Those who saw the Siamese twins," reported an English newspaper in 1870, "will have a vivid recollection of the pained look that their features bore, and the constrained movement of their bodies when they walked in any direction. There is a total absence of this in the [graceful] young lady," who was such a good draw that she was abducted and fought over by owners, promoters, a woman claiming to be her mother, and her actual slave mother, until she was free at last to be a "coloured individual," earning enough to retire in 1891 to a ten-room house built on the site of the plantation where she had been born. When the mansion burned down in 1909, she lived on in a cottage, speaking in a collective first person despite the old slander that Millie was a Baptist fundamentalist, Christine a good-time girl. In October 1912, Millie passed away. Singing hymns, Christine succumbed seventeen hours later. Their gravestone reads,

A soul with two thoughts;
Two hearts that beat as one.[28]

She died, as did Chang-Eng, in North Carolina. As would, by coincidence, the Hilton sisters Violet and Daisy, joined at the base of the spine. They had been, most of their lives, pawns: gifts to the midwife by their British mother who died in childbirth, 1908; exhibits at an Edinburgh wax museum, 1909, and at German circuses, 1912; talented minors singing their way across Europe, Asia, and America, in bondage to abusive managers who earned two million dollars from them; dual saxophonists on the Loew vaudeville circuit, 1920–30s; subjects of scientific experiments for discordance, 1927; controversial brides (bigamists?), 1936, 1941, soon divorced; doomed stars in *Chained for Life*, a film of passion and murder which made them out to be deadly opposites, 1950; owners of a Miami hamburger stand serving meals "on the double," 1955. They were stranded in Charlotte by another devious manager after a guest appearance in 1962 at a drive-in theater showing *Freaks*. They became clerks in the produce section of a supermarket, with a short stint promoting potato chips in twin-packs. When they died of the flu in 1969, sixty mourners attended services at Purcell United Methodist Church. Few came to gawk.[29]

Conjoined twins are disappearing, and amidst such praise for the surgeons that new ethical dilemmas face parents: "Siamese twins: killing one to save the other." The pressure to cleave them is not narrowly medical; it is broadly cultural. We resist evidence of their companionate relations because the Siamese alliance seems in so many (cinematic) ways unseemly: involuntary (*Chained for Life*); melancholic (*Freaks*); incestuous (even the "foxy vixen twins" Saber and Raquel, *Joined* by Mother Nature and sharing everything "including each other," must in Part Two be *Separated* to "enjoy sex-filled lives on their own"); mutually fatal (*Dead Ringers*). Our fictions allege, with some psychologists, that "Like bookends, conjoined twins remain fixed at opposing ends of a single continuum." John Barth's "Petition" of 1969 comes from a twin fastened belly to the small of his brother's back "by a leash of flesh heartbreakingly short. In consequence [my brother] never lays eyes on the wretch he forever drags about – no wonder he denies me, agrees with the doctors that such a union is impossible, and claims my utterance and inspiration for his own!" They must be separated; they must. "I, lifelong victim of his beastliness, he calls the monkey on his back!"[30]

It is the monkey-rope of Siamese twinship, rather than the papyrus of the vanishing twin, that entails an opposed and deadly consort. True, twins are never perfectly identical, and one is usually dominant. True, each of the two is nursed and reared differently by mothers, no matter how valiant the attempt at maternal equity, no matter the guilt and ambivalence – which in extremis can lead to parental projection of positive qualities onto one twin, negative onto the other. "Some parents call us when their children are as young as four days old," says the director of Twin Services in Berkeley, "and say that they already know which one is the 'bad' one." Yet dark twins become fateful only when they assume a Siamesed aspect: **Evil twin masquerades as his brother!** "Jealous Nicolas Klein stole his twin brother's life." **Stole his money & Porsche! Took over his big buck job! Moved in with his sexy wife!** or, "Inseparable as kids, their paths divided as they grew up," until now **MY EVIL TWIN WANTS TO KILL ME!**[31]

Lest we be inclined to dismiss such bombast, we must be alert to evil twinships that intrude even upon such academic works as David Crouch's *The Beaumont Twins: The Roots and Branches of Power in the Twelfth Century*. Waleran, the elder, with twin Robert, were equal heirs to Count Robert of Meulan, whose lands were divided equally between them, yet "In the end the twin aristocrats came to personify the two faces of medieval magnate power. Waleran was a magnate at his worst... unreasonably ambitious and dangerously powerful.... Robert was a magnate of the best sort: capable and judicious."[32] Crouch's bisection is not gratuitous. It refers back to a dangerously powerful Esau, the elder, and a capable Jacob. It sustains a classical need for rhetorical balance. But its bite is that of a double-headed monster, two ruling powers with, originally, a single territory.

So we can appreciate the bite of the *The Dark Half* (1993), a horror film about three other sets of Beaumont Twins, the twin daughters of two-sided Chad Beaumont, mild-mannered teacher of creative writing and, as George Stark, author of lucrative novels about a psychopathic killer. The third set of twins? Chad and his fetally absorbed brother — uncovered when brain surgery for throbbing headaches yields an eye and teeth from a twin long gone. Or is he? When Chad decides to end his career as George, the pseudonym will not be so peremptorily cut away. Stark begins to stalk Beaumont, his wife, and twin daughters. Is the Siamesed George perhaps "the spirit of the twin who never accepted his fatal fetal absorption?" The dark half, the evil twin, returns with a starker edge in our culture of the copy as we begin to fear that we are losing track of ourselves.[33]

Two Heads, Two Bodies

Only a *Man without Qualities* could be sufficiently not himself to freely take on a Siamese twin. In the third volume (1932) of Robert Musil's Austrian novel, Ulrich goes to meet his married sister Agathe, five years younger, whom he last saw ages ago. To their surprise, they have dressed alike. "I didn't know we were twins!" exclaims Agathe, who becomes Ulrich's co-conspirator, stealing the medals from their father's corpse, replacing them with replicas. Then she becomes his "self-love," a "certain tender relationship to oneself that seems to come naturally to most other people" and must come to the selfless Ulrich through another. Says Ulrich, "The point is that nobody knows which of all the halves at large in the world is his own missing half." Unless they are Siamesed. Siamese twins, though always of the same sex, are born with palms that mirror each other, right to left, left to right. "It goes back a very long way," continues Ulrich, "this desire for a Doppelgänger of the oppo-

FIGURE 2.4. Identical Twins as Doppelgängers. Advertisement, 1991. Reproduced by permission of the Suzuki-America Motor Corporation.

site sex, this craving for the love of a being that will be entirely the same as oneself and yet another, distinct from oneself." When Agathe urges that they disport themselves as Siamese twins, Ulrich wonders what it must be like to be physically Siamesed. "He conjectured that every agitation in the one psyche must also be felt by the other." They must "join forces" toward a devout incest.[34]

Doppelgängers were christened at the end of the eighteenth century in the novels of Jean Paul Richter. They are "double-goers," mirror-twisted twins without whom the other has neither past nor future, yet in whose present and presence tragedy must ensue. Every agitation of the one psyche is felt by the other. The gothic horror and romantic terror of the Doppelgänger is the horror and terror of a Siamesed bond: a life contravening yours, but its fate your fate. William Godwin traced the bond in 1794 in *Things as They Are, or The Adventures of Caleb Williams*: "Man is like those twin-births, that have two heads indeed, and four hands; but if you attempt to detach them from each other, they are inevitably subjected to miserable and lingering destruction."[35]

Titular Councilor Yakov Petrovich Golyadkin has met his match and his fate in "a different Mr. Golyadkin, completely different but at the same time absolutely identical..., so that if one were to take them and place them side by side, no one, absolutely no one, would have taken it upon himself to determine just who was the real Golyadkin and who the counterfeit, who the old and who the new, who the original and who the copy." A compatriot at work sees the resemblance, asks if Golyadkin has heard of "what do they call them? Oh, yes, Siamese twins. Their backs are attached to one another and they live like that, and eat and sleep together. People say they get big money."[36]

Fyodor Dostoevsky was writing *The Double* in 1845, for small change, after fifteen years of news about Chang-Eng and fifty years of Doppelgängers, during which period European authors transformed the old Scandinavian and Slavic Double from a shape-shifting figure of divine protection to a spectral presentiment of disaster. The Doppelgänger was incubus to the romantic soul, which exulted over and devoured its self. Poets like Novalis and novelists like Ludwig Tieck contemplated a world that was the construct of a transcendent self – or was it the self that was constructed by a world we cannot fully know? The Double was vertiginous, oneself and not oneself, like that fabulist who wrote incessantly of Doubles and whose identically named state official, E.T.A. Hoffmann, led a second life.[37]

Mr. Golyadkin the Second, busiest of bodies, a false friend, cannot be kept at a distance. He calls Golyadkin "brother," then cozens Golyadkin out of his state job, the copying of documents. The Titular Councilor gets mired in the making of dubious distinctions. "Well, what a marvel and what a strange thing; they say that Siamese twins.... Well, but why bring them in, the Siamese ones? So they are twins, but after all even great people have sometimes looked like eccentrics." Which is how Golyadkin will look, "annihilated," shamed by Golyadkin II.[38]

Dreams Golyadkin, in Dostoevsky's rewrite of 1866, shortly before Chang-Eng toured Russia: "with every thud of his foot against the granite of the pavement there would spring up, out of the ground, an exact likeness of the repulsive Mr. Golyadkin with his corruptness of heart. And all of these exact likenesses, immediately upon making their appearances, began running one after the other and stretched out in a long chain like a string of geese, waddling after Mr. Golyadkin Senior, so that there was nowhere to escape to from these exact likenesses." Nor can William Wilson escape from a whispering, admonitory William Wilson in Edgar Allan Poe's story of two William Wilsons born on the same day (January 19, Poe's birthday), "singularly alike in general contour," one the conscience to the other. Golyadkin tries to be the good conscience, penning a letter to Golyadkin the Corrupt, "Either you or I, but not the two of us! And therefore I am declaring to you that your strange, ludicrous and at the same time impossible desire to seem to be my twin and to pass yourself off as such will only lead to your utter dishonor and defeat."[39]

Which kind of self-defeating Double is this sinister twin, Golyadkin the Corrupt? A ghostlike self out of the past? The worse but seductive half of a self struggling to mature in the present? An unearthly self from the dreamtime, the future? Golyadkin II is the second, projection of the Titular Councilor's thwarted ambitions, his obsessions with honor and the extension of himself. He is the present *tensed*, a Double to whom Golyadkin is fatally Siamesed. "Here's a man perishing," Golyadkin panics; "here's a man losing sight of himself."[40]

Finally, as in stories by Dostoevsky's predecessor, Antony Pogorelsky, the Double himself becomes the staunch materialist, advocate of civility and exactness against uproar and ambiguity. Running beside the coach into which an unstable Golyadkin has been thrust, he sends "little farewell kisses" to the Titular Councilor, who sits twitching across from his calm old friend the doctor – "only not the previous one! this is another Krestyan Ivanovich!" – physician to those who are not themselves.[41]

Where there be two heads and two bodies, bound and counterposed, fact or fable, that way lies dis/grace and the asylum. Dis/grace: when the Double is a criminal, as law texts were wont to report of Capt. Atkins (d. 1811), who "had a double of this kind, that was the torment of his life; for this double was a swindler, who, having discovered the lucky fac-simileship, obtained goods, took up money, and at last married a wife in [Atkins's] name." Later in the century would appear Doubles of ambassadors, actresses, captains of industry – "human replicas. Nobody wants them, and the unfortunate who knows he has a 'double' somewhere by no means rejoices in the knowledge; or cares to be brought into contact with his counterfeit presentiment." The asylum: when the contact *is* made, as by Guy de Maupassant, whose heroes would marry to escape their shadow ("Lui," 1883) or burn down a house haunted by a figure obscuring their image in mirrors ("Le Horla," 1887), and who himself would confess, "Every other time when I return home,

I see my double. I open the door and see myself sitting in the armchair."
Hallucinating, de Maupassant died in an asylum in 1893 as another fin
de siècle wave of Doppelgängers washed through European fiction.[42]

One Head, Two Bodies

Where there be one head and two bodies, that way lies theater. For centuries, European performers had been struggling to inhabit a second
body. In 1536, for example, those of Bourges presenting a mystery play
were applauded as "sage men, who knew so well how to feign through
signs and gestures the characters they were representing that most of
the audience thought the whole thing real and not feigned." At issue,
of course, is how each society or era reconceives, and represents, the
naturally human. During the eighteenth century, actor-directors like
Aaron Hill in England began to demand a consistent stage presence, dis-
paraging those "who between their speeches relax into an absent unat-
tentiveness...looking round and examining the company of spectators."
Actors should stay in character, which implied absorption: on canvases
or on stage, figures had to be so "completely caught up" in their roles
that awareness of audience lapsed. As dramaturge, Denis Diderot insisted "that representations of action, gesture, and facial expression actually convey what they ostensibly signify." His principles of acting – *Unité*
of effect, *Naïveté* of feeling, *Instantanéité* of expression, *Oubli* (obliviousness) of spectators – were the principles of a *UNIO mystica*, the mystical union of one head and two bodies.[43]

But the passions driving each character were thought to be isolated
states, and onstage each passion – united in effect, feeling, and expression – was delivered discretely. Diderot's *UNIO* led not to the "grad-
ual unfolding of a personality" but to a series of *tableaux vivants*, group
poses held in striking likenesses of familiar paintings or literary scenes.[44]

Tableaux vivants spread from the French stage of the 1760s to aristocratic little theaters across the Continent, then to English drawing
rooms and American parlors. "Something indescribably weird and witch-
ing" there was about a good tableau, like "Waiting for the Verdict": outside a courthouse, every face wears "a look of strained anxiety"; at the
center of the group sits a woman, hands clasped over knees, bonnet
hanging around her neck, hair disordered, eyes wild with misery. In all
cases, "The great requirement on the part of the performer is...to
remain perfectly still – a feat which may be acquired to a wonderful
degree by practising before a mirror."[45]

Tableaux vivants were the special domain of those who regularly sat
before mirrors. In the same manner that women accomplished the com-
posure demanded of them, they practiced before looking glasses those
dramatics otherwise denied them in public. Anne Boleyn's "whole attitude expresses repugnance and refusal – head turned aside, left hand
raised to screen her eyes from the glare of the jewels, and right hand
extended with vertical gesture." Rehearsing such attitudes, integrating
them with a set of operatic gestures designed by François Delsarte in

FIGURE 2.5. *La Belle Marlène B.* by Cesario Rachador. Electrographic postcard, 1986. Reproduced courtesy Cesario Rachador.

the 1840s, Victorian women would express at once the freedoms they had on their minds, the passions they felt within, and the outward stillness society expected: two bodies and one mind, one soul.[46]

Emma, Lady Hamilton, hair loose, cashmere shawls wafting about an uncorseted body, was hardly still. Dancing in her private theater in Naples, she sent Goethe himself into transports of delight with her embodiments of classical statues. He who would satirize the static narcissism of tableaux vivants was genuinely moved by Emma's lithe progression from one attitude to the next. These *poses plastiques* of the late eighteenth century shared with the ballets of Jean-Georges Noverre a revolutionary impulse to "Smash the hideous masks, burn the ridiculous wigs, get rid of the awkward hoops," and end an ancien regime of mechanical gestures. Noverre's ballets, however, had been conducted in royal apartments with stately emotions and "regulated" motions. *Poseurs* on the outskirts of formal theater, like Henriette Hendel-Schütz in Germany and Andrew Ducrow in England, practiced that emotional fluidity we now find crucial to the convincing assumption of a theatrical role. An observer of "animated statues" in Dublin in 1828 wrote that Ducrow's act "far surpasses the 'Tableaux' which are in such favor on the continent." From fighting to fallen to dying gladiator, Ducrow "quitted his attitude from one gradation to another, of display of strength; but at the moment in which he presented a perfect copy of the most celebrated statues of antiquity, he suddenly became fixed as if changed to marble."[47]

Yet Ducrow was also disdained as a puppet jerked by unknown hands, and Goethe said that Lady Hamilton "lacked soul." Word was made Flesh more smoothly in mime. Denied spoken Words, performers on the Boulevard du Crime in Paris had made the most of Flesh, with buffoonery and acrobatics, with large and largely sexual or scatalogical gestures. Under eighteenth-century decrees of total silence or of nonsensical speech, French actors excluded from royal troupes had two choices: pulling the strings of eloquent marionettes or joining in a gallimaufry of grunts and grimaces, unspeakable as the Wild Boy of Aveyron, from whose life would be drawn the first successful stage melodrama. German playwright Heinrich von Kleist would have chosen the puppets. They, at least, put on no airs, wrote Kleist in 1801 (ten years before he and a lover, of one mind, committed double suicide). Self-consciousness, explained Kleist, would not obstruct a puppet's expression of its role or the grace of its limbs, moved from above by puppeteers who had to imagine themselves (one mind, two bodies) at the center of gravity of the wooden creatures.[48]

Soon there would be a figure of flesh and sinew who put on no airs, who moved not to and from but through emotions, and whose center of gravity was sustained, some said, from on high. When Jean-Gaspard Deburau made his entrance as Pierrot in black skullcap, white pantaloons and blouse, an admiring critic, Jules Janin, described Deburau as "an impervious stoic who gives way, mechanically, to all the impressions of the moment." That was a Kleistian compliment. "Mechanically" meant automatically, unreservedly, unrehearsedly. "Actor without passion, without speech, and almost without face, he says everything, expresses everything, mocks everything."[49]

Puffery aside, Deburau was certainly other than the swaggering valet Piero, chickenhearted bully of Italian harlequinades, and leagues apart from those with whom he shared the Théâtre des Funambules: axfighters, vaulters, physiognomists who contorted facial muscles to signify in rapid sequence rage joy sadness madness petition and prayer. "Far from adopting the tedious self-importance of those comedians who stop to underline each of their gestures," wrote another admirer, "Deburau on the boards acted as if he were involved in real life and had persuaded himself that he was going through everyday motions." Born into a family of tumblers and ropewalkers, Deburau moved with an acrobat's center of gravity and smoothly secured transitions, but his forte was doubleness: mockery, hypocrisy, shy bravado. He never stood aside from his second body.[50]

Silence was not the crux; rather, seamlessness. Deburau worked in a noisy world, cheered by hoi polloi shouting from the cheap balcony seats called "Paradise." He admitted to his plays sound effects, songs, and some dialogue. What silence remained was that of the unpointed transit between Deburau and Pierrot. No matter the interruptions from Paradise, on stage there was little breach between the mime and his second body. The fussy collar that had in the past guarded a player's head (and mind) from the character's heart (and body) was gone.[51]

When Deburau died gasping from asthma in 1846, he had given no lessons to his son and successor, Charles the utterly silent. With the too-worshipful stance of his son and subsequent caretakers, Pierrot became stylized and stiff, until mime had again to be reinvented around 1910 – in the theater and school of Jacques Copeau and Suzanne Bing, and from under the lights of Gordon Craig. Craig, like Kleist, sought an actor-puppet or *Über-Marionette*, for that which human actors give us, emotions ever in the way, "is a series of accidental confessions." One of the new mimes, Etienne Decroux, would "personally wish for the birth of this actor made of wood.... It must inspire terror and pity and, from there, rise to the level of a waking dream." Another of the new mimes, Jean-Louis Barrault, reflected upon a "problem that always stirs me to the depths: *the problem of the double*," a problem endemic to theater. "In man there is a double position: the first one is real, visible, palpable; the second is impalpable, only apprehended, present, yes, but invisible – that is the double.... The human being that [theater] brings to life on the stage is, in fact, *as double as he can be*."[52]

Because, in the best and worst of times, he is Siamesed. Barrault had become a mime upon the premise that "There is no actor who can act convincingly with his own genuine emotion. Hence actors who want to play by their emotions are obliged to invent a false one." Disciplined movements evolving from the gut were safer, for they did not risk the painful discontinuity between person and persona that was the threat of the Doppelgänger. "The more difficult the play the more the actor, behind his Character, should husband his own sincerity, for the risk of the Character being found wanting in 'authenticity' is greater." Was this bad faith? Barrault wondered aloud (with Jean-Paul Sartre) in 1941, shortly before he and Decroux mimed an homage to Deburau in a film of nineteenth-century bohemian life featuring *Les Enfants du Paradis*, the unruly "children" of "Paradise."[53]

To take on double roles, each body moved by its own center of gravity, and yet the same sincere mind at work inside both, this were thespian heaven.[54] Not to reveal that each of the two bodies is ruled by a single mind, this were the hell of bad faith, of imposture.

Imposture is never far from theater. Whether impostors are ceaselessly living out "an oedipal conflict through revival of the earliest definite image of the father" or working toward reality through a family romance in which they merit and receive the mother's love, their drama is seamlessness. Call it "non-ego ego" and despair of any therapeutic transference; call it "narcissism" and despair of any expression of true inner feelings. Either way, imposture is the incessant Siamesing of one's life. It is compulsive, it feeds upon itself, it is unrepentant.[55]

Compulsive: *Memoirs of a Social Monster; or, the History of Charles Price, otherwise Bolingbroke, otherwise Johnson, otherwise Parks, otherwise Wigmore, otherwise Brank, otherwise Wilmott, otherwise Williams, otherwise Schutz, otherwise Polton, otherwise Taylor, otherwise Powel, &c. &c. &c. and commonly called OLD PATCH,* "who piled as many schemes upon schemes as there were stones in the tower of Babel" and who hanged himself in jail, denying everything.[56]

Feeding upon itself: about to masquerade as a French servant named Caraboo, a young woman was taken for a Sumatran princess, a title she came to relish. With patrons clamoring to fête her, she pretended to "Hindoostanic" vegetarianism and the worship of Allah Tallah. Through gesture and gibberish she unfolded a story of seizure by pirates while strolling about her gardens at Javasu, of sale to the Captain of the *Tappa Boo,* and so rhyming forth until set adrift in England. Which last was correct, since she was (probably) Mary Willcocks, alias Baker, born in Devonshire in 1791, teenage vagabond, beggar in men's clothing, common-law wife to a man with supposed Malay connections. Accosted with facts (?) about her origins, she confessed but insisted that she had spent time in Bombay, and "more than once expressed a wish, that the tale might be dramatized; and nothing, she said, would have given her greater pleasure, than to have acted the part of Caraboo!" Forcibly retired, she died in 1865 in Bristol, "but there was a kind of grim humour in the occupation which she followed with much credit to herself and satisfaction to her customers. She became an importer of leeches."[57]

Unrepentant: *The Life of William Fuller, by original a butcher's son, by education a coney-wool-cutter, … by vote of Parliament an impostor, by title of his own making a colonel, and by his own demerits a prisoner at the Fleet* in 1701, and a self-disclosed spy, an Anglican, a Catholic, an apostate, a renegade Protestant hoping to persuade others he was yet Catholic. And an avowed double agent: in this too, Fuller was fool of himself.[58]

Repetitive, recursive, inveterate, foolhardy, imposture wears the mask of infernal comedy. Consider the devilish farce of George Psalmanazar, birthplace and baptismal name to this day unknown, hacking around Europe under Japanese papers, who between 1704 and 1711 reinvented himself and the island of Formosa, its customs, language, and rituals. Later he ran an English pharmacy, taught the art of fortification, clerked for a regiment of dragoons, sold fan paintings, and in 1728 converted (again) to Christianity, abetted in imposture by Rev. William Innes, a plagiarist who that year would publish as his own work a friend's treatise on *Moral Virtue.* To the last, Psalmanazar kept his pseudo-Assyrian name because, he said, he deserved no other fate than to be remembered as an impostor. He ended his days defending biblical miracles and writing articles on geography wherein he denounced his earlier "romances," still cited as authoritative sources on Formosa many years after his death in 1763.[59]

Impostures succeed because, not in spite, of their fictitiousness. They take wing with congenial cultural fantasies. Impostors persevere because any fear they may have of being discovered is overshadowed by their dread of being alone. Their perpetual reincarnations of second bodies arise out of a *horror vacui*, terror of empty spaces within and without. Manic, they are always beside themselves. They brook contradictions far more breezily than they can break with a Siamesed life.

Flash photography nor fingerprinting nor videotape brings impostors full stop. In a world of proliferant degrees and diplomas, impostors have more room than ever to move on from one half-life to the next. These days embossed papers substitute for personhood, identification cards for identity, licenses for learning, all of which were used by Stanley Clifford Weyman to establish himself as a lawyer, physician, naval officer, and the Roumanian consul general. Caught and jailed, he studied penology; upon release he showed up outside Sing Sing as an expert in prison reform.[60] At last, night manager of a motel, Weyman resisted a stickup and was killed in 1961.

That year, Tony Curtis starred in *The Great Impostor*, the true-lives film not of Weyman but of Ferdinand Waldo Demara, Jr., a man who said, "Every time I take a new identity, some part of the real me dies, whatever the real me is." Denied entry into the Trappist order after two years as a young novice, Demara became an itinerant ascetic. He shed his identity as a high school dropout to clothe himself in the robes of university professors and psychologists, a Royal Canadian Navy surgeon, a certified public accountant, a prison reformer, a teacher of the mentally retarded, and a member of "more Catholic orders and institutions than any Roman Catholic alive today." The quotation is from a biography published in 1959, when Demara was thirty-eight, in mid-career. Afterward, regardless of the biography and Hollywood celebrity, Demara under versions of his own baptismal name founded a New Life (!) Youth Ranch for delinquent boys, served as a Baptist pastor in Oregon, labored as a postulant at an interfaith monastery in Missouri, acted as pastor to a Conservative Baptist congregation in Washington State, and worked as a religious counselor at the Good Samaritan Hospital near Disneyland. "At first I was very skeptical," said a hospital co-worker, "but he sort of grows on you." The press seems to have lost sight of him after 1978, when he was fifty-seven. Has he since gone through another fifty-seven varieties of faith?[61]

Faith is a peculiar word to attach to those who violate our affections, yet it is we who expose them. Imposture is not imposture until its duplicity is laid bare, and when impostors persist, treading in their own footsteps, they are not deranged but faithful to a lifelong project that oscillates toward the spiritual. Although names and bodies change to project each fantasy, the head is true, as sensible to its lackluster singleness as to its need for the numinous unity of two-in-one. This is a good

description of the emotional state of the religious seeker, and a perfect prescription for religious conversion as we find it in the lives of
Psalmanazar, Demara – and Trebitsch Lincoln. Born of Jewish parents
in Hungary in 1879, Ignácz Trebitsch was a would-be actor, actual journalist, flimflam Christian convert, actual missionary, silent Member of
Parliament, fluent confidence man, World War I double agent spurned
by both sides, actual tutor to the son of a Chinese general, self-devised
Buddhist advance-man Anagarika Pukkusati "the Homeless One," and
truly ordained monk Chao Kung "The Venerable," the twelve spokes
of the Wheel of Becoming verily tattooed upon his skull. From Shanghai in 1939, he appealed for world peace, a peace to be assured by a
tribunal of Tibetan sages.[62]

Fastening upon the Western cultural fantasy of a restored faith – in
divinity, miracle, revelation, reincarnation – impostors this century
descend from the Himalayas or similar aeries as gurus, healers, psychologists, and personal trainers. Impostors who in their seamlessness have
subtly modeled faith and who in their inevitable betrayals have modeled
faithlessness now teach us, by positive precept and negative example,
how to believe in ourselves as something other than impostors.[63]

I distinguish here between imposture, the compulsive assumption
of invented lives, and impersonation, the concerted assumption of
another's public identity. Impersonators may lose themselves in their
roles, but their second bodies are rarely so intransigently bound to their
first. They may keep faith with the King, who had a stillborn twin, and
say that any dedicated Elvis impersonator "has to eat, sleep, feel and
act like the King," but they know more surely than any impostor that
after all is sung and danced, "you can't be Elvis!" Ever fearful of detection or defensive of reputation, impersonators labor against the odds
of archives, eyewitnesses, and competing claimants. An impostor lives
within lyric opera, weightless as the very generic figure of a modern
major (*alias Major Harrold, Major Maxwell, Major Grant, Major Cunningham, Major Winter, &c. &c. &c.*). An impersonator lives under the heavy
impress of historical biography: physicist Julius Ashkin writes to Marvin
Hewitt alias Julius Ashkin, asking Hewitt to resign his impersonation:
"I should then be willing to help you to relieve yourself of what must
have become an almost unbearable burden."[64]

Almost unbearable. For the advantages of wealth, title, love, or sheer
celebrity, impersonators have emerged out of thick air. They have stead-
fastly maintained their claims to being the (safely) shipwrecked heir
Roger Tichborne, the (casual) casualty Martin Guerre, the (un)murdered
brother-in-law Russell Colvin, the (nearly) executed Princess Anastasia.
The best impersonators, however, like the best double agents, are those
we know not of. When, during World War I, a U.S. judge decided a
case of plagiarism between a play and a novel about espionage, he noted
that "This war [has] added a new class of spies to fiction, and some say
to real life. Persons supposed to have been kindly and inoffensive, it
seems, are spies. . . . It is a sad revelation."[65]

Double agency, implying a singleminded performance of two opposed roles with silent devotion to a cause, is the impersonator's stock in trade. An impostor may be an abbot, a knight, a general in Morocco, an innkeeper in Denmark, a postmaster in Bohemia, an ambassador in Belgium, a doctor in England, a coachman in Sweden, a dentist in Italy, and a thief to boot, as was Jean Frollo in the 1700s,[66] but impostors are unable to bear the burdens of double agency. Impersonation, not imposture, is at home with quiet deceit and may breed underground. Both may be impeccably costumed, yet in the final dressing down, impostors want attention and love, and we betray them; impersonators want our money, our secrets, our family line, and they betray us.

The Quick Change

Dressmaker by trade, Mme M. during World War I added a new class of delusions to paranoid fictions and to real life – *l'illusion des sosies*. Sosia was servant to princely Amphitryon, who accidentally killed his uncle, King Electryon, to whose daughter Alcmene he was betrothed. In Plautus's aside to a cruel tale of blood guilt, Amphitryon is off at war when Mercury impersonates Sosia while Zeus, impersonating the prince, impregnates Alcmene, who will bear dioscuric twins, Iphicles by her human husband, Hercules by her divine seducer. *Sosie* became the French for Double and Mme M.'s term for all the Doubles she saw around her in 1914.

Like Alcmene, Mme M. had borne twins. Marrying in 1898, she gave birth the next year to a singleton, then was delivered of a pair of girls in 1903, a pair of boys in 1906. To her grief, four of the five children died very young. Unnerved, Mme M. began to believe that she herself was a changeling; switched at birth, she was really Princess Mathilde de Rio-Branco, Argentine heiress. Foreign adventurers who knew her true identity must have kidnapped her babies, substituting unbreathing doubles. War on the horizon, Mme M. found that enemies had stolen away her one surviving child, sending a platoon of young *sosies* to stand in the daughter's stead. For the duration of the Great War, a girl in the guise of the twin daughter would appear each day or hour and be replaced by a different pretender the next. Mme M. warned the authorities that beneath the streets of Paris lay cellars in which were to be found more than two thousand of these missing children as well as the eighty *sosies* of her husband, who had been murdered years ago or who "if in any event he is my husband, is more than unrecognizable, he has been totally transformed."[67]

Countless others were being lost or transformed, declared Mme M., and all underground. Regiments descending into the Métro disappeared. In the tunnels, other soldiers were being disfigured as if they had been to the front, itself a fraud, a battle of blanks. And if the subterranean world was a catacomb of hoaxes, aboveground her maids, her concierge, the constabulary belonged to a society of *sosies*, as did attendants in the Maison-Blanche, the asylum where Mme M. reigned when war was

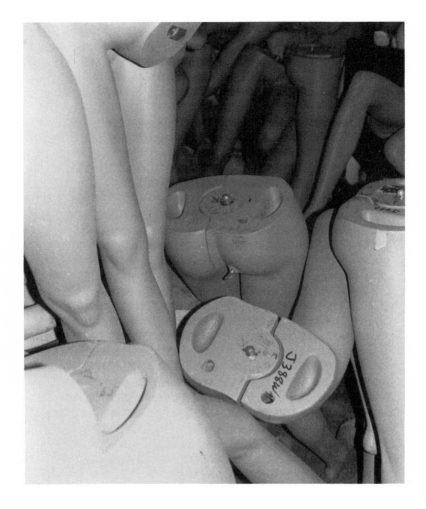

FIGURE 2.6. Mannequin legs with visible connections, Van Calvin Manikin Restoration Studio, Portland, OR. Photo by Linda M. Strauss.

done. There, she scrupulously described herself as singular, for any *sosie* of her could never be as elegant as she herself in her well-dressed fifties. She had, however, counted fifteen Doubles of the supervising physician, Jean Marie Joseph Capgras.[68]

Capgras presented a paper on her case at the asylum in 1923. Mme M. interrupted the discussion with a grand entrance after which she exploded his analysis, expanded upon her fortunes, and expounded upon *sosies*. It made no difference: the new syndrome would be named not after her, the persistent patient, but after him, the perceptive doctor, Capgras, chair of the Société Médico-Psychologique. Earlier, Capgras had co-authored a book on chronic delusions such as *fausses reconnaissances*, the mistaking of different people as identical. Mme M., conversely, mistook the same familiar persons for a series of impersonators. Her sense of their strangeness was due to guilt and anguish over recurrent loss. So many loved ones having vanished (and the war snatching up and changing the costume of so many others, drilling boys into lookalike soldiers), her greatest fear was that the rest would disappear. In her infinite scrutiny of daughter and husband, she could not be certain that they were exactly as she had known them. Desperate to hold on to those who survived, she lost them to a memory of what they had been when they were safe and she was sure. "A little mark on the ear, a slightly thinner figure, a longer moustache, a different shade to the color of the eyes" gave away the masquerade. This was, concluded Capgras, son of a civil engineer, a disorder of exactitude.[69]

More precisely, it was a disease of *chronic* exactitude, of double time. Each of us must admit that we are slightly older, slightly different each day. In social intercourse we allow for disruptions of mood and appetite, affect and demeanor, presuming an inner continuity by which we recognize friends regardless of fashions, frustrations, wrinkles, worries. The greater the exactitude of feature and character demanded of people over time, the more likely they will come to resemble "diverse apparitions of the same individual," Doubles each a little off the original. Mme M. and Mme H. (another case written up in 1923) could accept their own timeliness and aging, but not that of their loved ones, whose features and characters had to be set in what to us must seem unreasonably permanent detail. All other appearances of their loved ones could only be facsimiles, never the real thing. There was the pinch: to be protected under such strict tolerances, loved ones had to be unchanging objects, real *things*.[70]

Jacques Vié, Capgras's student, suggested that Mathilde de Rio-Branco's delusion was a vital defense against the loss of psychic integrity.[71] She had made the least painful of three choices to explain the absence of her loved ones: either her loved ones had changed beyond recognition and were no longer those whom she loved and who loved her; or she had so changed that she was no longer herself and all mutual bonds were broken; or doubles were impersonating her loved ones, whom they had kidnapped or killed. Everywhere she looked, in the years leading through the Great War, the seams of family life and national identity were unhappily jagged or torn. It was up to her to maintain a personal seamlessness.

Seamlessness was equally the ambition of the finest of impersonators during Mme M.'s time, Lepoldo Fregoli, who transmuted in the wink of an eye from man to woman, bass to soprano, in 650 theaters from Moscow and Paris to Manhattan and Buenos Aires. Son of the majordomo of a palazzo in Rome, Lepoldo was an aspiring musician but was apprenticed to a watchmaker. At sixteen he abandoned the profession but not the skill required to order those imperceptible transitions we call time. By twenty he was involved in shows imitating the Spiritualist acts of the Davenports, magicians with a penchant for disappearing and reappearing. Entertaining his fellow soldiers on an island in the Red Sea in 1887, Fregoli did his first theatrical solo, creating *Camaleonte*, Chameleon, who was one and then another famous person. By 1896 Fregoli had his own troupe, Compagnie Fin de Siècle, touring with twenty assistants for his one-man quick-change parodic operas. "I live surrounded by mannequins," he said, "who substitute for me while I am changing, all the while I continue to speak." He might do sixty characters and three operas a night, singing falsetto, contralto, and bass, this "multiple man," this "Parliament of people, this "Pantheon, swift as a cinematograph."[72]

High praise, that, and Fregoli must have liked the reference to motion pictures. An amateur photographer, he improved upon a projector he got from his friends, the Lumière brothers, and by 1900 had created twenty-six films to show during his performances. He collaborated with Georges Méliès, film pioneer of special effects, on *Lightning Transformations* – twenty changes of costume in two minutes in plain view of the camera. Fregoli (and his admirers, the Futurists) would boast that his films were the first to reveal "that dynamism, that rhythm, that rapid sequence of scenes, secured by 'changes almost in open sight,' destined to become the rule of the new cinematographic art."[73]

Fregoli's name spread from the theater marquee to the film screen on which the "frégoligraphe" repeated magical transformations, and to the artistry of the quick-change itself, called *le frégolisme*. His name was borrowed by imitators (Fregola, Frego, Frégoly) and in 1927 by two French psychiatrists. He who had performed at an asylum where after each change the applause was delayed until the inmates could be sure it was the same man, this identical Fregoli inspired the definition of a variant of Capgras syndrome in which people saw strangers as familiar. In the earliest reported case, a stagestruck woman believed she was being persecuted by her favorite actresses Robine and Sarah Bernhardt, who could pass under the skins of others and fregolify them. In 1930 Vié discussed the case of Mme B., whose husband was "a real illusionist, he changes his figure as he wishes" into the forms of her various lovers. Fregoli patients claimed that although the strangers bore no physical likeness to a friend or loved one, they were psychologically identical, just as Fregoli could assume the inner spirit of hundreds of famous people.[74]

All this – the quicksilver of the cinema, the seamlessness of theatrical impersonation, the chronic exactitude of the *sosies*, the insidiousness of double agency – came together on August 13, 1953, in the California town of Santa Mira. Becky, newly divorced, goes to Dr. Miles Bennell. She is worried sick. Tough-minded Cousin Wilma believes that her Uncle Ira isn't Ira. "She says he looks exactly like Uncle Ira, talks just like him, acts just like him – everything. She just knows it isn't Ira, that's all." Wilma isn't going crazy, is she? Wilma says her uncle's emotional responses are off; he's missing that special sparkle in his eyes. Soon Miles is shown the naked body of a man on a billiard table; "at one and the same time it looked unreal and theatrical, and yet it was intensely, overly real." The body is healthy and unused. It has no fingerprints. Its face is unfinished. Miles consults Professor Budlong: Could the body be a blank shaped from giant seed pods, awaiting the imprint of a specific person? No, lies Budlong, who has become one of *them*, alien spores, parasites with "the ability to reform and reconstitute themselves into perfect duplication, cell for living cell, of any life form." The original body disappears in a pile of fluff, and the alien spore takes over the replica body, human memories and mannerisms intact. Sterile, incapable of replicating themselves as humans, they are also incapable of anything but rote emotion. That greyness Wilma had remarked of Uncle Ira, Miles remarks at last of Becky Driscoll herself. In the book, Miles thwarts the plot. In the movie, Miles's warnings of an *Invasion of the Body Snatchers* fall aslant the blank faces of motorists as the aliens begin to export their pods across the highways of the Earth.[75]

Bad seed consumed good in this novel and film from the McCarthyite 1950s, during which "patriots" found Doppelgängers everywhere there had been "fellow travelers" and uncovered two-facedness among Hollywood's aliased actors. Who might not be a *sosie*? The Capgras syndrome was – and still is – spreading. The divorce rate is sustained by depositions that one's spouse is no longer the person one married. Plastic surgery makes for almost unmistakable substitute wives; the parallel universe of television produces proxy parents while asking the real Mr. Q to please stand up; the Other World of old-age homes fosters impersonated relatives. Reviewing the literature in 1987, a neurologist concluded that the Capgras syndrome was not rare. Indeed, so common to European, North American, and Japanese culture are delusions of substitution that the Capgras syndrome is sometimes demoted to a symptom – of an industrial society afraid for itself.[76]

If the paranoia of the Cold War led to nightmares of double agency and evil twins whenever the Balance of Power was upset, other inequitable power relations have led to other disturbing forms of double agency. We have witnessed the double agency of blacks passing as whites, Jews as Christians, gays as straights, women as men, colonial subjects as their colonial rulers. "We become what we see of ourselves in the eyes of others," wrote novelist V.S. Naipaul of his native Caribbean. "We pretended to be real, ... we mimic men of the New World." With these impersonations, people take on malign second bodies in order to escape hurtful demands upon the native body. They find themselves in tow to the Doppelgänger as one's mortal *fetch*, one's passing.[77]

Two Heads, One Body

Could one take into account each imposture and impersonation by people hoping to escape loneliness, tyranny, or intolerance, how many might not be leading double lives? A few paragraphs ago, this chapter seemed to have little to do with the general run of human beings; there were monstrous twins, compulsive impostors, pod people, spies. Of a sudden, we begin to suspect doubleness in us all.

Before he meets his Double, Titular Councilor Golyadkin is already ill at ease. Waking in his dirty room with its imitation mahogany chairs, he rushes to the mirror. He is unchanged. But something is up, he has hired a coach, he is riding along when his division chief spots him playing hookey. Thinks Golyadkin, "Shall I admit that it's me or not? or shall I pretend that it's not me but someone else, who strikingly resembles me, and look unconcerned? It's really not me, it isn't, and that's that!" At his doctor's office, a perplexing visit, Golyadkin says, "I don't like worthless two-faced people.... I put a mask on only to go to a masquerade." Canted from slight teetering to extreme imbalance by consistently civil steps, Golyadkin is troubled by the very notion of civility, which seems so...Siamesed.[78]

Where there be two heads and one body, that way lies the drawing room. Etiquette. Civility. Civility is the habit of masks, like its mirror image, hypocrisy (< Greek for "actor," he who pretends). During the Renaissance, civility was to the conduct of humanists what hypocrisy was to the conduct of courtiers; while Erasmus's manual of etiquette defended the humanist ideal of a noble congruence between outward manner and "inward mind," Ben Jonson's epigrams attacked the courtworm's dissembling silks and dishonest praise. Late in the Ancien Régime, civility was to *finesse* what hypocrisy was to aristocratic *duplicité*. The double man (*l'homme double*) tells himself he must always have the wits to appear an upright man but never the stupidity to be one. The double man deceives you; the elegant man (*l'homme fin*) allows you to deceive yourself.[79]

Civilization by mutual deceit became, in the nineteenth century, at once a requisite of compacted urban living and a sore point of the interior life. Civility was to politeness what hypocrisy was to artificiality. "A defence of artificiality may seem scarcely compatible with the warnings against its dangers with which from our childhood we are made familiar," commented an English essayist in 1888, and yet "Goodbreeding in itself largely consists of what, when it comes to be analysed, is essentially artificial. Civilisation may be said to consist in properly

FIGURE 2.7. Alchemical "double vessel" in the form of a double retort, for the production of a volatile antimony which, if it cannot double any object or transmute lead into gold, as can the Philosopher's Stone, will be a powerfully penetrative medicine. From *Basil Valentine His Triumphant Chariot of Antimony, with Annotations of Theodore Kirkringius* (1678).

understood artificiality." Tact, muffling of feelings, concealment of thoughts, was less selfish than honesty.[80]

Killing with kindness or with cunning, such two-facedness was gradually framed as double-mindedness. A studied uprightness may have produced an outwardly agreeable deportment to the body, but it left one with a host of contrary thoughts and feelings, reflected in the triple-faced German dolls of century's turn whose countenance changed from calmness to smiling contentment to tearful, noisy crying at the pull of a (heart)string. Deportment, carrying oneself as the person one wanted to be seen to be, meant that heart and mind had to be so managed that one did not give oneself away. "Never point at another. Never speak much of your own performances." Factitious continuities of deportment were exaggerated in public by gas and electric lighting and reflections off plate glass windows, in private by the mounting of household mirrors and photographic portraits. The body had to be of one piece, at home as on the avenue, but thoughts wandered, feelings contended.[81]

"At a time when stage-lovers were nearly all sixty, and dressed like waiters," the tender twilight love scene between genuinely young lovers during *Society* was a revelation in 1865. Thomas Robertson's insistence upon "natural" acting in his plays aggravated the sense of discontinuity between a disciplined propriety of body and indisciplines of heart and mind. Which could be trusted? "Madeleine dissected her own feelings and was always wondering whether they were real or not," wrote Henry Adams in *Democracy* (1880); "she had a habit of taking off her mental clothing, as she might take off a dress, and looking at it as though it belonged to someone else, and as though sensations were manufactured like clothes." Such doubleness was especially problematic for women, who had to negotiate more treacherous passage between private and public, and who were skinned of their old names, sometimes of their identities, when they married.[82]

Meanwhile, detectives were in hot pursuit of women and men who in very deed were leading darkly double lives. They who dramatized themselves as masters of disguise and "shadowing" would not be fooled by the civility of Allan Pinkerton's American "who for years moved in the best circles of society, who was universally respected, and regarded as a leading man in the community where he resided, and yet who was for years associated with hardened criminals, and actively engaged in criminal exploits." This could as easily have been the summary of a Scottish case, that of William Brodie of Edinburgh, deacon of the Wrights (cabinet- and coffinmakers), *and* a gamester, cheat, bigamist, and chieftain of a gang of thieves. He was hanged in 1788, then restored to double life by Robert Louis Stevenson in 1886 as the "polar twins" Dr. Henry Jekyll and Mr. Edward Hyde. "Though so profound a double-dealer," Jekyll stated, "I was in no sense a hypocrite; both sides of me were in dead earnest" – and had long been. Hyde, pleasure-loving, corrupt, was fully half of Jekyll. In the toils of a "moral weakness," Jekyll had to face "that truth, by whose partial discovery I have been doomed to such a dreadful shipwreck: that man is not truly one, but truly two."[83]

Brains themselves, reported anatomists, were dual. The two hemispheres were "in fact two distinct and entire organs," and "a separate and distinct process of thinking...may be carried on in each cerebrum simultaneously." One intelligent man, "haunted by himself," argued with his pertinacious other, who would "to his great mortification sometimes refute him," proof that we are physiologically capable of "distinct and contradictory trains of thought simultaneously." People evidently had Left brains and Right brains, and although the localizing of speech functions in the Left gave it higher status among wordy neurologists and wordier psychologists, trauma could bring the Right to the fore. From the basic duality of the brain, from the double-mindedness of everyday experience – and from accounts of stillborn monsters, one head black, one white – it was a short leap to cinematic retakes of Jekyll/Hyde and to novels with villainous doctors hypnotizing heroines in order to summon their evil alter egos.[84]

Everywhere one looked at the turn of the century, people were leading double lives. Perhaps not so brazenly as with the dandy Oscar Wilde or the rubber stamp manufacturer Théophile Longuet who knew he was the criminal Cartouche reincarnate. Perhaps not so ethereally as with the newly weighed (69.5 grams) astral body joined to the physical body by an elastic silver cable, each person Siamesed to *Phantasms of the Living.* But thoroughly and conclusively, with the scientific detection of an interior double life, deduced earlier in somnambulism, confirmed now by the distinctness of the hypnotic state. "I feel as if I were living two lives at once," says a sleepwalker in an 1884 "hypnotic romance," *Double Life; or, Starr Cross,* one of many fictions exploiting double-mindedness as "an ethical convenience, a psychological fact, a metaphysical reality." The French psychologist Jules Janet, discussing an easily hypnotizable woman, wrote in 1888, "It seems that there are in the normal person, or more exactly in the person exempt from hysteria, as with the hysteric, two personalities, one conscious and the other unconscious." What American philosopher William James called "the hidden self," his Boston friend Dr. Morton Prince called a "second personality," asking rhetorically, "have we all within us such a second personality... which observes, remembers and governs our actions more than we dream of?"[85]

Multiples

We are back where we should be: Doppelgängers as reflections of the strong discordance modernity has imposed upon Siamese twins. Monsters with two heads and two bodies compete side by side and go mad; monsters with one head and two bodies veer toward imposture or double agency; monsters with two heads and one body are multiple, and contrasting, personalities.[86]

Historian J.H. van den Berg, noticing the preoccupation with Doubles and plural existences during the 1790s and again during the 1890s, has suggested that images of a divided existence – of Doppelgängers and Doubles, the subconscious and unconscious – become most compelling when family relationships are most upset, workers most estranged from their work. Ian Hacking, a philosopher of science, has suggested that "split personality" became "a spontaneous way in which to express unhappiness" only after installation (ca. 1875) of the norm of the "whole person" as a "consensus of vital properties"; once the dominant medical, legal, and philosophical model of human beingness implied not an indissoluble but an *integrable* self, split personalities could be constructed as a psychological disorder and as "a possible way for a person to be." Elsewhere, I have suggested that our fascination with multiple personalities (given an etiology in childhood abuse) stems from societal fears of the loss of generational continuity, most acute at the ends of centuries.[87]

"Is it not quite possible, then, that other normal, ordinary people, possess a second personality, deep-down beneath their ordinary, everyday self, and that under conditions which favor a readjustment, this hidden subliminal self may emerge?" asked a New York physician in 1897. The conditions that favor such a readjustment seem to be growing ever stronger at this century's (and millennium's) end, as has the "haunting mystery" of "our seeming *duality* – the presence in us of another *person*; not a slave of ours, but free and independent" (wrote Mark Twain at

FIGURE 2.8. *Web of Time*, sculpture/hanging by Tsuneko Kokubo, co-artistic director of the Snake in the Grass Moving Theatre, for a performance, *Ghosts in the Machine*, December 1990, at the Museum of Anthropology, University of British Columbia, Vancouver. Reproduced by permission. Photo by Heidi Piltz Burton.

last century's end). With dangerously deciduous families, with estranged workforces of multinational economies, with fin de siècle apprehensions about the world our children will inherit, we seem to be leading double lives in unsettled times.[88]

Freud was drawn to the *unheimlich* or unsettling or uncanny, whose definition he borrowed from the philosopher Friedrich Schelling: that which "ought to have remained secret and hidden but has come to light." Psychoanalysis itself could seem uncanny, for it brought what was repressed into the open. Yet, "When all is said and done," wrote Freud, "the quality of uncanniness can only come from the fact of the 'double' being a creation dating back to a very early mental stage, long since surmounted – a stage, incidentally, at which it wore a more friendly aspect. The 'double' has become a thing of terror, just as, after the collapse of their religion, the gods turned into demons."[89]

That, in short, is what these first two chapters have been about: how the companionate, faithful, heavenly twins have become clashing antagonists. That is also, writ in several hands, the history of multiple personality. Since first seen in 1811, exuberant alternate selves have gradually become more cruel and self-destructive, and the few (3, 4, 5) have become the many (16, 24, 56, 90). What was a contest between ephemeral high spirits and fragile civility is now a conflict between a host of "sociopaths" and an "Inner Self-Helper." The transit from primary to alter ego(s), which occurred in the sitting room at needlepoint, now occurs anywhere and unpredictably. Where before the multiples could be taken as adolescent muddle, today they are taken as the muddying of generations, of injury done to children by adults who were themselves victims of early abuse, deepening that "something repressed which *recurs*," as Freud italicized during the violence and shock of the Great War.[90]

To his wayward disciple (Doppelgänger?) Carl Jung, Freud had written, "But you can read in Frazer's *Golden Bough*, Vol. I, in how many primitive peoples the placenta is still today the *brother* or the *twin* and correspondingly treated, fed and cared for – which naturally does not last long. If there is a phylogenetic memory, which unfortunately will soon prove to be so, then the uncanniness of 'doubles' has also this source." Jung himself did not shy from the Double, that primitive twin he knew as the Shadow, one of those Archetypes or "complexes of experience that come upon us like fate." Resident in phylogenetic memory or the collective unconscious, the Shadow was no less twinned to each of us individually, and would not vanish: "The encounter with the dark half of the personality, or 'shadow,' comes about of its own accord in any moderately thorough treatment.... The shadow is a tight passage, a narrow door, whose painful constriction no one is spared who goes down to the deep well... where I am indivisibly this *and* that; where I experience the other in myself and the other-than-myself experiences me."[91]

Controversy over Multiple Personality Disorder (is MPD for real? is it a charade?) has sharpened as we uphold a psychological concept of the person as a "consensus of vital properties" yet keep to the philosophical concepts of a unitary, responsible individual. While cases compound (thousands worldwide), hospital staffs, psychiatrists and psychologists, private and public counselors are bitterly divided over MPD. The more common the idea that each of us plays many roles, the keener the suspicion that MPD is a form of malingering. The more prevalent the notion that MPD is "a creative and highly effective strategy for preserving the integrity of the organism in the face of chronic catastrophic trauma," the more pervasive the mystique of alters. Does a society that encourages *The Search for the Real Self* make us "aware of our essential, separate, unique identity" or does it afford us practice in the acting out of Siamesed identities?[92]

One could make a fine brief for the dramatic, literary nature of MPD. Mary Reynolds in 1811, the first case to be fully reported, was well versed in the Doppelgängers of gothic fiction. Alma Z. in the 1880s had a clairvoyant "No. 1" who knew by heart the poetry of Tennyson and Browning, a "Twoey" whose vocabulary was limited by an Indian accent, and a "Boy" who popped up during a Beethoven concerto at the Met. Most spectacular in this regard was the case of Clara Ellen (Kavanaugh) Norton (Forest) Fowler (Waterman). Articulate and independent, she was a special student in English Literature at Radcliffe College in 1906 when her Boston therapist, Morton Prince, founded the *Journal of Abnormal Psychology* and earned international acclaim for his book on the multiples within "Miss Beauchamp." That pseudonym was taken from George Meredith's *Beauchamp's Career*, a novel co-starring a shrewd physician, Dr. Shrapnel, and Nevil Beauchamp, who, though male, shared a history of feminism and star-crossed love with Clara Norton Fowler, who had shed her Kavanaugh family name in honor of Caroline Norton, real-life novelist and feminist heroine of Meredith's *Diana of the Crossways*. "Miss Beauchamp" was also described in the *Ladies' Home Journal*, inspiring two dramatists, Edward Locke – who wrote *The Case of Becky* in 1912 – and Amelia Bachman, who sued Locke for stealing her play, *Estelle*. By 1915 Miss Beauchamp a.k.a. Becky a.k.a Estelle was Anna Anson in a two-reel silent film, *Her Other Self*, in which a Dr. Reed cures Anna of dual personality through the use of a dictagraph machine, confronting one self with the voice of the other. Just then, a writer of stream-of-consciousness short stories began to hit her stride under the name of Katherine Mansfield, born in New Zealand no other than Kathleen Mansfield Beauchamp, a.k.a. Julian Mark, Katherine Schönfield, Matilda Berry, Elizabeth Stanley. Given to gestures theatrical and identities carnivalesque, she had an "obvious – indeed, dazzling – talent," wrote an acquaintance, "for multiple impersonation."[93]

Multiple personality or multiple impersonation? Traumatic dissociation or conspiracy to deceive? Arguments against the diagnosis of MPD are arguments about delusion, collusion, and canniness. Those therapists who see MPD springing up all around must be, as it were, victims

of the Capgras syndrome, mistaking "borderline personality" for sets
of doubles. Those with MPD must be virtuosos of Fregolism; through
quick changes they impersonate themselves at different ages, different
crises. Elicited or elaborated under hypnosis, multiples must be artifacts of a *folie à deux* between commanding clinician and demanding
patient. Clients with fractious crowds of inner voices shed responsibility for their actions while therapists stake out "a gold mine for the study
of psychological phenomena," each personality a psychic entity, akin to
the old topography of phrenology. If Self-Esteem, Hopefulness, Domestic Propensities, Wit are no longer inked along the cranium, advocates
of MPD replot the faculties within the manifold neediness of patients
performing the Baby, the Outrider, Mother Hen, Comedian. These are
not uncanny figures exposing what has been repressed since childhood but crafty representations of how we believe humans, and human
memories, work. At its worst, the diagnosis permits the splitting of
headaches into several personalities; allows a teenage boy who has read
The Three Faces of Eve to invent for himself a fetal personality after failing to talk a girlfriend out of an abortion; allows a teenage girl who has
read *Sybil* to continue her chronic lying as a symptom of this new
"fascinoma"; lets murderers off the hook. At best, the multiple personality is a tragic Richard II: "Thus play I in one person many people,
and none contented."[94]

"After treating a considerable number of patients who have Multiple
Personality Disorder," wrote one psychiatrist in 1990, "I am still struck
by the play-acting quality of many of these patients. It's as if the whole
presentation is a monumental 'put-on.'" Yet he has become a partisan
of their sincerity, like the two thousand members of the International
Society for the Study of Multiple Personality and Dissociation, for "You
can *see* the identifications [with past experiences]; you can *hear* the
traumatic scenarios." The drama which renders MPD suspect to therapists with an antitheatrical bias is precisely that which renders MPD
so persuasive to those who establish an arena in which the multiples
may play out their play. Indeed, as another partisan has argued, patients
with MPD are more skilled at dissimulation – at hiding their multiples
from sight – than they are at simulation of the characters their alters
take on. That is why they remain so long misdiagnosed (seven years on
average) and why, when the alters come out of the closet, there are fireworks. MPD would be neither a comforting nor a comfortable fraud;
some three-quarters of cases attempt suicide.[95]

Why would anyone go to such mortal lengths to pretend to such
pain? Freud, having decided that his patients were telling him tales,
drafted a psychic architecture of screen memories, oedipal turrets, camouflaged emplacements, but some historians suggest that he was building a castle in the sky while patients were in harm's way down below.
Skepticism about the physical reality of abuse suffered by those with
MPD repeats an earlier era's disbelief in the extent of abuse – perhaps
because of the archaic quality of the life of a person with MPD, whose

biography is an archaeology, and whose history of treatment reenacts the myth of Osiris, killed by his brother, scattered across Egypt in fragments gathered up by wife and sister Isis, embalmed by Anubis, restored by his hawk-headed son, Horus.[96]

Predictable, isn't it, that multiples themselves, in archival records as on psychic scrims, should be so often crucially involved with twins, doubles, and pseudonyms? Clara Norton Fowler's career as Christina (and Sally) Beauchamp began when she held herself responsible for the sudden death of one of a pair of twin infant sibs, a guilt and trauma exacerbated when an infant sister later died in her young arms. Christine Costner Sizemore, the name behind the Eve Black and Eve White of *The Three Faces of Eve* (1957), was elder sib to twin sisters and as a child played house with her double cousin (their fathers brothers, their mothers sisters), each of them mothers to twins, spanking the "bad" child. Her papers, replete with notes on what turned out to be not three but twenty-two alters, bulge with correspondence about ghostwriting and pseudonyms. Subsequent cases have had twins as part of the very constellation of multiples: Toby tangled with five sets of matched twins as well as a triplet of Dark Ones sent by the Archangel Michael to watch over her spiritual progress.[97]

Progress in treatment of MPD has meant the integration of the personalities. Predominantly male therapists managing predominantly female patients have since 1875 worked toward "fusion," toward that whole person, that consensus of properties, and that continuity of personal history which industrialized societies at once demand and obstruct. Pressures to fuse have also been pressures to refuse parts of oneself inconformable to cultural expectations of gender roles, or to defuse legitimately rebellious parts of a gendered life. Some feminist therapists propose instead to move those with MPD in the direction of Siameseship and networks of "connectedness."[98]

Behind the disputes over the diagnosis and treatment of MPD lies the problem of power. Are therapist and patient allied in a long, talkative struggle against the powerful historical dysfunctions of the (modern) family and repressed evidences of an abusive society? Should we classify MPD as a psychosomatic illness, like hysterical paralysis, then look for its roots in the complex historical repression of women and children? Do multiples appear when a person is about to revolt against the mores of a culture or when a person is feeling cornered and powerless?[99]

Siamesed doubleness, like the vanishing twin, is an image and experience we have made our own. We commonly speak of "being of two minds," commonly *explain* our virtues and failings by reference to "left brain" skills and "right brain" intuitions. Though few of us are likely to have commissurotomies separating left brain from right (to relieve intractable epilepsy), our prominent philosophers now speculate, with writers of science fiction, that "the concept of a single person with a disunified consciousness will become less strange as science advances." And we do now appear to accept a culturally and historically peculiar sort of self-commenting, self-combative, doubled but estranged consciousness. Doubleness has become an inescapable element of modernity; yea, for some, its very definition.[100]

Hang on to that monkey-rope.

FIGURE 3.1. Womannequins, the middle one is fitted with an extra piece to appear pregnant, a device invented by Van Calvin, of the Van Calvin Manikin Restoration Studio, Portland, OR. Photo by Linda M. Strauss.

CHAPTER THREE

Self-portraits

> In one word... we wish to create man a second time, in
> the shape and semblance of a tailor's dummy.
> — *Treatise on Tailors' Dummies or the*
> *Second Book of Genesis*, by Bruno Schulz's father

Vanishing twins disclose our longing for a consummate companionship even as we exalt a unique personhood. Doppelgängers expose the
Siamesed factions of that person. Through portraiture we mean to anchor
and extend ourselves — for remembrance or reconnaissance, identification or indemnification, glory or vainglory.

At this fin de siècle, our self-portraits seem neither to anchor nor
to extend. Why? Perhaps because the fury of acceleration and the fatigue
of deceleration felt at each century's end, and most deeply in our 1990s,
make us desperate for new bodies. Perhaps because our likenesses are
as fragmented as our lives. Perhaps because our false intimacies lash us
on to a narcissism ever enamored of but ever discontented with likeness. Perhaps because we carom inside a "fictive culture" whose obsession with role-playing leads to a portraiture as clichéd as it is unstable.
Perhaps because, amidst a parade of electronic spectacles, all we make
of our selves is suspect. Perhaps because the best we can manage in a
world of simulacra is a visage unavoidably generic.[1]

Perhaps perhaps. My trouble with these explanations is that they
explain everything and all of a sudden. Apocalypses, or unveilings, are
banefully seductive at millennium's end, but I must bind us to the mast-
head of this chapter, and recall the tailor's dummy. "Can you imagine,"
asked Bruno Schulz's father, "the pain, the dull imprisoned suffering,
hewn into the matter of that dummy which does not know why it must
be what it is, why it must remain in that forcibly imposed form which
is no more than a parody?" What can explain, more gradually and specifically, how our culture of the copy has come to be so bewildered,
even terrified, by figures we shape in our own image?

Let us contemplate, by way of answer, a series of triplets in the cultural history of likeness: (1) miniatures, silhouettes, and portrait photographs; (2) embalmed bodies, waxworks, and wax anatomies; (3)

artists' wooden models, mannequins, and sex dolls; (4) puppets, ventriloquists' dummies, and automata. These will take us through realms
legal, religious, economic, and political, for they put our selves and our
likenesses in question as plaintiffs and defendants, mourners and celebrants, producers and consumers, subjects and rulers.

Dodging: Plaintiffs and Defendants

Giant stone ancestors at Luxor saw pharaohs to their coronations, where
new kings were joined to the eternal *ka* – the spirit-double of their
ancestral line. The great stones of archaic Greece stood in for unrecov-
erable bodies of the lost or dead, anchoring the absent to the heartholds
of *kol*, place.[2]

By their very mass, colossi assert that someone has *taken place*; by
their presence, they maintain the indelibility of power. In 1272, three
hundred pounds of wax were shaped into an image of Henry III of
England and arrayed atop the king's closed coffin. Over the next centuries, larger-than-life figures in wood, wax, gesso, or boiled leather
assumed the regalia of perpetual kingship and were paraded on triumphal chariots behind plain caskets holding the naked corpse of a king.
At the death of François I in 1547, his effigy lay in state, ritually fed by
French grandees. In 1610, at the same court, three effigies assumed the
royal Dignity as Henry IV's natural body decayed.[3]

Miniatures, subtle with the play-full-ness of character, extend us
toward second chances, times ahead and remediable. Egyptian dolls,
Roman puppets, jointed manikins in the studios of Renaissance artists
were less mass than energy, always *trading places*, being changed or
exchanged. The scale of the miniature encourages impromptu affections, banter, fantasy.[4]

By twelve months a child can match a miniature to its life-size original, yet relations between children and dolls are hardly one-sided.
As children separate from their mothers, they ascribe more independence to their playmates, until dolls are agents in their own right.
About the time that children begin to construct sentences, dolls become co-respondents, sharing small rebellions: "she says she doesn't
want her dinner." The colossus is entirely dependent upon an external
story; the miniature is that figure through which we collude with personable doubles.[5]

We find such a drift toward the personable in European portrait miniatures. From medieval pictures of churchmen, sketched according to
physiognomic rules that each must have looked his historical part, portraiture passed to "lifelike but anonymous faces" inked inside manuscript initials. Passed, next, to the identifiable double chin of John,
Duke of Bedford, drawn in his Book of Hours. Next, to idiosyncratic
faces on Renaissance medallions. Next, to the exquisitely particular miniatures of Henry VIII and his daughter Mary, and of François I and his
two sons, exchanged as gifts between these sovereigns prior to the
Treaty of Amiens (1525). Thence to the engraving of small noble por-

FIGURE 3.2. Pulp doll makers in early modern Germany, probably Nüremburg. Copperplate engraving by Christoph Weigel, 1698. From Karl Grober, *Children's Toys in Bygone Days* (1928).

traits and to the art of limning the distinctive features of merchant couples. By the 1700s, a London modeler in wax would promise "The Likeness of *any Person from common Shade* or DESCRIPTION ONLY, though the Original may have been dead Forty Years."[6]

"Shade," in Mr. Percy's time, denoted a ghost and a shadow portrait. The waxworker was vying with both, recalling one from darkness, lending substance to the other. Shades, cut from black paper and pasted on white board, or drawn with India ink on glass or ivory, became so cheap that they were renamed after a French finance minister, Etienne de Silhouette, who delighted in cutting profiles as he cut corners. A.A.C. Fidèle Edouart, who in 1825 turned from the snipping of faithful portraits using human hair to the snipping of silhouettes, cut a hundred thousand during his career in England and America. He produced, actually, two hundred thousand profiles, since, like many of his profession, he cut in duplicate and kept the double, "Primarily that copies may be supplied when the sitter is separated from friends by reason of place or death." So the "shade" could serve as ghost *and* as shadow portrait, but Edouart was responding less to a need for unchanging memorials than to a newer hunger for "CORRECT LIKENESSES taken with elegance and despatch" – *instant* likenesses of changeable people taken in 2–10 minutes. William King of New England had twenty thousand profiles under his thumb by 1806, each done in six minutes flat "with the greatest possible correctness."[7]

Correctness is a curious thing. As Erasmus had observed centuries before, "what an enormous amount of the real person is missing from the portrait!... Where are the brain, the flesh, the veins, the sinews and bone, the bowels, blood, breath, humours? Where are life, movement, feeling, voice, and speech? Where finally are man's special characteristics, mind, intelligence, memory, and understanding?" A portrait painter can detail a scar on a knuckle or eyebrow hairs askew, but no portrait can be utterly correct for long: styles change, the skin wrinkles, the spine slumps.[8] Agues and accidents of the body conspire against that correctness which, demanded overmuch, culminates in the Capgras syndrome, where all one's familiars seem unfamiliar.

Our hunger for likenesses has become insatiable due in part, despite Erasmus, to the ache for continual "correctness" under the impress of industrial economies anxious about the passage of time. Ruth Henshaw Bascom, who painted one hundred portraits a year and drew over a thousand profiles of New Englanders from 1828 to 1846, was directed to add new glasses to the face of Rev. Timothy Rogers, whose portrait she had done less than a year before. During a period of six years she was called upon several times to update the hair and dress of her painting of Lydia Burr. A losing battle, this finicky correctness, but it was strenuously fought, to the profit of artists who did fifty silhouettes or a dozen oil portraits a day. These were formulaic, but they had to catch each time some remarkable accidentals. "My portrait is quite recent," a later artist would brag, "and represents M. [Emile] Zola as he appears after having considerably reduced his weight by a complete system of dieting." The same artist was defensive about his portrait of Pope Leo XIII, "still a striking likeness, although His Holiness is now much more frail."[9]

Catching timely silhouettes with "uncanny accuracy," William Henry Brown proudly cut them "from sight alone with a pair of common scissors without the use of any machine whatever." As did in 1823 W.J. Hubard, sixteen, "who, by a mere glance at the face! and with a pair of common scissors! not by the help of a Machine nor from any sketch with Pen, Pencil or Crayon, but from Sight alone!!! cuts out the most spirited and striking Likenesses in One Minute." The Machine against which Brown and Hubard were racing was a profiling machine, invented by G.L. Chrétien, musician to Louis XVI, and advanced by his friend Edmé Quenedey, who in 1788 took the device into noble salons and to Versailles itself, where sat the Dauphin, very still. In five minutes the "physionotrace" did the youngster's profile, which could be engraved to yield two thousand copies, though twelve was the usual order. Furnishing quickly multiplicable miniatures, the physionotrace began as a "scientific" alternative to the painted portrait. Like scientists, Chrétien and Quenedey would redo the experiment when results were poor — when sitters had assumed uncomplimentary attitudes or had fussed and fidgeted. Together, machine and men finished thirteen hundred portraits in four years. Their invention was revamped by a refugee from the Revolution, Févret de Saint-Mémin, who took coach from one well-connected house to another along the eastern seaboard of the United States, charging Thomas Jefferson, Meriwether Lewis, and Aaron Burr $25–$30; by 1810 Saint-Mémin and his machine had done eight hundred portraits of judges, senators, and the merchant elite.[10]

Responding to a compliment on one of his physionotracings, Saint-Mémin denied all artistry, "since I made use of an instrument in order to obtain the most essential features, and since, if there is any merit in the delicacy and studied exactness of the likeness, the draughtsman owes his ability, so entirely independent of his efforts, to providence."[11] Mechanical providence, unspoiled by human hand, assured the vital momentariness of the likeness: altogether correct, yet instantly revisable.

Providence (upper case) frequently demanded the services of Isaac Wetherby, an itinerant American portrait painter summoned not only to alter outdated portraits but to paint postmortem. On June 28, 1842, he paid a sexton one dollar "for opening tomb in Park Street Yard for me to goe in & take sketch of dead child for Capt. Hodge." Months before, however, he had bought a new apparatus first released in France by L.J.M. Daguerre in 1839, and he had just painted postmortem from someone else's "very indistinct Daguerreotype miniature." Thereafter he alternated between painting from life, from death, from memory, and from photographs taken of the dead when they had been alive. "Secure the shadow ere the substance fade; / Let nature copy that which nature made," ran the daguerrean motto. It was a motto for human shades: 90 percent of daguerreotypes were portraits. By 1854, when Wetherby owned a profitable photographic gallery in Iowa City, there were eighty-six such galleries in New York City alone, twenty-five hundred people living off photography in London, three thousand in Paris.[12]

Behind the excitement of "immediately" obtaining "an exact *fac simile*," as Daguerre had promised, lay a technical problem. Depending upon the quality of light, these silver nitrate pictures took five, ten, fifteen, or thirty minutes and more (the Pyramids, twenty). At the opening of a Belgian railway in 1840, parading troops and dignitaries stood stock-still for seven minutes in hopes of one commemorative daguerreotype. With accelerating chemicals or quick-stuff, the process was shortened to fractions of a minute, but for the first decade or more, those who sat or stood in front of the camera had frequently to endure long exposures during which they were supported by headrests or classical columns. Hence the careful disposition of limbs, the straight necks, the compressed mouths, the eyes "fixed on some object a little above the camera" that made early photographs seem strangely colossal. Elizabeth Barrett, whose dearest brother had recently drowned, admired the ancestral tenor and fixity of these portraits. She wrote to a friend in 1843, "Think of every man sitting down in the sun and leaving his fac simile in all its full completion of outline and shadow, stedfast on a

plate, at the end of a minute and a half.... I long to have such a memorial of every being dear to me in the world." Less for art's sake, she
interrupted herself, than for *love's* sake. "It is not merely the likeness
which is precious in such cases – but the association and the sense of
nearness involved in the thing...the fact of the *very shadow of the person*
lying there fixed forever!"[13]

Alas, not so. Whatever the process, daguerreotype or cheaper calo-
type paper prints (1839–41) or speedier prints from glass negatives
(1851), the image often vanished as if a ghost. There were fixatives,
but visiting cards and paper prints seemed impossibly impermanent.
"They gradually fade, first losing their glossy blackness and sharpness
of outline; then all their early brilliancy dies away, they assume a yellow
tinge, and in time entirely disappear." Analogies to human mortality
were unmistakable in this essay of 1868, whose author had been looking
through albums only to find faces vanishing into a silvered darkness.[14]

The fading of images, the quickening of exposure times, and the use
of retouching techniques transformed the photoportrait from colossus
to miniature. That which had required a fine sensitivity to light and
shadow to conjure the *ka*, the spirit-double of a person, became as
mechanical as the silhouettes of Saint-Mémin. That which had been
unique (daguerreotypes could not be used to reproduce themselves)
gave way to millions of versions. That which had been costly became
so cheap that a prestidigitator promised to broadcast "200 photographs of himself" over a Boston playhouse; one hundred thousand
photos of presidential candidate Abe Lincoln were broadcast over a
house dividing.[15]

Photoportraits took on the properties of the miniature: repetitive,
recursive, revisable, phantasmic. Each time people changed stations or
partners, they rushed to romance the camera, sitting for new portraits
as they adopted new personae. They also sat holding photos of their
dead. Such photographs of photographs were poor memorials – they
lost scale and clarity – but they were fine evidence of that faith in successive incarnations through which miniatures work their wonders.
Hence the late Victorian intrigue with the photochemical *medium* – by
which those in the Other World were spirited onto emulsions to ratify
the Afterlife. These were long-lived illusions, since those who could
have exposed the hoaxes were themselves enchanted with the craft of
dodging. *The Book of Photography: Practical, Theoretic and Applied* revealed
to every shutterbug the methods of composite photos, "in which the
same person is seen talking to, drinking, or playing cards with himself."
One step beyond, a physicist at Duke University in 1897 made photos
of "Prof. Dowd playing chess with himself, with two of himself looking on."[16]

Singly and together, the living became other when they sat before
the camera, as shutterbug Lewis Carroll recorded in "Hiawatha's" studio, where the Father beside a massive pillar

would contemplate the distance
With a look of pensive meaning,
As of ducks that die in tempests.

His wife would hold a huge bouquet. His Cambridge son would have aesthetic curves, "Curves pervading all his figure." His eldest daughter would assume a "look of 'passive beauty,'" which

Was a squinting of the left-eye,
Was a drooping of the right-eye,
Was a smile that went up sideways
To the corner of the nostrils.

And his younger son would fidget...until at last the group was taken and "Each came out a perfect likeness."

Then they joined and all abused it,
Unrestrainedly abused it,
As "the worst and ugliest picture
They could possibly have dreamed of...."

Which of course could be retouchéd,
Painted over, colored finely,
'Til the family glowed divinely.
And, as wrote a French observer, not a single self-respecting camera professional could allow a portrait to be printed off a negative produced by light alone. The least a portraitist could do would be to brush the image free of blemishes, restore the line to blond and auburn hair and sight to eyes of blue or grey (to which most plates were blind). As well soften the shadows under the chin, round out the angular profile, eliminate with a Negafake Erasing Pencil the sagging flesh of middle age.[17]

Always, to be sure, retaining "in each face the peculiarity of character it possesses." Photographic portraits should not reduce an individual to a family resemblance, "a mere *map* – which may give a very good idea of a strongly marked outline, or even of an insipid regular beauty – but to every other purpose, is of little value," as John Randolph wrote about a silhouette of his sister Fanny in 1805. "Every individual is distinguished by certain peculiarities," stated a popular photo-retouching manual, "and these must be so treated that where they appear prominently as defective individualities they will remain, and yet not attract special attention." Retouching was thus an art of mutual accommodation between the individual and the camera. Retouch therefore that "fixed, staring and unnatural look, assumed by so many persons while sitting for a portrait, into an easy, natural smile." Head for the hills with lightweight "detective" cameras and catch persons "who are unaware at the time they are in the receipt of adventitious immortality," but supply the studio with a ten-pound prop piano and unroll a paper moon.[18]

Were not photographs true? Lady Elizabeth Eastlake in 1857 knew that photographs "give evidence of facts, as minutely and as impartially as, to our shame, only an unreasoning machine can give." While painters worked to the pulse of the beating heart, did not cameras objectively reflect the outer reality? Were not albums and mantelpieces now emboldened with sincere images of sincere people made abruptly immortal? Were not lockets and loveletters stuffed with black-and-white pictures as totems of unswerving honesty and undying devotion?[19]

No, photographs were hardly true, impartial, or objective. Not initially: dustmotes and shadows got in the way. Not mediately: from different angles came different profiles. Not in their final states: developing had its own pitfalls. The first high priest of American photography, Matthew Brady, did stun gallery visitors with his "Pictures of the Dead at Antietam" in October, 1862; did get "hushed, reverend groups standing around these weird copies of carnage, bending down to look in the pale faces of the dead, chained by the strange spell that dwells in dead men's eyes." But the *New York Times* reporter was misled who stated that the bodies "are taken as they fell...their lips set as when they met in the last fierce charge which loosed their souls." Brady and his assistants were not above moving bodies into better light, shifting Civil War loyalties (in black-and-white, Confederate browns were indistinct from Union blues), and posing live soldiers as if in rigor mortis. Shooting at Devil's Den, they achieved the most widely reproduced image of the war, "Fallen Sharpshooter," by dragging an anonymous body forty yards, putting a knapsack under its head, adding a severed hand, angling a prop gun against a nearby wall, and concocting a story that the man, wounded by shell fragments, had lain down to await his fate. Among the last of Gettysburg's unburied dead, the Confederate soldier's body had more probably been ravaged by wild pigs.[20]

Little wonder that courts were reluctant to accept in evidence the photograph so easily staged and regularly retouched. When the Supreme Court of Pennsylvania met in 1874 to consider a case in which the crux was the identity of a corpse as one A.C. Wilson or/and W.S. Goss, it confronted objections against the use of a photograph to pin down Wilson as Goss. The Court decided that since a painted likeness could be put in evidence, "There seems to be no reason why a photograph, proved to be taken from life and to resemble the person photographed, should not fill the same measure of evidence." Granted, photographic images were not traceable to a human hand, yet "the images on the plate, made by the rays of light through the camera, are dependent on the same general laws which produce the image of outward forms upon the retina through the lenses of the eye. The process has become...so common that we cannot refuse to take judicial cognisance of it as a proper means of producing correct likenesses." Then the Court sighed with relief: "happily the proof of identity is not dependent on the photograph alone." As another court had stated, photographers did not necessarily produce exact facsimiles, and photography was "at last a mimetic art, which furnishes only secondary impressions of the original, that vary according to the light or shadow which prevail whilst being taken."[21]

Taking *un*retouched portraits was, as a Paris police clerk would demonstrate, the art of detaching unique profiles from the masquerades of life and decay of death. Appointed chief of the Office of Judicial Identification in 1888, Alphonse Bertillon amassed a file of a hundred thousand photographs of adults and children, toward the end of identifying Jane or John Does at the morgue and criminals skulking under false names. Though "the lens of a camera would not know how to lie," cameramen and their subjects did; indeed, wrote Bertillon, sitters however adamantly opposed to adulterated images were never pleased with unretouched portraits. It was against the social habits of dodging that he brought to bear his grids and systematic compositions: the frontal shot, left profile, right profile. When courts grudgingly began to admit photographs in evidence, Bertillon was ready with a portraiture that had arrived at "exactitude."[22]

Which sort of exactitude did Bertillon mean? His Liberal father, excited by the work of the Belgian statistician Quetelet (he of the Normal curve), became a pioneer of criminal anthropometry; he married Zoé Guillard, daughter of a pioneering demographer. Alphonse was their rebellious but anemic child, beset by migraines. In and out of many schools, educated primarily by Zoé, he studied Quetelet, occupied himself with botanical classifications, and in 1876 did a metrical analysis of the 222 parts of the human skeleton. His father pulled strings to get him a police job copying out forms at a Paris prefecture, a job so stultifying he began to snip portrait photographs and juxtapose the features. In October 1879, at twenty-six, five foot ten, of haggard eye and raucous voice, and known to his family as "the Barbarian," Alphonse submitted a report on his snipping: no two faces are identical. Years passed before he convinced his superiors that he was other than a tall manic mumbler, but by 1884 his system had been used to uncover hundreds of disguised "recidivists."[23]

Convinced of his own and everyone else's unique appearance, Bertillon admitted that photos were unequal to the best canvases. Hurried police cameramen could achieve neither the liveliness nor the subtlety of likeness at which portraitists arrive after days of painting. This did not bother Bertillon. The exactitude he desired was as blatant as it was regular. Posed with a scientific sameness against a scaled background, people should become recognizable no matter what name or disguise they travel under, just as a thief in Lausanne had been apprehended after his daguerreotype was circulated in 1854. Bertillon's procedures, adopted and adapted across the world, assured the likeness of a unique, inescapable physical self. Bone structure was prominent, and the shape of the skull, but no entreaty to the soul – despite the first photos of Jesus, taken in 1898 from the Shroud of Turin, itself a kind of photographic negative.[24]

All around us now, thanks to Bertillon and to wars that have sent millions fleeing across borders and driven millions of others to bread lines, we have photographic miniatures of our selves which certify our correctness – national loyalty, financial solidity, academic standing, military-industrial trustworthiness, medical fitness, driver's probity. Without them, children are not adults and adults feel like children. None makes pretense to harboring the spirit-double while the body decays, but without them hospital rooms are barricaded and burial anonymous. None is as permanent as the tattoo (a form of identification which leapt from military chests onto civilian breasts with electric tattooing during the 1890s), but people carry them "on their person" and hurriedly renew them when they expire. None is as distinctive as fingerprints (which Bertillon researched and Galton classified), but when these miniatures are lost, uniqueness is at risk, identity questioned. When Louise Odes Neaderland found that her father, eyes sharp but body fragile and mind wandering, refused to give up his driver's license, she interleaved two identities in a series of photocopies: left, her father from youth to old age; right, the unyielded license. From page to page of her artist's book, the license, which "represented to him empowerment and freedom of movement," looms larger and larger in counterpoint to the aging, shrinking, dying man.[25]

Dissembling and Disassembling: Mourners and Celebrants

Bitumen, natron, and a kilometer of cotton bandages preserved the Egyptian dead. Romans, when they did not burn their dead, pickled them in brine. The Christian West, however, looking ahead to a resurrection in which bodies would be restored (or transmuted: there was debate), had neither the will nor eventually the skill to embalm. Even the corpses of medieval monarchs, preserved for a brief period of mourning and display, were left to rot inside their tombs. Across a humid Europe in which leprosy was long the scourge of souls, an undecaying corpse heralded a saint – like Teresa d'Avila (d. 1582), whose incorrupt body would be thrice exhumed to testify to her beatitude.[26]

For many reasons, embalming in the West was reinvented during the nineteenth century. The Art of Dying Well, five hundred years' wisdom on how to conduct oneself so that one's passing would be instructive to onlookers, gave way to an Art of Arranging the Deceased, recumbent in the "living rooms" of funeral directors whose professional euphemisms undertook the privacy of death. As deathbed scenes disappeared into Sunday School stories and funerals themselves became longer and more elaborate, bodies had to be embalmed, had to become euphemisms of themselves. Packed in ice or sealed in a coffin, the putrefying body had been kept aromatically distant from services; now the "Deceased," deprived of an active presence on deathbeds, became passive centerpieces. Made up and laid out in plush caskets as if at "eternal rest," the dead watched through open lids or glass windows as life (in mourning habit) passed dutifully before them.[27]

FIGURE 3.3. *Crossing Paths* by J. Seward Johnson, Jr. Life-size bronze sculpture, cast 1983. Reproduced courtesy of Sculpture Placement, Ltd., Washington, D.C.

"Eternal rest" implied a rest in perpetuity: another reason for embalming. Before, bodies interred in crowded churchyards or municipal burial grounds were periodically unearthed, their bones sent to charnel houses. Middle-class families, renting plots for ten or twenty years, were first allowed perpetual burial rights in 1804 at Père Lachaise, a Parisian burial ground whose landscaped paths influenced the layout of cemeteries as public parks detached from family land or hallowed soil.[28]

Unprotected by the spirits of ancestors or the Holy Ghost, the dead were taken under the wings of the law, which defended gravesites against the depredations of thieves seeking specimens for anatomists and medical schools. Embalming, and burial in cast-iron coffins molded to resemble the drapery around a corpse, would be symbolic, weighty protection against the mutilation of a body unlikely to rise anytime soon.[29]

As for mutilated bodies, they were more underfoot than ever, as a result of railway accidents, injuries at large factories, and the casualties of modern warfare — shell fragments from land mines and ricochet bullets from repeating rifles and machine guns. While vampires rose from coffins each night to take victims at erotically close range in late nineteenth-century paintings, novels, and plays, embalmers masked industrial disfigurement.

Picture-perfect, the embalmed body was counterpart to memorial photography. "We take great pains to have miniatures of Deceased persons agreeable and satisfactory, and they are often so natural as to seem, even to Artists, in a quiet sleep," claimed a pair of Boston photographers in 1846. Undertakers too arranged the deceased as still lifes in tableaux nearly vivants: the child on its sickbed; an old man fallen asleep while reading; Ophelia on the stream with "floating roses."[30]

Other tableaux common to memorial photographs – a dead daughter upright in a chair, a wreath of flowers in her hair or a rose in her hands; a boy sharing a bed with his dead baby brother – were improper to the funeral parlor, where death, no matter how healthy its aspect, should make no claims upon ongoing life. These instead rose up, like stone twins, at Victorian gravesides. In posh cemeteries, the simple winged soul on slate was surpassed by allegories of Faith and Hope, then by life-size portraits in soft white marble. At Laurel Glen in Cuttingsville, Vermont, a stone John Bowman visits his wife and two daughters, top hat between his arms. At Greenwood in Brooklyn, by her design, young Charlotte Canda (d. 1845, age 17) ascends to heaven flanked by books of music and two angels. At Staglieno in Genoa, the most extreme nineteenth-century necropolis, a wife with elegant earrings gazes anxiously at her dying husband, obviously a captain of industry; a mother in puff sleeves lifts up a daughter to embrace the dying father in his armchair; a grandson in sailor suit prays at the bedside of a frock-coated patriarch.[31]

Throughout Italy and Iberia to South America, and in some parts of North America, likeness was compounded by photographs embedded in the stone. "If on every tombstone there could be seen the life-likeness of the sleeper," wrote a Californian, "how much more inviting would be the lasting resting places of the departed." Embalmed body, trompe l'oeil coffin, life-size portrait in stone, embedded photograph...the nineteenth-century dead were rewarded with layers of likeness similar to the wrapped mummy, its cover portrait in gold leaf and tempera, its shaped case with carved head. Speaking in low voices, morticians imitated Egyptian priests who issued oracles through speaking tubes hidden in statues of the *ka*, but, like nineteenth-century physicians and magicians who also stood between life and death and were also investing in more formal costumes, they were less technicians of the sacred than technocrats of the quick change.[32]

Learning the secret of arterial injections that put an end to messy excavations of the viscera, embalmers first turned the substantial corpse into a colossus bulked up on a couch of satin and cherrywood, complement to early daguerreotypes. "I have attained to the power of preserving bodies," wrote the Frenchman J.N. Gannal in 1838, just as Daguerre was writing the brief for his camera, "...so as to admit of the contemplation of the person embalmed, with the countenance of one asleep." Then, realizing how rare were those bodies which must be permanently preserved (Lincoln, Lenin), morticians became masters of the miniature, of the deceptively healthy corpse glimpsed in part and in passing. They began to work toward a last correction of posture and countenance "to serve the living of our time...not to create museum specimens for the amazement of those who may populate the earth many centuries in the future."[33]

Two new kinds of burial grounds, laid out during World War I, harbor more of our known dead than any other ceremonial sites: the military cemetery with uniform white plaques and crosses in parade-ground formations – the "cemeteries for the living" rationalized by mining engineer Hubert Eaton. The six hundred Forest Lawns and Memorial Parks spread across North America by 1935 had much in common with war cemeteries – the spurning of chaotic "marble orchards" in favor of identical markers; the rigid control of offerings and inscriptions; an overarching faith in the virtue of repetition, from the immaculate ranks of thousands of identical graves (dug since 1949 by mechanical backhoes) to copies of famous art – "Nowhere else on earth may so many exact replicas of renowned statuary masterpieces be seen together." At both war cemetery and memorial park, portraits of the people are absent, and the wrack of death is dissembled.[34]

Dissemblance I take to be a soulless duplicity, that which becomes dissimilar through the very enactment of the sham. Headed for punctiliously spaced gravesites, the embalmed body in its casket has been emptied of *ka*. No longer does it lie as surety for an ancestral soul or individual spirit. No longer does it present in public, one last time, a personnage in its social relations ("Because everything is in one location, costs are lower and our mortuaries offer privacy and seclusion. There is no need for funeral processions through crowded city streets.") Unlike the plaster lifecasts set in tableaux by George Segal since 1962, and unlike the lifecasts in polyester resin painted with verist detail by Duane Hanson since 1965, the embalmed body makes no allusions. It does not impress "the living as the appearance of the original never perceived until now," as philosopher Maurice Blanchot wrote in the 1950s, meditating upon the cadaver as our mortal but estranged remains.[35]

It might as well be wax.... Which is how the *ex voto* figure came about, proxy for the sacrifice of a man, wrote Roman mythographer Macrobius, trying to account for the small wax figures given as gifts after Saturnalia, a December revelry that continued into the eleventh Christian century. Subsequently, as royalty were represented at death by wax effigies, Europeans of all orders began to make wax offerings, life-size images of loved ones who needed the mercy of the Church. By the fourteenth century, the Church of the Santissima Annunziata in Florence was hung over with heavy *boti* clad in cloth or armor, sometimes on wax horseback, hanging from cords stretched from hooks in the roof; by the seventeenth century, the cords were so worn that the six hundred figures came rotting, rotting, down to the Florentine floor.[36]

Another "Ragged Regiment" formed the first public museum of wax figures. At Westminster Abbey since the 1400s, "The Play of the Dead Volks" was a collection of funeral effigies of English monarchs, their wax features and finery twice restored (1606, 1760) from rags to richness. But in Renaissance Italy too, notables were commissioning lifesize waxes of loved ones with wigs of human hair, blown-glass eyes, tinted skin, fine raiment, to be put on public display. At the same time, between 1486 and 1610, a New Jerusalem of painted, costumed figures in wax, plaster, and wood was erected by the poorer folk of the Lake District of northern Italy. Through the many chapels of these "sacred mountains," life-size Magi rode on their stuffed horses, the Innocents were massacred, the Virgin gave birth. "How can an Italian peasant realize to himself the Annunciation so well as by seeing such a chapel?" asked the English novelist Samuel Butler three centuries later. "For the people delight in these graven images.... They like them as our own people like Madame Tussaud's."[37]

Before Mme Tussaud of Paris and London, there had been men such as Ambrosius Müller renewing the Reformation in Germany in 1605 with waxes of Jan Hus and Martin Luther. In England women took over the business: Mrs. Goldsmith and Mrs. Mills, doing kings and queens; Mary Salmon, with the Countess of Heningbergh and her 365 babies, born all at once. Patience Wright, come to London as a spy for the embattled British North American colonies, exhibited in 1779 wax likenesses of "many of the most exalted and respectable Personages of the Present Age." Visiting Mrs. Clark's galleries in 1793, a boy would be struck by the "hideous copper countenances" of Cherokee chiefs and by Renwick Williams, "called the Monster, cutting the Miss Porters."[38]

Monsters with sharp blades were everywhere in 1793, in gothic fictions, London streets, and abroad, where revolutionaries sliced off the head of Louis XVI and the Terror advanced through France. At the side of the guillotine, basket in hand, was Marie Grosholtz. Her mentor, Philippe Curtius, had been a court favorite with his museum of wax celebrities at the Palais Royal, and a popular favorite with his Den of Thieves on the Boulevard du Crime (and a lucrative sideline of "little groups of Wanton and Licentious Figures"). Daughter to his housekeeper, Marie learned the art from Curtius and cast Voltaire when he was eighty-four and she seventeen. Soon she was teaching a sister of Louis XVI how to work in wax and, once the Revolution got bloody, accepting decapitated heads of royal f(r)iends tossed at her by mobs demanding that the faces be cast in wax. By order of the National Assembly, she made death masks of Louis XVI and Marie Antoinette, of Marat and his assassin Charlotte Corday – a tableau viewed by Robespierre, whose unhinged head she would hold in her hands the next year. Curtius was poisoned in 1794. Marie married François Tussaud, an engineer, in 1795; sculpted Napoleon for a loving Josephine in 1801; left for England in 1802.[39]

Marie and her sons toured Great Britain for thirty years in the company of Voltaire, Rousseau, Benjamin Franklin, and a changing entourage of sovereigns, murderers, body snatchers, and mummies. On the road her sons did physionotracings; she did wax portraits of the living and of "PERSONS DECEASED, with the most correct appearance of Animation," but what distinguished her waxwork troupe was its historical drama. A Nottingham newspaper reported in 1819: "Instead of a number of unmeaning sallow faces, sitting in rows behind benches covered with green cloth . . . we were astonished on entering to behold a vast number of full-length figures, standing, sitting, and lying, in splendid attire, the whole bearing the appearances of real life." She who had modeled the last prisoner in the Bastille, and who herself had for some weeks languished in a French jail, would magnify that real life when she settled down in London in 1835 and built a dungeon for wax villains. This became known as "The Chamber of Horrors," complete with a blade from the original guillotine. "Wax-work!" wrote one Londoner in 1841: "The grace and benignity which we associate with the idea of a queen, . . . the tyranny of the Turk, the grimness of the murderer, the grotesqueness of the monster, are characteristics which may ordinarily be traced to the ineffaceable impressions received at the waxen exhibitions of the county fair, or from their better dressed, 'large as life' associates of the London sights" – especially Mme Tussaud's.[40]

Mme Tussaud made her own presence known as collateral to the historicity of her figures. Handling admissions, her manner was "easy and self-possessed, and were she motionless you would take her to be a piece of wax-work; *a dame of other days*." She was there again, in wax, "an excellent deception, and being placed at the entrance of the rooms, has caused many ludicrous mistakes." She was there, in the flesh, until her death in 1850.[41]

Few could command the prestige that gave Mme Tussaud access to an emperor's coach or the actual devices of a mandarin of murder. Other waxworkers worked upon such as "Daniel Dancer & His Sister, the Notorious Misers, who Starved themselves to Death in order to Save their Money" or "The Wonderful Maniac of Woodseats, Norton, Derbyshire; who was discovered, having remained in the position he was found in upwards of FOURTEEN YEARS," or the Siamese Twins who, wound up, began to fight. Gradually, waxworks were shunted away from historical impersonation toward theatrical imposture. Mrs. Siddons the actress and Liston the mime began to vie with Napoleon for pride of place in wax tableaux, appearing in costume in one or another of the characters they nightly assumed. Although a showman might earlier have been "careful to call his exhibition the 'Statuary,'" talking of biographies and "the moral lessons to be drawn therefrom," by the late 1800s the dignity of the figures was rarely a speaking point. The *ka*, the spirit-double, was vanishing from the wax.[42]

What had been a figure of annunciation bearing the Dignity of kingship or the dignity of personal faith had become merely an "agreeable" deception. Why? The skills of wax modelers had not declined. Their three-dimensional, expertly tinted productions were surpassed neither by two-dimensional black-and-white photographs nor by the "photo-sculpture" fad of the 1860s. But we know that figures were both shown and made by many women, among them Mme Tussaud and Catherine Andras, Modeller in Wax to Queen Charlotte. Waxwork declined in status during the nineteenth century at the same time that other "women's work" – in thread, shells, ivory, paper, foil, and wax flowers – was being demoted by a patriarchate intent upon defining an exclusively male public sphere. A century earlier, English connoisseur Horace Walpole had praised the work of the miniaturist Thomas Worlidge, then he had given equal time to the work of Worlidge's wife and other women who produced embroidered portraits from original crayon sketches. By the 1800s, any attempt on a woman's part to claim an artistic equivalence with men had ordinarily to be made under the guise of a male persona. Wax figures, in this context, were being reduced as women themselves were being reduced, to a confining domestic correctness.[43]

But the Musée Grévin in Paris, Eppmann's Panoptikum in Berlin, Gassner's wax figures in Monaco were not primarily women's work. A second explanation: as embalmers and mourners had to contend with the smell and sight of mortal decay, so waxworkers and celebrants had to contend with that smell and vulnerability of wax to which we are still sensitive in cheap lipsticks and bad candles. Europeans were becoming increasingly disturbed by personal odors and domestic effluvia even as their factories discharged volumes of untreated by-products into the water and air. The stillness of wax figures, once appreciated as dignity of bearing, began to be redolent of decay in poorly ventilated rooms. Dim lighting, necessary to keep wax from melting, had been acceptable in eras of candlelight; it seemed furtive or occult in eras of gas and then electric lamps. Those who had felt it an honor to be in the presence of wax eminences began to keep their emotional and physical distance as they also shied from the sicksweet smell of a made-up body preserved with formaldehyde.[44]

Left to the cold minutiae of correctness, wax figures today beg for our embrace but forbid our touch. The National Historical Waxworks Museum hopes that Lincoln's assassination "will look so real that spectators will feel impelled to do something to save the President's life." But the so-reality is too precious for intervention, the props too valuable, costumes too original. As investment, not investiture, wax museum figures now have what the nineteenth-century German poet Friedrich von Schiller called false dignity, which "destroys all the mimic play of the features by which the soul gleams forth upon the face."[45]

Correctness, thence to dissemblance. The Movieland Wax Museum at Buena Park, California, in 1984 invited visitors to "RELIVE" no momentous events but "scenes from Halloween, The Alien, and Altered States," tales of a soulless duplicity, of possession and regression in the name of nothing whatsoever. Movieland's Superman set was "an authentic replica" of actors playing characters in a mock-up of a scene from a film from a comic book. Elsewhere on museum platforms from France to Canada to Australia are transilient figures, celebrities with multiple identities or evaporating histories who are waxworthy because they are already other than who they were last year, requiring a rewrite and an "authentic replica" set to make them meaningful again. And none is actually made of wax.[46]

Undertaking the pilgrimage to Madame Tussaud's Wax Museum in London, you can piece together this history of wax figures. Mme Tussaud is there at the entrance as she was when last she took her own measure at the age of eighty-one. She is there also, younger, with the head of Marie Antoinette, in the historical section across from a hauntingly thin Voltaire and the most moving of the wax impersonations, the Comtesse Du Barry, loveliest mistress to Louis XVI, a gracile "Sleeping Beauty" cast by Curtius and placed now in a short casket of a bed, her small diaphragm rising and lowering almost imperceptibly beneath a faded white dress. But the crowd, which has posed for photos in the forecourt beside an actor choking a crocodile, is impatient with Du Barry, Lord Byron, and the hundreds of cast hands (Franz Liszt, Danny Kaye) on wooden pallets. The crowd wants the Chamber of Horrors, cries and whimpers through a foggy London street where stands John George Haigh, the Acid Bath Murderer, who bequeathed his suit to the museum before he was executed and whose wax figure was placed on exhibition, fully dressed, twenty minutes after. The crowd wants the correctness of the hall of dignitaries: Henry VIII with his unfortunate queens, the British royal family, a Mahatma Gandhi so out of place he would, if he could, bring down this raj too. Along the way, at every turn, has been dissemblance, people so detached from personhood that the best you can manage is a name, not an identity; a finger pointed at, oh, it's Joan Collins vamping down a staircase as gray plaster papparazzi crouch for glamour shots.[47]

Alone among hundreds of figures is one who has both weight and character: a middle-aged lady in a warm blue sweater, fallen asleep on one of the couches along the wall in the hall of dignitaries, blue plastic shopping bag at her feet. She is a tired nobody with a museum brochure – and a kissing cousin of the resin figures by Duane Hanson and bronze casts by J. Seward Johnson, Jr., artists who love to place in situ their maids, housepainters, picnickers, businessmen. "People will rush by one of my works in a public place," Johnson has noted, "and be fooled into thinking, 'That's a real person.' Then they try to come up with reasons or excuses for why they were mistaken." They were mistaken because, he writes, "In each case, I celebrated a moment when the individual had taken control of his or her life."[48] He has something there, for the loss of weight (literal and figurative) of modern waxworks is due to a loss of place and purpose. If the lady in the sweater has fallen asleep, she is at one with herself, while the dignitaries are posed as in life they were groomed to pose, looking neither themselves nor away.

Like the embalmed body, the waxwork has been evacuated of soul, losing first its public position, then its play-full-ness, and finally its Happen-Stance, that bond to events past and future. Lacking Happen-Stance, it can neither surprise us nor exact devotion.

Between the field of waxwork and the field of embalming lies a commons, the thing itself, unaccommodated man. Bare forked animal, its lendings off, the wax anatomical body appeared in Italy, heir of traditions memorial, artistic, and medical.

Memorial. From the mid-fifteenth century, "men began to make, at a slight cost, death masks of those who died, so that a number of these life-like portraits may be seen in every house in Florence over chimney-pieces, doors, windows, and cornices."

Memorial and artistic. Fond of taking plaster casts of body segments for his own painting and sculpture, Andrea del Verrocchio studied with a master waxworker and fashioned three grand waxes of Lorenzo de' Medici, who was rendering thanks to God after having narrowly survived an assassination attempt.[49]

Artistic and medical. Dubious of the customary use of ox and ape as models for human anatomy, the young Flemish doctor Andreas Vesalius in 1537 began public dissections of fresh human cadavers in Padua. His book of the human body, partly illustrated by one of Titian's students, was scorned by conservative anatomists when printed in 1543, and it did contain errors, but the figures were so exquisite that it was issued in an *Epitome* for art students. Layers of skin flayed away, the body was depicted in neoclassical poses as its systems of bone, muscle, veins, nerves, and viscera stood exposed on separate sheets. Clear of decay, clean of tissue, the erect body carried itself with dignity, aloof from the bloody incursions of dissection.[50]

Medical. At the medical school in Bologna, muscles were moulded in tow, wax, mustard, and turpentine, then laid over human skeletons. These figures substituted for scarce cadavers and allowed seventeenth-century anatomists to handle bodies without contracting blood poisoning from poorly preserved specimens or infections from victims of plague and syphilis, wax specialties of the Sicilian abbot Gaetano Zummo. Perfecting the life-size wax anatomy, Anna Morandi in 1776 finished what she and her late husband Giovanni Manzolini had begun under commission from the Archbishop of Bologna: a full series, new-born babe to aged man. Continental and American sculptor-surgeons pursued similar work, but it was from Italy that the finest anatomical models came. Under the initial supervision of the physiologist Felice Fontana, a workshop of Florentines created whole wax bodies and thousands of body parts, enough in 1794 to occupy twenty rooms in the palace of Fontana's patient, Leopold, Grand Duke of Tuscany.[51]

Jewel among wax figures was the pregnant woman, her abdomen peeled open, the fetus revealed. As early as 1730, one such was on display at a London pharmacy; in 1746 another was in Paris, eight months along; in 1788 Clemente Susini at the Fontana workshop sculpted a

woman whose uterus held removable fair-haired twins; in 1835 a similar woman was shown "to Ladies in private, and explained by a Female"
before being auctioned off – to a man – for the queenly sum of £195.
Parturience satisfied prurience. If the wax anatomy was "employed to perpetuate many transient phenomena of disease of which no other art could
have made so lively a record," it perpetrated as well a gravid pornography, private parts teased out, the lovely naked woman manhandled.[52]

Anna Morandi herself had done a pregnant wax woman as natural as
she was lovely – far lovelier than the papier-mâché figures produced in
the 1800s by Louis Auzoux, "not so much a corpse as a kind of toy,
horrible-looking, very spic-and-span, and smelling of varnish," but
even so instructive, the lungs "like two sponges; the heart like a large
egg." The female anatomical figure with removable parts, called a "dissembling doll or Venus," was truly a pedagogical tool, but in wax it also
suggested malleability, voluptuousness, and *morbidezza*: delicate flesh.[53]

A work of erotic art, warm white wax dripped along silk threads
(her lymphatic fibers), the pregnant wax anatomy was closest to life
because closest to desire: her disassembly was no dissembling but foreplay to ensoulment; her reassembly celebrated the act of reanimation.[54]
Sexual object and biological event, she nodded across to other genera
of reproduction, the artist's wooden manikin and the window dresser's
mannequin.

Making Out: Producers and Consumers

Male and female did the masters make them, articulated at ankles,
knees, hips, waist, wrists, elbows, shoulders, and neck. Their specialty
was to be unearthly. They hovered as angels and *putti*, flew to Heaven
as saints, descended from Mt. Olympus. But as subtly as they maintained
the proportions or distentions of a humanesque body on mercurial or
seraphic errands, they stood revealed when used as scaffolding for subjects who were meant, like most of us, to suffer the pull of gravity.
Under ten inches tall, these faceless little men or manikins (< Dutch
manneken) could be posed as diverse characters in the same scene, but
they could sustain neither the roundedness of social intercourse nor the
groundedness of the individual. Noticed first in the works of Masaccio
early in the fifteenth century, their (im)postures were most apparent
in sixteenth- and seventeenth-century pictures of tavern or table gaiety, whose Dutch and Flemish painters dispensed with preliminary
sketches, building up their canvases one manikin posture at a time. The
resulting obliviousness of relationship among figures may be seen in Jan
Miense Molenaer's *Atelier* of 1631. On our left stands the artist, looking
over his shoulder and directing our eyes to the dwarf (*manneken*) dancing with a lapdog. The dwarf, legs at unstable angles, is as emotionally
distant from and unsupported by the dog as he is distant from the others in the studio ❭ a bearded traveler with his back to the worldmap ❭
a short grinning courtier dandling his cane or rapier ❭ a tall woman (innkeeper?) looking at no one, her right hand raised, finger pointed in

FIGURE 3.4. *Atelier* or *Painter's Studio* by Jan Miense Molenaer, 1631. Oil on canvas, 96.5 × 134 cm. Reproduced courtesy of the Staatliche Museen zu Berlin, Gemäldegalerie im Bodemuseum (State Museums of Berlin, Painting Gallery of the Bode Museum).

admonition. The same figures appear within a finished painting aslant an easel to our right, their rearrangement implying a conviviality we now distrust. Bent awkwardly forward, the painter himself must be no more than manikin, unmuscled as the suit of clothes on the chair center stage.[55]

Joke on the production of art, Molenaer's *Atelier* took the wooden manikin through all four stages of likeness at a single ironic bow. There was impersonation, in the very image of the artist; there was imposture, the four oblivious figures, each a differently enlarged incarnation of a wooden miniature; there was correctness, the well-painted people on the easel carousing at a table without psychic force or emotional drive; there was dissemblance, the bodiless suit of clothes, and the studio itself, dispirited in the very enactment of the sham.

Through the tergiversations of the manikin or lay figure, painter and sculptor were relieved of the fatigue, the moods, the illnesses of flesh-and-blood models shivering in the studio. The lay figure (< Dutch *leeman*, *ledenman*, jointed or limb-man) was not a collaborator but an apparatus. Undisguised, lay figures were shown skewered with a rod from neutered cleft between the buttocks down to pedestals of wood, or they were sat down. Rarely could they stand alone. They were to artists what artists were to patrons: dependents. The manikin, read one definition in 1730, was "a little statue or model usually made of wax or wood, the junctures whereof are so contrived, that it may be put into any attitude at pleasure." Grown to two feet tall, and sometimes life-size, the lay figure would remain a miniature, subservient and manipulable: "that model who amid all the changes of artist-life remains ever true to its master." In a painting by Wilhelm Trübner in 1888: a life-size naked manikin, arms akimbo, stands with head tilted inhumanly back and torso in extremis, subject to the painter's every whim; a fully clothed live model faces us directly, proper, stiff, hands in her lap. Pablo Picasso's 1923 *Nude and Sculpture* contrasted a hysterical wooden manikin with a living model who keeps something of herself from the painter. One has double joints; the other has dignity.[56]

When at the start of World War I the Italian artist Giorgio de Chirico called his paintings of manikins "metaphysical still lifes," he was, with his cousins the Futurists, endowing mechanism with spirit, apparatus with vitality. Son of an architectural engineer, Giorgio was taken with the manikin, a blind construction one sets one's sights by. His centerpieces in *The Seer* (1915), *The Duo* (1915), *The Disquieting Muses* (1917), *The Condottieri* (1917), *Prodigal Son* (1922) were halfway between wood, cloth, marble, metal, and life. What the Futurists would paint in furious action, de Chirico drafted as human prototypes waiting to be set in motion along an architectural grid. This would be the status of the war itself – months of immobility for mud-caked soldiers crouched in trenches, interrupted by brief involuntary spasms of violence across a murderously industrial no-man's-land gridded with barbed wire and metal fragments. The shellshocked soldiers were treated like crash-test dummies, thrown into battle against obstacles of indefinite resistance to measure the success of a grand design.[57]

Today, in their most sophisticated form, lay figures may leap and jump in *tour jeté*, but still they cannot come to terms with gravity and the violent forces of repulsion and attraction. Like children's stick figures, lay figures on computer screens fail to appreciate their own mass and rarely socialize.

Some problems are technical. Skin presents a complex, semipermeable, unevenly sensitive, inconsistently elastic surface, so electronically imaged figures must remain as skinless as their wooden kin; their skeletons fleshed out geometrically with discs, spheres, or polygons, they cannot yet *feel* the ground. The processing time required to enable a parahuman body to check constantly its perimeters for evidence of collision or penetration is so great that interactions as simple as the shaking of hands are possible only with supercomputers. Moreover, the body is not a uniform solid. If one can establish its proportions, it is difficult to estimate shifts of weight as a dancer moves fluidly from a *plié* to a canted leap, more difficult yet to describe the contours of tissue surrounding a joint as a dancer changes position. Like manikins, computer-simulated bodies have no muscles, must be moved by rote or extrapolation. Electronic lay figures may take elegantly programmed steps and change pace or stride with inhuman precision, but a *pas de deux* threatens to become a Siamesed monster as soon as one dancer reaches for the other.[58]

Choreography using the program COMPOSE reveals another problem with digital figures that is as much cultural as technical: facelessness. Devised at Simon Fraser University by the Human Figure Animation Lab, COMPOSE has been used by Thecla Schiphorst in Vancouver and by the arthritic Merce Cunningham in New York City to choreograph dances and extend movement vocabularies. The lead dancer of COMPOSE was digitized out of a medical text from cross sections of a cadaver with poor posture and a short neck. All other dancers on screen must be replicas of him and, like him, they have no true faces. The face is a devil of a thing to model in motion because culturally central to our reading of character, emotion, intent. Alert to the least flicker of any of its many muscles, we scan the face for signs of boredom, disapproval, love, soul. The lay figure's countenance, wooden or electronic, is restricted to a simple geometry, blank enough to assume any character, any position.[59]

On the computer screen, figures running faceless and shadowless through a dance routine are liable to run blithely through each other. They run, eventually, through all four positions of likeness. 1st: The impersonation of a cadaver. 2nd: The imposture of its clones. 3rd: The correctness of twinned figures going-through-the-motions without internal impetus or spiritual engagement. 4th: The dissemblance of bodies which are not really bodies at all but simulations, weightless, emotionless, and spineless (in lieu of vertebra they have an algorithm

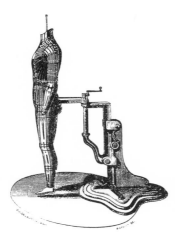

FIGURE 3.5. C. de Dunin's mechanical tailor's dummy, a "correct likeness to the Apollo Belvedere" but designed so as to accommodate most measurements, shown at the Crystal Palace, London, 1851.

for motion like the bending of an accordion). Computers may give lay figures a virtuosity admired by choreographers who chase after the modernist phantom of an impersonal grace, but they also confirm the historical anonymity of lay figures, protean and generic as the name they go by on the open market: "Life Forms."

Think of manikins as a means toward the interchangeable form, the One that fits the Many. If the history of technology is, as a New England poet wrote in 1843, a history of machines created in the image of Man –

> What are his machines
> Of steel, brass, leather, oak, and ivory,
> But manikins and miniatures,
> Dwarfs of one faculty, measured from him,
> As nimbly he applies his bending self
> Unto the changing world...?

– then manikins could be machines. That is how a jury in 1851 thought about the manikin exhibited at London's Crystal Palace. A headless version of the Apollo Belvedere, C. de Dunin's mechanical figure was composed of "875 framing-pieces, 48 grooved steel plates, 163 wheels, 202 slides, 476 metal washers, 482 spiral springs, 704 sliding plates, 32 sliding tubes, 497 nuts, 3500 fixing and adjusting screws, and a considerable number of steadying pinions," all dedicated to adjustments away from perfection toward the "peculiarities of form of any individual." Artists could use Apollo as a lay figure; tailors could adjust Apollo to alter suits for their clients "with as much facility as if the original person, whose measure had been taken, were present." Blessed with several Apollos, boasted Dunin, you could fit uniforms to an army of several hundred thousand men.[60]

That's one giant leap to mankind from the screws of a few headless men, but it was the smallest of historical steps from manikin to dressmaker's dummy. Medieval knights in the off season hung their suits of armor upon dummies called "dobbles." In 1464, the Florentine artist and architect Filarete situated his claim to having invented the lay figure within paragraphs about the need to dress sculpted or painted figures in costumes suitable to age and circumstance. Manikins who appeared as themselves were given atypically personable features in seventeenth-century engravings by Crispijn van de Passe, but even he recommended that they be used solely in studies of the draping of the human body. Common was the warning that "The Painter ought to avoid all manner of stiffness and hardness of folds, and be careful that they don't smell of the layman [lay figure]." De Chirico's metaphysical still lifes this century have vacillated between the atelier and the sewing room, between the jointed wooden manikin and the chalk-marked cloth dummy. *The Lay-Figure* in Ethel B. Van der Veer's one-act play of 1936 was "NOT one of those beautiful and costly affairs now used by some artists, but the old-type of *crude* figure made of stout muslin and stuffed with sawdust or upholsterer's cotton-wool. Even the face of the figure need not necessarily be painted in, but it should be fitted with a mohair wig of a color to match Sylvie's own hair" — Sylvie, model for the Angel of Light painted by her mad father, who had punished Sylvie as a child by stripping Lay-Sylvie and leaving it naked all night in the dark studio, and who now takes a bullwhip to the faceless figure, crying, "Are you my daughter? Are you my daughter?"[61]

"We should weep, ladies, at our own fate, when we see that misery of violated matter, against which a terrible wrong has been committed," says Bruno Schulz's father, who in fact did own a dry-goods shop. The story of the "Tailors' Dummies," by Bruno Schulz, a twentieth-century Polish drawing teacher and fabulist, is a Kleistian fiction, an explication of his father's supposed *Treatise on Tailors' Dummies or the Second Book of Genesis*. Wishing to perpetrate a Second Creation, wrote Father (wrote Bruno), "we shall not insist either on durability or solidity of workmanship; our creations will be temporary, to serve for a single occasion.... For each action, each word, we shall call to life a different human being." This, like Schulz's own drawings of men bowing before fashion-plate women, was a profound confusion of the mercurial lay figure, slave to transience of characters, with the stolid dummy whose padded torso is molded to accept one after the other a measured individual's many costumes. It was a confusion bred of an industrial world's incessant production and a throwaway culture's incessant consumption. Not marble but papier-mâché, not hardwoods but oakum and sawdust must be our passion. "In one word," concluded Father, "we wish to create man a second time, in the shape and semblance of a tailor's dummy."[62]

And woman a second time, in the shape of the dressmaker's dummy. Headless but familiar, breastless but full-busted, legless but self-standing,

bulky but insubstantial (bast, sawdust, cotton-wool, air), the dressmaker's dummy is pregnant with ambivalence to the degree that wax anatomies are pregnant with desire. She reproduces the contradictions
through which men have adored their mothers, lusted after maidens,
and dreaded matrons, as in the childhood of a boy passing each day the
shop of the Misses Scriven, who displayed dresses upon "headless, arm-
less and legless mock-ups of female torsos, having lathe-turned erec-
tions of dark wood in place of heads." From this came a recurrent
nightmare of "a calico-covered dummy, formidably breasted (without
cleft) and sinisterly headless," wrote Alan Watts in his memoirs. "This
thing would mutter at me and suggest ineffable terrors."[63]

Dummies embody the contradictions of the process by which modern societies dehumanize the labor whose products they extol, then
celebrate the "made to measure" individuality that factory labor and
mass-produced objects make possible, as in a 1990 advertisement for
"SEPARATES" − a stereo amplifier, tuner, cassette deck and compact
disc player, on their individual walnut stands, hooked up by earphones
to a faceless tailor's dummy before a backdrop of chalk dashes on dark
grey cloth: "Suit yourself."[64]

Such an androcentric image I must immediately regret. In women's
lives the dressmaker's dummy is touched with the power and glamour
of the shopwindow mannequin, which has achieved a substantial cultural authority through its command of FIT. Remember Mme M.? She
was a dressmaker. That she should have borne two sets of twins was
coincidence. That she should begin to suspect each living loved one
of being a rack of successive impersonators, like a rack of dresses misfitted to the same shopwindow mannequin, was more than coincidence.
Capgras never credited Mme M.'s occupation with relevance to her subsequent preoccupation, although she identified herself obsessively with
the dresses she could be known by. Women have worked out their
own meanings, their own sense of FIT, through dressmaker's forms and
womannequins. This is scarcely to say that women require the artifice
of a shopwindow. It is to say that women's portraits of themselves (like
the many self-portraits by painter Judith Leyster, wife to Molenaer) have
been and can be liberating.[65]

Visible since the fourteenth century, dolls with the newest coiffures
and dresses were sent from fashion centers in France, Flanders, and Italy
to courts throughout Europe. Democratized, they would be known as
"bagmen's dolls," packed in the saddlebags of pedlars. By the eighteenth
century, gentlewomen as far away as India and the Americas were relying upon these foot-tall dolls to keep up with European fashions.[66]

Companion to these *couriers de la mode* were other circulating figures, miniatures made to the exact proportions of women who sent
them off to distant designers, whose seamstresses extrapolated therefrom a life-size body and tailored a new wardrobe. Such womannequins
had a power that the generic dressmaker's dummy could maintain only
in part, the power to demand FIT. Unlike the artist's manikin whose

measurements were ideal or proximate, these womannequins bore the markings of a Double. FIT went beyond correctness; it was a closeness of relation between woman and doublet, a comfortableness of the self with her portrait. If the portrait was as seasonal as the womannequin was provisional (a woman could become stooped, gain or lose weight), FIT assured at least a successful, civilized impersonation.[67]

As womannequins became life-size public figures, FIT was also required of them. Under new social pressures for clean clothes, then under commercial pressures for window display, the vaguely contoured cloth-and-straw clotheshorse of the 1600s had to be more precisely human and supple, made of willow strips by 1750, of wire by 1810, of cane by 1848, of stitched cardboard by 1860. In public, working behind plate glass under better lighting, window dressers had to assure that womannequins seemed to be made for their costumes, especially when Charles Worth in the late 1850s began to employ live models to display his Paris originals, designed upon and FITted to breathing bodies.[68]

Turn and turn about, statuesque womannequins began to exert a personal spell known, after 1840, as glamour — "When devils, wizards, or jugglers deceive the sight, they are said to cast glamour o'er the eyes of the spectator." For women who could never make the trip to Worth's salon, who gazed into shopwindows imagining themselves in this or that outFIT, womannequins demanded that each body be FITted to their curvaceous *cartonnage*, shaped tight of corset and painted smooth of complexion.[69]

Hairdressers and hatmakers had been using pasteboard heads to display wigs and bonnets since the eighteenth century. Around 1850, while dressmaker's dummies with paper-cone heads appeared in New England storefronts, Professor Lavigne in Paris directed the first firm producing full-trunk mannequins. The Belgian sculptor Frédéric Stockman, working as a couturier for tailors in Paris, learned from Lavigne the manufacture of flesh-toned busts with surfaces of percaline. On his own he added limbs articulated at hip and knee. Farming out the heads to maskmakers, modeling the torsos upon live fashion "mannequins," Stockman and his son would found an industry that, thirty years later in 1900, was producing over 1.5 million complete life-size figures.[70]

They came in many dimensions, and from Rome, Brussels, Berlin as well as Paris. They came with improvements in the FITtings at their joints to extend flexibility. They came with character. It was the wax figure, introduced at the Paris Exposition of 1894, whose human hair, glass eyes, and wax face secured a commanding presence. Full-bodied (two-hundred-pound women in wax and papier-mâché, three-hundred-pound men in wax and cast iron), grounded (metal bases with a rod up one leg), articulated (at neck, waist, hips, arms, wrists), teeth gleaming (artificial or real), neck glowing with paste jewels or graced with foulard, the wax figure was no one to trifle with. Where before she had been adjusted to every style, now each womannequin, rouged and coiffed, owned an enduring persona which apparel and accessories had to FIT.

Photoengraved fashion plates usurped the role of dolls, but woman-nequins held their own by virtue of their glamour and their command of FIT. By 1900, FIT had connotations across the economic spectrum. It meant, on the high end, being FITted for a gown by an imperious couturier or being remeasured by one's haberdasher for "tailored" (closer-FITting) jackets and trousers. Midspectrum, it meant trying on ready-made clothes in a cramped dressing booth, struggling to FIT one's body to the sizings of an industry whose mass-produced fashions looked most alluring on wax figures. At the lower end, it meant achiev-ing at the kitchen table with pins, scissors, and needle the FIT of a dress seen on a womannequin. To all it meant a demanding exactitude, for as Social Darwinists said, in the battle for survival only the FIT would survive. Exacerbated by mounting anxiety over the sloppiness of body fat, by height-weight charts posted on penny scales, and by prescriptions for eyeglasses that at last corrected for astigmatism, FIT was becoming more than a matter of myopic fashion; it was a tenet of the virtuous life. The womannequin was the deity of FIT, features finely drawn, car-riage indefatigable, its body at one with its *mode* and milieu. Command-ing dramatic scenes comparable to the new tableaux in natural history museums, mannequins by 1900 stood at the center of things.[71]

"Self-contained" articles, complete in themselves, were best served by mirrors, wrote a Chicago window dresser in 1909; everything else needed livening up. You could borrow mirror effects from sideshows and get the bust of a woman to float in the air, wrote another window dresser, or hire live "mannequins" to change costumes every hour; what-ever you did had better have a spirit of motion to it, which was the spirit of promotion, without which "the modern merchant sinks into obliv-ion, the busy world forgets him, and he is left to himself – to rust, to vegetate, or to fail ignominiously." Thus L. Frank Baum, founder of the National Association of Window Trimmers of America (1898), editor of its trade journal, *The Show Window*, author in 1900 of *The Art of Dec-orating Dry Goods Windows* and *The Wonderful Wizard of Oz*.[72]

Baum was born in 1856 to a world fluid and theatrical, in which he would switch costumes as often as the mannequins in his windows. Youngest of seven children of a man who made a fortune in that slip-pery commodity, oil, Frank at fifteen was publishing with his brother Henry *The Rose Lawn Home Journal*, direct from the family estate out-side Mattydale, New York, twenty miles from the site where a laborer digging a well had struck a water-worn stone colossus and exclaimed, "Jerusalem, Nichols, it's a big Injun!" The brothers Baum speculated that during Noah's time, this Cardiff Giant found in 1869 must have drowned in waters he had said "ain't deep." P.T. Barnum bargained for rights to the Giant, who was drawing three thousand folks a day; when his terms were rejected, Barnum commissioned a sculpted copy and dis-played it as "the one, the only, the original Cardiff giant." The original was itself a hoax, carved in gypsum as the spitting image of a tobacco farmer, then buried for antiquity's sake (all 10′4½″, 2990 lbs.) under a stump here in this "Burnt-Over" District of revivalists and spirit-rappers, where a petrified Indian might prove attractive. As the perpetrators of the hoax moved on to uncover the Missing Link (clay baked with human bones and apelike legs), the young Frank Baum struggled to find his evolutionary niche: cub reporter in Manhattan; touring thespian in his own drama, *The Maid of Arran*, with scene changes that were a "triumph of mechanical art"; hawker of axle grease; proprietor of Baum's Bazaar in Aberdeen, South Dakota; publisher of the *Aberdeen Saturday Pioneer* (1888–90) with its praise for a commercial carnival of women "mannequins" costumed as diamonds, strawberries, typewriters; traveling salesman for crockery and fireworks; journalist at the *Chicago Evening Post*; author of *Mother Goose in Prose* (1897) and *Father Goose: His Book* (1899); novelist by the names of Edith Van Dyne, Floyd Akers, Laura Bancroft, Suzanne Metcalfe, Schuyler Stanton; playwright fascinated with special effects.[73]

Emerald City, suggests one historian, was an enormous show window; it and Oz were inspired, suggests another, by the Midway Plaisance at the 1893 Chicago World's Fair, a show window on the industrial Midwest. In that window glowed the womannequin, painted, posed, and FITted in secret, overnight, to emerge as resplendent as Glinda the Good, "the greatest sorceress of all," whose own story, *Glinda of Oz*, would be Baum's last, completed days before he died in 1919 in Hollywood. Most exegetes, however, would equate the mannequin with the Scarecrow, a straw man, "an assemblage of detachable parts" with "no interior originating center" and "an uncanny ability to become whatever it acquires, refusing to separate essence from accident." Or with the Tin Would-man, a lover who has maimed himself, "first a leg and then a finger and then an ear," until he is entirely prosthetic, a disheartened figure longing for the lubricity of Baum's axle grease, of motion and emotion, of endless desire and consumption. Or with the Cowardly Lion, all stuffed and nonsense, his roar as much a put-on as Baum's account (in the *Saturday Pioneer*) of an Oproar House where the singers "was all dummies with phonographs inside 'em." Or with the Wizard, projection of himself: "How can I help being a humbug when all these people make me do things that everybody knows can't be done?"[74]

Whatever else it does as economic or political parable, *The Wonderful Wizard of Oz* rehearses the history of manikins and mannequins. The Munchkins at the foot of the Yellow Brick Road are lay figures, cute but ineffective on the larger stage of modern merchandising. Scarecrow is the straw clotheshorse, his contours patchy, his static body powerless against crows of bankruptcy. Tin Woodman is the wire-ribbed dressmaker's form, hollow and clumsy. Cowardly Lion is the cloth tailor's dummy, stuffed with (h)oakum. The Wizard is the animator, the window dresser who sets the figures in apparent motion and gives them purpose, heart, and fortitude, but he is inadequate to the final task, the transduction of fantasy into fortune (the Emporia of Kansas). Consistent with Baum's feminism and theosophy, Dorothy must await a redemp-

tive woman, Glinda the new wax womannequin, to discover what perfectly FITted ruby slippers can do for a real girl.[75]

"I still remember the first day I saw her in 1912 (I was five at the
time), staring aloofly at a spot approximately two inches over my head,
as I peered through the glass of The Famous, Hannibal's biggest store.
She had a delicious pink-and-white waxworks complexion, the longest,
curliest eyelashes I'd ever seen, dainty little fingers that stuck out at
right angles to her hand, and she was wearing a dress that blinded me –
made of glistening beads with a parrot embroidered over the entire front
of it." So would be sewn the future career of Lester Gaba as a designer
of womannequins, but before we get to him (and long before we get
to parrots), we must take note of his implicit animation of the mannequin, central to the window trimmer's creed. Addressing an 1899 convention of his peers, one trimmer said, "You do not place that [wax]
figure in your work simply because it has a head. When you place it in
your displays you do so to represent life." A decade later a trade manual repeated the window dresser's creed: "Under his deft manipulation,
the mechanical device of wax, wood and iron is made to live – to assume
all the graces of the human figure. To him the form is not a lay figure,
but a living, breathing being."[76]

Pygmalion, king and sculptor, dressed and redressed his ivory woman,
laid flowers at her feet, embraced her nightly yet was wretched until
Venus was moved to make the figure live,

> as though ivory had turned to wax
> And wax to life, yielding, yet quick with breath.

If the wax womannequin was Galatea *redux* (Gaba turned to womannequins after sculpting in Ivory Soap), her power to enchant had in the
end to be the power to come alive, in show windows as in Ovid's *Metamorphoses*. Without the legend of animation, she could not make consumers "believe the unbelievable," which is the art of window dressing
as of other storytelling. Standing above eye level, she had to *in*spire, to
breathe each passerby in.[77]

Did it help that she was mortal? That as she took on character, she
became more sensitive and could melt under hot bulbs? That she aged:
"the older a wax head gets the more brittle and hard the wax becomes
until it is so brittle that you cannot do any patching or mending on the
head without great danger of its falling to pieces"? That she soon had a
name to go with each of her Parisian faces: Véra, Marjolane, Célimène,
matronly Adeline, Renilde of the eyeglasses? That she was caught smok-
ing by the Woman's Christian Temperance Union, which decried her
easy virtue in 1927 as it did her shamelessness, undressing in public and
showing, for a while, nipples? That she gloried in publicity and would
be seen on average by a quarter of the people in a town? That she was
at ease in the big city, escorted by Lester Gaba, her Pygmalion, to swank
nightclubs and a performance of *Madame Bovary*? That in 1941 she was

sued by a jealous woman who had sat as her prototype only to see herself outdone?[78]

Yes, it helped, but never enough to escape accusations of bad faith. Unlike the lay figure, the tailor's dummy, and the dressmaker's form, whose purposes are plain and whose plainness purposeful, the womannequin oscillates between favors material and sexual. Granted a first name, an age, physical confidence, social mobility, and legal standing (as a portrait), her self is all the same illusive. The womannequin may begin with impersonation, but she will be sculpted from a living model known not for her interior life, her wit, or her historic role but for a Look. She may be a steadfast impostor, but she is directionless, the show window "a dazzling lake, her heart bait." She may be posturally correct but has no backbone and is held up by a bumrod. Her limbs are interchangeable with the limbs of others in her set, but she has neither womb nor family name. It is this absence of ancestry which marks her as a dissembler and makes her invaluable to a "high intensity market setting" where what is imputed to things overcomes what they actually are.[79]

At the center of *things*, she can become all things: figure of a false labor, of work devoid of personal investment; figure of manufacture, an endless but sterile production line; figure of FITful fashion, momentarily correct in detail and proportions; figure of consumption itself, perpetually conditional and tensed.

Supercharged, she was one of the enabling fictions of Surrealism, which embraced the womannequin in all her manifestations — sleepwalker, found object, biomorph, dream subject. Surrealists stuck a womannequin's legs into the horn of a Victrola, her hand the armature for the needle; they mutilated large dolls; they sculpted humanoid figures as if long-necked womannequins.[80] In Paris in 1938, visitors to an International Exposition of Surrealism proceeded along a Surrealist Street whose streetwalkers were womannequins dressed by André Masson, Max Ernst, Marcel Duchamp, Jean Arp, Yves Tanguy, Man Ray, Hans Bellmer, Joan Miró. "One of the most admired was Masson's, the head of which was enclosed in a bird cage, the mouth gagged by a black velvet band decorated with a pansy; beyond that it was adorned with nothing but a G string made of glass eyes." There were pansies at the armpits, too, and a peacock mask curling up from the crotch, and a fracture line at the waist where top joined bottom.[81]

Assemblage was a word Surrealists applied to their womannequins, who were, in modern art as in the clothing industry, heirs to the readymade. While Marcel Duchamp elevated a hatrack to unique Art, womannequins framed above eye level would dissemble the mass-produced dress into a One-of-a-Kind. Indeed, the figures in Duchamp's *Nude Descending a Staircase, No. 2* and *The Passage from Virgin to Bride* (1912), with the curious swivel to their joints, rods to the pelvic girdle, patternwheel dots, and dressmaker's bastings, were those of a womannequin refracted through plate glass, like the womannequin with a skin of bro-

FIGURE 3.6. Fashion mannequin designed by Pierre Imans, 1924–25. Shown at the Fashion Pavilion of the Exposition Internationale des Arts Décoratifs et Industriels Modernes, Paris, 1926.

ken mirrors presented at the Salon d'Automne in 1911. Duchamp, who admitted to having stolen his Bride from mannequins in wedding dress at a country fair, once proposed that he be considered rather a *fenêtrier*, a window dresser, than a painter.[82]

Just as André Breton was issuing his manifesto on Surrealism, the womannequin herself became Art. "With forehead too large, eyes too vast, gestures [too?] literary," the Art Deco womannequin lounged or lunged in black wax, olive-toned papier-mâché, gold or silver or bronze carnisine in the windows along a street of shops at the Exposition Internationale des Arts Décoratifs et Industriels Modernes, Paris, 1925. Sculpted not after live models but from fashion drawings, these womannequins had elongated bodies and attitudes suited to Art Deco shop facades. "The old wax mannequins were too realistic to respond to the abstract form assumed by architecture and decoration," explained Victor-Napoléon Siégel, the Canadian "Mannequin King" now allied with the Stockman firm. Added André Vigneau, the artist with whom Siégel and Stockman worked, "What is surprising is that now that the mannequin is no longer an exact copy of nature, it has more life." Pierre Imans would insert a disclaimer in his catalog of the line he showed at the Exposition: "the photographic reproductions in our album-catalogs but imperfectly capture the impression made by seeing our mannequins *in the flesh*."[83]

Freed from the tyranny of the realistic mannequin, explained Imans, a designer could achieve the intensity of highly stylized figures driven not by the actual but by the ideal body of the modern woman, with her "supple grace and gracile charm." The nouvelle womannequin, molded in papier-mâché or carnisine (plaster and gelatin), was more than ideally slender. It was lighter, reduced from a solid two hundred pounds to a hollow forty pounds. It was more durable, withstanding greater heat from spotlights and rougher handling from window dressers. It was sinewy, with extraordinarily flexed fingers, arms, torsos. It was, it seemed, ready for anything – mounting a monumental staircase in evening dress (on the cover of a 1925 issue of Breton's journal, *Révolution surréaliste*); entering "ready-made daydreams" (1930s windows by Dalí and Jean Cocteau); going to war.[84]

World War I had enlisted cut-out figures for purposes of deception; World War II put rounded mannequins in tanks, measuring their reach, as earlier Henry Dreyfuss had put a plaster Joe in tractor seats and a plaster Josephine at switchboards. Like Raymond Loewy, who had dressed windows and mannequins before entering this new field of "human engineering," Dreyfuss put the human form at the center of industrial design, conforming products to the demands of the body. Surrealistically wired for sensitivity, what Josephine and Joe lacked in glamour they made up for by way of FIT, which was their raison d'être – a rather military FITness at that, intent upon mobility and degrees of freedom.[85]

Maury Wolf in 1944 sold his chain of Dallas clothing stores and went in pursuit of the perfect womannequin, who wouldn't just stand there but would *do* something. For years he had been dressing papier-mâché figures, whose plaster heads came from American factories "made up like a bunch of scarecrows in the field," like "a bunch of goddamn comedians." One of the first, nonetheless, to bunch as many as forty mannequins in a single window, he had found that their noses would break, hands crack, hips shatter. Worse, their sizes were unreliable because papier-mâché shrank. Worst, their proportions appeared stumpy from the angle at which passersby glance up into a window. European mannequins, he knew, were elongated, their features more finely detailed, but their waxiness and glass eyes made them seem "like dead people." The answer, he thought, was plastic, about which he had been hearing during the war, and from which Europeans had constructed dolls' heads.

He headed for the Southern California airplane industry, where plastics technology was most advanced. By 1946 he and his partner David Vine were deluged with orders for their inaugural line of lively plastic mannequins. Under lights, sadly, the innovative mannequins turned the same sort of green that formalin had turned corpses when first used by embalmers. This problem (with a glycerine plasticizer) dissolved upon the development of a polyester resin, and Wolf & Vine began turning out energetic "action" figures adapted specifically to postwar sportswear.[86]

Action mannequins had long been sought. Charles A. Tracy, successor to Baum as editor of *The Show Window*, had warned, "The greatest dangers in posing figures come from trying to get too much grace or from attempting too striking a position." But window dressers were ever straining after that semblance of motion which Felsenthal of Chicago and Roullet et Decamps of Paris achieved with automatic (but rarely full-size) mannequins whose descendants we find in windows at Christmastide. If, as Tracy wrote in 1909, it was unnatural for figures to be molded into positions that were by nature transitory, it began to seem unnatural in 1939 for figures to be so stately that they looked (to Wolf) "like they had a yardstick up their ass." In the spirit of flash photographers and the new "candid" camerawomen of the 1930s, whose aim was to make vivid the arrested motion of the Depression, the New York designer Cora Scovil and sculptor Lilian Greneker independently reconstituted the womannequin so that its joints and composition could express the New Woman's athleticism and nerviness. Selecting the faces of their womannequins from those of fashion models or movie stars, then reducing the weight of the figures while molding them tall and slender, Scovil and Greneker (and Gaba with his "Kandid Kamera Kids") convinced the most exclusive stores to use womannequins where before they had relied upon the abstractions of drapery or simple skirt forms.[87]

Wax mannequins went into eclipse after World War II. Under cool fluorescent lights stood Wolf & Vine's more adventurous figures of polyester resin, resin-bonded papier-mâché, or, soon, fiberglass. The character figure disappeared from windows, as did a variety of body shapes, ages, and social orders – the fat, the old, the stooped, the working stiff – in which wax sculptors had excelled. American manufacturers restaged the world with slimmer, taller, less vulnerable, less personable portraits of Cold War selves. Each had to seem "self-assured," said a display manual of 1953. "Just as with the human mannequin she must play the role.... She has to be grappled with at every performance, pampered and propped, twisted and turned before she is beau ideal." Should a dresser fail in this wrestling match with FIT, then "The look of the mechanical doll – frozen, staring, uncomfortable, arthritic – caught in the middle of a movement with its gears run down, communicates its discomfort."[88]

Over the past thirty years, the window dresser's creed of animation has risen to crescendo while FITness has become more cosmopolitan. African and Asian, suntanned and freckled faces compete with abstrac-

FIGURE 3.7. Mannequins and pregnant womannequin, from the Van Calvin Manikin Restoration Studio, Portland, OR. Photo by Linda M. Strauss.

tions in chrome or aluminum atop bodies "bent, stretched, doubled back, and otherwise thrown out of joint for the sake of high style." The reserve of society womannequins has given way to the relaxed poses of a Twiggy and the exoticism of a Helenka (found dancing in a disco), both sculpted by former prop designer Adel Rootstein, who believes that mannequins "should look like real people with real faces, faults and all." Nostrils and brows have become more well defined, nipples and genital mounds more prominent, the pelvis more dynamic. Vinyl ears and polyurethane hands complement fiberglass torsos in the workshops of the two hundred manufacturers worldwide who promote their wares as much more than "a bag of phoney bones."[89]

Self-assured, mannequins have made a Faustian contract: greater personhood, shorter lives. Before, manufacturers introduced different mannequin styles at irregular intervals; now, "revolutionary" figures are unveiled twice a year and seem obsolete several seasons later. It is not so much that fashion requires constant novelty of its (wo)mannequins as that trends in medicine and diet, recreation and travel, fashion and art gradually redefine the FIT body, and (wo)mannequins must have not only "the figure to wear the clothes" but must "far surpass the customer in the 'look' of the garment being worn." Without the body to FIT the clothes, a mannequin is dead in the water.[90]

Lester Gaba, when he got Cynthia home after the soirées and costume balls, would take her apart and put her in seven black sateen boxes. Despite his care and her "eerie, almost human quality," she toppled from a chair into "a thousand little chips of plaster." Other mannequins, cast off, become shooting targets for the police and for photographers (who call them zombies), or subjects for medical students to resuscitate and poets to place in realms of the undead. After the creed of animation comes the screed of death-in-life, that unsettling repose of the mannequin who is a slave to timeliness. If I also am waxing pathetic, that is revealing; as the poet Howard Nemerov has said, there should be no pathos where there has been no life. But her glamour and command of FIT entitle the cast-off womannequin to an obsequy.[91]

Womannequins have not been captives of a male imagination. Like earlier wax bodies, they have been shaped by women sculptors (Cora Scovil, Kay Sullivan, Tanya Ragir), produced by women designers (Lillian Greneker, Mary Brosnan, Adel Rootstein, Kathë Kruse), posed by pacesetting women window dressers (Cecilia Staples, Candy Pratt), and lifted into art galleries by Marisol Escobar and by Leza Lidow, whose painted mannequins become the cityscapes shopwindows reflect. While Mr. Gene Moor, a legendary display artist, would say of mannequins that "I don't think they are very realistic, because I never see people taking positions that mannequins take," Ms. Candy Pratt would confess that "Those people are very real to me," Adel Rootstein would give womannequins navels and say, "I never had any real children, but I have hundreds of fiberglass ones," and Evangeline Calvin would patent a snap-on "maternikin" for pregnancy. It is women who have felt most offended,

men most relieved, by the lifelessness of a womannequin. Wrote Sidonie
Gabrielle Colette in 1933: "I have often wished that the devil would
melt them in his crucible, these mummies with their stiff hair, their
Chinese smiles, and their bodies without breasts," and then she praised
Siégel's exquisitely vibrant womannequins, who seemed to breathe.[92]

Accustomed to being in control, men have given lip service to the
creed of animation but withheld their faith when it comes to the *man*-
nequin, "a disaster to this day," says Martha Landau after thirty years in
the business. Given the adventurousness of men's fashions in the last
decades, *man*nequins should have come into their own, but men still
take unkindly to such motionless figures, reminiscent of the effigies of
tyrants or traitors. *Man*nequins seem either too passive or too complicit,
too dull or too parodic for men who need to think of themselves as
producers, not consumers. And what to do with eyes whose eyelashes
will not be painted, lips that should not be glossed, cheeks that must
not be rouged? "Put a dress on a well-styled [wo]mannequin – a woman
will easily be able to see herself in the dress. But," wrote Maria Massey
on the problems of menswear display in 1951, "put a man's suit on a
mannequin and place the figure in a window with nothing but an eye-
catching prop beside it, and no man will consent to identify himself
with the figure in the window." Her answer was to put the *man*nequin
in action and give him character, but this proved unconvincing. In 1978
display artist Robert Currie declared it "a curious cultural fact that male
display mannequins are, almost without exception, nowhere nearly as
graceful or realistic in appearance as are their female counterparts. The
best female mannequins have an uncanny presence in a window.... The
male figures, by contrast, often appear to be ill or in pain." For men,
*man*nequin has been a pejorative term: a terrorist gas that freezes muscles; a pawn of media managers; an artifact for "therapy rooms where
facsimile humans are kicked, beaten, torn apart." Men, and the women
who shop for them and share the prevailing images of a virile manhood,
have found it impossible to sympathize with *man*nequins, so obviously
immobilized and impotent, whether posed double-fisted with legs
spread or going through Ralph Pucci's muscular workouts. So mis-
matched in aura and attitude are *man*nequins and womannequins that
we rarely see the sexes mingled. They do not FIT together.[93]

Bad faith, then, is a charge to be laid gingerly against womannequins,
who have never lied about their intentions. From fashion doll to display figure, the womannequin has represented woman as both creatrix
and consumer, shaping a culture she is also shaped by. The back and
forth of this collaboration is play-full, like relations between girl and
doll. While ceramic dolls have kept that beautiful fragility of which
French elites have been inordinately proud, dolls produced since the
mid-nineteenth century in Germany and America for less exclusive markets have become increasingly durable, manufactured with composition (rosin, wood, flour, starch), soft or hard rubber, then with the
vinyls and hard plastics that led in 1958 to Mattel's Barbie. Barbie was

not the first to have her own wardrobe (Effanbee's Patsy had hers in 1926), but she was and remains the doll with greatest command of FIT. Changing her styles – and her head, her joints, (gradually) her measurements – Barbie has been womannequin to an ever-expanding hope chest of clothes for the eight hundred million copies of herself around the world. The personalities that girls give to their Barbies, observes artist Lisa Herskovits, "usually resemble...the personalities that those little girls develop when they become adults." Given Barbie's glamour and her command of FIT, we should not be surprised when a woman dresser of womannequins says, "It's like playing with oversize Barbie dolls."[94]

Charges of bad faith should more forcefully be laid against *manne-quins*, who can sustain neither glamour nor FIT and do surely disguise their purposes. Designers and manufacturers know that men are ill at ease before realistically sculpted displays of themselves; *man*nequins tend hence to be abstracted and void of personality. If *man*nequins and womannequins are equally expressionless and close-mouthed (teeth become grotesque, laughing faces ludicrous or psychotic), they are not equally at peace with their cultural anatomy. Each of us is a consumer, each of us desires to be who we are not, speak the womannequins. "We are the hollow men," murmur the abstracted *man*nequins, who, ever fearing for their dignity, have no public say.[95]

Hollow women there are too, hidden in sailors' chests or bachelor wardrobes. Their silk stockings drawn up over shapely calves to swelling thighs under lacy gowns, life-size sex dolls with enamel eyes and ivory teeth were manufactured in France as early as the 1880s. As she sold her flesh-pink concubines, who could be ordered with eyes that rolled and arms that dropped in abandon, Mme Van der Mys of Lyons told tales of murderous jealousy: when a sea captain caught his first mate *in flagrante delicto*, he killed the adulterer but held onto the rubber adulteress. Madame's anecdotes stressed two of the choicest virtues of the sex doll – scrupulous correctness and perpetual willingness.[96]

Rebuffed by Alma Mahler (whose name and life were homonyms for "soul of the artist"), a doting Austrian painter in 1918 commissioned a life-size likeness of her from a Munich puppet-maker. Completed in every detail according to Oskar Kokoschka's quite anatomical drawings, the doll's dimensions were exact, its face correct, its surfaces finished with a soft down. Kokoschka would later explain that "I wanted to have done with the Alma Mahler business once and for all," yet he need not have sent to Paris for dainties and dresses were this cloth-and-sawdust Alma merely therapeutic. When it/she arrived in Dresden in the spring of 1919, Kokoschka was in "a state of feverish anticipation, like Orpheus calling Eurydice back from the Underworld." Earlier he had invented a daughter, written plays for marionettes, tried magically to animate a jointed doll he had dressed in "oriental" clothes; now, opening the crate, he saw a light such as he had never seen before, and (shades of Pygmalion) "the image of her I had preserved in my memory stirred into life." Competing with the likes of Eurydice and Galatea, the doll

FIGURE 3.8. *Similitudes II*, paper collage by Cal Bowser, Jr., 1993. Reproduced by permission.

itself could only be blighted, no matter how clever the beautiful rumors Kokoschka spread about the Silent Woman's mysterious origins. At her coming-out party, enriched with chamber music and sly questions from a courtesan (Did the artist sleep with her? Did she resemble anyone he knew?), Oskar lost track of Alma and Alma lost her head. Police pounded at the door next morning: a bloody body had been spotted lying in the garden. It was Alma alright, headless and wine-stained, whom the dust-man carted away. Catharsis and denouement, wrote Kokoschka in ret-rospect; this sex doll therapy had worked. But in 1922, when he finished *Self-Portrait with Doll*, Alma was sprawled naked in his lap, the painter pointing at her pubes with sober disappointment.[97]

Impersonation, imposture, correctness, Kokoschka's sex doll was made to shed one veil of likeness after another. As the sham unraveled, claimed Kokoschka, so did his infatuation. More likely, he was sham-ing a woman who had shamed him. He turned Alma Mahler into the best of puppets, brutalized it, then reversed the direction of his excite-ment and painted it into his public lap as if she had never been more than the coarsest of puns, a *lay* figure. Sadism (writes Leo Bersani, re-writing Freud and Mallarmé) depends upon these re-presentations. Pain and shame are screened as pleasure and desire. The "shared commotion" of sex becomes a private commodity, the Desirable no longer a person per se but a repetitious event that must be tortured into novel forms.[98]

Kokoschka's autoerotic episode was fact to the 1950s fiction of "Gogol's Wife," who was, supposed Tommaso Landolfi, a thick rubber dummy whose endowments changed at the Russian novelist's every puff. Inflating her to different volumes through her anal sphincter, greasing and powdering her, Gogol experimented with many incarnations, a "fresh creation every time," true creature of one man's fashions. What remained constant, and crucial, was her anatomical correctness: "Particularly worthy of attention were her genital organs... formed by means of ingenious folds in the rubber." Mated for a quarter century, Nikolai and Caracas had a falling out when he contracted syphilis from her and she began to assert herself, speaking brazenly, and announcing in polite company, "I want to go poo poo." Not that she could, but that she meant to embarrass Gogol, who finally blew her up beyond monstrous disdain to the surreal scatter of explosion. Was it the madness of syphilis that drove him to burn the fragments in his fireplace as he had (it was true) burned his manuscripts? Or was it her unaccountable aging? Or the rubber baby doll he held in his arms for an instant before tossing it in the flames, muttering, "Him too! Him too!"[99]

"There is no dead matter," Bruno Schulz's father taught; "lifelessness is only a disguise behind which hide unknown forms of life." But the sex doll is meant to be as selfless as it is willing, always and fully open to the boldest advances. If it speaks, it must vent upon command, crying out in phonographic orgasm when a man presses her lips with kisses: "Mon cheri! mon doux amour! mon trésor!" Her sex, and gender, has to be so safe that a man forgets how much he is the consumer in this intercourse, how thoroughly he is consumed by it, and how like the woman-mannequin is the sex doll with her promise of a sensual FIT. Should the sex doll become inflexible, argumentative, or fertile as Gogol's wife, its sexuality will appear as a treacherous disguise, telling on Gogol's tyrannies, Kokoschka's bad faith.[100]

"Hey — these are perfect ladies! They don't whine when you watch football & drink beer. They love all kinds of sex, even kinky!! They NEVER get headaches." Ms. Wonderful, $89.79, is made of 250-lb.-test rubber vinyl, lifesize with a "pump-action vibrating vagina," a "pulsating mouth," and "Lifelike 'velour' skin, silky blond hair, eyes that close." Aphrodite has "blue eyes that close. Sewn-in blonde hair. Full lifelike breasts you can even fill with warm water" for $69.95. Get hour after hour of SOLID PLEASURE from a "Life size revolutionary not inflated sex doll" who is nameless but comes "complete with Electronic Vibro-Vagina"; it is "Not a cheap toy or old fashioned inflatable, but the most Lifelike LOVE SLAVE Imaginable!... so lifelike she'll thrill you like you've never dreamed possible!" for just $12.95, an unprecedented LOW PRICE made possible by a "NEW, MASS PRODUCTION PROCESS." And Suzie, "the most exciting bed partner any man could desire," five-foot two with "three cushiony penetrable openings," is sent "absolutely free to all new customers."[101]

Privities exaggerated, Suzie, Aphrodite, and Ms. Wonderful are still less convincing than a Royal Classic vibrator erect in any of three skin shades, or the "ultra realistic SOLID PENIS" whose shaft is covered "with a thin independent layer of spookily lifelike skin," or the "Porno Star cock hand crafted to capture each vein, bulge & crease." Sex dolls dissemble in ways the age-old dildo does not, for although they have no retina, no nerve endings, no pulse, their fluttering eyelids imply more than a straightforwardly selfish pleasure; absent vocal chords, their custom deluxe "soft sensual voice urging you to do all those things that make YOU happy" and their moaning "in the ecstasy of repeated climaxes" are the hollowest of raptures, unmoved by the breathless words they may speak. This is the pinnacle of correctness, the discourse of *dis*engagement.

Sex dolls might as well be universal gyms – a Mouth Simulator ($29.95), a Madame X Artificial Vagina ($9.95 at "forced liquidation"), and a Sweet Ass with "sure grip buns" (also $9.95) – except that they prolong an illusion of sexual *relations*. They embody a system of liaisons through which, since the late eighteenth century, "drive" and "libido" have been substituted for affection, just as orgasm and "cathexis" have been substituted for communion. Male physiologists and psychiatrists of the nineteenth and twentieth centuries have found the female body to be an alien territory so ripe for scientific exploration that the modern sex doll can make an anatomical fetish of the vents of vulcanized women, turning sex into spelunking. In the dark, isn't it all the same?[102]

Impersonal but your very own, a sex doll may be "inspired by Candy Samples," goddess of the pornographic scene, but it is ultimately as anonymous and unreachable as womannequins on the silver screen. There, an unattainable woman is set afire in womannequin proxy by Archibaldo de la Cruz, who tries to kill those women of whom he is enamored, and who will marry one who exchanges clothes with a womannequin. There, an orthodontist orders from Japan a life-size doll with lifelike skin and protrudable tongue. Defiantly unresponsive, she earns his obedience and the envy of his wife, who begins to imitate her. The orthodontist goes off to marry (and so possess) the doll, then commits a double drowning. The doll floats to the surface like Ophelia.[103]

Possession is nine-tenths of the law of the sex doll; the other tenth is release. Through its command of FIT the womannequin appears self-possessed and can collaborate in singular escapes that go beyond itself – lying under blankets or standing at shaded windows as the live Double elopes. The sex doll effects only minor and repeated escheats, confiscations in the name of its lord and master. Whereas a womannequin has some purchase on fantasy and fashion, the sex doll *is* a purchase: price tags on a womannequin are for what she wears, on a sex doll for what it materially is. Assisted by a womannequin, who costs $800–$1000 wholesale and takes hours to make up, the retailer hopes to possess us to buy new fashions. At a twentieth of the cost, the sex doll is itself a commodity, ready-made. A shop owner asks how much a womanne-quin's window generates each week in revenue, the doll's owner checks the batteries and cleans the merkin. Lifting her with professional care by head and crotch, a window dresser takes the womannequin from warehouse nudity to public costume drama; if the womannequin has been well constructed, she will release a designer's creative impulses, as in the frothy movie *Mannequin* (1987). Built to be privately man-handled, the sex doll arouses feelings it cannot return – a beggar's opera: "Lifeless charms, without the heart."[104]

Inadequate to love, the sex doll is a shoddy forgery. Shoddy, because it belongs to that class of materials and persons "characterized by the endeavour to pass for something superior to what they really are." A forgery, because it isolates an act from its original contexts, social, his-torical, biological.[105] It circulates the false coin of a sex "disambiguated" of gender, a lovefaking detached from the personal rhythms of hormones and menstrual periods, from the social concerns of syphilis, herpes, AIDS. At best it is a soft but durable good which the shy and ship-wrecked, the sexually repressed and sexually oppressed can trust for a modicum of comfort and safety. At worst it is a Klein bottle, a geo-metrical figure that looks to be tubular yet has only a single side that neither gives nor receives. In the turn-out of the sex doll's limbs and the rictus of its open mouth we see the "frightening sadness" (said Bruno Schulz's father) of "violated matter."[106]

Mixing It Up: Subjects and Rulers

"Don't strike me too hard!" says the piece of wood. "Is it possible," wonders Antonio the carpenter, "that this piece of wood has learned to cry and complain like a baby?" He palms it off on a poor childless friend who wants to whittle a wooden puppet – "a really fine one, that can dance, fence, and turn somersaults in the air" – to take on tour and make some money. Why then does old Geppetto name the puppet, this simulacrum, after a family of beggars?[107]

Eldest son of a seamstress whose village name he would take as nom de plume, Carlo Collodi was a Florentine journalist who lost his father as a child and spent much of his youth in the political dueling for Italian independence. He was a more sedate bachelor of fifty-four and a transla-tor of French fairy tales when he wrote the first installments of *Pinocchio* for a new children's magazine, and the newly unified Kingdom of Italy in 1881 was scarcely twenty, making the mistakes of youth. Antonio in his shop chances upon a piece of firewood "just like any other piece of firewood" as the Italian poor were being denied customary rights to gather wood on local commons. Geppetto names his puppet after the pine nut, a poorbread, as the able-bodied poor were struggling against poverty with no public relief. Pinocchio first runs away and Geppetto is arrested under suspicion of childbeating, tacitly accused of having turned a stripling into a plaything, as newly enfranchised yet often illit-

FIGURE 3.9. Writing automaton designed by Pierre Jaquet-Droz, 1772–74, now at the Musée d'Art et d'Histoire, Neuchâtel, Switzerland. Photo by Linda M. Strauss.

erate Italians feared being turned once again into political puppets. Pinocchio is persuaded by the chummy Fox and Cat to sow his gold pieces in a Field of Miracles as parliamentary allegiances were being made neither by party nor principle but by faith in political miracle workers. While Pinocchio is watering the ground so that his gold will grow, the Parrot laughs "at those simpletons who are silly enough to believe all the nonsense they hear, and who are always cheated by those who are more cunning than they are."[108]

Yet if Pinocchio seems repeatedly under the sway of others, he also cannot abide being apprenticed, and if he does not know his own mind, he is rather a naive Wild Boy than a devil, however insensitive he may be to his conscience in the shape of a talking cricket. A French entomologist and fantasist, Charles Nodier, had written in 1842 in praise of puppets that they might be the noblest of actors. Devoid of interior life, marionettes (originally altar dolls or *Maries* who nodded their heads and moved their arms to bless the prayerful) could express any scripted or communal feeling with utmost purity. "I would go even further," wrote Nodier at the end of a life that had been repulsed by the Terror and distressed by the false spring of the republican Revolution of 1830: "marionettes are the only authentic tradition of the ancient democracies; and when people will have firmly resolved to gather republican institutions around a throne, it will be necessary to surround that throne with marionettes."[109]

Whether with *fantoccini* operated by strings and sticks from above, or with *burattini* operated by hands from below and within, motions from person to puppet seem always countered by motions from puppet to person. We can read *Pinocchio* (in four hundred versions in 87 languages) in the tradition of puppet-as-blockhead, as satirist Mark Morelli has done with "A Letter from Geppetto," the old man asked to carve a wooden puppet "with a big dumb face, its eyes vacant as an old steel mill," to run for vice president. Or we can read the story in the tradition of puppet-as-roughly-hewn-human, as has psychoanalyst Willard Gaylin, who finds Pinocchio moving from the dependency of a baby to the responsibilities of a growing boy – "not a fantasy of the human creation of life, but of the everyday miracle that is reproduced by human development." Or in the tradition of puppet-as-hireling, as has literary historian Scott C. Shershow, arguing that puppets like Pinocchio inescapably reflect a Western hegemonic discourse that associates diminutiveness with subordination, deceit, and sheer materiality. Or in the tradition of puppet-as-insubordinate, sharp and sliverish, as the translator Noel Streatfeild sees the story, written "to show how a bad little Italian citizen could grow up to be a useful man in the new kingdom."[110]

Emperor Marcus Aurelius, meditating in Rome in the second century, had advised himself, "Thou art an old man; no longer let this [body] be a slave, no longer be pulled by the strings like a puppet to unsocial movements." The strings of desire, he told himself, must be resisted, yet in one passage he also had to "Remember that this which pulls the strings is the thing which is hidden within: this is the power of persuasion, this is life; this, if one may so say, is man." Which was it? Man the puppet, slave to the senses, or man the lofty puppeteer, with his refined soul? "I confess," wrote James Ralph of Philadelphia early in the eighteenth century, at a time when puppets three and four feet tall were performing raucous Sicilian dramas as well as operas composed for them by Haydn, "I confess," he wrote, gradually losing himself in the puppets, "I confess I cannot view a well-executed puppet show without extravagant emotions of pleasure: to see our artists, like so many Prometheuses, animate a bit of wood and give life, speech, and motion, perhaps to what was the leg of a joint-stool, strikes me with a pleasant surprise and prepossesses me wonderfully in favor of those little wooden actors and their *primum mobile*." Wherefore the surprise and wherefrom the prepossession, unless doubts remained as to who the First Mover was – puppeteer, puppet, or some artistic force beyond them both? And who was First Mover to that piece of wood that cried out before any axe had descended and mocked Geppetto before the old man had laid a hand upon him?[111]

Effrontery is on the lips of puppets as soon as they speak. Their voices challenge the locus of power. Thirty feet tall and waltzing or three inches tall and pouring tea into teacups, puppets by their very nature move (are moved). Nothing about their motions has changed enough over the millennia to help us with the historical problem at the core of this chapter: how the portraits we make of ourselves have lost their capacity to anchor and extend us.[112] Over the last two centuries, on the other hand, the voices of puppets have been raised in a newly impudent chorus.

Or rather, their voices have been *thrown*. Puppets have always had their mouthpieces and interlocutors, profane or sacred. Egyptian statues for the *ka* and Greek oracular stone figures had been alive with voices spoken into them by priests and priestesses; voices had emanated mysteriously from Speaking Heads fashioned, in legend, by such mathemagicians as Albertus Magnus, Roger Bacon, John Dee. Not until the eighteenth century, however, did men publicly claim the credit for these redirected voices earlier framed as divine or demonic. Ventriloquists began to appear on stage in and of themselves, and in historical tandem with complex self-moving mechanical figures whose gears, tubes, and bellows enabled them to produce music and speech.[113]

Far-famed among the mechanical musicians was Jacques de Vaucanson's automaton flautist of 1738, a five-foot-tall faun who held a transverse flute to its mouth in enviable embouchure, blowing air through flexible lips, tonguing each semiquaver, and fingering the trills. As with his automaton duck that swallowed, digested, and shat, the "whole mechanism exposed to View," Vaucanson's declared ambition was to model physiology rather than to profit from a mystery; he "would not be thought to impose upon the Spectators by any conceal'd or juggling Contrivance." He therefore showed his faun, insides and out, to members of the Académie Royale des Sciences, to whom he read a technical paper stressing the vocal likenesses between flute-playing and speaking. An unabashed admirer of that "masterpiece of Mechanics, work of genius, miracle of Art" was most impressed by the inner quiet of the flautist's ratchets, and by its ability to produce an echo, a feature of which Vaucanson was especially proud: "Would you produce a soft Sound to represent an Echo? Place the Lips over the Hole quite to its Edge, by turning the Flute much inwards: then the Sound being able to be communicated but to a small Quantity of external Air, thro' so small an Hole, makes us hear a Sound that seems to be afar off, by its striking our Organs weakly." This was, sans flute, exactly how the Parisian grocer Saint-Gille in 1765 would have accomplished his ethereal voices, acts of ventriloquism performed in profile so that spectators (and a committee from the Académie Royale) would be unaware that one side of his lips was moving. Saint-Gille's miracle of Art, like that of Vaucanson's flautist, depended on an internal stillness during the production of sounds coming ostensibly from afar.[114]

"Thy voice shall be as of one that hath a familiar spirit, out of the ground, and thy speech shall whisper out of the dust." Quoting Isaiah 29.4, the nineteenth-century ventriloquist Antonio Blitz drew up an estimable genealogy for his profession, from Hebrew prophets and Greek "engastrimythes" (prophetesses who "spoke through their stomachs," whence the ventral prefix of "ventriloquism") to Eskimo shamans and a Dutch woman who spoke in voices during religious frenzy. Blitz misread Isaiah (he would have fared better with 1 Samuel 28, the "witch" of Endor), yet there was much to his genealogy, since the secret to ventriloquism was, as Blitz wrote, learning to speak upon *inspiration*. What modern ventriloquists do, while compressing the glottis and confining the distortion of the muscles of speech to a small part of one side of the face, is to redirect an ancient technique of healing and divination toward a less sacred theater.[115]

Inspiration for stagecraft, expiration for science. "I am not ... occupied in making the mute speak, nor, like Pygmalion, in animating a statue of ivory," disclaimed the physicist Christian Gotlieb Kratzenstein in 1782, "but for several years I have been occupied in my moments of leisure by a machine that can counterfeit the human voice and that can, like an instrument of music, articulate words by the aid of the fingers." His speaking machine and keyboard of vowels, winner of a contest set by the Saint Petersburg Imperial Academy of Science in 1779, was just one of several mechanical heads bleating across Europe in the late eighteenth century, all limited by flaps and bellows to Kratzenstein's Danish vowels, the Abbé Mical's French phrases, Wolfgang von Kempelen's Hungarian/French "papa, Roma, astronomie, opéra, pantomime, venez avec moi à Paris." The heads were basically pipe organs; when they spoke, they spoke *out*.[116]

Controlled by keyboards and foot pumps, the expiring machines made every effort to speak; ventriloquists, inspiring, pretended not to. The inventors called attention to ingenious assemblies of valves, membranes, and tubes as proof against hoax. The performers, conversing with wax busts or invisible strangers, recalled the speakers to themselves as proof that the voices came neither through tubes nor from small boys hidden in the bellies of large dummies. Mr. Fitz-James, in performances around 1800, would emerge from the audience, acting the part of a skeptic protesting that the voices came from cronies crouched under a dais. The voices responded indignantly from somewhere beneath the stage, he shouted back, and they, and he, and they, in furious exchange until Fitz-James claimed every voice as his own. He had learned the art of speaking during inspiration, he said, and each voice was formed in his lungs. He demonstrated anew. Twenty invisible men rose up to debate each other. A watchman crying the hour came down the street, closer and closer, to the very door of the theater.[117]

Key to the technical success of both speaking head and ventriloquist was intelligibility, a social quality. Discourse (as von Kempelen maintained) implied intercourse: auditors agreed to understand. But (as Descartes had maintained, anticipating von Kempelen) parrots could be intelligible. To be fully persuasive, ventriloquists needed something beyond vocal mimicry. It was, finally, insufficient to throw one's voice into different areas of the room and into gentlemen's hats, as did Richard Potter of Boston in 1811; insufficient to imitate, as did Nicholas Marie Alexandre in 1821 in London, the sound of a fire crackling or a lori-keet squawking. Ventriloquists had need of a more magnetic presence, something on the order, perhaps, of the Talking Turk of E.T.A. Hoff-mann's 1814 story, "Automata," in which the figure turns its eyes then head to each questioner, and with a "gentle stream of air" from its mouth, replies with words "cold and severe, or sparkling and witty; or painful and tragic and always strikingly apposite." No, on reflection, ven-triloquists needed something else, for figures of Hoffmann's sort were false automata whose noisy clockwork camouflaged a conspirator; false automata allowed magicians a wider ambit of responses to audience demands than did mechanical automata, but they were presented so that the mystery seemed to lie entirely within the clockwork.[118]

Missing was the give and take of real conversation, for which Vaucan-son had at least supplied an echo and von Kempelen a few interrogato-ries. To transcend mere mimicry, ventriloquists had more need of the take than of the give. Life *inspires* as it *exchanges*. Mechanical heads were as exclusively expository as they were expiratory; ventriloquists sought the semblance of dialogue with figures as active as themselves, who supplemented their acts with quick-change impersonations and acrobatics.[119]

How better to convince an audience of one's vocal powers than to play straight man to a brash puppet who interrupts, talks back, has a mind of its own? Ventriloquists had begun talking *through* wax busts and figures in the 1770s. Such "automata," rarely self-moving, were familiar enough in 1835–36 that P.T. Barnum, afraid that his prime attraction was losing her appeal, spread the rumor that Joice Heth, "161-year-old former nurse to George Washington," was actually an automaton and Barnum a ventriloquist; suckers returned in droves to see how they had been had. A decade later, while a speaking automa-ton was clearing three hundred dollars a week for Barnum, the English comedian Charles Mathews was talking *to* his "speaking Tommy" and Signor Blitz *to* his "wonderful 'Bobby.'" During the 1850s George Wash-ington Kirbye toured with an automaton whose head, eyes, and lips were moved by a spring manipulated behind its back with the fore-finger of the right hand. By the 1870s, stages were redundant with the "Wondrous Living Heads" (false automata) of magicians; with the "automata" or "figures" (later called "dummies") of ventriloquists; and with the speaking heads machined by inventors such as Alexander Graham Bell, intent upon modeling the processes of human speech. Audiences could never know whether they would be encountering an offstage voice, a mechanically produced voice, a thrown voice, or a mechanically reproduced voice from a newfangled phonograph — as they would never know which Signor Blitz was ventriloquizing on stage. In America alone, wrote the real Blitz in 1871, men were "not only assuming to be the *original* Blitz, but in many instances claiming to be a son or nephew." Blitz himself had been "denied my own personality, and termed 'Bogus.' "[120]

Occupational hazard, I guess, of men who make their living talking to themselves: in 1889 the *Boston Post* reported that Blitz was confined in a lunatic asylum, although the *Philadelphia Ledger* had given him an obituary in 1877 and a burial in Cypress Hills Cemetery. Another ventriloquist, "a little, old man, with a bald head and a wrinkled face," was his own prisoner in a city of emerald spectacles under the glower of a papier-mâché Great Head whose mouth opened and eyes moved at the pull of a thread. Back in Omaha, the Wizard had trained with a master ventriloquist before he became an advertising balloonist. He had, in other words, exchanged the art of inspiration for the practice of puffery, but his balloon had torn loose from its moorings, as advertisements still do, and he landed daze later in Oz. If I too seem to be drifting from my tether, it is only to return home with the firmer conviction of a vital link between "vent" and vehicle, and to find there, in turn-of-the-century London music halls and New York vaudeville, Fred Russell, Arthur Prince, and Harry Lester with wisecracking Irish dummies seated on their knees, taking the limelight and laughs. The dummy was becoming what the vent had been before, a trickster getting people in trouble, pandemoniating. Where the ventriloquist Valentine Vox in a 1904 novel disturbs Parliament with phantom voices and imparts wit to the British Museum's statue of Memnon, the dummy will turn the tables, make the vent the butt of its jokes, and ask again and again, "Who's in charge here, anyway?"[121]

Playing second fiddle, the "vent" treats his (recently, her) "figure" with respect, looking at it when it speaks onstage, arranging it on a chair offstage. The Stradivarius of figures, sculpted in plastic wood by the brothers Glenn and George McElroy during the 1930s, has fourteen or more face and hand movements orchestrated through a keyboard in its back. Superior craftsmanship aside, the figure attains to its powers by virtue of a "game of make-believe in which you act as if the puppet actually had a life of his own" — a life more unabashed than your own. In the take and give of ventriloquism, the dummy is passion and revolt: "Let your hidden desires be expressed in your dummies."[122]

Long ago, it may be, all of us were dummies to our own ventriloquy, and forces of light and darkness spoke to us through a bicameral brain. That was a time, suggests Julian Jaynes, when to hear was to obey, when inner voices were neurological commands, when the words and world of gods and demons occupied the right hemisphere, the words and world of women and men the left. Across the anterior commissure linking the halves of the brain came directions to build wide-eyed speaking statues through whom the wishes of the gods could be made public.

Over the millennia, reorganizing for self-consciousness and psychology, we have lost bicamerality.[123] Most of us, neither inspired nor possessed nor "out of our minds," must seek authorization for our acts from voices less implicit than those heard by schizophrenics. Holding his dummy couched upon his left hand, side of the gods, and keying its motions with his right hand, side of humanity, the ventriloquist may be replaying the historical breakaway toward a civilization of introspective individuals. The dummy, shaking off the authority of the voice that inspirits him, appears to talk independently, held back only by the embrace of an antique conscience whose lips and throat are still. We reward the stillness of the ventriloquist but what sticks in our minds is the half-child face of the uppity dummy.

Dummies likely cannot bear the full weight of such a grand history, yet it is remarkable that when the Scottish inventor John Logie Baird in 1926 tested his television transmitter, he chose two ventriloquists' dummies for the first true television broadcast.[124] If ventriloquist and dummy do not between them replay a cultural revolution in the balance of functions in the brain, they do replay a technical revolution in the almost-simultaneous transmission and reception of voices.

Habituated as we are to the disembodied voices emanating from radios, telephones, and loudspeakers, or floating off records, audiotapes, and laser discs, we also take for real the voices thrown into figures moving across screens, even though much of cinema speech and song (all of it, in Italy and India) has been dubbed, often by people other than those on screen. The problem is not simply that foreign films and videotapes may be mistranslated or misinterpreted but that the anonymous voices we hear are not engaged with the drama, and are directed never to be: "Dubbing is a mechanical technique, like typing."[125]

From the duplicity of cinematic ventriloquism it is the quickest of jumpcuts to *Girl You Know It's True*, an album lipsynched on video by the (dis)award-winning (un)singing duet of Milli Vanilli. And to the dissemblance of ghostwritten speeches read by political figures managed like dummies by media consultants. Or to the egregious dubbing of Senator Joseph Biden, a presidential hopeful who spoke the speech, assumed the manner, and adopted the autobiography of a British party leader.[126]

Professional ventriloquists enact, in good faith, that puppetry which electronic media and the political process, in bad faith, now make invisible or, so to say, inaudible. Ventriloquists' dummies bespeak both subjection and resistance: our fears of being manipulated by the demonic keyboards of a technological society or of being possessed by the foreign voices of advertisement or propaganda; our dreams of defiance, of talking and acting from the gut. Granted, the dummy's destiny is finally determined from above, but meantime it makes one articulate gesture after another in the direction of free will. Together, ventriloquist and dummy allude to power and powerlessness through stand-up comedies of insolence. Insofar as insults are "an inherently democratic form of address," the irreverent figure in the lap of the ventriloquist makes its master into its accomplice. A "vent" who did not suffer himself to be sassed would be deadly.[127]

Comic upstart, the half-pint theatrical dummy is child to the industrial robot, an adult colossus, a life-size or oversize worker ever threatening, in sociological and science fictions, to usurp its maker. The master's voice, thrown into the dummy, is always about to be thrown off by the robot, a figure of terror or tragedy. The dummy's exercise of freedom is an exercise in talkback and leveling; the robot, the laboring automaton, has been an exercise in feedback and rebellion.

One historian, Otto V. Mayr, has proposed that the complex clockwork inside automata (out of which sprang the machinery of the Industrial Revolution) was retarded from practical deployment by a long association, economic and philosophical, with tyrannical regimes and individual slavishness. Automata could be shifted down to James Watt's centrifugal governor and Jacquard's card-programmed looms when, in the later eighteenth century, clockwork was reconceived as self-regulation. In England, where industrial growth was well capitalized, the engineering of feedback systems was nicely coincident with an economic theory of dynamic balances of trade and a political theory of checks and balances.[128]

Checks and dynamic balances were clearly in evidence in a former English colony when John Randolph in 1794 went to see two automata, Mr. Aristocrat and Citizen Democrat, in Philadelphia. A wise twenty-one, he explained to the younger Fanny Tucker, "An Automaton is an artificial person, who by means of machinery, performs many actions similar to those of a rational being. It differs from a puppet inasmuch as it performs its tricks, not by the assistance of external force, but by powers contained within itself." These were probably false automata, but their manager made a great show of winding each of them up. "The musicians played ça ira, upon which Mr. Aristocrat shook his Head, and appeared much displeased. On the contrary Mr Citizen Democrat showed evident signs of Joy and danced in a most spirited manner for about ten minutes, when the tune being changed he stopped, appeared offended and sat down: not so Mr. Aristocrat, who recognizing it to have been a favorite tune of the late Queen, began to dance also, but in a more genteel style than his neighbour had done." Back and forth they danced for an hour, "no tune ever pleasing both." The next year, in Boston, a Frenchman exhibited M. Sans Culotte and M. L'Aristocrate; in the nick of time appeared a talking Mrs. Moderate.[129]

Halfway between Frontierland and Fantasyland, in Liberty Square, inside the Hall of Presidents, Abraham Lincoln is the most emancipated of figures, clearing his throat, grasping the arms of his chair, rising to speak in a voice wrongly resonant. Outside the Magic Kingdom, however, we see few such political automata. Since 1800 most have been entertainers – musicians, dancers, acrobats, fortune-tellers, magicians – each of whose flesh-and-blood models had greater freedom of movement and a (reputedly) looser style of living than the people in the audience. While bourgeois children created fantasy worlds with an increasing variety of erratically self-propelled wind-up or friction-driven toys and talking dolls, adult observers of public automata seemed as taken with quick obedience as with motions toward improvisation and independence. Mareppe's Automaton Violinist may have played "supremely well" with a live orchestra, "But the *chef-d'oeuvre* is the manner in which the figure is made to obey the direction of the conductor, whereby it is endowed with a sort of semi-reason." If von Kempelen's automaton chess player amazed spectators with endless victories and its mechanical cry of *"échec et mat!"* (this "check and mate" added by J.N. Maelzel, inventor of the metronome), the most widely repeated compliment to its intelligence concerned not its chess tactics but its sweeping refusal to condone the cheating either of Catherine the Great or Napoleon Bonaparte.[130]

Too sharp a demonstration of independence led to suspicions of "*a man within a man*," that is, of machinery screening a little boy, a dwarf, an amputee. The more whimsy there was to mechanical actors, the more their innards were suspect. Strict obedience was what prompted admiration for the makers of automata, as it did with governess Nelly Weeton in 1814 when she saw Haddock's Androides in Liverpool. There, a man stood before a dollhouse in front of which sat a very little dog. The man placed a tiny plate of toy fruit before the dog and "told it to take care of it; and do you know, the little dog said 'bow wow!', and... when the man stole some of the fruit, it howled and barked and whined, in a most piteous manner! How ingenious the man must be, to make such a dog; for I suppose it was nothing but wood. A little doll," she continued, writing to her charge, Sarah-Anne, "not so big as yours, stood at the door, and when the man told it to fetch any fruit, it went in, shut the door, and in two minutes, came out again, bringing whatever it was sent for." The obedience school went on. "The man called for a chimney-sweeper, and bid him go sweep the chimney. A little figure, about two inches high, dressed like a chimney-sweeper, came creeping through a side-door, went in at the front door, and in five or ten minutes, popped his head out at the top of the chimney, held up his brush, and shouted 'sweep!' Then he went down again, and bye and bye, he came out again with a bag of soot, and went away."[131]

Grimy Hephaestus at his forge had had equally obedient automatic assistants, a score of self-inflating bellows to serve his divine metalwork and a set of life-size maidens, voluble golden automata on whom he leaned as he hobbled about. Although automata have appealed to both sexes (fully three-fifths of an Albany audience were female and delighted with the show, as Weeton had been in Liverpool and Marie Antoinette at Versailles), it is the case that ventriloquists' dummies and automata since the days of Ctesibios and Hero of Alexandria have usually been given body and voice by men — men who, like Jackson Knickerbocker Van Horne, tangle love in the wires of servility. Van Horne buys a young girl, names her Zero, isolates her, trains her up inside steel-wire dress-makers' dummies to shape her proportions, and weds her after she falls, as she must, for him. "I want your caresses precisely the same this instant as I have ever desired them," he tells her. "I merely intend to teach you...that hereafter you are to be an automaton, that my exact desires may be carried out," for which reason he locks her up in a wire dummy and shocks her whenever she feels "like asserting the liberties that wives usually practice." At the end, he finds that loving compan-ionship is incompatible with servility; she consents to be his ideal wife only when he consents to be her ideal husband.[132]

Zero, the *Automatic Wife*, was a pale contemporary to the brilliant Hadaly, *Tomorrow's Eve*, created by a wizardly Edison under the pen of Auguste, comte de Villiers de l'Isle-Adam. A Breton Catholic who in 1863 applied for the vacant throne of Greece, impelled by his family's decrepit nobility and its motto, "Go Beyond," the not-quite Count then went beyond himself in pursuit of an English heiress who thought him a lunatic. In a bare room in Paris in 1885, impoverished by a contradic-tory life of monasticism and debauchery, Villiers de l'Isle-Adam wrote of an aristocrat's disinfatuation with a lovely but spiritually lifeless actress who seems to Lord Ewald a luminous temple profaned by "mechani-cal fidelity, unconscious coldness of heart, a superstition of unbelief." Through virtuoso electronics, Edison merges Hadaly, a spiritually rich magneto-electric entity, with a body photosculpted from the vain ac-tress. Previous automata, says Edison, have been miserable failures reeking of rancid oil and gutta-percha. "Their animation, as of wigmak-ers' dummies! That noise of the key in the mechanism! The sensation of vacancy!" Until now: "The techniques of reproduction, of *identifi-cation*, have been rendered more precise and perfect.... Henceforth we shall be able to realize – that is, to MAKE REAL – potent phantoms, mysterious presences *of a mixed nature*." Asks Ewald: "Will she know who she is? Or rather what she is...?" Answers Edison: "Do we know so well ourselves who we are and what we are?" Of no less a mixed nature than we are, his automaton does seem to go beyond the cylin-der of gestures and the discs of the two golden phonographs by which she can converse for sixty unrepeating hours. Hadaly becomes Eward's equal, only to drown with him aboard a sinking ship, the *Wonderful*.[133]

Thirty-five years later, after the wonderful Belle Epoque had sunk in the mud and gas of World War I, robots made their entrance on the world stage. They came with a mixed nature, obedient but self-regulating, mechanical but intuitive. Meant to liberate human workers, they were driven finally to liberate themselves. By derivation they were servile labor (< Slavic *robota*, Czech *robit*). By historical origin they had been guardians of pyramid tunnels and subterranean labyrinths. By technological extension, they became railway crossing guards, electric flagmen, mannequins at the windowed entrances to department-store mazes. By psychological extension, they were people who made invol-untary motions, those automatisms associated with nervous tics and the repetitious actions of workers on assembly lines. By literary extension they became Tik-Tok, Frank Baum's "Patent Double-Action, Extra-Responsive, Thought-Creating, Perfect Talking MECHANICAL MAN," guaranteed to work for a thousand years. By dramatic conclusion, in Karel Čapek's play, *R.U.R.* (1920), they were laborers, Rossum's Universal Robots overthrowing their human masters and rediscovering romance.[134]

"Today's astonishing Robots are a race misunderstood," wrote E.E. Free (!) in 1929. The new prototypes, Electric Eric ("RUR" inscribed on his chest) and Televox, deserved better. "If Robots had emotions such indignities might be resented. One might think them no better than imitation men. In truth, they are creatures of an altogether different kind; relatively new on earth and not improbably as potent for the future" as humankind itself. They would turn the tables on us (wrote one science fiction novelist after another), become a new gender or our new species (speculated Olaf Stapledon in 1931), transform us into them, who do "good and evil indifferently" (protested Georges Bernanos in 1945, after watching mechanized, routine killing and mass murder). We who have called robots into being cannot call them out of being as a kabbalist might halt the golem in its tracks. If we give them speech, we must also give them a conscience – or else.[135]

"Automation," a word for the deskilling processes of industrial capitalism after World War II, is heir to the or-else of automata as obedient yet self-regulating, artificial yet self-moving figures. The numerically controlled machine tools and remote-controlled arms developed in the 1940s and 1950s, the spot-welding and paint-spraying robots introduced in 1969–70, the colossal Fujitsu-Fanuc robots of the 1990s making other robots for the twenty-first century, all may bear scant physical resemblance to human beings, but we still replay with them our ambivalences about power and displacement, dominion and alienation. What do we lose (or gain) of ourselves when we give them voice? Do we thereby delegate our humanity or abdicate it? What would we do with the replicants of *Blade Runner* (1982), "more human than humans," manufactured as slave labor but angrily aware that a built-in obsolescence will shut them down after four years, when they revolt and cry out for "more life"?[136]

Haven't we too been crying out for "more life"? Our self-portraits now neither anchor nor extend us because we are no longer sure of our selves as originals, no longer sure of what it means to be inspirited. The more uncertain we have become of what colossus could possibly anchor our selves, of what miniature could without mortal danger extend our selves, the more we have demanded correctness and the more we have finished in dissemblance.

Walter Benjamin, a theorist who for some readers must have been lurking behind each of these pages, did not say it best when he said that through replication the Original has lost its aura. He was wrong to claim that the ritual distance which we keep, or by which we are kept, from unique works of art had been diminished by modern industrial processes. What withers in the age of mechanical reproduction is not the aura, the Happen-Stance, of works of art but the assurance of our own liveliness. Benjamin got it as sidewise as he got the solution to the First Mover of von Kempelen's automaton chess player, whose cabinetry was occupied by no devious hunchback (of "historical materialism") but, for twenty years, by a stooped man six feet tall whose endgame was a little weak. Philosopher of the snippet, Benjamin confused misdirection with deformity. It is not that we ourselves are of a sudden monstrous, but that we look misguidedly to our creations to find our animation and learn our fortune. Only in a culture of the copy do we assign such motive force to the Original. What we intend by "Original" these days is that which speaks to us in an unmediated way, an experience we seem to believe we have lost between ourselves, human to human. If Benjamin the collector of books rightly saw that "Every day the urge grows stronger to get hold of an object at very close range by way of its likeness, its reproduction," he failed to comprehend that such possession is ultimately pentecostal, a desire by way of our pained likenesses to be translated in our very nature and speak in tongues.[137]

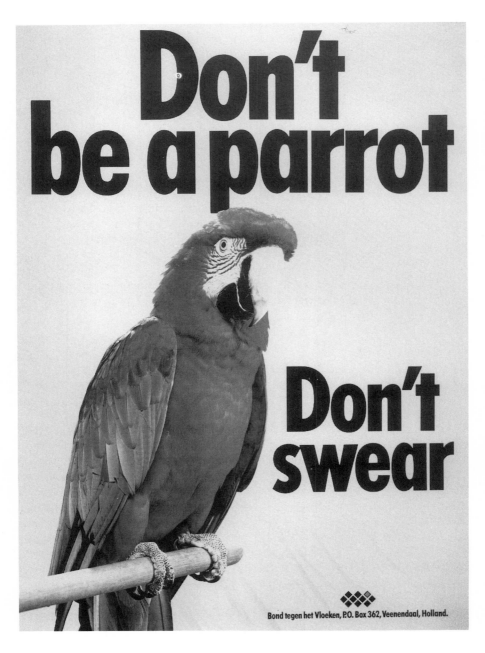

Bond tegen het Vloeken, P.O. Box 362, Veenendaal, Holland.

FIGURE 4.1. English version of a Dutch poster, distributed throughout the Netherlands by the Bond Tegen Het Vloeken (Society Against Profanity), 1990.

CHAPTER FOUR

Second Nature

> Every man carries on his left shoulder a monkey, and on his
> right a parrot. Though Guillaume made no effort, his par-
> rot repeated the speech of a privileged class, his monkey
> imitated its gestures.
>
> — Jean Cocteau, *Thomas the Impostor*

Parrots

The tongue of the parrot is nearly human, wrote the naturalist Ulisse
Aldrovandi four hundred years ago. Could that account for its human
speech? Of all birds, the parrot's tongue *is* uniquely fleshy and mus-
cled, but its strength and finesse are rather for working at nuts than
nouns. Humans talk through the larynx, shaping speech with teeth and
tongue; parrots talk with the syrinx, farther down the windpipe, as if
ventriloquists.[1]

In native habitats parrots are screechers whose "truly awful 'Crrah!'"...
goes through you like a knife," wrote the twelfth Duke of Bedford in
1929. An admirer and advocate of parrots, he yet doubted "if the whole
realm of nature contains another sound so incredibly harsh." Only in our
keep, bonded to us in lieu of a mate, is their gift of tongues manifest.
Until this century, Europeans slit parrots' tongues "to render speech
more fluent." This was a cruel deed of transferral. Wild, parrots were
rude noise and rare plumage, riots of color to which an ancient Vedic
hymn entrusted the hues of the fading moon at dawn. Chained, parrots were sentinels, as in French forts during World War I, squawking
early warnings of enemy airships. Tamed, their tongues split, parrots
were initiates into civil discourse. A "loosed" tongue translated parrots from sheer noise into our next of kin, beings who second us and
take us, for better or worse, at our word.[2]

Known best for the nonsense of *The Owl and the Pussycat*, Edward
Lear also did the first book of color lithographs dedicated to parrots. He
was also among the first to draw from live parrots and to depict each
bird with its own personality. In 1831, completing his *Illustrations of the
Family of Psittacidae, or Parrots*, Lear observed, "for the last twelve months
I have so moved − thought − looked at − & existed among parrots −

that should any transmigration take place at my decease I am sure my soul would be uncomfortable in anything but one of the Psittacidae."[3]

Flippant remark, maybe, of a nineteen-year-old who had taught himself art by copying all the plates of animals in the Count de Buffon's forty-four volumes of natural history. Or maybe not: images of the soul's migration from human into parrot have served many cultures. Birds, of course, have been natural choices for flights of the spirit; among the Kaluli of Papua New Guinea, the passage from life to death is danced as "becoming a bird";[4] the Egyptian *ka* separated at death into two birds, the *akh* and the *ba*; Christian saints acquire wings on their way to heaven. But, of all birds, parrots have been unusually endowed with powers to mediate and transform; their flights of eloquence take us, and our culture of the copy, beyond our twins and our self-portraits to what may be our second nature. Let us follow them as they weave through India, the Americas, and Europe.

Sacred to Hindu deities of love, Indian parrots have been totems of courtesans and companions to lonely wives. Taught to speak of love in the *Kama Sutra*, parrots are inviolate messengers between women and men, between sisters in lands of famine and brothers in lands of plenty.[5]

Along the plenteous Amazon, "the Bororó believe that their human form is a transitional state: between that of a fish (whose name they have taken as their own) and that of the macaw (in the guise of which they will finish their cycle of transmigrations)." Thus Claude Lévi-Strauss, who did work among the Bororó and hoped to fix "the line of demarcation between culture and nature, not in tool-making, but in articulate speech."[6]

Félicité is an inarticulate servant, "a simple heart" (wrote Gustave Flaubert) whose half-century of sacrifices for others goes unrewarded. The final object of her devotions is a gray parrot whose voice is all Félicité can hear as she grows deaf. When Loulou dies, she has it stuffed and kneels before it to say her prayers. She confuses Loulou with that aspect of the Trinity charged with the gift of tongues – a fair confusion, since the dove, traditional emblem of the Holy Spirit, cannot talk. Breathing her own last breath, Félicité sees, as the heavens open, "a gigantic parrot hovering above her head."[7]

"I am not a messenger of God though I am wearing green [like descendants of Muhammad]," says Tuti the parrot, who knows the Qur'an as he knows events ten days ahead. Tuti is closer to Allah than he will admit when an Indo-Islamic merchant buys him for his beauty, eloquence, and foresight. Off for business, the merchant leaves his wife in the care of Tuti and Tuti's consort, a female myna. Husband gone, Khojasta falls for a prince. The myna, adjuring chastity, mocks Khojasta, who beats the bird to death. Tuti sagely promises to act as go-between and keep things hush-hush. On his return the merchant learns of the affair. Khojasta blames innocent Tuti for the betrayal, plucks the parrot naked, and throws him out on his beak. Angrier at the mistreatment of Tuti than at the infidelity, the merchant expels Khojasta, who runs in tears to pray at a shrine where Tuti, hidden, is recuperating. In the voice of the shrine's saint, Tuti commands Khojasta to tear out her hair and pray for forty days. On the forty-first day, "when like a gold-winged parrot the sun came out of its cage in the east," Tuti in full feather reappears to the merchant and declares himself restored by the shriven Khojasta, who must be forgiven.[8]

Pure example of the "prelogical" nature of the "primitive mentality," the Bororó believed themselves to be red parrots, meaning not only or simply that they became scarlet macaws after death, but that they the Bororó actually were parrots, in a "mystical community of being" alien to modern minds. Thus the French philosopher Lucien Lévy-Bruhl, who in 1910 was citing a German account of an 1887 expedition to Brazil. Karl von den Steinen himself had shied from such conclusions, but he did portray the Bororó as imitative, repetitive, and noisy, and his photographs showed them naked except for ritual costumes of parrot feathers along arms and shoulders. The Bororó word for parrot, he wrote, was "the word for a complex that includes parrots and themselves," and they said (or was this von den Steinen?) that they were to red parrots as caterpillars were to butterflies.[9]

Green was the color of resurrection for Europeans. Psytacus, son of Deucalion who restored humanity after the Flood, asked to be relieved of human cares after a good long life in Ethiopia. The gods transformed him, wrote Boccaccio, into a parrot with emerald plumage, symbol of virtue and renown.[10]

Once the troops of Alexander the Great returned triumphant from India with plum-headed parakeets at their wrists, parrots became the darlings of the Hellenistic world. The Romans later had a regular trade in Asian parrots and a parrot-teachers' association. So much in aristocratic fashion were parrots that Ovid composed a mock elegy for one:

> ...Parrot is dead, humanity's echo,
> the talking gift from the Far East

whose last words were to his mistress: "Goodbye, Corinna."[11]

Four or five villages of Eastern Bororó survive; the Western Bororó have been extinct for three generations. Parrots, the sole pets for which the Bororó express affection, are taken as fledglings and fed from the mouths of their owners, who name them as persons yet disregard their ability to talk. Playmates for women and children but closely identified with Bororó men, macaws are never traded or sold; they descend to the heirs when owners die. Since spirits often temporarily lodge in macaws, these red parrots are neither entirely celestial nor animal; they are as betwixt and between as Bororó men, themselves considered only partial, temporary vehicles for spirits. Thus an analysis by J. Christopher Crocker. "We are macaws" is an assertion of belonging through displacement, continuity through flight.[12]

Riding through a forest, young Gaius Julius was addressed by a swooping parrot, *Ave Caesar*, "Hail Caesar," foretelling his later glory or, rewrote Christian theologians, the glory of the Virgin, hailed by the angel Gabriel (Luke 1.28): *Ave Maria*. It was Saint Jerome, intrigued with Mary-full-of-grace, who in the fourth century made of the Annunciation a miraculous paradox, the announcement of Mary's divine pregnancy and of her perpetual virginity. Depicted at his desk translating the Bible into Latin, Jerome in miniatures and paintings was regularly accompanied by a parrot, symbol of the Word at once pure and generative.[13]

Actually, the Bororó do not so much mean to say that they are araras (macaws) or become araras as that they *make themselves* araras in order to become Bororó. *Aroe*, the word for the red parrot plumes vital to the men's ceremonies, is also the word for soul, spirit, ancestor, and for "Bororó"; the plumes are "the material medium through which the Bororó play the role of spirit toward themselves. By covering themselves with arara plumes, the Bororó create themselves *in the form* of creators of social form," for only as overflying birds can one see society as a whole. Thus, wrote anthropologist Terence Turner in 1987, for the Bororó "to 'become araras' is to become fully human, in the sense of a social being capable of transcending and recreating the structure and meaning of social life."[14]

Arthur, who organized the Round Table, was also the Chevalier du Papegau, Knight of the Parrot, for in combat he won "the best bird in all the world, who sings the sweet, pleasant song of love." The French *papegai* (< Arabic *babaga*) became the English popinjay or fop, target for witty barbs and for the arrows of archers aiming to pierce a parrot effigy swung on a pole. The parrot was as much a being of touch as of tone, of lechery as of language. Shown perched on a woman's wrist, biting her thumb, the parrot was emblem of eloquence and sensuality.[15]

Living in peace, the Tupi and the Guarani quarreled over a talking parrot. Found by one woman but given to another who reared it, their kin battled so heatedly over the parrot that the two peoples had to separate, the (elder) Tupi staying, the Guarani moving on. And on, restlessly, throughout Brazil.[16]

With the fifteenth-century Norman and Castilian conquest of the Canary Islands off the northwest coast of Africa, the most talkative of parrots, African grays, joined Asian parrots at European courts. In West African mythology, the parrot had brought words to men; nesting in the tallest trees, it was of all beings nearest to heaven. Pope Martin V himself appointed a Keeper of Parrots at the Vatican while a story about an African gray reciting the Apostles' Creed vied with Renaissance poems in which parrots magnified the name of the Lord.[17]

Still, Europeans wrote of parrots as marvels of the Orient, as did the English poet John Skelton around 1522, describing Parrot as "a bird of Paradise" driven by the Flood into India, there honored with silver cages by ladies who ask courteously, "Speak, Parrot, I pray you." Parrot learns all languages, acquiring the wisdom that comes of speech. "Above all others birds, set Parrot alone," wrote Skelton, who set Parrot against an ambitious Cardinal Wolsey and a decaying political landscape. In Parrot's name, features, colors, and fortunes the poet found a miniature of Paradise itself, gorgeous and green. Earliest to call a popinjay a "parrot," Skelton was playing upon the French *Perrot*, diminutive of *Pierre*, derivative of that Greek stone (*petros*) from which the apostle Peter took his name. "Parrot" alluded as well to the alchemical Philosopher's Stone, transmuting corruptible to incorruptible matter:

> When Parrot is dead he doth not putrefy;
> Yea, all things mortal shall turn unto nought
> Except man's soul, that Christ so dear bought;
> That never may die, nor never die shall:
> Make much of Parrot, the papegai royal.[18]

Which hath done Cristoforo Colombo, whose own name he took to mean the "Christ-bearing dove." Sailing from the Canaries to benefit from the trade winds, which made the air smell as sweet "as April in Andalusia," Colombo noted twice in his log that all that was missing was the (heavenly) song of the nightingale. On October 7, 1492, about to sail beyond the northern limit of the trades, he saw "great multitudes of birds [probably puffins, called sea parrots] passing from north to southwest, which made it seem likely that they were flying off to sleep on land." Aware that "most of the islands that the Portuguese hold they discovered through birds," Colombo fortuitously changed course, turning west-southwest; five days later he was on Guanahaní.[19]

Colombo was as prepared to make much of Parrot as he was to hear nightingales, which he and his men did, impossibly, in the Caribbean, where there were none. Nightingales intimated at a Spanish paradise; large colorful parrots heralded the Orient of Marco Polo. Parrots were not native to Europe, and the African parrots Colombo knew from Guinea were the size of pigeons, gray with short red tails or green with gray heads and yellow vents. The handsome people swimming out to his launch that first day with three-foot-long scarlet macaws on their shoulders as gifts had to be an Annunciation of Asia, of an Indies pregnant with spices and gold ("where parrots, gold," went the proverb).[20]

As parrots mediated the encounter between Europe and these "Indies," so "Indians" were melded with parrots. Receiving the macaws with deep pleasure, Colombo and his sailors handed out in return tiny bells and glass beads reminiscent of the bells and mirrors Europeans hung in the cages of parrots. That day of initial contact, October 12, Colombo wrote of the friendly natives, the Taino, as if they were no less, and no more, than clever parrots: "They should be good and intelligent servants, for I see that they say very quickly everything that is said to them; and I believe that they would become Christians very easily, for it seemed to me that they had no religion. Our Lord pleasing, at the time of my departure I will take six of them from here to Your Highnesses in order that they may learn to speak." Next sentence, same thought: "No animal of any kind did I see on this island except parrots." Clever parrots – and caged parrots: on October 14, Colombo wrote, "whenever Your Highnesses may command, all of them can be taken to Castile or held as slaves (*captivos*) in this same island; because with 50 men all of them could be held in subjection and can be made to do whatever one might wish." Finding that some wore small bits of gold in their pierced noses (flashing like the beaks of scarlet macaws), that some painted their naked bodies (like the plumage of parrots), that most had large and "very beautiful" eyes (like the eyes of parrots), and that they slept on hammocks suspended in the air (like parrots in trees), early Spanish colonists rounded up "Indians" for sex and slave labor in much the same mode as Colombo collected macaws for the pleasure and evidence of having reached an exotic outpost of India. On his triumphal return to Spain, Colombo paraded with his prizes: cotton, spices, a few gold masks, six painted *Indios* wearing golden trinkets and bright feathers, and forty magnificent parrots. Before the admiral's death in 1506, mapmakers would be designating the New World by red macaws, the Portuguese would be calling Brazil the *Terra de Papagaios*, and artists would be painting Americans as reddish brown people sporting parrot feathers. In 1569 Gerardus Mercator would hint at yet another new continent, somewhere in the South Indian Ocean: *Psittacorum Regio*, Parrot Territory. That would be Australia – which when found did truly abound with parrots.[21]

"Flocks of parrots obscure the sun," Colombo had noted in his log. Every Caribbean island he came upon likely had its own variety of red parrot. These are extinct. Of the three hundred thousand Tainos in Hispaniola in 1492, only five hundred remained in 1548. The Columbian Exchange by which syphilis and sotweed reached Europe wrought the devastations of smallpox and gunpowder upon America. Amidst this uneven exchange, parrots were the sign of the New World as Second Nature. Much of the cultural baggage the parrot carried from India through Europe to the "West Indies" was deployed in the exploitation of the American peoples, who had their own myths centered upon red parrots and who, like the Zapotec of Mexico, revered them as oracles.[22]

Second Nature: an Other World, the Indies, or a New World, the Americas, both fronted by splendid parrots. Second Nature: outlying islands of the Orient, as Colombo for years insisted, or continents lying between Europe and the Indies, as others saw, finding meanwhile mermaid manatees, armored armadillos, pouched opossums, cowled flatnosed monkeys – creatures who seemed to cross species as speaking parrots cross the boundary between birds and people. Second Nature: an afterWorld where the Ten Lost Tribes might be found and the souls of "Indians" be claimed for Christ through the parroting of catechisms and confessions. Second Nature: an inferior world, a wilderness of screaming parrots and uncouth people suitable only for hard love and harder labor (the parrot's skull is so thick, wrote Pliny, that to be taught anything "it wants an occasional crack with an iron bar"). Second Nature: doing what one always does (*consuetude est altera natura*, "custom is second nature," ran the Latin maxim), making the New World in the image of the Old, with parrot-towns repeating the names and political forms of the homeland, from New Brunswick to Nieuw Amsterdam, Nouvelles Orléans to Nueva Armenia. Second Nature: despite everything, a second life – for the poor, the punished, the persecuted, the prophetic, a place to redeem humanity and transform oneself as the brilliant parrot, conflated with phoenix or saint, redeems and resurrects. Second Nature: parrotdise, seas brimming with fish, lands teeming with game, skies vivid with scarlet macaws.

Exploring the Amazon in 1800 to "find out about the unity of nature" among an extravaganza of "fantastic plants, electric eels, armadillos, monkeys, parrots," Alexander von Humboldt met up with an old parrot speaking the literally dead language of the Atures, a tribe thirty years extinct. Fact or Germanic fantasy, it was Humboldt's gift to recapitulate through his story the Second Nature of parrots as our mouthpieces and messengers, as it would be Flaubert's gift to contemplate parrots as our Second Coming. "Do you know what I've had on my table in front of me for the last three weeks?" wrote Flaubert in July 1876, at work on the story of Félicité. "A stuffed parrot.... The sight of it is beginning to irritate me. But I keep it there so that I can fill my head with the idea of parrothood."[23]

Parrothood is not easy to define. It is too mixed up with our ideas of humanity, especially when we begin to take pride in our skill at perfect replication. Even classifying parrots has been a struggle, for they appear more distant from other orders of birds than we make ourselves distant from other mammals. Found as fossils thirty millions years old, parrots "stand alone as a peculiar group" with 7 subfamilies, 75 genera, 326 (or 332, or 333) species. More may be discovered, or lost forever. The entire family "of this very natural group of birds" may be re-sorted once more, as it has been, time and again, since the fourteen varieties of parrots known to Europeans in 1555.[24]

Whatever the schema, parrots have popularly been put at the head of the class of Birds, due to their large forebrains and the gift of tongues, their footedness and use of a grasping claw to feed themselves. Most parrots perch on the right foot, eat with the left – an expression of laterality otherwise unique to simians and Homo sapiens. That parrots mate for love and for good is so much a part of the lore that their pining away at the passing of a loved one, avian or human, has been taken as evidence of soulfulness. When the Duchess of Richmond died in 1702, her finely costumed funeral effigy did not fool her parrot; collapsing of grief, he was stuffed and placed at her wax side in Westminster Abbey. When Mr. Jennings of Essex died later in the century, his parrot devoted himself "to the most exquisite grief, until the day of his master's interment: when, after moaning and lamenting, in a manner so audible and impressive as to increase the affliction of the family, he sunk down and died." A dying parrot, versa vice, will cry out for its human. J.J. Sprenger, in the premier issue of *Audubon* magazine, 1887, eulogized his cockatoo companion of twenty-two years for laughing like a man, whining like a puppy, crying like a baby. Doddering at fifty-two, Polly fell off the back of a chair and uttered "the most pitiable of cries, evidently trying to say 'Papa' (meaning me)." Sprenger sprang up the stairs. "A few gasps, a convulsive tremor, a closing of his jet black eyes, and Polly was no more!"[25]

Death scenes such as these are the more plausible given the lifespans of parrots, their aging and illnesses. "Common report [in 1861] says that Polly, like the phoenix, sees out its century; but from fifty to eighty years is the term of its natural life" – the term of human life. As parrots age they lose their memories with their feathers, become silent or muddled, "decrepit and doting like a very old man." Wrote a wry observer in 1930, "We know of no old birds' home for parrots, for did not Long John Silver say, 'They lives for ever mostly, and if anybody's seen more wickedness it must be the devil himself.'" Satanic or angelic, parrots, especially scarlet macaws, share with humans, notably Edward Lear and Gustave Flaubert, fits of epilepsy, "the sacred disease." Long thought a demonic or divine possession, the disease is peculiarly apt to birds known for playing dead, for cursing to high heaven and reciting the Apostles' Creed, for being the pets of pirates and parsons (parakeet < *perroquet* < *parrochetto* < *parroco*, Italian for parson, or < *parochus*, Latin for curate, a dubious derivation). Parrots may also communicate disease to human beings, so that we may succumb (with Félicité) to a type of pneumonia known as psittacosis or parrot fever.[26]

Parrothood is a parabolic humanity. From birth (both parents feeding their infants colostrum) to death (and transmigration), parrots trace the stages of becoming human. If they have represented the visible Second Nature of new and other worlds, they have also been our audible Second Nature.

They begin, as we, "screaming horribly." Then they imitate, as infants do, the sounds around them; in our company, they practice the jabber on the radio, the wrinkling of cellophane, the squeak of my swivel chair – even as we in turn have made Artificial Aviaries with mechanical birds singing as they hop from branch to branch; have put Disney lyrics into audioanimatronic macaws, the songs of nightingales into automatic red parrots.[27]

Real parrots move on to repetition and memory work, ABCs, multiplication tables, and daily prayers. "Parroting" is a primary skill, a stage we all go through. The issue, wrote John Locke in 1690 amidst debates about memory and language, is to get past the parrot: "because by familiar use from our cradles, we come to learn certain articulate sounds very perfectly, and have them readily on our tongues, and always at hand in our memories; but yet are not always careful to examine, or settle their significations perfectly.... Nay, because words are many of them learned before the *ideas* are known for which they stand: Therefore some, not only children, but men, speak several words, no otherwise than parrots do, only because they have learned them, and have been accustomed to those sounds." So an English gent would be skeptical of youth who

> With words and sounds...idly play,
>   But never exercise their mind;
> Such talents as these boys display,
>   In gaudy Parrots we may find.

"The education of a parrot has been compared to that of a child," wrote the Count de Buffon, from whose natural history a young Edward Lear had copied the plates; "it frequently had been more just to compare the education of a child to that of a parrot." The preface to an American primer, *The Teaching Parrot* (1809) began: "Great pains have been taken with many parrots, by children of all sizes, to teach them to speak; but I never knew one that could read in a book: therefore, as I know how much a parrot would be valued, that could read, and how pleasant it is to hear little children read, I have given a new set of letters and an alphabet," each letter a bird. Romantic reformers have disdained such rote learning, "the parrot method of sticking incomprehensibilities into the memories of Children as you would do pins in a pincushion." Despite them, parroting has been as fixed a part of schooling as of growing up; Peter Pan, who "won't grow up," doesn't want to go to school "Just to learn to be a parrot / And recite a silly rule."[28]

But parrots, like young children, play with the rules and the words, adapting them to context and personality. Mrs. Cassirer's African gray "asked questions and returned answers, made requests, and returned thanks; and used words correctly in relation to time, place, and persons," noted the nineteenth-century British authority, Dr. William T. Greene. Countless anecdotes made it clear to Dr. Karl Russ, his German counterpart, that "It would be very unjust to maintain that the parrot merely chatters words mechanically without ever having any idea of the meaning. How coaxingly it begs for some tit-bit, how angrily it can scold if it does not get it, how joyfully it chatters when its master returns after a long absence, and cries welcome to him."[29]

Imitation and playful repetition may be much more than the sincerest form of chattering. They may be prerequisites to reason and preamble to invention, as the American philosopher Josiah Royce thought in 1894. Our "imitative functions," he wrote, are "absolutely essential elements of all our rationality, for all our mental developments, of all our worth as thinkers, as workers or as producers...the necessary concomitant and condition, and instrument of all sound originality." At one extreme, idiot savants, leading lives of echolalia, can repeat with exact intonation any language spoken to them yet be otherwise incapable of coherent speech. At the other extreme, mockingbirds (mistaken for nightingales by Colombo) can refine their own tunes and also perfectly mimic the calls of fifty other species of birds, mystifying ornithologists seeking functionalist explanations. Between the two extremes are most of us – and parrots like Sparkie of Bournemouth (531 words) or Toby of Washington, D.C. (350+), who use their impressive vocabularies with "intelligent intention, malice, and volition," teasing and apologizing ("Ouch!" after biting you), protesting ("Stop that! I said stop that!") when you clean the cage. As tongues of parrots were hung from the necks of pupils during the legendary Vedic Age, so an Indian educator insists in 1987 that "parrotry is the first stage of Foundation Education," proceeding, as do parrots in folktales, to a privileged wisdom.[30]

From imitation and repetition, then, to a higher ordering that requires not simply a coincidence of event and phrase but a sense of categories. We know today that parrots can reason across permanent categories, thanks to the researches of Prof. Irene Pepperberg. Or rather, thanks to her experimental subject, Alex, an African gray born in 1976 who has proven to be able to distinguish more than sixty objects by color, shape, and texture. Unless bored with rounds of simple (stupid) questions, Alex can correctly name, request, refuse, or comment on "paper," "chair," "grape," "shower"..."shoulder"; can discern the relationship between a green pen and a blade of green grass ("color"); can tell the difference between identical pieces of paper ("none") or the similarity between a green wooden key and a blue rawhide key ("shape"). Alex has shown that he also understands that objects once in his grasp continue to exist out of his sight. When he himself wants to be out of sight, he announces, "I am going to go away," then turns his back. And once, just once, himself in sight, regarding the mirror in his cage, *he* asked a question: "What color?" "Gray," a trainer said. "That's gray; you're a gray parrot." Alex rehearsed the words. "Gray," he said to the face in the mirror. "Gray parrot."[31]

How we see ourselves, in myth and literature, in philosophy and science, is tied up with parrots, for we have given them, as they have taken, our voice. "The parrot is its owner's diary – nothing can be said of one without implicating the other," writes essayist Alexander Theroux, his Double a Mexican yellowhead. We refer to parrots in therapy – they feel and remember cruelty, cannot comprehend violence. We look to them for friendship – something about them "makes them very difficult to claim as one's property," writes novelist Paul Bowles. "A creature that spends its entire day observing the minutiae of your habits and vocal inflection is more like a rather critical friend who comes for an indefinite stay." We train them to praise us and abuse our enemies. We depend on them for love – they are a "huddle species" with a penchant for closeness, and make lifelong bonds with us. We mourn them in poetry and funeral march as they mourn us, calling our names after our passing. And our storytellers tell stories, for children and for adults, of the human spirit migrating into parrots.[32]

"A vociferous symmetry of green and gold and ruby red, with eyes like jewels, with their identical irresponsibility of fire,...and a beak of such a fine curve of cruelty as was never excelled," Martha's parrot "was the link with that which was outside her, and yet with that which was of her truest inwardness of self. This tropical thing, screaming and laughing, and shrieking out dissonant words, and oftentimes speeches, with a seemingly diabolical comprehension of the situation, was the one note of utter freedom and irresponsibility in her life." If parrothood is a parabolic humanity, parrots must be heard to hold dear their liberty, as we do ours. So we hear in the jungle "the wild glad mad cries of flocks of wild parrots," at sea we think of parrots swearing with "outlandish oaths," and in good society, wrote Eliza Haywood in 1746 in the name of a new journal of social commentary, "the *Parrot* will cry out against the *Vices* and *Follies* of *Humanity*." Parrots are resolutely improper; to our immediate aggravation and ultimate relief, they remain rude and parodic, and resist speaking on cue. "A Thing sent by the Gods, and by them inspired to utter only sacred Truths," parrots are equally inspired to the desecration of manners and antiques, the violation of decorum and carpets. Inveterately messy, they cannot be housebroken and pluck out their feathers when abandoned or mistreated. "Every *Parrot*," concluded Haywood, "is King of himself, and obliged to obey no other Laws than those of Nature."[33]

Second Nature: that which seconds us, stands beside us – parrot as *para*, "by the side of," or "to one side of, amiss," or "side by side, simulated." At each stage of our becoming audibly human, the parrot is there. Paraphrasia (incoherence, noise). Parallelism (imitation). Paraphrasis (translation, playful repetition). Paralipomena (supplements, innovations). Parrhesia (frankness, freedom of speech). Parabasis (an aside, a bold insight). Paraclete (the Holy Spirit, giver of the gift of tongues and translator of souls). And parallax: the mutual inclination of two lines, two lives, meeting at an angle.

Monkeys

"Pretty, Pretty Poll," said Parrot. "Chatter, Chatter, Chatter," said Monkey. Poll sang, Pug the monkey danced, "full of tricks, an ingenious copyist of the actions of the human race, so that, at times, he almost did away [with] the distinction between it and him." Félicité, childlike before Loulou, dreamt of a monkey carrying off a demoiselle, as Flaubert had dreamt of walking as a boy with his mother and being encircled by monkeys, one of which caressed him and pulled at his hand. He shot it. Wounded, it howled. His mother scolded: "Why did you injure him? He's your friend. What's he done to you? Can't you see that he loves you? And that he looks just like you!" The monkey kept looking at him. "I felt my soul being torn apart and I woke up...feeling as if I was at one with the animals."[34]

While parrots have spoken for the living and the dead, for lost tribes and newfound continents, monkeys have enacted our lovelessness and

FIGURE 4.2. *The Monkey Sculptor*, attributed to Jean Antoine Watteau, early eighteenth century. Reproduced courtesy of Musée des Beaux Arts, Orléans. Photo from la maison Bulloz, Paris.

our melancholy, our long-lost cousins and newborn children. Parrots echo our humanity, monkeys mirror it. Equally "gregarious, mischievous, noisy, and irresponsible," parrots and monkeys appear in art and literature in our and each other's company more often than in the company of other animals, perhaps because, as the Count de Buffon claimed, we most admire those animals who most resemble us, the monkey in features, the parrot in language. Even "savages," wrote Buffon, "so insensible to the great spectacle of Nature, so very indifferent to all its wonders, have been struck with astonishment at the sight of parrots and monkeys." Parrots and monkeys share (with us) an alphabet of talents: aping, bandying, climbing, deceiving, escaping, fooling, grasping, helping, inquiring, jeering, keeping faith, laughing, mimicking, naming, obsessing, pondering, questioning, recalling, self-sacrificing, and tool-using. Viewing them in the crowns of trees, our culture of the copy

has placed parrots and monkeys with us at the crown of creation, para-
gon and apex.[35]

"Monkey" here is a covering term for simians, including the apes
(gibbons, gorillas, orangutans, chimpanzees). Linnaeus in the mid-
eighteenth century reserved his order of Primates for sloths, monkeys,
great apes, orangutans ("tailed men"), and Homo sapiens, segregating
these from other mammals, Secundates, and from all other animals,
Tertiates, but long before and well after Linnaeus, apes were mixed up
with monkeys and monkeys enchained with human beings. While parrots have been exalted as a risen humanity, simians have been taken for
a primitive or fallen humanity. They have been the monstrous races
inscribed upon empty regions of maps; the hairy wildmen and wild-
women woven into medieval tapestry and ritual; the devils tempting
Saint Anthony in painted deserts or tormenting sinners in hell; the half-
human murderer in Poe's Rue Morgue and the giant abductor of Fay
Wray in King Kong. Transmigrating, we become parrots; transgressing,
we become monkeys who leap from fool to infidel to Antichrist, or from
mischievous mimic to sinner, lecherous, miserly, proud.[36]

Linnaeus's order of Primates was a family reunion, an ingathering
of wildmen and apes – between whom, he admitted, it was hard to dis-
criminate. His contemporaries used both as test cases for the Enlightenment doctrine of educability, which put less emphasis upon voluble
speech than upon innate rationality. A British anatomist, impressed by
the large brain of the orangutan (actually, chimpanzee) he had dissected,
wrote that "The Animal of which I have given the Anatomy, coming
nearest to Mankind; seems the Nexus of the Animal and Rational." If
ape and monkey had larynx and pharynx but did not talk, perhaps their
organs served other purposes, or perhaps, like wild children, they had
not been taught. "Speak, and I will baptize you," said Diderot's cardinal to an orangutan, but this was unfair, for newborn babes, speechless, were baptized regardless, and, as Rousseau would argue, speech
could be no key to humanity for those born mute. Would the cardinal
baptize a parrot? And why did Buffon mistake the name usually given
African gray parrots, Jaco or Jocko, for the name Africans supposedly
gave chimpanzees? How did it happen that Mozart's apish wildman in
The Magic Flute was the feathered "Pa-pa-pa-pa-pa-pa-pa-pageno" (< German papagei, parrot)? Was this because orangutans and apes acted as if
they could, or should, speak the speech set down for them?[37]

Apart and together, monkey and parrot were the finest puzzle that
philosophers, naturalists, and Masonic musicians could pose for themselves among the topmost loops of the Great Chain of Being. Peaceful,
nomadic, isolated, the orangutan was Rousseau's model of the unsocial-
ized human, suggesting that language and civilization might be corrupt
artifacts of each other in the same way that art and society were mutual
distortions in Watteau's painting of The Painter, a monkey artist completing the portrait of a decked-out dummy. Meanwhile, simians in
rococo or Chinese dress cavorted on the walls of French châteaux,

Dutch townhouses, English fishing houses. They danced with parrots in French ballets. They played German chamber music in clockwork facsimile. They stood on London stages in the flesh, like the female chimpanzee or "Mockman" in 1738 who drank tea and "hath a Capacity of understanding & great Affability," or Yo-Ho, three years old in 1801, "a grave old Man" with the "face of an old Ethiopian." The verdict was ambiguous: simians were the bare forked animals that humans had been, without lendings; they were drolleries of what people had unthinkingly become.[38]

During the nineteenth century, as private menageries yielded to public zoos with monkey houses, apes were given Christian names and taught to turn the pages of large tomes. In books of natural history or jungle adventure, orangutans and chimpanzees skillfully handled clubs and carried off beautiful women. When the chain of fixed species yielded to an evolutionary tree, lines of kinship among primates became as historically tight as before they had been structurally proximate. Embryologically, wrote the biologist T.H. Huxley, man was much nearer the ape than the ape was to "man's best friend," the dog. Retrojecting a common ancestry for simians and Homo sapiens was controversial, but the monkey-rope between ape and human bound them in the familiar relation of savage to civilized. Friedrich Engels traced the dialectics of human nature to our posture, more comfortably erect than apes (often depicted with walking sticks, lest they seem insolently stable on two legs). Down from trees and easily upright, Homo sapiens found their hands free to refashion the world, from which came labor, the reworking of the very structure of the hand and the land, and collaborations in which "men in the making arrived at the point where *they had something to say* to one another." Stance and grasp were prior to the emergence of society, the development of the larynx, language itself. "In a state of nature, no animal feels its inability to speak or to understand human speech," as now, in our company, an animal may. Exemplary of such yearning was the fact that "it is the bird with the most hideous voice, the parrot, that speaks best of all." Simians were those unachieved beings we might yet be, had we not descended from golden boughs, stood up, and gone to work.[39]

Such logic underwrote the long success (1911–54) of the hoax of the Piltdown Man, contrived with what has turned out to be the lower jaw of an orangutan. A critic of the skull wrote in 1921 that Darwin had foreseen a time when "doubts must arise as to whether we are dealing with ape-like men or man-like anthropoids." Had Darwin also foreseen an age in which scientists experimented upon monkeys and apes as our chief natural surrogates? At century's turn there were cadavers enough to put paid to the practice of dissecting apes as human proxies, a practice begun two thousand years earlier by Greek physicians who dissected once-sacred hamadryas baboons (Barbary apes) but spoke of human organs. Excepting undergraduates and prisoners with life sentences, however, live humans were unwilling to subject themselves to the rigors

of experimental medicine and social science, disciplines newly confident of themselves and eager to amass results of trials set for human-
seeming beings. Once Darwin in *The Expression of the Emotions in Man
and Animals* (1872) had shown that simians were truly our senti/men-
tal cousins, they were a connection ripe for the mazes and probes of
psychologists and neurologists. Ironically, the Darwinian and Mende-
lian discoveries that confirmed new forms of equity between Homo sapiens and simians opened up new forms of exploitation.[40]

Darwin placed at the disposal of his scientific ally George Romanes
the notes on animal intelligence he had been collecting for forty years.
In 1881 Romanes decided that animals who learn from experience have
minds. This included parrots, who can *recollect*, "that is to say, they
know when there is a missing link in a train of association, and purposely endeavour to pick it up." Monkeys and apes, the only animals
other than parrots who imitate for the sheer joy of imitation, were
praised by Romanes for their "tireless spirit of investigation" and for
their curiosity about life-size models and mirror images of themselves.[41]

Neither his mindfulness of nor admiration for simian mimicry and
curiosity was novel. Rather, that "spirit of investigation" and those powers of imitation were being fitted to a new cultural program by which
apes and monkeys could be made to appear as much collaborators in as
objects of scientific research. Richard Lynch Garner, camped on lake-
shores in the French Congo to observe great apes in 1893 (do they make
things? do they believe in private property? do they understand death?),
had with him a rifle, a native boy, and as "companion" in a wire cage a
young chimpanzee he named Moses, from whom he learned twenty
expressions and to whom he taught four. His choice of the four words
was no less apt than the choice of names: Moses, who came within
sight of but never entered the Promised Land, spoke of family (*nkgwe*,
"mother" in Nkami, *mamma* in English), of scientific method (*wie*,
"how" in German), and the inventiveness of technology (*feu*, "fire" in
French). So began the deliberate observation, injection, and incision
of monkeys, baboons, gibbons, orangutans, and chimpanzees, who were
being set up as comradely positivists, solving science's puzzles with concern for the repetition of "how" and "fire" but unconcern for "why?"[42]

How warmly convenient: scientists could believe that they were
enlisting primates as assistants in trials that would materially benefit
humanity. Apes and monkeys stood for what scientists stood for: repeated inquiry, practiced technique, (statistical) acts of association,
evolution, technological progress. The closer that monkeys and apes
came to humankind, the more human-unkind demanded their surrogacy. Should they stand before us as our Second Nature, then they
shall stand *for* us when we are poisoned, syphilitic, poliomyelitic, psychotic; when we have been abused or abandoned; when we feel disori-
ented or confused.

Late-eighteenth- and nineteenth-century sideshows billed apes, especially orangutans, as wildmen; twentieth-century drama and cinema

have more often billed men as apes, from Eugene O'Neill's *The Hairy Ape* through *Tarzan of the Apes* to *Planet of the Apes*. In a transitional French play of 1906, the title character Narcisse is so ugly that a friend advises, "You look too much like an ape. Become a real ape and exhibit yourself." He does, and is invited to afternoon teas to be petted and courted, a social success. Franz Kafka's ape a few years later lectures a learned society upon the significance of a handshake and the meaning of freedom. Soirées since 1901 have seen suave men in formal dress known as "monkey suits." Cued in part by a rising respect for pets, by outcries against the general mistreatment of animals, by thoughts about the moral capacities of other species and our own duties to them, the shift of perspective from ape-as-debased-man to man-as-gifted-ape has been prompted as well by feelings that simians are at once our ancestors, our co-respondents, and our children. Nicolas Pike, describing baboons for the *Scientific American* in 1891, knew that "Many people refuse to shoot them, for if not killed outright it is so terrible to see their death agonies.... A little gray monkey I saw accidentally shot made so powerful a scene before it died, its appealing looks, actions, and cries were so exactly those of a badly hurt child, that I vowed never to shoot a monkey, and I never did."[43]

Carl Akeley did, for he was on a mission to collect and mount the best specimens of wildlife for American museums. But here too, in the art of taxidermy, a comparable change was coming about. Mummified bodies had anchored early cabinets of curiosities, which also displayed the remains of such hybrids as basilisks, contrived from manta rays, dart-shaped tongues, and enamel claws – a subterfuge like those favored by the Japanese artisans who made P.T. Barnum's mermaids. Bones missing, colors fading, eyes a-glint with glass: actual preserved fauna were scarcely less composite. It was an eighteenth-century French innovation to steep eviscerated birds in spirits of cognac and lavender, then wire them into position and allow them to dry; after this was done at the British Museum, a visitor of 1748 would be impressed by "stuffed birds" that "often stood fast on small bits of board as naturally as if they still lived." The birds were eaten by insects because not truly "stuffed": some flesh had been left on the frames to keep the bodies solid. Methods slowly improved. Slitting the skin lengthwise, the French removed all soft tissue, cleaned the skeleton, substituted hemp for muscle, looped wire around the sternum to support neck and wings, and sewed up the skin, which had been bathed in an arsenical soap; or they filled the skin with plaster and inserted artificial eyes and beaks.[44]

Nelly Weeton, touring Bullock's Museum in Liverpool in 1808, found "The birds, beasts and fish all stuffed in a surprising manner. Entering one room you see a huge rhinoceros almost as large as life, and would be quite so, but that the skin is shrivelled in the drying"; in another room, she saw "a panther just ready to spring upon you, its attitude is so natural." Its attitude may have seemed natural to a governess who could only have known panthers from paintings or drawings in books, yet it was an isolated figure, as out of its natural context as a lion crouching in a nightmare. What inspired a crucial transformation in taxidermy were the attempts of bird illustrators to depict unstuffy birds against appropriate backdrops. Parrot expert François Levaillant in 1804 complained that any paintings after birds in captivity, live or stuffed, were so disparate in hue and attitude from wild birds as to represent oddities rather than true types. John James Audubon, who had practiced taxidermy, sketched from freshly killed birds before they stiffened and their colors faded; then he painted them into *scenes*, one of the most famous of which had branches interlaced with Carolina parakeets, sole parrot native to the United States. At the same time, during the 1820s, taxidermists for European collectors began to place birds and small mammals against shrubs and blue skies painted on the inside panels of glass-fronted wooden boxes. At his museum in Philadelphia, Charles Willson Peale distributed ducks "on Artificial ponds, some Birds and Beasts on trees and some Birds suspended as flying."[45]

Animal figures still appeared "stiff, gaunt, erect, and angular," wrote one museum curator in retrospect. The Yorkshire naturalist Charles Waterton therefore appended "original instructions for the perfect preservation of birds &c." to his *Wanderings in South America, the North-West of the United States, and the Antilles* (1825). As testimony to his own skill at taxidermy, the frontispiece showed a wildman's face modeled from the skin of a red monkey and captioned "A Nondescript"; in his text Waterton asked "whether it be possible that the brute features of the monkey can be changed into the noble countenance of man?" Taxidermy could, it seemed, challenge taxonomy. On his wanderings, Waterton had been as annoyed by the howling of the red monkeys of British Guiana as he had been moved by the grandeur of the Brazilian scarlet macaw, who "will force you to take your eyes from the rest of animated nature, and gaze at him." He brought back the skins of red monkeys, red macaws, and hundreds of other birds, whom he mounted along the staircases in his ancestral home. His taxidermic technique did away with rigidifying wires; instead, he soaked the whole skin in a dangerous solution of perchloride of mercury, modeled the body from the interior so that he could "hit the character of an animal to a very great nicety," then let it harden. He spent days scraping out the hands and feet of monkeys until he could display them with as much lightness and finesse as the soaring of birds.[46]

Others too abandoned "the old wooden school of taxidermy." At London's Crystal Palace, Herman Ploucquet of Stuttgart showed groups of well-clothed kittens and rabbits posed in cute fables. The groups "gave a considerable impetus to the more correct and artistic delineation of animals," observed Montagu Browne, curator of Leicester's Town Museum in 1884; the German school of taxidermy, "though it may perhaps be decried on the score of misrepresenting nature in the most natural way possible, yet teaches a special lesson by the increased care necessary to more perfectly render the fine points required in giving animals that serio-comic and half-human expression." After this Great Exhibition of 1851, and after Darwin in 1859 (working from preserved specimens) had placed the struggle for survival in dramatic biogeographic settings, British taxidermists began to embellish their bird and animal tableaux "with natural grasses, ferns, &c., and with representations of scenery and rockwork, in the endeavour to carry the eye and mind to the actual localities."[47]

Most museums continued to show stuffed animals behind glass on squares of plain white paper in a kind of Platonic quarantine. Painters had for centuries delighted in hunting scenes and bovine panoramas, but that was Art, as were the small avian tableaux prepared by taxidermists for Victorian country houses and imitated by makers of mechanical aviaries and designers of large hats. Modern science, contrariwise, demanded an undistracted contemplation of single, mature, pristine individuals.[48]

Or did it? Again, birds inspired a flight of imagination. Frank Chapman, who at the age of fourteen shot and ate the only two passenger pigeons he ever saw in the wild, seven years later met master taxidermist John Bell, ancient aide to Audubon. Impressed by Bell and informally taught by two other men equally good at collecting and mounting birds, Chapman at the age of twenty-three was hired to sort the eight thousand bird specimens recently bequeathed to the American Museum of Natural History in New York. The museum, which already had twelve thousand mounted specimens and its own department of taxidermy, needed to catalog its collections, but what it needed more was someone to plan public displays of its magnificently dead birds and mammals. Chapman, at heart a field ornithologist, began arranging exhibits of birds that could be found on the wing within fifty miles of City Hall, birds in native foliage (of wax and cloth, "in close imitation of the natural plants"), birds beside nests, birds always in context.[49]

Among the first curators, therefore, to make a point of natural camouflage, Chapman was also the first to base exhibits upon photographs of bird colonies. His Bird Rock group of 1899, the result of a photographic expedition he and his wife took to the Gulf of Saint Lawrence, reproduced "in facsimile" a part of the rock with specimens of all the birds, including their young. "I wanted to bring into our halls the illusion of outdoors," he said in his autobiography, "and, by placing the bird in its own setting of land or water, vegetation and air, retain its charm as one of the most beautiful of animate creatures, at the same time showing its character in relation to its haunts." With theatrical lighting and scenery, the Bird Rock group and the 1901 Cobb's Island (Virginia) group violated curatorial custom, "which made an exhibit presented to the public as formal as the papers they read before their confrères," but Chapman's "habitats" won out. They were popular; they were, as the president of the museum said, "*very* beautiful"; and they were family.[50]

Potent illusions of a natural world in which all was in its place and no creature crippled or outcast, "habitats" imposed upon the animal kingdom Western and male notions of continuity, integrity, family, and gender. The first to achieve a coherent vista of related taxidermic dioramas, Chapman in his 1903 Hall of North American Birds grouped them on shore and in the woods by nesthold, matching specimens of the young to adult pairs. The "habitats" implied, if not the legendary monogamy of parrots, then a spousal loyalty, a maternal attentiveness, and a paternal protectiveness dear to men who were at century's turn as anxious about social anarchy as about cultural decadence, racial degeneration, and the extinction of noble species. Men who spoke of themselves as conservationists or "oecologists" applauded the "habitat" although it justified the collection (the killing) of immature birds usually safe from hunters. Captured complete with nest, plants, and sod, these units of papa, mama, junior, and hatchlings were skinned, wired, and stuffed, their nests cast in plaster, the leaves and branches subtly reproduced. Through his taxidermic theater Chapman was creating shrines to an unspoiled family, an unbroken history, and an unending vista.[51]

Larger, more awkward birds — ostriches, emus, cassowaries — had molds taken of their leg bones, then the skin was stretched over a dummy figure, glued, and sewn shut. It was Carl Akeley who had devised and would further refine the manikin method of taxidermy as well as the casting of specimens whose size, like that of Jumbo, made stuffing too laborious. As a taxidermist at Ward's Natural Science Establishment in Rochester, New York, from 1883 to 1887, the young Akeley had worked over the corpse of P.T. Barnum's favorite elephant, applying what he had learned about treating the skin with salt, alum, and arsenical soap, and stuffing the torso with straw. The results were, as usual, "awkward, stilted, unnatural," but when Akeley tried something more expressive with a zebra, it was trashed. Invited by his friend William M. Wheeler (founder of the discipline of animal ecology) to ply his trade at the Milwaukee Museum of Natural History, Akeley there devised some of the first mammalian habitat groups — a Laplander driving reindeer over the snow; Borneo orangutans in jungle branches. His fame was such that in 1894 the British Museum was courting him, but he was sidetracked by the allure and revenge of preparing the enormous number of specimens Chicago's Field Museum had just bought from Ward's. Akeley became chief taxidermist for the Field Museum and in 1908 for the American Museum of Natural History, where he "revolutionized taxidermy," bringing "his genius to bear upon those subtleties of feeling and expression which make his works vibrate with life and individuality."[52]

Akeley's highest quarry, as hunter and as sculptor, was the gorilla, for, wrote Akeley, "the gorilla is still comparatively unknown," and he feared that its kind would vanish before much was understood. Moreover, explains anthropological critic Donna Haraway, the male gorilla was to him the epitome of manhood and of natural man, like the Giant of Karisimbi, a great silverback he mounted for the American Museum's Hall of African Mammals. In 1926 Akeley was buried on Mt. Mikena, near where he had first killed and skinned a gorilla, in exactly that "habitat" he was preparing for a gorilla "family."[53]

"I live to remember the animals undisturbed and untamed, living without fear or care of man, as wild and free and as beautiful as was the country," Akeley said, and he did come to use a camera more than a rifle. The quotation however is posthumous, the Akeley African Hall was opened posthumously, and taxidermy is a posthumous art. What Akeley constructed were living corpses; what Akeley perpetuated was a Second Nature of animals reconstituted in tableaux of societal utopias; and what Akeley put in motion with his papier-mâché manikins was the progressive disincorporation of stuffed animals, such that our museums of natural history now surround us with molded replicas suffused with polyurethane foam. Less and less of the original animal remains. With polyester resins in lieu of skin, there may be nothing animal left but a shock of hair — and that, sometimes, the hair of a less endangered mammal. The original has become a vanishing twin, photographed, measured, sculpted in plasticine, and discarded in favor of a fiberglass body sometimes threaded with hydraulic tubes and electronic wires. Where taxidermy was once the art of mounting a kill, in modern museums it is the art of manufacturing second skins.[54]

Our second skins. The nearer we allow parrots and certain primates to approach human beingness, the more we have insisted that they be as we desire ourselves to be, with strong males, motherly females, family-minded youth, or, currently, with sensitive males, resilient females, inquisitive youth. At this century's end we describe simians, preeminently chimps, as if they were self-reflective and empathic, recognizing themselves in mirrors and comforting friends in pain, appreciating the notion of a persona, creating (sign language) metaphors, enjoying the drama of play-acting and the success of a deceitful limp. The fact that simian larynxes are incapable of fluent human speech holds them no more distant from us than the fact of a macaw's red feathers. A single difference in the sequence of 141 amino acids stands between the alpha chain of human and gorilla hemoglobin; Chimpanzee DNA, it turns out, is a 99 percent match for human DNA. We are now blood sisters, blood brothers, and like identical twins, our bodies seem willing to accept some of the organs transplanted from baboons and chimpanzees.[55]

Yet, warns primatologist Jane Goodall, "we must not forget, not for an instant, that even if we do not differ from the apes in kind, but only in degree, that degree is still overwhelmingly large." Our speech and intellect apparently distinguish us just enough to impel us toward a responsibility for saving primates from an in-pressing, oafish world — all primates, including us. As our Second Nature, apes and monkeys stand for what the naturalist now stands for: empathy, ecological sensitivity, urgent conservationism. Projecting upon simians our fin de siècle fears for our own immunity and generativity, we must redeem them, return them to the oxymoron of a protected wilderness, so that our transgressions become not theirs. They may at last redeem us, as rhesus monkeys have been meant to do since the 1930s, and as the pig-tailed macaque may yet do, found in 1992 to be a "cheap and unendangered" species on which to test vaccines for AIDS.[56]

Sex

Parrots are to primates as eunuchs are to Eve and Adam. Many parrots cannot be visually sexed; most apes and monkeys instantly raise issues of gender. Parrots are sensual, simians sexual. The redemption parrots offer us is neutered; gorilla suits and monkey glands promise to restore virility, chimpanzees and douc langurs (who pass a newborn from female to female) renew the energies of motherhood. Parrots will commune with us if mated to us alone in an articulate civility; simians we study in their colonies, troops, pairs, or treat as one of the family.

True, parrots flap into sight at erotic moments, but in painting as in poetry theirs is the eroticism of foreplay or afterglow rather than coupling. A gorgeous yellow parrot, wings spread, has flown from its wooden perch to the left wrist of an auburn-haired woman sprawled naked on a cream-coloured sheet in her boudoir. Is this parrot heir to an iconographic tradition of bird as phallus and escaping bird as the

FIGURE 4.3. Lovers with monkey to the side of the man, parrot to the side of the woman, who caresses the man with her right hand while her left is picking his purse. German woodcut, 1470–80. From H. W. Janson, *Apes and Ape Lore in the Middle Ages and the Renaissance* (1952). Reproduced courtesy of the Warburg Institute.

breach of a maidenhead? No, this parrot is a voyeur, thrall to the same
review of pleasure as jealous Venus, who, cockatoo on upraised left arm,
has found Psyche asleep, naked and beautiful. *Woman with a Parrot* was
the culmination of Gustave Courbet's earlier *Study of Two Women (Venus
et Psyche)* and his *Portrait of a Woman Holding a Parrot* (Solange Clésinger,
daughter of George Sand, holding a dazzling macaw). Hung in a coveted
space at the Paris Salon of 1866, *Woman with a Parrot* marked the start
of Courbet's career as a fashionable painter, and for years he carried in
his wallet a small photograph of the painting, thought by contemporaries to be the portrait of a courtesan.[57]

Whoever she is, and whether drawn from live model or lay figure
(the pose was awkward, and Courbet had just had his father send him a
female manikin to be retouched), the woman trusts the parrot as her
intimate. If its beak and spread wings remind of sexual conquest, the
parrot's immediate presence is as voyeur and confidant, as it was in
nineteenth-century English paintings where, for the single woman, a
parrot is a safe object "round which to twine the loving tendrils that
stretch from her heart." Herald of assignation or party to secrets of the
breast, the unfettered parrot is the eunuch in the harem; like a spectator
at a Salon, the parrot can achieve communion, never consummation.[58]

It must be "an absolute rule," counsels *The New Parrot Handbook*
of 1986, "never to leave a baby alone in the same room with a large,
uncaged parrot." Parrots as intimate observers may read your character
("You have a sensitive nature, and are frequently misunderstood by your
close companions"), carry out a lover's revenge, testify at divorce trials,
or be sought as witnesses to murder, but they are rarely represented in
Western societies in the proximity of infants, of whom they can be
fatally jealous. Parrots bespeak Annunciation, but the mess of parturition and the burdens of motherhood have been left to monkeys.[59]

For while Pietro Aretino dedicated his lewd, satirical sixteenth-
century *Dialogues* to his Darling Monkey, and while monkey testicles
early this century were transplanted into men aching to reassert their
manhood, it is the female primate who has been seen as most human,
given her menstrual cycling, her childrearing choices, her "dual careers"
as mother and provider. We call apes and monkeys "simians," not from
the masculine *simius* but from the feminine *simia* (< Latin, those appearing to be what they are not). The natural history of simians has led
most powerfully to parables of motherhood. Believed always to bear
twins, simian mothers were observed to carry one in their arms, the
other on their backs. Hence the classical parable that the female ape
hugs the one she loves, smothering it to death, and spurns its twin,
who lives. Or, chased by (medieval) hunters, the female monkey drops
her beloved child (the Flesh), who dies; the unloved child (the Christian Soul), clings to her and survives. Or, by the weight of the unloved
child (Sin) on its back, the mother is caught — whence "a monkey on
one's back."[60]

Not without a substantial cultural momentum, then, have psychologists in laboratories and primatologists in the field been concerned with vanishing twins, that is, with lost infants and mother love. To this day, Jane Goodall is shocked by the cannibalism witnessed among one band of chimpanzees in Gombe, where two females seized and ate the babies of others in the band. Just as attempts to teach nonhuman primates human language have been less about the physiology of speech than about the sociology of knowledge (how do they *know*? can they *invent*?), so experiments upon and observations of ape and monkey mothers have been less about the physiology of maternity than about the andropology of womanhood and the politics of reproduction. Are good mothers possessive or "restrictive"? Can good mothers be high-status females? Does division of labor by gender grant evolutionary advantages? What does it mean to talk of a division of "labor" when nonhuman primates work equally toward subsistence but the female alone gives birth? Is the experience of being baboon or being human, of being man or being woman, entirely, or essentially, or eventually, biological?[61]

Susan Sperling and Donna Haraway, separately reviewing this century's study of simians (much of which has been done by women, from the founding of primate colonies to the following of groups in the wild), have quite recently pointed out that the gender diformities drawn for nonhuman primates reproduce the sexual oppositions of the how-so stories and how-come agendas that women and men have been telling about themselves. We have used our near-replicas, our Second Nature, to ratify our own ideologies. Where before the simian female was living proof of the naturalness of a gendered and inequitable division of labor, power, or initiative, now she is the mover and shaker of simian society. "The new female primate is dressed for success," writes Sperling, "and lives in a troop that resembles the modern corporation; now everyone goes to eat power lunches on the savanna." The danger is a blindness to or disrespect for the complexities of both simian and human behavior and, they agree, an "implied obliteration of the border between human and nonhuman."[62]

Years earlier, the experimental psychologist Clara Harlow recognized this danger with respect to the anthropomorphic assumptions of her more famous husband, Harry F. Harlow, who at midcentury conducted the infamous experiments depriving monkey infants of their mothers and substituting either frightening, neutral, or welcoming figures of wire or cloth. Harry himself had been raised by his mother, his paternal grandmother, and two childless aunts, one of whom created life-size puppet dramas in a backyard theater. "Not everyone grows up," wrote Clara Harlow, "with three surrogate mothers plus a biological mother and then proceeds to make the surrogate mother famous."[63] But Western society has long used simians as sites for reproduction of its past, whether as barbarians, wild people, lost sinners, missing links, or an ancestral species. Animals in (almost) our own image and apt at imitation, monkeys and apes this century have been made to reproduce not only our gestures and words, our ways of loving and

A NONDESCRIPT.

FIGURE 4.4. From the frontispiece to the 1852 edition of Charles Waterton's *Wanderings in South America*. Is it possible, he asked in his discussion of this figure, whose head and shoulders he claimed to have cut off a mysterious creature he had found and killed in South America, "that the brute features of the Monkey can be changed into the noble countenance of man?"

learning, but the full trajectories of our lives, from crying baby to contentious sociobiologist.

We confide in parrots; they are our sensual present and a heavenly presence. We entrust our protohumanity and our terrestrial future to monkeys, who sign to us more eloquently through their sexuality, their procreation, their mothering, their child's play than through American Sign Language. Not parrots but apes and monkeys do we call our progenitors; not parrots but apes and monkeys test our future earth-worthiness. Should our closest kin die out, how dare we go on?

Something Else

"My apes were trying to become something else," said Gertrude Lintz, whose trained chimpanzees worked in Tarzan movies and whose gorilla Buddy performed for the Ringling Brothers. "I cannot express it differently."[64] The more systematically we have exploited "lower" animals to tell us about ourselves, the more they lay claim in their own right to personhood. My syntax, of course, begs the question, granting animals the subjectivity, political motives, and feelings of moral outrage now (more than ever) at issue. Even as we have perfected machines that hum on the verge of their own independence, we have gathered the species two by two, beginning with parrots and monkeys, around an arc all of whose tangents imply humanity.

Asking, *Can Animals and Machines Be Persons?*, Justin Leiber has noted that Mary Wollstonecraft wrote *A Vindication of the Rights of Women* in 1791 in the English house of Thomas Taylor, author in 1792 of a *Vindication of the Rights of Brutes*. Taylor argued satirically that, given the criteria by which Tom Paine vindicated the rights of all men and Wollstonecraft the equal rights of women, we must admit animals to the same precincts, since they display enough apparent intelligence to demand no less standing than thoughtless maidservants assuming the airs of their mistresses. What Taylor meant to be a ludicrous argument in 1792 would today be taken as a slur against women and, in some quarters, against the other beings with whom we share the planet.[65]

Although Aristotle had conceded everything but reason to animals, and although Neoplatonists (whose works Taylor translated) had sometimes posited animals as human souls being scourged, the inferiority of animals was not sharply contested until the seventeenth century. If animals had souls, as Thomas Aquinas said, they had mortal souls. Rats, mice, moles, locusts, weevils, bees, and caterpillars were impounded for devouring crops, and pigs (in theory) sentenced to death for eating babies, but such medieval judgments determined quasi-legal culpability, not moral capability. Animals after all were (Aquinas) "intended for man's use in the natural order," to plow his fields and bear his burdens, even unto apes and parrots, wrote *Batman upon Bartholome His Booke De Proprietatibus* (1582), who were ordained "for man's mirth."[66]

Even so, Galen in the second century had used pigs or goats as subjects for dissections of the brain, rather than the Barbary apes on which he ordinarily worked, because "you avoid seeing the unpleasant expression of the ape when it is being vivisected." Experiments upon live animals, revived in the sixteenth century upon the recovery of Galen's *On Anatomical Procedures*, would in the seventeenth century lead to questions about the plausibility of analogies between animal and human anatomy and about the extent of animal suffering. Medical excitement around the newly demonstrated pneumatics of blood circulation, for which William Harvey had dissected or vivisected 128 different animals, engendered investigations of the similarly dynamic respiratory system, toward which end Robert Boyle and Robert Hooke sacrificed larks, mice, vipers, ducks, cats, dogs, and wolves. But Hooke, who cut away a dog's thorax and diaphragm to observe its beating heart, was already writing to Boyle in 1664 that "I shall hardly be induced to make any further trials of this kind, because of the torture of the creature." Under friendly pressure, Hooke in 1667 did repeat the experiment for London's Royal Society, where John Evelyn found it "of more cruelty than pleased me." Europeans at the vivisecting table were having a case of nerves.[67]

Literally. Animal spirits, "Particles of the Blood so exceedingly Rarified...as to be Capable of a Swifter Motion, and of a free Passage through such Parts of the Body as are Impervious to the other Particles of the Blood," flowed through the nerve canals from animating soul to tips of claws. This was, for René Descartes as for later "mechanical philosophers," a precarious neurology, devised to affirm the sensibilities of animals yet quarantine them from a rational soul. The Cartesian debating point that animals were mere automata, or sensing machines, invested them with a full palette of physical sensations so as better to delimit animal from human in terms of something peculiarly incorporeal, a self-reflective, reasoning soul.[68]

To just such a soul would appeals be made to stop the manhandling of animals. Early in the seventeenth century, the medical humanist Jean Riolan the Younger had opposed vivisection on the moral and methodological grounds that it should not and could not be possible to ascertain the truth via tortured, dying animals. Early in the eighteenth century, as Europeans began to define their own noblest natures in terms of a balance of sense and sensibility, creaturely pain began to seem less instructive or entertaining. The eternal torment of Hell itself appeared suspiciously vicious and unchristian; Hell had to be transitory, remedial. Prospects for an eventual "universal salvation" of humanity shone brighter, not only among pietists and deists but among the very revivalists who delighted in depicting dramas of damnation but made every effort to draw every dangling sinner up from the burning pit. Salvation (and, for John Wesley, an immortal soul) seemed also to extend to animals, whose (lamb's) blood had been successfully transfused to humans in French experiments of 1667–68 and who, as pets, were regularly included in eighteenth-century family portraits. At death, beloved animals would on occasion be buried in sarcophagi, as was Ver-Vert the

naughty nunnery parrot, though suspected upon his decease to be transmigrating from nun to nun,

> Transmitting to all ages hence
> In them his deathless eloquence.[69]

Communing with animals, sympathizing with their plight, mourning their deaths, none of this implied their sapience or equality. The
philosopher David Hume thought animal intellect distinguishable from
human only by degree, but animals had as yet been granted no intrinsic dignity. Protests against bloodsports recalled people to their own
nobility rather than invoking the nobility of dogs, cocks, bulls, bears.
In the same manner that early abolitionists meant to prove that slavery
brutalized the souls of slaveholders, antivivisectionists in the eighteenth
century hoped to show that habits of cruelty toward animals subverted
human nature. Samuel Johnson contended that a person "buys knowledge dear, who learns the use of the lacteals at the expence of his
humanity." Wrote Immanuel Kant, "he who is cruel to animals becomes
hard also in his dealing with men."[70]

Kant, however, defended experiments on live animals as a justifiable
cruelty, "since animals must be regarded as man's instruments" toward
(an implicit) Greater Good. In rebuttal, turning Kantian ethics against
Kant, Arthur Schopenhauer insisted that animals be treated as ends in
themselves. Humanity was to be defined by the ambit of its humani-
tarianism: if animals had mortal souls, then their deaths were final and
we must not kill them casually or cruelly; if they had immortal souls,
they were entitled to the respect due every human being. In this spirit
was founded, in 1824, the London Society for the Prevention of Cruelty
to Animals. The Victorian zeal for animal welfare deflected attention
from the bestial treatment of industrial laborers, or it was an outgrowth
of movements for the reform of working conditions. It reflected a bourgeois desire for a more sanitary, bloodless world, or it was an ingrowth
of evangelical campaigns to sanctify children. It was an extension of feminism from one household "object," the wife, to another, the pet, or
the distention of Romantic, anthropomorphic, leanings. It was an avenue for the social discipline of the lower classes, or it was their embrace
of the likenesses (discovered through physiognomy and phrenology)
among orders of creation.[71]

Or it was, almost, an act of Providence. So wrote George T. Angell,
yes, Angell, founder of the Massachusetts SPCA (1868) and editor of
its newsletter, *Our Dumb Animals*. Son of a Baptist minister from Providence, Rhode Island, Angell in 1869 went to Zurich to address an international congress of animal protection societies. He told the assembled
delegates that his American society was now, four years after the brutal
Civil War, striving "to unite all religious and political parties on one
platform, for the purpose of carrying a humane literature and education into all the schools of the country, and thus not only insure the

protection of animals, but also the prevention of crime, unnecessary wars, and forms of violence. When the leading minds of all nations shall act together on this subject, and the nations shall be humanely educated, wars between nations will end."[72]

War between this Higher Purpose and the scientific Greater Good was, for a while, anaesthetized. With the introduction of ether to surgery in 1846 in Angell's Boston, the subsequent British promotion of chloroform, and injections of morphia through the new hollow-needle syringe of 1853, it became convenient for science to accommodate the modern cultural sensitivity to creaturely suffering. In fact, animal advocates had generally left scientists alone, more upset with the *thoughtless* cruelties of the working class. Claude Bernard, the premier French experimental physiologist at midcentury, was free to study the effects of curare and strychnine on live animals, free to vivisect large numbers of frogs, rabbits, goats, and dogs, and yet remain attached to a pious wife active in the *Société protectrice des animaux*. After English scientists in the 1860s began to follow the vivisecting lead of continental physiologists like Bernard, they were rather pleased with an 1876 Cruelty to Animals Act that legislated the use of anaesthetics as a prerequisite to the licensing of experiments upon live animals. Anaesthetics legitimated what otherwise might seem, as the antivivisectionist Frances Power Cobbe wrote, a "calm, cool, deliberate" barbarity.[73]

Over the long run, the war between the Greater Good and the Higher Purpose has dug two deep trenches with a killing ground between. The trenches are amazingly parallel, and have been so since the 1870s, when the Scottish neurologist David Ferrier adopted monkeys as paradigmatic experimental subjects, examining the physiology of *the* (their, our) brain. // In order to justify methodologically their work upon animals, experimenters have alleged that animal and human cells, organs, systems, or behaviors are similar enough to allow for extrapolation from one to the other. "I shall prove," wrote Claude Bernard in 1865, "that results obtained on animals may all be conclusive for man, when we know how to experiment properly." The formula Harry Harlow used in his rhesus monkey experiments was that "If human behavior can be replicated in the monkey, the results of the study would generalize to human behavior." Upon these bases most drugs and many social-psychological theories are still tested on animals. The logic opposing animal experiments is identical: as our similarities and not our differences sustain the principles of human rights and dignity, so the many similarities between us and other animals constrain us to affirm the rights, or at least the intrinsic dignity, of animals. "We have freed the black population of Africa," wrote an overly sanguine admirer of the African gray parrot in 1861, "– why shouldn't some zealous philanthropist ... take up that of her gray forest-people, kept slave to our pleasure in a solitary dwindled-down existence?" // Along one side scientists argue that they cannot decipher complex physiological responses without watching the reactions of an entire living organism; along the other side the same stubborn holism is used to call for respect for the life-direction of every animal.[74]

Late last century, amidst a budding interest in wilderness ecology and outdoor life on a vanishing frontier, controversies erupted over "nature fakery," by which was meant the sentimental misrepresentation of wild animals. The naturalist John Burroughs and his friend Theodore Roosevelt then attacked the works of Jack London, Ernest Seton, Beatrix Potter, and William J. Long for putting human words in the mouths, human emotions in the hearts, and human tragedies in the lives of wolves and dogs, bears and woodcocks, moles and rabbits, even as docile white mice were replacing wild rats in laboratory mazes. Late this century, animal feeling, reasoning, and communicating are again tender points, made most tender by the tragedy of extinction. During the eighteenth and nineteenth centuries, perhaps one hundred species of living beings became extinct; now, six species every day.[75]

Faced with a vanishing Second Nature, we the next of kin are going through the stages of mourning on both sides of the killing ground.

ANGER. About to address the Public Relations Society of America in 1989, Harold Burson was interrupted by Susan Rich of People for the Ethical Treatment of Animals, who presented him with a blood-stained rabbit-fur jacket and bloodstained money as memoranda against the work done by the firm of Burson-Marsteller for the Fur Council. PETA had been founded by Ingrid Newkirk and Alex Pacheco in 1980. The next year, working undercover at the Institute for Behavioral Research in Maryland, Pacheco saw that experiments being done "on surgically crippled primates to monitor the rehabilitation of impaired limbs" were conducted with such cruelty as to warrant (as happened) the liberation of the mutilated macaques. Angered by the successes of the chief experimenter in legally retrieving the macaques to continue their trials, Pacheco and others sued as "next friends of seventeen non-human primates." An appeals court in 1986 ruled that the International Primate Protection League et al. did not show "cognizable injuries" to themselves and had no standing to sue to enjoin research upon primates, research which in the past (according to an amicus curiae brief filed by alarmed scientific and medical organizations) had led to the diphtheria, hepatitis, and polio vaccines, and in future might help cure AIDS. Despairing of legal recourse, the Animal Liberation Front during the 1980s secretly raided ninety laboratories in Europe and the United States while others led public campaigns forceful enough to persuade cosmetic companies to stop using animals for toxicity tests, to make wealthy women self-conscious about wearing furs, and to reduce by 15 percent the number of university psychology departments in the U.S. maintaining animal labs. // Angered by the success of antivivisectionists, Frederick K. Goodwin, Director for the National Institute of Alcohol, Drug Abuse, and Mental Health, urged the research community in 1989 to take action to defend itself, as *any* animal, and every simian, would: "We know that in the animal kingdom, when an animal is faced with a predator, the worst thing that animal can do is freeze. The best thing the animal can do is scream, like the monkeys do, and adopt an aggressive posture."[76]

DENIAL. However well simians or dolphins imitate our behaviors (or we theirs), and however much they resemble us in neuroanatomy or cerebration, they are not conscious in the way we are conscious, say those with the Greater Good in mind. Animals do not query the nature of other animals, do not feel responsible for other species, and do not feel pain like we feel pain. "As a concerned scientist and as a practicing neurosurgeon," writes Robert J. White, whose research team in 1964 was the first to maintain an excised primate brain outside its body, "I am simply unable to plumb the depths of a philosophy that places such a premium on animal life even at the expense of human existence and improvement." // However much frogs, rodents, dogs, cats, and primates duplicate us in their various parts, and however many we use up in order to replicate results (200,000,000 worldwide each year, 750,000 rhesus monkeys alone for the creation of vaccines before 1970), it is in vain. Transpositions to human behavior are not credible: few humans are born and raised in cramped cages under artificial light or in reserves threatened by poachers. Transpositions to gross human biology are shaky, especially with lethal-dose tests, and can be grotesquely misleading.... Such systems of denial, for the Greater Good or a Higher Purpose, run contrary to the social, methodological, and philosophical needs along each trench to pull humans closer to a Second Nature. That isolation, of course, is what happens in denial.[77]

BARGAINING. "Would you sacrifice the entire species of chimpanzees for the entire species of *Homo sapiens*? I hope most of us would," encourages Willard Gaylin, a psychoanalyst for the Higher Good who fears that "animal-rights arguments diminish the special status of *Homo sapiens*." But, recognizing the appeal of the notion of stewardship, should not the biomedical community work toward "(1) reduction in the numbers of research animals used in general, (2) their replacement with alternatives to animal use as they become identified and verified, (3) refinement of experimental design to minimize pain or suffering and to substitute species of lower phylogeny where possible"? // Is there a technical middle ground that is not a killing ground, where mannequins, automata, computer simulations, in vitro tissue cultures, microorganisms, or plant cells may serve as our models or "guinea pigs"? Some ethological middle ground where humans and other animals experiment cooperatively for a Higher Purpose? Some moral middle ground where we agree to consider animals as moral objects if not moral agents?[78]

GRIEF. As early as 1946, Clarence Ray Carpenter of the School of Tropical Medicine at Columbia University was calling attention to the plight of rhesus monkeys being imported into the United States from India (15,851 in 1938). Sacred to Hindus and Buddhists who resented the capture of monkeys for the "rejuvenation of decadent Westerners," more than a third of the monkeys died en route from suffocation, thirst, internecine violence in crowded cages, or the climatic violence of a shift from the heat of a Bombay August to the cold of a Boston October. If some scientists, like some slave owners, have been benevolent masters, the traffic in animals as of slaves has been cruel, as much for those animals we make our pets toward some Higher Purpose as for those we slowly (and painlessly) destroy in the name of a Greater Good. Shipments of thousands of contraband parrots and other exotic birds from Africa or the Caribbean arrive in Europe, Japan, or North America with few survivors; for each alive, ten others have died. Of the million live parrots on the market each year, a large number will be bought and later abandoned or "put to sleep" when they become, as is their nature, raucous, messy, jealous, and demanding. Second Nature: that which is more like us than we want, less like us than we hope. Second Nature: that which lives as if a person and dies as if a thing.[79]

ACCEPTANCE. We cannot accept the disappearance of our Second Nature. Were parrots and apes, dolphins and monkeys to vanish, they would haunt us as vanished twins now haunt surviving singletons. Like Félicité's stuffed and transmigratory Loulou. Like the chimpanzee, "such a brutally responsive exact imitator of its human cousin's attitudes that an average sensitive man watching a chimp will pause and wonder and sometimes grow fretful at the resemblance."[80] Second Nature we cannot well live without. We need our Seconds beside us. We need the parrot on our right shoulder, the monkey on our left, active echo, imaginative ape. Second Nature poses more problems for us more acutely than ever before because we have come to realize at once the extent of our dependence upon it and the extent to which our demands could be deadly. If we need parrots and apes, dolphins and monkeys, they may also need us, for the time being, to leave them alone — the classic dilemma of living twins.

8. The largest of
the flock picks her
up by the skirt.

5.

Just as he reaches a small grassy point of land, another fish
attacks him, lashing furiously with his tail.

FIGURE 5.1. Top: *My Wife and My Mother-in-Law*, by cartoonist W.E. Hill (1915), frequently used to illustrate the reversibility of figure and ground. Bottom: *Standing the World on Its Head*, from cartoonist Gustave Verbeek's *The Terrors of the Tiny Tads*, published in the *Toronto Star Weekly*, 1906–14. Turn this book upside down for a clear view of the bird.

CHAPTER FIVE

Seeing Double

Only a part of what is perceived comes through the senses
from the object; the remainder always comes from within.
– Matthew Luckiesh, *Visual Illusions* (1922)

"I am bird crazy and that's the truth," confessed Abbott Handerson
Thayer, painter and naturalist. He took his family on birding trips to
Florida, Europe, the Caribbean. In 1903 at the age of fifty-four he was in
the West Indies, tasting butterflies. "This," wrote his daughter Gladys,
"was in order to disprove what his very dear friend, Professor Poulton
of Oxford, has written many lengthy books to *prove*, the theory of mimicry, trying to show that harmless butterflies...had through natural
selection acquired similar patterning and coloring to those of bad tasting butterflies for their protection."[1]

All the butterflies tasted the same; Poulton must be wrong. Thayer's
own theory was that of Obliterative Gradation and Protective Coloration: birds (and butterflies) sport patterns and colors that blend with
their environs and reduce tell-tail shadows. In 1896 Thayer had demonstrated his theory before Frank Chapman, curator of "habitats" and
editor of *The Auk*. Like Chapman, Thayer collected bird skins for study
and was hopping mad about massacres by milliners' agents who "sometimes have got 144000 birds to one boat with three men and a barrel
of ammunition." That was a biblical exaggeration: in the fourteenth
chapter of the Book of Revelation, 144,000 stand redeemed on Mount
Zion. Protective Coloration was a saving grace for birds, and for Thayer
too, who got religion on the wing – "The beauty of a bird's patterns,
etc. simply thrills me and my immense color progress and decorator
progress is greatly due to this passion in me and the hundreds of hours
spent in looking at my bird skins."[2]

He who painted angelic wings on female figures could show how
a peacock's feathers " 'melt' him into the scene to a degree past all
human analysis." He who painted larger-than-life portraits of women
as half Psyche, half sky, could appreciate how the wildest colors neatly
commingled with Nature: "What wonder, then, since the macaw's
banquet-hall is forever hung with one gorgeous tapestry of fruit and

foliage scenes with sky-glimpses between, that his costume proves to be such as marvelously dissolves him into the scene, as he climbs about, burying his head in cluster after cluster of the brilliant fruit?"[3]

In flannel shirt, golf knickers, and high boots, Thayer blended best with the wooded slopes of New Hampshire's Mt. Monadnock. On the streets of Manhattan, Oxford, London, and Florence he was a highly visible crusader for the invisible. His nephew Barry Faulkner's earliest vivid memory of Thayer was of his uncle placing a pair of wooden ducks in the dust to demonstrate the principles of Protective Coloration to a drawing teacher. One duck, its back dark, its belly light, had "no more solidity than a cobweb." A cat ignored it, mauled the other. The luckier duck had been countershaded according to Thayer's Law: "Animals are painted by nature darkest on those parts which tend to be lighted by the sky's light, and vice versa." A bird seen from below disappears into sky light; seen from above, it fades to earth tones. On this principle he offered to make U.S. battleships "semi-invisible" during the Spanish-American War of 1898. Scorned by the Navy, Thayer did see the British put his ideas into practice during the Great War, while his nephew, a muralist, enlisted seventy-nine artists to apply Uncle Abbott's principles in the belated American war effort. Thayer himself went over to assist the British and fell ill from, of all things, exposure. Returning to New Hampshire, he died in 1921, one of the fathers of what was by then called "camouflage."[4]

Camouflage has a compound paternity and a complex maternity. Its swift baptism during the Great War lay at the juncture of several long paths of historical changes and questions about the visuality of Western society: To what extent can we trust to our eyes for the truth? What should we make of a cultural field on which so much is seen double? Camouflage takes us beyond our flesh-and-blood doubles (the identical twins of Chapter I, the Siamesed pairs of II), beyond our crafted doubles (the wax figures, mannequins, and automata of III), beyond our animal doubles (the parrots and simians of IV). With camouflage we broach our replication of the entire natural world.

Trompe l'oeil

Lecturing in Boston in 1893, the Scottish theologian and naturalist Henry Drummond considered the natural world: "[Thomas] Carlyle in his blackest visions of 'shams and humbugs' among humankind never saw anything so finished in hypocrisy as the naturalist now finds in every tropical forest. There are to be seen creatures, not singly, but in tens of thousands, whose every appearance, down to the minutest spot and wrinkle, is an affront to truth, whose every attitude is a *pose* for a purpose, and whose whole life is a sustained lie.... Fraud is not only the rule of life in a tropical forest, but the one condition of it." How had such a comprehensive accusation of fraud come about?[5]

Pliny, discussing "similitudes" in the first century, was intrigued with a stone on which could be seen Apollo and the Nine Muses. For medi-

FIGURE 5.2. Wilson's Snipe on its nest, obliterated by countershading and patterning. From Gerald H. Thayer, *Concealing-Coloration in the Animal Kingdom* (1909). Photo by Herbert K. Job.

eval Christians, humanity as well as divinity was everywhere refracted in the Creation Adam had named. As manuscript illuminators began to take pains with flora and fauna, Nature herself was celebrated as *Natura pictrix*, painter of ruins on veins of marble, scorpions on jasper, seascapes on agate or porphyry. Renaissance and early modern trade in such "picture stones" was a trade in signatures: the impress of one realm upon another. All parts of Creation could answer to each other, by sharing a place ("convenience"), by emulation, by analogy (a walnut, creased like a brain, will cure headaches), or by sympathy (a "weeping" willow). Centuries later, Edward Lear in *Nonsense Botany* would travesty such anthropomorphism with his drawing of the rare Manypeeplia upsidownia, but Nature's exuberance has never provided as hearty a theory of likenesses as the hint of a meaningful mimicry between stones or plants and people. The dramatist August Strindberg, peering through a microscope in 1896, saw in a walnut "two tiny white hands, white as alabaster, raised and clasped as though in prayer."[6]

To find ourselves and the world repeated back to us not just by parrots and monkeys but by walnuts or the great potoo is only...natural. Human societies work, play, and speak in metaphor; our rituals dance to elaborate sets of likenesses between people, animals, plants, colors. Writes the French philosopher Roger Caillois: "Why suppose that to claim to find elsewhere the characteristics of [man's] nature, or, on the other hand, to rediscover in him the laws that one sees operating in other species, is necessarily cranky, delusion or a mirage?" We would do more justice to all living beings were we not cowed by injunctions against anthropomorphism. "The accusation of anthropomorphism ends, in the long run, in isolating man in the universe and in refusing to admit that the other creatures are in the remotest way connected with him and, in some respects, his brothers."[7]

Henry Drummond's imputation of fraud against the creatures of the tropical forest was, of course, strongly anthropomorphic. He meant thereby to counterpose the cruel "Struggle for Life" to an ennobling "Struggle for the Life of Others." Darwin had found the first axiom of evolution but missed the second: self-sacrifice. Those similitudes so classically delightful, so complementary to Renaissance microcosm and macrocosm, so corroborative of Strindberg's mysticism, were for Drummond a diorama of deceptions against which were played out scenes of altruism and mother-love. Animal mimicries were ruses for species survival, the dark side of that sympathy and unselfishness which were "the direct outcome and essential accompaniment of the reproductive process." Fraud competed with faithfulness for the heart of natural selection.[8]

When Abbott Thayer in an old suit and rubber boots hurried Frank Chapman outside the American Museum of Natural History, he was about to perpetrate a fraud. His countershaded wooden models resembled decoys, but Thayer was using them against their nature, for decoys are meant to be seen, and Chapman saw them not. The word "decoy" comes from the Dutch for duck cage, *eende-kooi* — hunters since Tutankhamen have used captives to lure wild ducks. Live decoys "by seeming kindness trained to snaring" or tethered to a post ("stool pigeons") were European bait; crafted decoys were a North American tradition, beginning with canvasback ducks woven of tule and plastered with feathers by Nevadans around 800 A.D. Lake Champlain tribes in the 1600s stuffed duckskins with hay, tied them to floating logs. White hunters, wanting decoys more permanent than those (de)composed of beaks, wings, or skin, carved schematic wooden birds, no literal reproductions "but rather a symbol which will suggest the bird to its mates circling high overhead."[9]

Armed with rifles and shotguns, market hunters during the 1870s–80s tied hundreds of machine-made "dollar ducks" in rigs to attract circling flocks of waterfowl which they killed for their plumage. It was no feather in one's cap to take 144,000 birds in this fashion, and the greedy deceit of such decoying was expanded in the 1890s by the use of "confidence decoys," replicas of other species placed among decoys of the birds being hunted so as to float a familiar scene: swans bobbing among wooden widgeon, a heron rising above manufactured mallards. To these

eye-cons were joined unusually limber decoys, "leaning into the wind."
Just as Thayer was countershading his simple stiff wooden models,
decoys were being implicated in far more ignoble deceptions.[10]

Dead ducks, hung from a flat nail by the feet or neck, were also
conspicuous at century's end in smaller, framed deceptions. Two-
dimensional art that persuades the eye of the immediate three-dimensional presence of birds, mice, flowers, or hatpegs goes back to the
peapods and filberts apparently scattered over a second-century mosaic
pavement. For the classical world, achievement of this effect was proof
of supreme craft; on interior walls of Roman villas such frescoes extended closed rooms into garden vistas. Resumed during the Renaissance, illusionism pointed toward a Christ-like crossing of borders: as
pilgrims had pinned badges and tokens onto the pages of tiny devotion-
als to hold to the blessings received at shrines, and as noble travelers
pressed flowers or insects into illuminated books of hours to remind
them of their excursions, so objects began to break the pictorial plane
of illustrated manuscripts and figures leaned out from behind the curtains that seemed to hang in front of oil paintings. Taken up into the
domes of baroque churches, illusions of sky and angels drew the eye
from the visible toward the transcendent.[11]

For the Dutch and the Danes of the seventeenth century, illusions
were exposures of vanity, of the sham of those pleasures of the flesh
abounding in societies embarrassed by riches. Cornelis Gysbrechts of
Antwerp and Copenhagen alone innovated half a dozen illusionistic
motifs: *quod libets* or what-have-yous on half-grained backgrounds, hap-
hazard racks of half-opened letters, overflowing cabinets seen through
half-closed glass doors, half-stuffed hanging pockets, paintings half-
turned to show backsides of raw linen, and the *vanitas* niche of skull
and candle revealed to be a painted canvas half-peeling off its frame.
Gysbrechts promoted as well the *chantourné* figure, a life-size painted
flat of a person, braced upright at the dark summer firesides of châteaux,
in the corners of English country homes and American vestibules. These
figures became eighteenth-century "deceptions," refreshments in the
most refined of senses, bringing fresh sights into a room. Other illusionistic pieces played upon the Enlightenment intrigue with paper –
with scrip, scripture, tracts, books, letters, tickets of admission, newspapers – metonyms for reason, education, liberty...serious refreshment
indeed. Christened around 1800 as *trompe l'oeil*, such pieces would steadily lose their status as moral summons. By 1900 they were a disrepu-
table "fooling of the eye," evoking the same uneasiness as did rigs of
machine-made decoys: a mean-spirited trick. Trompe l'oeil seemed no
demonstration of craft but of craftiness: the killing of two innocent
birds with one stone.[12]

From the start, birds and flight have been implicated in trompe l'oeil.
Pliny's tale of the grapes of Zeuxis had birds flying up to peck at fruit
painted by the master. Too often to be mere ornament, parrots perch
on illusionistic balustrades, their hooked beaks and claws teasing us

toward a visual field that begs to be entered for its depth and touched for its bodiliness. Bodiliness, above all, is put up for grabs. Hence the presence, in Eastern as in Western trompe l'oeil, of a fly, a fly motionless in a corner or on someone's nose. Like trompe l'oeil itself, the fly is obsessed with our minutiae, Christian or Confucian. The fly moves between the cracks of houses and bones, waiting upon feasts and misfortune; it generates – it was long thought – spontaneously, coming from nowhere to live briefly on that which we leave behind. It is the afterimage of flesh.[13]

"Painters assure us that the object most difficult to imitate is the living human skin," wrote a contributor to *All the Year 'Round* in 1880. "There have been painted draperies whose folds we could probe, goblets we could place to our lips, perspective interiors we might walk into, water we could bathe in, flowers and fruits whose perfumes we might inhale; but no face or form depicted upon a canvas has ever so far deceived the eye as to be mistaken for the reality." The trompe l'oeil artist was good at surfaces but not at *our* surfaces – a startling obverse to hypocrisy, where outwardly kind expressions hide malice. Now the superficially human resisted artifice as firmly as the human heart. Regardless of the black, blue-black, white, lake, yellow ochre, carmine, orpiment, and ultramarine used with restraint by Joshua Reynolds or the riot of pigments used by Renoir, and regardless of the new range of cosmetics applied by thespians, shop girls, and society ladies, painted faces were painted faces.[14]

What then of the green faces on banknotes and stamps, when they turned up in paintings by William Harnett and John Haberle in the 1880s in Chicago, Boston, Philadelphia, New York City? Well, despite his protest that "I do not closely imitate nature," Harnett in 1886 was arrested for counterfeiting. His $ paintings (like those of other $ artists of the era) were impounded by the Treasury Department, whose agents were cold on the trail of a superlative forger who *was* hand-finishing banknotes. This "Jim the Penman" would not be identified until the 1890s as Emanuel Ninger of New Jersey, a former sign painter who pressed genuine notes onto moist, coffee-stained silk-fiber paper, then traced over the lines and filled in the colors. One calligrapher dismissed Ninger as "parrot-like," another praised him as "a first-class impressionist." Harnett's $ paintings were dubious sensations during an era when counterfeiters grew rich; when forgers were thriving, especially in Russia, where a gang issued half-rubles captioned, "Our money is no worse than yours"; when American politicians debated a gold or silver standard. Harnett's $$$ were spurned by collectors in favor of the many versions of his *After the Hunt* (1883+), a soothingly antique trompe l'oeil of the paraphernalia of a hunt with its fine trophy, a wild duck.[15]

As for the $5 and $10 notes of John Haberle's *Imitations* (1887), *Reproduction* (1888), and *Changes of Time* (1888), these were accused of being hoaxes, actual bills pasted on canvas or board to look as if they had been painted. Forced by law to desist from his one-sided $, Haberle painted on the front of one canvas the back of one bill, which in 1889 carried a stern warning against ANY imitation of Federal banknotes. From a poor family, Haberle had worked both sides of the trick of reproduction, bullion and biology: he had trained as a silver engraver; he had served the Yale paleontologist Othniel Marsh, making casts of bones, mounting skeletons for display. He knew what he was doing with his scrupulous humbugs of $, of French postcards, of a pamphlet "How to Name Baby" scandalously legible in *A Bachelor's Drawer*. Eyes failing after forty intricate paintings, Haberle desisted, except for *A Japanese Corner* (1898), toward one side of which could be read the label "Do Not Touch."[16]

"One reaches to touch as if in spite of oneself," wrote a backhanded admirer of a work by Haberle's contemporary, John Frederick Peto, another painter of $. "One is seized with the notion of...denuding the picture of its objects. In short, if you put this board in the right light, the illusion is complete." Right light was as critical for the visual tolerances of the microscope as for the misleading tactility of trompe l'oeil. If Haberle's work was, as one catalog put it, "Painted with microscopic detail," and if Haberle himself hung a (painted) magnifying glass above historical species of (painted) currency in *Changes of Time*, we are obliged in this account of camouflage to consider the historical significance of the assisted eye and the immense cultural power of the (mediating (interfering)) lens.[17]

Eyeglasses were invented around the 1260s, or so it is inferred from the drawing in a book of psalms of a crane wearing spectacles, the verses of German poets, the regulations of the Venetian guild of crystal workers, and a Florentine sermon of 1305. Ever since, glasses have been worn with ambivalence. On monkeys, doddering men, usurers, courtiers, and bewigged judges they have been emblems of folly, senility, avarice, preciosity, blindness of justice; on scholars, jesters, notaries, and unmarried women they have been emblems of learning, acumen, punctiliousness, off-putting intellect. For centuries they had greater value as emblems than as optical aids; convex, they were simple magnifying lenses, of some help to the literate who felt more acutely the handicap of presbyopia as printers around 1475 began economizing with smaller type. Although concave lenses (for shortsighted hunters) were produced after 1450, and Venetians began to grade the power of lenses around 1600, only by chance would eyeglasses have exactly compensated for a personal blur. Lucia, patron saint of restored vision, lost little business to spectacle-makers.[18]

Given the strain of reading by inconstant candlelight through a streaky lens, bookish men like the sixteenth-century historian Justus Lipsius would complain lifelong of poor sight and poorer spectacles. His contemporary, the Milanese physician Girolamo Cardano, feared that curved lenses distorted rather than corrected vision. Cardano's fears derived from three long-lived debates: the first, on the reliability of the senses vis-à-vis the reasoning mind; the second, on the comparative nobility of sight (painting), touch (sculpture), and hearing (music); the third, on the unnaturalness of lenses (as an oculist of Dresden wrote in 1583, "It is much better and more useful that one leaves spectacles alone. For naturally a person sees and recognizes something better when he has nothing in front of his eyes than when he has something there"). Did *spectacula* (eyeglasses) produce the same sorts of ghosts as the *specula* (mirrors) of Roger Bacon, who had warned in 1267 that "those looking will run to the image and think the things are there when there is nothing but merely an apparition"? Could one trust reports of the world that struck not the naked eye but came filtered through wavy glass? Why believe that a device contrived from the same imperfect lenses could suddenly reveal, sixteen hundred years after Resurrection and Assumption, heavenly bodies heretofore invisible?[19]

Historians dispute the degree to which the new devices and procedures of the Scientific Revolution implied a turn away from thought experiments to a hands-on testing of theories about the natural world. Any new device by definition was nonstandard and could seem canted to show whatever its handlers wanted it to show; if it failed at the hands of strangers, as did the air pump built by Robert Boyle and Robert Hooke and the prism used by Isaac Newton, then whose trials or hypotheses could be accepted? Historians similarly dispute the degree to which the seventeenth century witnessed an exaltation of sight as a superior path toward truths about the physical world. Vasco Ronchi has argued that the invention of the telescope had to await a milieu in which one trusted one's eyes to see the truth: not until the seventeenth century could people have been convinced that what lay beyond the lenses was other than optical illusion. When investigators entrusted their visions to their vision, they abandoned the double image of light as either sensational (*lumen*) or psychic (*lux*, that light in Genesis prior to the creation of the sun) and focused upon light as strictly a physical presence, sight a physical process. The laws of optics adumbrated by Newton were no casual offshoot of other pursuits; they were at the crux of modernity.[20]

But the natural philosophers of the Scientific Revolution did not so much learn to trust their sight as they did push to develop theories of light which made the physical aspect of light more presentable. Francis Bacon, disturbed by "the manner in which light and its causes are handled in Physics...as if it were a thing half way between things divine and things natural," encouraged his peers to experiment more and contemplate less, yet he doubted the prospect of *seeing* ephemeral events. What was distinctive was less a new regard for sight than a new system of methodical manipulation. If scientific observations took on an authoritative cast, this was because they were to be repeated and confirmed, not because the eye could now be trusted.[21]

With the disappearance of plague from most of Europe and the refueling of the middle-class larder in the eighteenth century, average lifespans grew. Grew then the numbers of the aged, who gradually lose their capacity to focus upon such near and dear objects as faces, lines of scripture, pages off the penny press. Grew too the number of laborers with eye diseases contracted from factory fumes or dust, and others with eyes weakened from closework as seamstresses, copyists, painters of wax flowers. Diseases of the eye, "eminently diseases of the poor" according to an 1828 Boston report, were in 1898 not only the occupational hazard of women shellacking pencils and of metal polishers unprotected from the spray of sharp particles but also of telephone operators, college students, anxious businessmen, and wealthy neurasthenics.[22]

It was in the context of an increasing awareness of and frustration with poor eyesight – most distressing to those who now worked at typewriters, high-speed drills, and deafening rotary presses – that eyeglasses were improved. Glass for spectacle lenses had been a by-product of other glass manufacture, its impurities disguised by rosy tinting. The Swiss conceived and Germans perfected a process to ensure the homogeneity of molten glass. Higher-quality glass yielded clearer lenses just as the ophthalmoscope (1850) enabled specialists to tell by examining the retina itself the extent of distortion produced by each eye. Prescriptions for the separate grinding of the two lenses of a pair of glasses were advanced when the Snellen sight test was disseminated in 1862 and when Frans Cornelis Donders in 1864 alerted oculists to the prevalence of astigmatism. By the end of the century, while Thayer waxed evangelical on Protective Coloration and Haberle painted trompe l'oeil $, effective eyeglasses had become generally available, their cylindrical lenses ground to counteract individual presbyopia/myopia and astigmatism.[23]

They fit, too. Until the eighteenth century, the problem of poor lenses had been exacerbated by the problem of keeping eyeglasses in front of the eyes. Pinched to the nose or tied to a headband, hung by ribbon from the neck or mounted on a short stem and held up to the eyes, spectacles were better suited to looking up than down. The strain of keeping them in place matched the strain of looking through them for any length of time.[24]

"Temple glasses that allow one to breathe easily," the French called the new spectacles with rigid arms reaching back to press against the side of the head. If it was not yet fashionable in 1727 to promenade with eyeglasses perpetually before the eyes, it was more practicable. Diverse sorts of spectacles, including Benjamin Franklin's bifocals, were to be found in eighteenth-century business offices as in artists' studios, where Jean-Baptiste Chardin during his far-sighted seventies painted portraits of himself in temple glasses or pince-nez. Goethe in 1805 was resisting a see-change in attitudes when he felt miffed at the approach of a sociable stranger wearing spectacles: "What can I know of a man whose eyes I cannot see when he speaks, and who has the mirror of his soul veiled by two pieces of glass that blind me?" Once peculiar, bothersome, and unnatural, by the mid-1800s eyeglasses seemed ordinary, convenient, and, in portraits of such matriarchs as Mme Tussaud and Queen Victoria, natural. What had been scary (bespectacled surgeons performing circumcisions) was in 1876 "the rich second sight of modern man."[25]

Looking through eyeglasses without frown or blur, peering through opera glasses or binoculars (*jumelles*, "twins" in French), people of means began to look to the lens as more than a prosthesis for failing eyes. It was a teller of profound truths. Having telescopically revealed unknown moons, stars, and by the 1880s the Martian canals, lenses microscopically revealed the terms of earthly existence. Antoni van Leeuwenhoek late in the seventeenth century had described human hair and blood with good microscopes of 24x power; his descriptions were difficult for eighteenth-century observers to confirm with their lenses of poorer quality though greater magnification. Everyone saw something different. Felice Fontana, the Italian anatomist, wrote in 1781 that any fool could look through a microscope, but few could be sure of what they had seen. Much of what scientists did think they saw through composite microscopes was an illusion due to diffracted light; eight different aberrations afflicted the compound microscope, the optics of which were not set out until 1873. With the manufacture of banded test plates, the use of aniline dyes for staining transparent matter, and the achievement of a resolution as fine as .2 microns (500x), late nineteenth-century crystallographers and microbiologists could proceed to define their disciplines and discoveries upon a standard micrometry. If the president of the American Association of Microscopists still warned in 1883 that "Even the well trained eye is in danger of projecting the mental preconception...into the focal plane of the objective, and seeing...not what is really there but what some theory demands shall be," the cultural *sense* of the microscope was that through its eyepiece one could see the inner truth.[26]

Like Sherlock Holmes with his magnifying glass scouring sills for fingerprints, like muckraker Jacob Riis with his flash photography exposing misery in dark tenements, the microscopist was engaged in a looking *down-and-in* which, though staged and manipulated, was also probative. With their lenses, detectives, newsmen, and bacteriologists could reveal the darker processes of crime, despair, disease. Men might settle the most taxing, hidden questions of identity and origin – as had (he said so himself) the American gynecologist Marion Sims, whose use of a basting spoon to hold open the vagina he would improve into a speculum. But first: "Introducing the bent handle of a spoon, I saw everything as no man had ever seen before.... The walls of the vagina could be seen closing in every direction, the neck of the uterus was distinct and well-defined, and even the secretions from the neck could be seen as a tear glistening in the eye, clear even and distinct, and as plain as could be." Thus in 1845 was Sims's aggressive look down-and-in returned with poetic justice by a teardrop. Vision was pressed farther inward in 1896 when the X-rays of Wilhelm Röntgen spread from Germany, making visible your inner being and, it was said, your very thoughts.[27]

Under these circumstances, surrounded by this spectacular technology, trompe l'oeil was a disease of the eyes, epitomized not only by that speck in the eye, the fly, but by a tradition of advertising art in which a pane of (painted) broken glass stood between the viewer and, say, a stuffed green parrot, or a maiden with a songbird at her wrist, or a matron taking Brown's Iron Bitters. Trompe l'oeil was to high art as the infirmity of neurasthenia was to the healthy body: a debilitating excitement of the (optic) nerves with symptoms of vertigo, hypersensitivity, and exhaustion. It was an "embarrassing fact," an induced hallucination like that from mescaline, on which the pharmacologist Ludwig Lewin first reported in 1886, or from cannabis, whose tincture gave a medical student of the Jekyll-Hyde era two personalities, one a patient and one a doctor, whereupon he examined himself. To set out purposely to fool the eye in such a world, amidst millions of electric light bulbs, hundreds of thousands of fitted eyeglasses, thousands of microscopes, and hundreds of X-ray parties whose live wires came to see each other's glowing bones – this had to seem ill willed, or at least misguided.[28]

"Sight," wrote Abbott Thayer, "is the sense by which at the last moment the quarry's fate is decided...a *single instant of successful disguise suffices to protect an animal from a swiftly passing marauder.*" Trompe l'oeil, like Protective Coloration at its visible best (with bold mimicry rather than countershading) is most deceiving to the quick glance. It was, in 1900, correlative to misleading headlines whose **LARGE BOLD FONTS** & Dramatic Leads!! seduced workaday readers to buy newspapers whose curtailed paragraphs and p*i*c*t*o*r*i*a*l*s were short on substance but bustling with ephemera, like picture postcards. They read the "rags" at a glance while commuting on crowded omnibuses, learning to expect swift incident and sudden disaster.[29]

Quick glance gave way to quick image, at the movies. The novelty of moving pictures allowed at first for sustained medium shots of relatively slow motions, but audiences were most excited by a replication on screen of what was going on inside the projector – images in rapid succession: workers streaming out at *Dinner Hour at the Factory Gate*, horses running the English Derby, *Arrival of the Paris Express*, stripteases, chases. Cinema provided another lens for seeing truly and for seeing what could not truly have been seen before. Many early films, like those of the quick-change artist and impersonator Lepoldo Fregoli, were devoted to the disrobing of false identities, the unveiling of deceptions. Not that people remained naive about the degree to which films were staged: editorial jump cuts and directorial close-ups of high-profile performers defined movies as artifice. As early as 1901, *The Countryman's First Sight of the Animated Pictures* made fun of a bumpkin who confused the pictures with real life. Rather, acceding to the virtues of an assisted eye (the photographic Eye, wrote Henry Drummond, was superior to the evolutionary organic Eye), people (putting on glasses to read the captions or see the picture) trusted the cinematic lens to reveal higher (or more intimate) truths.[30]

Of course, the motion of every film was illusory. The apparent continuity from one frame to the next relies upon the physiology of the
afterimage, that fraction of a second the retina holds to an image, and
upon the psychology of the *Gestalt*, our tendency to see things as a
whole. At the same time that the lens-assisted eye was compiling cabinets of microscopic cell cultures, photographic albums of "pure" abo-
rigines, cinematic records of sexual congress, and telescopic clues to
the solar system, the unassisted eye was proving to be unreliable. Subject to industrial injury and nervous blackouts, it also suffered irre-
mediably during epidemics of measles and chicken pox. Yet a healthy,
protected eye was hardly better off, for experimental psychologists were
finding that human beings tend to see a world more permanently skewed
than any but trompe l'oeil artists would expect. We overestimate verticals; we think parallel lines bowed when diagonals pass through them;
we select for or bind parts of a figure that constitute a familiar whole.
"Of all the senses none is more frequently the seat of...deceptive judgments than that of sight," wrote the English scientist and popular lecturer Silvanus P. Thompson in 1880. Vision was no straightforward
response by excited rods and cones; it was a matter of *attention*, of *lux*
as well as *lumen*.[31]

Attention organized perception, even the perception of color. We
seek visual order, symmetry, balance. We insist upon a background, a
foreground. We credit objects with motion, constancy, persistence.
We are dynamically involved with what we see. Insight is a shift of
attention, wrote the German gestalt psychologist Wolfgang Köhler,
director of the Canary Islands Anthropoid Station; apes learn by *Geistes-
blitzen*, "fitful flashes of novel thoughts," sometimes the product of
visual errors, that mistaking of one thing for another which poets
call metaphor.[32]

In Germany, where the gestalt principles of perception were elaborated before World War I, strategists ransacked Abbott Thayer's work
for guidance in military concealment. Thayer himself had a gestaltist
sensibility: "every changed point of view on the beholder's part makes
all the [peacock's] details assume new colors and new correlations to
each other and to the scene." The culture of the copy was coming to
rest upon experiences and theories of vision in which the unassisted
eye was untrustworthy, where figure and ground were no longer stable,
and where the confusion of the two could be fatal.[33]

Dazzling

On the ground, waiting their turn at death or disfiguration, soldiers of
the Great War rarely saw the enemy. They had imagined heroic hand-
to-hand combat, like the French in Champagne in 1915 who began their
assault behind military bands. What they got was artillery barrage from
guns miles behind them (their own) and miles across from them (the
enemy's). Neither the men tending the howitzers nor those caught in
the curtains of dirt thrown up by bursting shells could see much of any-

FIGURE 5.3. Retouched photograph of a cardboard zebra among imitation reeds, from Gerald H. Thayer, *Concealing-Coloration in the Animal Kingdom* (1909). In its natural environment, argued Abbott Thayer and his son Gerald, the zebra's stripes made for invisibility. "Zebrage" naval striping, attempted during World War I, was meant not to render invisible but to confuse U-boat commanders as to the silhouette and direction of a ship. During World War II, zebra striping was used on PT boats and heavy cruisers.

thing. When infantry advanced, they were in a crouch, apelike, sixty pounds of food and equipment on their backs. Beyond the mud, the mines, the legless bodies, the wire, the enemy was dug in with machine guns. Lucky to survive the first minutes going "over the top," a soldier might glimpse through dense smoke the enemy's forward line, a few figures no more visible than ghosts. And many ghosts there were. Epidemics of typhus along the fronts took thousands of men through fevered hallucinations of Doubles to final oblivion.[34]

Did a man rebound from typhus or from chlorine fumes, there remained, inescapable, the pounding of shells: at the Third Battle of Ypres, a preparatory barrage of 4.5 million shells exploded nearly ten thousand pounds of shells upon every linear yard of front. The pounding battered the nerves of the sturdiest soldiers. "There is no man on earth who can stick this thing forever," declared one who had owned to a joy in war but now was panicky about being buried alive; twice he almost died under mounds of debris. "Shellshocked" men could not stop trembling, heads shaking so much they could neither walk steadily nor see straight.[35]

Camouflage reproduced the visual experience of troops at the front: doubling, obscurity, displacement, disorientation, fragmentation, vertigo. If the nightmarish hallucinations, amnesia, deafmuteness, fugue states, tremors, and dizziness of the new disorder of shellshock were sometimes suspect as the creations of terrified men, the symptoms of such malingering or "sinistrosis" reflected in a left-handed way the tactics of *camoufleurs*: mimicry, obliterative gradation, decoying, masking, disruption, and dazzling. War trauma and war trompe l'oeil were of a piece.[36]

Unclear were the origins of that "confusing and baffling name Camouflage, that has been recently adopted in our language," wrote the *camoufleur* Maurice G. Debonnet in 1918. Was it from French underworld slang for candle, *camoufle*, alluding to dark deeds "hidden by the smoke of the old tallow candles"? From French theatrical jargon for make-up and disguise? Or, as Prof. Poulton suggested, from the military *camouflet*, a mine "placed in a wall of earth between the galleries of besieged and besieger, so as, in exploding, to bury, suffocate, or cut off the retreat of the miner on the opposite side"? The derivations fell into the two camps of camouflage strategy, hiding (invisi lity) and showing (ddeceptive *V*isibility).[37]

Out in the open, the war saw the end of bright battledress meant to embolden one's own troops and dishearten the enemy. In the sights of machine guns firing three hundred rounds per minute, ranks of soldiers wearing starched whites or splashy reds did not intimidate. Native Americans and English colonists had faded in and out of forests in what amounted to Protective Coloration, but the first intentionally inconspicuous uniform was that worn by the paramilitary Indian Guides of 1846, dressed in khaki (dust, in Urdu). British regulars dyed white tunics khaki during the Afghan and Egyptian Wars, 1880–1882, then had field order khakis for the Boer War, 1899–1902 — by which time the smokeless small-bore rifle, accurate from a mile off, was changing the optics of war itself: "the old terror of a visible foe had given way to the paralysing sensation of advancing on an invisible one." The khaki of the British, the yellow-green of the Japanese in Manchuria in 1905, the silver-green adopted by the German army in 1910 became the footsoldier's cloak of invulnerability. French regiments entering battle in 1914–15 in red pantaloons switched quickly to "horizon" blues. Wrote a Russian colonel, after the war: "Everyone who took part in the last war knows that to be unseen is more important than to be protected." The practical goal was to be invisible, not invincible.[38]

Considering the smoke and the mud, the color of soiled uniforms meant beans in the trenches on either side of no-man's-land. Although the first use of camouflage at the front was the German placement of black bags in sandbagged breastworks to distract fire from actual gunholes, these were minor feats of trompe l'oeil, as were the papier-mâché mock-ups of horse carcasses into which snipers crawled, and the flat silhouette "Tommies" raised from the trenches to decoy enemy snipers.

What war camouflage was truly about, what gave rise to its mystique, was not the concealment of one side across from the other but from an assisted eye looking down-and-in. From observers with binoculars, hidden in what passed for trees on jagged battlefields: dummy trees whose tops had been blown off, with bark of beaten iron, an inner core of bullet-proof steel, and steps leading to an eye-slit beneath artistically splintered branches. From observers with telescopes in balloons and blimps. Above all, from pilots snapping photos. At the height of the war, the French printed ten thousand aerial photographs nightly; during the Meuse-Argonne offensive of 1918, some fifty thousand photographs were delivered to the American Expeditionary Forces in four days; before war's end, the Germans had in place two thousand cameras which at full aperture and short exposure could resolve footprints from two miles up.[39]

Wherefore, all-too-aware of "the all-seeing, all-recording photographic camera" on high, the Cossacks painted white horses green to match the foliage. Wherefore the English designed netting garnished with fake leaves to cover guns, trenches, depots – seven million square yards of netting unrolled against aerial lenses that showed the front to be no traditional set of parallel lines but the tangled nets of "defense in depth." Wherefore the English and French painted sheets of canvas with splotches of color matching grass, earth, chalk, debris. Wherefore the French, who publicly credited themselves with the first unit of *camoufleurs*, erected canvas roofs painted like quiet country roads, beneath which troops could march unseen. The Germans, clever enough to keep their own cleverness a secret, had begun camouflaging anti-aircraft shelters before the war on the basis of what would be seen *from the air*. They built immense false arcades over their encampments and "covered miles of roads and acres of fields with rigid hangars coloured and modelled to represent the original scenery"; they built, near an actual landing site, two (2) decoy airfields, one done poorly so that enemy analysts would jump to the conclusion that the other (decoy) airfield must be the true target. Solomon J. Solomon, the portrait painter who directed British efforts to make "aerodromes look like lakes, and gas-emplacements like cabbage-fields," waged a futile campaign to get his Air Ministry to appreciate the extent of German deceptions. Of all camouflage during the war, said a veteran of the 40th Engineers Corps (U.S. *camoufleurs*), 95 percent on both sides was done to deceive aerial reconnaissance.[40]

Above, if you knew how to look down and in – if you understood shadow like a painter, projections like an architect, pattern like a zoologist, reflections like a physicist – the war might make sense. Artists depicting the war for propaganda at home drew people and machines with qualities of power, vigilance, and endurance; others closer to the front privately drew portraits of men struggling against a mechanical anonymity, faces dark with *le cafard*, the silence of a brutal waiting. Meaning, pattern, plan were not to be found close up. The gestalt had to come together from above, from aircraft surveying fronts so vast that no general on a promontory could take them in with the sweep of a spyglass. Camouflage therefore was meant to hide from the aerial assisted eye the fact of war (What war?) or to make the land seem as crazy as the broken lines of the war itself (What land? Isn't everything below – the shadows, the fragments, the false trenches of four million zigzag lives – isn't it all the war?)[41]

"Really the composition of this war, 1914–1918, was not the composition of all previous wars," wrote Gertrude Stein, "the composition was not a composition in which there was one man in the center surrounded by a lot of other men but a composition that had neither a beginning nor an end, a composition of which one corner was as important as another corner, in fact the composition of cubism." Large guns painted black on top, white below, with brown and green here and there "and presto!" wrote Debonnet, "the futurist composition blends so well with the landscape that only occasional flashes of fire remain as tell tales." Yet of the twelve hundred men (or more) and the eight thousand women working in France under the insignia of the chameleon, and the thousands of others in Germany, few were Cubists or Futurists. Only post hoc was the war a "Cubist War." Ad hoc, French camouflage was instigated by Guirand de Scévola, an academic painter as was the British Solomon and the American Lt.-Col. Homer Saint-Gaudens, son of the sculptor Augustus Saint-Gaudens. Americans spoke of Protective Coloration and "Indian fighting," the English of Dazzle and discipline, the French of Cubism and "an art bordering on the miraculous," the Germans of *die Tarnung* (masking and screening). In all camps camouflage was created by portrait painters, mapmakers, cartoonists, make-up artists, prop men, plaster modelers, seamstresses, carpenters, engineers, architects, and scene designers. "The cubists rubbed elbows with the disciples of Ingres" – and with the discipline of trompe l'oeil, of *chantourné* figures and ostensible broken glass. Emotionally, visually, the Great War was a war of illusion and disillusionment, a disease of the eyes whose sole cure, it seemed, was the sense one could make from high above through lenses more reliable than the naked eye.[42]

And more deadly. To be seen from above was to be bombed. While British planes struck at the Zeppelin works in Düsseldorf in October of 1914, Germany was launching the first of fifty-one airship attacks and fifty-two airplane bombing raids over England. The bombings behind the fronts and across the Channel had greater psychological than strategic effect. Far from the front, civilians had become decoys leaning into the wind as the enemy's "light bright silver insects" flew over. Inside those birds, pursued by other birds of prey and dodging the spray of bullets from anti-aircraft batteries, airmen had the briefest of moments in which to spot a target and release their ordnance. Casualties from bombing were casualties of the quick glance down-and-in. If photo-analysts needed an expert eye and the lens of a camera to make sense of warscapes, pilots and bombardiers had to depend upon a swift recognition of landmarks. On the approach of a plane, Russian infantry

were taught to lie in circular groups at the side of the road, rifles concealed, to give an impression of heaps of stone used for road repair. Like
an animal's disappearance into the brush *at the very last moment*, camouflage was the art of confusing the glance that led to the pounce.[43]

This was as true on water as on land. Primitively, naval deception
amounted to flying a false flag. Yankee whaling ships, fearing piracy,
had impersonated warships with a band of white painted at their girth
and black squares spaced along the white as if gun ports. During the
War Between the States, the Union's Admiral David Farragut had substituted trees for the upper spars of warships, plastered mud on their
sides, and attacked at night; Confederate ports welcomed English block-
ade runners, their sides painted dark gray, their smokestacks telescopic,
their masts hinged. The white battleships of the British, Germans,
French, Italians, and Americans gave way at century's end to ocean
grays, for the range of naval guns had so increased that it was possible
to sink ships glimpsed on the horizon. Only those blithely confident
of intimidation, like Theodore Roosevelt's fleet touring the world in
1907–08, kept to glaring whites. The grays, however, were themselves
often too dark, defining ships as obvious solids. In 1902 a patent was
issued to Thayer and his friend, artist George de Forest Brush, for a
painting scheme that would blur the definition of ships, which, they
said, *should* maintain white upper decks so as to merge with the sky,
not with the water.[44]

Their argument was prophetic. The threat to navies during the Great
War would come not from above but from across and below. Few aircraft had the range to attack on the high seas; naval camouflage had to
defend against views through binoculars across choppy waves and, most
urgently, against glances through periscopes. From periscopes, the top
eight feet of a ship were sharply etched against the sky; a vessel painted
to blend into the waves stood out mightily against daytime sun or night-
time stars. In "this great game of hocus-pocus," the Allied and German
navies tested each species of camouflage. Mimicry: the upper section
of the U-boat *Deutschland* was painted blue-green with white caps, so
that when it surfaced it was just another wave. Obliterative gradation:
the British tried Thayer's countershaded whites and pearl grays, Americans the pale violets, stippled grays, blues, and greens designed by
muralist William A. Mackay to match the spectra of light radiating from
water. Masking: battleships were given the silhouettes of destroyers;
English tramp steamers were outfitted like battleships. Decoying: the
British and Germans disguised attack vessels as cargo ships or commercial liners. Disruption: since torpedoes would speed innocently away
if a 5 percent error in targeting could be induced, British and American painters distorted ship profiles using wavy lines with blurry edges,
falsely outlined bows, harlequinade. Dazzling: proposed (after Thayer's
"razzle-dazzle" of "ruptive" and "secant" patterns) by John Graham Kerr,
a Scottish embryologist, and Hugh Cott, a Cambridge University zoologist, thick verticals and diagonals (*zébrage*, in French) were applied

across the sides of ships to befuddle German U-boat captains looking through the range-finding parallel lines etched on periscope lenses. By 1918 the Allies had, one way or another, camouflaged forty-two hundred ships.[45]

We have no clear-cut proof that dazzling saved ships. We do know that troops aboard bedazzled ships had better morale, as did troops beneath camouflage nets on land. Camouflage officers were called "window dressers," but, wrote Barry Faulkner, soldiers liked that window dressing, "for it gave them a sense of protection, false yet comforting." Magazine articles spread "Fantastic notions as to the character and efficacy of camouflage." A military impostor claimed to be a camouflage officer who made "things appear to be what they are not." Camouflage was becoming a wider metaphor: "We *camouflage* our trenches now, when we cover them with wire, and then put grass on them. Later on we shall *camouflage* our thoughts. Politicians won't talk with their intimate friends of how to conceal their actions, but how to *camouflage* them." Or manufacturers would conceal shoddy products under the camouflage of extraneous decoration, wrote a young architect, Le Corbusier, decrying an industrial "consecration of camouflage" that ignored human needs. Wasn't this what Freud with his migraines and spectacles had been seeing and saying about transference (mimicry), sublimation (obliterative gradation), screen memories (masking), symbolization (decoying), condensation (disruption), and displacement (dazzling)? War, politics, mass production, and neuroses had to do, didn't they, with seeing double? Of all *Civilization and Its Discontents*, the commandment to "Love thy neighbor as thyself," wrote Freud, "is impossible to fulfill." It was, however, possible to deceive our neighbors as we, one way or another, and from childhood on, deceive ourselves.[46]

Stand-Ins

After the War to End All Wars, in 1921, Freud received a letter from Moscow that "had on it stamps to the value of 10,000 rubles – a glimpse into our future, perhaps into yours, too," he wrote to his son Ernst in London. That monetary inflation, which did in the economy of postwar German liberalism as, almost, of Soviet communism, was a glimpse into *The Future of an Illusion* (infantile inflations of a religious "as if") and into the dazzle of the Roaring Twenties, the ersatz of the Depression Thirties. What seemed on the surface to be valuable and substantial would turn out to have been synthesized – a skill at which Americans were surpassing Europeans. So thought the German poet Rainer Rilke, himself fatally ill and feeling "like an empty place." He wrote to his Polish translator in 1925, "From America empty, indifferent things are crowding over to us, sham things, *life-decoys*.... Animated things, things experienced by us, and that know us, are on the decline and cannot be replaced anymore."[47]

Sterling Leather, in the lingo of American advertising, was patent (imitation) leather; Iceland Fox, lamb; Brook Mink, dyed muskrat;

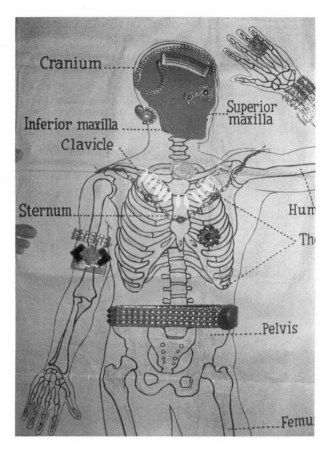

FIGURE 5.4. *Stand-in*, mixed media collage by Donna Sasso, 1993, featuring glass, cut glass, rhinestone, brass, alloy, and plastic costume jewelry imitating diamonds, pearls, malachite, aquamarine, gold, gold leaf, silver, and ivory. Reproduced by permission.

Parisian Ivory, celluloid. Celluloid was cousin to collodion, a solution of cellulose nitrate used to coat photographic plates. In 1863, amidst fears that riflemen were killing off African elephants at the same rate they were killing men at Gettysburg, an American manufacturer offered a ten-thousand-dollar prize for an artificial ivory. John Wesley Hyatt of New York in 1869 patented celluloid, a solid collodion and the first synthetic plastic. Though kin to gun cotton and very flammable, celluloid had a tensile strength ideal for stiff collars, false teeth, piano keys, buttons, and billiard balls. Formulated to mimic ivory, celluloid never escaped its stigma as a "cheap imitation."[48]

Bakelite did. Leo Baekeland, a Belgian chemist settled in New York, had already invented and in 1899 sold to Eastman Kodak a photographic

paper yielding good prints under artificial light. In his Yonkers laboratory he pursued and in 1907 found a way to direct the reaction of phenol
with formaldehyde, producing a moldable resin that, when thermally
set, was permanently solid. Unlike celluloid, dark Bakelite and other
more tintable plastic resins such as Marblette and Formica were at the
front edge of consumer technology, in cars, telephones, refrigerators,
hearing aids, radios. Not always cheap and not necessarily imitations,
these plastics were ideally conformable to modern fashion.[49]

"Costume jewellery – that's a fine way of labelling a string of false
pearls," says Old Ashe in Agatha Christie's *A Murder Is Announced*. The
phrase was fresh to the 1930s; the trade was old. Ancient Egyptians
glazed ceramic beads to look like turquoise; Roman sardonyx was more
often fake than real. When wealth and status began to be asserted
through lush portraits by Titian or Tintoretto, Renaissance sitters (or
the artist himself) added imitation jewels to their robes for a lustrous
presence, as did many a monarch whose crown held fake gems, false
pearls. "Doublets," precious stones fabricated from glass and crystal, had
a regal history, and mock pearls were especially fine after a seventeenth-
century rosary-maker began to coat alabaster beads with an iridescent
paste. However, given the brighter wax candles flickering in rooms lined
with larger and larger mirrors, the diamond rather than the herring-fish-
paste pearl now caught the eye: first the Dutch rose-cut diamond of
the 1640s with its twenty-four or thirty-six facets, then Italian and
French "brilliants" with as many as fifty-eight facets. Beryl, amethyst,
and citrine quartz, customarily shaped and sold as diamonds, lacked the
"fire" of these novel cuts, but in 1728 artifice met up again with art
when Georges Frédéric Stras, jeweler to Louis XIV, concocted a lead-
glass paste that could be cut and polished to sparkle like brilliants. By
1767 a guild of three hundred "makers of false jewels" were at work
for the French aristocracy.[50]

Mounted in gold or its stand-in, pinchbeck (an alloy of zinc and copper, called by Germans Similor), in sterling silver or its stand-in, German silver (zinc, copper, and nickel), these costly fabrications were
expert decoys. The naked eye of a highwayman could not tell a brilliant-
cut diamond from a paste version or a polished spinel (a metallic oxide
with natural crystals). In the nineteenth century, he might more easily
tell genuine from fake by the mount, for jewelers were leaving the backs
open to admit light to stimulate the brilliance of a true gem, while paste
jewels were mounted with closed backs lest their foil linings corrode.
As large numbers of foil-backed rock-crystal "rhinestones" were ex-
ported from Bohemia and as ceramic reproductions of antique cameos
were taken to heart, deceptive imitations came within reach of the
middle class. While a single piece of well-worked costume jewelry was
a treasure to a poor working girl, a mounted fake was common enough
to the more prosperous that they learned to want matched sets, *parures*.
The matched set was an operating principle for an industrial world of
mass-produced table settings, electroplated silver or gold utensils,

machine-stamped trompe l'oeil pins of (yes) houseflies, xylonite (celluloid) coral, fish-scale-and-nitrocellulose pearls. *Parures* implied the reproducibility of that which had long been assumed to be irreplaceable: the gem, a unique stone of rare beauty.[51]

Nonethesame, when designer Coco Chanel in the 1920s flaunted outsize jewels of Catalin and row upon row of pearls as accessories to casual dress, her playfulness was shocking. Marshall Field's department store in Chicago halfheartedly told its customers that "The imitation is no longer a disgrace." *Vogue* in 1927 looped "costume jewelry" around suntanned necks: "Fashion itself has decided that all we need ask of an ornament is to adorn us and that neither our complexions nor our gems are to be natural." Diamonds galore had come from South Africa after mines opened in the 1870s, synthetic diamonds from Switzerland in the 1890s, cultured pearls from Japan in 1896 after Kokichi Morimoto patented his method for distressing oysters, and paste-makers had scurried to imitate the best of each, natural, synthetic, or induced. However, when Chanel in 1928 launched a line of diamonds too-large and pearls too-even and when Elsa Schiaparelli followed suit with surrealist pieces of "junk" jewelry for hats and dresses, then costume jewelry had become *ersatz* – no longer an imitation but (from German military jargon) a replacement.[52]

So from America and from Europe came sham things, *life-decoys*, compensating for the loss of substance during a worldwide economic failure. As gold was taken out of circulation, plastic jewelry glided up the arms and glowed on the necks of those who had time to play. Was it forgery or frivolity when someone copied a New Zealand jade pendant using celluloid from a toothbrush? *Life* noted that in the 1920s paste jewelry had been called "fake," for "Then the aim was to make the imitation look real"; in 1938 enormous diamonds and pearls were, blithely, "costume jewelry," with no claim to precise imitation or precious investment. A rhinestone-and-simulated-emerald bracelet might go for a hundred dollars, but most women could afford only knockoffs of designer originals. Chanel was flattered. Indeed, through two of those reversals in which our culture of the copy exults, exclusive costume jewelry was intrinsically plastic and imitable, and it could be detected by the very implausibility of its *parure*: "The six clear, perfectly matched pieces of glass in the bracelet obviously couldn't be emeralds."[53]

By 1938 the range of plastics had expanded beyond cellulose nitrates (celluloid) and phenolic resins (Bakelite) to include cellulose acetates (Tenite, in safety glass), urea formaldehydes (Plaskon bottle caps), vinyl resins (Saran film, phonograph records, fabrics, inflatables), styrene resins (wall tiles, toys), acrylic resins (American Lucite and German Plexiglas for eyeglass lenses and camera lens filters, gun turret and cockpit enclosures). Bakelite's New Jersey plant, covering 128 acres, was responsible for just a small proportion of the fifty thousand uses to which plastics were being put. In the middle of World War II, with the production of melamine, polyethylene, and silicone, the "Plastics

Age" was hard upon J.H. DuBois of General Electric, who stood amazed by "The drama of raw materials such as petroleum, coal, water and air, or waste products like oat hulls, peanut shells, corn-cobs, insect secretions and bits of cloth, being transformed into...combs, buckles, buttons, brushes, jewelry, radio cabinets...and even the huge transparent 'noses' of bombing planes, looking like glass but shatterproof."[54]

Drama of war momentarily aside, the drama of chemistry was also transforming the most plastic and transparent of all media, motion pictures. Without the nitrocellulose strips we call "film," there would have been no "films" as we know them, but many early films have gone up in flames. During the 1930s, the more stable and less flammable cellulose acetate (used in protective goggles) became the standard film stock. On screen too, as on the reel, synthetics were central to the survival of illusion. Costume designers for actresses in sequined satin must receive equal billing with Chanel (herself in countless newsreels) for the popularity of costume jewelry – and for the elegant lines of crease-resistant trousers (synthetic resins impregnating natural fibers, 1929), and for the seams rising up legs contoured by the first completely synthetic fiber, nylon (1938).[55]

Films made a point of being synthetic. Most features reveled in artifice: miraculous escapes, leaps of the calendar, outbreaks of singing and dancing. As plastic in the manipulation of person as of place and time, films transformed men into monsters, women into interchangeable chorus girls who (said director Busby Berkeley) "matched like pearls." Films in fact fabricated celluloid twins out of skin-and-sinew singletons: Mae Murray was both Daisy and Violet White in *The Twin Pawns* (1919); Grace Cunard played the twins Nell and Jo and their double, Grace the Crook, in *The Twins' Double* (1914); Louis Hayward played Louis XIV and his twin brother in the *Man in the Iron Mask* (1939) – mimicking himself to perfection (wrote a reviewer), chasing himself down the road from Fontainebleau "with thoroughly commendable skill." Double roles of lost brothers or sisters, tragedies of mistaken identity had long tested the mettle of stage performers; cinematic editing lifted theatrical twinship away from the flimflammery of the quick change to that of the close-up and the skills of make-up artists, who delighted in the step-by-step synthesis of Mr. Hyde out of Dr. Jekyll.[56]

Like stage producers, movie directors had cast actual twins for other twin roles: Robert and William Bradbury in *The Adventures of Bill and Bob* (1919), Marion and Madeline Fairbanks as Coca and Cola in *The Beauty Shop* (1922), and Ted and Fred Williams as orphaned African-American twins who were a modern Abel and *A Modern Cain* (ca. 1925). Came the Talkies in 1926–27, biological twins were shunted to the proscenium in front of the screen, leftovers from the novelty acts of vaudeville. This was crystal clear in the forty minutes of live prelude to movies shown in the Fox West Coast Theatres during the summer of 1930. A touring show starred the acrobatic Electric Twins, singing Elca Twins, tap-dancing Clute Twins, toe-dancing Nolay Twins, jazz-playing Maltby

Twins, all prefaced by a dozen twin-beauties posed in reversed positions within the full-length frames of (pretend) mirrors. They sang the theme song, "Seeing Double."[57]

Audiences in moviehouses were, every which way, seeing double. Even where plots entangled no twins, film was a medium for duplicities as complex as producer (and spy) Alexander Korda's postwar espionage classic, *The Third Man* (1949).[58] If the tabloids caught movie stars off-screen acting more amorous than glamorous, rarely did they betray that cadre of secret agents without which stars could hardly be celestial – stuntpeople, doubles, stand-ins.

"Whenever unusual physical exertion is required of a player, a perilous fall, or a desperate leap, a trained gymnast is usually engaged as double," explained a theater reviewer in 1873. He told the story of the actress Mrs. Mowatt, who, as the tragic heroine of *Ariâne*, must leap from a cliff and plunge into the sea. It was a ballet girl in identical costume who climbed the rock, and a "most life-like lay figure" that hurtled into the abyss, but "The illusion was so perfect that on the first night of the representation, a man started up in the pit, exclaiming in a tone of genuine horror, 'Good God! she is killed!' "[59]

On film, other than in newsreels, accidents could not just happen; off camera or in outtakes they could. After Harold Lloyd nearly lost two fingers to an explosion during a gag as Lonesome Luke, insurance companies began insisting upon doubles for adventurous cowboys, daredevil women, and pratfalling comics. Thus came together in 1915 the Suicide Club, the first stuntpeople. Of the seventy-five original members, untrained, all but one had died violent deaths by 1935. "In the making of a serial, a double will probably risk his life about thirty times," said stuntman Cliff Lyons in 1936, who was in large part responsible for designing safer movie stunts. Hollywood then insisted upon ever-more death-defying feats for both villains and heroines, and upon ever-greater anonymity for stunt doubles with their specialties (Mary Wiggins for auto accidents, Ione Reed for horse tricks), lest they shatter those illusions of prowess that sustained the stardom of actors and actresses. When Scarlett O'Hara tumbled down the stairs in *Gone with the Wind* (1939), not Vivien Leigh but Aline Goodwin, for two hundred dollars, took the spill.[60]

Less perilous moments had Barbara Jones as Leigh's double and, as her hands, Millicent Miller, chosen over hundreds of others in a national contest for her stand- or hand-in. Originally, while lights were being set and camera angles adjusted, silent-screen star Pola Negri had retreated from the heat and turmoil, leaving a dummy in her stead. Dummies were too glossy or too dull, and they melted. Enter the stand-in, patient human placeholder and silent twin of the superhuman star. Next came the double, also silent but intermittently visible on screen: stooge to practical jokes, corpse to the hero, ghost to the heroine, fleeting side or backside when both players must be shown in the suspense of confused identity or the hilarity of double-takes.[61]

Stand-ins like Sylvia Lamarr, for Hedy (no relation) and later for Joan Crawford, identified with their stars; as a *focus artist* "you knew the script, you knew the star's part by heart and you knew the star – all her foibles and idiosyncracies.... You even copied the star's mannerisms." The status of the focus artist, much lower than that of the movie double, was elevated by a 1937 comedy, *Stand-In*, with Humphrey Bogart as the producer of an over-budget epic, *Sex and Satan*, starring a vamp whose stand-in, Joan Blondell (herself stood in for, anonymously, by Connie Rae) teaches financial analyst Leslie Howard to respect the technicians and stand-ins who keep studios going. Doubles the same year were abetted by *It Happened in Hollywood*, with two stars of silent Westerns, Richard Dix and Fay Wray, trying to make it in the talkies. In one scene they lasso a passel o' stars fer a shindig fer a crippled kid who adores Dix; the stars are all doubles – Frank E. Farr for Eddie Cantor, James May for W.C. Fields, Carol Dietrich (no relation) for Marlene, Virginia Rendell for Mae West, and the best, Eugene De Verdi, who made a career impersonating, with his permission, Charlie Chaplin.[62]

Few "focus artists" (Troy Donahue, June Kilgour) and fewer doubles and stuntpeople made it out of trompe l'oeil into frames of their own. They were, truly, vanishing twins. What was notable if unnoticeable about them was that they tended to appear in precisely those cinematic instants which became *the* visually memorable instants – body-doubles (also, here, called stand-ins) for risqué nude scenes; stunting doubles for the risky exploits of a Betty Hutton or a Tyrone Power, for displays of athleticism by cowboys and iceskaters. As the hocus of dubbing was integral to 1930s musicals, so the pocus of doubling made the most sensational scenes elaborate exercises in being taken.[63]

You could not believe your eyes. Hugo Münsterberg, professor of psychology at Harvard, had written in 1916 of motion pictures as "more than any other art destined to overcome outer nature by the free and joyful play of the mind." Earlier, however, he had pondered that play of the mind through which eyes and witnesses lie. "Only recently," he noted in 1908, "passengers in a train which passed a courtyard were sure, and swore, that they had taken in at a glance the distinct picture of a man whipping a child; one swore that he had a clean-shaven face, a hat, and was standing, while another swore that he had a full beard, no hat, and was sitting on a bench." Both were probably wrong, for when Münsterberg gave his students time for much more than a glance at less complex images, their reports were still discrepant. The professor himself, after a break-in at his house, gave testimony that mixed a few truths with "a whole series of confusions, of illusions, of forgetting, of wrong conclusions." Confessions could be the false results of fatigue, doubt, or disrupted memory occasioned, say, by "sharp sunlight reflected from [a doctor's] eye-glasses." One woman "felt it like a shock, [her doctor's] eye-glasses seemed to become large and uncanny, and from that moment on her consciousness was split and her remaining half-personality developed a pseudo-memory of its own." Münsterberg, who wore glasses, looked forward to the time when experimental psychology, with its sphygmographs and galvanometers, would become "a magnifying glass for the most subtle mental mechanism, and by it the secrets of the criminal mind may be unveiled."[64]

Studying the 1896 conviction of a down-and-out adventurer named Adolf Beck, a British Royal Commission in 1904 warned that "Evidence as to identity based upon personal impressions is, unless supported by other facts, an unsafe basis for the verdict of a jury." (On the similarity of mustaches, Beck was mistaken by many witnesses for one William Augustus Wyatt, alias William Thomas, Dr. Weiss, Lord Wilton of Willoughby, a charmer who defrauded women of their jewelry.) Despite the warning, "identification parades" became standard constabulary procedure, less because line-ups gave reliable results (they do not) than because they imitated controlled experiments and reproduced in vivo the social habit of looking down-and-in at photographs in albums. Through to the 1960s British eyewitnesses were shown snapshots of the prime suspect prior to a line-up. Used to seeing wanted posters, newsphotos of accused criminals, and mugshots circulated by detectives, people were prone to consult an assisted eye before making up their minds about what they had seen. Thus it was not so odd that before the 1921 trial of Nicola Sacco and Bartolomeo Vanzetti, no eyewitness to the robbery and shooting on the main street of South Braintree, Massachusetts, could identify Vanzetti until repeatedly shown his face in photographs.[65]

"The human eye is a mighty poor camera," wrote lawyer Asa S. Herzog and photographer A.J. Erickson in *Camera, Take the Stand!* (1940). Cameras, they argued, saw more clearly and never forgot. That was the issue: visual memory. The prey evades the pounce, the brigade the bomb, with split-second deceptions. In a world of glances, we rely upon the lens for the long study; the snapshot snaps shut on the moment. Two-thirds of American families in 1936 had a camera, but their appetite for Kodak film was weak; the creative people at Kodak's advertising agency were briefed that December: "It is the procrastination in picture-taking that we have to work against. Situations that people want snapshots of pass before they realize." Hence the hook for a Kodak advertisement in 1937: "Your baby – you'll never forget how sweet she is...(that's what *you* think)." Below was Sara Delano Roosevelt, the president's mother, holding a snapshot: "Not many of us are able to remember as we'd like. We do need something definite to start the recollection, or some of the pleasantest days and happenings are soon entirely lost.... I never feel quite at home unless I have pictures of my family around me."[66]

Promoting its Kodacolor home movie camera in 1930, the company had capitalized on the problematics of visual memory and the joy of the re-view. Capture "your children *exactly* as they are today – your mother just as she is today." The movie camera made people "alive forever" in "60 Seconds you'll never forget." In 1935 Kodak had produced the Retina, a camera capable of thirty-six exposures "at lightning speed," 1/500 second. And in August 1939, right before the German blitzkrieg (twenty-eight days of lightning strike the Poles cannot forget), Kodachrome color movies would hold "you spellbound when you see them flash on the screen," so real you had "*actually* to see them to get 'any idea.' "[67]

Five miles up and five miles away, a World War II bombardier releasing his bombs never *actually* saw the targets; he recognized them. Flying at 200–400 mph, he had thirty-five seconds to adjust his bombsight to what he had been taught to recognize by studying aerial photos. With color film and filters, magnifying stereoscopes, flash bombs, and (in 1942) false-color camouflage-detection film, it was close to impossible for ground or naval forces to be invisible under clear skies. In good weather, day or night, photographs could detect objects two feet wide from thirty thousand feet; white faces of soldiers, turned skyward, glowed half a mile up. New infrared cameras revealed stark differences in vegetation that escaped the naked eye. "The aim, then, is not so much to prevent an object from being seen, but admitting that it must be seen, to prevent it from being recognized for what it is, and preferably to make it seem to be nothing out of the ordinary." True to its numerals, World War II was a war of replicas and doubles.[68]

German camouflage units built dummy V-1 rocket launch sites, set small fires on factory roofs to detour bombers from buildings "already" hit, and painted repaired runways to look cratered. These were minor efforts compared to their work on the port of Hamburg, where they planked over 225,000 square yards of open water with wood painted to resemble, from the air, blocks of Hamburg rooftops and streets; to the north they built a fake causeway half a mile long in direct line with ersatz railroad tracks, trains, and train station, while painting out the true station and port, visually shifting strategic targets away from the city center. The British knew what was going on, but the *momentary* disorientation of pilots flying over the two Hamburgs in 1941 was all that German anti-aircraft batteries needed.[69]

British doubling was equally extensive. Working with movie designers, camouflage units created dummy aircraft for dummy aerodromes, the real hedges around them "trimmed to look like the artificial hedges used to camouflage real aerodromes." A film company built a huge oil depot and dock out of old sewer pipe, fiberboard, and canvas. "Wrecking parties" painted buildings as if they had already been hit. On the attack the British dropped dummy parachutists who, hitting the ground, triggered wire recordings of gunfire. The XX (Double Cross) section of MI-5 had a chorus of 120 double agents, German spies who had been "turned" to give the Nazis disinformation, particularly about the British 4th Army in Scotland (Operation Skye), with its chickenwire navy, wooden bombers, and frantically meaningless radio traffic.[70]

Far to the east, Japanese infantry, hands and faces dyed green for jungle fighting, shouted in English, "Buddy, help me! I am badly hurt!" to entice American platoons into ambushes. The Japanese navy painted carriers and destroyers at dock as if an extension of the Honshu landscape; the air force had so many imitation Zeroes and Mitsubishi bombers that by 1945 one-quarter of the planes visible on Japanese airfields were dummies.[71]

Still farther east, on the vulnerable West Coast of the United States, American camoufleurs – using methods that would be adapted for Disneyland – hid an airplane factory under the replica of a Southern California suburb. U.S. aircraft were painted in dark browns and greens or ocean grays after misfortunes with the B-17, its shiny bare metal alerting Japanese lookouts forty miles away. Truth to tell, Americans had to put back in place habits of camouflage lapsed since 1919; troops learned from stage designers like Harry Horner, who had done the set for *Lady in the Dark*, while lyricists struggled to convince the men that

> The ruses
> One uses
> Are nature's own scheme....
> Though we're like mirages,
> We're all camouflages –
> Things Are Not What They Seem.[72]

Back in Washington, D.C., organizing camouflage battalions, Homer Saint-Gaudens was besieged by applicants; his best officers, he wrote, were architects, his best corporals movie prop men, "resourceful, disciplined, with an eye for the look of things." At the Army School of Camouflage in the Jefferson (Missouri) Barracks, courses were directed by a stage designer, an interior designer, a fabric designer, a painter, and an architect, all well known. Jane Berlandina, famous for vast murals and her painting of *Three Stand-Ins* (a Picasso clown, a cardboard woman, a Napoleonic impostor), applied to war matériel the tricks she had learned as a painter of backdrops for dance and opera.[73]

Not only was camouflage the art of standing in; willy-nilly everyone was a stand-in. "Don't we all spend half of our lives standing around waiting for cues?" asked Berlandina. Color advertisements for Calvert Whiskey had been featuring pheasants in fields perfectly and protectively "blended." Louis Philippe's Angelus Rouge Incarnat in 1935 had the gift of matching "Human Blood Tones" so well that "**Only an Expert with a Magnifying Glass Could Detect** That the Color of Your Cheeks Wasn't *Natural* Color." Warned that the noncombatant "for the first time in history [is] in almost as dangerous a position as the soldier" and "cannot expect to be entirely safe from aerial bombardment," civilians studied camouflage in art schools and colleges. Camouflage, said one observer, "is the glamor girl of civilian defense."[74]

Glamour for the Americans; magic for the British. Magician John Nevil Maskelyne, maker of false automata and creator of the illustrious Box Trick in which two people seem to change places instantaneously, had shared with the War Office during the Boer War his experiments with balloons. During the Great War, his magician son Nevil trained five spies to practice the black art so convincingly that they would be taken for holy men by Arabian tribes and prophesy a future congenial to the plots of arch-spy T.E. Lawrence. In 1939, the grandson, Jasper Maskelyne, who had spent his life "making things appear to be precisely what they are not," offered the military his trompe l'oeil skills but was rejected. He pestered the War Office, promising that "I can create cannon where they don't exist and make ghost ships sail the seas.... I can make the Nazis see guns where they expect to see guns and soldiers where they believe soldiers might be." Since his grandfather's time English and German magicians had improved their inventory of disembodied heads (using finer mirrors), disappearing bodies (setting matte-black objects against black curtains), speaking ghosts (prerecording "The Girl with the Celluloid Mind") and double bluffs (in which, with a dazzling show of electrical devices, nothing happens but audiences think it did). So, when at last his services were accepted, Jasper Maskelyne in 1940 set to work with a movie stuntman, an optician, a perfumer, a comic-book illustrator, a carpenter, a painter in oils, and a former thief, manufacturing "Warships that disappeared... thirty-six tanks drawn out of one Army truck like rabbits out of a hat...aerodromes that weren't there...ships at sea whose entire appearance changed, on the pulling of a few levers, like a transformation scene in a pantomime."[75]

Under such conditions, within a world ordinarily accustomed to celluloid stand-ins and plastic doubles and where, in extremity, one trusted one's life to decoys while suspecting one's enemy of illusion, how difficult it was to believe any pictures, let alone the rumors, of mounds of eyeglasses and gold fillings.

The Cult of the Surface

Wrote Oskar Schlemmer, a German dancer and artist who painted figures resembling manikins, "In the days to come I shall devote myself to the cult of the surface." Commandeered into camouflage service, Schlemmer in 1940 knew that "nowadays artistic neutrality, camouflaging one's real intentions, is necessary or appropriate; one should convey one's message through the universally comprehensible medium of landscape." The Cult of the Surface was a survival tactic for this former member of the Weimar Bauhaus, whose philosophy of art the Nazis denounced as "cultural bolshevism" while stealing its principles of total engineering. The Cult of the Surface also underlay the devotions of camoufleurs during World War II. When the war was over, the Cult of the Surface ordained the program of much of modern art.[76]

Another Bauhaus teacher, the Hungarian Constructivist László Moholy-Nagy, had been an artillery officer on the Russian Front during the Great War, and one can see along the curves, tangents, and circles of light in his subsequent work the arc and flash of shells. In 1917, wounded, delirious, he began a poem to himself, "Learn to know

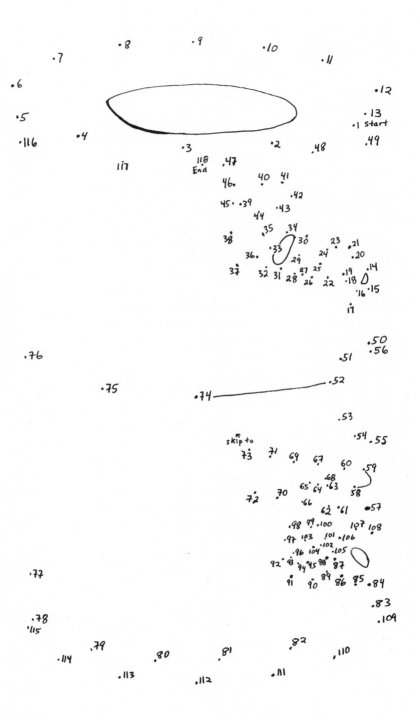

FIGURE 5.5. *Connect the dots. Please.* Designed by Cal Bowser, Jr., 1993.
Reproduced by permission.

the Light-design of your life"; aching to escape those black spiral fila-
ments of barbed wire he drew around the dying in charcoal or grease
pencil sketches, he continued,

Light, ordering Light, where are you? Far away.
A luster that illuminates mere being.
Come over me, proud Light, fierce Light, burn deep,
Ferocious Light, spread through me, cleanse my eyes.

He survived to commence a lifelong series of trials with lenses, perfo-
rations, translucencies. Proud Light shone through his photomontages,
advertising layouts, watercolors, window displays of shirts on headless
mannequins, collages of celluloid strips, sculptures of nickel and glass,
"light-space modulators" of punctured discs and metal lattices. Zealous, bombastic, he confessed that "It's a good thing to know the art of
camouflage. God, how much hurt pride and self-conscious embarrassment I've covered up with shows [of cockiness]." He tried out new
luminous materials: Rayon, Rhodoid, Plexiglas. In Paris, he knelt over
a white sheet with Piet Mondrian, rearranging strips and bars of black
and red paper whose tensions were harmonized only when both men
jumped up on chairs to look down from a height at the design on the
floor, a design expressive of living a "future life – more real, more pure."
Thus Piet to László in Chicago in the fall of 1937, where Moholy-Nagy
was opening The New Bauhaus under the auspices of department store
magnate Marshall Field II, to educate "what you might call the art engineer," an artist adept at window displays and stylish jewelry, earnest
about lacquers, serious about factory layout. The New Bauhaus failed to
keep to its economies, but Moholy-Nagy resurrected it as the School of
Design. During World War II the school gave instruction in camouflage,
taught by Moholy-Nagy and his colleague, Gyorgy Kepes, a painter and
designer whose theories about light led to novel methods for mounting jewels as for mounting optical illusions. Moholy-Nagy died in 1946,
at fifty-one, inside the cellophane curtains of an oxygen tent.[77]

Taken together, Schlemmer's Cult of the Surface and Moholy-Nagy's
Ferocious Light may help us understand the degree to which the hab-
its and tactics of war camouflage were carried into the postwar world.
The zoologist's nets and mottled surfaces for the Protective Colo-
ration of foxholes and artillery were reproduced on the spattered,
netlike canvases of Abstract Expressionists, in whose vanguard was
Arshile Gorky, who had set up a civilian camouflage course in New
York and who knew that "the unconscious is, so to speak, the domain
of camouflaged objects." Thayer Blue and Sea Blue for Obliterative
Gradation of ships were reproduced in duochrome paintings by Mark
Rothko, disruptive patterning on the dazzling silkscreens by Ellsworth
Kelly, who learned his art in the 603rd Engineers Camouflage Bat-
talion.[78] The catoptrics and box tricks for the deceptive visibility of
phantom armies were reproduced in the vortices of Op Art. Dummies

for the decoying of airfields and depots were dandified in Pop Art.

Schematic as this thesis is, I mean it to be suggestive of continuity rather than of causality. Leaving World War II behind, people had good reason to distrust the unaided eye — blinded *to* crematoria chimneys thinly camouflaged as industrial smokestacks, blinded *by* unprotected visions of atomic fireballs. Postwar painting and architecture seem often to have been intended to be seen from above, by aerial photographers, or from far away, through telescopic or microscopic magnification.

"Splotchography!" exclaimed Oskar Schlemmer in his diary in 1941. Laboring on camouflage projects, he was "Inspired by what appear to be microscopic photographs of natural objects such as sponges, bark, etc., but are actually splotchographies," like the patterns painted on tanks. Jackson Pollock, inspired by the sandpaintings of Native American healers who ritually sprinkle colored sands in symbolic designs on flat ground, began in 1943 to splash paint at his murals and then in 1947 to drip thin house paints, lacquers, aluminum emulsions over canvases on the floor. These "action paintings" presumed an aerial perspective; art was an act of looking down-and-in. Pollock said he felt "nearer, more a part of the painting, since this way I can walk around it, work from the four sides, and literally be *in* the painting." Surface *was* all, light *was* furious, image *was* ground, motion *was* meaning, as every camoufleur had learned and every photoanalyst knew. Pollock and other action painters became at once bombardier and target. What resulted was an elemental drama of camouflage, the battle between revelation and privity.[79]

Jasper Maskelyne had mixed Worcestershire sauce with spoiled flour, cement, and camel chips to produce his own sandpaintings, camouflage for tanks in the North African desert; Yves Klein, mixing pigment with synthetic resin, would claim exclusive rights to an International Klein Blue, sole object and medium for many of his works. Coatings chemists had concocted nonreflective steel grays and forest greens; Ad Reinhardt laid black upon matte black in cruciform patterns which could only be detected — in my case, in 1961, at the Art Institute of Chicago — from twenty feet away, as if through telephoto lenses. Jan Purkinje, a Czech psychologist, had found that red objects fade faster from our visual field than blue objects, a principle that the DuPont Company used to produce a naval camouflage paint; Mark Rothko and Joseph Beuys would make large expanses of a single color appear to shimmer and float upon the surface of another. These postwar abstracts were "silent" surfaces on which "pure" color was turned toward the meditative, the obliterative, the quiet invisibility of snipers in white suits lying patiently on fields of snow.[80]

Surface would be everything — and nothing — to the glass-and-steel corporate skyscrapers designed after the war by Mies van der Rohe, former director of the Bauhaus, and to the explicitly reflective glass buildings inaugurated in 1962 by Eero Saarinen. Arguments in favor of such architecture answered to the dreams of camoufleurs who through two wars had sought structures that, season to season, appeared to blend into clouds, trees, neighborhoods. The reflections, said advocates, made the building at one with its world; reflections, said critics, isolated the building, shielding its occupants from social intercourse as if democracy were a Medusa. Like postwar fiberglass mannequins and polyurethane foam dolls, the new buildings were essentially hollow; like the monumental steel sculptures anchored to barren stone plazas, the new buildings were stern and impersonal. Glass skyscrapers were meant to be glimpsed from afar or from on high, where they maintained a skyline of deceptive visibility and proximity; up close, they pretended to be invisible, denying community while mirror-mimicking fragments of urban stone and chrome around them. A carnie's house of mirrors from the outside, a shrink's one-way mirror from the inside, the glass-and-steel building was to the Cold War what the fake-dead-tree/observation-post had been to the Great War and what the camouflaged reconnaissance plane had been to World War II, an epitome of seeing double. And at sunset or sunrise, brashly duplicitous, its glass flashed a light as ferocious and faceted as the light glancing off the foil of paste diamonds.[81]

Facade and luster were the lifework of bespectacled Andy Warhol, who would "always think about what it means to wear eyeglasses." It meant, he said, that vision is standardized. His best friend as a child was Charlie McCarthy, the doll version of the monocled dummy (who in real life had a bedroom to himself next to ventriloquist Edgar Bergen's other child, Candice, and who on movie sets had his own stand-in). Warhol's earliest art jobs, 1947–52, were backdrops for display windows and footwear illustrations for *Glamour*. His designs for shoe ads during the 1950s got him known as "the Leonardo of the shoe," but he envied the fame of Roy Lichtenstein, who did large-dot versions of the photomechanical processes behind the bam! zap!! zoom!!! of color comics. Warhol's own Pop paintings initially appeared behind five mannequins in a Bonwit Teller shopwindow in 1961. His first fifteen minutes of fame came in 1962 with his cans of Campbell Soup (at which the Company was miffed but from which it would soon derive great profit; Warhol complained twenty years later that he had never received any nod from the Company for what he had done for its cans). Around 1963 Warhol learned how to transfer a photographic image onto a canvas in his choice of colors at the blink of an eye by pressing paint down-and-in through a porous screen, whence sprang twenty-three squeegeed Marilyn Monroes and *Eighty Two-Dollar Bills*. Like the mirrored spheres spinning from discotheque ceilings, Warhol's Factory was papered in silver foil, as if all images must be repeated. Like Claes Oldenburg's soft sculpture of a *Giant Good Humor Bar* (1965), Warhol's Coke bottles, Campbell Soup cans, and Brillo boxes were dummies; like the targets and flags painted by Jasper Johns, they were decoys. Warhol's approach to celeb pix and Name Brands was what an adman called the Seventh Technique, Camouflage: "*borrowing* believability from all the places in our society where it is stored up."[82]

Diamond Rabo Karabekian, rich and famous artist, as a youth had thought that believability lay in the perfect counterfeit. He entered World War II commanding a platoon of camoufleurs; he left with one less eye and no patience for a draftsmanship too easy and empty in an era of aerial photography. He took up with Pollock, Rothko, and Terry Kitchen the spray-painter, and committed himself to Abstract Expressionism, rolling acrylic wallpaint over vast canvases. He never achieved what his friends at their best achieved, the presence of life and death, the "pure *essence of human wonder*." He had tried, applying strips of colored tape to fields of Sateen Dura-Luxe, each strip "the soul at the core of some sort of person or lower animal"; the tape peeled off. As did the paint from all 512 sq ft of *Windsor Blue Number Seventeen*, his premium painting. In his barn, the eight panels stood newly virgin, white with sizing. Karabekian forsook art, then returned to create a panorama of where he was "when the sun came up the day the Second World War ended in Europe." The panorama had an aerial photographer's realism, the look down-and-in, its largest figure "the size of a cigarette, and the smallest a flyspeck." Still, if you knew where and how to look, everyone was there, Japanese, Americans, the queen of the Gypsies, Maoris, a Canadian bombardier, a Gurkha, a concentration-camp guard.[83]

Karabekian (with Kitchen) is himself a stand-in, fictive hero of *Bluebeard: A Novel* (1987), in which Kurt Vonnegut shows how the twentieth-century habit of camouflage has been working itself out after the war, oscillating between obliteration and dazzle, invisibility and hypervisibility. More than ever we distrust the unaided eye, which has been dizzied by regimens of pain relievers, antidepressants, reducing pills, low-calorie fasts, to say nothing of intoxicants and hallucinogens. As glasses (and sunglasses) have become fashion accessories, make-up "corrective," and dressing (for success) illusionary, the Cold War, the Vietnam War, the Afghan War, the "War on Drugs," the wars in the streets of Los Angeles and Sarajevo have seemed to demand an optic of surveillance through shatterproof lenses. The assisted eye of the late twentieth century has been an eye on the defensive, protecting from nuclear missiles, subversives, guerrillas, or from rapists, snipers, ultraviolence, ultraviolet. We watch our backs with rearview mirrors, our storefronts with parabolic mirrors, our prisoners through one-way mirrors. We watch newsfootage shot by helicopters overhead, their cameras zooming down-and-in as casually as we have glanced down at the hour ever since the Great War, when officers wore wristwatches to synchronize attacks up and out of the trenches into shadows of no-man's-land.[84]

Up and out, studying distant galaxies to determine our origins, astronomers – the first to discover astigmatism – have abandoned the eye altogether; they sweep the heavens with devices that "listen," count, and remember. On the witness stand are infrared telephoto cameras that can "make" a face in the dark 250 feet away and X-rays of dark bands representing core DNA sequences in the "minisatellite" regions of a human gene, sufficient to identify a rapist from a drop of semen. Who we uniquely are and where we ultimately come from are invisible to the naked eye.[85]

Photorealism, Super Realism, Verism are styles of commentary on the inadequacy of the naked eye in an epoch of Life-Decoys. Late-twentieth-century painters and sculptors have given us two- and three-dimensional surfaces at which to be astonished in the same way that postmodern architects and interior decorators have resurrected the trompe l'oeil facade. The camera that from the air had yielded the abstract expressionism of a Pollock could yield, face front, the "Really Real," the "Radically Real," or whatever one calls an art that works exclusively from photographs.[86]

Now It's the Women's Turn was the title of Rabo Karabekian's aerial panorama of the last day of World War II. In the postwar years, women whose domain has customarily been that of the Everyday have turned with enthusiasm to arts of heightened realism, the garbage of Idelle Weber (photographed on the street, then rendered on canvas), or the glass and jewelry of Audrey Flack, who remembers "going to Europe and being very shocked at how dull the work looked compared to the reproductions and I thought I never wanted that to happen to my work." A fine photographer, Flack paints from color slides. Her meticulous paintings glow as do the honey jars painted by Janet Fish, whose work demands such scrutiny, month after month, that only a photograph will do. For only a photograph assures the painter of the same weather, same quantities of dust, qualities of light. This species of realism is the most idealist of pursuits, presuming a clean permanence to lustrous surfaces our eyes cannot confirm. Janet Fish: "This effort for verisimilitude is made the more engaging because I do not consider that the appearance of the world has been established." And while painters use acrylics and alkyd enamels, sculptors (Jane Sinclair, Kathleen Calderwood, Marilyn Levine) use latex rubber, roplex, polyester resins, and decal transfers to re-present a synthetic society whose very bodies have been tattooed, from snapshots, in "single-needle photorealism."[87]

Trompe l'oeil is no longer a trick. It is how we negotiate our lives, how we enlarge them, how we propose that things and bodies be re-membered. That which has been dismissed as dishonest art, superficially clever art, or all-too-devout "working-class" art is in fact as central to the way we make our peace as the way we conduct our wars. Trompe l'oeil has shifted so assuredly from the motif of vanity to the contrary motif of the vanishing twin — of truths unseen until seen double — that the Starn Twins in the 1980s could make of their collaboration a proof of heightened perception. Scotch-taping photos of famous paintings, scratching at exposures in various stages of seaminess, the Starns collaged both sides of camouflage, the astutely hidden and the deceptively re-vealed. Sons to the owner of a supermarket chain, their self-presentation as twins was a "marketing" decision, but toward the 1990s, prefer-ring to be spoken of separately as Mike and Doug, they still created *Double Stairs, Double Chairs, Double Mater Doloroso, Double Stark Por-*

trait in Swirl. Unlike Miguel and Geronimo García, twins who collaborated in the 1600s on wooden statues, the identical Starns made the multiple imagery of twinness — and the artistry of double negatives — the method *and* the madness of their art: the method, reproducing Jan Asselijn's *The Threatened Swan*; the madness, splitting it into a hissing *Two-headed Swan*.[88]

Bird crazy, that's the truth. If paper birds and parrots yet fly and perch as painted illusions, they are icons of the bird's-eye view, a view that has expanded to encompass the Earth entire. From aerial reconnaissance photos taken during the Great War, one could see the hidden trenches of the Great War; from RAF photos taken in 1921–22, the overgrown path leading past the heel stone of Stonehenge toward the point of the solstice sunrise on the summer horizon; from Charles and Anne Morrow Lindbergh's photos taken in 1929, the flat tops of pre-Columbian pyramids crumbling in Central American jungles. From space now, computer-linked cameras reveal subterranean mineral deposits, the streets of submerged cities, the planting patterns of fields last plowed five hundred years ago. The assisted eye, looking down-and-in, lays further open our presence and our past even as we grow more skillful at the invisibility of "stealth" bombers and the deceptive visibility of plastics, stand-ins, simulacra. It is not that such remote sensing tells us the literal truth but that we have greater faith in the virtues of the artificial lens than we do in the naked eye. "Seeing double" has become perplexing, for it refers at once to the illusions we foster or fear *and* to our faith in a second sight through discs of polished glass we place so willingly before our eyes. Looking down-and-in, our astronauts tell us that our globe is a "jewel," a fragile ornament in a darkened room. We want to believe them as we look at orbital photographs of an Earth too true a blue to be paste.[89]

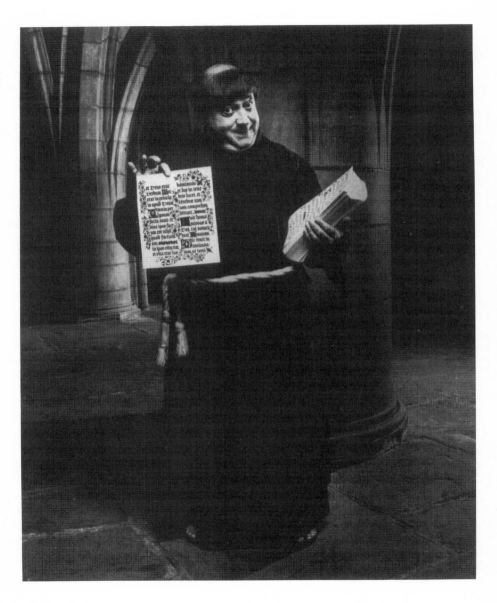

FIGURE 6.1. One of a series of advertisements playing upon the figure of the
monastic copyist and manuscript illuminator. This 1980 advertisement, for the
XL-10 Imaging Process, was captioned, "Xerox has come up with another miracle."
The legend read, in part, "XL-10 copies aren't just positively beautiful. They're
absolutely faithful." Reproduced courtesy of the Xerox Corporation.

CHAPTER SIX

Ditto

"Ditto," said Tweedledum.
"Ditto, ditto!" cried Tweedledee.
— Lewis Carroll / Charles Dodgson,
Through the Looking Glass

1900: "After spoiling years of canvases through foolish persistence while I kept noticing that somehow all my successes came, as it were, out of the side of my eye, or rather came in the *first three days*...I now keep reverently every *start*, have it copied by an assistant while I paint something else or go up to Monadnock or write on birds, *anything* to get as far as possible from my work, and then pounce on the copy and give it a three day shove again and actually have that furthered result copied again and so on." Abbott Thayer called this his "old master" system, several replicas going at once so that he never risked obliterating any "achieved beauty."[1]

1922: With graph paper and a factory's color chart at hand, László Moholy-Nagy rang up the foreman and ordered five original paintings. He wanted one done in three sizes and two others of set dimensions, painted to scale following the shapes and colors on his grid. "In an industrial age," he declared, "the distinction between art and non-art, between manual craftsmanship and mechanical technology is no longer an absolute one."[2]

1973: "Mr. Herron's work, by reproducing the exact appearances of Frank Stella's entire *oeuvre*, nevertheless introduces new content and a new concept...by actually representing the actions of someone other than Frank Stella. That is, in their real meaning, these objects are Stellas *plus*, Stellas and *more*."[3]

Copying is pedestrian. Copying is peculiar. On the one hand, copying makes us what we are. Our bodies take shape from the transcription of protein templates, our languages from the mimicry of privileged sounds, our crafts from the repetition of prototypes. Cultures cohere in the faithful transmission of rituals and rules of conduct. To copy cell for cell, word for word, image for image, is to make the known world our own.

On the other hand, we are not identical, nor do we wish to think of ourselves as clones. Copying is ultimately imperfect, our errors eventually our heirs. The more widespread the act of copying, the greater the likelihood of significant mistranscription. Genetic slip or evolution, scribal mistake or midrash, whatever we call it, miscopying raises hard questions about identity, security, and integrity. The same technical advances that render our skill at copying so impressive also intensify the dilemmas of forgery. We use copies to certify originals, originals to certify copies, then we stand bewildered.

What are we about, who take so easily to ditto marks yet look so hard for signs of "individual touch"? Whose work was a painting by Thayer after his labor upon a series of assistants' copies of previous versions? Whose work, and of what singularity, were the paintings ordered over the phone by Moholy-Nagy? Dare we espouse, as did Hank Herron (a critic's hoax), the supremacy of copy over original?

Last chapter focused upon the optics of seeing double. This chapter refocuses upon the act itself, the duplicating of our own words and artifacts, from the handcopying of manuscripts to the digitizing of art. Such copying, inherently flawed, always begs for ratification even as we look to copies themselves for assurance of continuity, value, and authenticity. Anything unique is at risk of vanishing: we make a twin – a notarized copy, a plaster cast, paste diamonds, Thayer's working replicas. An object uncopied is under perpetual siege, valued less for itself than for the struggle to prevent its being copied. The more adept the West has become at the making of copies, the more we have exalted uniqueness. It is within an exuberant world of copies that we arrive at our experience of originality.

Practical distinctions between the unique and the multiple have historically been entrusted to theologians, notaries, connoisseurs, and curators. None of these now seems to be able to keep the One apart from the Many. Can we still uphold – or is it time to abandon – any distinction between original and replica?

Original Sin

Questions of a similar nature had already come to a head in the fourth century: What exactly is the relationship between God and Jesus the Christ, also called God? Are the two identical, or of the same essence, or of separate essences? In sermons on Proverbs 8.22–31 and in songs for sailors, Arius of Alexandria maintained that God and Jesus were separate essences, the Father precedent to and creator of the Son. Otherwise, as a commonsense philosopher, Arius could not see his way clear of a disturbingly double God, "composite and divisible and mutable and a body." His sense of a too-common Jesus was condemned in 325 by the Council of Nicaea, which espoused a Son identical and coeternal with the Father. Arius died in 336, but five more councils would meet and three centuries pass before the Eastern Church decisively articulated the personhood of Christ, fully divine yet so fully Incarnate that

FIGURE 6.2. Addressograph advertisement, captioned, "Expensive Lesson for Businessmen to Learn," 1961. Reproduced courtesy of the Data Card Corporation.

humanity might share in the grace of His sacrifice. Time and again, the Western Church too would be upset by hitches in the correspondence between Father, Son, and Holy Spirit, and by questions of what it meant that Man had been fashioned in the likeness of God, or what it would mean to live in imitation of Christ.[4]

Central as was supramundane copying to Christian theology, no less central was the practice of mundane copying to Christian and European life. In 418 a Carthaginian churchman, Apiarius, accused of malfeasance and removed from office by a local African bishop, appealed to Rome. The new Pope, Zosimus, was already at loggerheads with the North Africans over theses about the effectiveness of good works; he had been siding with the Pelagians, whose faith in man's moral will to overcome the stain of Original Sin had been denounced by 220 African Church Fathers. Responding to Apiarius, Zosimus asserted Rome's right to intervene, citing canons from the Council of Nicaea. Finding no such canons in their copies, the Africans insisted that Zosimus consult at Constantinople, "where authentic copies of the Nicene statutes are said to be kept." The pope's canons proved to be later impositions, and

Zosimus had to withdraw from the side of Apiarius as he would, shortly, from the side of the Pelagians.[5]

It was fitting that a contest over papal authority, fueled by controversy over how closely humanity could approach divinity, was settled by recourse to "authentic copies." The Intact Copy was a root metaphor in late classical as in Christian patristic culture, central to political reassertions of the glory that was Rome, artistic reproductions of the sculpture that was the grandeur of Greece, and Christian realignments of the Faith with the grace that was Apostolic. Seven years earlier, in the wake of the sack of Rome by (Arian) Visigoths, a momentous debate in Carthage between 286 Catholic and 279 Donatist bishops had hinged upon Intact Copies and the nature of transcription. Donatists, believing that the validity of the sacraments rested upon the personal holiness of the man administering them, objected to the reading of shorthand minutes, for those who read from stenographic marks could stray from the truth without anyone being the wiser. They demanded the reading aloud of a full fair copy of the previous day's debate – as they demanded the full integrity of each priest. The Catholic bishops, led by Augustine and persuaded of the virtue of the Church to transmit God's grace through imperfect clergy, were content with the reading of minutes from speed-written (tachygraphic) signs. Imperial Commissioner Flavius Marcellinus decided the debate about the copyists, and about the priesthood, in Augustine's favor: the Church was not a reserve of perfectly pure men but a holy institution whose servitors, like Augustine, had perpetually to struggle toward the City of God.[6]

Within the City of Man, those schooled in taking dictation advanced to the making of law. From mere copyists, archivists, or public scribes, they became notaries, executive secretaries, administrators, and, by the fourth century, senators. Irked at the voting presence of these "ink-coolies," one Roman senator whined that sons of sausage-makers were being admitted to the Senate solely on the strength of their tachygraphy, a mindless labor. But the shorthand route to power was so clear that the title of notary would mark rather a political than tachygraphic skill. Petronius Maximus, Emperor in 455, had started off as a notary.[7]

In late classical and medieval culture, the notary was more than amanuensis. He (sometimes she) was a swift copyist, trusted witness, strict stylist adept at preambles and appeals. Attached to landowners, bureaucrats, churchmen, or merchants, notaries extended the law as they extended legal language with runs of synonyms to make intent infernally clear. On their own, they advised citizens, wrote out contracts, prepared affidavits. Required to keep copies of the instruments they drew up, they became the chief repositors of legal precedent.[8]

Stenography transforms the spoken word into the written. Copying transforms the One into the Many. Notarizing transforms the private into the public, the transient into the timely, then into the timeless. The emblem of French notaries was the gnomon at the center of a sundial, its shadow tracing the edge of time. The notary was a symbol of fixity in a world in flux, yet the making of copies is essentially transformative – if not as the result of generations of inadvertent errors, then as a result of the generation of masses of copies whose very copiousness affects the meaning and ambit of action. The notarial motto was *Lex est quodcumque notarius*, "whatsoever we write is the Law."⁹

Had we paper enough and time, we could follow notaries from the merchant exchanges of medieval Lombardy to the law courts of England and France, serving expansive economies. We could watch how, as towns grew, notaries produced charters confirming urban independence. We could observe the recopying of crumbling title deeds unearthed by abbeys under threat of expropriation. We could sit with notaries at childbed as they legitimized heirs and at deathbeds as they put codicils to wills. We could consider their role as historians reconstructing events from rough memoranda, inserting concocted speeches into formal documents. We could, lastly, track the course of civil and canon law through their accounts of trials and judgments; rarely verbatim, their records determined what was memorable at law. Whatsoever they did not write down was   lost.¹⁰

"If men were able to remember all and singular by heart, which is absurd, then it would clearly follow that to write is nothing else than to anticipate labour with labours," wrote Nicholas Grantham as he took his scrivener's oath in 1573, "– writing therefore, often calls to mind [matters] which sink and stagger through the instability of human nature." It had been the duty of monastics to fix themselves upon the utter stability of Christ by copying scripture while reading it aloud or by subvocalizing. Through copying a monk would hear and hold to matters eternal; through copying a nun would come to know by heart as by hand the slow turn of the Word. After the parchment had been prepared (or, later, the paper secured), the sheets cut to size and scored with lines for lettering, the reed pen (later the quill) cut, the ink mixed, a monk or nun writing six hours a day six days a week for a year could have copied out a Bible. That was two to three columns of text a day, a dozen or so characters a minute, an exhausting task where any error meant the corruption of holy writ. Writing, wrote the scribe Florencio at the end of a text he had copied in 945, "extinguishes the light from the eyes, it bends the back, it crushes the viscera and the ribs, it brings forth pain to the kidneys, and weariness to the whole body.... Know ye how sweet to the sailor is arrival at port? Even so for the copyist is tracing the last line."¹¹

Each line, first to last, was to be compared with the original by a Corrector, but the greater the emphasis upon speed the less time spared for proofreading. And late medieval society owed many of its copies not to monastic scriptoria but to university stationers who rented out eight-page (sixteen-column) portions of texts, week to week. These portions or *peciae* would be copied speedily, as fast as 374 lines (seven columns) a day by a medical student in a rush. Usually, the copying went about half that fast, 160 lines a day. Hastily or not, students would copy successive *peciae* from whatever exemplar was then available, each with its own errors. A completed copy would reflect a congeries of variants, further debased by ambiguous abbreviations. Of three thousand extant manuscripts of the widely read works of Thomas Aquinas, nary a handful take us back to a fair copy made by the secretary to whom he dictated. What we have, and what the students had, was neither intently fresh nor intentionally foul.[12]

Handwriting itself was not mastered until one's teens. Medieval university students were still tutored in quillmanship, which they learned as a skill of faithful transcription. Writing was primarily for taking down the spoken word — a technology, in lecture halls, for the simultaneous multiple copying of a text. During the fourteenth century, however, instructors who had dictated from received texts began instead to read their paraphrases, and then to speak from their own work on the subject, especially in the faculties of medicine, law, and theology, whose professors at Paris and Heidelberg were directed to lecture to advanced students at a pace faster than could be transcribed. A tactic to forestall the dissemination of new works universities hoped to monopolize, fast talking also indicated a shift in the primary function of writing. From a method of fair copying, handwriting was to become a vehicle for innovation and personal expression. Advocating a simple hand learnt by tracing letters through transparent vellum, Erasmus in the sixteenth century was nonetheless sure that "A man's handwriting, like his voice, has a special, individual quality" that went beyond the newly dotted *i*'s.[13]

Part of Renaissance "self-fashioning" was to fashion a script that showed one's devotion to a social order yet signaled one's personal presence. To the faithfulness and legibility of monastic ideals of penmanship were superadded ease and expressiveness. Writing masters of the sixteenth century, claiming to model the forms of civility, did teach a running ("current") hand for the rote production of legal and business documents, but they prefaced the slender verticals of their copperplate-engraved letterforms with disquisitions upon character. A noble person must command a courteous hand. Courtesy required civility, which was a way of carrying oneself and, literally, italicizing oneself — in that new hand, *italic*. A graceful hand began in homage and ended, like a paraph spiraling off the end of a signature, with a public flourish irreproducible by any printing press.[14]

During the first fifty years of printing, 1450–1500, more books were issued than had been copied by Christian hand over the previous five hundred years. There were some 100,000 manuscripts in Europe in 1450; by 1500 there were perhaps twenty million copies of printed books and pamphlets. Much of the travel of medieval scholars had been in search of unique volumes they would laboriously copy out. Some catalogs did exist for locating manuscripts — 1412 different titles for the Franciscan libraries in the British Isles — but such numbers shrank in comparison to the 42,000 different titles issuing from presses at 300–600 copies an edition between 1454 and 1500, or the 575,000 different titles issued during the sixteenth century (or the 200,000,000 copies of the novels of Harold Robbins sold between 1948 and 1981).[15]

This is not to say that printing assured the survival or accuracy of every text. Many incunabula titles have been lost, and as early as 1478 a sheet of errors was prepared for a printed book. Despite a papal bull excommunicating any printer who mangled the Vulgate Bible authorized by Sixtus V (1585–90), so many errors cropped up that the first edition had to be destroyed. Books in seventeenth-century stalls had typographical errors on neatly every page, doubled doubled lines, mixΣd-up signαtures. If, as historian Elizabeth L. Eisenstein suggests, printed books had a "typographical fixity" which changed the patterns of discourse, that fixity was neither eternal nor absolute.[16]

Such was the stubborn position, at least, of Abbot Johann Tritheim's *In Praise of Scribes*, written in 1492, set in type in 1494. The late fifteenth century saw a resurgence of manuscript copying among Benedictine monastics; Tritheim was writing in their defense. "It is the scribes who lend power to words and give lasting value to passing things and vitality to the flow of time. Without them the Church would see faith weakened, love grown cold, hope confounded, justice lost, the law confused, and the Gospel fallen into oblivion." Even in the age of the press? Yes. "The printed book is made of paper and, like paper, will quickly disappear. But the scribe working with parchment ensures lasting remembrances for himself and for his text." Yet one could print on vellum, as Gutenberg did with his first Bibles. Many manuscripts after 1460 were in fact copied from printed pages. The key was not the medium but the method, for a monk copying sacred passages "is gradually initiated into the divine mysteries and miraculously enlightened."[17]

Ironically, Tritheim's handwritten original of *In Praise of Scribes* has vanished, while 108 copies of his books, printed five hundred years ago on rag paper, sit on the shelves of North American libraries. Yet the tradition of handcopying did survive the printing press. It has survived as a spiritual practice and, in Jewish communities, a religious prescription, each Torah to be written out (200–500 lines a day) by a scribe whose scrolls must be free of errors. It survived as a covert means of transmitting heretical, occult, and erotic works, and as the policy of courts, chanceries, and embassies whose documents had to be indited in duplicate or triplicate. It survived as the copybook method of teaching penmanship and as the methodical labor of scholars copying out from archives those passages they will embed in their own pages. The book before you is based upon some 16,000 notecards handcopied from manuscript and printed sources.[18]

The Fair and the Foul

Trust me that my notes are verbatim? Edmund Gosse, editing the works of the eighteenth-century poet Thomas Gray, boasted that he had transcribed Gray's letters directly from manuscript; in fact he had hired a copyist who, tiring, secretly chose to copy by hand (and inaccurately)

FIGURE 6.3. As she thumbs her nose at her pursuer, the woman is saying, "Nuts to you, pretty boy!" Supposedly an illustration from a classical Greek vase, this fake of the early nineteenth century was taken for the real thing in the *Journal des savants* (1829). Reproduced most recently in Gilbert Bagnani's article, "Fakes and forgeries," *The Phoenix* 14 (1960).

from an earlier printed (and botched) edition of Gray's letters. Tritheim himself, abbot of Sponheim, copying documents for his *Chronicon Sponheimense*, falsified deeds and invented personages to deepen the antiquity of Sponheim.[19]

I had meant here to pursue the fair copy, not the forged, thinking that forgery has to do with intentional misattribution, fair (and foul) copying with inadvertent error. That distinction is tenuous. Forgery has been complicated by ideals of selflessness. Since antiquity, authors of obscure, heterodox, or imitative works have stood in the shadows of names more prestigious. Ascriptions could be devout (the 900 sermons attributed to John Chrysostom) or devious (Pelagian tracts masquerading under the name of Saint Jerome, an enemy), playful (the 105 extra comedies of Plautus) or portentous (Paul's *Third* Letter to the Corinthians). Was it piety or self-interest that led monks to create originals, in archaic script, of charters whose fading copies were all that stood against a loss of lands? Two-thirds of the ecclesiastical documents extant from before 1100 A.D. are, in part or whole, forgeries. After the Crusader treasure-hunts, the same could be said of relics — so many and multiplied (the six bodies of Saint Madeleine, the four heads of Gregory the Great) that Saint Juliana of Mont-Cornillon in the 1200s acquired the beatific power of discriminating true relic from false.[20]

Forgery is but the extreme of copying: the extreme of fair copying, when what is forged is indiscernible from the original; the extreme of foul copying, when what is forged is a fabrication passed off in the name or style of another person or era.[21]

Against such extreme copying we have long had the indenture of personal seals, whose authority derives from the promise that each successive impression will be the same. Peculiar, that our modern culture of the copy should opt instead for the authority of the signature, since no two signatures by the same person are exactly the same. (Experts discern forged signatures by the absence of *sprezzatura*, that offhandedness by which we sign a bit differently every time.) Children rarely practiced signatures in premodern schools; it was a needless accomplishment when an X and witnesses stood one in better legal stead, and where a seal had more fixity. If a few early antiquaries did collect "Original Letters, and other matter of the proper Hand-writing of persons of all ranks, eminent in their generations," signatures acquired their full authority only with the Romantic celebration of genius, when devotees of the autograph snipped signatures from letters and mounted them beneath engraved portraits as if the hand underwrote the face. "Autographs are indicative of the movements of the mind as well as of the pen," wrote the handwriting expert Dawson Turner in 1848. "I never met with the man who was not gratified to see how Newton wrote, or how Milton and Bacon formed their letters; who did not love to trace... the lucid clearness of Franklin, the lightning rapidity of Napoleon.... Indeed, so universal is this feeling, that an autograph appears at the present time a no less indispensable accompaniment to biography than a portrait; and both for the same cause, as clues to the decipherment of character."[22]

Commanded throughout the nineteenth century to follow copybook forms, students meanwhile learned the lesson of uniqueness from textbooks featuring famous people whose autographs, reproduced below their pictures, proved the virtues of a distinctive script. Pious lovers of autographs were meanwhile and innocently confusing the historical record, sponsoring the publication of series after series of well-reproduced commemorative facsimiles that would soon circulate on their own as true originals.[23]

Given the paradox of unique signatures reproduced in thousands of facsimiles, a profitable career could be had from both extremes of forgery. Extreme foul copy: Denis Vrain-Lucas, who had apprenticed in a notary's office and had clerked for a genealogist who hammered coats of arms out of thin air, exploited a rich mathematician's enchantment with the autographs of famous people. During the 1860s Vrain-Lucas sold him 27,472 letters from such celebrities as Alexander the Great (to Aristotle), Judas (to Mary Magdalene), Mary Magdalene (to Lazarus), Lazarus (to the apostle Peter), Joan of Arc (to her family), and Pascal (to a young Isaac Newton), all written in modern French on sheets of paper watermarked with a fleur-de-lis. When found out, Vrain-Lucas was unrepentant. "Whatever is said or done, my conscience is calm," he said. "If to reach my end [of exalting France] I did not act with perfect discretion,... if I used a trick to strike the attention and to arouse the curiosity of the public, it was merely to recall certain historical facts which are easily forgotten or unknown even to the learned."[24]

Betwixt fair and foul: Alexander Howland Smith, a sallow copy clerk in an Edinburgh lawyer's office, wrote out letters from Mary Queen of Scots, Sir Walter Scott, and the Scots poet Robert Burns. He took advantage of "published *fac-simile* reproductions" of their script, creating in their hand and style on genuinely old paper "battalions" of forgeries. His career as "Antique" Smith (1888–92) had begun when he found in his office documents actually signed by Scott, which he sold to autograph hunters until he had no more. Then he invented.[25]

Extreme fair copy: Charles Weisberg of Philadelphia, who had posed for the figure of the patriot on an American Legion medal of honor, for years forged on the most genuine of papers and sold with aplomb the signatures of such as George Washington, Thomas Jefferson, and Abraham Lincoln. Paroled from prison in 1943, "Baron" Weisberg opened a bookstore. He called it Jabberwocky.[26]

Spirit Masters

> One, two! One, two! and through and through
> The vorpal blade went snicker-snack!

Ah, if 'twere that simple. But with a mobile, litigious, industrial society keen for copies have come technologies that can run all originals through a looking glass. To see how copying has gotten out of hand, we must go galumphing back from the Baron to his bandersnatched Secretary of State, Thomas Jefferson.

Those qualities of handwriting required of modern secretaries and "Secretaries" of State were the qualities necessary to factory work: speed, legibility, faithfulness, and ease. Industrialization meant, in essence, the replacement of handcopying by machine-copying – machines whose work was "rapid, regular, precise, tireless." An essay on handwriting in the *Encyclopédie* stressed not calligraphy but the efficiency of a "mechanical art" producing a "clear, neat, exact, distinct, elegant, and easy" hand – like that executed "precisely and rapidly" by a life-size boy built by the Swiss automaton-maker, Pierre Jaquet-Droz.[27]

Another eighteenth-century automaton writer was tinier and more restricted in repertoire, but his Viennese maker, Friederich Von Knauss, had geared him to social convention: he could write his messages in a heavy **fraktur** or a blithe cursive. Europeans were accustomed to two tiers of script, public and private. Official documents and invitations had been penned in a relatively slow, ornamented hand, while a faster, plainer hand was reserved for letters between friends, family, or lovers. This double system was undercut by the "round, even, flowing busi-

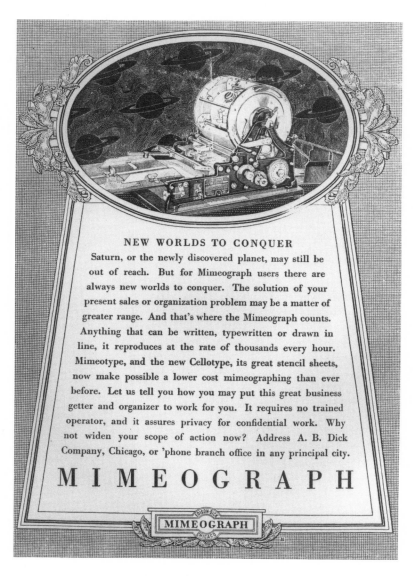

FIGURE 6.4. Advertisement for Mimeograph machine, 1930. Reproduced courtesy of the A.B. Dick Company.

ness hand" of new copybooks, which tacitly promoted a single "clear, neat, exact" script. Grievances sent to Paris from the provinces just before the French Revolution may have been inked in a formal notarial style, but the standard of different hands for different occasions and orders of people gave way before the democracy of a commonly legible hand (and shorthand) by which to transcribe fiery speeches on behalf of the common people.[28]

That estimable democrat George Washington "wrote readily, rather diffusely, in an easy, correct style." So noted Thomas Jefferson, a prolific correspondent who, after the American Revolution, was wont to keep close records of his letters. Twice, Jefferson's papers had been lost, once in a fire, again in 1780 during a British raid on Richmond. Sensitive to the precariousness of originals, Jefferson tried any device that might redeem the hours he spent entering into journals a précis of each letter he wrote. In 1803 he endorsed the pantograph, by which he would eventually make copies of more than 5700 letters. "I only lament that it had not been invented thirty years sooner."[29]

Monkeys, or polygraphs, or perspective machines, or pantographs had in fact been around since the 1500s as apparatus wherewith draftsmen produced simultaneous copies of drawings. A 1631 German version consisted of a wooden frame from which hung a horizontal parallelogram of pivoted rods with two pencils fitted vertically at proximate corners such that, by adjusting the angles of the rods, the second pencil would simultaneously reduce or enlarge on a separate sheet the design being drawn with the first. With this and with pen-and-ink pantographs there were problems: maintaining consistent pressure for both writing instruments; preventing the second instrument from slipping off its sheet; sharpening or re-inking the instruments. The process was therefore tedious; a "double-writer" patented in 1648 "was found to take considerably more than twice the time to produce its copies that the common pen took to produce one." European and American tinkerers reworked the pantograph, which was perfected to Jefferson's satisfaction in 1803 by preacher-clockmaker John Isaac Hawkins, inventor also of a device for tracing profiles. Hawkins teamed up with the artist and showman Charles Willson Peale, also of Philadelphia, whose painterly son Rembrandt praised their "polygraph" as a

Triumph of art! amaz'd I view
A transcript fair of all I drew.

The polygraph (or pantograph) was, "in fact, writing two original letters at once, with as much ease as one."[30]

Previously, Jefferson had been using a "copying press" patented by James Watt, he of the steam engine. Watt resented the time it took to copy for his records the letters he sent daily to his partner, Matthew Boulton. In 1779 Watt devised then refined a portable press whose impressions were made not by inked metal type but by ink alone — a special compound of Aleppo galls, gum arabic, green copperas, and alum. A letter written in such ink could be pressed upon a second, tissue-thin sheet moistened with a solution of borax salt, vinegar, crushed oyster shells, bruised galls, and distilled water. This yielded a copy in reverse but transparent, so the text could be read aright on the verso.[31]

Overcoming fears that his copying press "may be made a bad use of" by counterfeiters, Watt was employing the method of print transfer, itself not unanticipated. A century earlier, progenitors of the Royal Society had hoped that through print transfer, abetted by stenography and double-writers, a global intellectual community could be sustained. When "a book can be transcribed within an hour even if it is a large one, and no matter in what language, including Oriental tongues, it is written," then the members of an Invisible College might commune across all borders. That cosmopolitan printer Benjamin Franklin had tried a gum arabic ink on smooth paper, sprinkled with iron powder then transferred to a copper plate, but his copies were "far from beautiful." Watts too had problems with the ink, which had to be thin enough to flow, vibrant enough to yield an impression hours after written, and harmless to the original.[32]

Even so, the copying press was attractive. Washington owned two. Franklin in Paris ordered three. James Boswell, scribe and biographer to the copious Samuel Johnson, "regretted that there is no invention for getting an immediate and exact transcript of the mind, like that instrument by which a copy of a letter is at once taken off." Jefferson wrote from Paris to James Madison, advising him to get a copying press; Madison wrote back, "I am led to think it would be a very oeconomical acquisition to all our public offices which are obliged to furnish copies of papers belonging to them." Weeks after becoming the first U.S. Secretary of State, Jefferson installed the copying press at the heart of American bureaucracy and diplomacy. "The utility of these Presses is too obvious to require any recommendation," said the *Federal Gazette*. The copying press could produce a whole sheet "in less than two minutes, the copy as fair as the original" – five times as fast (and twice as faithful?) as a scrivener.[33]

When Jefferson set aside his copying press for the polygraph or double (or triple, sometimes quadruple) writer, he was returning to the ancient stroke-by-stroke mode of copying even as he made the modern choice of the simultaneous over the consecutive. Bartleby and other stubborn scriveners perpetuated that post hoc stroke-by-stroke copying of texts practiced since antiquity, but two hybrid modes of copying would come to dominate officework: 1) copying as one went along, s/t/r/o/k/e/-/b/y/-/s/t/r/o/k/e, mechanically, with parallel pens or, by 1880, with typewriter keys striking through layers of carbon paper; 2) copying an ENTIRETY after the fact, chemically, fullsheet by fullsheet.

Choices between the two modes were choices between two philosophies of copying. Copying s/t/r/o/k/e/-/b/y/-/s/t/r/o/k/e as one went along approximated the actions that produced the original, except that what had been the scribe's task was now done by visibly conjoint twins. Copying an ENTIRETY all-at-once scarcely resembled the original process; one arrived at the result not step by step but through a fluid, seamless, and invisible act of twinning. The distance between the two modes of copying was that between a certain gorgeous writer and a certain lovely warbler.

Constructing an automaton writer in the 1840s, the magician Jean Eugène Robert-Houdin commissioned an artist to sculpt a head for the mechanical figure. He got what looked to be the visage of a saint: no good. Commissioning another, he got "a family likeness to those Nuremberg dolls made to act as lay figures in [art] studios." As unhappy with manikins as with immaculata, he turned to a mirror and shaped (unconsciously, said he) "an exact likeness" of himself which, when first it moved, penned the name of its First Mover, Robert-Houdin. Enthused, he had the automaton sign "Robert-Houdin" a thousand times. Since audiences "generally understand nothing of the mechanical effects by which automata are moved; but they are pleased to see them, and often only value them by the multiplicity of their parts," he added a whizzing noise to the mechanism so that they could hear as well as see the writer repeating both the series of motions *and* the effort necessary to pen a signature or missive. This was copying as s/t/r/o/k/e/-/b/y/-/s/t/r/o/k/e reenactment. However, with another automaton, a nightingale, the copper tubing and steel piston by which his bird sang had to be silent and hidden, for the bird's appeal was its outward ease. This was copying as the reproduction of an ENTIRETY, without visible or audible means.[34]

Elegant writing was one of the Enlightenment's signs of Reason, of thought made clear and public, step by logical step; it followed that an automaton's s/t/r/o/k/e/-/b/y/-/s/t/r/o/k/e penmanship be shown to proceed from a systematic arrangement of ratchets and geartrains. Sublime singing was for Romantics a sign of Art, of voice and soul entwined, mysterious as the (unexposed) nightingale. Techniques for copying paintings and drawings in their ENTIRETY fell in with Romantic visions of the union of body&soul. Lithography, stereotyping, and (later) photography were oriented not toward reenacting the original process (painting on a second canvas, or engraving, or resetting type in facsimile), but toward appropriating complete images, all at once, through chemical resists or molds. If the pantograph, like Robert-Houdin's automaton writer, caused people to admire the smooth concurrence of imitation, the copying press, like Robert-Houdin's automaton warbler, led them to expect a sudden wholeness.[35]

S/t/r/o/k/e/-/b/y/-/s/t/r/o/k/e reenactment implied subordination, an unequal collaboration between leader and follower, originator and copyist. The taking of an ENTIRETY implied appropriation. The two modes of copying became gender-specific in the late 1800s, but the transfer to the "second sex" of the domain of copying↔as↔reenactment had begun in Jefferson's era. Pantography, rang out the Peales, was so easy that "on the first trial the feeblest female hand, to her astonishment, produces two original copies." The American architect Benjamin Latrobe, early owner of a Hawkins-Peale pantograph, lent his machine to Jefferson, "much to mine and my Wife's inconvenience, whom I have now returned to her former post of Copying Clerk." Hired by the Patent Office in 1854, American women copied documents at home as piecework; when they and then European women entered the office workforce, they entered as copy clerks, as s/t/r/o/k/e/-/b/y/-/s/t/r/o/k/e transcribers (up to 108,000 words per month), as stenographers, as "typewriters" – wo/man and machine called by the same name.[36]

Not that men entirely abandoned copying. Rather, they held to the prerogative of copying ENTIRETIES. What men valued was copying→as→appropriation, taking instant charge of a whole – as in the new practice of franchising, the licensing of reproductions of the entire format of a business, for example, the Bryant Business Schools, which across America instructed females in shorthand, typing, and the operation of office machines while preparing male students for accounting, finance, and merchandising. In 1890s print shops, American and English unions fought to keep women from operating linotype machines, which cast type a full line at a time; a master printer might hire a woman but would restrict her, testified one man, to "straight composition [setting character by character], to make as much as possible an automaton of her."[37]

The more zealously men defended their prerogative of copying ENTIRETIES, the more they devalued s/t/r/o/k/e/-/b/y/-/s/t/r/o/k/e reenactment as "merely mechanical." In *The Marble Faun* of 1859, Nathaniel Hawthorne's heroine (as was his wife, Sophia) is an art copyist whose paintings are endowed with "that evanescent and ethereal life – that flitting fragrance, as it were, of the original" – yet in her own life she is incapable of apt invention. "We won't complain," said a Frenchman, an art critic, about female copyists, "if their talent serves only to reproduce the old masters.... This modest task is certainly suitable for women."[38]

Male was to female as original was to copy, ever since, yes, the second account of Creation in Genesis 2.22. Adam's rib was reconceived in 1866 by the German morphologist Ernst Haeckel: "every individual organism repeats in its own life history the life history of its race, passing through the lower forms of its ancestors on its way to maturity." For Homo sapiens, maturity was a rational individuality, which man alone reached; woman was stuck at the stage of the imitative child and the childlike savage: "in ontogeny she represented eternal adolescence, in phylogeny she recalled the ancestry of the race."[39]

Biblical biology and Victorian social science played themselves out not only in museums but in libraries, where men remained the masters of rare books and manuscripts while women became the mistresses of mass media. Public libraries were increasingly staffed by women and the stacks stocked with novels by women. Librarians tried at first to impose some moral order upon the reading habits of their patrons, but, as Agnes Hill commented in the *Library Journal* in 1902, "It takes some degree of personal courage to urge the exclusion of a book when you know that the library ten miles away has just put in twenty or thirty copies." Learning a fine "library hand" for labeling the spines of books and copying catalog entries, women who were trained to do "monotonous things over and over in a mechanical way" became promoters of the copy rather than priestesses of the original.[40]

Ontogeny recapitulated this edition of phylogeny in court rooms and legislatures, in business, law, and newspaper offices. A male stenographer protested in vain in 1864 that "the work of the short-hand writer is much more responsible than is commonly supposed. To say that it is merely mechanical is absurd." Within forty years, though, stenography was thought a woman's job, the stenographer a "safe, efficacious, labor-saving device." Other "merely mechanical" tasks – tabulating, typing, telegraphy – also fell to women, in part because single, educated women were choosing officework over lower-paid, more socially restrictive jobs in teaching and nursing, in part because s/t/r/o/k/e-/b/y/-/s/t/r/o/k/e reenactment was tied to womanual dexterity. The first practicable American typewriters were manufactured in the 1870s at the Remington Company's sewing machine plant, and 1890s dictaphones were run by sewing machine foot treadles, a neat conjunction of three technologies given over to women, who were supposed to be intrinsically suited to detailed, repetitive work. Stenographer Ida C. Murray explained in 1906 how she pleased a difficult employer: "It was my aim clearly defined in my own mind that he should find me a perfectly working, smoothly-ordered, thoughtful machine ready for his serving – not a woman."[41]

If women in offices had to become "thoughtful" copying machines, copying machines in turn required the presence and gradually took on the personae of women, whose "tendency is toward reproduction, while man's is toward production," wrote a man in *Popular Science Monthly* in 1895. What made the "typewriter" the necessity it and she became was less the speed than the clarity and consistency of the typed characters and the compatibility of woman and machine with duplicating processes. Although a skilled typewriter of 1907 could manage about twice as many words per minute as a fluent scrivener (50–60 typed wpm on average and 87–95 wpm for World Champions, compared to 25–30 longhand wpm or 40–60 less legible wpm under duress), the typewriter's virtues were supreme in the preparation of simultaneous copies. Demands for efficiency from new layers of middle management reporting to home offices produced an endless belt of time-and-motion studies, schedules, wage and sales statistics, memos, and letters, which had to be copied quickly, accurately, cheaply – and cleanly.[42]

Cleanliness, brightness, and endurance were the industrial ideals of the perfect library, perfect office, perfect home, and perfect copy. Cleanliness and brightness were still being promoted in 1962 in ads for Thermo-Fax copies as "sparkling white" as eggshells. Spotlighting brightness and endurance, James River Graphics in 1981 declared that "The only mistake you'll ever make with a TECNIFAX Diazo film is when you try to distinguish it from the original. In fact, the TECNIFAX Diazo Film 'second original' is so exact you can put your original away – file it indefinitely – and use your second original for any part of the job." The original was vanishing twin to a pristine, glowing, long-lasting "second original." And as identical twin women had become the center-pieces of vanishing-twin (before-and-after) advertising, the pure twin-ship of copying would be closely identified with beaming women in white blouses.[43]

Women: who knew how to handle carbon paper so that it would not smudge or wrinkle. Whose use of Lebbeus H. Rogers's new one-sided carbon paper in typewriters supplanted the copying presses and bound letterpress books with their wetted sheets of tissue copies interspersed with protective but messy oiled paper. Whose ability to produce good clean copies simultaneously with a good clean original was, as histo-rian W.B. Proudfoot has argued, "an outstanding step in the history of copying."[44]

Women: whose costuming and copying were brightened by the in-tense aniline (coal-tar) dyes applied in the 1860s to textiles, in the 1870s to inks and to the hektograph (< Greek *hekaton*, 100, i.e., 100 copies from a single image), in the 1880s to stencil duplicators. Who could prepare stencil masters for rotary "Mimeographs" so that no extraneous marks would spoil six thousand violet copies run off at sixty a minute.[45]

Women: who learned to "strike and lift" away from the keys of the "literary piano," the typewriter, with the same celerity as at the musi-cal piano. A pianist could buzz through the *Flight of the Bumblebee* at 700 notes per minute; a touch-typing demon could clatter through 500 characters per minute of lower-case English. Adeptness at touch-typing led not only to speedier but to "cleaner" copy: left-hand margins with none of the careless or frivolous indentations of handwritten text; less underlining (less tedious back←spacing); abandonment of superscripted abbreviations (hangovers from church Latin or business Italian, such as d° for *ditto*, "the aforesaid"); regular spacing.[46]

Producing rectangular blocks of clean text, the "typewriter" with her/its carbon copies was in effect a miniature printing press, much as rotary duplicating machines were miniatures of the giant cylinder presses responsible for the splurge of newsprint by 1900. Like mass-circulation dailies, the mass of typewritten carbon and stencil copies did more than prompt the rearrangement of files from horizontal to ver-tical or the adoption of paper clips. Typewritten copies affected the very nature of expression. Because two pages of handwritten text could be fitted legibly on one single-spaced page, and because typed text seemed to occupy less territory on a plain white sheet than handwriting on the blue-tinted sheets from an office letterpress, the new copies became visual proof of expedient language, concise and collared as the shorter

sentences of modern journalism. Because stenographers taking dictation omitted most marks of punctuation, restoring them sparingly as
they transcribed at the typewriter under deadline, typed texts would
seem particularly definitive, untempered by pauses and parentheses.
Because it was awkward and time-consuming to make simultaneous corrections on a typed top sheet and its carbons, typewritten texts had
about them a special air of conclusiveness; not only did typed lines
resemble lines *set* in print, but the presence of as many as twenty back-
ing copy-sheets intimidated typists into more resolute transcription and
composition, the fewer strokes the better. Because the interval between
notes or drafts, formal transcripts, and fair duplicates was so brief, typewritten carbon and stencil copies seemed to narrow the gap between
forecast, event, and report.[47]

Efficient copying machines and strong stencil (and tracing) papers
were cultural partners to a theory of audience which projected a flaw-
less, breathless transfer from action to record. While news came hot
off the wire and copies flew from typewriter platens or mimeo cylinders, experimental psychologists were exposing the subtle motions by
which we physiologically transcribe every stimulus, such that one more
species of polygraph could be imagined – the "lie detector" whose pens
would scratch across bands of smoked paper a graph of inmost reactions,
s/t/ro/k/e/-b/y/-/s/t/r/o/k/e. *This* polygraph made of the human body
itself a working model of fair, accurate, indelible transcription.[48]

Working models intimated at an adroit transfer from prototype to
multiple. Moving beyond miniature sewing machines and electric trains,
working models took center stage in more adult arenas during the 1890s.
As girls tested the stamina of walking-talking dolls and boys screwed
together Meccano grain elevators, architects began making models that
could be used to study last-minute changes and were "an honest statement of facts which cannot mislead any one.... From such a miniature
the client can get a perfect idea of the building."[49]

Copying↔as↔reenactment, like model-building, could be instrumental. It made the One real to the Many – perhaps more real, because
cleaner, brighter, less ephemeral. Given the slavish reproduction of each
stroke and the simultaneity of transcription, typewritten pages and carbon copies were acceptable as legal documents. Paymasters sat down
to large pantographs, ten (newly reliable) fountain pens attached, and
signed five thousand paychecks an hour, further automated in 1916 by
the autopen, which reproduced s/t/r/o/k/e-/b/y/-/s/t/r/o/k/e any signature. As slaves had become Roman senators by dint of tachygraphy,
so office workers engaged in copying became invested with the power
of transforming the One into the Many. She who certainly must have
perceived the exploitation of repetitive labor would study typing and
shorthand, then hire herself out, Eleanor Marx, daughter of Karl, as a
public stenographer.[50]

As office women became "thoughtful" copying machines, and as
duplicating devices began to depend for daily upkeep upon the know-

how of women, stenography and typing were transmuted by a secretarial subculture whose status and wages for women remained relatively high until World War II. Neither typewriters nor Dictaphones nor adding machines nor Multigraph copiers de-skilled office work, for each demanded a greater versatility. Despite the ambitions of managers to simplify tasks and segment workers into single-task pools, typists and stenographers partook of that paradoxical power of individuation which acts of copying can bestow in our culture of the copy. By 1903, an "old legend" had it that you could tell apart typed pages by personal patterns of errors, the darkness of impressions, the wear of the type – a legend soon confirmed by criminologists and later by a critic of the [expletive deleted] Watergate transcripts. Similarly, it was clear by 1895 that no two stenographers long at work used the same marks; that each mark came to stand for an expanding set of words (| for "it, do, day, dollar," &c) and each stenographer used differently expanded sets; that therefore it was perilous for one veteran to transcribe the notes of another. Shorthand transcription relied upon personal vocabulary and a personal memory of the spoken context. So was reintroduced to s/t/r/o/k/e-/b/y/-/s/t/r/o/k/e copying that personal expressiveness which would seem to have been overridden in the industrial pursuit of speed, legibility, accuracy, and ease. When photocopiers took pride of place in offices, these too would be transformed into expressive media.[51]

Mooning the Machine

Photocopying, like photography, is copying→as→appropriation. It reproduces of a sudden, oblivious to the historical steps that gave rise to what lies before it.[52] Photocopying takes, as it were, without homage. Its fealty is not to matter but to light. Like the Victorian "photogram" and the engineering blueprint, photocopying bears a platonic relation to substance. Taking all in all, patently indiscriminate, it demands spotless originals, free of creases, thumb smudges, wisps of hair, any of the embarrassments of bodiliness. Copying↔as↔reenactment follows close upon anatomy; copying→as→appropriation surveys the empyrean.[53]

Electrographic copying is all the more heavenly, originating with tiny stars that appeared mysteriously in 1777 on dusty cakes of resin left carelessly uncovered. The cakes were inductors for an electrical generator in the laboratory of a thirty-five-year-old professor at the University of Göttingen, Georg Christoph Lichtenberg, who determined that the dust stars had appeared when light struck the (photoconductive) resin and electrically charged the surface. Strewing dust more thickly, he found "whole Milky Ways and greater Suns." Astronomer, physicist, mathematician, geologist, Lichtenberg was also a critic and satirist who entered lecture halls sideways, like Groucho Marx, face to the audience. He had made his name as a pundit in 1778, ridiculing four volumes on physiognomy by the Swiss Protestant mystic, poet, and doctor's son Johann Kaspar Lavater, who looked to the shapes of faces for proof of

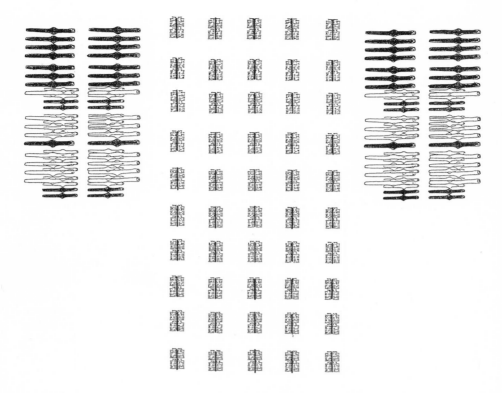

FIGURE 6.5. One sheet of a series of electrographic permutations of a wristwatch, replicated and reduced, from Wolfgang Ziemer-Chrobatzek's *Autogenese*, Cologne, 1987. Reproduced by permission.

dullness and genius, vice and virtue: the more deformed or apelike the visage, the more debased the person.[54]

Himself hunchbacked, Lichtenberg's denial of any fixed relation between bone and moral bent was understandable, or so wrote Lavater's allies. Lichtenberg did feel keenly the pain and embarrassment of his twisted, rachitic spine: "My body could have been made better by a bad artist drawing in the dark." But shyness of a figure that "laughs him to scorn" led to a scrutiny and sketching of others. Years before Lavater's *Physiognomic Fragments*, Lichtenberg prided himself on discerning qualities of mind in facial expressions, but Lavater supposed that anatomical contours followed an immutable character, and "he jumps, or rather stumbles, from similar noses to similar mental dispositions and — an unforgivable presumption — from certain deviations of the external form...to analogous changes in the soul." For Lichtenberg, character was "a very neatly constructed totality" always in motion, its expressions decided by the play of internal affect and external effect. "The whole man must move together"; superficies could change as the moment was charged. Those electrostatic images still called "Lichtenberg figures" were apposite to a life fixed not by anatomy but by personal energy and resilience.[55]

No less apposite was a severe arthritis of the spine which afflicted Chester Carlson around 1935 as he was studying reports about electrostatic images from eighteenth-century Göttingen and photoelectric effects from twentieth-century Göttingen. Even before the onset of the arthritis, Carlson had deplored his own bumbling in laboratories, his "lack of skill in manipulation of apparatus." Constant pain made him fear "the specter of total disability" from the same spinal arthritis that had crippled his father, a tubercular barber who in search of a healthier climate for himself and his consumptive wife had moved from place to place – Seattle (where Chet was born in 1906), Los Angeles, Yuma, Abuya (Mexico), San Bernardino. At fourteen Chet was the family's mainstay, working after school and summers in canneries and the testing lab of a cement plant. At seventeen his mother died; over the next three years, his father, "a bent, emaciated wreck of a man who was to spend the greater part of each day lying flat on his back, wracked by coughing spells and defeated by the world," had a breakdown: "Pa gone crazy 1924–26." Was it so unlikely that the son, at twenty-four a physics graduate of the California Institute of Technology but, in his own words, "too slow and inaccurate" for lab work, should file the basic patents for a method of copying that required no manual dexterity; that avoided "the bent and crabbed form of the scribe"; that invoked, in lieu of the bodiliness of things, the light above them?[56]

"I have an ambition," Carlson confided to a diary in 1928 while at Cal Tech. "It is to avoid attachment to worldly things and also to 'heavenly' [established religious] things.... To evolve new ideas and stimulate people with them by publishing them. I think free verse would be best." As, for example:

> And scientific lore tho' good,
> Call not religion.

This, from an Epilogue to a theme he wrote on the moralizing English poet Arthur Hugh Clough, who had considered what it meant

> To spend uncounted years of pain
> Again, again, and yet again,
> In working out in heart and brain
>   The problem of our being here....

Carlson had been reading under the guidance of Howard H. Bliss, a contemplative professor of electrical engineering. As much as he knew that he wanted to be another Edison, Chet wanted to be an artist, planned an *American Dictionary of Quacks and Fakes*, and contemplated a poem "satirizing American money worship." At ten, already aspiring to publish, he had had "a consuming desire" for a typewriter. As a teenage janitor for a printer, he used a small discarded press to print up an issue of a chemistry newsletter only to be struck "with the difficulty of getting words into hard copy." He faced parallel difficulties once out of Cal Tech and in the New York labs of Bell Telephone: How well could one hear and transcribe words over the static? Then, readying specifications for the patent department of an electrical firm, he found himself perpetually short of the requisite number of copies. Everywhere, in his reading and printing, his ache to expose imposture, his testing of telephones and vetting of data, he came up against problems of transcription and duplication.[57]

Fast, clean, true, painless copies resonated with the life Carlson meant to pursue above the body. In his second marriage and, really, his second life, after electrostatic photocopying was baptized xerography (< Greek, "dry writing"), Carlson would fund pathways East and West to explore the incorporeal imaging of bodies and transcendental publishing of thoughts. He subsidized American Zen Buddhism, J.B. Rhine's laboratory on ExtraSensory Perception at Duke University, programs of the American Society for Psychical Research, the Shanti Foundation's study of auras, interviews on out-of-body and near-death experiences. He who listed in a 1932 notebook under "Invention Wanted" one process after another for painless transcription and faithful duplication – a new method of color photography, a faster way to animate cartoons, a better facsimile receiver – wrote in 1961 to a poltergeist-minded friend that in his own house in Pittsford, New York (thirty miles from the house in which the Fox Sisters first heard spirit-rapping in 1848), he had been witness to "spontaneous pk [psychokinesis]" for some years. "Occasionally a rap will occur at a time as if to emphasize a thought one of us has had, or a statement just made or read. At other times it seems to be a call to duty, particularly when it is time to go and meditate."[58]

Two years later he was meditating upon an "electrodynamic theory of life – electric field charges at or near surfaces of living beings" which changed under the impress of emotions in a sort of biophysical xerography, so he supported biophysical research. In 1965 he clipped an article on "Extrasensory electroencephalographic induction between identical twins," as if their immaterial bond might provide another clue to true painless copying for an only child who "for many years ... was close to being a scientific materialist." In 1967 he confessed, "I want a theory of psi but am baffled as to how to proceed except by relating it somehow to my crude ideas of sensory perception."[59]

Problems of transcription yet again. For Carlson, psi was shadow energy to the charged plate of earthly existence, and he, like psi, still needed grounding. He seemed to be making the xerographic principles of light, conductivity, charge, and imprint into hypotheses of a higher-order life. Vice versa, xerography could reflect a higher-order transcription, its metamorphosis of light into charge into image into record akin to the metempsychosis of spirit from one body to the next.

Am I making too much of this? Lichtenberg, playing upon his name ("Light mountain"), took as pseudonym its Greek synonym, Photorin, when attacking Lavater's arrogant attempts to convert the Jewish philosopher Moses Mendelssohn to Christianity. In aphorisms and essays, Lichtenberg stood against any bullying confidence in received Truth, religious or scientific: "I see such hypotheses in physics as nothing else but convenient *pictures* that facilitate the conception of the whole." Kierkegaard, Nietzsche, and Wittgenstein would applaud his stance. Freud, who read his work "with great delight," cited Lichtenberg in regard to slips of tongue and the compoundedness of motives. Subconscious images became manifest through Freudian analysis much as Lichtenberg figures come to light in the dirt on charged surfaces. "Only this is gain," wrote Lichtenberg: "To make *latent* things *sensible*."[60]

Nearly two centuries pass, and Carlson appears to take "psi" as totem both for the xerographic process and for the One World program he supported through the United Nations. "Psi" implied the potential unity of minds. It implied, too, a universe of latent images waiting to be dusted with a metaphysical lycopodium as Carlson (in a kitchen behind a beauty parlor above a bar & grill) had dusted the sulfured surface of a zinc plate with powdered spores of moss to reveal the markings of a celluloid ruler and a date inked on a glass slide, "10-22-38 ASTORIA." In this our culture of copying, where copies sustain the fabric of lives, those emotions and notions which led Carlson to xerography were little distant from his political and spiritual devotions.[61]

Born in 1906, like Carlson, but on the other side of the country and down the road from Eastman Kodak, was a firm formed to manufacture photographic papers prepared with haloid salts. By the 1930s the Haloid Corporation's "Copylite" and "Record" photocopying papers were so profitable that Haloid could buy up its Rochester neighbor, the Rectigraph Company, producers of a camera that transferred text or art directly onto their papers. Rectigraph had been founded, also in 1906, by a man employed at handcopying real estate documents executed in quadruplicate. "It was the tiring, painstaking drudgery of endless making of abstracts which caused [George C.] Beidler to wonder whether some quicker, accurate means of copying legal documents could not be found," explained a Rectigraph brochure. "In 1903 the answer came to him – photography!... No other copy could be as fast – for nothing is as fast as light." His photostat camera succeeded, but Rectigraph remained small despite testimonials from Los Angeles city engineers, who did 41,179 Rectigraphic copies in one year. During World War II, Rectigraph in tow, Haloid throve as a supplier of cameras and camera papers for photo-reconnaissance. In 1945, facing retrenchment and casting about for other products, the company chanced on a Kodak abstract of an article about electrophotographic copies made by Chester Carlson, with whom Haloid would soon share the light of a revelation and a revolution.[62]

That's hype. The revolution in copying, taken broadly, had begun in the 1920s, when copying was already in the air. In the airwaves – as the Radio Corporation of America in 1926 began transatlantic radio facsimile service for transmitting news photos. In the rarefied air of national libraries and archives – as the Library of Congress, British Library, and Bibliothèque Nationale used photostat cameras to acquire rare materials or create catalogs, and as scholars and curators microfilmed manuscripts for research or preservation. In the most rarefied air, out past Saturn, around that new planet, Pluto, located in 1930 near the star δ-Geminorum, close upon the stars named Castor and Pollux – where the A.B. Dick Company of Chicago saw "NEW WORLDS TO CONQUER" for their Mimeograph machine: "Anything that can be written, typewritten or drawn in line, it reproduces at the rate of thousands every hour."[63]

Thousands an hour were needed, especially in the U.S., as the New Deal multiplied regulations and federal agencies filed millions of mimeo'd memos. The Works Progress Administration, aided by historical and genealogical societies, set bands of citizens to copying colonial records. A century before, starting in 1833, Peter Force had paid pen-and-ink copyists to transcribe manuscripts for a documentary history of the American Revolution. In 1933 the copyists used typewriters and carbon paper, Hunter Electro Copyist machines ("Now ANYONE can make Fast TRUE COPIES of Important Documents"), photostat and Lumastat cameras. Now ANYONE could, and many did, produce not merely transcripts but facsmiles ("no chance of error in LUMASTAT facsimiles – every copy is an EXACT photographic print of the original"). Intermediate between copying↔as↔reenactment and copying→as→appropriation were popular gelatin duplicators – in America, the Mimeograph, the Speedograph, the Ditto; in England and France the Gestetner Neo-Cyclostyle; in Germany the Roto. These had demanded a complex stencil master; simplified, they too gave the impression that anything could, and everything should, be duplicated. "The Original Writing says do it!" said Ditto, Inc., in 1935, but "The Copy gets it done – Orders filled, Instructions carried out, Statements analyzed, Salesmen inspired, Records kept."[64]

At one hundred copies a minute, "No longer need live facts lie buried for want of an easy, quick method of reproduction." The Ditto motto: One Writing. The Ditto method: Reincarnation. At 5¢ a hundred copies, who could afford not to d°? Prof. Robert C. Binkley, charged by the Social Science Research Council with reviewing all office reproduction devices, wrote in 1937, "When books and papers can be copied in this price level, the result is to make all records of civilization mobile to a degree that could not otherwise be imagined."[65]

An equally momentous result was to make it seem that the appropriation of entire texts was of itself an intellectual assimilation. The speed, volume, and sheer habit of copying photochemically, as prevalent in Nazi Berlin and Conservative London as in New Deal Washington, encouraged the illusion that to copy was to comprehend. Did the American researcher who returned with 80,000 microfilmed documents after a summer's descent upon Europe around 1935 ever read those documents, or had duplicative edacity become self-deception? Medieval monks had gained at least a familiarity with scripture when copying texts at 4700–5500 characters a day. Office copyists in 1917, held to a standard of two typewritten lines (100 characters) per minute, reproduced perhaps 48,000 characters each day and scarcely remembered what passed before their eyes. Scholars running off Lumastats of ENTIRETIES at one page every four minutes, could copy up to 288,000 characters in eight hours and be beguiled into thinking they had assimilated texts when they had only, if grandly, appropriated them at sixty times the pace of a scribe. Prof. Marcus W. Jernegan, researching the emigration to colonial North America, photostated every pertinent archival document in Europe and America, then filed these along the walls of his office at the University of Chicago. He never wrote his book, never read many of the 'stats, but the history was *there*, wasn't it? Lovingly shown the walls of files by a feeble Jernegan in 1946, historian Edmund S. Morgan has since made it a rule "never to xerox anything until after I have read it and after I have taken notes on it. Otherwise the xeroxed material, copied in full because it seemed at a glance to be so crucial, never gets full attention."[66]

"Xerox," as the Corporation has been apt to protest (hoping to keep the word from becoming as generic as kleenex), is not a verb. But "xeroxed" *has* become a participle, "to xerox" an infinitive, symptoms of the power of copying→as→appropriation to confuse the object with the act, copy (*n.*) with copy (*v.*). The more instantaneous the copy, the more complete the confusion. The electrostatic process which Carlson was inclined to interpret as a prototype for spectral transcriptions between spirit and matter inclines the rest of us to believe in copies as both actors and subjects. "From Original to multiple copies in 3 minutes" was more than a slogan for the Haloid xerographic copier of 1953; it was a decree of eminent domain.[67]

What happened with Carlson's copier happened also and in parallel with Land's camera. Though born on opposite edges of the continent to opposite sides of the social spectrum, Carlson and Edwin Herbert Land (b. 1909) had both decided to be inventors by the time they entered university (Carlson at Cal Tech, 1928–30; Land at Harvard, 1926, 1929–32). They had sat in the New York Public Library paging through scientific journals (Land 1927–28, Carlson 1935–38). Development of their camera and copier began during World War II (Land's "one-step dry photographic process" with his Polaroid Corporation, Cambridge, 1943; Carlson's "dry-picture" copying process, with the Battelle Memorial Institute, Columbus, Ohio, 1944). These were financed after the war by firms that had prospered with instruments and materials for aerial reconnaissance (Polaroid's vectography for three-dimensional images that could expose camouflaged sites, Haloid's enlarging camera). Working models were first presented to the Optical Society of America, by Land in February 1947, Carlson in October 1948, where Land's camera *made* dry sepia pictures in a minute, Carlson's *made* black-and-white copies in two. Land, for demonstration, *took* a series of self-portraits; Carlson *took* engineering schematics.[68]

Which was it – *making* or *taking*? At the 1948 debut, Haloid's president predicted that "the stenographer of the future will not have to make carbon copies.... [She will] simply type the original, slip it into a xerocopying machine, set the dial to the desired number of copies, push a button." Land, after his 1947 debut, wrote that photographers now could "think of the art in the taking and not in making photographs." Instant copier and instant camera so sped up (and disguised) the steps of wholesale transcription that you seemed to take and make at two and the same time. Like the instant copy, the instant photo had a halo of instant absorption. In the postwar consumer-driven economy, instant copier and instant camera were proofs positive that perception was apperception, that to see was to grasp.[69]

Land told his staff that they were developing a camera "for the mothers of America," by which he meant inept females as impatient with f-stops and shutter speeds as with the long delay for processing. This was a doubly peculiar statement, for like the bumbling Carlson who "in desperation" hired an engineer (Otto Kornei) to prepare the plates for his 1938 experiments, Land from the start had hired others to do his labwork. Moreover, Land's projects were regularly staffed and headed by adroit women – Emily Wheelwright, Eudoxia Muller, Meroë Morse, Lucretia Weed, Nan Buddy, Caroline Hunter – women whom Land trained and trusted, as he had trained and then married Helen Maislen.[70]

Haloid's "Manhattan Project" for xerography had enlisted thirteen males and just one female, but the new copier was also to land in the hands of duennas of reproduction. "Over my dead body – it's our last copy!" exclaims a secretary in a striped dress belted at the waist, pad and pencil in her right hand, arms outstretched to protect sixteen cabinets of carbons. This Kodak ad offered a "free copy" of the booklet *How I Learned the Verifax of Life*, so we can be pretty sure that rapid reproduction was being offered as an escape from rape by the copywriters for the 1957 Signet Copier. The Verifax of Life were that an original could remain intact if women with loops of costume pearls at V-necks could run off with cheerful promiscuity "5 copies in 1 minute for 2½¢ each." An orgasmically smiling woman, her eyes closed, urgently extends herself – and a four-second copy – between a 3-M "Secretary" Thermo-Fax copier and her boss's desk. Below, "The Thermo-Fax Copying Machine Story" of 1956 is a four-frame filmstrip: "← ... in / ← and / → out / in 4 seconds." Sing that body electric: a joyous secretary in a tight sweater-blouse and tight skirt, right palm to her cheek in amazed rapture, stands behind a Xerox 914 copier, holding in her left hand a Lincoln penny that makes up the economical **o** of the headline: "makes copies on ordinary paper." The ordinary was then, of course, extraordinary; the copier itself was as omnific as Old Abe: "Copies in seconds anything written, typed, printed, stamped, or drawn...Copies often look better than the original."[71]

With the Xerox 914, introduced in 1960, xerography became at once commonplace and extraordinary. Despite the improvement of the technology by the substitution of selenium (< Greek, "moon") for sulfur as photoconductor and the use of corona discharges to produce the electrostatic image, xerographic copiers had been user-unfriendly. The Model A of 1950 demanded 12–14 manual operations for each copy and a week's training to achieve consistently clean images. If xerography had no imitators in its ability to reproduce thick- or thin-paper documents of various inks, its competition during the '50s was hardly out of the picture. Reflex contact processes (where light is shone through sensitized paper, then reflected back onto the copy paper by the white areas of the original document), known since 1839, were so improved that 3-M's Thermo-Fax machines were faster, cheaper, and more compact than the Model A. So also were gelatin-process Verifax machines and the Apeco, Copycat, and Duplomat machines using a silver diffusion transfer process. As late as 1955, Chester Carlson was still making carbon copies of his own letters.[72]

Crumpled, dirty, the used sheet of carbon paper on the left-hand side of a two-page advertisement was the Before: "This was the beginning of office copying." Spare of line, the Xerox 914 copier stood alone in a field of white on the right: "This is the end." The After world: "The 914 makes permanent copies on ordinary paper. Your great grandchildren will be able to read Xerox copies." Resurrection: "The 914 is a dry machine. Bone dry." Last Judgment: "Adjustments for light and dark originals? There aren't any." Second Coming: "Turn the knob past '15' and the copies will keep coming until you return and say stop." New Jerusalem: leased, not sold, and weighing 648 pounds, "That means you'll have to come to *our* offices.... (People representing thousands of organizations, from United States Steel to the White House, are glad they made the trip. You will be, too.)" Eternal Gospel: "This is the end. At least for the time being."[73]

Omega, & alpha. At the end of the Eisenhower era and the emergence of John F. Kennedy's New Frontier, the Haloid Xerox Corporation projected the end as the beginning. On TV spots in 1961, a man handed a document to a six-year-old girl who skipped over to a Xerox 914, pressed a button, waited ten seconds, and skipped happily back with a copy. In 1965 appeared the Xerox 2400, capable of 2400 images an hour, 40 pages each minute, almost one copy a second. By 1971, some 24,000,000,000 pages were being "xeroxed" each year in the U.S. alone; by 1979, perhaps 90,000,000,000, with worldwide revenue for the copying-machine industry pegged higher than that from moviemaking; by 1986, 234,000,000,000. Most of these billions (worldwide, trillions) of pages were being copied not by little girls but by working women who were and are the secretaries, the copy-room clerks, the managers or owners of retail copy shops.[74]

High-speed plain-paper copiers, voiding the office manager's distinction between copying (directly from an original) and duplicating (through impressions from intermediate plates or masters), gave women guardianship of a medium that undermined any hard-and-slow difference between transcription and publication. The pantograph, gushed Benjamin Latrobe in 1805, "never betrays the confidences it receives, for though it *repeats* every thing entrusted to it, it never publishes a hint of its master's secrets, and in this respect sets an example not always followed by confidential clerks." The typewriter, wrote Elizabeth Waddell in 1916, could be a seductively private secretary: "You can certainly tell it things you wouldn't tell an amanuensis." The Mimeograph, pledged the A.B. Dick Company in 1930, "requires no trained operator, and it assures privacy for confidential work." Mimeo and Ditto did, however, become tools for labor organizers in the 1930s and student protesters in the 1960s; the dry-writing of xerography would be tinder to *The Pentagon Papers* of 1972. From the 1960s on, ads for copiers rarely bespoke privacy; even a cloistered monk now held in his arms a stack of xeroxes. In 1989, the Soviet Ministry of Interior Affairs, *glasnost*algic but also finding it impossible in an age of faxes and computers to keep the lid on copying, announced that after forty years it was removing the double locks from the steel doors barring access to *kseroks* machines, which had been used surreptitiously for *samisdat* or "self-published" criticism of the regime.[75]

Access to leased Xerox copiers or, after 1968, to the plain-paper (portable, privately affordable) copiers manufactured by Canon, would enable "all men to become publishers," pronounced that guru of communications, Marshall McLuhan. But it was women in particular who found their voices therein, beginning in the 1950s with the artist Toni Linowitz, wife to Sol, general counsel for Haloid Xerox. Sonia Sheridan of Chicago's Art Institute, having collaborated on 3-M's 1968 Color-in-Color copier, conducted the first course in copy art in 1970. Louise Odes Neaderland, trained in printmaking and photography, one day in 1972 at the Women's Studio Workshop in New York "just happened to put my photo of a High Falls diver on the Xerox machine, and realized I had found my true art form" – an art of unique grays and saturated blacks, of tantalizing distortions from a shallow depth of field, and of intriguing immediacy in the (de)generation of images; in 1982 she founded the International Society of Copier Artists, the majority of whom are women. Pati Hill collected everyday objects in a laundry hamper then let them fall as they might across a Xerox window for mysterious two-dimensional images; her work was featured in 1975 in the first gallery show of copier art.[76]

"Mail artists," it is true, mostly male, had been using xerography to create sheets of fanciful stamps for artistic and political purposes ever since the advent of the Xerox 914. It was Ken (Anderson), Wolfgang

(Reitherman), Hamilton (Luske), and Clyde (Geronimi) who used xerography to facilitate the 450,000 drawings required for that animated Disney epic of replication, *101 Dalmatians* (1961). It was Jürgen (Olbrich) in Germany who collected discarded copies (mis-taken impressions) as exemplary of the multiple surprises of xerography. It was Christian (Rigal) who thought to preserve two thousand quixotic works of copy art by founding, with the Universidad de Castilla–La Mancha, an International Museum of Electrography in Cuenca, Spain, in 1990.[77]

And, true, it was the male artist Timm Ulrichs who in 1967 wittily "reprographed" one hundred (de)generations of the original 1936 title-page of "The Work of Art in the Age of Mechanical Reproduction," a repeatedly cited essay by Walter Benjamin, the German-Jewish literary philosopher who died in 1940. Contemplating the culture of the copy from his library of first editions, Benjamin the collector (for whom "not only books but copies of books have their fates") proposed that mass-produced texts were dislodging the authority of original manuscripts to the same serious extent that photographic reproductions were dissolving the aura of original works of visual art. Finding authenticity and power in multiples, such that "Every day the urge grows stronger to get hold of an object at very close range by way of its likeness, its reproduction," the masses might liberate themselves from outmoded industrial relations as they sloughed off a ritualistic (and now suspiciously fascist) aesthetic tradition of uniqueness and genius. But he to whom "the acquisition of an old book is its rebirth" did admit the childlikeness of his own faith in reanimation, and what must here pique our curiosity is the degree to which Benjamin's life, like the lives of Carlson and Lichtenberg, was haunted by the figure of a hunchback.[78]

Benjamin's *bucklicht Männlein*, hunchbacked little fellow, was a folk scapegrace blamed for the clumsiness of a child who spills wine, topples a lamp. This German "Mr. Bungle" appeared in 1930 in the last chapter of *A Berlin Childhood around 1900* as summary figure of Benjamin's youth, awkward and myopic; he reappeared in the first lines of Benjamin's last major essay, the "Theses on the Philosophy of History," written in response to the start of World War II. There, a *buckliger Zwerg*, a hunchbacked dwarf, is seen to be the (hidden) chessmaster guiding the moves of a Turkish (false) automaton. One must not be lulled or gulled into amazement at the machinery of history, wrote Benjamin; rather, one must embrace the emergency of event, "For every image of the past that is not recognized by the present as one of its own concerns threatens to disappear irretrievably." The hunchback recalls to us, and recalls us to, a life needfully contingent.[79]

Effective historical understanding was photoconductive: "It means to seize hold of a memory *as it flashes up* at a moment of danger." Had he known of the electrographic experiments by Paul Selenyi in Budapest in the 1930s as well as he knew the experimental Marxism of the Hungarian György Lukács, would Benjamin have seen in my flashing italics the parallels between his method of historical attentiveness and the new methods of capturing the instant? Benjamin in 1932 did write a playlet during which researchers from the Moon hear testimony from Lichtenberg that he alone of all Terrans, true philosopher, is no puppet to Fortune, so can see clearly the state of the Earth. Like Lichtenberg, who proposed an archive of children's early attempts at writing and who in his own writing sought "Brevity with force and thunder after the flash," Benjamin was a gatherer of sparks and shaper of aphorisms, ambitious to publish a book composed solely of striking quotations. Like Lichtenberg the sketch artist, Benjamin the strolling observer regarded physiognomy as a precious mode of insight: "Sudden shifts of power such as are now overdue in our society," he wrote in 1931, "can make the ability to read facial types a matter of vital importance." Like Lichtenberg, Benjamin walked with a stoop. "I don't think I ever saw him walk erect with his head held high," said a friend. "There was something unmistakable, deliberate, and groping about his walk, probably due at least in part to his nearsightedness."[80]

Can we blindly let pass these striking likenesses? Was it happenstance that our foremost theorist of the copy and our progenitors of the modern copier should each be haunted by a bent spine and stumbling body? That each should dismiss the plodding additiveness of event in favor of the flash of history that for Lichtenberg was the passage of spirit across the planes of the face, for Carlson the transfer of energy from a physical to a spiritual plane, and for Benjamin a plain "shot through with chips of Messianic time"?[81]

Or might we gingerly take the bearings of Lichtenberg, Carlson, and Benjamin as indicative of the way in which Western men have approached copying? How copying must transcend the little hunchback, his strange gait, his lack of prospect, his deformation. How the act of copying must be elevated to an empyrean perspective – Lichtenberg at his window sketching faces in the street below, Carlson calculating time in "microcenturies" (52.8 minutes), Benjamin excited by the vertiginous motion picture and bird's-eye views of the "masses." How copying as a political act of appropriation, taking all-in-all, is also an eschatological program "to double our witness, and wait."[82]

Perhaps, then, we can apprehend the sadness in so many works by male copy artists, who battle to make the copier an instrument of total salvation and arrive so often at absence, nowhere moreso than in George Mühleck's utterly black works, *Copy of the Moon* and *Copy of the Stars*, the copier's glass left open to night skies. Whether degrading an image beyond recognition, as in Wolfgang Ziemer-Chrobatzek's 1987 sequences of detached watchbands, or blowing an image out of all proportion, as in Céjar's 144-meter-long tape measure laid along the Great Gallery of the Louvre in 1982, the works seem exhausted by their bodiliness, the artists less proud of the resultant image than of their struggle with the machine to realize it. "And so I hang in the world suspended...between the most spiritual vistas and the most sensual feelings," wrote Lichtenberg the hypochondriac, "and stagger from those into these until after a short struggle my twofold self will come to rest some future time, and I shall, totally divided, rot here and evaporate into a pure life there." Jakobois may photocopy his genitals, David Secter may film a couple making love atop the glass of a flashing copier, but these are unconsummated acts of reproduction whose titles tell us as much: "Desperate Art," "Blow Dry." Joseph Kadar and James Durand may tackle the insides of (mal)functioning machines to obtain unique refractions from the light within, as if the photocopier were the Source of singularity, yet their work seems driven by an obsessive desire to match wits with the soul of the machine, that Benjamite hunchback hidden from sight by a system of mirrors.[83]

For women artists, the photocopier is not a self-defeating or melancholic device, nor is it an autocratic presence holding them to its "planimetric universe." Rather, it is a companion bright with surprises, much like the alchemist's Philosopher's Stone, capable not only of multiplying what lies upon it, but also of purifying that which is the object of its projections. Taking *and* making, women copy artists have looked to electrographics for a new embodiment, not disembodiment. "It repeats my words perfectly as many times as I ask it to," says Pati Hill, "but when I show it a hair curler it hands me back a space ship, and when I show it the inside of a straw hat it describes the eerie joys of a descent into a volcano." The photocopier becomes a partner in a happy personal exploration, the color copier in particular, for its "color is expressive, not imitative," and with it Connie Fox can discover a new beauty to oil cans and whisk brooms. Women have used the photocopier's capacity for appropriation less to lay claim to uniqueness than to celebrate multiple identities, as in the cards exposed in Sarah (and Seth) Shulman's *Xerox Wallet* (1987), or to question identities imposed, as in Margareth Dunham Maciel's *Enregistrement* ("Registration," 1975), which advances from a birth certificate to the microphotographed cells of the Margareth for whom the certificate stands. The higher truth sought by men trying to elude the hunchback becomes, for Claude Torey, an other truth, images from *la machine-mère*, the machine-matrix, as she presses parts of her body to its face and returns with unforeseen images of herself, freed from traditional representations of the female body.[84]

Copied face down (until recently), the shapes or pages reproduced by a photocopier have come, as it were, from the dark side of the moon. "It is the side of your subject that you do *not* see that is reproduced," observed Hill. The photocopier takes life-size but unexpected portraits, and "I would prefer," she wrote, "that the original of my work have no value." Conclusion to an historical process: the original as vanishing twin.[85]

After-words, After-images: Statutes of Imitation
The Verdict in 1982 swung between the virtue of a copy and its dark twin, the original. Attorney Paul Newman's case on behalf of a woman rendered comatose from botched surgery comes down to the admis-

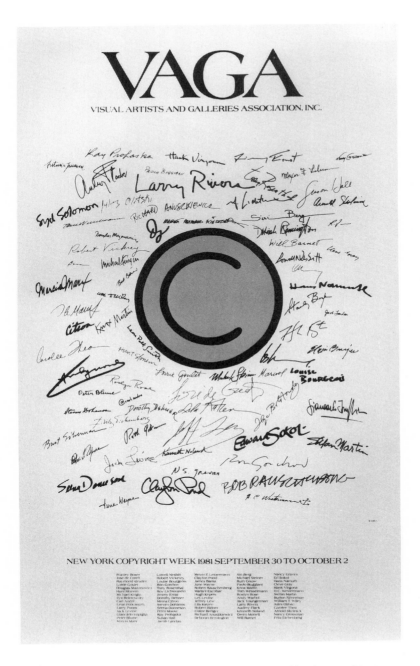

FIGURE 6.6. Poster, 1981, signed by the artists represented by the Visual Artists and Galleries Association, Inc., New York, with the international copyright symbol at the center. Reproduced courtesy of VAGA, which labors to protect its artists from unauthorized use or piracy of their works of art, and to inform the public about artists' rights.

sibility of a photocopy of an intake sheet that a frightened but ethical nurse had made before obeying orders to alter it. At law, an original takes precedence over a copy; to the jury in the film, as now in copy art and the copyhold of our hearts, the intact copy takes precedence over originals.[86]

Subversive as are high-speed plain-paper copiers of the absolute ranking of original over duplicate, so they subvert the the absolutism of copyright. In 1934, American librarians were already anxious about the legal ramifications of photocopiers. It was suggested that there be a test case involving the copying of a large part of a copyrighted work

1. By longhand by a scholar for his own use;
2. By the scholar with a camera, for d°;
3. By typist/stenographers hired by the scholar, for d°;
4. By camera by an adjunct hired by the scholar, for d°;
5. By a copyist, for others too, not d°,

and so on, effectively rehearsing the entire history of copying. When did one cross over from transcription to publication, from innocent remaking to disingenuous taking?[87]

Copyright law is neither natural nor universal. First formalized in England in 1709, it was still being resisted by China in the 1970s. An Englishman was bemused in 1903 by the attitude of the Chinese, to whom copyright law "was but the haggling of the harlot over the price of shame." For a Chinese writer, "If his views are copied out and passed around, he is delighted.... If they are seized upon, printed, and scattered to the furthest corners of the Empire, he folds his hands and dies triumphant. He has said what was in him to say, and men have listened."[88]

Since copyright law always lags behind the technologies of copying, it can seem as hoary to Westerners as it is incomprehensible to the Balinese and whorish to Confucians. Its warrant derives from a wager that writers or artists will be discouraged from their efforts if society does not vouchsafe their works. This wager is less about uniqueness or plagiarism than about insecurity. For Anglo-American jurisprudence, the insecurity has been economic, the loss of investments of time and prospects of income from the sale of a physical property. In 1774, as the law was being adjusted after a spate of conflicts among publishers, Catharine Macaulay wrote sardonically against those who, in the name of the free spread of ideas, would reserve to (starving) writers a sole reward, fame: "authors, it seems, are beings of a very high order, and infinitely above the low considerations of the useful, the convenient, and the necessary!" While English courts affirmed written work as private investment property, continental courts were confirming the enduring moral rights of authors, so had to confront spiritual and aesthetic insecurity – the tampering with a work expressive of an individual's spirit. At issue either way was, and is, the assertiveness of a personal signature in societies that thrive upon multiples but disparage imitation. "In a religious sense," wrote Barbara Ringer of the Library of Congress in 1974, "it is man's creative acts that bring him closest to the godhead, and it is precisely these acts that copyright is concerned with."[89]

Sacred or profane, copyright law must handle the politics of what happens when the One becomes the Many. "Why are we all socialists where [the author] is concerned?" asked one bellettrist in 1900. "The answer is easy. It lies in the fact of Publication; for what is publication but an invitation to enter and enjoy?" Moreover, "Property which has to be published and can be reprinted is indeed no property at all and never has been so regarded." As history, this was off; as signpost to the easy trespasses of our culture, in which copying is ever faster and cheaper and more public, it was right on.[90]

Socialists and Situationists, on the copyLeft, have held that the benefits of easy, timely, communal access outweigh an individual's need to profit from the (re)circulation of a text. Marxists have disputed the commodification of ideas which copyright-as-property-law indulges. "Developing" countries have resented the monopoly on information; to enforce foreign copyrights would be to serve as sheriff for "developed" powers, to perpetuate colonial tyranny, or at a minimum to collude in a scale of prices that mocks the common people. This last was the position of one developing nation, the United States of America, which with Russia and China rejected the Berne Copyright Convention of 1886 – and would not be in full accord until the 1990s.[91]

CopyCentrists like the French novelist Emile Zola have been willing to agree that "the great artists and the great writers would be unworthy of having been elected to glory if they did not consent to shine for the whole world like the sun" and should not take shelter under the umbrella of copyright law, so long as "our present capitalistic society be suppressed and replaced by the socialistic or anarchistic society"; until then, we must protect the creations of artists and writers.[92]

CopyRightists – like the publishers Williams & Wilkins, who sued the National Library of Medicine for freely providing thousands of photocopies of journal articles to its patrons, and writers' unions like the 1893 Congress of Authors or 1993 PEN International – fear that sales will be softened and context lost through our habit of piecemeal copying. They imprint on the verso of title pages increasingly complex warnings against piracy, similar to the anathemata in medieval manuscripts cursing sloppy copyists and to the INTERDIGITUR of early typeset books warning against infringement of exclusive printing privileges.[93]

Back in 1934, the Joint Committee on Materials for Research, representing U.S. scholars, reached a gentlemen's agreement with the National Association of Book Publishers that "a library can make a photographic reproduction of a part of a copyrighted book for a scholar, if the scholar represents in writing that he wishes to have the reproduction made in lieu of a loan or in place of manual transcription and solely for purposes of research." Photocopiers were stand-ins for scribes, nothing more. But, as we all know, photocopiers entice us to copy texts we would otherwise blanch at transcribing, entreat us to make second copies (just in case), and encourage us to copy artwork we could never manage by hand. The agreement ignored the addictive, transformative, ungentlemanly nature of copying in our culture of the copy.[94]

Put into triple jeopardy by other magnificent copying machines – the computer, digital scanner, and color printer – copyright law now finds itself defending distinctions irreconcilable with the new electronic media. Lawyers shoring up copyright briefs for software, algorithms, neural networks, or databases conflate private monopoly with public good, market economy with moral economy, signature with social imprint. The more incorporeal or contingent an original, the more often copyright will be ambushed between a painstaking s/t/r/o/k/e/-/b/y/ -/s/t/r/o/k/e reenactment and the immediacy of electronic appropriation. Medieval scribes knew each line of text, as do their remnant, music copyists who still dip steel nibs into ink bottles to copy four or five pages (40–50 staves) an hour on heavy paper that will not flop off a music stand. Copyshop attendants are scantly aware of what they are copying at 135 copies per minute with the Xerox 5090 Duplicator; word processors (the *people*, not the machines) lose sight of the very act of copying when with a single stroke they SAVE TO DISK. Copyright law intends the circle around its © to be an embrace and an enclosure, rewarding the creatrix and protecting the copies; but when copying is second nature, that circle comes to resemble a snake devouring its own tail.[95]

Novelist John Hersey, sitting on the U.S. National Commission on New Technological Uses of Copyrighted Works, protested in 1979 against a majority decision granting copyright to computer programs, which are sets of instructions to a machine *and* systems for dialogue with human beings. The decision, said Hersey, in principle equated humans to machines as species of information-processing systems and, in the long run, would diminish "those aspects of the human spirit which can never be fully quantified...courage, love, integrity, trust, the touch of flesh, the fire of intuition, the yearning and aspirations of what poets so vaguely but persistently call the soul." Since one begins by copying a program into the computer, and since computers shine at the swift making of copies, would we not be led irrevocably to confuse the act of creation with the act of copying? A writer of documentary novels, Hersey was guarding that border between fiction and transcription around which he had made an estimable career. He was arguing that computers copy by rote, not by right, what they are given byte by byte, and can no wise appropriate the ENTIRETY that is self-reflexive Homo faber.[96]

Ah, but our neurophysiologists, philosophers, and pandits more and more frequently equate the computer's binary acquisition of data with processes of human memory and learning. The metaphors of machine reasoning and computer linkage have become our own: our brains are parallel processors, our thinking is signal processing, our lives are databanks, and we need "downtime." In the company of laser copiers, faxes, and scanners, we are drawn to assume that what we copy instantly we know intimately.[97]

Creation and imitation, invention and repetition may become as indistinct as knowing is from copying. A number of artists in the 1980s contended that copying *is* assimilation, reenactment *is* appropriation, appropriation *is* creation. In works more ideologically potent than emotionally moving, they alleged that willy-nilly we move within a cosmos of recycled words, cysts of images. What therefore we make of the world is bound to be quotation, unavoidable if unwitting trespasses upon copyright. To quote is by definition to use out of original context, so copyright is a presumptuous assertion of the right to control what is, philosophically, uncontrollable. Fighting rearguard actions against such anarchy, the courts have severely restricted "fair use" of quotations, advantaging the claimants to (obsolete though momentarily privileged) property rights in words scribbled or printed, but the courts themselves flounder when asked to restrict the use of images which have become such icons (Mickey Mouse, Marilyn Monroe) that freedom of expression demands liberal access to them. We have thus the irony of the executors of the Warhol Estate announcing in 1988 that they will prosecute anyone stealing Andy's images, when it was Andy who pioneered the transfer of others' photographs to his silkscreen canvases, Andy who "infringed the copyrights of everything and everybody," and Andy whose methods underlay, for example, the use of Arnold Newman's photograph of Picasso in Larry Rivers's *Homage to Picasso* (1974). "I didn't even use the whole thing," said Rivers, "only across the forehead and down to the nose. The rest is drawn in. It's like a quote, that's all. He says I didn't give him credit. Where am I supposed to put the credit? On the bottom? 'Eyes by Arnold Newman'?" Art in this context is a Kafkaesque vaudeville of one-liners: like jokes, images float through our culture with blustery anonymity, jerked loose from whatever moorings they have within museum galleries, magazine racks, slide libraries.[98]

Slides, video documentaries, art magazines, advertisements, artbooks – all differently untrue to the hues, textures, and proportions of artistic masterpieces – have conditioned the ideas of "appropriationist" artists. Like most of us, their familiarity with Great Art was originally through discrepant reproductions, wherefore David Salle would locate his originality "outside this question of personal 'style.'... Put simply, the originality is in what you choose" to borrow. He was sued by two artists for choosing to borrow from one of their collaborative drawings, itself based on another man's Pulitzer Prize–winning photograph. When Sherrie Levine in 1979–81 photographed reproductions of the photographs of Edward Weston, signed her name to them, captioned them "After Edward Weston," and displayed them in a gallery, she was having fun with our mounting confusion of reenactment with appropriation. Her "After" was a woman's cackling homage to the Western canon, but it was also on the verge of violating copyright – the statutory right of Weston's heirs to profit from copies of his signed photographs, and the moral right to have one's photographs protected from mutilation. Levine's re-photographs "by" Edward Weston, Eliot Porter, and Walker Evans were provocations; her re-drawing and re-painting "after" art-book reproductions of the drawings and paintings of Leger, Mondrian, and Schiele were, she explained, "distillations" emptied of that "male desire" which infests Western art: "Succeeding the painting the plagiarist no longer bears with him passions, humors, feelings, impressions, but rather this immense encyclopedia from which he draws." Or *she* draws, as did Elaine Sturtevant, from works by Marcel Duchamp, Roy Lichtenstein, Andy Warhol, on an identical scale. "People will say that [my] work looks better than the original. Then I say," says Sturtevant, "that's totally wrong, it's not supposed to be better." No?[99]

Let this be said another way: "Originality is not the urge to be different from others, to produce the brand new; it is to grasp (in the etymological sense) the original, the roots of both ourselves and things." I am quoting from William Morrow quoting Nick Waterlow quoting Herbert Read quoting Max Raphael. Quotation at the fourth remove is as common in painting as in criticism. "The pictures I make are really ghosts of ghosts; their relationship to the original images is tertiary, i.e., three or four times removed," said Levine, M.F.A. in photo-printmaking who worked first in advertising, where, "If [artists] wanted an image, they'd just take it.... There was no sense that images belonged to anybody; all images were in the public domain and as an artist I found that very liberating." Making *as* taking.[100]

Without closure, philosophers, historians, and connoisseurs have debated the moral and aesthetic problems of the "After" as

(1) second and subsequent states of a painting or print, each by the original artist;

(2) versions created by a school of painters following a master's style;

(3) copies of a work executed by apprentices learning their craft under a master;

(4) copies of the work of one artist by another, equally gifted, in homage or to try out a style;

(5) copies executed by apprentices under supervision of a master, who signs and sells them as his originals,

and so forth, from Rembrandt's studio copying to Abbott Thayer's reworking of interim copies done by assistants. Problems of the "After" are acute in our culture of the copy, torn between our premium upon the unique and our egalitarian pride in good cheap reproductions, but the problems have been a long time coming.[101]

Briefly, from the Renaissance on, artists adept at imitating classical models in whose After-world they lived came also to think of themselves as avatars. They began to sign their works and ward off predators upon their styles. Buoyed by an increasingly secular art market that demanded more of the same in the name of their fame, artists capitalized upon the familiar uniqueness of their hand through techniques and technologies for a faster reproduction of their art – factories of apprentices, copperplate engravings, etchings.... Each leap up the ladder of reproduction was accompanied in self-defense by louder claims for the originality of true art and stronger actions against "fakes," which in their own way were accommodating the demand for originals. Appeared then the connoisseur, whose aesthetic function was to profess the irreproducibility of great art but whose economic function was as Aftermathematician, subtracting fakes or copies from the oeuvre of an artist, dividing greater from lesser originals, multiplying the repute and prices of favored art, and adding up "how much is every man's own, and what is not so."[102]

While "genius" was invoked in the eighteenth century to transform writers into *authors* (< *auctor*, originator) and make copyright a defense of inspired intellect, nineteenth-century connoisseurs began to defend the legal and aesthetic uniqueness of works of artistic genius. "A great picture," it was claimed, "has no resembling twin." Like the written page, "more emphatically [an author's] own creation than any material product of labor can be," art was emphatically of the spirit. The brushstrokes of the best copyists or forgers must inevitably appear slavish in contrast to the spontaneous strokes of a master, a genius.[103]

"Badly drawn, obscure in style, complex, illogical, and often incomprehensible," laws of artistic copyright since 1800 have gradually emboldened an almost-supernatural distinction between an original and a copy. "A copy," said Justice Bailey in 1822 in the most widely cited of definitions, "is that which comes so near to the original as to give every person seeing it the idea created by the original." Upon this basis copyright would be slowly conceded to paintings, engravings, sculptures, lithographs, drawings, and architectural plans.[104]

Of course, it has been the aim of much Western art to give "the idea" of the original – of a ruin, an antique sculpture, a landscape, someone else's painting of a landscape. Working "after" other artists has been an education for artists from Leonardo and Michelangelo to Levine and Sturtevant. Edgar Degas, who met Edouard Manet while both were etching copies of Velázquez's *Infanta Marguerite*, would execute more than 400 copies from 290 sources. Vincent van Gogh made at least 520 copies after other artists, for insight and, toward the end of his life, for emotional security. The history of art is the history of copy rites, of transformations that take place during acts of copying. When artists do not copy others, they may copy their own work over and over to deepen "the idea" of *their* original, like Ingres, who, chided for repainting *Raphael and La Fornarina* (four times) and *Paolo and Francesca* (eighteen times), wrote in 1859 that "the majority of those works of mine whose subjects I like have seemed worth the trouble of being perfected through repetition and retouching" – as "the great Poussin" had done in the 1700s. "Is not a good copy worth more than a bad but original painting?"[105]

Indeed, as some would argue, that which made any person an individual made every handcopy unique; slavish imitation was not human but "mechanical." Amid industrial reproductions of Chinese painted porcelain and East Indian textiles, connoisseurs began to distinguish "inspired" copies by such as Marcantonio Raimondi from uninspired copies by such as Peter Shee, a Dublin painter "almost Incapable of anything but Copying," who promised in 1765 to forfeit his fee "if the Original shall have any Advantage of his Copy, excepting what the former may have acquired by Age." While Victorian parlors flowered with reproductions – mezzotints, photogravures, halftone images clipped from magazines, plaster casts of the Venus de Milo at fifty cents a crack – and while schoolrooms displayed "original size" Assyrian Reliefs, artists and art teachers would dedicate themselves to the proposition that no handcopy is created equal but that each has something of its very own. "By imitation only," wrote Joshua Reynolds in 1774, "variety, and even originality of invention, is produced"; Picasso and Robert Rauschenberg have since extolled the copyist as a blessed deviant, lest Art find "glory in making servile machines out of free spirits... until at length there appears a mother Marionette leading a Marionette daughter."[106]

The Museum of Copies

Leading a daughter through an art museum, what should a mother expect to see? Is not a museum a knowing collection of illustrious or illustrative originals, stocked by connoisseurs, cleaned by restorers, annotated by historians? Ummm. Natural history museums have become playhouses of animated dinosaurs rather than rooms of stuffed animals. Museums of archaeology present replica relics. Tourists to the Lascaux cave paintings have been rerouted since 1983 to nearby Lascaux II, "five hundred tons of modeled concrete reproducing every little bump and hollow of the original, with a precision of a few centimeters" assured by stereophotogrammetry and a palette of natural colors achieving "the patina of time." A few actual artifacts at the Nixon Library have been infiltrated by scores of replicas, "meticulously torn, tattered and aged." The Diaspora Museum in Tel Aviv, tracking Jewish life across history, is all copies and makes no bones about it. Why should art museums be any different?[107]

Curators at the J. Paul Getty Museum in Malibu will display only original paintings and are reluctant to display any in bad condition, but some frames have been carpentered, wormholed, and banged up to look as if they had come down the years in company with the paintings whose aura they share, although it is rare for older paintings to rest in their original frames. A frame that van Gogh did specify for a painting of his now at the Getty was found to be too simple, however, and a more elaborate frame was substituted. Toledo's El Greco Museum asks a stiff fee to view the master's works – in reproduction; after all, El Greco had a workshop making copies of his more popular paintings, some labeled "This is the original." Worried about sculptures in European gardens,

FIGURE 6.7. Calligraphy and drawing by a writing automaton displayed by Henri
Maillardet during the first half of the nineteenth century, now at the Franklin
Institute Science Museum, Philadelphia. Reproduced by permission.

conservators have removed marble originals from the outrages of birds, smog, and acid rain, replacing them with antiqued copies treated to attract the algae that lovers of old gardens look for. Are we not letting go the ideal of an art museum as a fortress of the first-hand?[108]

Shrines with their relics, cabinets of curiosities with their mermaids, antiquarian cases with their runes were stocked with fabrications purporting to be ones-of-a-kind. When private galleries became public, noble sponsors did not hesitate to commission copies of works they coveted. Passions for true-blue originals overtook the con-assured museum, but its Double, the Museum of Copies, has itself a not ignoble genealogy.[109]

Duchess Louise of Savoy, for example, presented to the town of Amiens in 1517–18 an illuminated manuscript of forty-seven miniatures, copies of votive pictures in Amiens Cathedral. This artbook was to the cathedral what a seventeenth-century *kunstkamer* painting was to the "art room" of a wealthy Dutchman: a catalog – which, like most museum catalogs, is a celebration of the sponsors, a missal for devotion before each picture, a restaging of the art toward ideological ends, and an aide-mémoire. Art historian Gary Schwartz suggests that the last was most important. Showing in virtuoso miniature on a single canvas as many as fifty-six paintings ostensibly from one "art room," such canvases invited viewers to engage that Art of Memory by which the world entire could be recollected through images arranged room by room in one's mind. In Catholic Antwerp, where most *kunstkamer* paintings were made, the Art of Memory was a Jesuit exercise, a way to see oneself through to the Imitation of Christ.[110]

Then the Art of Memory was diverted to the Commemoration of Art. Rather than finding the arrangement of the world in the arrangement of works of art, connoisseurs called upon the world to witness to art. Sitting before copies of paintings or casts of sculptures in "study" galleries, connoisseurs and aspiring artists would try to catch the drift not of the world but of *pieces* that came from a certain school or period. Under the regimen of the Art of Memory, copies in their place were evocative of the full scheme of things; under the regime of the Commemoration of Art, copies had to be kept in their places. These were contrasting intuitions, the former shaping the Whole from the Many, the latter pulling the Singular from the Multiple. The contrast lay between those who "can't help thinking that when a Copy reaches such a degree of Perfection, as to deceive both the Practitioners and Judges of the Profession, it ought to pass as an Original" (like Don Juan Bautista del Mazo Martinez's copies after his father-in-law Diego Velázquez), and those who can't help seeing with their trained eyes "a perfect and natural force of grace in the originals, whereas in the copies they can see nothing but an imperfect and borrowed comeliness."[111]

Nonetheless they *were* comely, and forthcoming from workshops meeting early modern desires for small bronzes of classical statuary and etchings of famous oils, full-size bronzes and paintings procured by Velázquez for Philip IV of Spain, full-size marble copies and casts ordered for Louis XIV of France. The power to command the making of fine copies seemed no less exalted than the power to commission originals. As art critic David Robbins observes, "Inventing an event or an object is a wonderful thing, but inventing it *again* has more to do with power than it does with invention: you are proving that you are powerful enough to arrange the same conditions." Study galleries of the 1800s, with their copies and casts, were as much extensions of empire as were ethnographic museums with totems uprooted from exotic lands and "primitive" tribes. Anthropologists took stock of distant peoples; artists recaptured Antiquity, the Renaissance. The Prix de Rome sent French artists to Italy for five years, their fourth year to be spent making copies of Renaissance and Baroque pieces to send back to Paris. In Rome, an avid Ingres proposed a "museum of copies of the most celebrated paintings" of every era.[112]

Museums of Copies, whatever they did for the education of artists or, in Canada in 1845, the education of educators, were edifices of indoctrination. Aesthetic indoctrination, against slapdash art. Political indoctrination, toward pride in the past and faith in the future of a country. Social indoctrination, against too great a love of novelty, fashion, foolish revolt. Moral indoctrination, toward the virtues of humble anonymity, the copyist an unsung but unsullied hero who must have "both the dexterity and discernment of a consummate artist, and at the same time that resignation, that submissive patience and naive faith...found only among the most gifted young."[113]

Influenced by a naive faith in photography ("Great works of Art are now, when once photographed, imperishable"), the conservatism of the Museum of Copies was translated into conservationism and thence, paradoxically, into a celebration of the unique. With architectural historians lumbering off to photograph crumbling monuments and art historians scurrying to click the shutter on fading frescoes, the Museum of Copies could become a chapel of saving graces. Titian's *Martyrdom of St. Peter* went up in flames in 1865; France thanked its lucky stars it had a good copy the size of the original. As the camera spread the refinements of Art "by multiplying excellent copies of the highest works of human genius with a cheapness which brings them within the reach of thousands who can rarely see, and never possess, originals of the highest merit," so, wrote a critic in 1880, "the possession of a few first-rate copies of first-rate originals...is likely to do more to engender and foster a real love of Art than any amount of wearing and tiring 'doing' of Art galleries is likely to accomplish." One might actually prefer copies, in a social democratic sort of way, to originals; anyhow, in the long run, photos and painted copies might be the last deserving kin of art lost to fire, war, pillage, hoarding. Damaged, destroyed, disappeared, originals were again being cast as vanishing twins.[114]

Partly from this prospect, and partly from the plush of that other Museum of Copies, the bourgeois parlor, can we appreciate the first commercial exhibition of copies, "*D'Après les maîtres*," at the Galerie Bernheim-Jeune in Paris. On display in 1910 were 116 paintings "After the Masters" by predominantly male painters who had copied without "false reverence" the work of male forebears. Art critic Octave Mirbeau had earlier said of van Gogh's copies that "one should not really speak of copies in reference to these imposing re-creations. They are, instead, interpretations through which the painter is able to re-create the work of others and make it his own without abandoning the original spirit and special character of his model." Now, all styles of artistic copying would be authorized as transcendent acts. Unintimidated, or Oedipally conflicted, or anxiously defiant copying was the special talent of the Cubist *collagistes* – as it had been for decades the talent of Victorian women arranging colored papers and cut-outs into illusionistic screens and famous scenes amidst the chromolithographs, postcards, and photo-reproduced etchings pinned to the walls of *kunstkamer* parlors.[115]

Regardless of the subsequent precisionism of photographers using Ektachrome or Kodachrome, reenactments s/t/r/o/k/e/-/b/y/-/s/t/r/o/k/e have not ceased. Some have been what courts and connoisseurs call forgeries but what convicted forger David Stein would call *tours d'esprit*: "Once he had composed his work (he never made a direct copy of any master's painting but merely stole elements from each and fabricated his own creation that had a striking resemblance to the artist's style), David was convinced that the piece was exactly what the painter himself would have painted." Some have been outrageous gestures: Mike Bidlo re-painting, from scratch, in public, Jackson Pollock's *Blue Poles*. Some have been student works, often Japanese. Some have been works of supreme technique and art-historical homage: from 1971 to 1976, Barrington Bramley re-painted the thirty-five known paintings by Jan Vermeer "in what he believes to be their original condition" and put them on exhibition in a Museum of Copies in Vermeer's home town of Delft, where the great forger of Vermeers, Han van Meegeren, had studied architecture. Bramley then turned to Leonardo, Jan van Eyck, Diego Velázquez, Manet, taking their most famous paintings "back in time to the day when they were first executed" and signing them BB in *their* style, so producing *origenes* that fall between the easels of reproduction, restoration, forgery, and appropriation.[116]

Some s/t/r/o/k/e/-/b/y/-/s/t/r/o/k/e reenactments, finally, are in every sense investments. Today one can stroll into a Paris gallery to discover nothing but copies of Corots, Renoirs, Modiglianis, Cézannes, Pissarros, or Morisots (Berthe Morisot herself a grand *copiste* whose copies were shown to much praise in 1910). The copies in the Galerie Daniel Delamare are not those "multiple originals" which since the 1950s have wreaked such havoc among buyers of prints. Nor are they pastiches in the style of Chagall or Miró as sold by True Fakes Ltd. of New York. Each copy here is certified unique: no one else will be entitled by the painter's estate or the French government to paint and sell such another near-exact copy of the original. The copyists themselves, a corps of thirty artists, sturdily attest to the uniqueness, for despite their anonymity, despite the sales price on the commissioned work (US$10,000-$40,000), the making of the copies is as truly personal an investment as it is, ultimately, a compromise: "When I painted *The Olive Trees*, I quit the solitude of my own creative work to enter a dialogue with van Gogh, who must have felt himself far more desperately alone than I, and far more haunted by failure. And I thought of van Gogh copying Millet, seeking perhaps as I was seeking, an impossible communion." Buyers, accepting the compromise, want precisely this uniqueness: the value of the copy will then double or triple when resold. A number have been purchased by those who own the original, not merely for a monopoly over this Lautrec or that Turner but for purposes of insurance, since originals are worth too much to risk on casual display. So the copy goes up on the wall, the original goes back to the vault, and both, certifiably unique, signed with one celebrated signature by two separate hands, appreciate. How expertly do the economic and aesthetic forces of our culture of the copy converge to drive originals out of sight even as we demand of our own lives visible proofs of authenticity.[117]

Under construction as I write is a new Museum of Copies, the outcome neither of new copying techniques nor of an art copying industry that profits from "limited editions" of ten thousand signed prints. The new Museum of Copies will house only s/t/r/o/k/e/-/b/y/-/s/t/r/o/k/e reenactments of select pieces of Western art since Leonardo, drawing upon the corps of artists assembled by Daniel Delamare. The Museum of guaranteed unique Copies is in Osaka, financed by the Japanese, for whom the monkey and the mirror are central cultural symbols, and who for a century have been dismissed as imitators of Western technology. Commissioning European artists to complete copies of European masterpieces, the Japanese meanwhile place high bids for the West's most famous originals. Derided as a country of copyists, Japan is now the nation Westerners beg to copy, seeking in Japanese industry (copiers, computers, fax machines, robots) a model for their own production and research. Americans in particular speak of Japan in terms of a thankless twin given a healthy constitution in the protective womb of post–World War II Occupation, nourished in peace with low trade barriers, now a selfish, devouring ogre. So the West has begun to frame itself as a vanishing twin, making copies for the Japanese as its own originals deteriorate.[118]

Irretrievably. After years with microscope, scalpel, solvents, and large Polaroids for comparison, Pinin Brambilla Barcilon can hope only to make the *Last Supper* again "readable," not stable: the experimental primer Leonardo used was already, in his day, detaching from the plaster on the wall. Like Technicolor movie film and early photocopies, artistic experiments with the new paints, plastics, and adhesives available after World War II are decaying before our eyes. And the more we look, the more the art decays, for while we are looking we are scuffing museum floors into flurries of particulate matter, releasing noxious

chemicals from perfumes and deodorants. In 1992, artists and archaeologists finished a six-year project to restore the Tomb of Nefertari; if
the Egyptians leave it open, two thousand visitors a day will come to
gawk and the tomb will for all historical purposes be literally rubbed
out before the year 2000. More sophisticated about contaminants, more
alert at century's end to the ravages of time, curators must struggle
against inclinations to remove from public view the art and artifacts
they love and are paid to preserve. Where originals are guard-railed
and glass-cased, and where museums of originals operate under the
twin commandments Thou Shalt Not Touch and Thou Shalt Not Get
Close Enough for a Good Look, there shall arise many another Museum
of Copies.[119]

Kept at harm's length from those originals we have learned from connoisseurs or constant reproductions to respect as masterpieces, we turn
not unreasonably to facsimiles. For we want to see the brushstrokes,
feel the stone. The popularity of the copy need not be dismissed as a
"fetishism of the signifier" or, less pompously, as a mistaking of the messenger for the message. Honoring the skill and devotion it takes to hand-
craft or machine a replica whose features I may trace with my finger,
what offense do I commit against a fragile, inaccessible original?[120]

Arose therefore Museums of Copies from within museums of originals. By 1859, London's South Kensington Museum, founded as a Museum of Manufactures, was selling photographs and casts of artwork
from its halls, the Louvre's, and the British Museum's. The Louvre
itself had five thousand plaster casts for sale. The British Museum began retailing reproductions during the 1920s while the Metropolitan
Museum of Art was setting up its own reproduction studio. Like the
exotic displays of vast department stores, museums of originals have
themselves engendered the desire for re-creations, their curators the
advance agents for reproductions of Tanagra sculptures, Moghul miniatures, ancient wood-fired Japanese pots. In 1985 the Met grossed
$34,000,000 from sales of reproductions while "museum stores" in-
vaded malls with reproductions from art museums across America. Traveling exhibitions now arrive with crates of copyrighted replicas and
poster-size reproductions, sold as memento to a once-in-a-lifetime
glimpse, from a crazy distance between the bobbing heads of a noisy
crowd, a few water lilies or jewel-encrusted eggs.[121]

Rich or poor, replicas and reproductions end up in our living rooms,
bedrooms, bathrooms, and dens. If Victorians had C. Arthur Pearson
Ltd.'s Famous Pictures of the World, "fac-simile reproductions (large
size) in colour" at ONE SHILLING for each set of nine, we have eight
hundred paintings and drawings scanned, digitized, color-adjusted by
microprocessor, and laser-transferred to canvas for sale by the Ethan
Allen home furnishings chain at $120 to $1800 apiece; cast aluminum
versions of the cast iron bamboo furniture made by Victorian craftsmen
to bamboozle gentlefolk; real imitation baroque chamber pots; "mel-
lowing reproductions" of eighteenth-century desks; sculpture from the

private hoard of Nelson Rockefeller, cast in facsimile to "look like the originals, imperfections and all!"[122]

What we want, imperfections and all, from "the entire system of replicas, reproductions, copies, reductions, transfers, and derivations, floating in the wake of an important work of art" is as confused as what we get. To love and admire? To prove that we love what it is *de rigueur* to admire? To study? To remind us of an occasion, a person? To get close to, and touch? To be assured by? To compare? To own, in spirit?[123]

Rumor or humor has it that Sherrie Levine appropriated her *After Mondrian* from a forgery of a Mondrian: on whom was the joke? Is it not seriocomic in our era to protest a decision by the Barnes Foundation ("one of the last places in the United States where it is still possible to see a Matisse or a Renoir or a Cézanne as if it had just been created!") finally to permit color reproductions of its holdings – lest people lose the chance "to see a masterpiece for the first time: true of color, honest in scale, its once-onliness intact"? Is it not a bit foolish to think enforceable, in light of replicas machined under numerical control with data from 3-D laser scanners, a regulation that art reproductions must differ "in at least one major, visible, and unalterable characteristic from the original"? Is it not somewhat hilarious that our legal world should be divided as to whether granting copyright in a mannequin may lead to the "monopolization of the basic human form"? It *was* a laughing matter (wasn't it?) when a man offered $3500 for a motorcycle he saw in a photo, only to be told by Revell, makers of "perfect reproductions of the real thing," that it was just a model, four inches high.[124]

Truth in labeling would scarcely resolve the comedy, since our labels themselves are looney, as any researcher from the moon would know upon buying a carton of I Can't Believe It's Not Butter, a T-shirt from the Counterfeat Clothing Company, or a "crystal pavé faux pearl clutch bee pin, inspired by Tiffany & Co.," from an Impostors Copy Jewelry franchise. The bottles and styles of lettering are identical, but the difference between Mattei and Matté is that the original Corsican wine does *not* have on its label *La Vraie marque*, "Authentic Trademark." Sly or fly, counterfeits make up 3 percent of world trade, probably more, since, according to a Designer Imposters perfume commercial, "If she likes Giorgio, she'll love Primo." Giorgio, the costly original, must vanish before Primo the twin, "Number One," just as years of counterfeits have made the apéritif Byrrh vanish under sixty other labels, Bhyrr, Tyrrh, and backwards (almost), RRhyb. "180 imitations of our bottle since 1925," boast the makers of Suze, the Pernod liqueur. "There is surely something to this appetite for Suze.... Taste Suze. People will imitate you." Sketching a bottle of the liqueur, Picasso pasted a Suze label onto the canvas, "implying that there was little point in approximating to a reality by arduous academic exercise when we could just coopt fragments of reality and incorporate them in our works," writes philosopher of art Arthur Danto. Accept no limitations.[125]

"Our history," says the firm of Pierre Vuitton, "is a history of being copied." I second that. Copying is what we are now about. The expansion from museums of originals to the Museum of Copies to museums of counterfeits cannot be laid at the stained-steel feet of machines. Machines simply do blest what we do for better or worse. In our post-industrial age, the copy is at once degenerate and regenerate.[126]

Consider the modern potter who insists, like Karen Kames of Vermont, that "Only a [unique] piece thrown by hand has the particular quality of transmission of spirit from maker to receiver." Yet other potters use slab machines and hydraulic RAM presses to produce two thousand pots a day. "Now, one may comment, 'all those lousy thousands of pieces with little character. No imagination, no variety, like the copy from a Xerox machine; the marketplace is being flooded with drones.'" Or, continues potter Wallace C. Higgins, the RAM press can free one to experiment with uniquely "mutilated multiples." Clay, writes William Hunt, editor of *Ceramics Monthly*, is "capable of being a liar if there ever was one, or of being as faithful as can be." Which is the *faithful* pot? Hand-thrown and slightly imperfect? Machine-pressed and identical to every other from the same mold?[127]

We who in so many myths come from clay and who slip so swiftly from expressions of faith *in* the unique to faithful expressions *of* the unique, we perpetually transfigure what and when we copy. By heart, by hand, by art, by ROM or RAM or the light of a Lichtenberg moon.

FIGURE 7.1. H.G. Wells playing with toy soldiers, ca. 1913. From H.G. Wells, *Little Wars* (1913).

CHAPTER SEVEN

Once More, With Feeling

> Is there repetition or is there insistence. I am inclined to
> believe there is no such thing as repetition. And really
> how can there be.
>
> — Gertrude Stein, in *Lectures in America*

You can see him kneeling on the lawn, a giant in white trousers bent over footsoldiers and cavalry. He has set in motion a time machine, an invisible man, a new woman, a war of the worlds, but in 1913 has composed *Little Wars: A Game for Boys from Twelve Years to One Hundred and Fifty and for that More Intelligent Sort of Girls Who Like Boys' Games and Books*. A year before the guns of August roar and H.G. Wells is playing at "tin murder." Little War, he writes, has been refined. Men of opposing flags are still equally brave and strong; any two, meeting up, kill each other. But "so desperate is the courage and devotion of lead soldiers, that it came to this, that any small force that got or seemed likely to get isolated and caught by a superior force, instead of waiting to be taken prisoners, dashed at its possible captors and slew them man for man." Such heroics were inhuman, so new rules of engagement had to be sworn: generals must play for total points rather than the pointlessness of total war.

How much better were Little War the only war, Great War the banished twin. "You have only to play at Little Wars three or four times to realize just what a blundering thing Great War must be." Little War is war "done down to rational proportions," with "no smashed nor sanguinary bodies, no shattered fine buildings nor devastated countrysides." Great War is "a game out of all proportion."[1]

Most of us, I trust, would with Wells prefer rehearsals in miniature to the monstrosity of a first night. The issue before us is how our culture of the copy deals with event. We are moving on from the doubles of our selves past the doubling of our sensible worlds to the redoubling of our times. At risk are history, science, and documentary: how we tattle on the tales of our lives, confirm what we see and feel, play back the remains.

Does practice at "tin murder" cure players of bloodlust, as Wells hoped, or does it deceive them about battle, desensitize them to death, destine them for wars where winning is accountancy? The wargame immediately confronts us with the dubiousness of simulation, dilemmas of replication, disorders of repetition. Is simulation a mode of insight or escape, recall or denial? Is replication a policy of insurance or an instrument of hegemony? Is repetition rhythm and intensity or is it fever and illness?

Real Time

The antiquity of simulated combat and toy soldiers lies beyond our horizons, but we can distinguish the strategic display of tournament from the tactics of chess. Strategy is the marshaling of wealth, political will, diplomatic wiles, technical skills, and military mettle toward intimidation and conquest; tactics is the art of maneuvering armed forces in combat.

Between strategy and tactics is drill, which shunts men back and forth from display on parade grounds to deployment on killing grounds. Modern military drill was introduced during the 1590s. Responding to mobile cannon and lighter musketry, Maurice, Prince of Orange, captain-general of Holland, ranged battalions of men in ranks six to ten deep, drilled to break formation and return swiftly. When four battalions could re-form in twenty-three minutes, wheel smoothly "right face" or left, and countermarch the front rank rearward to reload as the next came forward to shoot, their flexibility and firepower could be decisive.[2]

Subdivided into platoons, Dutch, Swedish, English, French, Swiss, and German soldiers learned to move with exactitude and alacrity at the shout of a single voice. If they became clockwork units wound up by drill sergeants, they also became a community of the "rank and file." Drill, which assured morale amid the tedium of standing (waiting) armies, insured against desertion amid the chaos of battle. Drill entrained: it aligned the bodies of the many and made them into one, set them in motion in unison, and geared them to fire regular volleys at close range.[3]

Tabletop wargames, repeated day after day, would be the equivalent of drill for officers. Brigades of grenadiers, dragoons, and cannoneers sped over the 1666 squares laid out in 1780 for the Duke of Brunswick; in 1797 they crossed the five terrains and 3600 squares of a New Wargame, or *Kriegsspiel*. The Baron von Reisswitz, Prussian war councilor, substituted eskers of sand and plaster for these flatlands, but it was his son, First Lieutenant in the Prussian artillery, who in 1824 put wargames at contour-mapped green tables overseen by umpires judging the feasibility of commands. He also drew up charts on the effect of fire and weighted the casualties incurred after the die were cast. War was chancy, but the wargame, played and replayed over the same grids, was meant, like drill, to leave little to chance on real battlefields where time was more precious than life.[4]

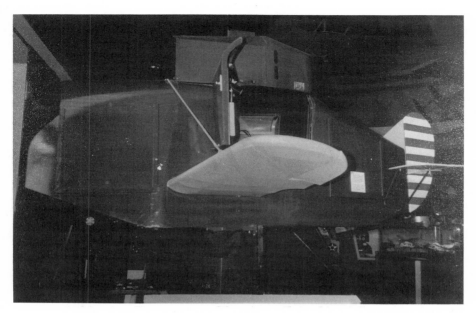

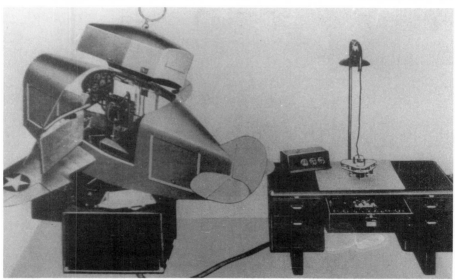

FIGURE 7.2. Top: Early flight simulator, the Link "Pilot Maker," for training U.S. Army Air Corps mail-delivery pilots in all-weather flights, 1934. Bottom: Schematic illustration of the "Pilot Maker" with remote control operations desk. Reproduced by permission of the San Diego Aero-Space Museum.

Wargaming entrained two compressed realms, a Game Time with rounds of two minutes each, stutter-stepped with intervals of Gainsaying Time. Game Time was more punctual than war has ever been: troops were either vigorous or dead – no walking wounded, no malingerers or deserters. Gainsaying Time was retrospect in media res, concerned less with clean victory than with clear-headed debate over means and opportunity. Game Time was a stopwatched burst of rivalry; Gainsaying Time was pedagogical, collegial. Like boxers whose cornermen by 1812 could "call time," wargamers reduced the vertigo of combat to a time in and a time out.[5]

Not exclusively theoretical, wargaming found a partisan in Helmuth von Moltke, for thirty years (1857–87) chief of the Prussian General Staff, who replayed so many variants of a Bohemian *Kriegsspiel* that when war against Austria came in 1866, he confidently deployed his troops – for a campaign won in six weeks. Napoleon before him had been seen "leaning and sometimes lying on his map, where the position of his army corps and those presumed of the enemy were marked off by pins of different colors." John Clerk's naval tactics, explained to British countrymen via "small models of ships with which he demonstrated new battle maneuvers on table tops," had enabled Nelson's victory at Trafalgar in 1805. If von Moltke warned that "War cannot be conducted from a green table," it could surely be prospected, staked, and mined.[6]

In action, von Moltke meant, do not presume to repeat move for move a tabletop action. Sixty-four 'ere he braved an active battlefield, the Field Marshall nonetheless saw that modern war required the flexibility of semi-autonomous units led by decisive men using rapid communications. Therefore his adoption of the "free" kriegspiel proposed in 1876 by the chief of staff to the 1st Army Corps. Aides during the Franco-Prussian War (1870–71) had collected data to recalibrate wargaming manuals, but Col. Julius von Verdy du Vernois outflanked platoons of clerks with a faster game in which umpires decided on the spot the fatigue of troops, passability of roads, results of battles. With such limber kriegspiels Alfred von Schlieffen, von Moltke's successor, rehearsed the Great War, against whose double front east and west the die always turned. After defeat, enjoined from military exercises, German generals had no recourse but the kriegspiel, a habit so strong by World War II that response to D-Day was tardy because coastal commanders were standing at yet another green table.[7]

Vacationing in Germany in 1873, the son of a pacifist British banker bought a tract on the kriegspiel. He who had rarely seen a soldier returned to university to fight his brother across maps of Oxfordshire with porcelain cavalry. In 1876 he organized the Oxford Kriegspiel Club. In 1878 he drilled for home defense as a civilian Volunteer. In 1881 he formed the Manchester Tactical Society. In 1882 he started writing newspaper analyses of foreign campaigns. All, said Spenser Wilkinson, from no bloodlust but from patriotism and pursuit of the "art of command."[8]

European refinements in the art of command were prompted by

·reports of deadlocks and massacres across the Atlantic. The Civil War (1861–65) had made full use of modern weaponry, including the machine gun, "an Army in six feet square" which put thousands of men six feet under. Wargaming blocks called the Automaton Regiment and the Automaton Battery had been designed by a Union captain and may have been used by Union General Irvin McDowell, charged with the first Virginia campaign. But

> it takes time to mold your men into blocks
> And flat maps turn into country where creeks and gullies
> Hamper your wooden squares. They stick in the brush,
> They are tired and rest, they straggle after ripe blackberries,
> And you cannot lift them up in your hand and move them.

So, at Bull Run, wrote the poet Stephen Vincent Benet,

> The General loses his stars and the block-men die
> In unstrategic defiance of martial law
> Because still used to just being men, not block-parts.[9]

Tactics and unstrategy wounded 5 percent of U.S. white males ages 18–45 — some of whom, amputees with wooden legs, became, in part but literally, blocks. For a brief moment, war did not seem to be a game, but the kriegspiel reemerged in the 1870s at the headquarters of the Battalion of Engineers in New York Harbor and then at West Point, where officers in four hours could finish an Information Game, jockeying troops into position on a map of Gettysburg, or a Mischief Game, maneuvering men in combat. Novices would be disappointed in the lack of drama, warned a captain in the Corps of Engineers, for the kriegspiel was no longer a game with "a clear and definite conclusion, one party being declared the winner and the other the loser." As slow as it was indefinite, a four-hour wargame of 1883 might represent just thirty-two minutes of field action (a ratio of Gainsaying Time to Game Time twice that at football games in 1983). Spectators thought American wargames "stupid in the highest degree," which led adjutants to advocate the speedier free game, but those engaged in the games found them "extremely fascinating."[10]

Their fascination, was it with the 96 topographical blocks, 1252 pasteboard pieces, pointers, calipers, and firing boards of a kriegspiel? Or was it with the oxymoron of reiterable novelty that lay behind it? Von Verdy du Vernois: "War brings forth new pictures and, though the situations appear very similar, they are hardly ever so." The kriegspiel had to consist of attacks whose repetition led to unintended results. "No mortal can ever eliminate that ultimate *uncertainty* with which the God of Wars turns the scale to suit other ends than those of earthly strategists," wrote Lt. Charles Totten of the 4th U.S. Artillery about his 1880 game, Strategos. Like Major Livermore (U.S.), Major Kitchener in Britain, and Captain Naumann in Germany, he introduced subtleties that made the wargame more pragmatic *and* more incalculable: periods of reconnoitering, chances of flinching after severe losses. "The subject of 'casualty in action' is of paramount importance in the problem of modern warfare," wrote Totten; "it is well nigh impossible to keep apace of it, and, perhaps, hopeless to anticipate its furthest reaches."[11]

Would he have flinched from the thirteen million killed in World War I? the fifty million in World War II? Kriegspiels were simulations whose atmosphere of close personal combat, captain versus captain, kept commanders psychologically distant from the deadliness of repeating rifles, Gatling Guns, Hotchkiss Revolving Cannon...a technology that, ever compounded, itself made killing reiterable and impersonal. Capt. Philip Colomb of the British Navy, who introduced the first naval wargame, was convinced by 1879 of "the growth of mechanism – if I may use the expression – in future sea-fights. We seem to be losing every day some page in that large chapter of accidents which made past sea-fights so romantic." Broadside artillery and bow guns had become so effective that fightingmen on deck were "neither here nor there," merely waiting to jump overboard in their cork vests. One might as well "play ship-sinking without the men."[12]

Which they did, the British, Germans, French, Italians, Japanese, and, despite defeats by most fleets put on the table, the Americans. As of 1894, the naval wargame was anchored to the curriculum of the U.S. Naval War College, taught by Capt. William McCarty Little, who believed that the art of command had to become "instinctive, through continuous practice and repetition." He also believed that kriegspiel was "like the 'Music of the Future'; while it is the 'top of the heap,' most people have to be led up to it gradually, and love of music is best kept going by a plentiful use of lighter kinds for every day," so smaller finger skirmishes must prepare men for the symphonic "big game." Small or large, wargames must train officers to give orders rather than to issue commands; the orchestration of modern warfare demanded an intelligent use of subordinates and the preservation of personal responsibility down the line. It was the peculiar aim of wargames to achieve through "instinct" that individual presence dulled by a bass line of mortar shells or, at sea, by the pounding of a ship's engines. "Life on ship board is almost like spending one's days and nights in an iron foundry," said W.B. Norris of Annapolis in 1916; hardened by the drone, men come to act as if machines. "Personality then drops into the background and the necessity of man's being a source of inspiration to those he commands is forgotten." While drill for the ranks produced an oiled "fighting machine," wargames were to produce an echelon of charismatic officers unafraid of making semiautomatic decisions.[13]

"Material is soulless," warned a lecturer at the Naval War College; "it cannot be pushed to an endurance beyond that which the mind of man designs for it." So, yes, fascination with the detail of the kriegspiel did lead Fred Jane in 1912 to design diminutive firing devices to simulate the "moral effect" of combat excitement upon the accuracy of gunners. And, yes, a wargame created in 1912 at Fort Andrews, Massachusetts, did have officers with field glasses surveying coastal relief maps on which were set tiny electric searchlights, cannon, and balsa ships, while other officers scouted opaque projections of silhouettes of enemy warships. Yes, the more monstrous the behemoth guns, the more appealing the Lilliput of the wargame, manageable in a Wellsian sort of way. Yes, the more obscene the firepower, the more seductive the intellectual distance and miniature ingenuities of a simulation, pure and hopeful in an Orwellian sort of way.[14]

Still, "Because of the imperfections that must naturally exist in this mimic warfare, its results cannot be accepted in their entirety," warned the president of the Naval War College in 1897. The imperfections: not the blur of detail due to reduced scale, but the blur of unpredictable human beings. To the wargame as boardgame was thereupon added another simulation, this in real country in almost Real Time: field maneuvers.[15]

Although soldiers and sailors had long performed ceremonial battles, only after 1870 did officers go on staff maneuvers or squadrons train against each other at sea. Thinking big, McCarty Little in 1891 had in mind "utilizing [a] whole island, and having combined regular autumn maneuvers, military and Naval, laid out just as a play at a theatre, with full explanation of the reasons of each move." Board or chart maneuvers were "cinematographic" diagrams, he wrote in 1912; field maneuvers, "carried out just as a play is," would be "war brought within the grasp of the ordinary individual." By World War I, as theater ushers practiced "fire drills" to control stampeding audiences, the dramatic practice of splitting a corps into opposing divisions for a sham battle was familiar enough that two French soldiers thought the Great War "not a real war, but a test run (*une guerre d'expérience*)." During the interwar years, as the U.S. admiralty gamed its tactics against Japan on three hundred occasions on a 428-square-foot board (and as the Japanese gamed against the U.S. at their Total War Research Institute), the U.S. Army began large-scale maneuvers. The 1940 maneuvers of the Third Army, across 2800 square miles of Louisiana, were transitional between the green table and field greens. Directives made it plain that the maneuvers were "*not* intended as a competitive test of troops or individual commanders.... Every effort will be made to prevent close contact and the intermingling of units in so-called sham battles." This was a tightly muzzled kriegspiel with divisions of men and (too many) mules as pieces on maps. Maps are not the territory, said critical observers: "Staff officers tended to regard the maneuvers as more of a map problem or wargame and, hence, failed to get out and reconnoiter the terrain" — much of it swamp, tortuous for tanks and formidable to infantry, who kept to paved roads with the same stubbornness that tacticians kept to the tried if untrue grids on green tables.[16]

Freed up by roving umpires, the next year's maneuvers sent 400,000 men fighting over 30,000 square miles of Louisiana and Texas. Halfbreed of display and deployment, the well-publicized maneuvers were the first open field tests of anti-tank groups, of paratroops, of coordinated attacks by army, navy, and marine planes working their propaganda in the clouds, then strafing troops unpersuaded of the virtues of camouflage. Medics treated fake wounds; trucks broadcast prerecorded battle noises. The "realism" of this Game Time was maddening, an illusion trickier than some could abide. Elite paratroops, feeling their oats, would not stay captured; infantry, most still carrying bolt-action Springfield rifles from World War I, would not hide from planes firing blanks. Crossing a bridge flagged as blown up, a squad was accosted by an umpire shouting, "Hey! Don't you see that bridge is destroyed?" A corporal shouted back, "Of course I can see it's destroyed. Can't you see we're swimming?"[17]

After World War II a new form of kriegspiel, disembodied, would rely upon machines built originally to crack enemy codes and calculate trajectories, but not before American (and Soviet?) troops were exposed to the extreme realism of high doses of radiation during 1950s tactical atomic maneuvers. The men were there in the flesh, ironically, because maneuvers had been reconceived as a means for "the training of people who, in the final analysis, won the battles – small units and the individual airman and front-line soldier." As the Cold War heightened the intensity of sham battles, staged with live ammunition, officers were drilled in the stages of "escalation," a word that strains the qualities of mercy. Rocket and H-bomb were twice blessed by strategists seeing in them deterrence and dominance, twice cursed by tacticians who could practice effectively with neither. Feature films recreated holocaust, from game to war to postnuclear numbness, in ninety minutes. Computers programmed by "game theorists" presented World War IIIs that could begin and end in a period so compressed by the flash of multiple warheads that there would be few two-minute rounds and no pauses for gainsaying. Nuclear war was repeatable only on electronic grids.[18]

Computers exacerbated the scientism of the kriegspiel, whose repetitions had persuaded politicians of the science of warfare as much as they had drilled captains in the art of command. Reflecting the German refinement of laboratory techniques during the nineteenth century, kriegspiels were the equivalent of assays of toxicity, tests of vitality, trials of reflex and perception. Wargames this century have been propounded, funded, conducted, and defended as experiments presuming replication. Wargamers commence with hypotheses about troop strength and terrain; they conceive methods of investigation (rigid or free, green table or open field); they calculate the parameters; they study the engagement; they gainsay the results and come to tentative conclusions; they begin again, revising hypotheses and parameters until they are as sure of victory as sure can be. On such a scientist basis Germany followed the Schlieffen Plan into World War I, the Japanese attacked Pearl Harbor in World War II, and the Americans responded, shocked but not surprised. "The war with Japan had been reenacted in the game rooms here by so many people and in so many different ways," claimed Admiral Chester Nimitz, "that nothing that happened during the war was a surprise – absolutely nothing except the kamikaze tactics toward the end of the war," which H.G. Wells had dismissed as untenable even for Little War. After Hiroshima it was only courtesy of computer programs that the strategies of Mutual Assured Destruction could be projected.[19]

While computer screens preempted green tables in the Kremlin and the Pentagon, war itself became stagestuck and pixellated. The U.S. lost the Vietnam War, said some critics, because its generals relied on tactics plotted against a Red Team of American colonels and civilians and placed too much faith in "gaming-table analysis over GIs-in-jungles reality." GIs-in-jungles had, for their own part, a sense of unreality, of watching themselves in a movie; GIs-back-in-the-States suffered cinematic flashbacks of the war. Later, in 1984, five days after Pentagon wargamers played out a "real-time" computer scenario in which Iran closed the Straits of Hormuz, Iran closed the Straits of Hormuz.[20]

If theaters of war were being experienced as repeat performances of wargame theater, wargames played at electronic grids have become indistinct from field combats fought through radar screens, video monitors, infrared gunsights, and the visors of helmets whose electronic systems track pilots' eye movements to produce synthetic images. Sonar training equipment can "so realistically simulate reality that [submarine] crew members cannot tell the difference between a real target and one that has been synthesized by a computer." A 1979 NORAD wargame instigated a nuclear alert: someone inadvertently switched the game's tape into the active warning net, and NORAD screens (as in the 1983 film *War Games*) confirmed a Soviet attack on the U.S. Writes a military historian, "As the battlefield becomes more automated, the battle itself becomes more like a war game."[21]

Wistfulness for the chivalry of male champions in single combat? The complement is truer: The more automated the wargame, the more a war, like the Gulf War against Iraq in 1991, can be represented as a perfectly clean replication of a game. Zigzagging through wartorn towns built from scratch with craters, rubble, and bombed-out houses, marines use MILES, a Multiple Integrated Laser Engagement System that allows rifles to register laser "hits." With death itself a radiance and life instantly recuperable, officers and senators speak with ever-more distaste about "dirty wars" that drag on past any reasonable Game Time.[22]

Pubescent children in video arcades or at home at the keyboard of an F-19 Simulation Game, with "real-time" views of the terrain beneath them, experience the visions of pilots some six years older firing "smart bombs" from a distance so antiseptic that they must trust long-range sensors to tell them what they have done to pulsing targets. The flight simulator, supposed to give safer, more economical training in a cockpit, has been from its start, like the wargame, a tool for psychic distancing, and like the wargame, it had its roots in entertainment. America's pioneer flight simulator was produced in the 1930s by Edwin A. Link, son of a manufacturer of rolls for player pianos. The hands-off automatisms of the player piano were built into the hands-on gyrations through which Link Trainers took their trainees atop a revolving octagon with four bellows that spun, twisted, and lifted the blue box of the cockpit. Advances during and after World War II in computing, feedback engineering, and electronic imaging have made flight simulators so authenticative that commercial pilots after months at the controls of jumbo jets must return to the simulators for testing. But now the experience can seem too real: inside a simulator a pilot can sweat to death, having forgotten that the event is bogus, the sound canned, and the controls at which he sits the toggles of an expensive toy.[23]

Is the wargame any longer a plaything? asked German analysts in 1979, apprehensive of the growing coincidence, as much visceral as technical, of *krieg* with *kriegsspiel*.[24] My answers must be equivocal and unsettling, for simulation and dissimulation are, in our culture of the redoubled event, congeners.

‡ The wargame is an escape, a well-rehearsed folly like televised wrestling, where "The very visibility of the faked violence acts as the guarantor of the outcome." Or a less vicarious entertainment, like Paint Wars, spread by a Wall Street broker in 1981 and fought by camouflaged teams named Gang Green or Grim Reapers toting Assassinator II pistols firing paint-balls once used to mark cattle. Says one player, a banker, "We live in such a controlled society. War games are just an opportunity to let everything go and shoot people."[25] † The wargame is a means to insight, a training tool for "in-your-face" business management or face-to-face moral conflicts in social work, medical triage, political activism. It forces you to confront feelings of anger, weakness, shame, guilt.[26]

‡ The wargame is a mode of denial, like one satirist's facetious Venus 360b Relationship Simulator, each loving or unloving sensation "digitally reproduced and enhanced." Or denial more gruff, as in Brigadier Peter Young's forward to a manual for war boardgames that "cover the period when war as an instrument of state policy was at its height, before it got too dangerous to be either useful or attractive. One has yet to see an enjoyable evening's play based on the destruction of Nagasaki."[27] † The wargame is a mode of perfect recall, from the Battle of Kadesh in 1288 B.C. to the tank battles of World War II: "If the battles are so reconstructed that both armies are of historically accurate, scaled-down strength, pursue the same tactical plans, use the same weapons and fight in a manner of their day, it is highly likely that the table-top encounter will follow its historical course."[28]

‡ The wargame is a method of insurance, of consolatory advice from experts, translated into flow charts to handle all "conceivable" crises.[29] † The wargame is a method of establishing hegemony, large contingents just happening to mass for maneuvers across the border from turmoil or recalcitrance.

‡ The wargame is a gamble. "No two games or battles are ever alike," though you begin as they historically began. Between 1939 and 1945, "The tapestry of the whole war was dark to its creators, its final outcome obscure and inevitably the result of a panoply of individual efforts." Play by mail, then, with 129 others, in an "unprecedented theatre of alternate history," a second Second World War whose battles redevelop across the 20,000 hexagons of a world map 120 feet square.[30] † The wargame is a fevered repetition of figures and shadows, not unlike paranoia, a mental state that computers simulate most persuasively. With "eerie atmospheric sounds," wargames may encourage policies evermore "extreme and absolute," predilections ever-more omnipotent: "Fling disasters on the non-believers. Volcanoes, floods, swamps, earthquakes. If you've enough power – Armageddon!"[31]

Real Time II: Memes

Wild rains flooded the four thousand Scots in the grandstand and pelted the seventy thousand waiting by the riverbank, all of whom had come to Eglinton Park in Ayrshire on a Wednesday at the end of August, 1839, to watch a medieval procession of swordsmen and bowmen, trumpeters, heralds, the King of the Tournament in velvet and ermine, the Queen of Beauty under a silken canopy. When the sky cleared, a baker's dozen of assorted knights jousted in the soggy lists. Thursday, Prince Louis Napoleon, later Napoleon III but for the nonce a dashing socialist and pacifist, went a-tilting. On Friday the 30th, eight champions flailed at each other with broadswords. Invited guests attended a banquet: flagons of malmsey, bowls of syllabub, quarts of hippocras, pots of swan, primrose tarts, dilligrout, posset, flummery. For £40,000, however, the affair was nowhere as splendid as had been imagined by Archibald William, 13th Earl of Eglinton, Lord Montgomerie, Lord Seton and Tranent in Scotland, Baron Ardrossan of the United Kingdom. Eglinton's castle was Gothic Revival, its foundations laid less than seventy years before. His Middle Ages had been given color by *Ivanhoe* (1825) and the Waverly novels of Walter Scott; tonality by an opera, *The Tournament* (1838), from the pen of a friend, Lord Burghersh; nomenclature by a relative, Samuel Egerton Brydges, editor of *Collins' Peerage* and claimant to a vacant barony through descent from the Merovingian kings, proved with forged papers.[32]

Ian Anstruther, to whose *The Knight and the Umbrella* I am here indebted, would have us draw from the Eglinton Tournament a stern lesson, "That the past can never be brought to life, and that ancient pastimes and decorative arts should never be imitated in a different age." It was a lesson that Eglinton, who lived to read news of the disastrous Charge of the Light Brigade during the Crimean War, could have learned before he died of apoplexy in 1861, for "to revive chivalry in the Age of Steam was only to invite an absurd catastrophe."[33]

By 1861 the medieval tournament – taken up by Frederick the Great of Prussia in 1750 for martial display; by Gustavus III of Sweden in 1777

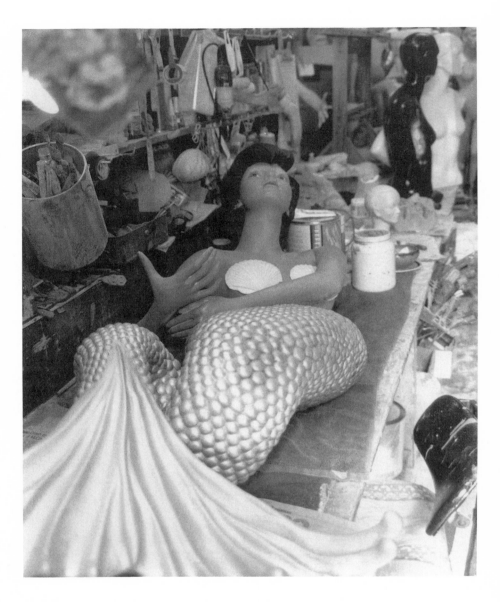

FIGURE 7.3. Mermaid womannequin from the Van Calvin Manikin Restoration Studio, Portland, OR. Photo by Linda M. Strauss.

to counter the "effeminacy" of the age; by the Viennese in 1814 in honor of the Allies who had defeated Napoleon; by the highborn of New Orleans in 1839, and across the antebellum South, in honor of honor – seemed to be winking out, but it emerged again at century's turn with another round of Knighthood in Flower and the resumption of the Olympic Games. The chivalry of the games ("the aim is not to conquer but to struggle well") and the contemporary celebration of prowess, "spontaneous, irreproducible, unique, and conspicuous moral acts, undertaken for honor and not for utility," were rebuttals to the Darwinian story of life itself as war, the economy of nature subject to a "severe competition." From that same rebuttal we inherit an obstinate idea about the obstinacy of event, embodied in the philosopher George Santayana's epigram that "Those who cannot remember the past are condemned to repeat it."[34]

History – as vestige and natural selection, as atavism and screen memory, as anachronism and political confection – must outlive the past, or so it has seemed since Darwin, Santayana, Freud, and our other best dramatists. Past may be prologue, but history is, as one usurper said after a tempest, "in yours and my discharge." Wherefore, whilst domestic Museums of Copies were transformed around 1900 from closed parlors in which one displayed one's fixed *character* to open "living rooms" in which one deployed one's changing *personality*,[35] the dark cabinets of Museums of Originals and the tightly held copyholds of Original Manses were opened to pageantry and public education.

Museums were now to have "life." Before (said a new corps of self-congratulatory curators), museums had been collocations of the dead, arranged perhaps by century or species or style, but all in all "a necropolis." Cincinnati's Western Museum had banked on the thirty-nine-year run of its Infernal Regions, a hell of animated wax figures, and P.T. Barnum's American Museum had had its share of automata and shrieking missing links, but these were clockwork, bluff, and brilliantine. The new museum was to take on life and strong personality in twelve ways. It would be organic, developing from hall to hall to hall. It would breathe, its exhibits less dense, its ceilings lofty. It would respond to stimuli, to the desires and questions of visitors. It would communicate through informative labels and bolder murals. It would engage people with dynamic displays. It would be active, not august and funereal but playful and forward-looking. It would be sensitive to time, to weekends and seasons. It would be productive, as much an active center for the promotion of modern arts and crafts as a treasure hoard in vitro. It would be purposive, sending missions into the hinterlands. It would pass along its wisdoms through series of object lessons. It would be soulful, drawing from folklife. It would, like the irrepressible folk, be self-repairing, practiced in conservation. And it would adapt, balancing new technologies against old traditions.[36]

Most alive and personable would be the Living Museum, conceived by Dr. Artur Hazelius, linguist, folklorist, and son of a Swedish general.

His was a national romance which, like a child's family romance, fantasized for Sweden an other, uncorrupt parentage, perhaps the Dalecarlians on the Norwegian border, from whose villages he removed entire rooms to repopulate them with wax figures within a Museum of the North, founded in Stockholm in 1874. Transplantation had been tried before, notably in London's India Museum, where visitors passed before a law court of the Raj, peopled with mannequins in native dress. Less an imperial Liberal than a liberal impresario, Hazelius sought scenes more evocative and energetic. Rather than demonstrating the reach of an empire on which the sun never set, he engaged Scandinavians with a northern ancestry on which the sun no longer seemed to rise. To a deer park on an island in Stockholm he transported a Lapp village (with reindeer), wooden bell towers and churches, old farmhouses (with crops), chalets and huts, windmills and workshops (with tools). Throughout would walk and work Dalecarlian peasants and Lapp reindeer-herders, paid to inhabit this limbo between Game Time and real time.[37]

Skansen Park in 1891 was a refuge for the endangered folk and a spa for the Swedish spirit. The Living Museum defined a people not by military conquests or political treaties but by those aspects of daily life – anonymous, unwritten – that transcend annal. Through folk songs and sensibilities, a decadent fin de siècle society could be reminded of its pristine self, howsoever ground down by modern life. The healing impulse and national romance of the Living Museum spread quickly to Norway, Finland, Denmark, then to the Netherlands, England, and the United States.

National romance nurtured both ends of folkishness, the brusque vitality of the "uncultivated" and the perseverance of a noble "original stock." The romance was most extreme in the U.S., where exhausted men went West to inhale frontier air while Daughters of the American Revolution aired the houses in which their great-grandmothers had led lives of quiet decoration. Out in the Dakotas, guided by mountain men, Easterners thrilled to the ancestral hunt; back in Philadelphia at the Centennial Exhibition of 1876 (to which Hazelius sent six folk tableaux), ladies in their grandmothers' gowns guided visitors through a colonial New England Farmer's House. Lawyer Theodore Roosevelt and novelist Owen Wister (*The Virginian*, 1902), Harvard men both, first entered the Wild West through dude ranching, which restored their patrician vigor; the pedigreed Catherine Rankin, descendant of one of Albany's first families, learned what was expected of the mistress of a 1787 estate by touring other manors kept meticulously old in Boston, Lexington, and Concord. Out in the Wyoming Territory were puma and primitive living; back in Morristown, New Jersey, was a house that had been a Revolutionary War command center, where "The same oaken doors open to you as they did to Washington.... The floors he trod in anxious thought and with wearied brain, you may tread.... The mirrors used by General and Lady Washington you may see your faces reflected in." Out there, primeval vistas; back here, period rooms and calendar photographs of a virtuous past, women in colonial dress perched on antique rockers over hooked rugs. Out there, open country and the preserved wilderness of the first National Park, Yellowstone, "a great breathing-place for the national lungs"; back here, a tightly laced string of National Battlefields and Old Houses preserved by the bequests of founding families.[38]

Preservation, no matter what theorists said, *was* restoration. People rich or middling chose to preserve that through which could be restored a sense of personal, ethnic, or national integrity and purpose. English architect George Gilbert Scott, lover of gothic churches, insisted in 1850 that the restorer "should forget *himself* in his veneration for the works of his predecessors," but such selflessness ran up against evangelical desires to retrieve "original detail" so as to rekindle an original faith. Wrote the most influential gothicist, French architect Eugène Emmanuel Viollet-le-Duc: "The term Restoration and the thing itself are both modern. To restore a building is not to preserve it, to repair, or rebuild it; it is to reinstate it in a condition of completeness which could never have existed at any given time." What fired his imagination was the "reinstating in its entirety and in its minutest details, of a fortress of the middle ages, the reproduction of its interior decoration, even to its furniture; in a word, giving back its form, its colour, and — if I may venture to say so — its former life."[39]

Architects centuries before, reworking structures during the "Middle Ages" and throughout the Renaissance, had debated the choices. Should they defer to a building's age, replacing with painstaking pastiche those elements of sculpted stone or stained glass no longer legible? Or did a new age demand a new edifice surpassing but incorporating the original, with a "concordance and harmony of the ancient and new work"? Victorians, restoring medieval cloisters and churches to "former life," blocked over restorations done with care by medieval masons themselves.[40]

Giving a house back its "former life" seemed to demand, by 1900, both divestment and investiture. Divestment: of the hodgepodge a house gathers unto itself; of that incoherence of styles common to well-off households furnished with a variety of replica pasts and unique heirlooms. Investiture: of the house as a dated Creation, with artifacts equally and impeccably old; of the house as a *home*, warm bodies taking on its airs. Like other ceremonies of confession and coronation, this was high theater.

At theaters, in fact, audiences had become anxious about anachronism. As early as 1802, drama critic Washington Irving had complained of thespians "dressing for the same piece in the fashions of different ages and countries, so that while one actor is strutting about the stage in the cuirass and helmet of Alexander, another dressed up in a gold-laced coat and a bag-wig...is taking snuff in the fashion of one or two centuries back." Directions written into eighteenth-century scripts had sometimes asked for performers "dress'd in the habits of the times"; by the 1820s, with James Planché's scrupulous designs for Shakespearean histories, actors and audiences began to attend to consistency and accuracy in the outfitting of historical dramas. "It was not requisite to be an antiquary," wrote Planché in hindsight, "to see the absurdity of the soldiers before Angiers, at the beginning of the thirteenth century, being clothed precisely the same as those fighting at Bosworth at the end of the fifteenth."[41]

Wasn't it? Wasn't it antiquarianism "When the curtain rose and discovered *King John* dressed as his effigy appears in Worcester Cathedral, surrounded by his barons sheathed in mail, with cylindrical helmets and correct armorial shields"? Wasn't it antiquarianism that led Charles Kean to excuse aforehand his 1853 production of *Macbeth*, whose costumes were surmised from those of Danes and Angles, since uncertainty about "the dress worn by the inhabitants of Scotland in the eleventh century, renders any attempt to present this tragedy attired in the costume of the period a task of very great difficulty"? By 1894, Great Birnam wood to high Dunsinane hill must come in the most archival of guises, to carry "the spectator involuntarily back to the very period itself by process of artistic and very justifiable illusion."[42]

Audiences were further persuaded toward completeness of illusion by vast historical panoramas with special effects, by detailed historical paintings, and by subtler theatrical lighting. The English playwright Tom Robertson taught audiences to be as impatient with unbelievable sets as with histrionics. "In a comedy which aims at realism, and the essential character of which demands *vraisemblance*," observed a London critic, "the furniture and accessories are of great importance" – so great that in Robertson's transatlantic successes of the 1860s and 1870s, the rooms for the first time had ceilings, the doors locks. "The ivy to be real ivy," instructed Robertson for Act III, scene 1 of *Birth*, "and the grass to be grass matting – not painted."[43]

From the "justifiable illusion" of theaters, from the investiture of old houses as ancestral homes, from national romance with frontier life and family trees, from the chivalry of tournament and the endowment of folkways with the power to heal, came the historical pageant. Its reenactments of episodes in the biography of a town or state were often modeled upon historical paintings, scripted by professional playwrights, performed by men who regularly dressed and skirmished in antique style, by women who dressed and furnished their houses in the fashion of bygone days. The historical pageant conflated recounting with restoration and, hoped one pageant master, commemoration with collective service. Maybe, thought Percy MacKaye, who co-directed a cast of seven thousand in the 1914 Pageant and Masque of Saint Louis, maybe the ritual and rhythms of pageantry could sate the hunger for a national drama that would otherwise be met by bloody repetitions of valor and fortitude. As historian David Glassberg has noted, the pageants tended to show Americans as at their finest in wartime.[44]

Like the kriegspiel, the pageant drilled and deployed forces to reenact events within a time frame too compressed to tolerate equivocal ambitions or double-edged outcomes, strikes, anarchism, indolence, indifference. Arising around 1900, when it was vital to clarify the transit to another century, pageants in the United States were dedicated to the purity of progress. English towns hosted strictly medieval anniversaries. In Germany, Everymen walked a late medieval tightrope between seduction and ignorance. American pageantry went beyond tournament medievalism (knights in lace-curtain chain mail), tournament colonialism (Minutemen and Redcoats reenacting the Battle of Concord), and tournament frontierism (circus Injuns circling Wagon Trains) to prove a community's vitality. To reenact was to be alive.[45]

After World War I, which recruiters made out to be another scene in an epic of American virtues, commercial companies began to stage standardized pageants of American history into which any town's times could be smoothly basted. The operative word was "smooth," as in the cinematics of D.W. Griffith's *America* (1924), filmed on National Battlefields and in Old Houses; as in smooth-talking advertisements for Victor Talking Machine recordings of "Henry Ford's Old Time Orchestra" through which barn-dancers in 1926 could "Recapture the Old-Time Communal Joy in Music." So smooth that pageants would glide from frontier folk to flappers, skipping gladly past the Civil War, ethnic rivalries, racism.[46]

Precisely the smoothness of such historical compression made the Living Museum appealing. To alight from an electric trolley into a pioneer village, a frontier trading post, or Washington's parlor was to make instant contact with what each American was already supposed to be, at root. The pioneer caravan of 1937–38 that retraced the path of colonial settlers leaving Massachusetts for Marietta, Ohio, crossed many a ridge, but the ox-drawn wagons were not crossing much of a psychic divide. The two millions who cheered the caravan as it passed, like the hundred thousand who saw the Pilgrims land again at Plymouth Rock in 1920, were reciting a credo of personal authenticity and social continuity.[47]

Call it "custodianship" of houses, "stewardship" of remaining wilderness, or "husbandry" of threatened species, acts of preservation were defensible only when felt to be a refreshment of inner life. Given an industrial capitalism that prided itself in its capacity to reproduce *anything* material, antiquarianism was inadequately persuasive, as were protests that uniquely old or lovely buildings "once destroyed can never be replaced." As sites of pilgrimage, houses and wildernesses had to promise more than righteous furnishings, rambling fauna. They had to hint at miracle, confirmations of faith, moments in which past and present precipitate vision: epiphany and resurrection.[48]

Resurrection as an American architectural program had begun with the Touro Synagogue, finished 1763, abandoned 1791, restored 1827, reopened (for tourists) in the 1850s, and visited by the teenage poet Emma Lazarus in the 1860s. The Rhode Island temple stood even then as a "relic of the days of old" when (from 1677) Newport had harbored a prosperous Jewish community, but Lazarus standing in the empty hall had an epiphany:

> Again we see the patriarch with his flocks,
>   The purple seas, the hot blue sky o'erhead,
> The slaves of Egypt, – omens, mysteries, –
>   Dark fleeing hosts by flaming angels led.

Composing a family romance of testamental ghosts, Lazarus sensed the need for inspiring presences. Too rigorous a fidelity to the original could lead to an inclement orthodoxy, as it would in 1908 when Boston's oldest house was restored not to the eighteenth-century home Paul Revere had made his own but to its 1680 plan, for the sake of a prim authenticity.[49]

What was required, as Lazarus intuited, was liveliness rather than literalness. Rescue the door of the Old Indian Home, last remnant of a 1704 massacre in Deerfield, Massachusetts, sure, then reenact the massacre itself in 1910, '13, '16. Move the 1685 John Ward House next to Salem's Essex Institute (with its own glassed-in 1750s kitchen), sure, then in 1909 instruct Sarah Symonds and aides, clothed in homespun, to guide visitors around the house in which, if "original furniture or utensils of the period have not been available, reproductions have been made, and the finished result is believed to be highly successful, giving much of the atmosphere of *liveableness*." Or – you are John D. Rockefeller, Jr. – commandeer a whole town and return it to the era when it was The Cradle of the Republic.[50]

Colonial Williamsburg and its eight hundred imitators in North America – Historic Deerfield, Mystic Seaport, Old World Wisconsin – feature "live interpretation" with smithies making barrel hoops, yeomen plowing fields. Living Museums propose to restore more than environments; they propose to restore behaviors that are a peculiar blend of folkways and aristocracy – the grace of the deserving rich, the nobility of the hardworking poor, the sturdiness of the farm wife, the competence of the plantation mistress. The time compression is so alluring that we admire (as at Fort Langley, British Columbia) a mother in colonial dress rocking her own infant in an antique cradle. At the Women's Museum in Aarhus, Denmark, you were "not a mere spectator, but a 'true' guest visiting your grandmother's, your mother's or your own youth. A maid sitting on her bed in her small room with her embroideries, a kitchen smelling of coffee and fried sausage, and a bedroom with a woman in childbed already in labor...showed the public what a living museum was all about."[51]

It was, and is, all about memes. Memes, proposes zoologist Richard Dawkins, are the cultural corollary to genes, transmitted in the tunes, tricks, visual tags, and catchphrases that spiral through a society. Archaeologists, costume-dramatists, and Living Museologists identify and transcribe for us the memes of distant epochs, interweaving those mne-

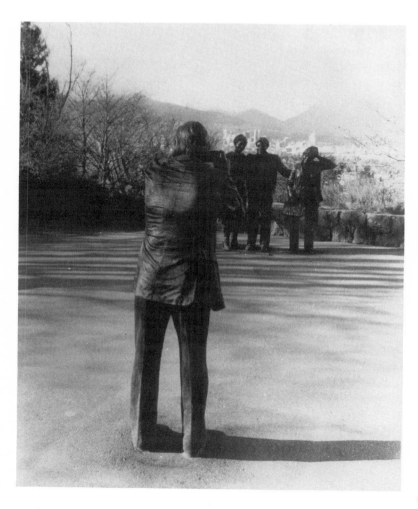

FIGURE 7.4. *Photo Session* by J. Seward Johnson, Jr., 1983. Life-size bronze sculpture of photographer *and* of tourists posing for photograph at Queen Elizabeth Park overview of Vancouver, B.C. Reproduced by permission of Sculpture Placement, Ltd., Washington, D.C. Photo by Heidi Piltz Burton.

monic strands by which we generate a familiar past. Memes pervade our travel diaries, proving that *we were there*. Memes are what tourists listen for to assure themselves that they have been in an other but authentic time – the creak of a castle drawbridge, the clang-clang-clang of a trolley. Memes are reconditioned in billions of picture postcards and in snapshots neatly aligned to postcard views. Memes circulate as airport exotica and folk art, what "first worlders" buy from canny "third world" artisans who recast or invent for them a series of objects redolent of "backward" lands.[52]

Granted that "tourism is the largest peacetime movement of people in the history of mankind" and constitutes the most global of industries, imperatives for preservation, restoration, and reenactment are likely to come less from curators than from tour guides, decorators, politicians, and filmmakers on the alert for memes – the purest of memes: that worn-through, picturesque look of objects made neither for markets nor museums but for daily use, matching images of the folk as a root cellar of practical wisdoms, an ecological preserve, an asylum of the spirit, a treasurehold of beauty. Come with us to the Kara Kum desert, invites the Travel Corporation of America. "Khiva, only recently opened to tourists, is a museum of woodcarving – almost every house is adorned with carved doors and columns with decorative patterns.... We explore places unchanged since the beginning of time."[53]

Living Museologists, like travel agents, have become memetic engineers, recombining our memes. At Williamsburg, whose directors since 1937 have put on sale seventeen hundred different replicas of colonial artifacts that "harmonize handsomely with either traditional or modern decor," the Public Hospital (1773, redone 1985) has cells with rancid straw and stained walls. "In the past," explains Dennis O'Toole, director of historic-area programs, "the criticism of Williamsburg has been that it's too clean, too spic and span." Now ox droppings are left unswept, the yards littered with oyster shells. Slave quarters have been restored and with them, at last, the greater presence of (acting) slaves.[54]

Inglorious color. Called upon to reenact the worst with the best, the Living Museum turns paradoxically to ersatz things, ersatz events. "If you are really going to tell an historical story," says one curator, "you have to be willing to use reproductions." We do have old furniture, collected until recently more for its patina than its workmanship, but rarely do we have the original upholstery, so we have become used to faking wear and tear. While eighteenth-century forgers and restorers varnished Old Masters back to "what must have been" their golden tones and made polished new limbs for antique sculptures, we intrude wormholes, knock the arms off the Venus Belvedere. The very paper on walls poses serious problems: "Do we leave a historic paper on a historic wall to insure a coequal integrity although the paper may be in only fair, perhaps poor condition? Do we in turn leave alone a historic wall that would be better repaired in order to leave untouched a historic paper in good condition?" Should they opt for legitimate decay or a lively, reviving reproduction? Living Museums tend to choose that which *authenticates* over that which is authentic, a culturally congenial deceit. Those who repeat history are condemned to repaper it — with vanished or varnished twins: the Living Dead.[55]

Who are coming to get us. As historian Pierre Nora has observed, "Since no one knows what the past will be made of next, anxiety turns everything into a trace, a possible indication, a hint of history that contaminates the innocence of all things." Almost anything can be a collectible, and recollectable. The antiquity of antiques is in steep decline. (A computer of 1984 vintage, isn't that an antique?) Advertisers and reviewers speak of "instant" classics. In a world market of products with "lives" of three or four years, nothing takes long to become History. Not even us: "You're history," we say, the moment we break up.[56]

This is not to imply, as some of late have been implying, that we are losing our grasp on history or our stake in it. That sort of critique springs from the typical tizzy at century's end over what seems to be the dizzying acceleration of events. Our problem lies not with the end of history but with a history of loose ends, a problem merely aggravated by technology. Electric pumps made possible the restaging of the 1900 Galveston Flood every half hour at Coney Island, and Victrolas encouraged "encore fiends" at the Metropolitan Opera in 1901 to demand the repetition of the entire scene in *Rigoletto* in which Nellie Melba sang "*Caro Nome*," but before the electr(on)ic world was well connected, we had already been petitioners of simulation and encore. Publishers had issued multiple editions, builders had mixed Mrs. Coade's artificial stone to simulate marble, and exposition stucco housed people simulating bygone lives.[57]

Nor are our memories, like old wallpapers, coming unglued. The everywhenness of our lives has, rather, jumbled the memes. Habits of reenactment undermine our subjunctives, confusing wish, intention, imminence, doubt; customs of simulation give us pasts as ongoing "recreations." Not a single original home stands at Plimoth Plantation; in houses recently handhewn, thirty women and men act out "learned fabrications," assuming seventeenth-century personae "invented according to probability." They go blank if you speak of MTV, but seem inured to the anachronism of half a million visitors a year thronging a Massachusetts village which in its heyday held two hundred souls. These Pilgrims have been as schooled in their present-day pasts as graduates of the Isabel O'Neil Studio for the Art of the Painted Finish have been schooled in faux marble, faux tortoise, and distressing.[58]

Distressing is the art of worrying surfaces to make them appear older. It is the mirror-opposite of the art of applying cosmetics to make ourselves look younger. That we should countenance both arts reflects an ethic of reversibility, another consequence of historical compression in our culture of the copy. We tell ourselves that we should be able to renew as we reenact, to be reborn as we recall. We look to refreshen what we play again, Sam, and to be refreshed by it. Reversibility pervades our theories of conservation (work so that "we can undo tomorrow what we did today"), of environmental action (recycle so that the Earth may return to health), even of Sequels (remake villains and heroes so that they may fight new-old battles). Irreversibility feels to be a doom, reversibility a noble contrition.[59]

When, for the centennial of the War Between the States, men of 1961 reenacted the Battle of Bull Run, it was that ethic of reversibility which drove the North and South to join on the battlefield and sing "God Bless America" at the end of what had been in 1861 a bitter rout. The ethic of reversibility drives American soldiers traumatized in Vietnam to return there and "find peace." The ethic of reversibility drives therapists to claim that "what we most fear has already happened"; they work to bring dark pasts and patterns to light and so begin recovery.[60]

Light itself turns the glazed greens of seventeenth-century paintings to gardens of bright blue. Sulfur dioxides in the air we breathe dissolve stone sculptures. Ammonia in our sweat produces a whitish bloom on antique bureaus. Mere proximity to a human body, its heat equal to that from a hundred-watt bulb, can dessicate a work of art.[61] The more that exposure is unavoidable in a democratic age, the more that deterioration threatens to be irreversible, and the more our culture of the copy insists upon some form of reversibility. What's done, if it can't be undone, can be redone, once more, with feeling.

Unlike wargames, whose excitements and repetitions have been male, the simulations of Living Museums have often been promoted and practiced by women, who have sustained our ethic of reversibility. As decorators by custom or by trade, women have shaped the market in reproductions and antiques, which come into their own through household acts of restoration: "No rare and precious objects are locked up here; they are touched, enjoyed, alive." As seamstresses and designers, they have given authenticity of detail to costume dramas. As experts at cosmetics and calisthenics, they have taken charge of our techniques of rejuvenation. As therapists and social workers, they have been responsible for much of our optimism that lives can be "turned around." As political activists they have sought to restore women to historical visibility and to reclaim a public presence. Yet, as Kathleen D. McCarthy notes in a study of American women philanthropists in the arts, there has been a disparity between their wealth and their power, and she asks why. This question I must pass over, but I cannot pass up the assumptions of her concluding sentence: "This question remains to be explored by those who would seek to know the past in order to better overcome it."[62]

What the Documeant

Shades of Santayana! Those who cannot remember the past are condemned to repeat it; ergo, those who can remember the past may overcome it? What does it mean, in a society replete with simulations and reenactments, to overcome history? Is it to reverse inertial forces? To

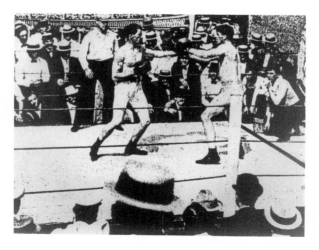

FIGURE 7.5. Kid McCoy (on left) boxing in a filmed reenactment. From Nat Fleischer and Sam André, *A Pictorial
History of Boxing.*

detach our lives from unwanted influences? To liberate ourselves from
punishing traditions?[63]

George Santayana was born in 1863 to a man of fifty-one and a woman
of thirty-seven whom he saw rather as grandparents than as father and
mother. Images of a missing generation haunted him as a Harvard student and professor, and as an independent philosopher who sought
always the moral and temporal continuities of life. He scorned the idea
that each era recasts history in its own light, for what he wanted of the
past could be neither fugitive nor fashionable: "Interesting as may be
an improvised reconstruction of things past, and fascinating the learned
illusion of living again the life of the dead, it distracts the mind from
mastering whatever the past may have mastered."[64]

A "detached, ironical, pessimistic aesthete" who preferred monastic order to modernist chaos, Santayana after World War I doubted that
outrage at the slaughter of a generation could fund an enduring peace.
He expected no change in human nature: "An ancient city would have
thought this war, or one relatively as costly, only a normal incident;
and certainly the Germans will not regard it otherwise." Although his
famous epigram has been wielded to incite breakaways from vicious
cycles, what Santayana hoped for was ethical wisdom derived from per-
petuities: "in point of truth concerning human history, any tradition is
better than any reconstruction. A tradition may be a ruin, broken unrec-
ognizably, or shabbily built over in a jungle of accretions, yet it always
retains some nucleus of antiquity; whereas a reconstruction, say a new
Life of Jesus, is something fundamentally arbitrary, created by personal
fancy, and modern from top to bottom. Such a substitution is no mere

mistake; it is a voluntary delusion which romantic egoism positively craves: to rebuild the truth nearer the heart's desire."[65]

His heart's desire was for imperturbable essences, "crushing all things in his heart as in a winepress, until his life and their secret flow out together." This was the wine, as he wrote, of a "disintoxication" of memory: "Progress, far from consisting in change, depends on retentiveness. When change is absolute there remains no being to improve and no direction is set for possible improvement: and when experience is not retained, as among savages, infancy is perpetual. Those who cannot remember the past are condemned to repeat it. In the first stage of life the mind is frivolous and easily distracted; it misses progress by failing in consecutiveness and persistence. This is the condition of children and barbarians," for whom Santayana, precocious, withdrawn, refined, had scant sympathy. "In a second stage men are docile to events, plastic to new habits and suggestions, yet able to graft them on original instincts, which they thus bring to fuller satisfaction. This is the plane of manhood and true progress," so long as "ideal identity" and "spiritual unity" remain. But "when the foundation itself shifts, when what is gained at the periphery is lost at the centre, the flux appears again and progress is not real." One must make the most of a cumulative civilization by "substituting articulate interests for animal fumes and for enigmatic passions. Such articulate interests can be shared; and the infinite vistas they open up can be pursued for ever with the knowledge that a work long ago begun is being perfected and that an ideal is being embodied which need never be outworn." No overcoming of history, not here. "Retentiveness, we must repeat, is the condition of progress."[66]

"History repeats itself," said the American lawyer Clarence Darrow, he who defended economic revolution and scientific evolution. "That's one of the things wrong with history." Darrow was litigating as history *was* being repeated before his eyes, in the shape of newsreels and the filmed "documentary," a word that appeared in English on February 8, 1926, a few months after the trial of Tennessee biology teacher J.T. Scopes. In the Darrow defense and in the *New York Sun* review of *Moana*, the issue was the same: How do we arrive at the truth? Darrow the workingman's advocate — and Scopes's counsel — arrived at truth by increments of evidence, then appealed to the spirit of a human, evolving law; his aged adversary William Jennings Bryan, "The Great Commoner," arrived at truth as he had lifelong arrived at oratorical climax, by passion and inspiration, then appealed to the letter of God's unchanging Law. Bryan died within a week of the conviction of Scopes, but it would have been fun to escort both men to the premier of *Moana*, for like the "Monkey trial," Robert J. Flaherty's film of a youth on a South Sea island posed questions about social evolution. The reviewer for the *Sun*, John Grierson, had come over from England on fellowship to study the effects of mass media upon public opinion; in his opinion *Moana* was a great film, "a poetic record of Polynesian tribal life...of man when he is a part of beautiful surroundings, a figment of nature, an innocent primitive rather than a so-called intelligent being cooped up in the mire of so-called intelligent civilization."[67]

Moana as an "account of events in the daily life of a Polynesian youth and his family" had "of course," wrote Grierson, a "documentary value," akin to the tattooing by which Moana's entrance upon manhood was certified. But *Moana* achieved greatness "primarily through its poetic feeling for natural elements." When Flaherty crossed the Atlantic to make a documentary, he went to the Aran Islands — to find a story in the location itself. He spoke to Grierson "almost mystically of the camera's capacity for seeing beyond mortal eyes to the inner qualities of things," and admired the spontaneity of children and animals, "the finest of movie actors," but talked also "of the movements in peasants and craftsmen and hunters and priests as having a special magic on the screen because time or tradition has worn them smooth."[68]

There was the rub. Another Englishman, devoted as was Grierson to documentary as "the creative dramatization of actuality and the expression of social analysis," took Flaherty's films to task as archaic idylls, "man against nature; cruel, bitter, savage, and heroic but unrelated to modern society." Ignoring the harshness of oppression and then Depression, said Paul Rotha, Flaherty "reconstructs native life of a past or dying generation. The heroes of both *Nanook* and *Man of Aran*, for example, were waxwork figures acting the lives of their grandfathers." Indeed, *Nanook of the North* (1922), funded by a French fur-trading company and subtitled *Man of Primitive Times*, was equal parts museum diorama and taxidermic drama. Filmed with cameras developed by that museum hunter and stuffer Carl Akeley, scenes of walrus hunting had been restaged with the help of Inuit men wearing only the best furs. The seal Nanook pulled out from under the ice after a long struggle had been, he knew, dead from the start, but Nanook also knew the conventions of comedy and tumbled head over heels in his tug-of-war with the prop carcass. The wife and children he embraced were unrelated to him and to each other. Two years after *Nanook* opened, Nanook died of starvation.[69]

Truth, "documentary" truth, played fast and loose with time and substance in order to catch the soul of a people, the genius of a place. "Sometimes you have to lie," said Flaherty, who got *Moana* islanders to resume tattooing, a rite they had abandoned. "One often has to distort a thing to catch its true spirit." By the 1920s, all but some home movies were cinematic events distorted and/or repeated for the camera, whether produced by Hollywood studios, civic boosters, industrialists, trade unions, socialists, or communists. "The basic fact was true, and remains true to this day, that the juxtaposition of two separate shots by splicing them together resembles not so much a simple sum of one shot plus another shot — as it does a *creation*." Thus Sergei Eisenstein in 1942, whose films *Potemkin* (1925) and *Ten Days That Shook the World* (1928) have such a documentary feel that clips are shown as if they were archival footage of the Russian Revolution.[70]

Before "documentary" was short for "documentary film," the French had applied "*documentaire*" to travelogues, and the English had "documentized," lecturing with magic lantern slides of exotic lands. *Nanook of the North* and *Moana* belonged to the tradition of the travelogue and to photographic practices in which transplanted walls and refurbished costumes stood in for "primitive," diminishing societies. The candid figures on the screen were, or would soon be, sole survivors to vanished twins pressed flat by an expanding industrial world. Such practices had been applied as early as 1870 in the Pacific Northwest, where Richard and Hannah Maynard photographed a Haida washerwoman against a plain backdrop, then rephotographed "Haida Mary" against the backdrop of an abandoned Haida village. By 1915, when American photographer Edward S. Curtis arrived to "document" the Haida, their elders enjoyed posing for photo portraits in suits and top hats, and their craftspeople used news pictorials as models for designs carved for the tourist trade. Curtis had the men wear long wigs over their short hair and asked everyone to pose in clothes less modern. The Haida themselves equated the camera with the wooden mask; both were for "copying people." On the glass backs of cameras, they saw "copies" of people appearing like masked dancers.[71]

Mask-dancing may serve as simile for making "documentary" pictures. Was it not mask-dancing to pose kids dressed as street urchins in before-and-after scenes so as to raise money for orphanages? "Once a Little Vagrant! Now a Little Workman." ❖ The Inuit of British Columbia carved animal transformation masks whose faces would split to reveal another, protective, animal or spirit within. ❖ Was it not mask-dancing to pose boys picking the pockets of a drunk, staged in the 1890s after an 1840s *Police Gazette* woodcut, so as to propel slum reform and the redemption of children whose faces were those "of animals, the souls being gone"? ❖ A Haida photographer went around taking pictures with an empty camera: what was vital was the ritual posing before the camera, not that spoor, the photograph.[72]

Behind the mask dance lay insignia or scenery guaranteeing that the documentary had been taken on location. To be "a transcript of real life," the documentary had to appear to be both on time and in place. One could photograph nude men or women running and jumping against black-and-white grids, as did Eadweard Muybridge in the 1880s, and one could film Fred Ott sneezing full-on, as did Thomas Alva Edison's crew in 1894, but such plain-Jane physiological (and erotic) documents were quickly superseded by cinematic narratives that required *situation*.[73]

Early films situated themselves through a process as crazily circular as any chase by Keystone cops. The first movies showed simple incidents: a waterfight on a lawn, a runaway horse, a kiss, a mounted police charge, people disembarking to attend the Congress of Photography. Then, filmmakers more ambitious and audiences more demanding, cameramen worked atop roofs or in black-box studios, shooting scenes in front of theater sets and refining special effects: ghosts, vanishings, Doppelgängers. As plots grew more complex, with indoor and outdoor scenes in the same film, action on stock sets began to seem unreal in contrast to action in the open air. Sets were rebuilt to ensure continuity between an inner electrically-lit world and the outer daylit world; a critic in 1911 would "never forget the honest joy with which the Vitagraph producers in the early days of that company's higher art endeavors, succeeded in producing a studio setting of a forest scene that deceived spectators into thinking it was genuine." By 1914, movie interiors could seem equally genuine, their detailing as exact as period rooms or as the sets supplied by producer David Belasco, who transported an actual boarding-house bedroom to the Broadway stage in *The Easiest Way* (1909). Exterior scenes were then taken to new extremes. For the climax of *Way Down East*, shot and reshot by an exacting D.W. Griffith during the winter of 1919, Lillian Gish and her valiant double nearly froze the hands they had to dangle in the icy waters of the Hartford River as they struggled on a (wooden) ice floe carrying the heroine over a(n intercut) waterfall to her death.[74]

Could a "documentary" be any more persuasive? any more real? It could, if it were news. Almost from the start, filmmakers manipulated props and actors to recreate events no movie camera had caught. Edward Amet redid the naval battles of the Spanish-American War of 1898 with ship miniatures set up in Waukegan, Illinois; Siegmund Lubin refought the *Fighting Near Santiago*, Cuba, near his optical shop in Philadelphia; the American Vitagraph Company filmed *The Battle of Manila Bay* on a Manhattan rooftop using pinches of gunpowder and a bay an inch deep. All sold their films as news footage. James Williamson recreated the Boxer *Attack on a China Mission* (1900) in his Sussex garden; Georges Méliès did the same outside Paris. After the Boxer Rebellion had been crushed, two American cameramen restaged the Western assault on the South Gate of Peking – in Peking itself.[75]

Back again, it seems, to wargames. Although other events (the San Francisco earthquake and the eruption of Mount Vesuvius in 1906) would be restaged for movie cameras, the odds-on favorites were battles and prizefights, in part because early film audiences were fascinated with the display of "accidental, arbitrary, and absurd" postures and movements, in part because club-room tacticians and barroom gamblers would *want* to re-view and gainsay them. The first peep-hole movie (kinetoscope) shown by Charles Chinnock in 1894 was a boxing match. The first offering from the Latham Kinetoscope Exhibition Company was also a boxing match. Jim Corbett and Pete Courtney met at Edison's New Jersey film studio in 1894 in a ring half as large for rounds a third as long as usual, so the action was concentrated. Said the champ, Gentleman Jim, who earned most of his money simulating matches in stage melodramas, "It is stipulated that I must put the guy out in six rounds or I get nothing; for, as I understand it, the machine is so arranged that a longer fight is undesirable."[76]

Fixed by the length of reels or by prearrangement, boxing films were punchdrunk about the ropes separating exhibitions from title fights, reenactments from originals. A few bouts, like that in 1897 at which Bob Fitzsimmons won the title from Corbett, were clearly filmed at original ringside; most early cinematic fights were foggier. Lubin by 1905 had an inventory of over 150 fight films, the majority recreated by doubles or by the boxers themselves shortly after the real thing. "BEWARE OF IMITATIONS," read an 1899 Lubin advertisement. "We Have the ONLY Reproduction of the FITZSIMMONS-JEFFRIES FIGHT.... The fight from start to finish is most realistic, true to nature, and full of life and action." In 1900, Lubin boasted that his "reproduction of the MCGOVERN-DIXON FIGHT was ready the day after the fight took place. Don't be a clam and buy pictures of a fight which are made four weeks after the fight took place and called original. Which is the fake, the one SHOWN the day after the fight or the one MADE four weeks after?" Such befuddling. Which *was* the fake – a reenactment filmed in Lubin's studio, ostentatiously copyrighted and ready for distribution the next day, or a film of the actual event, processed and on sale a month later? Beware that slippery word "reproduction," which Lubin seemed to be using as a synonym for "moving picture." As one of Lubin's cameramen wrote, "We faked championship bouts by using matched doubles for the boxers and staging the round-by-round action from newspaper accounts. We then sold the picture as the actual championship fight with the real boxers." After Corbett defeated Kid McCoy with suspicious ease in the fifth round of their match in 1900, the two fought a cinematic version which Lubin promoted as the real McCoy. Whether Corbett was to "lie down" but reneged, or whether McCoy had been lax because he was to take the fall, the two were condemned to repeat blow-by-blow what reporters remembered of what boxing afficionados suspected was a fixed fight.[77]

Lubin's cameramen were among the first to shoot front-line fighting during World War I, but the footage was "too horrible to be shown." Hoping perhaps to keep Americans out of the war, Lubin explained that "such pictures would be anything but neutral in their effect on an audience." The thousands of German films taken at the Front would be shown only to the military. And despite the brutalized bodies of his *Birth of a Nation*, D.W. Griffith had the *Battle of the Somme* rerun across Salisbury Plain; what he had filmed on the Front he had found, like Lubin, to be unsuitable, even for purposes of propaganda.[78]

Tell me if it is real,
    This life I have lived,
    This death I am dying,

went the death chant of Chief Buffalo Child Long Lance at the height of his fame in 1930, days before his exposure as an impostor and two years before his suicide. What documentary does is (re)construction work, personal, social, political. One may cry foul, but documentary truths are not instantaneous; they are the truths of action done double. In this culture of the copy, repetition and simulation make our life, our death, real. In 1913 Jack Binns, a shipboard wireless-telegraph operator, did win a suit against the Vitagraph Company for having depicted without permission what purported to be a "a true picture of him" signaling for help when the *Republic* collided with a steamship in 1909. The force of the legal injunction, however, was ultimately unequal to societal forces favoring the reenactment in *C.Q.D. or Saved by Wireless*. A Vitagraph director testified, "Our method of reproducing current events which I have described as news matters, is by getting all the data, all the matter in hand, from every reliable source and weaving it into what we call a picture story," written "just as a playwright writes a play" and filmed on sets. What was underhanded about that? Or about play-by-play radio narrations of baseball games during the 1920s, the plays phoned in to announcers who mixed crowd noises with their own pretense of sitting in the stands. News, like history, must be recreated. "Those who do not remember the past," as Santayana is repeatedly misquoted, "are condemned to relive it."[79]

Long Lance himself, popular authority on and filmstar of Native American life during the 1920s, seemed entirely unable to remember the past until he relived it. Born in Winston, North Carolina, in 1890, of Cherokee, Croatan, white, and likely black ancestry, Sylvester Clark Long was a good boxing reporter but an incorrigible liar about his life and an unreliable informant on the Plains Indians for whom he claimed to speak as "Big Boss." Circus brave, Indian School athlete, Canadian war hero, Blackfoot Chief, he put on one mask after another in order to pass as the noblest of savages in a white society that had made him ashamed of his (repudiated) black heritage and of a mother born a slave. Pass he did, his specious autobiography of 1928 praised by Paul Radin, a leading ethnologist, as "an unusually faithful account" of a Plains Indian childhood. The apex of his career was *The Silent Enemy* of 1930. In the tradition of *Nanook of the North*, Long Lance played Baluk, great Ojibwa hunter whose Silent Enemy, before White Men, was hunger. The documentary style of the film told him and his audience that it *was* real, this life he had hungered for as a red-blooded American Indian.[80]

During the Thirties, ideologies of social realism underwrote the power of documentary to affirm the dignity of people beaten down or displaced. Western filmmakers learned from a decade of social-revolutionary Russian documentaries; they watched peasants telling Dziga Vertov, The Man with a (Movie) Camera, "We don't know life. We haven't seen life, we've seen our village and ten verst around. Show us life." While March of Time newsreels collaged stock footage, impersonations, and reenactments with the real McCoy under the spell of "voice of God" narration, documentarists of all ilks went around capturing the spirit of the folk, broken or indomitable, to make points about loss or electrification, the disintegration of the family or the nobility of (organized) labor. Workers' newsreels in Holland, Germany, Japan, and the U.S. pursued themes of class warfare. Leni Riefenstahl's *Triumph of the Will* (1935), a lyrical record of the Nuremberg rally in 1934, did for the Nazi Party and German people what the Farm Security Administration wanted its documentaries to do for Americans: inspire a collective work of social reconstruction.[81]

Through repetition and reenactment, documentary elevated last testaments into testimonials. "Consciousness raised to the second power, [which] is repetition," noted Søren Kierkegaard in an essay on repetition translated into English around 1940. Life was repetition, and that was the beauty of it. "Indeed, if there were no repetition, what then would life be? Who would wish to be a tablet upon which time writes every instant a new inscription? or to be a mere memorial of the past?... Repetition is reality, and it is the seriousness of life." A theology of transcendence for a young Danish philosopher in 1843, repetition a century later was a strategy of iridescence employed by advertisers, behaviorists, journalists, and propagandists. Reality, many of them believed, was a vector of repetition and simulation. What the woman of the house did again and again made her what she was, or would be; what the man on the street heard over and over constituted what he knew, or loved. Hence the repetition of print ads and radio jingles and the launching of one documentarist magazine after another: *Life, Look, Click, Focus, Foto, Photo, Picture, See*. To assure their own documentariness, people began to carry club membership cards, library cards, driver's licenses – credentials that for the jobless during the Depression would become critical proof of identity and integrity.[82]

Whatever documentary photographers said about the integrity of their images of common people, they were rather "participant observers," the research personae of the 1930s. Walker Evans, shocked to hear that fellow photographer Arthur Rothstein had moved a steer skull from an alkali flat to scrubgrass near cactus so as to highlight the impact of overgrazing, exploded: "that's where the word 'documentary' holds; you don't touch a *thing*. You 'manipulate,' if you like, when you frame a picture – one foot one way or one foot another. But you're not sticking anything in." Oh? Working with James Agee on *Let Us Now Praise Famous Men* (1941), Walker rearranged subjects and objects. He set the beds at photogenic angles and cleared clutter from tables in sharecroppers' homes, intent on "the order and beauty that he believed lay beneath the surface of their poverty." Dorothea Lange, coming upon Florence Thompson and four of her seven children at a California pea-pickers' camp in 1936, took what became the icon of the Depression, *Migrant Mother*, but only after rearranging the children, excluding the teenage daughter and asking the woman to lift her right arm up to her face – a gesture since seen as a spontaneous expression of weariness and endurance. Nor was Florence, as many thought, one of the millions of poor whites displaced by the Depression; she was Cherokee. Forty-seven years later and forty-some miles from the same pea fields, speechless after a stroke, she died of cancer, in debt, uninsured.[83]

So a tradition of simulation was in place for the famous World War II flag-raising at Iwo Jima: never was that U.S. flag raised under fire; never do we see the forty men of Easy Company who did the original flag-raising (delayed while a photographer reloaded). The shot that became paradigmatic of American heroism was that of the anchoring of a larger flag, hours later, in front of a second photographer, Joe Rosenthal, from whose composition in 1945 (replicated in the hundred tons of Felix de Weldon's bronze statue of 1954) are missing the many other Marines relaxing atop Mt. Suribachi and the 150 Japanese who had suicided in a cave just below them. The tradition was in place for the simulations of the CBS TV series *You Are There*, 1953–57, where "All things are as they were, except YOU ARE THERE!" scripted by two blacklisted writers, who used others as their fronts, and narrated by Walter Cronkite, who would soon anchor the evening news. The tradition was in place for the televised docudrama, *Roots*, from a novel that won a special Pulitzer Prize and was praised for its loyal tracing of one man's African-American ancestry. Described by the author, Alex Haley, as "a faction," a "literary social document based upon exhaustive research and characterized by the presentation of historical fact through the medium of fictionalized dialog," *Roots* was, it turns out, an exhaustive fiction.[84]

Rectitude nor turpitude is the issue before us, but our increasingly indiscriminate acceptance of the commingling of act and reenactment, until a writer for a 1991 docudrama, *The Heroes of Desert Storm*, could crow that "The alchemist's dream in television, the turning of lead into gold, was to remove the wall that distinguishes reality from illusion. We achieved the alchemist's dream." With combat video segued to video reenactments segued to news clips, "You cannot tell where the various gradations of reality and reenactment cross paths." While televised news uses archival footage to grace fresh tape with an historic mandorla, feature films like Woody Allen's *Zelig* (1983) and Carlos Saurin's *The Nandu Era* (1987) intermix old newsreel with newly scratched, grainy footage to historiate a fiction. Oliver Schmitz's *Mapantsula* (1989) imitated documentary style – handheld motions, deep focus, longer takes – to feed "an audience starved of actuality footage" under South African censorship. Oliver Stone, in his *JFK* (1991) and his *Nixon* (1995), intercut "home" movies, videotape, and television news coverage with fictive "home" movies, specious videotape, and historical reenactments shot in black-and-white or fading color so as to meld his actors and actresses into still-unsettled contemporary dramas. In 1994, for soap-operatic effect, Robert Zemeckis digitally insinuated *Forrest Gump* (Tom Hanks) into the visual archive of some of the most memorable events of the last half of this century. At the American Archives of the Factual Film, "factual" itself remains a term as ambiguous as the alternate term, "non-theatrical."[85]

Theater or actuality – which was it? – when documentarist Mike Hoover staged guerilla battles for a CBS special, "The Battle for Afghanistan" (1987). Theater or actuality – which? – when ABC's *World News Tonight* in 1989 aired a tape of an alleged spy handing a briefcase to a KGB agent, both impersonated by men at ABC, whose news president apologized that a "technical failure" had left the simulation looking more real than the news producer (*sic*) intended. A news producer at NBC, asked to comment, said that the recreation of events was "a natural step in broadcast news. It is an idea whose time has come."[86]

Predicaments moral and political, deriving from the theatricality of event in an electronically mediated world, have been widely addressed. I am here addressing a different predicament: our habit of relying upon reenactment and repetition to establish the truth of events and the authenticity of people. Despite the rhetoric of uniqueness and once-in-a-lifetime experiences, our culture of the copy mocks that romanticism which seeks out the irreproducible as the source of Truth. The makers of Waterford crystal are wise (and wealthy) when they tell us, "Once in a lifetime moments don't just happen once in a lifetime." It is unwise (and unhealthy) to claim, as did the producer of *Roots*, that "You don't go back and refer to [a docudrama] for information. You see it once and whatever you remember of it stays with you. If what stays with you is the truth, how you got there, to me, is not overly relevant." For a decade now, schools have been teaching African-American history with *Roots* as archival centerpiece; since the advent of the VCR, we play back *Roots* more often than we read Haley's books (except perhaps *The Autobiography of Malcolm X*, which Haley ghostwrote). If constant repetition renders some events surreal (the filmed assassination of John F. Kennedy, the videotaped beating of Rodney King), singularity now surrenders events to apparition, evanescence, insignificance.[87]

Technologies of visual replay – movies projected in slow motion, the Polaroid camera, videotape, computer digitizing – accommodate our predilections for perfecting the instant. If a referee's call is dubious, instantly replay the moment until he gets it *right*. If a wedding ceremony is too messy, reenact it on the spot until the vows are *right*.[88] "When people see that the camera is turned on," director Bill Cran told writer Ved Mehta, "they start behaving like their real selves." Then, directing a documentary in India about Mehta's elderly first cousin, Cran refuses to accept the man's real self. Impoverished Chachaji would hardly arrive in a village in a horse-drawn trap. But it's so "Chachaesque," says Bill, who says that "whatever looks good, or can be made to look good, is fine in a documentary." Chachaji's arrival must be restaged, with trap and emaciated horse, for light and camera angles. Disappointed when a hailstorm does not flatten Chachaji's village, Cran finds the man's life too repetitive. "There's no progression. It goes round and round in circles." Repetition as restaging is fine; repetition that is "stoical, dogged" is not. Our culture of the copy wants every replay to transcend the original. Chachaji, watching the finished video on a VCR, turned to Ved Mehta: "Wonderful! Was that really me? Was it a dream? It seemed as if I was having a holy audience with myself in Heaven."[89]

Double Blinds

"To observe a recurrence is to divine a mechanism," wrote Santayana, who trusted that history could be a natural science if not a celestial audience. The historical currents of this chapter have been driven by a modern wellspring of faith in replication, confluent with our economy, technology, law, politics, and fine arts. What is reproducible seems profitable, patentable, provable, improvable, imperishable...and true. Repeatedly enlarging one detail in a picture, the fashion photographer of Antonioni's *Blow-Up* (1967) comes upon a crime. Reconstructing the scene of a crime, detectives solve murder mysteries and lawyers elicit confessions in courtroom dramas. Replicating experiments, scientists confirm an hypothesis, shore up a theory.[90]

Tacked to the door of Dorothea Lange's darkroom was a quotation from Francis Bacon's *Novum Organum* of 1620:

> The contemplation of things as they are
> Without substitution or imposture
> Without error or confusion
> Is in itself a nobler thing
> Than a whole harvest of invention.

The first half of the quotation is equally apt: "And yet (to speak the whole truth), as the uses of light are infinite in enabling us to walk, to ply our arts, to read, to recognize one another – and nevertheless the very beholding of the light is itself a more excellent and a fairer thing than all the uses of it – so assuredly the very contemplation...." But Lange had copied "substitution" for "superstition," a Freudian slip revealing, perhaps, the guilty retouching that takes place in the darkroom, where Lange had an assistant rub out Florence Thompson's unsightly thumb from a tent post in *Migrant Mother*.[91]

Bacon would have forgiven the mistranscription, for he had anticipated errors: "this is of no consequence, for such things must needs happen at first. It is only like the occurrence in a written or printed page of a letter or two mistaken or misplaced, which does not much hinder the reader, because such errors are easily corrected by the sense. So likewise may there occur in my natural history many experiments which are mistaken and falsely set down, and yet they will presently, by the discovery of causes and axioms, be easily expunged and rejected." If methods were made clear, others could repeat experiments to get them *right*.[92]

Natural philosophers (scientists), lawyers, and historians of the seventeenth and successive centuries, seeking good replications, devised probabilistic methods of adjusting discrepancies in observation, testimony, and annal. If no experimental results could be taken as true unless

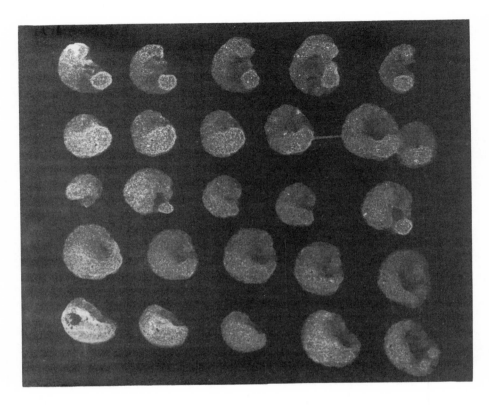

FIGURE 7.6. Photograph of the effects of N-rays, discovered by Prof. René Blondlot of the University of Nancy in 1903. Blondlot's directions on "How the Action of 'n' Rays should be observed" insist that one should "in no way try to *fix* the eye upon the luminous source, whose variations in glow one wishes to ascertain. On the contrary, one must, so to say, see the source without looking at it, and even direct one's glance vaguely in a neighbouring direction. The observer must play an absolutely passive part, under penalty of seeing nothing.... In fact, the observer should accustom himself to look at the screen just as a painter, and in particular an 'impressionist' painter, would look at a landscape. To attain this requires some practice, and is not an easy task. Some people, in fact, never succeed." Frontispiece to R. Blondlot, *"N" Rays: A Collection of Papers Communicated to the Academy of Sciences* (London, 1905).

replicated, it also seemed true that no two experiments yielded exactly the same results, no two participants or witnesses reported exactly the same thing. Astronomers had customarily dealt with such inexactitude by opting for the median — that figure below and above which lie an equal number of different results. Gradually, as scientists accepted the idea of inevitable inconsistencies regardless of instruments or methods, they preferred the mean or average. Supported by a mathematical theory of errors, the mean in the nineteenth century became the linchpin of that law of averages beloved of demographers and economists. Although (as today) the Average Man and Average Woman probably stuck with the mode — the most frequent result — as most reliable because most recurrent, social statisticians looked to the Average Person with a gleam in their eyes. The president of the Société de Statistique de Paris waxed poetic in 1886: "It is the mean that rules our life, our rent, our pleasures, our clothes, in a word our budget.... The physical world submits to this same influence. The stars balance themselves in space around their mean position with a rhythm as harmonious as the vibration of a string beneath a bow or the heave and shiver of a wave beneath a breath of wind.... So the universe aspires to the mean, which is but another expression of equilibrium."[93]

Equilibrium shaken by a newly relativistic physics and psychology, the mean this century has given way to a statistics of variability, levels of confidence, and "personal equations" describing unique rhythms of response to stimuli.[94] In a universe where no experiment is perfectly repeatable and observers affect what they observe, results and observations have had to be hedged with assurances of objectivity and neutrality or invisibility. These assurances were being given everywhere at century's turn. In journalism, the assertion of the objectivity of reporters. In baseball, the introduction of objectively neutral umpires. In psychiatry, ethology, advertising, criminology: the invisibility of analysts behind couches, fieldworkers behind bushes, market researchers behind polls, investigators behind one-way mirrors.

Double blindness was best. The double blind procedure was first used in the testing of drugs reputed to relieve cardiac pain. Long before modern psychophysics, in which pain is a half-truth either of sensation or perception, healers and torturers knew that pain is unrelievedly subjective. Wavering between careers as a physician or zoologist, Sigmund Freud wrote to a friend in 1878, "I am preparing myself for my real profession: 'flaying of animals or torturing of human beings,'" alluding to the cartoon terrors Max and Moritz, who tormented geese and people alike. The truth told by a patient's torment, wrote *Doctor* Freud in 1894, was hidden by the "neuro-psychoses of defense," but it was as revealing as it was personal — in his case too, with his migraines and the "stabbing pains" of tachycardia. Later, subject to the chronic pain of a mishandled oral cancer and a badly fitted prosthesis, he would fit mental disorders to an overarching theory about the obliqueness of unresolved pain — the pain, above all, of separation from Mother. Human beings might have similar "nociceptors" to sense acute pain, but their chronic pain was as much the pain of isolation as it was isolating. He from whom many had sought the meaning of their pain would write, shortly before his death in 1939, that his world was "a small island of pain floating on an ocean of indifference."[95]

Question: Where each person *is* an island, how can we test – objectively, impartially, invisibly – the effectiveness of an analgesic? Answer: play a double confidence game in which neither experimenter nor subject knows what is being taken, the test drug or a placebo. *Placebo Domino in regione vivorum*, "I shall please the Lord in the land of the living," reads the Vulgate version of Psalm 114.9, recited during vespers for the dead. In the Jerusalem Bible, "distress and anguish gripped me, / I invoked the name of Yahweh," and He rescued me from death, so "I will walk in Yahweh's presence / in the land of the living." From such gratefulness toward God, *placebo* in English was turned toward one's superiors; flattering servants "sang a placebo" in the fifteenth, sixteenth, and seventeenth centuries. By the eighteenth, a placebo was any soothing courtesy and, said Motherby's *New Medical Dictionary* (1783), a common course of medication – defined by a dictionary of 1811 as "any medicine adopted more to please than to benefit the patient." That was not quite so, for to please *was* to benefit. "One of the most successful physicians I have ever known," wrote Thomas Jefferson, "has assured me, that he uses more bread pills, drops of colored water, and powders of hickory ashes, than of all other medicines put together. It was certainly a pious fraud."[96]

Fraudulent? Placebos shrink tumors and mitigate asthma, arthritis, seasickness, depression. For pain, placebos can be more salutary than any pharmaceutical. They are to active drugs what docudramas are to cinema vérité, relying upon (dis)simulation. "I believe these pills may help you," says a doctor warmly if misleadingly, and patients, willing to please and be pleased, find relief. Like docudramas, placebos succeed because they show that someone has *taken time* for you, and taken you out of that time which feels interminable when you are in pain. The ritual prescription of simulacra may be all we need to be healed.[97]

Reviewing the history of the placebo effect, Arthur Shapiro in 1960 began by quoting Santayana: "Those who forget the past are destined always to repeat it." Shapiro had substituted destiny for sentencing, a telling error, for the destiny of modern science is, it seems, to surpass the past by acts of replication. Any field now that aspires to be a science must organize itself around an ideology of replication, such that learning itself becomes a process of replication: "as students in psychology condition the reflexes of an albino rat, so you – as students in sociology – will be asked to replicate sociological research. Hopefully, through the method of replication, you will develop a feeling and appreciation of the elementary methods of sociological research as well as an opportunity to convince yourself that sociology has a body of empirically verified knowledge."[98]

Verification in the sciences and social sciences, as in daily life, is a social process. Agreement must be reached on the terms of a satisfactory replication, and on what discrepancies may be ignored. In established fields, those terms are defended by Old Hands who draw lines in the sand of this imperfect world, where the height of a bench or light bouncing off a ring could conceivably make every difference. New Hand challenges to methods or styles of verification will be dismissed in a voice as impassive as the voice of this paragraph, which also discourages the publication of reports of "false starts, time wasted, paths to nowhere." That science should find pain so refractory is no shock, for scientific truth is meant to be exactly what pain is not: replicable and impersonal. "A scientific finding cannot be a purely personal experience," write a pair of social scientists in a college text, "it must be reproducible."[99]

Must be. Even the sociologist Harry Collins, who for years has teased out the cultural warp from the scientific whoop about replication, cites parallel studies that confirm his own analyses of battles over criteria for replication. Tasked with self-contradiction, Collins resorts to a double negative: "the permeability of replication does not mean that it is still not the only criterion of what is to count as a natural regularity (or social regularity). It is the only one we have." Among those Collins has cited in support of his work is Neil Friedman, who concluded that, like the physicists Collins has interviewed, "Psychologists do not in practice ever try to replicate 'the same' experiment. They just talk that way." They "can vary rooms, times, days, seasons, sexes, regions, experimenters, tables, and chairs and still be engaged in replicating, so far as their colleagues are concerned, the same experiment" – although no one has proven these variables irrelevant. What epigraph did Friedman place at the head of *The Social Nature of Psychological Research*? "Those who do not understand their past are doomed to repeat it."[100]

Incomprehension and doom: the misquotation is funny. Friedman let slide a corrupt text with the ease that psychologists let variables slide. The epigram itself has become exemplary of forgetfulness and fate. We splash the hyssop of Santayana upon our doorposts to save us from avenging angels, but inside our paper houses we worship idols of repetition and replication, no matter what. Philosophers observe that exact replication is implausible. Grant committees admit that proposals to replicate experiments are rarely funded. Biochemists explain that in research upon lively organisms, replication is fuzzy. Sociologists of science show that the rules for replication are never impartial and that, among themselves, scientists know "that exact compliance with another's methods and exact replication of their results is virtually impossible." Historians of science reveal that even when replications are successful, results could be as illusive as those confirming René Blondlot's N-rays, "a new species of light" which traversed aluminum, steel, and gold leaf, but whose action in 1903 could be seen only by looking away ("one must, so to say, see the source without looking at it, and even direct one's glance vaguely in a neighbouring direction"). No matter. Given the flimsiness of memory and fishiness of documentary, we feel condemned to repeat things to get them right. Better: in our era of redoubled events we are fated to believe that we can get things right only by repeating them. The uniqueness we value in matters of the spirit is what we most suspect when it comes to the cold truth.[101]

Cold fusion, for example. Within months of the press conference on March 23, 1989, at which chemists Martin Fleischmann and B. Stanley Pons announced the achievement of nuclear fusion at room temperatures, their results were confirmed by labs in Georgia, Texas, California, India, Hungary, and Japan: passing an electrical current through a beaker of lithium and heavy water (deuterium) via a platinum wire anode and a palladium rod cathode did seem to yield an excess of heat and a safe but non-negligible level of neutron emissions from a fusion reaction.[102]

Came a-doubting Nathan Lewis of the California Institute of Technology, who failed to replicate their results with apparatus identical to that depicted in photographs of the experiment. Ah, but the photographs were publicity fakes, so Fleischmann and Pons were momentarily off the hook. Others proposed that the palladium had been polluted, or that the heat had been measured with a faulty calorimeter, or that the results, so far as they went, could be explained without allusion to fusion.[103]

Placebo effects haunted the whole shebang. The first flurry of experiments ratified cold fusion in much the same way that a new drug is most therapeutic in its first public trials. Cold fusion was a wondrous remedy for the chronically painful problem of radioactive waste. It was a marvelous substitute for fossil fuels, which, during a fin de siècle worried about exhaustion, seemed dreadfully depleted. And it promised relief not just from pain and fatigue, poisonous waste, and depleted fuels, but from the dreadful complexity of modern technology. If the theory behind cold fusion was arcane, the apparatus itself was about as simple as a battery and more appealing than a multiple vitamin. Who could not want cold fusion to be true? From start to (near) finish, cold fusion was all about pleasing and replicating. "We recognize the desperate energy needs that will confront the 21st century," said Fleischmann, then he and Pons showed us the path toward a safe, controllable, rich, RENEWABLE reaction.[104]

Eighteen months after the press conference, what was left of practicable cold fusion was a scattering of inexplicable neutrons that, "like the grin on the Cheshire Cat...show signs of lingering long after the rest had gone." Pons himself was abroad and incommunicado, Fleischmann ill at home in England, and both stood accused of having practiced "pathological science." Not the forging of data so seductive to those racing for priority of discovery; not the fudging of results so common in undergraduate labs; not the cooking of good data and the trimming of bad data by veteran physicists (Galileo, Newton, Millikan) who are sure they are right; not the bolder fraud of experiments published but never carried out by young physicians (a glowing radiologist, an over-stimulated endocrinologist). No, not the deceiving of others but the pathology of self-deception, a diagnosis that transmutes the scientific community's shame (at having been gulled) into pity for those who had been shameless and self-deluding.[105]

Did the principle and habit of replication here prove its merit, turning cold fusion out into back alleys or even onto the pillory of satire, as with the scientific humor magazine *The Journal of Irreproducible Results*? A year later, in 1992, reputable men were reporting a fortyfold excess of heat from cold fusion cells and levels of particle emissions more compatible with an hypothesis of fusion. In 1994 Japanese and U.S. firms were continuing cold fusion research, a field still hot enough for the University of Utah to find a buyer for rights to exploit its cold fusion patents. Experiments at Stanford and Osaka confirmed the occurrence of cold fusion, apparently proving that it was not, as one hostile nuclear chemist wrote, "The Scientific Fiasco of the Century."[106]

Contrary to collegial confidence "in a system that operates in a highly effective, democratic, self-corrective mode," acts of replication cannot be relied upon to keep science honest.[107] "The hoax, the hum, the bam, the flam, and the bite," as the English mathematician Augustus De Morgan ran them off in 1859, have hardly seen their fare-thee-well. Journals are reluctant to print retractions; data publicly discredited reappear years later in textbooks. Concluded one set of academic investigators in 1987, "Replication, once an important element in science, is no longer an effective deterrent to fraud because the modern biomedical research system is structured to prevent replication – not to ensure it." When an experiment *is* redone, it is done inexactly, either because the researchers mean to improve on the original or because replication of experiments employing new devices demands an improbably close collaboration with those who designed the originals. Write two freelance investigators of scientific fraud: "The notion of replication, in the sense of repeating an experiment in order to test its validity, is a myth."[108]

Repetition, replication, simulation are the enabling and disabling myths of our culture of the copy. Boon and bane, they steal from us that for which they are the guarantors: insight, integrity, inheritance. Like placebos, they please us as they deceive us. In kriegspiel or newsreel, pageant or experiment, events must take place twice to take place at all.

"It's déjà vu all over again," says Yogi Berra

"Now – the place being without a parallel in England, and therefore necessarily beyond the experience of an American – it is somewhat remarkable that, while we stood gazing at the kitchen, I was haunted and perplexed by an idea that somewhere or other I had seen just this strange spectacle before. The height, the blackness, the dismal void, before my eyes, seemed as familiar as the decorous neatness of my grandmother's kitchen; only, my unaccountable memory of the scene was

FIGURE 7.7. The kitchen at Stanton Harcourt, built 1460–83, as Nathaniel
Hawthorne would have seen it in 1856. From an illustration in J.H. Parker, *Some
Account of Domestic Architecture in England*, III (1859).

lighted up with an image of lurid fires, blazing all round the dim interior circuit of the tower," wrote Nathaniel Hawthorne in 1856. "I had
never before had so pertinacious an attack, as I could but suppose it,
of that odd state of mind wherein we fitfully and teazingly remember
some previous scene or incident, of which the one now passing appears
to be but the echo and the reduplication."[109]

Hawthorne would attribute his odd state of mind to a subreptitious
recall of a page in which Alexander Pope had peopled the kitchen of
the fifteenth-century manor of Stanton Harcourt with witches, "engaging Satan himself as head-cook." Rare is the person lucky enough to
locate the origins of such oddness – and we must suspect Hawthorne's
luck, for he had arrived in England in 1853 prepared to experience déjà
vus: "I feel as if I might have lived here a long while ago and had now
come back because I retained pleasant recollections of it." Attacks of
déjà vu, however well met, are still inexplicable; what has changed since
Hawthorne's visitation is the feeling about them. Once provocative of
"uneasiness and actual discomfort," today they stir a casual wonder;
once symptomatic of psychosis or epileptic fit, today they point to

metempsychosis or to the split-second lag between sensation and cognition. The immediacy and clarity of a déjà vu may still be so striking that we interrupt to point it out, but déjà vu is readily assimilable to our habit of instant replay. Where before a man troubled by déjà vu concluded that he must be leading a singularly double life, now we joke: "Wow, there it is again... the feeling that I've used this mustard before: Dijon Vu."[110]

"Déjà vu" was first used in its present sense by a philosopher at Poitiers (across from Dijon), who wrote in 1876, "It has happened that, seeing for the first time a monument, a landscape, a person, I have suddenly and despite myself arrived at this conviction: I have already seen [*déjà vu*]) that which I am seeing." The convictions grew stronger over time, which Professor Boirac likened to the experience of an opera audience hearing lyrics more keenly because the sung words fuse with mental residues of words just read in a libretto. Boirac might better have compared déjà vu to the photographic enterprise, as did German psychologist Emil Kraepelin, who described "pseudo-reminiscence" as the state "where a new experience appears as a photographic copy of a former one," except that in déjà vu other senses (hearing and smell) may also be involved. The already-seen, déjà vu, is in its full effect *déjà vécu*, the already-lived.[111]

Louis was an unbelievable example of this, noted the French psychiatrist Pierre Janet, realizing that déjà vu, like hypnotic trance, was too intriguing to be passed up by people already delusive. A patient of Dr. Arnaud's in the 1890s, Louis thought that each event in his life repeated an event of the year prior. Arnaud showed that Louis was suffering not from an onslaught of déjà views but from an obsession with the very idea of déjà vu. Janet's own patients adopted the oxymorons of déjà vu – estranged familiarity, blasé excitement – only after learning about the new droll disorder. Déjà vu was a result of *déjà entendu*, the already-heard-of, by people half-asleep.[112]

Dreams, nocturnal or waking, were too insubstantial to account for déjà vu, Janet decided in 1905. Nor did he believe that one half of the brain was misfiring messages to the other half; neurologically healthy people also had déjà vus. The essence of déjà vu, he wrote, was a denial of the present. To feel that you have seen-it-already is to significantly reduce the intrusiveness of an occasion or event. For the insane, déjà vu was asylum from the jaggedness of time; for the sane but fatigued, déjà vu put reality on hold.

Hold on, wrote the French philosopher Henri Bergson three years later. Déjà vu is no mere gambit. Its intensity and sense of inevitability are consequent upon living, as all humans do, an integrally double life present *and* past, actual *and* virtual. Déjà vu is *un souvenir du présent*, a memory of the on-going, a slight catch in the flow of time, an intersection between our two inherently oscillating points of view.[113]

Freud wavered. In 1901 déjà vu meant to him a moment when "something is really touched on which we have already experienced once before, only we cannot consciously remember it because it has never been conscious." In 1914 it was equivalent to a screen memory of a repressed event. In 1919 it was the urge to return to the womb, to utter with confidence, "I've been here before." In 1936 it was a positive illusion "in which we seek to accept something as belonging to our ego, just as in the derealization we are anxious to keep something out of us." What Freud was seeking to accept was his Mother, whom he had seen naked when he was a child and whom he had seen-again-for-the-first-time "in the flesh," Greece, Mother of Western Culture, when he was forty-eight. Analysis itself begins and ends with déjà vu: begins with identifying what is repeated *as if by chance* with what has been seen but lost; ends with the analysand announcing, "Now I feel as though I had known it all the time."[114]

Problem is, déjà vu puts us in double jeopardy. When we look to repetition and replication to get things right, we may try ourselves more than once for the same crime. It is telling that our laws against double jeopardy are currently in a tangle. Axioms of psychoanalysis, of "Remembering, Repeating and Working-through," reflect strategies of healing and social justice, but also of torture and political repression. On the bright side, to make clear the repetition, through transference or déjà vu, opens the way for a recovery of, and from, memories and fantasies. On the dark side, repression is repetition breaking down resistance; as in George Orwell's *1984*, new states or levels of suffering must come to feel as if they have ever been the norm.[115]

Extraordinary as it may seem, the déjà vu has become our line on place, time, and truth. In a society of free-floating placards and postcards, of "repeats" and "repisodes," to experience a sense of familiarity without context is disturbingly common. Our remembrance of things present is induced by advertisements and soundbites, held in place by videoclips. The déjà vu brings us together ("Haven't I seen you somewhere before?"), gives us second chances ("Old reliable X, new and improved"), confirms self-knowledge ("Now I feel as though I had known it all the time"). Its displacements and repetitions take us from repression through reassurance to revelation and redemption.[116]

Echo homo

Experiences of déjà vu seem as involuntary as stuttering or echopraxia, disorders of repetitive speech and repetitive motion which often frame acts of prophesying. Involuntariness proves the purity of prophecy, untainted by the will of humanly imperfect prophets who may act as if, and sometimes are, epileptics, reputed since the 1500s as visionaries and known since the 1880s to have frequent déjà vus, seeing-again-for-the-first-time.[117]

My aim is not to make prophets of us all but to suggest that our attentiveness to disorders of involuntary repetition is synchronous with a culture of the copy in which repetition is psychologically, physiologically, cinematically, and commercially compelling. If tics, automatisms,

FIGURE 7.8. The nymph Echo pining away into the rock wall of a cave, cursed by a jealous Hera and disappointed in her love for Narcissus: an engraving by Abraham van Diepenbeeck (1596–1675) for Michel de Marolles, *Tableaux du temple des muses* (1655).

                 Through restless carke and care
Hir bodie pynes to skinne and bone, and waxeth wonderous bare.
The bloud doth vanish into ayre from out of all hir veynes,
And nought is left but voyce and bones; the voyce yet still remaynes:
Hir bones they say were turnde to stones.

                 Ovid, *Metamorphoses*, III, 493–97 (trans. Arthur Golding, 1567).

and larger "stereotypies" put time in suspense, the jerkiness of such disorders mirrors our wryneck lives within industrial society, just as stuttering reproduces the fragmented discourse in multimediated society.[118]

Classified since the 1880s yet described in 1985 as "*terra incognita*, sitting uneasily within the uncharted borderlands of neurology and psychiatry," tics are "rapid, coordinated caricatures of normal motor acts." That is, they are at once repetitions and simulations. So too stuttering, whose dysfluency is usually "attended with convulsive motions of the lips, tongue, and muscles of the face" and which starts when the normal process of learning speech through trial and error is beset with anxiety, second guesses, and horrible déjà entendus. Like the déjà vu, the jitters and shimmers of tics and stuttering have been mistaken for a bad conscience, winks and stammers for a body-of-truth at odds with indifference or dissemblance. We have tended to explain tics and stuttering the way we explain déjà vus, as "devices to control the intensity of anticipatory anxiety," or as "remembrance spasms" in which childhood trauma suddenly kicks in. Anticipatory *and* memorial, tics and stuttering, like déjà vu, are supposed to lay bare those events at which they shy.[119]

It follows that, more than other interventions psychoanalytic or behaviorist, modern therapies for ticqueurs and stutterers should have invoked the curse of repetition as the cure. Ticqueurs and stutterers since 1800 have been "mirror-drilled" to simulate calm motions and clear full words until these become real. Drilled contrariwise to repeat inapt actions or inept syllables until so bored that they overcome them. Drilled bass-ackwards to reverse sequences of irresistible movements or insurmountable sounds. Drilled back and forth by metronomes to keep a steady rhythm. Drilled into opposing speech and motor patterns – drawls or singing tones, relaxed or military postures. When, at last and as usual, drill seems bootless, scientists proffer biochemical explanations that turn these disorders of repetition into the kindred error of genetic misreplication, with attendant drugs that reemphasize the involuntariness of the spasms.[120]

On the one – the mechanical – extreme of disorders of repetition is Carpal Tunnel Syndrome (CTS), whose numbness, night pain, weakness, and stiffness result from repeated identical motions of hand and forearm. Symptomatic of the technology of a culture of the copy, CTS at last century's end was the "dystonia" of telegraphists making five hundred muscular contractions each minute as they pressed and re-pressed the key. In the 1940s and 1950s CTS was the "spontaneous compression" of the median nerve in the wrists of fast-order cooks, assembly-line workers, accountants, machinists, and typists. At this century's end CTS afflicts secretaries at keyboards, checkers at cash registers, meat cutters in packing plants. Already CTS accounts for half of all reported work-related illnesses in the United States, and it will become more common yet, not only because people tend to try out newly publicized syndromes but because a disorder of repetition is eminently appreciable in an era of replicas and replays.[121]

On the other – the animal – extreme is Tourette Syndrome, whose twitching, shrugging, cussing, and barking are symptomatic of the biology of our culture of the copy. Since 1884, when Georges Gilles de la Tourette grouped convulsive tic illnesses into one diagnostic category, the frequency and importance of the symptoms of echolalia and coprolalia have been exaggerated by observers. That may be due to the memorable spectacle of men (more than women) repeating questions instead of replying, or blurting obscenities in the course of a quiet tête-à-tête. But the focus upon echolalia and coprolalia has a further origin in the cultural figures of the ape and the parrot.[122]

Accounts of the "extraordinary and terrible contortions of countenance" of stutterers have resembled our most novelistic descriptions of apes; surgery on nineteenth-century stutterers to cut the frenum (the bridle) on the underside of the tongue was strikingly like the custom of slicing a parrot's tongue to improve its speech. Fascination and disgust with the adroit mimicry, obsessive intimate touching, and dirty words of a Tourette ticqueur matches our fascination and disgust with the imitativeness and shamelessness of primates; amazement at the echoed phrases, ejaculations, and cursing of a Tourette ticqueur matches our amazement at the mimicry, screeching, and outrages of parrots, messy birds who tend to fix upon those words we would not have them say in public. One ticqueur was indeed driven to assume a psittacine attitude, his tics cued by a nose that seems to have become an obtrusive beak, "to avoid which I turn or raise my head: I can now see the object I am facing, but, at the same time, naturally, I see my nose again at the side, whence one more tilt of the head, and so on," like a parrot's sidewise glances.[123]

We have been drawn/repulsed by echolalia and coprolalia because these are the boldest symptoms of aping and parroting, disorders of repetition to which we fear we are most susceptible. At railway stations in the Netherlands in 1990 were large color posters of a parrot on its perch beside the bold advice: "Don't be a parrot. Don't swear." If swearing makes us parrots, becoming parrots damns us to the animality – or humanity? – of imitation and repetition. Our linguists and information theorists tell us that redundancy is crucial, **crucial**, to communication. Historians recount the liberating effects of profanity as personal protest and social subversion, from Martin Luther to Lenny Bruce. Literary and music critics explain how vital is repetition and scatology to postmodernism and punk. Some bioscientists have guesstimated that 15 percent of the population carries a gene for Tourette Syndrome; one physician, David E. Comings at the City of Hope, has gone so far as to suggest that Tourette Syndrome is "a common, hereditary disorder that provides insight into how we and our children behave and misbehave and why some of us can't read, learn, or pay attention; compulsively do things including eating and abusing drugs or alcohol, spouses or children and are angry, short-tempered, anxious, afraid, depressed, or feel different and all alone."[124]

Ticqueur as all-encompassing dark twin? "My mind and body are constantly going at it," says a ticqueur. "Both are incredibly strong, like two bulls with locked horns, and if one side gets the upper hand I tic. If the other side gets the upper hand, I go crazy with these thoughts and urges." Says another, "There seem to be two persons in me: the one that tics, the son of the one that does not, is an *enfant terrible*, a source of great anxiety to his parents, who become a slave to his caprices. I am at once the actor and the spectator; and the worst of it is, the exuberance of the one is not to be thwarted by the just recriminations of the other." As with stutterers who shudder through solo speech yet sing flawlessly, it is the suddenness of the reversal of character in ticqueurs that lures us and them toward images of a double and redoubled personality.[125]

Echo, Greek nymph, daughter of Air and Language, was "alone chosen for the world's wife, for that is the true philosophy which echoes most faithfully the voices of the world itself," wrote Francis Bacon. But we hear Echo also as Ovid's Roman nymph cursed to repetition by a jealous Juno, spurned by Narcissus, and wasting away to a hollow, fragmentary voice. Echo may sound out what is implicit or she may mock us, distorting our words.[126]

Ultimately, what is most disturbing about Echo, about the stutterer and the ticqueur, is that they confront us with versions of ourselves as prisoners to redoubling and reenactment. Like apes and parrots, they threaten to become our second nature.

The Hard Stuff

"Next to the simple imitation of sounds and gestures, Quotation is the most natural and most frequent habitude of human nature," said James Boswell, whose fame derives less from his own quotability than from taking down the bons mots of the ticqueur and wit Samuel Johnson, who suspected quotation of drifting toward "downright pedantry." Boswell himself lambasted eighteenth-century Germans for books that resembled a beggar's gown, "in which there is no large piece of the same cloth, but an aggregate in various rags," yet that was flat-out the plan of the twentieth-century German most quoted on the subject of repetition. Walter Benjamin projected a critique of commodity capitalism consisting exclusively of quotations from nineteenth-century French sources. Through the seaminess of a beggar's gown, we might be disabused of our fetish for novelty, hoped Benjamin; instead, critics ponder the novelty of his plan and his ambivalence about tradition.[127]

Toward whatever mecca we hope that repetition and reenactment will take us, the path seems to veer into bramble when it does not double back on itself. It commences innocently with such replays as paint-by-number oils of Old Masters or Grandma Moses, lipsynched performances of songs by Elvis or Madonna, patchworks of direct quotation from Shakespeare or Gertrude Stein. These are examples of platonic repetition, the emulation of an Ideal: a painting, a ballad, a sentence perfectly done.[128] Such repetition was the classical method of teaching

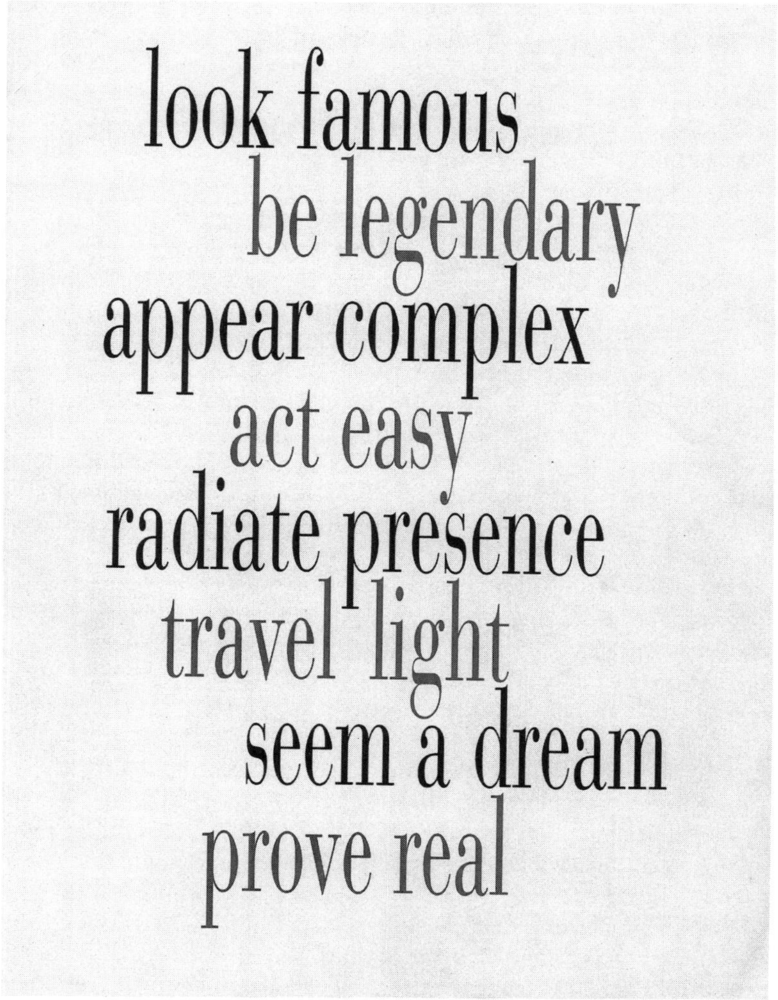

Figure 7.9. Go Silk advertisement, 1990. Reproduced by permission of Lazinger International.

rhetoric and the Christian method of homiletics: quotation as persuasion. It was the monastic method of teaching manuscript illumination and the studio method of teaching art, each apprentice copying masterworks or coloring in the outlines.

Temptations are great here to take credit for what others have said and sung, to pride myself in the quality of my covetousness and the seamlessness of my reenactments. I sign my name to paintings-by-number: "Yes, even if your artistic talents are zero, you'll be able to decorate your house from wall to wall with fine paintings and be able to say: 'I did it myself.'" I win celebrity by mouthing voices better or more famous than my own. And I earn immortality as the voice-under the wit of others: "It could be said of me," wrote Michel de Montaigne, "that in this book I have only made up a bunch of other men's flowers, providing of my own only the string that ties them together," but it is his *Essais* I quote centuries later, and it is with him that we begin the chronicles of the self-constituting individual.[129]

__Farther along the path, you get hooked on colorizing, pornography, indirect quotation. These are fledgling examples of Nietzschean repetition, phantasmic, progressively ungrounded. You digitize a black-and-white-and-gray movie to a more colorful palette such that the replay is as different as day from night. You mistake a volcanic physicality for passion or romance. You lose the sense of a thought to paraphrases and abridgments.

Distortion, contortion, misproportion are less crimes than quandaries. To what shall you compare the colorizing of a summer's day? To the repainting of Greek sculptures, most of which you know from white marble copies but which the Greeks painted blue, brown, and pink? To a Scarlatti air played at the piano with an expressiveness impossible to his clavichord? To the cropping of a Matisse for the squarish frame of television? To the make-up on a corpse, obscuring reality with a tinted afterglow, when summer's lease hath all too short a date?[130]

Hard-core in color can seem too slick. Events in pornography must appear as primitive and unrehearsed as in black-and-white documentary. In color films and videos you may need to be assured of the earnestness of intimacy by erratic zooms, stark lighting, naked wires, the lens trembling before sweaty palpitations. Amateurishness, clumsiness, sweat substantiate the sincerity. A zaftig woman in her fifties responds to a cameraman's audible directions, knocks over a lamp, awkwardly swings a loop of imitation pearls: you can trust her self-pleasuring in *Oldies But Hornies*. Men calling for telephone sex interrupt to be assured that what they are getting is not a recording but the real skinny (from women adept at sound effects). Pornography works to make every reenactment the First Time, Only Better. The truth of the Passion is in the Second Coming, for repetition is the gospel of pornography, proving male virility or female insatiability. Was it not apt that an adult-theater owner and a XXX star, Marilyn Chambers, would be at the forefront of investors in another new technology of replication, releasing as their first video laser disc Chambers's film, *Insatiable?*[131]

Insatiability, Boswell admitted, was a general problem of intercourse. "It is, I own, exceedingly difficult to avoid an excess in Quotation," he wrote, twelve years after the appearance of the last of the nine volumes of *Tristram Shandy* (1759–67), a novel Laurence Sterne larded with paraphrase and quotation from Robert Burton's *Anatomy of Melancholy* (final revision 1651). Sterne had mocked his own excesses: "'Tis either Plato, or Plutarch, or Seneca, or Xenophon, or Epictetus, or Theophrastus, or Lucian – or some one perhaps of later date – either Cardan, or Budaeus, or Petrarch, or Stella – or possibly it may be some divine or father of the church, St. Austin, or St. Cyprian, or Barnard, who affirms that it is an irresistable and natural passion to weep for the loss of our friends or children." Seneca, it was Seneca, Lucius Annaeus Seneca, father of the philosopher, and this too was paraphrased from Burton.[132]

In Sterne's wake, the historian Thomas Macaulay would write to a friend, "I feel a habit of quotation growing on me; but I resist that devil – for such it is – and it flees from me. It is all that I can do to keep Greek and Latin out of all my letters. Wise sayings of Euripides are even now at my fingers' ends...." Authors and orators had become apologetic about the habit, worried that sedulous quotation (worse, in dead languages) might appear supercilious. By 1919, Thomas Mann was referring to an "earlier age" in which "quoting was perceived as an art," this in preface to a collection of his youthful essays replete with "endless quotations and appeals to co-jurors and 'authorities.'"[133]

Today you learn from the earliest grades that "to reproduce in your own words" an encyclopedia article or magazine story is the essence of *re*search. Half-quoting ("paraplagia," "compression") prevails in high schools and schools of journalism. You use inverted commas and "air quotes" to report dialogue or acknowledge a debt, but also to signal disdain, skepticism, personal exemption, emotional distance. While literary philosophers and sociolinguists theorize that your private linguistic hoard is a weakbox of misremembered or excogitated clauses, radio and television interviews now spread epidemics of what one critic in 1757 (quoting another) called "licentious Paraphrase."[134]

Abridgment itself is no longer epidemic. It is endemic.

• First, and still, digests of statutes and decisions.

• Later, and still, digests of scripture, made by monks.

• Came professional digesters, indiscriminate, insatiable. "These gormandizers will eat you the very life out of a copy [a text] and so soon as ever it appears," wrote a London printer in 1705, "for as the times go, *Original* and *Abridgment* are almost reckoned as necessary as man and wife."

• Sustained by legal decisions that "a fair abridgment is not piracy," nineteenth-century gormandizers gutted *Robinson Crusoe* and *Paradise Lost* of moralizing and meandering, cutting to the chase. George Saintsbury, who bewailed an abridgment of his *Mr. Midshipman Easy,* abridged a novel by Samuel Richardson with this excuse: "There comes a time when, with all but the very greatest works which have been originally executed on a large scale, it is a case for presentation in some shortened form, or for lasting exclusion from the knowledge of generations of readers."

- Thus did abridgments gain favor as democratic acts on behalf of the Common People, who would read the *Reader's Digest* (1922–) and its Condensed Books (1950–) in preference to the digressions of an aristocratic, time-consuming "whole."

- Abridgment was what being popular and modern was all about, no? News, expeditious. Letters, cursory. Speech, contracted. Sound, bitten. Call this, in the 1990s, "data compression," which is either *lossless* or, at less cost(?), *lossy*.[135]

- Until you lose the personality of what you began with. You see a 1975 paperback by Michael Jahn, *The Invisible Man*. Based on the Universal Television pilot, "The Invisible Man." From a teleplay by Steven Bochco. From a television story by Harve Bennett and Steven Bochco. From the novel (remember that novel?) by someone called H.G. Wells.

Citation is what is left. As substantive notes fall away under the flensing knives of editors, or are eliminated altogether so as not to weaken your resolve "to say anything fresh," mere citation takes on the authoritativeness that full quotation once had. The status of scientists appreciates sheerly with the number of times others refer to their work. Yet citation, like namedropping, may simply be your way of rewarding a friend, honoring a mentor, injecting yourself into the mainstream, hitching your wagon to a star, deflecting doubt onto a stranger, disclaiming responsibility for a risky idea, proving fairhandedness, or demonstrating erudition in lieu of brilliance.[136]

————Down the path, irrevocably, toward sampling. Citizens this century have come to accept the part for the whole, not simply as the heart of the matter (a digest or abstract), but as the soul of a nation, the center of a person, the crux of an era.

Impelled by newly legislated state health insurance and pensions, by economic pressures to predict crop yields, and by political fears of unemployment, late nineteenth-century statisticians developed methods for representative sampling. The sampling was "purposive": one chose a sample according to assumptions of what/who would be exemplary enough to stand in for, and up against, the totals of expensive, exhaustive censuses. Rough sorts of such sampling were used by American newspapers polling voters at election time (since 1904) and by market researchers like Herbert W. Armstrong, who by the 1920s had conducted surveys "based on the law-of-average principle, obtaining, analyzing, and classifying facts on business and social conditions, problems and opinions from hundreds of people of all classes." Systematic proportionate sampling (1 in every 100 or. . .) was employed by British sociologists assaying unemployment insurance systems, by American engineers testing telephone equipment, and by Japanese officials estimating the displacement wrought by the 1923 Tokyo earthquake. The massiveness of the Depression supported a more profound abstraction, *random* sampling, secured by new tables of random numbers and complex equations of probability.[137]

Gathering cultural as well as mathematical momentum, random samples – from a target group or from the population at large – have supplanted the full enumeration. It has become a "general civic duty," more honored than voting, for people to respond when selected as part of a sample for political polls, health surveys, or market research. One may frown at the smallness of samples on the basis of which new products or political faces are launched, but then, to be sampled is all the more to be chosen. One may pale before leptokursis and interpenetrating replicate subsamples, but then the mysteries of the final prophetic extrapolation make for dicta all the more revered.[138]

An edict was issued not long ago that the entire history of art, not just the collages of Cubists, Dadaists, and Surrealists, is a history of sampling. Borrowing images, wrote art historian Leo Steinberg in 1978, is vital to "the abundant spiritual intercourse between artists and art," and "there is as much unpredictable originality in quoting, imitating, transposing, and echoing, as there is in inventing." Whatever artists do, they are held in the loose but loving embrace of artists past.[139]

Digital sampling, the electronic scanning and manipulation of images or sounds, presumes upon a similar largesse. In its simplest visual form, digital sampling is painting-by-number, reproducing pixel by pixel on a bit-graphed screen what passes under a scanner. Because scanners have only a probabilistic accuracy, the image is a sample that must be electronically retouched to match a mental picture or medical data. Less simply, digital sampling is surgery and colorizing (whose process derives from medical imaging): a 1985 advertisement showed four boys jumping through spray from a fire hydrant in front of a red wall painted with a "Coke is it!" sign, but Coke had not been *it* until the red was brightened and the hopping right foot of the boy in white shorts was digitally cloned from the boy in green trunks. Least simply, digital sampling is the pornography of rearranging images to one's desires. Changing the complexion of an actress, the race of a model, the placement of a diplomat is as easy as 0, 1, 10. Said Ben Blank, art director for ABC TV News, "There's no real concern about putting figures where they aren't as long as you don't alter the news itself."[140]

Neutering time is the real concern. Digital sampling does not merely give an artist the power to "graft picture elements to conjure up the most 'mind-blowing' special effects." Its seams, defying detection, also defy death. One reconstructs a mummy's face, "making Wenu-hotep human again." One resurrects Humphrey Bogart and Louis Armstrong to promote Diet Coke: it's the Real Thing. Freed from the technical problem of generational loss, where "you dupe a photograph, then dupe the dupe, then dupe the dupe of the dupe," one clones and ages the faces of boys and girls missing for years. If our technologies insure the reversibility of time presumed by quantum physics and our culture of the copy, digital sampling undoes the fullness of the times.[141]

"Enhancement," photo editors and art directors call it; "sweetening," audio editors called it, when forty years ago they began adding laugh tracks to televised comedies. As early as 1935 a (sampled) survey showed that listeners liked radio humor more when they heard an audience laughing, but live audiences were often groggy from a day's round of radio studios or, touched by the television lights, they yucked it up too much. Wherefore radio's use of canned laughter and American television's reliance upon Charles Douglas and his Laff Boys, with their 320 samples of giggles, guffaws, oh-ohs, snorts, and titters on 32 tape loops, keyed to be sounded singly or mixed for any occasion. "The fact is," said a television comedy writer, "real audiences sound phonier than the laugh track." "We're manufacturing a reaction to our own creation," said comedian Jackie Cooper. "It's the put-on of all time" – of neutered time, since the laugh one hears in 1995 may have been laughed at a television gag of 1955 or, mixing media, at radio shenanigans of 1945.[142]

Once digital synthesizers became commonly available in the 1980s, one could sample a century of recorded sound to produce a duet with Nellie Melba and Miriam Mikeba or a concert performance with "John Coltrane's sax, Gene Krupa's drums, Paul McCartney's electric bass, Carole King's piano, and the voice of Billy Holiday." Tom Lord-Alge won the 1987 Grammy for Sound Engineering when he sampled the clapping and foot-stomping of the Supremes as background to a Steve Winwood album. Steve Stein, who insists that "you want the thing, you don't want the almost thing," jockeys samples of Otis Redding, Walter Cronkite, and Led Zeppelin to produce dance music for clubs. Claiming that art progresses by "chameleonization," the composer John Oswald has baldly sampled Stravinsky's *Le Sacre du Printemps* to produce "a stylized state of strangely familiar angst."[143]

Angst more familiar than strange. "Sometimes I feel guilty when people spend time getting their sounds just right, and I just take them," says one sampler and drummer. At one and the same neutered time, sampling is a signal of respect for and rebellion against those templates by which one's time is fitted to one's times. Says Mike D. of the Beastie Boys: "One of the positive things about sampling is that you're incorporating a musical and cultural history into what you're doing." Kris Parker of Boogie Down Productions says, "Black people have been sampled for years, not only in music but in art, literature, everything," and turnabout is fair replay. Jon Hassell, collaborator with the Talking Heads, explains: "In African villages musical instruments are made from things that are closest at hand. In Bed[ford]-Stuy[vesant], it happens to be shards of James Brown or other cultural artifacts that are rearranged and recombined." Sampling is what imperialists did when they colonized "undeveloped" lands, calling theft "development"; sampling is what ghettoized colonies do in revolt against property laws wired around them.[144]

Should a note, a scream, a drum roll be proprietary? The question is more than one of ownership, for sampling ultimately erases the line between the quick and the dead. "It takes the playing out of the music," complains a rock critic, "the life out of live performance." Literally: the music at a "live" concert may be an electronic collage from recordings made by dead performers, or from previous concerts by the dead-tired performers onstage. Is sampling a ghostly disease of repetition, or the art form of reiterable novelty? "Art form?" says Lester Sill, president of Jobete Music. "Goddamnit, it's plagiarism!"[145]

--------Finally, at the dark end of the path: plagiarism, forgery, ennui. States of obsessive, sometimes fatal repetition.

Of plagiarism, little new can be written. Although concern for plagiarism has been used as a sign of the transition from the communality of an oral culture to the competitiveness of literate society, charges of plagiarism were leveled by their contemporaries against classical Greek philosophers, Roman poets, medieval illustrators. Vice versa, despite their love affair with originality, nineteenth-century Romantics excused their own many plagiarisms by alluding to that genius which transforms the plebeian into the extraordinary. "The man of genius does not steal; he conquers," declared the novelist Alexandre Dumas: "and what he conquers, he annexes to his empire." A partisan of Dumas and Edgar Allan Poe wrote in 1888, "Those from whom they borrowed have no more right to claim the resulting works than has the spectator who lends a coin to a conjuror a right to consider himself a partner in the ingenious trick the conjuror performs with it. If this be plagiary, make the most of it."[146]

Those who have raged most against plagiarism have tended also and ironically to make the most of it. William Warburton in 1762 decried thefts of literary property but burgled from Milton the concluding paragraph of an essay on miracles. Samuel Taylor Coleridge rabidly charged others with theft, but his own perpetual plagiary he considered a form of spirit possession: "I regard truth as a divine ventriloquist. I care not from whose mouth the sounds are supposed to proceed, if only the words are audible and intelligible." Objecting that one of Hawthorne's *Twice-Told Tales* he had told first, Poe would filch his later tale of Arthur Pym from Benjamin Morrell's factitious *Narrative of Four Voyages*. Hawthorne's "Howe's Masquerade" (1838) was supposed to have been taken from none other than Poe's "William Wilson" (1839), whose agonist finds in another of the same name a haunting double, "*and his singular whisper, it grew the very echo of my own.*"[147]

Again and again, plagiarism has surfaced precisely where doubling and repetition have been at issue.[148] One eighteenth-century scientist after another quietly saw his way to stealing a certain passage on seeing double. The first American book on photography retouched an English book, *Photographic Manipulation*. Sermons on honesty were read out from the pulpit by Victorian ministers who had handcopied them from printed books so as to seem to have an original text at hand. A *Boston*

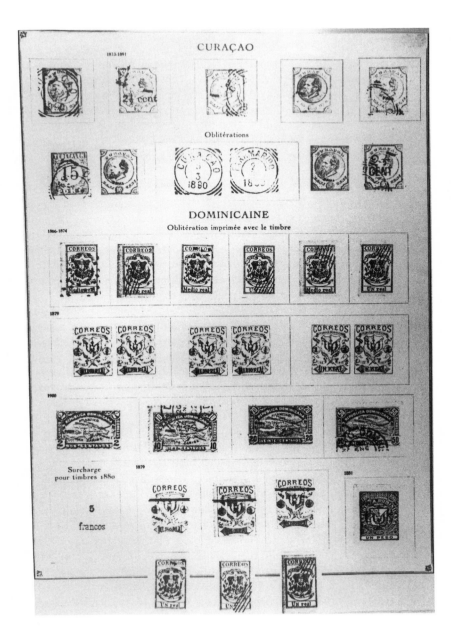

FIGURE 7.10. Page from François Fournier's *Album of Philatelic Forgeries*, compiled in 1928 by the Swiss Philatelic Society, which bought up all of Fournier's own "facsimiles," "restorations," and outright forgeries (nearly 800 sets of stamps in 3671 varieties) that remained after his death in 1914, to stop them from falling into unscrupulous hands. To this day, however, his "facsimiles" inhabit most major collections of stamps, for he was not exaggerating when he declared that "Their exact likeness to the real and genuine stamp causes them to be 'unequalled.'"

Globe story on the swiping of a commencement address in 1991 was allegedly swiped by the *New York Times*. Lexicographers responsible for defining plagiarism have been accused of plagiarizing definitions. A University of Oregon booklet plagiarized its section on plagiarism.[149]

Given this compulsion to repeat that which bears on repeating, plagiarism in our culture of the copy appears inevitable. Inevitable, as one famous estimate had it, because the number of different ideas the human mind is capable of is 3,655,760,000, and while there may be a slight hope that all the ideas have not yet been bespoken, there is a high probability of coincidence or unconscious repetition. "As if there was much of anything in any human utterance, oral or written, *except* plagiarism!" wrote Mark Twain. "The kernal, the soul — let us go further and say the substance, the bulk, the actual and valuable material of *all* human utterances — is plagiarism." He was writing to Helen Keller, who herself at the age of twelve had unconsciously (re)written and published as her own a story read aloud to her years before.[150]

Inevitable, because, like déjà vu, plagiarism is recursive, unsolicited, irrepressible. Inevitable as a recipe constantly resurfacing, such that Aunt Anne's scrumptious spongecake may be the economical 1934 spongecake of the Cook County Hospital Ladies' Auxiliary may be the 1896 spongecake measured out by Fannie Farmer may be the spongecake reported by Mrs. Mary Cole who in 1788, "like the sages of the law," struggled to cite her sources "where the receipt is not original," as hardly ever it was.... To an equally folk-anonymous tradition belonged Dr. Martin Luther King, Jr., who in his Boston University thesis quietly integrated a few lines from theologian Paul Tillich and fifty sentences from another's thesis even as he would smoothly merge the rhetoric of evangelical preachers to emerge with his own voice in Montgomery. King's academic adviser had told him, "all modern theology which is competent is 'essentially derivative,'" and King was willingly "led up and away from the world, on wings of aspiration," by the words of others with whom his heart kept warm if uncited company.[151]

Where the traditions of the recipe and the sermon hold, or where media replays make it hard to be certain what is original, "second storey work" seems not only inevitable but needful. Plagiarism may be "a species of multiple verbal personality," an individual pathology of claiming to do for the first time what others have done before, but plagiarism more broadly is collateral to acts of replication by which we prove our sensations, our suspicions, and our times. Right, center, left, our culture of the copy tends to make plagiarism a necessity, and the more we look for replays to be superior to originals, the more we will embrace plagiarism as elemental. Survivalists and screenwriters learn how to steal plots. The automotive and electronics industries rely upon "reverse engineering" to get ahead. U.S. Senator Joe Biden, who in stump speeches during 1987 borrowed the life and the rhetoric of U.K. Labor leader Neil Kinnock, failed less because he had failed to learn the lesson of his F-for-plagiarism in a legal methods course at Syracuse

Law School than because he failed to make Kinnock's life subservient to his own.[152]

Leftward, the 1988 Festivals of Plagiarism in Glasgow, London, San Francisco, and Berlin exalted plagiarism as a defiance of capitalism, whose commodification of the world and of art proceeds upon the pretense of originality and the projection of uniqueness. A century before, in 1888, the literary critic Louise Imogen Guiney had foreseen the day, "not too distant, either, when authors Mongolian, Caucasian, and Ethiopian will be seized with kleptomania;...when the possessive pronouns of art will get knocked smartly on the head, when ideas will disperse hourly under the auctioneer's hammer, and the individual pretensions alike of Dante and of Mr. Tupper will be ground to powder in some huge scrimmage of a comedy." Designing a program of subversive knockoffs or *détournements*, the Situationist International during the 1950s and 1960s hoped to realize that scenario, as did Asger Jorn with his later Institute for Comparative Vandalism and then the festive plagiarists. All, however, would reject "kleptomania" as an imperialist syndrome, the needless taking of what belongs to others; plagiarism must be a thoughtful assault upon privilege, retaking that which should belong to everyone.[153]

Necessary, inevitable, profitable, politically elemental, plagiarism is hardly as dead an end as Guiney thought. "Indeed," wrote an advocate of plagiarism back in 1927, "it is difficult to see how anything more advanced than primordial protoplasm can be free entirely from all taint of the hackneyed, and in that stage of existence scope for originality must, it seems, be rather circumscribed." For students especially, the way out of the ooze is difficult to see. "Everyone seems to know that this is a grave term, which is as it should be since the word comes from a Latin word meaning kidnapper or seducer (*OED*, 'plagiary'), but," noted a Vassar College handbook in the 1980s, "many students are unsure about when it applies." When a young performance artist can ask, "Are there any originals left or is everything an original? Or is everything a copy?" – sure they are unsure. When a young historian, shown to have plagiarized his first book, becomes a Program Officer at the National Endowment for the Humanities, is a high school girl to blame for reworking a magazine piece on who was to blame for Pearl Harbor? "I rewrote it. I cut out some stuff and added some new stuff. That's not plagiarism." A Rutgers University student, asked to write a paper using only his own ideas, "went to the library and copied a few of those things into my paper. I guess it was plagiarism. Only it's funny. I didn't really think of it that way.... I really felt like they were my own words after I'd written them down!"[154]

Precisely. Plagiarism in our culture of the copy is sticky with feelings of originality-through-repetition, revelation-through-simulation. That plagiarism should be taken up on all sides – as a means for subverting the System *and* as a means for getting an edge in business, science, or politics – is proof of its centrality and the reason why plagiarism is treated so gingerly, defended so boldly, resumed so intemperately. Like forgery, plagiarism is a personal addiction: Laurence Sterne, who borrowed so thoroughly for his fiction, sent his mistress love letters copied from those he had sent his wife years before. Plagiarism is, moreover, a cultural addiction, and I use that word with malice, for the ubiquity of the metaphor of addiction is itself a clue to our embrace of the rhetoric of replay despite a professional anxiety about disorders of repetition.[155]

The difference between forgery and plagiarism may not always be clear. C.S. Eccles, rector of Birt's Norton near Bath, copied out long-hand, with apt erasures, the full text of an influential book, *The Man of Feeling*, published anonymously in 1771. Wounded when Eccles then presented himself as the author, Henry Mackenzie had a devil of a time proving that he had composed what Eccles had, literally, written. Was it forgery or plagiarism when Sebastien Bourdon (1616–71), seeing an unfinished canvas by Claude Lorrain, rushed off to reproduce, finish, and sell the painting as the original before Lorrain completed his own?[156]

With less involuted cases, the difference is clearer. Plagiarists hope that their thefts will be taken for inventions; they make their name by standing on shoulders buried in sand. Forgers hope that their originals will be taken for classics; they make a career by standing invisible behind names or styles in demand. The timeline of the plagiarist starts *now*, the timeline of the forger ended *ago*. But the forger is alive *today*, so the act of forgery relies on ricochet: what is represented as the past is what the present maintains that past to be. Usually the forger follows in the footnotes of the historian; sometimes the forger leads, as did François Fournier, whose stamp catalogs philatelists in 1900 studied religiously for listings and facsimiles of counterfeits, but who did such a good business restoring stamps to mint condition that by the time of his death in 1914 he and his expert assistants had created (and authenticated) 796 "facsimile" sets of stamps of 3671 varieties – so many and so well executed that any serious collector to this day will have some stamps identified as canceled originals but actually what Fournier called his "art objects." Other forgers, equally artistic, have recreated in persuasive detail the lives and works of a person or era with which they feel an unusual bond. "I was born in our time," said Alceo Dossena (1878–1937), "but with the soul, taste, and perception of other ages" – particularly of the early Renaissance. Whether a daring inventor or a living anachronism, the forger is a master of the déjà vu, producing what the archaeologist or historian is already looking for, artifacts or documents quite familiar and a little strange. The familiarity makes the work meaningful, the strangeness makes it valuable.[157]

Over four thousand years forgeries have become no easier to spot. Our experts have been gulled recently by Hitler diaries, Mormon letters, and a copy of the first work printed in English North America, *The Freeman's Oath*. They are still uneasy about many paintings dissociated from the oeuvre of Maurice Utrillo: "Can anyone be quite certain that none of the innumerable fake Utrillos at present on the market was painted by Utrillo?" They so disagreed on the authenticity of some of the 2369 artworks forged by Edgar Mrugalla that he was acquitted after a trial in 1983. To this day, withstanding X-ray fluorescence and thermoluminescence, microphotography, infrared spectrometry, scanning electron microscopy, neutron activation autoradiography, and proton milliprobes, our finest historians, connoisseurs, and scientists alike remain perplexed by the "Vinland Map" showing the outlines of the New World but datable before Columbus.[158]

Supposing, asked Emily Lawless in "A Note on the Ethics of Literary Forgery" in 1897, "that for once [a forger] did *not* fail – supposing that he succeeded in producing so ingenious an imitation, so steeped in the colours of his elected period, so discreet in its modifications, so slyly, delicately archaic in all its details as to deceive the very elect – what then? Would his guilt be thereby lessened?" No, she answered: the guilt was great. Can we be so adamant? Accustomed to mass-producing interchangeable objects, can our society condemn in the forger what it urges in the entrepreneur? Isn't a temporarily persuasive forgery the confirmation of temporarily persuasive historical reconstructions? Doesn't the look and feel of a passable forgery, such as the many medieval chastity belts made in the 1700s, convince us of the coherence of our take on some time past?[159]

Vicious, this circle around from genuine article to forgery to genuine, and now more than ever. In our "culture of the second-hand, the imitation, the replay…the simulacrum," the absence of forgeries from an era (the Atlantean) or a place (the center of the earth) may itself be evidence of suppositiousness. Forgers collaborate in the work of magnification and replication, often wanting to be caught. What is the value of a dirty joke if no one gets the joke or sees that it is dirty? Found out, forgers irk us toward exactness in the look and feel of a style or period, even as they disturb us with their reverent irreverence. History, and life, would be drab and fuzzy without them.[160]

"Chiefly, I wrote the book to escape from boredom," confessed Magdalen King-Hall, referring to her *Diary of a Young Lady of Fashion in 1764–65*, published (and written) in the 1920s as if by an eighteenth-century girl, Cleone Knox. The editor of the diary protests, "Surely it is enough to realise that Cleone Knox *must* have existed"; consider King-Hall as Knox's ghostwriter or reincarnation.[161] Instead, let us consider the nature of (King-Hall's) boredom and its relationship to plagiarism and forgery.

Being bored is perpetual déjà vu, so perpetual that what is familiar is neither comforting by its presence nor provocative by its recurrence. The plagiarist usurps time, the forger reverses it, the bore ignores it, she who is being bored resents it. In boredom, repetition is not a symptom but a state of being from which may spring every sort of masquerade. Anything rather than to be oneself. Even suicide.

Abridg'd, the history of boredom from the *taedium vitae* of Seneca's

Rome to the condominimalism of Southern California is a history of nausea. Nausea as class vertigo: the disempowerment of traditional elites (Spanish caballeros, German burghers, French aristocrats, British gentlemen) left in place without effective position. Nausea next as the bitter regurgitations of individuals whose sense of self-worth is poisoned by society's indifference to what they can do: thus the vapours of the wealthy lady, the bile of the intellectual, the spleen of the romantic poet, the causticness of the critic. Nausea also as waves of regret or interminable waiting, experienced by exiles, outcasts, kids in summer school. Nausea lastly as surfeit.[162]

Alternately, the history of boredom is a history of the loss of vocation, from the acedia of the monk (dryness of soul) to the anomie of the assembly-line worker (brittleness of attachment). Here, routine is a tactic imposed from above, so that work becomes busywork, dedication mere attendance, devotion consistency, livelihood numbness. As Jacques Offenbach's comic operas were a "mutual insurance company for the struggle against boredom" of the nineteenth-century bourgeois, so Muzak is this century's cure for the bored weariness of the alienated laborer; it reduces fatigue by pumping the environment with blandly upbeat tunes, not by being memorable nor by reducing the physical repetition.[163]

Seen from space, says a Canadian astronaut, "there's no boring place" anywhere on earth. The "fiend Ennui" shuttles not through our heavens but shuffles through our hell; what was in Ancient Israel and Greece a dark and quiet place has become (after periods of fireworks and baroque slaughter) a place where absence of novelty is the ultimate torment. A waiting room with kitsch reproductions and no exits. A prison cell with loops of Muzak. A closed ward: "Consistency Is Consistency Is Consistency...And when you prescribe Thorazine or Stelazine, there's only one way to get the consistency that you and your patients can count on...Specify: No substitution."[164]

Such an oxymoron: no substitution for that which makes all things flat and indistinct. It is the way of our "placebo" institutions to make everything at once unique and substitutable. Modern ennui arose, says the critic George Steiner, at the end of the Napoleonic era, when each day was no longer aquiver with revolution, when life was no longer lived on the edge, when it came to seem that "one can do nothing but repeat words already spoken." By 1903 the French sociologist Emile Tardieu found ennui "more or less in all of our actions," a cry of pain at an existence drained of meaning or blocked at each turn: "the poignant feeling of an impossible happiness." Ennui was as typical of frustrated anarchists as of monotonously married women, of geniuses as of imbeciles. Postmodern boredom is said now to be completely diffuse and diffused, arising from overload and saturation; experience has no context other than replay. Been-there/done-that is ultimately no less desperate a feeling of boredom than going-nowhere/done-nothing.[165]

Or is boredom a feeling? "A wall of rain separated me from the rest of the world, far from any passion, far from life," says a bored character in André Gide's *Isabelle* (1911). To feel bored is to feel upset at not feeling at all, or, for the dandy, to feel superior at feeling nothing. And once the heart is gray, you become an automaton. "There is no other recipe against ennui than exercise of the body, and employment of the mind, or occupation of the heart," wrote the *ennuyeuse* Mme Du Deffand in 1767; "to get along without any of these three is to be an automaton; but we are all turning into one, or at least we must all turn into one." Boredom becomes the despondency of the tin human whose chest is hollow, whose employment is mindless. Absent a wizard, the jaundiced road of boredom leads on to suicide, the final, unique, personal, and irreproducible thrill.[166]

Except that suicide too is usually stereotypical. A suicide is a "copycat." The word is demeaning, but within our culture of the copy it fits suicides no less than plagiarists and forgers. Minted in the 1890s, the word deserved to be made "dictionary-official," wrote an English commentator in 1927, for copycats "do great harm, these unconscious caricaturists.... They have no judgment, no sense of proportion, no power but to reproduce. What they hear in jest they repeat in earnest.... With them the incidental becomes the essential."[167]

He could not have defined more acutely the suicidal state of mind as we profess to understand it. In 1840 the French doctor J.-B. Cazauvieilh lamented that one suicide would be followed madly, sadly, by others, proof that people have a "blind tendency" to repeat what strikes them most deeply, even to the point of self-destruction. "No other fact is better established by science," wrote Dr. Amariah Brigham in Boston in 1845, "than that suicide is often committed from imitation.... A single [newspaper] paragraph may suggest suicide to twenty persons." Dr. A.J.F. Brierre de Boismont in Paris in 1865 was astonished by the exactitude of imitative suicides, who attempt "the most bizarre fidelity to the reproduction of the act they are copying. This fidelity extends not only to a choice of the same methods, but often to a choice of the same place, at the same age, and with the most detailed representation of the original scene."[168]

Stories of imitative suicide, whether morbidly excited or melancholic, make for rows of statistics that continue to convince us of the copycatness of self-destruction, endemic to the pressures of modern life or epidemic among teenagers listening repeatedly to Ozzy Osbourne's "Suicide Solution." The numbers, usually for successful suicides, are multiplied by including attempted suicides and suicidal behaviors like drunken driving. One way or another, our sociologists and psychologists discover surges in suicide after television specials on teen suicide or headlines about stars who have killed themselves.[169]

Yet, if death at one's copycat hands be an extreme result of boredom, so the killing of time may result in revelation. Like plagiarism and forgery, boredom has come to seem as necessary as it is inevitable. Arthur Schopenhauer early last century ennobled boredom as a state of self-recognition: disabused of the fatuous world, one found one's will. Since, boredom has gathered unto itself the meditative reflex of the monk praising silence and the rebellious antinomies of the punk cater-wauling "A Boring Life." Boredom has become a vital downtime, a "window of opportunity," an "initiatory pretext" to the creative act, a means to "save ourselves from spiritual materialism." Boredom, wrote Saul Bellow in *Humboldt's Gift*, moments after indicting it as an instrument of social control, boredom is also the opposite, the Resistance, the noncaring of a "painfully free consciousness." It can be, suggests Wolf Lepenies at the end of a fine book on the history of boredom, "the heroism of standing still."[170]

Real Time in our culture of the copy is reel-to-reel time. Instant replay begins at birth and continues through second childhood. What we get from the déjà vu is the hint of loss and the prospect of gain; what we take from the replay is collateral and confidence. "At births," say two anthropologists, "we always did a playback of the baby's first cry for the family, and that re-experiencing was invariably an occasion for relief, laughter, and satisfied remarks about the successful outcome of the birth." The 1984 U.S. Supreme Court decision condoning the use of videocassette recorders for the home taping of televised programs was a vindication of a mature desire for and, as the Court wrote, a new facility at "time-shifting," the rearranging of the world's calendar to accommodate our own. An art therapist gives residents of a retirement manor Polaroid cameras whose "instant feedback" may produce a "heightened awareness of self." Documenting their environment and the responses of those around them, they see themselves as interactive human beings. A final photographic exercise asks them: "What can you give up and still be you?"[171]

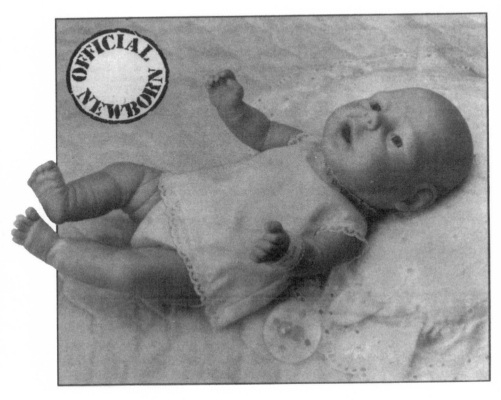

FIGURE 8.1. "True-to-life 'infant' doll" advertised for sale for five dollars by the RBM Company, Westbury, New York, 1990. Reproduced by permission.

CHAPTER EIGHT

Discernment

Who can be wise, amazed, temperate and furious,
loyal and neutral, in a moment? No man....
— *Macbeth* II.iii

Walking up from the heart of Souillac, a small town in the south of France, I find myself at a cemetery atop a hill. It is the second of November, All Souls' Day. I have been to a museum of automata where I have seen a girl feeding a sparrow, a clown dancing on the forehead of the Man in the Moon, a jazz trio running through its riffs, all mechanical and moving with the peculiar grace of the half-alive. I step inside the cemetery. This day the custom is to lay bouquets upon graves in solemn commemoration (says the Roman martyrology) "of all the Faithful departed in which the Church, their common Mother, after being careful to celebrate with due praise her children already rejoicing in Heaven on All Saints' Day [November 1], strives to help all those who still long in Purgatory." Everywhere are chrysanthemums, violets, begonias, peonies, and roses, but the violets are silk, begonias ceramic, peonies wax, roses plastic. On the gates of a crypt, bronze vines of forget-me-nots; on a tomb, an urn of granite lilies. Against a headstone leans a Plexiglas oval of dried daisies. From a dirt plot stretch the long green wire stems of dimestore tulips. Enameled photographs of the dead hang from crosses. *Que ton repos soit doux comme ton coeur fut bon*, reads a plaque — "May your rest be as sweet as your heart was good."

Between the photographs and flowers, in this limbo of silk, plastic, wire, granite, and bronze under a midday sky clearing after morning downpour, on the second of two successive days of the dead, I lose what remains of any outrage at artifice. The earnest of wrought-iron wreaths and marble perennials reminds me that we are impermanent creatures making claims upon permanence. Intimations not of immortality but of virtuality. Of struggling always, somehow, to be present....

Like the woman in the rust-colored ensemble surveying herself before a full-length mirror at the Musée de l'Automate. She turns her head to look at me, turns back to the mirror, lifts her veil, and powders her face, breathing almost imperceptibly. The freestanding mirror, its car-

touche advertising the PARFUMERIE NIVOSINE PARIS, is that sort
known as a psyche. Psyche was so beautiful that Venus envied her, and
Cupid, sent to punish her, instead took her secretly as his bride. Making love in the dark, he forbade any glimpse of his godly figure. Psyche
stole a look at Cupid as he lay asleep, but a drop of oil from her lamp
scalded him awake. Cupid fled wounded to Venus, who set Psyche
ordeals of perspicuity and of curiosity restrained. Still enamored, Cupid
appealed to Jove, who made Psyche immortal, as only fitting, for she
whom Eros would take as wife was the Soul.

In Jean de La Fontaine's version of 1669, written when large panes
of mirrored glass were coming into production in France, Psyche for
the first time admired herself in a mirror. The mirror, ever lengthening,
became her companion and emblem in paintings and ballets of the
eighteenth century, poetry and prose of the nineteenth. Freestanding,
full-length, mobile, reflective: the mirror before the soul, the automaton before the psyche.[1]

"Almost nothing, I am every thing," goes the riddle whose answer
is mirror. "More than anything, I am almost what you are," goes the
riddle whose answer is automaton. The mechanical woman before the
mirror and photographs on the headstones pose problems of discernment, of knowing what spirit speaks through them, true or false. Discernment is also the act of recognizing ourselves. It's time to take up
the chapters of this book one by one, in reprise, with their most disturbing implications about

    I. who we are
   II. whom we make ourselves out to be
  III. whose body we inhabit
  IV. what we are making of the animate world
    V. how we remake all the rest
  VI. where we are going
 VII. whence we believe we have come.

To sit *shiva*, or seven (for seven days, or chapters), is, in the Jewish tradition, to make peace, or to make the pieces fit. Here, I mean us to
see how the days become a week become a life become our lives, in
this our culture of the copy.

I. Vanishing Twins / Reprise: Celebrity

> the times have been,
> That, when the brains were out, the man would die,
> And there an end....
>
> — *Macbeth*, III.iv

Major Monarch and Mrs. Monarch, their means reduced, want employment. They are shy in the foyer, but the Major is emphatic that "We
can still hold ourselves up." Should an artist undertake to illustrate certain Society novels, he and his wife could prove ideal. Mrs. Monarch,

FIGURE 8.2. Vignettes of artists' models from *Century Magazine* (1883). Upper left: Model posing as a soldier falling from a horse. Upper right: "Do you want a model, sir?" Lower left: Model inspecting the painting for which she has been posing. Lower right: Live model (?) bowing to a lay figure (a manikin).

known in her youth as the Beautiful Statue, is well preserved, and Major Monarch is the very model of the general modern major. The pair have been photographed *immensely* and have, surely, the "demonstrable advantage of being the real thing." In the studio, however, the artist's renderings of Mrs. Monarch look "like a photograph or a copy of a photograph." The same photograph. "She was the real thing, but always the same thing" – while with blowsy Miss Churm, his regular model, "how odd it was that, being so little in herself, she should yet be so much in others." And that ragged Italian, Oronte, how intuitively elegant his English gentleman to Churm's lady.

Then let us be your servants, plead the Monarchs, bowing "in bewilderment to the perverse and cruel law in virtue of which the real thing could be so much less precious than the unreal." No, the artist can't let *them* do for him, for they have nearly done him in, got him into the "second-rate trick" of mistaking artfulness for art. The true artist's model is the No One who becomes Everyone, the Miss Churm whose value "resided precisely in the fact that she had no positive stamp." The true celebrity is the One-of-a-Kind that Anyone can become. The Monarchs are Someones who cannot be drawn as just Anyone, and are not drawn to One-of-a-Kindness; they hold themselves up to a position rather than holding out for personality. On canvas they come off dauntingly "colossal." The artist gives them money and sends them away.[2]

Story: "The Real Thing." Author: Henry James, a London "personality." Year: 1892, when people could earn a living as professional models – "a purely modern invention," observed Oscar Wilde. Artists earlier had drawn apprentices, whores, watermen; now career models were striking new social positions, the women known both for "their extraordinary prettiness and their extreme respectability." Erotic bonds between male painter and female model ran from Botticelli and his Venus (La Belle Simonetta) to Modigliani and Jeanne Hébuterne (who suicided the day after his death), and the genre of a painter, an unfinished painting, and his half-dressed model was full-fleshed long before Ingres painted *Raphael and La Fornarina* (1860), but it had taken centuries to define a profession of modeling apart from professions of love.[3]

Caravaggio in the 1590s was among the first to employ a variety of live models for his paintings. Life drawing classes were however quite rare until the 1700s, when nude models, male and female, stepped up to the platforms of European art academies. By the 1790s some had steady jobs holding complex poses; others came to modeling in relief from prostitution. With the photographic demand for figural realism and the Romantic search for ethnic variety, modeling in the 1800s would be a semilegitimate occupation for "the poorer sort," who sat in costume at the stoops of art schools, waiting to be called to the dais.[4]

After 1870 the status of the female model rose as women artists gained access to life drawing classes and as women everywhere became used to posing in public. "Mannequins" demonstrated fashions in Paris salons and, by 1910, on runways at Chicago trade shows. Society matrons froze onstage for charity tableaux, sat motionless for photographic visiting cards. Younger women arranged themselves more loosely for studio cameras in imitation of the glamorous Lily Langtree or in hopes of winning newspaper beauty contests. Dress reformers, cyclists, and swimmers posed for publicity shots, bold and unashamed.[5]

Copyists, dressmakers, country girls, dancers, when they turned to modeling, rarely succumbed to the hypnotic Svengali in George Du Maurier's fin de siècle novel about the model *Trilby*. Figural artists sought out women who could withstand their gaze, like Margot, the daughter of a French laundress, known in 1892 as *la petite Jeanne d'Arc*. "Her figure was young, virginal, and perfect, and there was a look in her clear gray eyes which drove every artist mad with a desire to put it on canvas." If art bolted from the figural toward the abstract, the painted and sculpted figures that remained were rarely forced into myth-historical costumes; more often, in the works of Schiele, (Gwen) John, Pearlstein, (John) Koch, Picasso, Neel, Gillespie, models have been represented *as* models, anonymous but themselves. Fashion models, who must inhabit clothing with the insouciance of a lay figure, hope some day to be celebrated for themselves, and by their own – single – names, like illustrious artists.[6]

Celebrities and models must learn the art of posing, as it were, au naturel. "There is a big difference between being natural and acting natural," says a guide to posing. "One is a happy accident and the other is a studied and consistent talent. Once you know how, this pseudo-naturalness can be called forth over and over again at command." Being an easily delineated celebrity requires practice. Asked a theater reviewer in 1896, "Is it character, or lack of character, that causes such ease of delineation?" It is knowing how to look *in character*, so that endorsements as a "personality" or attitudes on the dais seem to be the real thing. "When I am on the model's stand," says Cleo, a model for sixty years, "there is a spirit that comes over me."[7]

Spirit of the devouring twin. A celebrity's earlier identity vanishes as quickly as given names vanish under stage names, William Henry Pratt under Boris Karloff, Tula Finklea under Cyd Charisse, Nguyen That Thanh under Ho Chi Minh.[8] A model's identity vanishes as quickly as birthmarks are airbrushed out. Even under their given names, celebrities are disembarrassed of their origins, entering a pseudonymous state where they become that which we need them to be, No Ones elevated into Ones-of-a-Kind. Modeling is a state of anonymity; when models themselves are celebrities, they can no longer pose as just Anyone.

Pseudonymity insists upon the visibility of a mask, anonymity upon rings of invisibility. In either case the (un)real thing subsumes real people.[9] The indigenous being becomes vanishing twin to the celebrity or to the painted figure, whence the horror of Wilde's *The Picture of Dorian Gray* (1891), in which a portrait ages unmercifully as a celebrated Gray goes youthfully on. And cameras hasten the vanishing. Delacroix and successors worked from daguerreotypes, often preferring them to bodies in living color. Artists' models in the 1890s hiked their fees if photos were taken, for the camera bilked them out of hours of income posing for Toulouse-Lautrec, Munch, Khnopff. By the 1960s, Alberto Giacometti despaired of portraits done from live models, telling one sitter, "Ingres could do it. He could finish a portrait. It was a substitute for a photograph and had to be done by hand because there was no other way of doing it then. But now that has no meaning. The photograph exists and that's all there is to it." As if photos do not simply compete with paint but steal away the soul.[10]

To fear that one's soul may be stolen away is a fear as modern as it is primal. Samuel D. Warren and Louis D. Brandeis in 1890 resorted to ancient, priestly language when they held up a nightmare image of the theft of the self, of photographers and reporters invading "the sacred precinct of private and domestic life." Arguing in the *Harvard Law Review* that the intensity of modern living made solitude and sanctuary more essential than ever, Warren and Brandeis pointed to laws against public nuisances and laws protecting mental labor as tacit acknowledgments of a "right of the individual to be let alone." The right of privacy relied not upon the hidebound principle of private property but upon the newly uncovered principle of "inviolate personality."

Neither truthfulness nor absence of malice excused a violation of "inviolate personality," for the issue was neither injury to character nor intent to libel but rape: "being dragged into an undesirable and undesired publicity." Without consent you could not publish someone's diary; why, asked Warren and Brandeis, should you be free to publicize someone's life? On their minds were snooping reporters with "detective" cameras: "since the latest advances in photographic art have rendered it possible to take pictures surreptitiously, the doctrines of contact and of trust are inadequate to support the required protection, and the law of tort [civil wrong] must be resorted to."[11]

Strangely, the pivotal case broaching "inviolate personality" was a suit on behalf of an infant-at-law, Abigail Roberson, who could not legally have consented to the distribution of twenty-five thousand lithographs of her likeness as (unknowing) poster girl for Franklin Mills Flour. Yet if anyone's soul could be stolen in 1900, it was a child's, given the fin de siècle surge of stories about changelings, babies spirited away, girls abducted into white slavery, boys *Kidnapped!* (1886). Abigail's innocence had been stolen by the "Flour of the Family." Her young adolescent face, an image of purity, had been plastered on barrels in warehouses and saloons across the country. "[G]reatly humiliated by the scoffs and jeers of persons who have recognized her face," she had suffered nervous shock. Her guardians petitioned for her relief from such unwanted and unwarranted publicity.[12]

New York's Supreme Court granted the petition. Albeit the theory of a right to privacy was new, reasoned a unanimous bench, it was "an established principle of the common law that the person and property of every man is inviolate" and, as Judge Cooley had said in 1888, every

person has "the absolute right to be let alone." Property and personhood
met at that crossroads, the body, in which one has both a proprietary
and a spiritual interest. "If the face of a woman by reason of its beauty,
is especially valuable as a model, from which the picture of a Madonna
could be painted," wrote the court, "there can be no doubt that any
attempt by photograph to reproduce her face, so that it might be sold
to a painter, thereby depriving the owner of the opportunity to obtain
for herself the profit arising from it, would be a violation of her right
of property." Similarly, "The peculiar formation which made the Siamese twins unique was undoubtedly exceedingly valuable to them, and
the courts would without question have protected them against any
efforts made without their consent to photograph or by picture to
produce a counterpart of that formation for the purpose of exhibition." Extending the logic from monster to maiden was the heart of
equity at law.[13]

But the Court of Appeals, New York's highest court, reversed the
decision in 1902. Chief Justice Alton B. Parker, writing for a narrow
majority, argued that to accept a right of privacy would result "not
only in a vast amount of litigation but in litigation bordering upon the
absurd." Trouble would come if a man should have the right, Parker
exaggerated, "to pass through this world, if he wills, without having
his picture published, his business enterprises discussed, his successful
experiments written up for the benefit of others, or his eccenticities
commented upon either in handbills, circulars, catalogues, periodicals,
or newspapers," or even in neighborly gossip. And besides, "Who can
draw a line of demarcation between public characters and private characters, let that line be as wavering and irregular as you please?"[14]

Protested the editors of the *Yale Law Journal*: So unwavering a denial
of a right to privacy strengthened the insidious claim "advanced by the
sensational press of to-day, of a right to pry into and grossly display
before the public matters of the most private and personal concern."
New York legislators sided with Yale; in 1903 they enacted a statute
prohibiting the commercial use without consent of a person's name,
portrait, or picture.[15]

Parker ran for president against Theodore Roosevelt in 1904, during
which campaign he tried to declare a moratorium on "promiscuous"
photography of himself and his family. "I reserve the right," he warned
the press, "to put my hands in my pockets and assume comfortable attitudes without being everlastingly afraid that I shall be snapped by some
fellow with a camera." Abigail Roberson sent him an indignant letter,
for the right he was invoking was precisely what he had denied her.
Printed on the front page of the *New York Times*, her letter commiser-
ated with Mrs. Parker, obliged to quit her house to escape "ubiquitous
photographers," but Abigail knew "of no reason why you or your family have any rights of the nature suggested which do not equally belong
to me. Indeed, as between us, I submit that I was much more entitled
to protection than you," for Abigail was a poor working girl who had

never courted publicity while Parker was Democratic candidate for president. How scandalous that she should have been ruled unworthy of legal protection while the Judge should assume his own right to privacy.[16]

Georgia's Supreme Court must have agreed with Abigail. In 1905, in a separate case, it concurred with Justice Gray and the two other appellate judges who had dissented on Roberson: there was a right to privacy, with or without precedent. The Georgians quoted Gray: "Instantaneous photography is a modern invention, and affords the means of securing a portraiture of an individual's face and form [against the will of] their owner. While, so far forth as it merely does that, although a species of aggression, I concede it to be an irremediable and irrepressible feature of the social evolution." Must shutterbugs have their way? No, wrote Gray: "if it is to be permitted that the portraiture may be put to commercial, or other, uses for gain, by the publication of prints therefrom, then, an act of invasion of the individual's privacy results, possibly more formidable and more painful in its consequences than actual bodily assault."[17]

Aggression, assault, and, added the Georgians, enslavement. Finding one's face in advertisements or on placards in bars and brothels would bring "even the individual of ordinary sensibility, to a realization that his liberty has been taken away from him, and . . . he can not be otherwise than conscious of the fact that he is, for the time being, under the control of another, that he is no longer free, that he is in reality a slave without hope of freedom, held to service by a merciless master."[18]

Strong words. It helped that the case at the Georgia bar, *Pavesich v. New England Life Insurance Co.*, was blatant. Paolo Pavesich had been reading the *Atlanta Constitution* when two photographs in an advertisement popped out at him. On one side was a robust man identified solely by the caption, "Do it now. The man who did." On the other side was a sickly man: "Do it while you can. The man who didn't." The man who did, who had bought insurance and was quoted as being happy with New England Life, was Paolo. Who didn't, hadn't, wasn't. A photographer had sold the negative of Paolo's portrait to the insurance company, which used the picture because, I suppose, Paolo had the physiognomy of a provident man. An artist, Pavesich was doubly offended: his features had been appropriated and his person misrepresented. A photograph, with its many easy duplicates, had taken over his body, the copy traducing the original.[19]

Predictably, the devouring twin, celebrity, would refashion the right to privacy into a right of publicity. The right to privacy was an intimate redoubt against the invasions of the camera; the right of publicity, as expounded in the last forty years, has become a bastion of profit-taking, of the marketing of a valuable commodity, a persona that lives by the camera. The right of publicity has turned the right of privacy inside-out.[20]

Clearly something had to be done when Sanford Productions in 1921 distributed the first of a series of films starring Charlie Aplin. Chaplin, who in 1913 had perfected his "look" (mustache, decrepit derby, shoes too large, coat too tight, rascal cane) sued successfully to enjoin not the impersonation of himself the citizen but the impersonation of that other self by which he was making his name – *Charlie*, known world-wide, as the California Appeals Court noted in 1928, by costume and manner alone.[21]

If it was clear that one could have property rights in a publicly achieved persona, was it clear that one could assert those rights over against another living person coincidentally born to the same Look or Name? Woody Allen won a suit to enjoin commercials featuring a man who had grown up to be his Double, horn-rimmed glasses and all; the man (actor Phil Boroff) complained that "You cannot escape a person you look like. All the associations that a person has, good and bad, for a celebrity they have for you."[22] Edward V. Sullivan, he of the Ed Sullivan Show with fifty million TV viewers every Sunday evening, hoped to restrain the use of that name to which another had equally been born, Edward J. Sullivan, owner of Ed Sullivan Radio & TV, Buffalo. New York's Supreme Court ruled in 1955 that "There were 'Ed Sullivans' without number long before plaintiff was born – there are thousands of 'Ed Sullivans' alive today – and there will be, without doubt, many 'Ed Sullivans' in the future, all of which forces the conclusion that unless palpable fraud is shown, the use of such a common name cannot be restrained." Again the Appeals Court overturned the ruling: "Ed" could not be adjoined to Sullivan where confusion might prevail between the celebrity (who did endorse a brand of TV) and television sales or repair.[23]

Lawyers determined that lookalikes, natural or cosmetic, could earn money *as* lookalikes so long as they did not sign the name of the celebrity or act to deceive. But was it clear that onlookers or lookalikes did not deceive themselves? "When you're dealing with unreality," said Ron Smith, who in 1978 founded the first commercial lookalike agency, "you're in step with the times. Most people today aren't in touch with reality, either. They tell themselves they're seeing the really famous one." Vice versa, "It's when someone who *doesn't* have a strong identity gets wrapped up in his likeness," said another in the biz, "that there can be [real?] trouble."[24]

Finally, if it was clear that celebrity itself is an act – "The thing about Marilyn," says one Monroe lookalike, "is that she was really doing an impersonation herself,"[25] – it was not clear that there could be rights in a public persona like Marilyn Monroe or Bela Lugosi once the body it had taken over was overtaken by death. Lugosi's heirs argued in vain before the California Supreme Court in 1979 that the rights to his Dracula were descendible, and that they, not Universal Pictures, should control the vampire whom Lugosi had suffused with life in 1931.[26]

Vampirism is a most intimate invasion of privacy: the sucking of life-blood. What right of privacy, or publicity, remains to those no longer alive? Is there blood left to suck? Yes, said Philip Schuyler, nephew and stepson to the blueblooded Mrs. George Schuyler, in a suit brought way back in 1891 against the Woman's Memorial Fund Association, which had without leave commissioned a statue of his late stepmother. The association soon forsook the idea of "an actual likeness," but Philip and other surviving relatives still pressed for an injunction against displaying the statue, as intended, at the 1893 Columbian Exposition, where a life-size Schuyler, "Typical Philanthropist," was to stand alongside a life-size Susan B. Anthony, "Typical Reformer." In this, the first action grounded upon the Warren-Brandeis article, Philip asserted that his very retiring stepmother, fourteen years dead, had been opposed to the methods of Anthony, and that "notoriety in any form was both extremely distasteful to her and wholly repugnant to her character and disposition."[27]

As in the Roberson case, New York's lower courts smiled upon a right to privacy and extended it beyond death. "It cannot be that by death all protection to the reputation of the dead, and the feelings of the living in connection with the dead, has absolutely been lost." Yet again, the appeals court disagreed: "Whatever right of privacy Mrs. Schuyler had died with her"; it was actually "the right of privacy of the living which it is sought to enforce here," and the court found it "wholly incredible" that their feelings could be hurt by a project so benign.[28]

Only in the 1990s, the right of publicity completing its absorption of the right to privacy, can the "Deceased Personality" reach out phantom limbs and lay legal claim to the use of its image. A Kentucky court at midcentury did allow parents of dead Siamese twins to recover damages from those who without permission printed a photograph of the dead twins, but the twins alive had not labored to create a "personality," and to some extent the court was striving to defend "the essential dignity and worth of every human being," alive or dead. Worth, more than dignity, is what matters to the right of publicity. The heirs of Bela Lugosi wanted in on the profits to be made from licensing his Dracula for reproduction on toy pencil sharpeners and swizzle sticks. The court denied them: Lugosi's personal rights as Dracula were dead and buried. These were resurrected, by legislative kiss, in the California Celebrities Rights Act of 1985, which specified such rights as property rights, terminating fifty years after death. "Personality" outlives the body by half a century.[29]

Personalities have become surpassing legal fictions. In the name of an ogre twin, they threaten with oblivion the original embodiment of ourselves. Since the 1700s, when political rights were generalized in terms of the "rights of man" and private rights were consequently seen to emanate from one's "personality," a person (observes legal scholar S.J. Stoljar) "was no longer just a man with legal rights, he had legal rights because he had personality." Corporations and associations, gaining definition as organic persons, presumed "personality" as bodies politic, conscious of image, purpose, and action. More coherent than the personalities most individuals can muster, celebrity and corporate "personality" seem to bask in a higher reality.[30]

Bluntly put, artificial persons, juristic personalities, and deceased personalities have been invested with greater presence than any indigenous embodied person. If such there be. Sociologists, psychologists, and image consultants now collude in making of the person such a moveable feast that cartoon characters in *Who Censored Roger Rabbit?* (1981) speculate that "certain humans – Babe Ruth, Mae West, the Marx Brothers, and, of course, Lindbergh – were really humanoid 'toons who had crossed the line" into humanity. That narcissism and neuroticism which Freud identified with the quivering personhood of modern life is a concomitant of the cartoonishness of our culture of the copy, which looks forward to the perfection of holograms, three-dimensional doubles of ourselves reproducible in their entirety (like salamanders and celebrities) from any part, and entirely insubstantial.[31]

II. Doppelgängers / Reprise: Duplicity

> And be these juggling fiends no more believed,
> That palter with us in a double sense;
> That keep the word of promise to our ear,
> And break it to our hope.
>
> — *Macbeth*, V.viii

When Calvin combines his duplicator with his transmogrifier, he gets a machine that "instead of merely making a reproduction on paper... actually creates a real duplicate!" He makes a duplicate of himself to be his slave and clean his room, but it refuses to do his dirty work. Instead, it starts talking back to Calvin's mom, getting him in hot water. Then it duplicates itself into a gang and goes on a rampage for which Calvin is the dupe: "I'm being framed by my own doubles!" At last, he manages to retransmogrify all his doubles. He turns them into worms.[32]

Worms survive bisection. Excepting pairs of Siamesed twins now surgically divisible, we do not. If few of us find Doubles leaping from mirrors or copiers into our lives, we are each of us twinned inseparably to a body of lies whose biography decides our own. We learn to lie at the same time we learn to speak, says the editor of *The Penguin Book of Lies*. It is well-nigh impossible to live without lies in a culture of the copy where the lie is jape, jeer, jitters, jive, joke, and justification. "We live in an era of cacophonous misrepresentation," says a sociologist of scientific fraud, and the news we make, says a journalist, is promulgated by a "Culture of Lying."[33]

Modern lying has its roots in the sixteenth century, with the caginess of Machiavelli's Prince, the posturing of Castiglione's Courtier, the empty boasting of Spenser's Braggadocchio, and with the false promises of Luther's bugbear, Johann Tetzel, huckster of indulgences. Throughout the Reformation and Counter-Reformation, the Wars of Religion and civil war, religious beliefs had often to be dissimulated under threat of persecution. Lying to preserve one's state or status was not new to

FIGURE 8.3. Portrait of the Baron von Munchausen, supposedly sculpted by
Antonio Canova in 1766, drawn by Gustave Doré in the mid-nineteenth century.
The Latin motto reads, "In falsehood, truth." From the frontispiece to an 1865
edition of *The Adventures of Baron Munchausen*.

diplomats and dictators, nor was lying to save one's skin new to peasants, but in the 1500s lying was exalted to policy.[34]

Casuistry, to be exact. The art of dealing with knotty questions of
conscience (should one lie to a murderer who asks where the hatchet
is?), casuistry became a policy of half-truths on behalf of those faithful
who would otherwise be martyred, then equivocations in defense of
contradictory dogma. Allied to a doctrine of "mental reservation" propounded in the mid-1500s by Catholic theologians but readily deployed
by Protestants and by Jews acting outwardly as Christians, casuistry
justified not only the keeping of mortal secrets but also the making of
secret amendments to public statements, like a child crossing her fingers behind her back. According to the doctrine of mental reserva-

tion, "it is not lying to make a spoken assertion which you believe to be false, and which you believe will deceive your audience, provided you add in thought some words which make the whole truthful." Language was already a corrupt means to make your way among other fallible humans who mistook the plainest of words or who (in sickbed, for example) deserved the placebo of sweet untruths. What then was wrong with using words so that others heard what they had in mind to hear, when in fact you meant something else, perhaps quite parlous? Did not Bible passages themselves require commentary before they came clear?[35]

Followed to its logical end, this "New Art of Lying" would have made as much a mockery of oaths and contracts as it did (said critics) of morality and religion, but its true consequences were as little obvious as its reserve clauses were unspoken. Although Pope Innocent XI condemned casuistry in 1679, the policy of lying to protect the truth had over the years led to a habit of handling all writ with a sense of contingency. Where before casuistry had been a mode of evasiveness, it became a principle of interpretation "that militated against the authority of final answers" and supported intrepid acts of criticism, including the Higher Criticism of scripture. After casuistry had shown up the unholy arbitrariness of truth, arguments were less attractive when erected upon appeals to authority, any authority.[36]

Scribbler and physician John Arbuthnot, abstracting (his own?) *Treatise of the Art of Political Lying* in 1712, cautioned "the heads of parties against believing their own lies." Lying should be what one did, not who one was — a social grace, a political skill, not an uncontrollable habit or a clasp holding one's person intact. Dear to the author was a "Project for Uniting the Several Smaller Corporations of Lyars into One Society" to manage lies and invent one or two each day, with regard for the month and the weather and with the assistance of a Committee for Whispers. Still, he put forward some strict rules of *Pseudology*: one must not defame unbelievably, lest the libel fall flat; one must spread terrifying lies sparingly, since they travel at high speeds, above ten miles per hour. Nowadays, wrote critic Robert M. Adams in 1977, alluding to Arbuthnot's *Treatise* and to the Watergate scandal, "The whole scale of modern lying seems to have gone beyond this sort of petty needlepoint — which was appropriate enough as long as the aim of lying was to convince, but which became obsolete when the purpose of lying was to confuse and bewilder."[37]

Needlepoint and confusion, that is the difference between the conditional and the "constitutional" liar, between the malingerer and the Munchausen. Malingerers lie about a singular pain or wound so as to persuade physicians that they are incapable of going back to the front or the factory. Those with Munchausen Syndrome lie about everything (names, jobs, symptoms, medical histories) for the pleasure of confounding physicians and securing a scar from another unnecessary exploratory surgery; their diseases, like their lies, enfold their identities.

Medalist in an essay competition of 1836 on how best to detect "Feigned and Fictitious Diseases," Hector Gavin, surgeon to the London Orphan Asylum, cited many French sources, for during the severe conscriptions of the Napoleonic Wars "the art of feigning disease was brought to such perfection, as to render it as difficult to detect a feigned as to cure a real disease." Malingerers exaggerated or aggravated a minor problem. They reproduced a serious malady from observation in hospital wards or the study of textbooks. Desperate, they mutilated themselves. Mostly, they simulated disorders for which a doctor around 1800 had to rely upon a patient's word or behavior: chronic pains, deafness, shortsightedness, tics, mutism, lameness, palpitations of the heart.[38]

Ophthalmoscopes, blood-pressure cuffs, and X-rays limited the variety of masquerades at century's end, but they could not hold off "the dark side of human nature," said Sir John Collie, a Medical Referee for the government and for insurance companies in 1910. Under the impetus of workmen's compensation laws, cases of malingering had grown remarkably, he claimed, and malingerers seemed to know that some complaints, such as "railway spine" (back pain), "drumming in the ears" (tinnitus), and "traumatic neurasthenia" (our Post-Traumatic Stress Disorder) were (and are) devilishly hard to dismiss. Two American physicians described the malingerer as a clumsy caricaturist: "he sees less than the blind, he hears less than the deaf, and he is more lame than the paralyzed." Sir John was less sanguine about detecting medical lies; having found "the methods of the conscious deceiver so ingenious, and the mental outlook of the unconscious exaggerator so difficult to deal with," he warned doctors to be alert.[39]

Especially during the Great War, where "shellshock" could be either the cause or the result of hysteria, and where hysteria itself "sometimes predisposes to malingering." The circularity of such theory was reflected in practice: military doctors and psychiatrists used electric shock as a means both to provoke confessions of malingering and to recall a shellshock victim, mute or paralyzed, to himself. Elmer F. Southard, Harvard professor of neuropathology, found that "a number of patients upon recovery of speech are apt to believe that they may have been malingering. Functional disorder," he concluded, "may simulate malingering," just as the gas and shelling of the war produced perfect evidence of hallucination and tremor. Which was the "sinistrosis" — the war? the attempt, conscious or unconscious, to escape it by taking on the qualities of the war, as if in camouflage? or the diagnostic circularity?[40]

Gradually, malingering has come to be understood as a cry for help. Claims of impaired memory and chronic pain may have venial ends in personal injury suits or disability hearings, but the tendency in regard to malingering is toward a legal and medical casuistry. The disapproving tone of Sir John and other M.D.s, who associated malingering with a degenerate working class and who used their powers of discernment to protect industrial magnates against union clamjamfry or the military against mass desertion, can yet be heard among criminologists,

army examiners, and insurance investigators. Today, however, the malingerer is more often seen as someone who, like the rest of us, from time
to time has need of the "sick role" or the consolations offered to one
bereft – of, most recently, a (suppositious) twin. The chronic malingerer suffers, it is said, from "personality disorder," marked by extreme
narcissism, histrionics, and a feeling of helplessness.[41]

Lying, in our culture of the copy, must be what we cannot help.
Indeed, lying may be the charter of human society. Says Mr. Chaffery,
who makes it a rule never to tell himself lies but who cheats as a spirit
medium in H.G. Wells's novel *Love and Mr. Lewisham* (1899), "I am prepared to maintain... that communities are held together and the progress of civilisation made possible only by vigorous and sometimes even
violent Lying; that the Social Contract is nothing more or less than a
vast conspiracy of human beings to lie to and humbug themselves and
one another for the general Good." Had the world really come to this?[42]

Unhappy with the extent of our "white lying" to preserve the peace,
carry on experiments, spur sales, and promote healing, the philosopher
Sissela Bok in 1978 published a tract against lying, recognizing that "The
social incentives to deceit are at present very powerful; the controls,
very weak." A white lie, said a certain Lady of the highest quality in
1741, is intended "only to gratify a garrulous Disposition and the Itch
of amusing People by telling Them wonderful Stories," but lying of all
stripes has since become so prevalent, wrote Bok, that we are now being
denied, or denying ourselves, the opportunity to make moral choices.
"The ghastly truth of things," says Mr. Chaffery, is "that the warp and
the woof of the world of men is lying."[43]

Hieronymous Karl Friedrich, Freiherr von Munchausen, having served
in the Russian Army and fought the Turks, retired to his German estate
in 1760 and regaled friends with tales of fantastic adventures. Rudolf
Raspe in 1785, and other hacks for decades after, turned that nub of
fact into flights of fancy: the Baron lifted skyward by a brace of ducks;
the Baron leaping into Mt. Etna to visit Vulcan's workshop; the Baron
sailing to the moon. This liar's gallimaufry was borrowed in 1951 for a
new syndrome. On the wards of many English hospitals, Dr. Richard
Asher had met "widely traveled patients with dramatic and untruthful
stories" who discharged themselves, despite ostensibly grave illness and
against medical advice, after quarreling with hospital staff. "The most
remarkable feature of the syndrome is the apparent senselessness of it,"
wrote Asher. Their complaints did have a nub of fact, "a real organic
lesion from the past," but medical Munchausens used that to get themselves the pain and scars of a series of needless surgeries.[44]

Asher speculated that these Munchausens might be lying to escape
the law, to get free board, to obtain drugs, to work out a grudge against
doctors, or to be the center of attention. None of these etiologies satisfied him; they fit badly the distinction he made between malingerers, whose lying has ulterior motives, and Munchausens, whose lying
is their life. Subsequent studies of the "hospital hobo," that "itinerant

fabricator of nearly perfect facsimiles of serious illness," have been in awe of the fidelity of the imposture and the marvelous indeterminacy of the invented illnesses, life-threatening yet indecipherable. The malingerer assumes the role of a patient with an eye to relief or reward; the Munchausen's reward lies in being forever a patient, telling whatever story it takes to be put under the knife.[45]

Ego weakness, superego defect, fear of intimacy, anger projected back upon oneself – all sorts of psychological mechanisms have been advanced to account for the Munchausen patient.[46] What is clear is the compatibility of the syndrome with a culture that finds lying about oneself to oneself to be almost as natural as lying to each other.

III. Self-portraits / Reprise: Generativity

> I dare do all that may become a man;
> Who dare do more is none.
>
> — *Macbeth*, I.vii

She is with child.	He announces, "We're pregnant!"
She gets morning sickness.	He feels nauseous.
Her belly swells.	He gains weight.
She sleeps uncomfortably.	He gets toothaches, hemorrhoids.
She changes her diet.	Suspecting ulcers, so does he.

They practice for labor, breathing together.

She has contractions.	He times them, feels faint.

Bearing down,

she focuses upon an image;   he focuses the video camera.
She tells him how much the baby looks just like him.

He says, beaming, "We did it."

Anthropologists debate the nature and function of couvade in "primitive" societies, but we have it before us in the 1990s: men expressing the symptoms and assuming the roles of pregnant women. If Western men do not mimic childbirth directly, they may strap on a thirty-three-pound Empathy Belly to experience the heavy abdomen and swollen breasts of an expectant woman. If civilized husbands do not release tethered animals and unfasten moored boats to allow the birth energy to flow, they do cut the umbilical cord.[47]

Is couvade a magical activity meant to double the vitality of the forthcoming infant? A trick upon demons who, mistaking father for mother, miss their chance at the baby? The symbolic transfer of a man's ancestral life-spirit? The competitive bonding of a father with a baby who for nine months has bonded to the mother? A claim to the value of the man in societies of "low male saliency" where a husband absents himself from childcare? A form of ritual bargaining for men who lack legal, scientific, or economic means to prove paternity in a newborn? A case of womb envy, of men desperate to claim the powers of parturi-

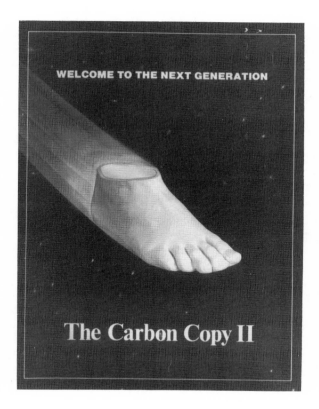

WELCOME TO THE NEXT GENERATION

The Carbon Copy II

FIGURE 8.4. Cover to brochure from Ohio Willow Wood Company, 1992, manufacturers of prosthetics. Reproduced by permission.

tion? Or, as folklorist Alan Dundes suggests, a reenactment of male creation myths, man as progenitor of all life, Adam as the source for Eve, "bone of my bones, flesh of my flesh"?[48]

Dundes goes further, submitting that "the rationale behind the current popular interest in cloning, actual or imagined, may be similarly motivated. A man can, through cloning, represent himself with no genetic input from woman!" In the context of the culture of the copy, the entailments of couvade are indeed profound, from the naming of children to the labors of artificial insemination; from plastic surgery and prostheses to cross-dressing and transsexualism; from genetic engineering to cloning. These are efforts at regenerating our selves in our own image through acts of surrogacy, dodging, substitution, and preemption.

Zaccheus Higby, Junior, and Oliver Bush, commissioners of highways for the town of Turin, surveyed a road in 1809, but the town clerk refused to record their survey because, for one thing, Zaccheus Higby, Junior, had signed himself Zaccheus Higby. New York's Supreme Court ruled that "The addition of 'junior' is no part of the name of the com-

missioner. It is a mere description of the person, and intended only to
designate between different persons of the same name. It is a casual and
temporary designation. It may exist one day, and cease the next." As it
had, and did, for John Padgett Jr. of Oxford, New York, contracting
for a deed in 1816, when there were three John Padgetts – a boy, his
father, and his grandfather, who died the next year. In 1843 the Court
of Chancery had to decide who had title to this deed, made out to "John
Padgett Jr.": the father (known by 1824 as the Elder) or the son (the new
Jr.)? It was evident to the court that the Jr. on the 1816 deed was the
same as the Elder of 1824, for "The word 'junior'... is merely descriptive of the person."[49]

Hardly so. A son named for his father bears the burden and blessing
of replication. He is *his father's child*, offspring of couvade. Should the
Elder falter, the Younger is to be what his father had aspired to be;
should the First die young, the Second must make of himself what the
father had yet to become; should Senior succeed beyond all measure,
Junior must not do less.

Powerful stuff, these namesakes, despite our insistence that individuals make their own waves in the world. Given a culture that reveres
originals yet trusts that copies will more than do them justice, the blessing of a name is inadequate to its burden. That burden is heavy even
when the name descends from a family friend – "a brilliant, admirable
person, and we hoped our son, by having the same name, would be the
same." In Renaissance France, and through to this day, the choice of
first names is said to fix a child's destiny: *Choisir son prénom, choisir
son destin.*[50]

Prénoms or first or given names were, at first, the only names given.
During the European eleventh century, family names were gradually
adjoined, and the stock of *prénoms* grew, accommodating a surge in population and, perhaps, an early "Renaissance of the Individual." Not until
the French Revolution was it illegal to change first or last names at will,
whether to dispose of a past or predispose a future. Abolishing noble
titles and frowning at the high-flying surnames assumed by social climb-
ers, the National Assembly in 1790 declared that citizens must keep to
their original family names. Henceforth, in France and across Europe,
prénoms would be the banners of parental and personal fantasies, ambitions, pieties, and pride.[51]

Those suffixes too – Jr., 2d, II – have been suffused with fantasies
of eternal life, or at least of empire. "It would be nice," says a man in a
commercial, "to have a IVth in the business – very official and important sounding. Sometimes I kid Jim about wanting to pass on his 'empire'
to his son." The Latin "Junioris" had appeared by the fifteenth century;
as an abbreviation (jun., junr, Jr.) during the sixteenth; as a flourish to
a signature (three signers to the Declaration of Independence) in the
eighteenth; as a 2d., at the start of the nineteenth; as II, III, and IV, at
the end of the nineteenth, when such regal numerals were appropriated by other elites. By the twentieth, Junior had become a name all

its own. In 1995 we can have, redundantly, a Junior Williamson, III.[52]

Was it the "Jr." of Ferdinand Waldo Demara, Jr., that set him up for his life as The Great Impostor? If he fled in his teens to the anonymity of a monastery, that was no less appreciable an escape from the burden of replicating a father than his subsequent impostures were appreciable attempts to become the spitting image of a fatherly professor, a fatherly psychologist, a priest (a "father"), a counselor. Descriptor *and* person, Jr. is, like a father's pregnancy, full of itself and yet achingly empty — which accounts, conversely, for the case of Mrs. G. Her first husband was Ronald, first son Ronald, Jr; second husband Lem, second son Lem, Jr.; third husband Theodore, third son Junior. Later still, she got romantic with a guy called Junior. In therapy during the 1970s for dissociation verging on multiple personality, Mrs. G. confused fathers, sons, and lovers, owing to sexual abuse as a girl and a lovingfury for all men, who wanted only one thing (her alter, "Candy"), but her confusion had surely been compounded by the aura of juniority, which identified the men in her life as extensions and figments of one another.[53]

Naming a child after the father establishes presumptions of personal consanguinity, continuity, and consequence — tenuous presumptions in a contemporary world whose ethics say that "all men are brothers," whose sciences say that "each of us contains genetic contributions from practically everybody who ever lived," and whose demographics say that life is a scatter. Namesakes assert a full transfusion of essence from father to son; Jrs. stake the persistence of individuals to the persistence of a lineage. This may explain the popularity of namesakes and Jrs. among white households during the Depression, when men were torn from their families and parents were anxious for any sign of continuity. It may also explain the prevalence of Juniors among black families in the decades since, the father so often achingly absent.[54]

Mere coincidence that one of our more advanced techniques of couvade should have led to a legal battle between Mary Sue Davis and her husband *Junior*? Mary Sue had had five tubal pregnancies, after which one fallopian tube had ruptured and the other had been tied; she then had seven failures with in vitro fertilization (IVF). During the last IVF attempt, nine eggs gathered from her ovaries had been placed in a petri dish with Junior's sperm; two of the inseminated eggs were implanted in her womb, the others frozen for later use, if need be. In 1989, still childless and now divorcing, Mary Sue and Junior wrangled over custody of the frozen embryos. Mary Sue, twenty-eight, said that the embryos were living beings and that she as mother had the right to decide whether to have them thawed and implanted. Junior, thirty, spoke of the embryos as property and of his right to veto their use, lest he be forced to sire a child against his will; he feared that he would be saddled with an unwanted fetus (as he had lifelong been saddled with a Junior). The Circuit Court in Maryville, Tennessee, awarded the embryos, clusters of four or eight cells, to — but wait. In what sense is IVF a technique of couvade?[55]

From the start, it has been men who have concocted the culture fluid in which insemination occurs, and men who have laid embryos in their nests of liquid nitrogen – five thousand such embryos in the U.S. alone by 1989. That year, a Virginia physician refused to release the frozen embryos of a couple moving to California. The embryos, said Dr. Howard Jones, were in his jurisdiction...as if *his* children, and Risa and Steven York but petitioners for an adoption. *He* was the fertile one, sitting defiantly on the eggs (*couvade* < French *couver*, to brood or hatch).[56]

Biologists and breeders who artificially impregnated fish (1742), frogs and dogs (1780), and horses (early 1800s) were making good on the myth of the fetus as a penis. John Stoltenberg writes that "Men control women's reproductive capacities in part because men believe that fetuses are phallic – that the ejaculated leavings swelling up in utero are a symbolic and material extension of the precious penis itself." The male in this scenario is not only seminal but parturient. America's premier gynecologist in the 1860s, J. Marion Sims, who used a metal apparatus to make fifty-five injections of semen within six women, spoke of artificial "fructification," sounding out the vicarious sex and virility of his instrument. The pleasure was all his. Sims succeeded with one woman, whom he injected with sperm on ten occasions, the last and best just after she and her husband had had sex. By 1866 he had abandoned his experiments, but he would remain devoted to clearing the way for the erect penis and its "fructifying agent." His opening of the vagina with his duckbill speculum and his opening of the cervical canal with surgical incisions were openings to male extension, just as his eldest sons grew to be his extensions, specialists in surgical gynecology. Implicit juniors, Drs. Harry and Granville Sims changed their last name to Marion-Sims for more complete identification with Father.[57]

"Ethereal copulation," Father had called it, that turning of a piston rod within a mechanical penis so that half a drop of semen was deposited within the cervical canal. Or so said a friend, Dr. T.M. McIntosh of Georgia, replying to a provocative letter printed in 1909 in the *Medical World*. Dr. A.D. Hard of Minnesota had just revealed that it was twenty-five years since Prof. William H. Pancoast, M.D., of Philadelphia had performed the first successful artificial impregnation of a woman. McIntosh defended the priority of Marion Sims (whose one success had been incomplete: the mother miscarried); other texts of the time referred to French successes going back to 1838.[58]

The sharper provocation, however, was in Dr. Hard's claim that Pancoast's procedure ca. 1884 had been kept secret so long because in this case the husband had been sterile and the sperm had come from another man. Pancoast had taken semen from the best-looking of the six (male, masturbating) members of the senior class of Jefferson Medical College, then injected the sample into the uterus of the woman, who lay chloroformed before them. The students were sworn to secrecy, and the woman was never to know that the child she brought forth was not her husband's.

Suspiciously, this first donor insemination proved to be a blatant case of couvade, for the baby boy "had characteristic features, not of the senior student, but of the willing but impossible father." Of course, wrote Hard; since "The mother is the complete builder of the child," and an infant's features are determined by the "mental ideals prevailing with the mother," she out of love or propriety would so shape the fetus that it resembled the putative papa. Outrageous, exploded Dr. C.H. Newth of Oregon; Pancoast "was a gentleman, and would not countenance the raping of a patient under an anaesthetic." Hard's brain must have been soft when, even as he gave the woman all the credit, he wrote that the spermatazoon "*generates* the ovum." Was that a slip of Hard's pen, or was penis-as-fetus so potent an image that it had to irrupt? Thanking his critics, Hard confessed that "while the article was based upon true facts, it was embellisht purposely with radical personal assertions calculated to set men thinking on the subject of generativ influences and generativ evils" such as using artificial impregnation to uplift the race. He himself "would not wish to own a child that was bred with a hard-rubber syringe." To own: to possess, or own up to? "And I do not care to think that my child bears toward the millennium no traces of his father's personality, humble tho it be."[59]

How comforting for a humble man to have at hand two biological myths to bolster the couvade of artificial insemination: for insemination of one's partner with one's own semen, the penis blossoming into a fetus; for insemination of one's partner with semen from another man, the mother building the fetus to flatter her spouse. That these are myths does not mean, once the technique had become more common – 100,000 births by donor insemination by 1957 in the U.S., 20,000 a year during the 1980s – that the number of namesakes would decline, or that grandparents would stop looking for striking likenesses between parents and child. Even the features of an adopted infant are likened to adoptive parents by friends or relatives ostensibly in the know.[60]

Junior and Mary Sue had also failed in an attempt to adopt a baby. IVF had been their last recourse. A generation earlier, they would have had no such recourse. The first "test-tube" baby had started out in a glass dish in an English laboratory on November 10, 1977. The dish held an egg from her mother Lesley ("from the grey fort," her fallopian tubes blocked) and sperm from her father John ("God's gracious gift," paying for the procedure with winnings from a football pool). An eight-celled embryo was transferred to Lesley's womb, and on July 25, 1978, in Oldham, Lancashire, Louise ("famous in battle") was born.[61]

Other men before Patrick Steptoe, gynecologist, and Robert Edwards, physiologist, had fertilized a human egg outside the body. Steptoe and Edwards themselves had done so in 1969, but together they had brooded over eighty imperfect "test-tube babies" until they got one perfectly reimplanted. Men were at work here, as it had been Saint Jerome who propagated the doctrine of the Virgin Birth and medieval churchmen who conceived of the male seed as the active force in a passive womb.

It was men who, in the main, directed the four thousand IVF births by 1989, as they had directed the hundreds of thousands of hysterectomies since the 1940s. It was Dr. Ronald Eric*sson*, former cattle rancher, who founded human sperm banks, and Dr. I. Ray *King* who had performed the IVF procedures for the Davises and was storing the embryos. It was Dr. Jerome *Lejeune* ("the younger"), director of the French National Center of Scientific Research, who testified in Maryville that a human being is created as soon as an egg is fertilized by sperm. And it was a man, Judge W. Dale *Young*, who granted all seven of the remaining frozen embryos to Mary Sue.[62]

Young was not denying male generativity. Basing his judgment upon the "fact" that fertilized ova are instantly alive and human, Young was affirming the central myth of couvade, that the enlivening and design work of creation is done by males. Junior was done with his labors; Mary Sue should now be the carrier for the offspring, whose best interests were to be born(e). Higher courts overturned Young, not so much refuting as ignoring his logic; fair was fair when it came to marital property, so they insisted on joint custody and on Junior's right to prevent Mary Sue from bringing any of *their* embryos to term. King gave the embryos to Junior in June 1993, as if to say that the right to determine their fate was a phallic rite. Junior, who had said after the initial Maryville decision that he was being "raped of reproductive rights," destroyed the embryos.[63]

Mary Sue (now Stowe, now in Florida) had in the meantime changed her mind about how the embryos might be used: she had been hoping to donate them to a childless couple. That a woman might carry a fetus genetically unrelated to her was feasible once IVF procedures allowed for the safe collection of eggs from ovaries, their fertilization in vitro by any healthy sperm, and their reimplantation in any healthy womb. A baby had been so born in 1984 to an Australian woman. By 1990 a single mother with one child of her own had been implanted with an embryo of and for a California couple: Crispina Calvert (who had had a hysterectomy) and her husband paid Anna Johnson ten thousand dollars to carry *their* child.[64]

Surrogacy, a form of female couvade, has a tradition reaching from scripture, the barren Sarah sending her handmaid to Abraham that Hagar may conceive a child in her stead (Gen. 16), to feminist science fiction (Margaret Atwood's book – and ensuing film – *The Handmaid's Tale* [1986, 1991]).[65] Aside from queens, empresses, mother-daughter lookalike contestants, and Nancy Sinatra, Jr., however, Western women have no strong tradition of senior and junior. Girls have been named after aunts, grandmothers, or mothers (if mothers die in childbed), but rarely has the public import of these namesakes been as grave as it is with boys; patrilineal laws of inheritance and customs of name change at marriage have colluded against female namesakes.

What women have had instead is spiritual motherhood. Louise Brown, the first IVF baby, saw light on the outskirts of Manchester, the same city in which a woman of thirty, two centuries before, lay as if dead after a hard delivery. Recovering, she declared that she would never copulate again. Then, seeing this her fourth child die in infancy as had all three earlier, she found her soul breaking forth to God, "which I felt as sensibly as ever a woman did a child, when she was delivered of it." That year, 1766, Ann, wife to Abraham Standley but known by her maiden name of Lee(s), and called Mother after her spiritual maternity, began to direct the small Protestant group called the Shakers. Merging with the Spirit while in jail for having disrupted a Manchester congregation, Mother Ann Lee became Ann the Word, Christ's bride, restoring woman to her original equality with man. Purified by Mother Ann and henceforth, like her, celibate, the Shakers crossed the Atlantic in 1774 to establish American enclaves. They prospered, adopting into their communities foundlings, orphans, and the children of parents who chose to join their society. Through Mother Ann Lee and successive women elders, believers were truly delivered.[66]

Closely allied to spiritual motherhood has been spiritual pregnancy. Saintly women of the thirteenth through fifteenth centuries, swallowing the Eucharistic wafer, felt themselves become pregnant with the seed of Christ; in 1814, Joanna Southcott announced in London that she was to deliver Shiloh, the Savior himself. "This year, in the sixty-fifth year of thy age," the Holy Spirit told Joanna, "thou shalt have a SON, by the power of the MOST HIGH." Her breasts and belly swelled up. Women friends were "well-satisfied as they can feel the Child as strong to move as they ever felt one of their own outwardly"; seventeen of twenty-one examining physicians were persuaded of the pregnancy. As crowds flocked to London, disciples distributed engravings of a "Striking Likeness" of Joanna, lest believers fall prey to the many impersonators soliciting gifts for Shiloh, who was to arrive in October, then in December. Joanna lay abed for months, taking opium pills and little else. Her bed was a deathbed, two days after Christmas.[67]

False, phantom, spurious, or hysterical pregnancy is the pejorative label given (by men) to less mortal episodes of this form of female couvade, whose bond between mother and wished-for infant (and redeemer) is no less robust and no more false than that between father and wished-for heir. Pseudocyesis, the technical Latin for false pregnancy, still troubles clinicians. Hormonal changes do occur, sufficient to pass pregnancy tests, produce amenorrhea, provoke bloating, and initiate spasms simulating fetal movement. Whether prompted by religious fervor, social demands for progeny, or a dread of menopause, such pregnancies mislead nurses and doctors into performing "missed abortions" – the removal of a vanished (nonexistent) fetus.[68]

"Fatty pregnancy," another of the pejoratives, hints at a newer form of female couvade. Since the 1930s, male therapists have analyzed female obesity as psychosomatic; a woman's abdominal fat, they suggest, *is* her fetus, compensating for a lack or loss of love. This analysis, ostensibly out of vogue, underlies a formidable belief that dieting releases the "real" person, the thin person, crying to be let out from within the fat woman or, yea, the fat man. As a process of midwifery, dieting is our most vibrant image of couvade, and most fraught with frustration, for no diet can fully deliver on the fantasies that inspire it.[69]

Men's fantasies of themselves as both creator and deliverer intrude upon female couvade. In the 1986–87 dispute over custody of Baby M between Mary Beth Whitehead, the surrogate, and Elizabeth and William Stern, the elements of female and of male couvade were unusually well drawn, for the features as well as the given names of the two women were similar, and William had been impelled to the arrangement as the last of a "bloodline" of a family of Holocaust survivors, to whom children were a crucial sign of re-generation. In Anna Johnson's case, California's Supreme Court ruled in 1993 that Anna as "gestational surrogate" had no rights to a child whom she had carried for nine months, to whom she gave birth in September 1990, and whom she wished now to rear as her own. She could not renege; surrogacy contracts were enforceable. The Calverts' lawyer, after whom they once thought to (re)name the child, was triumphant: "Today the Supreme Court has rendered a decision that changes how we determine parentage." Gestation, said the six-man majority, was not "the sine qua non of motherhood." Rather, in line with the male economy of couvade, maternity may also be established by contractual intent: "she who intended to procreate the child – that is, she who intended to bring about the birth of a child that she intended to raise as her own – is the natural mother under California law."[70]

In whose best interest was this? asked the lone woman on the bench and the lone dissenter, Justice Joyce L. Kennard. "A pregnant woman intending to bring a child into the world is more than a mere container or breeding animal; she is a conscious agent of creation, no less than the genetic mother, and her humanity is implicated on a deep level." Feminists had been protesting that "surrogate mother" is a patriarchal, capitalist misnomer, devaluing women while profiting from their work; an "unrelated" woman who labors to give a child birth is as much the "real mother" as she from whose ovaries the egg came. The inverted commas crowding this debate point up the degree to which, as sociologist Barbara K. Rothman writes, new reproductive technologies tend to make motherhood "fungible" and mothers interchangeable.[71]

By means of ectogenesis (fetal development outside the womb) or by means of artificial wombs implanted in men, childbearing could be spread across society as a whole. Such an egalitarian babyscape, envisioned in 1970 by Shulamith Firestone with the aim of "freeing women from the tyranny of their reproductive biology," is technically plausible. Infants born five months prematurely can now be rescued, and "the time span between the viable fertile ovum and the viable human fetus is being shortened, giving rise to the not-too-distant possibility of conceiving and gestating a child in an artificial womb." Or in a male womb: embryos implanted within male baboons have begun to grow. Meanwhile, commercial surrogacy coming under attack as the running of a "reproductive brothel," changes were being rung upon the happier couvade of a couple's embryo carried to term by the woman's (twin) sister, mother, even grandmother, cementing bonds between women as they share between them the birth of, often, twins.[72]

"Can feminism reconstruct a joyful sense of childbearing and maternity without capitulating to ideologies that reduce women to a maternal essence?" asks Rosalind P. Petchesky. Can contemporary acts of couvade lead to stewardship and spiritual motherhood on the part of women and of men? Or must we accept the disconnection and dismemberment by which men are referred to as "Prime sperm (Caucasian)," women as "endocrinological environments," "alternative reproduction vehicles," "therapeutic modalities"?[73]

With the reverse spin so characteristic of our culture of the copy, couvade has become an experience as much of physical and emotional detachment as of imaginary and passionate attachment. In this frame, it is the resultant of an historical alphabet of artificial arms, breasts, chins, ears, elbows, eyes, feet, hands, hearts, hips, kidneys, legs, lungs, muscles, noses, penises, retinas, skin, teeth, toes, vaginas, wrists. Autobiography, that art of re-creating oneself through narrative fictions (the rights to which can be sold separately from one's ongoing life), has a companion method now in what might be called autobiology. "By the turn of the century," predicts a physician at the Institute for Artificial Organs, "every major organ except the brain and central nervous system will have artificial replacements."[74]

As a process of detachment, the new technologies of couvade would seem to prepare us to accept the transplantation of fetal tissue on almost equal terms with eyes, kidneys, hearts. Our culture of the copy encourages us to believe that, where replication is yet imperfect, substitution is always possible. Our very definition of death as "brain death" accommodates the timely harvesting and recycling of organs.[75]

Beyond signing donor cards that fray in our wallets beneath snapshots of children, few of us will ever confront decisions about giving a hand or receiving a heart. Few of us will have to make the delicate decision to bring an anencephalic (brainless) fetus to term for the sole purpose of providing organs for transplant to other, dying infants.[76] Let me turn therefore, and curtly, from re-creations heroic and sacrificial to re-creations prosaic, selfish, and far more common.

Coming soon to a beauty salon near you is Permanent Make-up, eyeliner and lipliner applied to last as long as you do, through pigment implantation — "not just a beauty treatment, it's a way of restoring a person's self-confidence."[77] Cosmetic re-creations of ourselves are becoming less superficial, less transitory. The art of make-up (laboring for a Look) is merging with the art of plastic surgery as plastic surgery merges with autobiology.

Disfigurements congenital, accidental, martial, or medical have for ages prompted surgeons to try to restore appearance. Last century, reconstructive surgery became less perilous and more pleasing: anaesthetics gave surgeons time to work upon a placid patient, and habits of asepsis reduced the risk of infection. Reconstructive procedures were then employed to compensate not only for a harelip, a burn, or an unsightly surgical scar, but also for social and psychological scars, especially for those whose noses made them out to be, in physiognomic texts and political caricature, insensitive brutes, liars, micks, or kikes. Drs. Jonathan M. Warren of Boston and John O. Roe of Rochester, New York, refined the pug noses of the Irish; in Berlin Jacques Joseph reduced the size, thickness, and hookedness of the noses of Eastern European Jews. As he had gone from the glaringly Jewish name of Lewin to a circumspect Joseph, so he transformed noses to what would pass inconspicuously as gentile.[78]

Surgery on the physically healthy demanded a strong rationale in 1898. Joseph said he was curing severe depression. It was not that, as Lavater had supposed a century before, a hooked nose denoted a melancholic character, but that melancholy stemmed from the social disability of a hooked nose. Freud's friend Dr. Wilhelm Fliess operated on the swollen noses of 144 Jewish women and 12 Jewish men to cure their nervous (sexual) disorders; Joseph operated on the large or hooked noses of hundreds of Jews to cure them of melancholy and shame. Even an actively Zionist woman would benefit from such surgical camouflage – to avoid anti-Semitic harassment, advised her doctor in 1908.[79]

One year earlier, the first book devoted to cosmetic surgery had been published by Charles C. Miller of Chicago, an expert at surgery upon baggy eyelids, crow's feet, and general facelifts "to restore the contour of youth." The youthfulness of a French actress returning with a facelift after a 1912 American tour inspired the Parisian physician, Suzanne Noël, to develop her own techniques, perfected during World War I as she and many another surgeon worked upon bodies shredded by shrapnel. These opportunities for facial reconstruction, and for the smooth fitting of skin flaps from stumps of living flesh to artificial limbs, provided "aesthetic surgeons" with a wealth of experience. Able to remove flesh from ears, wrinkles from the forehead, bags from beneath the eyes, sags from cheeks, and folds from double chins, all without visible scars, cosmetic (aesthetic) surgery during the 1920s was more extensive than ever, extending to the reduction of women's breasts and the cutting away of fat from the belly. Dr. Max Thorek of Chicago performed "adipectomies" to restore "mental poise and vigor" in young American dancers, singers, and housewives; Dr. Noël worked on older French actresses and fashion models to return their youth to them – annually. If a woman must retint her hair regularly and exercise daily to keep in shape, then why not come to Noël's offices once a year for upkeep?[80]

"With the tremendous changes in the character of the people, and the developing of a pleasure-loving race in place of the more serious types of the past," wrote Dr. Miller in 1924, "there has come more or less of a demand for cosmetic operations." That was the faintest of explanations, for the operations had painful aftermaths, the skin tender for months. Miller was closer to the mark when he wrote that "The most beautiful women of middle life cannot charm American audiences. Signs of maturity in women must go." Life insurance charts were sullenly denying healthy weight-gains after age thirty, and "the fashion of non-motherhood" threatened (said conservative males) to reduce women to female eunuchs or to slip them into the ranks of slim-hipped men.[81]

Full on the mark was the coincidence of *plastic* surgery with the commandeering of pregnancy by gynecologists and the cloistering of death in hospitals; like life and death, beauty was a medical matter. And the coincidence of an *aesthetic* surgery with fashions that shed Victorian layers of clothes. And the coincidence of *cosmetic* surgery with cinematic and industrial streamlining that referred as well to the human body as to roadsters. So many coincidences, verily, that cosmetic surgeons could appear to achieve what a certain Mr. Jeamson had promised for his cosmetics in 1665: "Though you may look so *pallidly* sad, that you would be thought to be dropping in your *Graves*; and though your skins be so devoid of colour, that they might be taken for your winding sheets; yet these *Recipes* will give you such a rosie cheerfulness, as if you had new begun your resurrection."[82]

We are not, any of us, the Practically Perfect People that Pamela Barber sold nationwide in the 1980s, photos of customers' faces imprinted on the light-sensitive fabric heads of life-size cloth dolls. Cosmetic surgery promises practical perfection, a resurrection consistent with fairy tale mirrors. "I look in the mirror and what I see isn't me. I feel young inside. I just want to look as young as I feel." Social psychologists, therapists, and surgeons warn against too-great expectations and the tendency toward "polysurgery," a third, fourth, fifth operation to get a body part exact, to fix "that strange look – not old, not young, just tight," or to amend other body parts that seem suddenly old or odd in proximity to what is now youthful or perfectly normal. Obsession with cosmetic surgery may be an attempt to make one's body an alibi for the course of one's life. It may come at last to resemble "delusional reduplication," a state in which people imagine that for any defective body part they have four or five practically perfect others.[83]

Warnings go unheeded, so attractive is the promise of resurrection, so perfectionist the computer projections of what I will look like after the knife or laser finishes with me. "Give of yourself, give to yourself," begged a CosmetiCare advertisement for liposuction in 1993. The next year, the American Society of Plastic and Reconstructive Surgeons recorded 393,049 purely aesthetic procedures and another 1,373,059 procedures involving both reconstructive and aesthetic surgery. But these apparently precise numbers are far too low – many surgeries go unreported, and we have no data on the ratio of repeats to remedy a defect from previous surgery, as with breast enlargements, a problem since 1899. "In this age," said one woman, "with all the technology possible, changing something less than perfect about one's looks seems so easy, so normal." Gift certificates are available.[84]

Couvade as the carrying of a junior or a 2d has become, courtesy of plastic surgery, the creation of one's own second, with a second chance in life, as in the 1966 film, *Seconds*, where deaths are faked and plastic surgery performed so that adults bored with their lives may begin anew under different faces. Or so that those born in the wrong body may begin again, as adults, with the right body. If reconstructive surgery has to do with correcting disfigurements that impair a person's "efficacy as a moral agent," and if cosmetic surgery has to do with the "accomplishment of gender," assuring men of a culturally constructed masculinity and women of a culturally constructed femininity, then sex change operations are the penultimate form of both, and of couvade itself. Through transsexual or "sex reassignment" surgery a person becomes that Other, carried within and all along.[85]

Early in the 1700s, as homosexual men in London began to convene a distinct subculture and as masquerades became popular entertainments where wo/men eagerly cross-dressed,

> Where sexes blend in one confus'd intrigue,
> Where the girls ravish and the men grow big,

aristocratic men of the "molly" clubs would put on female garb and "try to speak, walk, chatter, shriek, and scold as women do, aping them as well in other aspects," including mock births with groaning "mothers," midwives, and wooden babies. The same European society that instituted ever-harsher penalties for sodomy sought out the seductions of cross-dressing. The same society that now preferred women to boys in female stage roles applauded the Chevalier d'Eon, thought to be a woman acting as a man on the political stage. The same society that was skittish of hermaphrodites was fascinated with the tangle of cross-sex twins.[86]

Historians read all this as the origin of the "modern challenge to traditional moral and psychic strictures" *or* of the modern dogma of two opposite sexes defined by inescapable biologies; as the emergence of the "sexually ambidextrous" subject *or* of its repression by science; as the deepening of gender ambiguities *or* the fetishizing of gender; as the articulation of "a space of possibility" for a fluid identity *or* the chaining of individual character to reproductive physiology.[87]

Sex change surgeries intensify the scholarly ambivalence and popular anxiety about gender (re)construction. If "transvestism, like repetition, puts in question the idea of an 'original,' a stable starting point," transsexualism puts in question the idea of a conclusion, a resting point to gender. If "transvestism, like the copy or simulacrum, disrupts 'identity' and exposes it as figure" rather than ground of being, then transsexualism, like the mirror image, reverses identity and...and what? Does "sex reassignment" surgery confirm or subvert the biological bases of maleness and femaleness? Confirm: The transsexual does not feel fully male or female until invested so far as possible with the organs of a man or a woman. Subvert: The transsexual as a metamorphic figure proves that neither genetics nor physique locks in the sensations and convictions of masculinity or femininity. Transsexuals seem at once to defy and to define a system that makes sex characteristics the basis for the assignment of gender. Defy: Even before operations on the genitals, breasts, and Adam's apple, the transsexual is sure that s/he is in the "wrong" body for ter gender. Define: Even after the operations, their extent often invisible to everyone except sex partners, some transsexuals are only convinced of the surgical success by enacting the most conventional roles of the gender to which s/he physically, more than less, now belongs.[88]

Passing for a wo/man is the transport of the cross-dresser, who must emphasize those qualities of fe/maleness exaggerated by the society at large. The thrill of transvestism is the thrill of trespass, whether keeping it secret or defiantly camping it up. The transsexual moves beyond trespass to a new birth certificate, a new passport, and may live as any sort of woman he or man she wishes, tennis player, minister, or, with the utmost faith in this form of couvade, nightclub stripper – reenacting the discovery (the uncovering) that s/he was all along "a beautiful woman trapped in a fat man's body."[89]

Both the M→F cross-dresser and the M→F transsexual, gay or hetero, nurture fantasies of being pregnant, of giving birth to children as they have given birth to the woman within. ("There is buried within every man a composite 'woman,' " say the male cross-dressers of the Society for the Second Self.) Most transsexual operations have been from male to female, conducted by midhusbands who redouble the couvade, for it is usually a male surgeon who delivers the inner woman out of the man and nurses her toward her new life. So, in 1929–30, undergoing one of the earliest M→F operations, Lili Elbe, formerly the painter Andreas Sparre, regarded her surgeon Werner Kreutz as a Deliverer: "I feel so changed that it seems as if you had operated not upon my body, but upon my brain." When she revisited Sparre's Danish birthplace, she felt like a stranger. "I am newly created," she wrote to Kreutz. "I was born under your auspices at Dresden," on the banks of the Elbe. But to be truly female she felt that she had also to give birth. In June 1931, the Lily returned to the Cross (Dr. Kreutz) for another operation, "to make it possible for her to become a mother." She died that September of a "paralysis of the heart," having "long since realized that the life of a woman consists of sorrow and yearning."[90]

Sorrow: For that male twin who had been the ogre and was at last being supplanted... Lili spoke of Andreas that way, as a receding twin. Yearning: For a baby, as a M→F transsexual in 1980 would yearn for a baby after he had become Mrs. James Noyes, the couple contracting with a surrogate for a child by artificial insemination. Transsexual surgery turns the clock back *before* birth, in endocrinomythological terms, to a time when the hypothalamus of a female fetus was insufficiently protected against male neurohormones and the male chromosome push was weak. M→F surgery deals with "gender dysphoria," a restlessness about sexual identity, by correcting an "intrauterine hormonal error."[91]

Where transsexuals begin as females and give birth to themselves as males, the couvade is less a fetal correction of gender than a postpartum usurpation of personhood. Since 1880, when Herman Karl changed his name from Sophia Hedwig and his sex from female to male after genital surgery, there have been few F→M transsexuals. This, argues cultural historian Marjorie Garber, is due to a Western reluctance to admit that it can be as easy to construct a man as a woman. What with their wigs and cosmetics, breast implants and permanent eyeliner, women are obviously artifacts; men (say men) are the *real* people, whole, stable, and inimitable. Womanliness itself may be a masquerade, but surgeons will not let that masquerade get out of hand by designing workable, aesthetic penile attachments for women avid to be men.[92]

Ultimately, we have the clone. The folklore of couvade tells of being half-pregnant; the lore of cloning tells of being beside ourselves, of birthing others who are at once our juniors, twins, cellmates, and co-evals. This is impossible. The cells of an adult are specialized; only within the first days after fertilization can any cell within an embryo become any type of cell. After that, we are never totipotent and cannot, like the shape-changers of John Brunner's fiction, *Double, Double*, reproduce ourselves by fission and twinning. We can bisect a two-cell embryo, place the two in culture mediums, let them grow, then implant them in separate wombs, producing identical twins from different mothers. We can freeze one or both of the cells for later implantation, producing genetically identical babies born years apart. We will be able, soon, to practice parthenogenesis, transferring the nucleus from one blastocyst into another from which the nucleus has been removed, producing twinned embryos (without the mother's chromosomes or the father's sperm) ad infinitum. But we cannot guarantee that our virtue, intelligence, artistry, or stamina will ride along with these embryonic clones through to adulthood, or that other traits carried genetically will be expressed to the same degree. Granted the vagaries of environment and event, wrote a biologist in 1979, "I never expect to witness the construction of carbon-copy humans."[93]

Once more that phrase, "carbon copy," which has been with us from page 11. The phrase should have receded before biology as carbon papers have receded before xerography. But no. Today we have Ohio Willow Wood Company's Carbon Copy II, "recreating the human leg...a lightweight endoskeletal system featuring a modular, energy-storing foot." Beyond prosthetics, carbon copying guides our understanding of the "natural" sequences in the reproduction of living things: the very metaphors of molecular biology are of complementary pairs and exact transcription. The DNA double helix is stabilized by the "pairing of bases" between its two strands, a pairing achieved through "hydrogen bonding"; the DNA "master blueprint" is "transcribed" via the synthesis of messenger RNA – all to assure an "extreme copying fidelity."[94]

Carbon copying is, for us faithful carbon-based life forms, a prime analog of the process of replication, the posture of couvade, and the promise of cloning – of impressing ourselves into another in the midst of making something of ourselves. The carbon copy restores to us a companionate twin, running happily along with us, just as sympathetic fictions find clones in the closest of communion, expert at sharing, "inexpert at solitude."[95]

Not the prospect of cloning itself, of cloning as couvade, but the prospect of cloning gone wrong, cloning as the creation of a Doppelgänger, turns the halcyon into the horrible. Rollin D. Hotchkiss of Rockefeller University, who drafted the term "genetic engineering," warned in his seminal contribution of 1965 that, attempting "to produce the noblest Roman of all, one might unwittingly produce a Dogberry, a Caliban," a being of no social conscience. Finally the objections to cloning are to its (my) disposition toward such selfishness that one of me will never seem enough, that my Doubles will claim for themselves the eminence of a multiple me, scornful of the rest. What is most to be feared in our world of 2ds is a world of second-to-nones.[96]

IV. Second Nature / Reprise: Diversity

> And that distilled by magic sleights
> Shall raise such artificial sprites
> As by the strength of their illusion
> Shall draw him on to his confusion....
>
> – *Macbeth*, III.v

However insatiable for the charms of the unique and the original, our culture of the copy threatens everywhere to reduce diversity. We are not far enough along with the engineering of human beings to see a decline in our own variety. We do see this in the strains of wheat and white mice we have shaped.

Alexander Pope, poet and gardener, deplored the vogue for topiary, that pruning of shrubbery so that "Any Ladies that please may have their own Effigies in Myrtle, or their Husband's in Horn beam." Topiary had blossomed in England during the reign of William III and Mary (1689–1702), whose native Holland was populated with yew trees clipped into birds, dogs, men, and women, but the ancients whom Pope admired had carved cypress into hunting scenes, Renaissance gardeners had tamed leafy dragons, and baroque groundskeepers had hedged their mazes "In Satyrs, Centaurs, Whales, and half-men-horses." The topiary garden had the exuberance of an Eden all in privet – privet, "so apt, that no other can be like unto it, to bee cut, lead and drawne into what forme one will," wrote an enthusiast in 1629. Pope in 1713 was not amused; he

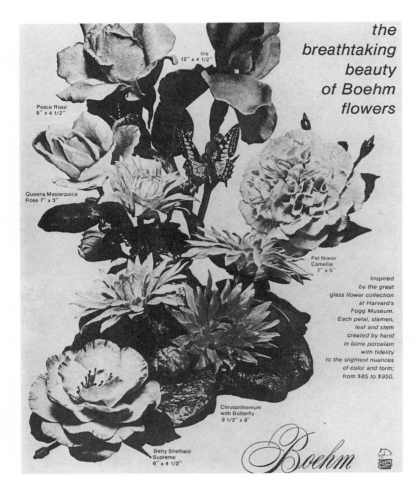

FIGURE 8.5. 1972 advertisement for bone porcelain flowers, modeled not upon living flowers but "with fidelity to the slightest nuances of color and form" of the glass flowers at the Fogg Museum, Harvard University. Reproduced by permission of the Edward Marshall Boehm Company.

disliked the "monstrous attempts beyond the reach of the art itself: We run into Sculpture, and are yet better pleas'd to have our Trees in the most awkward figures of Men and Animals, than in the most regular of their own."[97]

Although the English "wilderness" of twisting paths was less regular than the geometric walks of the French garden, its art lay in the disguise of artifice. "In a word," advised gardener Timothy Nourse in 1700, "let this Third Region or Wilderness be Natural-Artificial; that is, let all things be disposed with that cunning, as to deceive us into a belief of a real wilderness or Thicket." If this cunning was too blatant for Pope's Augustan tastes, it was well suited to the Natural-Artificiality that ravished the Victorians: "I love the topiary art," wrote one such, "with its trimness and primness, and its open avowal of its artificial character," for it was "the properest transition from the architecture of the house to the natural beauties of the grove and paddock." As gentlewomen arranged delicate wax and satin flowers around trompe l'oeil fruit, estate gardeners turned outdoor greenery into cats, swans, and gates of Heaven.[98]

Hell it was, not Heaven – "The Tartarus of Maids" – that Herman Melville visited in 1851. While children and women in Paris, London, and New York molded blossoms of taffeta, batiste, silk, velvet, or cotton at long tables in rooms suffused with the bloom of arsenic, mill girls sat at "blank-looking counters" in the Devil's Dungeon paper mill by Blood River – "rows of blank-looking girls, with blank, white folders in their blank hands, all blankly folding blank paper." Out of city tenements came women dressed in "tawdry shams, taking brass for gold, galvanized iron for silver, cotton for seal-skin," to paint the petals of asters, violets, fuchsias, camellias, dahlias, hyacinths, pansies, carnations, forget-me-nots; from farms and small towns came the factory girls, to sort rags, feed the Fourdrinier machines, and fold paper in white-washed buildings, their faces "pale with work." The flower makers labored at "miraculously perfect imitations – every crease, vein, spot, tint and filament in the natural creation being reproduced with such minute fidelity that a magnifying glass is needed to detect the artifice." Each day mill maids in pairs counted each of forty thousand finished sheets of paper, which others then folded into envelopes.[99]

For seeds. Yes: from the "sheet-white," virginal maidens to the white envelopes of seed companies, an irony Melville intended, and an irony compounded: the celibate Shakers were the first to sell seeds in paper envelopes. Through to the 1870s, the seed business was a major Shaker enterprise. Their 1836 sales catalog advertised, among other vegetables, six varieties of beans, five of cabbage and turnips, four of cucumber and peas. Renowned for the trueness of their seeds, Shaker sisters at New Lebanon (NY) put up 36,000 paper bags and envelopes of seeds in 1851 (the year Melville visited the Old Red Mill in the Berskhires), 110,000 in 1855 (the year his story was printed).[100]

Paper envelopes from pale maidens for seeds disseminated after 1836 by the government too, by the Commissioner of Patents, who funded plant collecting expeditions, built a national greenhouse, and posted packets of seed to farmers across the country – a million free packets, 1850–55; a billion in the year 1897.[101]

With the rediscovery in 1900 of the work of Gregor Mendel, plant breeders at U.S. agricultural stations could purposefully crossbreed plants to transfer desirable traits from exotic to established species. "The plant breeder's new conception of varieties as plastic groups must replace the old idea of fixed forms of chance origin," wrote a Department of Agriculture cotton breeder in 1905; "...it is no longer necessary to wait for nature to supply the deficiency by some mass seeding."[102]

Mass seeding to find useful plants was replaced by a massive search for germplasms with useful genes and by an agrindustrial program to produce hybrids, which by 1936 were mixes of two inbred lines, with high yields but no regenerative ability. The paradoxical result of the breeders' vision "of creating organisms different from any now in existence" was to reduce the available number of open-pollinated varieties of seed and to make farmers more dependent on a few companies controlling elite seed lines. Hybrid corn, whose genetic uniformity made it very vulnerable to pests and disease, and whose stiffer shanks made ears harder to handpick, presupposed larger farms that could sustain the cost of additional spraying and mechanical harvesting. A constriction of varieties was also seen in wheat, cotton, cucumbers, cauliflower, onions, tomatoes. By 1969, all but 4 percent of U.S. acreage under peas was planted with one of two varieties, and the United Nations was worried about "genetic erosion," the worldwide disappearance of unique cultivars due to land clearance and monocrop planting with seeds patented by multinational corporations.[103]

Patented? Well, isn't every seed "a mechanism as surely as is a trolley car"? The Plant Patent Act of 1930 said it was, and any seed "invented" (through asexual reproduction) had only to be shown to be new and distinct. Another Act in 1970 mandated seventeen-year Plant Variety Protection Certificates for new-made sexually reproduced plants. In 1985 the U.S. Board of Patent Appeals ruled in favor of the commercial protectability of plant parts – roots, tubers, leaves, fruits, and flowers – as well as seeds. In 1990 Biotechnica International received the first patent on a plant (maize) genetically modified by the insertion of a foreign gene (to improve protein content). Those seeds which had been slipped into the millions of paper envelopes folded by mill girls are now sealed within the proprietary envelope of agribusiness and the biodegradable polymer envelope of genetic engineers. Our culture of the copy has conflated the reproduction of life with lifeless reproduction, under the oxymoron of "artificial seeds." If there be (as yet) no artificial human ova, there are, courtesy of in vitro culturing of tissue from seed embryos, billions of clones each within a gel and polymer coating, ready to sprout identical seedlings of coffee, rice, Douglas Fir. Second-growth forest may truly be of a Second Nature.[104]

Second Nature, so constituted, relies on us for everything. Hybrids with lives of three to ten years need our chemicals to survive; in profitable circularity, companies engineer seeds with outer coatings that resist ever-denser concentrations of their own herbicides. Reintroduced to Asia and Africa, whence the West originally obtained the seeds for most crops, this Second Nature may impoverish countries already being depleted of a wealth of germplasms and unprepared for the cost or consequences of rampant spraying. Our tendency to treat Nature as a standing reserve where "Everything everywhere is ordered to stand by, to be immediately at hand, indeed to stand there just so that it may be on call for a further ordering" (as Heidegger wrote), is shadowed by a tendency toward mistaken identity, those living things we have engineered taken to be "the best that nature had to offer."[105]

Genetically engineered seeds may be unstable, like other creatures of ours – Caliban, Frankenstein's "monster" – kept from reproducing themselves. They may provoke dangerously simple changes in pests or pathogens that need but a single mutation to defy an entire family of chemical agents. They *do* lead, by force of economic circumstance, to reduced genetic diversity within germ lines. Can we fulfill our obligations to future generations by presenting them with practically perfect seeds which, but for a technological topiary, would be sterile and indefensible?[106]

New to the world in the 1970s was a pure culture of *Streptomyces vellosus* Dietz, neither plant nor animal but a useful microorganism. The U.S. Patent Examiner approved a patent for the process by which *Streptomyces vellosus* produces the antibiotic lincomycin; there were precedents back to 1873 (Pasteur's purified yeast) for awarding patents to manufacturing processes using single-celled organisms as catalysts or as microscopic factories; there were also prospects for using other bacteria to synthesize large quantities of insulin, interferon, human growth factor. The Examiner, however, denied a patent on the bacterium itself. Had not the Plant Variety Protection Act explicitly removed from consideration any fungi or bacteria? Besides, *Streptomyces vellosus*, mayhap impure, did exist in the wild and was, as such, uncoverable, lest, as a commissioner had cautioned in 1889, patents be obtained "upon the trees of the forest and the plants of the earth, which of course would be unreasonable and impossible." The Court of Customs and Patent Appeals reversed his decision and in 1977 allowed the patent, arguing that "biologically pure cultures of microorganisms...are much more akin to inanimate chemical compositions such as reactants, reagents, and catalysts than they are to horses and honeybees or raspberries and roses." Microorganisms were frequently "a kind of tool" used to ferment beer and digest sewage. "In short, we think the fact that microorganisms, as distinguished from chemical compounds, are alive is a distinction without legal significance." Judges Miller and Baldwin dissented: the distinction of a bacterium from a honeybee or a rose was "purely gratuitous and clearly erroneous."[107]

Erroneous, probably, but given a culture of the copy in which all life seems driven by replication and transcription, no longer was it impossible or unreasonable to patent living things — so long as they were *our* creatures. The 1977 Court pretended not to be deciding whether "living things in general" were patentable. That decision came three years later, in the affirmative: a genetically engineered bacterium (a virtuous one, capable of breaking down crude oil after oil spills) was indeed patentable, decreed the Supreme Court. The bacterium in question was the handiwork of Ananda Chakrabarty of General Electric, the company with the slogan, "We bring good things to life."[108]

Far from bringing a being to life, Chakrabarty had mere?ly reconfigured its innards, planting four different oil-degrading plasmids inside one *Pseudomonas* bacterium, where they were quite comfy. That was enough for a patent; like other inventions, the new bacterium did not need to be novel in every aspect or origin. (Bacteria, after all, were growing and columnizing 3.5 billion years ago.) It had only to be a non-obvious adaptation or improvement — like polyploid oysters, produced by making multiple copies of genes, for which a patent was granted in 1987, or like a special mouse, patented in 1988.[109]

OncoMouse, so trademarked by DuPont, was, evolutionarily, a failure. It carried two copies of a gene disposing it to breast cancer. We who as primates genetically diverged from rodents rather recently, about sixty million years ago, are now engaged in shaping mice for our own evolutionary ends, as test animals born and bred to a human and serious disease. Since 1907, biologists had been culturing simple animal cells; since 1943, they had been able to culture chick embryo and rodent tissue; since 1974, they had been inserting genetic material into embryonic mammalian cells to see if foreign genes would be expressed. Some were. *Transgenic* animals could transmit to offspring foreign genetic information that would be reliably expressed. With mice, argued two biologists in 1985, this was natural: "all mice are transgenic in the sense that foreign DNA, especially of viral origin, has stably integrated into their germline throughout evolution." In 1989, the U.S. Office of Technology Assessment expanded the argument: "nature makes it clear that there is no universal or absolute rule that all species are discretely bounded in any generally consistent manner." To insert a foreign gene in raspberry, horse, or honeybee did not violate the integrity of a species. It was another step in that topiary by which we breed and shape dogs, cows, horses, rats, and white mice.[110]

And other human beings? No, said the head of the U.S. Patent Office, Donald Quigg, in 1988: his agency would not patent human beings. Some sort of gel around *our* species protects us from our own logic — despite anticipations of gene therapy to remedy human genetic defects that code for debilitating diseases like Lesch-Nyhan Syndrome, in which children mutilate themselves, compulsively, toward death. "When people talk about manipulating animals and changing their genetic essence," cautioned a historian of science in 1993, "that is different than just breeding animals," but by 1993 transgenic animals were as far out of the closet as transsexuals. Three more gene-altered mice and a rabbit (inclined to AIDS) had been granted patents, and 140 other animals were patent-pending, most also "living laboratories" for the study of a specific human disease. [111]

The European Patent Office had turned down such patents, doubting that they were as "morally neutral" as averred an attorney for Monsanto Chemical Corporation. If the OncoMouse "reliably develops neoplasms within months," it was the first animal ever born solely to self-destruct. "We can now produce animals with essentially any genetic disorder," gleamed one medical researcher. Could us animals, Homo sapiens, be far behind? [112]

DNX Corporation of New Jersey, having engineered pigs with human hemoglobin, hopes to develop swine with hearts, kidneys, lungs, and livers acceptable to human bodies. Baboon hearts have been implanted in (dying) children. In 1994, genetically engineered mice were reported to be producing human antibodies. [113]

Hanging over our culture of the copy are a blade and a claw, both sharp. The blade of eugenics would reduce our diversity in the name of a practically perfect body rearranged in embryo to eliminate such "imperfections" as albino skin, a sixth finger, left-handedness, shortness, femaleness. The claw of the chimera, classically a lion in front, serpent behind, goat between, and now, biomedically, any transgenic animal, is no less dreadful in its implication that through our search for the practically perfect, we ourselves may lose all definition, may become a collage of assorted animals or a cross between a mammal and a machine.

V. Seeing Double / Reprise: Virtual Reality

> Thou art too like the spirit of Banquo: down!
> — *Macbeth*, IV.i

"Can machines think?" asked the mathematician Alan Turing in 1950. He proposed a series of "imitation" games, the first of which puts a man and a woman in a room separate from and unseen by an interrogator. The interrogator must ascertain from teletyped responses to teletyped questions which is the man, which the woman. The man's job is to deceive the interrogator. The woman tries to help the interrogator toward the truth. [114]

Strange, that our current debate over the difference between human and machine intelligence should begin with guessing the difference between male and female where the man is pretending to be a woman. No less strange, for all that Alan Turing was gay, and his suicide by poisoned apple in 1954 a consequence of life within a homophobic British society to which he had revealed his homosexuality in 1952 and whose courts had put him on a regime of female hormone treatments

FIGURE 8.6. *Staff Choir*, by C.T. Chew, 1990. Mixed media self-portrait using Photobooth, Canon Color Laser, and hand coloring with pencil and acrylic paint. Reproduced by permission.

C. T. CHEW, CHEF DE CUISINE, AND STAFF CHOIR
DAVENPORT HOTEL, U.S.A. FEB. 1927.

tantamount to "chemical castration." If it would occur most poignantly to a gay man to put gender at risk, it did not follow that he would in the next "imitation" game substitute a machine for the man (and a man, it has usually been presumed, for the woman). That substitution was rather a response to millennia of debate about automata.[115]

Very briefly, that debate had always stipulated to technical (magical) competence at shaping a golem, a creature who looks and moves like a human. The question posed by a golem was never about its skin or breath or blood; it was about the extent to which looks may deceive. Babylonian Jews long ago imagined a golem, sent to trick Rabbi Zera, who spoke to him, but received no answer. "Thereupon he said unto him, 'Thou art a creature of the magicians. Return to thy dust.'" Not physiognomy but responsiveness, sociability, sincerity have been at issue, whence the shock as von Kempelen's chess-playing automaton swept the pieces off the board if opponents cheated; whence the drama of Rossum's Universal Robots as one falls in love; whence the smiles of audioanimatronic figures at Disney World. The more agile we become at replicating animate beings, the more we look to qualities social or immaterial (loyalty, love, despair, boredom, competitiveness, confusion) to tell ourselves from our creations — or the more pride we must take in their equivalence to us.[116]

Turing saw "little point in trying to make a 'thinking machine' more human by dressing it up in...artificial flesh." To be deceived by such cross-dressing would prove nothing about the mentality of a machine. Indeed, he wrote, it would be harder for a person to carry off the pretense of being a mechanical calculator than for a disguised electronic computer to carry off the imposture of being a thinking person. An intellectual uneasy with small talk and oblivious to many social conventions, Turing reframed the debate about the limits of mechanism in terms of the limits of our ability to see through social simulation.[117]

Without surgery but from close-up, onstage or at a party, a woman can pass as a man, a man as a woman. What we think we know about maleness and femaleness is a social knowledge. The sociologist H.M. Collins takes the next step: computers have an "isolated upbringing"; how can they know, think, converse, when they do not live in society? To the extent that we attribute thought to a machine, are we not welcoming the machine into our culture as, at least, "a social prosthesis"?[118]

Vice versa, what if the interrogator during a Turing test mistakes every human being as a machine? Isn't our tendency to muddle the two rather an historical than a philosophical problem? "The great difficulty in deciding whether a machine is behaving like a human is that humans have spent so much of history behaving like machines," writes philosopher Mark Halpern; "it is not yet clear what human behavior will turn out to be when actual machines are universally available to relieve us of the need to impersonate them." We grant machines humanity by default. Once we have such perfect servants as intelligent machines promise to be, then we may discover who we really are.[119]

Whether we have been mechanical for so long that we cannot tell our discourse from that of our better machines, or have begun to admit to our company machines socialized to be intelligent in ways that we recognize intelligence among ourselves, the Turing test continues to provoke us because of the momentum in our culture of the copy for replicas to transcend originals. A revealing version of the Turing test would replace the human interrogator with a machine: do we know enough about ourselves to program a computer capable of discriminating by words alone between a well-groomed machine and a man or a woman?

In 1949, the English neurosurgeon Sir Geoffrey Jefferson declared that "No mechanism could feel... pleasure at its successes, grief when its valves fuse, be warmed by flattery, be made miserable by its mistakes, be charmed by sex, be angry or miserable when it cannot get what it wants." Turing wrote in rebuttal that recourse to such inner states is shaky. For social harmony, and not because other people can more cogently than machines prove to us that they are thinking or feeling, do we accept standard signs of pleasure and grief as the real thing. "The original question, 'Can machines think?' I believe to be too meaningless to deserve discussion," Turing said, for thinking presupposes itself. (I am thinking, believe you me, ergo I think.) "Nevertheless I believe that at the end of the century the use of words and general educated opinion will have altered so much that one will be able to speak of machines thinking without expecting to be contradicted." Presto change-o, a 1985 ad: "IF YOU'RE THINKING OF A NEW KITCHEN, CONSIDER THE KITCHEN THAT THINKS – General Electric Appliances. Good looks, well built, and brains too." Children today work with computers as thinking companions, with a friendliness Turing did not anticipate, considering "the difficulty of the same kind of friendliness occurring between man and machine as between white man and white man, or between black man and black man."[120]

He dropped the analogy, but the innuendo – from this son of a colonial administrator in India – was biting: the vehemence of objections to a *thinking, feeling* machine was the vehemence of racism, which denies to those dissimilar a refined intelligence, refined emotions. Questions that Turing did consider meaningful in 1950 were especially so in light of India's recent independence and the decline of a British Empire to which the Turings had been devoted since 1638, and for which Alan had worked – in British Intelligence – during World War II: Can machines learn? (Isn't inferiority fixed?) Can they originate? (Aren't lower races mere apes or parrots?) Can they surprise us? (To advance, mustn't underdeveloped nations – or primitive peoples – follow our lead?)[121]

There is little difference, come to think of it, between the passing of a man for a woman, a machine for a human, an Indian for an Englishman, or a black man for a white man in a Turing test. An epitome of our culture of the copy, the test appears to be a fine filter for the uniquely human but presupposes, as did Turing, that passing is profitable, that complex acts of copying are advertisements for an unconfined humanity. We are being warned against "regarding ourselves as abstract reasoning machines" or "wetware," but the approach of artificial intelligence is less a problem of loss of identity in the face of reasoning machines (or of self-replicating cellular automata) than of seeing what we want to make of ourselves next. To speak of the "liveliness of a logic element," to model microchips upon human neural networks, to work "toward some circuitry of ethical robots," is a conscious (and predominantly male) act of couvade, redoubled by computer programs constructed around small sets of algorithms from which may emerge the properties of life.[122]

Artificial intelligence and artificial life are metaphors to explain to ourselves what we are about. If we cannot yet make good upon the metaphors, our failures may be due to our habit, at each success, of raising the ante. We keep redefining intelligence and life in tandem with our experience of hardware and software and their bioelectronic diseases – voracious worms, recklessly replicating viruses. The philosophers Georges Canguilhem and Didier Deleule explain that we are in the midst of reversing the Cartesian equation: from human being as a devout thinking mechanism to machine as faithful ambassador or conquistador for the evolutionary human. Investors speak of "generations" of computers; cognitive scientists investigate "evolutionary robotics"; psychologists study computer-simulated organisms that "evolve" "motivational units"; bioscientists contrive "animats," engineered from what we know of Second Nature, animals, and from what we think we know about ourselves.[123]

Alan Turing never confused simulation with duplication. His test was meant to show that a camouflaged machine could approximate, not duplicate, those aspects of ourselves we take to betoken thoughtfulness and responsiveness. Machine intelligence, Turing knew, would always be virtual – but that should be enough to unpeg our arrogance.

We have before us now the converse prospect, or project. Virtual intelligence shows us what we expect to see, similar to aerial photographs of dummy squadrons; virtual reality dazzles us, making us unsure of what we see, feel, or hear. Like the disinformation of counterintelligence, virtual intelligence orients us treacherously; virtual reality leads us to regard "the real world itself as simply one last run of a simulation."[124]

Virtual reality is older than sin. It is the hallucination of heaven, the peyote vision, the dionysiac stupor. It is the play, the novel, the film, the radio mystery, the panorama, the pastoral symphony, the soap opera, any system devised for losing ourselves in another world. The tactile glove and optical goggles of what Jaron Lanier in 1989 dubbed "virtual reality" are no more freeing, and no less (hopes Lanier), than meditation.[125]

I find it striking that the wraparound devices of these virtual reality (VR) systems should so resemble the mindreading *and* the brainwashing machines of futuristic fictions. Derivative of medical imaging techniques and prosthetics *and* of the flight simulators and satellite robots of our astronomilitary, VR draws upon one field devoted to forcing bodies to yield their particular secrets *and* upon a second field devoted to the defiance of gravity and bodiliness. VR comes to us Siamesed in the same manner that the man/or woman and the man/or machine are Siamesed during Turing tests: one working to be (thought)fully incorporated in the other, the other working for total divorce. The "virtual" of VR may refer to practically perfect communion or to practically perfect camouflage. VR may unlock our secret desires, freed of time and gravity, but it may also permit us to assume deceptive personae, free of those commitments that ground humanity. Entering upon VR spaces, we must be chary of that ogre which wants always to unhinge us from the messy world we are born into, a world we neglect to our peril.[126]

Whatever we make of VR — whether we "recreate the commons" across cyberspace (hopes Jaron Lanier) or construct self-pleasuring digital copies of ourselves "In Hot Pursuit of Happiness" (speculates Stanislaw Lem) — VR is already making cyborgs of us, circumstantially if not substantially. To the extent that we follow our money, we become invested in that electronic network which maintains our stocks, credit cards, debts, futures. To the extent that we follow our entertainers and muses into the mazes of computer simulation, we become "live action" or human-machine "interfaces," binary visionaries, half here half not.[127]

Of course, the world itself is only half here, maybe less than half. Describing the quantum behavior of the electron, the French physicist Paul Dirac in 1928 arrived at an equation with two solutions, one positive, one negative. Classical physics had routinely discarded negative solutions as artifacts of the operation of the $\sqrt{}$ and the ^{2} ($\sqrt{n^2} = \pm n$) but Dirac took seriously this "ghost-entity," a mathematical figment with real consequences. "On my new theory the state of negative energy has a physical meaning," he wrote; by acknowledging the ghost-entities, or "anti-electrons," he could preserve for quantum physics the principle of the conservation of energy. Such positively charged, negative-energy particles entailed some physical absurdities. No matter: he postulated a "world of negative-energy states uniformly occupied by an infinite number of electrons" — a "Dirac sea" — or ocean, for by 1933 he thought that for every particle there should be "a corresponding anti-particle."[128]

Some physicists objected that this was *meta*physics, but cloud chambers in 1933 revealed the shadowy paths of electron/anti-electron pairs created under the impact of cosmic rays, and Carl Anderson renamed the ghost-entities "positrons." Physicists and fiction writers began speculating about parallel universes and planets made of mirror matter; Isaac Asimov (chemist and novelist) conceived of androids with positronic brains. In 1955 another "nuclear ghost," the antiproton, was caught out in a Bevatron maze; in 1956 the antineutron. By 1990 there were, on paper, antiquarks with anticolors (antired, antigreen, antiblue). The nuclear ghosts of positron emission tomography were helping physicians

locate brain tumors and study, of all things, schizophrenia. And physicists were anticipating the synthesis of antihydrogen for the storage of
what is called "antimatter."[129]

Common to stage magic and "lost wax" casting, to the graphics of
M.C. Escher and jewelers' molds, negative space and disappearing acts
are, as I have steadily insisted, the other side of twinning. It is not for-
tuitous that we are moved by a cosmology whose course and recourse
are dark or vanishing twins. Like the sense-antisense strands of DNA,[130]
the visibility/invisibility of the cosmic stuff reflects the actual/virtual
dynamic of twinship – and of our culture of the copy, where, afloat in
a Dirac sea, we seem to be searching always and everywhere for the
shadow, dark, strange, or mirror matter that *must* be there to explain
how anything, or everything, bears its opposite. "Wherever we see luminous matter," writes physicist James Trefil, "we should expect to find
dark matter as well."[131]

VI. Ditto / Reprise: Fidelity

> *All*. Double, double toil and trouble;
>   Fire burn and cauldron bubble.
> *Second Witch*. Cool it with a baboon's blood,
>   Then the charm is firm and good.
>
> – *Macbeth*, IV.i

A thief, in lieu of crucifixion, agrees to act as the double of the mortally
wounded warlord he closely resembles. The thief becomes a Shadow
Warrior, *kagemusha*, for the Takedas, one of the great clans doing battle
during the troubled sixteenth century. In Akira Kurasawa's 1980 film,
the conflict is internecine, but the Shadow Warrior may stand also as
the figure of Japan vis-à-vis the West. Westerners, who forced themselves upon the Japanese in the 1850s only to be stunned at their skill
at doubling what they wanted of the West, have been of two minds
about Japan. The West has applauded and derided Japan's aptitude for
imitation, doubting yet dreading that Japan might overtake it, the thief
making off with the Real Thing, the copy transcending the original.

Treating Japan as a Shadow Warrior had begun with the Chinese,
from whom the Japanese of the sixth through eleventh centuries acquired Confucianism and Buddhism, their calendar and bureaucracy,
their codes of law and ranks of nobility, their census-taking and tax
collecting, and their tea. To the Chinese, the Japanese were the Wa,
"Eastern Barbarians" who dwelt on mountainous islands and borrowed
their few virtues from China. When Nippon (Cradle of the Sun), as
the Japanese called their land, began to go its own way in matters of
state, art, alphabet, and poetry, the Chinese regarded it as an imperfect shadow, less slavishly faithful than Korea. The Japanese were not
simply barbarians, but shadow-boxers with whom, on occasion, the Chinese had to do battle.[132]

Most honorable machine

FIGURE 8.7. Advertisement for an electronic facsimile printer, 1962. Reproduced by permission of the Addressograph-Multigraph Corporation.

Westerners from much farther West had access to Japan between 1542, when Portuguese merchants landed on Kyushu, and 1640, when the Tokugawa Shogunate (which had turned back the swords and arrows of the Takeda clan with musketry and cannon) expelled all Europeans and forbade Japanese to leave Japan. During that century, Jesuits brought spring-driven clocks, printing presses, and Christianity, and the Dutch brought Western science; Europe got Japanese swords, silk, ceramics, woodwork, and textiles. The commerce, however, was limited. Japan lay in the shadow of China, not Europe. It was from a Chinese translation, for example, that Japanese artists in the eighteenth century studied Andrea del Pozzo's *Perspectiva Pictorum* and tried out linear perspective. They succeeded with some trompe l'oeil interiors, but painting the *ukiyo*, the floating world, they kept to those bird's-eye scenes they had from the Chinese and their own floating points of view. Their backgrounds had a European sense of horizon, their foregrounds a Japanese sense of detail. Such art resembled montage – a still life against a landscape, a portrait against a prospect, with no middle ground between.[133]

Scurrying to Japan in the 1860s, Westerners sought out a middle ground and found discontinuity, Japanese distinctiveness set against

Western vanishing points. The modernizers of the Meiji Restoration (1868) made this into policy: *wakon yōsai*, "Japanese spirit, Western technology." Francis Hall, correspondent for the *New York Tribune*, arrived in Kanagawa shortly after the port was opened in 1859 and saw the discontinuity instantly: "No Japanese treads on their mats till he has left on the ground his sandals. We Americans were less particular, leaving our footprints wherever we stepped, for it was inconvenient to draw off our boots." Tall, booted Westerners *must* leave their mark on the land, but what exactly would the Japanese absorb? From a rich Connecticut family of farmers and merchants, Hall believed that Japan should have been left alone to ask the West in, rather than humiliated by Commodore Perry's gunships steaming into Edo Bay in 1853 with demands for a trade agreement. Nonetheless, Hall had learnt enough Japanese to know, he wrote in 1860, "just what heartless souls are concealed under the smooth exteriors of this people" – like the mechanical hollows of their festival automata. He marveled (as did P.T. Barnum, a steady customer) at the seamless deceit of a mummified mermaid in Yokohama, with the "grinning skull of a hideous ape, fleshless and eyeless, an ape's shoulder and breast, clearly joined to a fish body," and he deplored the picturebooks of seamy sexual joinings offered him at every turn. The Japanese were polite yet shameless, refined yet raw. And less taken with a delicate music box than with visions of themselves in Hall's large glass mirror.[134]

Amaterasu, goddess of the sun, angered by the adulteries of the god of the netherworld, closeted herself in a cave, leaving the earth in darkness. The other gods reasoned with her, then tricked her. Constructing a metal mirror, they sang its charms: it was as beautiful as Amaterasu. Jealous, she peeked, and the gods thrust the mirror into the cave. Stunned by her reflection, Amaterasu allowed herself to be brought out into the open. Light returned to the earth, and Amaterasu sent the celestial mirror down to Nippon, to be regarded "exactly as if it were our August Spirit; reverence it as if reverencing us and rule the country with a pure luster such as radiates from its surface." The mirror their imperial emblem, Japanese mirror makers improved upon and ornamented what had been a Chinese technology. They developed the *makyō*, or magic mirror, made to reflect one's face and also to cast a figure of the Buddha on white surfaces. These small light-transmitting metal mirrors would be as intriguing to the West as European full-length freestanding mirrors were to the Japanese, who in the 1880s resurrected the Shinto ritual in which one bowed before a mirror while scrutinizing one's reflection to cleanse the soul. Occidental magicians and spiritualists used Japanese magic mirrors to project faces from the Other Side; Japanese, looking into Occidental psyches, found themselves.[135]

By the 1890s, Japan's fleet was western and extensive enough to present a challenge on the boards of European wargamers. If, as Westerners thought, the Japanese were unlikely to be military innovators, the West already feared/admired Japan as, not so metaphorically, a Shadow

Warrior. The sixteenth-century *kagemusha* had stood in for warlords at tedious ceremonies. After victories over China in 1895 and Russia in 1905, Japan was a warrior more combative and would not be thrown from the warlord's horse so quickly as Kurosawa's *kagemusha*, revealing his impersonation. Those scars the Japanese carried from the prying open of Nippon in the 1850s they inflicted upon their neighbors as indelibly as Chyo tattooists pricked Japanese lizards and demons into the white skins of thousands of Western sailors.[136]

Some Westerners chose to become inscribed in Japanese life. As European artists, actors, dancers, designers, and puppeteers were deeply impressed at century's end by the subtlety of prints, patterns, and performances reaching them from the Hidden Kingdom, Lafcadio Hearn came to Yokohama more than willing to sacrifice his "original self" (Greco-Irish-American) to Nippon. One of the few Westerners to become a Japanese citizen, he would write thirteen books in fourteen years extolling an "Unfamiliar Japan" on the verge of vanishing. "The sight of a superb Japanese iron-clad at Mionoseki the other day, filled me with regret," he wrote soon after arriving. "That splendid monster appeared as an omen of some future so much more dismal and artificial than the present." He died in Japan in 1904 during the Russo-Japanese War.[137]

Hearn had loved the eyes of the Japanese, and their eyelids, "in which the lid-edge seems double," for the effect was a "softness and shadowiness difficult to describe," but he had looked on Nippon with the eye of a Westerner (his left eye blind) see(k)ing "the old Greek soul again. To escape out of Western civilization into Japanese life is like escaping from the pressure of ten atmospheres into a perfectly normal medium." Or like staring at a projection of the West as it had been, Japan as shadow to his Ionian birthplace: "How marvelously does this world resemble antique Greece — not merely in its legends and the more joyous phases of its faith, but in all its graces of art and its senses of beauty." He had worked at being Japanese more through reverie than through study of the language, in which he was never fluent, relying upon tales told him by his Japanese wife. He wrote ghost stories, "glimpses," "shadowings"; never invested in Japan as it was in the present, Japan was never fully present to him.[138]

"We must do things in the Western way, since our future must be industrial and commercial," a Japanese student told Hearn. "If we should try to do things in the old way, we should always remain poor and feeble." Hearn could say nothing; Japanese youth wanted what he had hoped to escape by embracing Japan — "here the individual does not strive to expand his own individuality at the expense of that of everyone else." But the direction was clear: modernity and competition. In 1871 Yamagawa Kenjiro boarded the *Japan*, the most advanced steamer of its day, to embark upon a Yale curriculum; he came back to become Japan's first professor of physics. Francis Hall sent Iwasaki Yanosuke to be educated in the U.S. in 1872; Yanosuke, returning, would make the Mitsubishi Company an industrial giant. Meiji Japan's railway and navy were in the British mode, parliament and hospitals German, sales techniques American, films French. Kitasato Shibasaburō, who discovered the plague bacillus, assumed the mannerisms of his mentor, German bacteriologist Robert Koch, whose wife noticed that Shibasaburō's "actions and gestures are just like Koch's. They even hold a pointer the same way when they're lecturing." The Japanese, wrote the French sociologist Gabriel Tarde, proved the Law of Imitation: the inferior imitate the superior.[139]

Mere apes the Japanese were not. The transplantation of a Western-style economy in the 1870s failed, for Japan lacked the infrastructure; economic growth before World War I was due largely to the development of traditional industries supplying a world market. The transfusion of Western culture was pinched short by nativist intellectuals and by an educational system aligned to older values. Where the Japanese explicitly borrowed Euroamerican know-how to set up laboratories, they did original research in seismology, immunology, reproductive biology. Yet their contributions often went unrecognized, for they were disregarded as a society of copyists. "It must be remembered," wrote a British diplomat in 1900, "that Japan has never originated anything."[140]

Galen Fisher, a Christian missionary to Japan, was willing to debate the point after World War I. "It is customary to speak of the Japanese as strong in imitation but weak in invention," he wrote in 1923. "But... they have never adopted ideas or institutions from other countries without so modifying and adding to them as to create something new." If they were imitative, wrote the journalist Miriam Beard, so were we all: "After England developed modern industry, her methods were copied by her neighbors on the Continent as assiduously and as closely as the Japanese ever borrowed from the West."[141]

Japan's military successes during the 1930s and again during the Great Pacific War should have disabused the West of its notion of the Japanese as mimics. Yet U.S. admirals insisted that they had anticipated every move of the Japanese but one, and that, the kamikaze attack, was evidence of blind, mindless fidelity. Allied propaganda depicted "Japs" as automata of a military machine or helmeted monkeys grinning as they swung from jungle vines. After the war, producing toy robots and cymbal-banging monkeys, Japan endured an Occupation meant to transform it into a democratic America yet to keep it as a Jr., a tamed ape.[142]

"Japanzees," the English called them in the eighteenth century, gawking at "mockmen" or chimpanzees. Prof. Charles Richet, awarded the Nobel Prize for Physiology in 1913, implied that the Japanese were exactly that, mockmen, chattering intermediates between monkeys and human beings. This Darwinian insult Japanese would have taken quite differently than a Frenchman, for they had no trouble with Darwinism, even with the slogan that Man had descended from monkeys. East Asian Buddhism was rich with tales of monkeys seeking enlightenment in the Buddha's company. The monkey deity appears in the oldest Japanese writings, "his eyeballs glowing like an eight-handed mirror," welcoming the sun goddess in the same way that macaques at dawn welcome the sun. The medieval Japanese had trained monkeys to dance and bless rice crops, counterparts of shamans; macaques, "the beast in every body," were sacred Shinto messengers from the mountain deity, and Monkey Deity was the guardian of the Tokugawa peace in the seventeenth century. Mori Sosen's eighteenth-century paintings of simian society, affectionate and tender, were widely copied in the nineteenth. Social and emotional, monkeys seemed to weep as humans wept, and to this day the Japanese address them as *san*, a form of address otherwise reserved for human beings. If monkeys rarely transformed themselves into people, monkeys held up a mirror by which the Japanese saw themselves and their society.[143]

Between one Japanese and the next, monkeys were respectable mediators; between the Japanese and the foreigner, monkeys were symbols of a forced, distorted, or foolish imitation. The more ambivalent were the Japanese about Westernization, the less popular were the antics of monkeys who tried to be what they were not. Studying macaques in the wild, however, Japanese ethologists after World War II had no qualms about attributing to them emotion, thought, innovation (washing a sweet potato in sea water), and society. Kinji Imanishi wrote in 1957 that monkey troops represented "prehuman society," marked as was Japanese society by rules of deference, incest taboos, and family lines – the young, when they matured, honored their mothers. Monkeys, he wrote, had culture, which was "a problem of the whole troop in full activity" across time. Through identification (imitation), young monkeys acquired culture. The "acquisition of culture means the absorption of another personality into one's own personality."[144]

Wasn't that what happened in the 1950s, '60s, '70s, and '80s, when Japan, with its smog, its noise, its tourists, became (said some critics) more Western than the West? Wasn't it consistent with the supposed automatism and monkeyishness of the diminutive Japanese that they should surpass the West specifically through processes of miniaturization and products for replay: transistor radios, audio and video tape recorders, calculators, copying machines, cameras, faxes, industrial robots? Wasn't it paradigmatic of the imitativeness of Japanese culture that Akio Morita in the 1950s built the Sony Corporation upon the profits from manufacturing tape recorders for the playing of language tapes by which Japanese students could repeat the words of those nations they would later follow in their fashions, music, and merchandising? Wasn't it illustrative of Japanese mimicry that "One constantly sees businessmen on crowded station platforms practicing the motions of a golf-swing, or students endlessly repeating a baseball throw, just the movements, that is"?[145]

Just the movements. As the Japanese had gone through the motions of Western reform during Occupation while shaping a distinctively Japanese political and industrial system.... As Japanese plastic surgeons in the 1960s and '70s had removed epicanthic folds and given clients larger noses, while Japan impressed the face of its own capitalism upon Southeast Asia and, in the '80s, upon America itself, building "virtual carbon copies" of its auto plants in the West and Midwest.[146]

Today the Eastern Barbarians – monkeys, automata, copyists – seem poised to transcend the original. However Eurocentric, Atlantocentric, and racist the belief that the West is the original, that belief lies at the root of Western ambivalence toward the Japanese as amoral if masterful thieves *and* as an ancient, noble people who make others feel inadequate. The ambivalence of one of America's deans of East Asian history, and a professed Japonophile, Edwin O. Reischauer, was unmistakable in 1977. Even as he strove to reverse the impression that the Japanese were intellectually uncreative, even as he argued that they were not "a nation of pliant, apathetic robots, meekly conforming to one another," he ended his chapter on mass culture by writing of Japanese commuters, "To the foreigner especially, these vast throngs, clad alike and looking very similar to the outsider, all moving determinedly but in orderly fashion to their destinations...seem to be a vision of the robot-like future that may await us all." New York executives in the '80s looked desperately to Tokyo for the secrets of industrial management while corporate lawyers accused the Japanese of software piracy; California technicians disassembled Osaka toys in a quest for new components while Japanese microchips were said to be a stolen technology. Japan, said *Time*, that "student-nation, famous for raiding the inspirations of others," having run out of countries to raid, had turned to itself as a model. A Japanese economist, examining patterns of industrial development, concluded that "pre-eminence of industrial technology stemmed not from early innovative work, but from conscious emulation of early starters"; what America had done best in the nineteenth century, Japan had done best in the twentieth. Asked *The Economist* in 1989, "Who are the copy cats now?"[147]

Where before Japan had been a kimonoed woman following several steps behind and deferent to the masculine technology of the West, now the West bowed to Japan. "I do not believe," wrote the American author of *Made in Japan: The Methods, Motivation, and Culture of the Japanese, and Their Influence on U.S. Business and All Americans* (1987), conceding Japanese headship, "that we should mindlessly ape Japanese society to the extent that we lose the wonderful qualities that have made Americans both unique and (for a long time) the envy of most of the rest of the world." But the tendency was there, in science fiction and fact, to invoke Japan as the Future – Japan, which every twenty years for a millennium has razed the shrine at Ise and, meters away, built another, identical shrine to Amaterasu and the celestial mirror. As Japanese ethologists had defined culture in terms of a copying machine, so Japan was apparently copying in order to transcend. What to the West is often a rampaging Frankensteinian ROBOT is to Japan an Einsteinian GO-BOT or friendly go-between – one office or industrial robot to every five hundred Japanese in 1992, millions more on toy shelves. What the

West calls "virtual reality," the Japanese call "intimate presence."[148]

Odo Makoto, on a Fulbright fellowship to the United States in 1958 and visiting twice in the 1960s, wrote a Japanese best-seller about America as "the extreme form of civilization on its dead-end street." He hoped that it could reform itself, for "To think about America is synonymous with thinking about Japan," and both needed renewal. America, he said, was a constant presence in Japanese life; years after Occupation the Japanese carried with them an "internalized America."[149] During the 1960s, such twinning was a sign of enculturation – but in Japan, parents have long believed that twins are unnatural and unlucky, and have abandoned them at birth or sent one off to be adopted by another family. In the '90s that "internalized America" has become the very image of a vanishing twin.[150]

VII. Once More, with Feeling / Reprise: Authenticity

> All our service
> In every point twice done and then done double
> — *Macbeth*, I.vi

Chester F. Carlson, who rarely went to the movies, died of a stroke in 1968 at a Manhattan matinee. Whiling away the time before a board meeting, he had been sitting through *He Who Rides a Tiger*, a British art film in black and white "with a kind of ersatz modesty," wrote one disdainful reviewer. Another admired its portrait of a soulsick criminal with two sides: a violent, impatient cat burglar; a nice guy, kind to orphans and loyal to cronies. At the end, which Carlson did not see, the eight-time loser spurns the love of an art teacher to return to his fumbling career of crime. He who rides a tiger cannot dismount.[151]

The film was no apt summary of Carlson's lives as inventor of xerography and seeker after higher planes. That would have been too artful a coincidence – as was, perhaps, the story that before entering the theater, he had bought some helium balloons from a vendor and "released them to fly high in the sky over the city. The balloon seller had asked him why he did that, and Chet replied, 'I wanted to set them free.'"[152] But the cat burglar, who keeps trying to snag the baubles of the upper class through windows into upper stories, does confuse reenactment with appropriation, appropriation with a truth higher than love. He is incorrigibly xerographic, replaying a scenario in hopes that it will become the brilliant original he had in mind.

Grand may be the rewards of repetition: the children's book learned by heart, the symphony savored, the novel reentered as a familiar. The pleasures of repetition coax us toward eternal return; the aesthetics of repetition open us up to the appeal of worlds where simplicity is rich or where richness has the simplest of initial conditions.

Recidivists or prodigal daughters, we have been drawn to those who show us our origins in a rich *and* simple world. Hence the resilience of

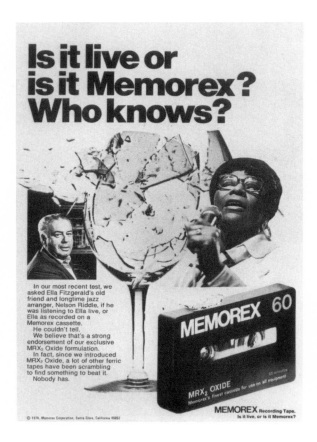

FIGURE 8.8. One in a famous series of advertisements for Memorex audio cassette recording tape. This, from 1974, implied that a tape recording of Ella Fitzgerald's high C could be so true that it too, like her voice, would be pure and clear enough to shatter a crystal goblet. Reproduced by permission of Memtek Products, Inc.

a fantastic archaeology, where what is retrieved through fossil, mound, or rune is a monkey-rope from antediluvian creation to postdiluvian pall, from isolated Himalayas to crowded malls. Hence the resilience of a fabulous anthropology where what is restored to us through dank cave or shrunken skull leads us from the shamans of worlds that knew themselves well to the hucksters of a world that cannot seem to find itself at all. So strong is our desire to link up with what we must have been, to redeem ourselves through vanished twins, that hoaxes are always more appealing than history, though as glaring as the Assyrian sphinx unearthed in Wyman, Michigan, in 1891, along with tablets inscribed in "a horrible mixture of Phoenician, Egyptian, and ancient Greek characters." Neither naiveté nor gullibility fuels ongoing debate – popular, scholarly – over the Kensington runes, the Glozel neolithic tablets, the *Book of the*

Hopi by Frank Waters, the tales of Mexican magus Don Juan by Carlos Castaneda, the discovery of the "stone-age" Tasaday by Manuel Elizalde, Jr. Naiveté and gullibility imply a misleading passivity; we actively perpetuate fantasy when it knots the ends of the monkey-rope.[153]

Naiveté is not what kicks us off but what lures us on. It is what we want to find: authenticity. The designs that the naïf reproduces on stone, cloth, bark, or clay must be faithful to an "inherently harmonious, balanced, self-satisfactory" culture "in which nothing is spiritually meaningless, in which no important part of the general functioning brings with it a sense of frustration, of misdirected or unsympathetic effort." So wrote the anthropologist Edward Sapir in 1924, exalting the culture of the Pacific Northwest natives: "The Indian's salmon-spearing is a culturally higher type of activity than that of the telephone girl or mill hand because there is normally no sense of spiritual frustration during its prosecution, no feeling of subservience to tyrannous yet largely inchoate demands." As much could be said, and has been, about the Folk, that protean re-source from whom comes the lore of authenticity and the illusion of innocence.[154]

Folklore, or "fakelore"? Hellenistic artists archaized their work to recall the idols of an earlier, purer Greece. Clambering over Roman monuments, Renaissance antiquarians invented many of the Latin inscriptions they "copied" from the ruins before them, anxious "to revive the glorious things which were alive to the living in antiquity but had become buried and defunct through the lapse of ages and persistent injury at the hands of the half-dead." James Macpherson published *Fragments of Ancient Poetry* in 1760 to restore to an Anglophone civilization the vowels and virtues of a tribal Gaelic world he made up as he went along. While Macpherson's measured prose ("Dark rolls the river through the narrow plain") was proved to be a fabrication rather than a translation, the verses of professional writers became the treasures of folksong – or "fakesong," like nineteenth-century ballad anthologies whose words were cleaned up to suit a Romantic image of the Folk as childlike and pastoral. Having published a collection of olden Scots ballads, James Hogg was told by his mother, "Ye have spoilt them awthegither. They were made for singin' an' no for readin'; but ye have broken the charm noo, an' they'll never [be] sung mair. An' the worst thing of a', they're nouther richt spell'd nor richt setten down."[155]

Were there *any* certifiable originals to scruple over? *any* First Words, "handed down by long-repeated tradition," which, though distorted over the years, could be reconstructed? Postmodern critics have lost faith in the fidelity of Folk traditions of song, saying, and craft. Appeals to the indelibility of "tradition" seem tendentious. No longer do we esteem the fidelity of memory: we do not bring before the bar people who, "by unassisted memory of performances," have supposedly carried away and later repeated verbatim the plays or lectures they have watched and heard from a seat on the aisle. We wonder whether the memories of abuse elicited in therapy or under hypnosis are artifacts of the process. Our neurologists no longer conceive of memories as tracks laid along the ganglia of brain cells or as permanent installations in our cranial cavities; the matter is grayer. Spies cannot boast of "photographic" memory — an impossibility. "That we keep copies of thing in our memory, that we can in some sense riffle through them," say philosophers, is "a simple and convenient enough notion, but a little too puerile." Those recollections to which we give most credence have been recorded apart from us, by video cameras in ceilings, bugs on telephone lines. Our culture of the copy externalizes memory. [156]

Therefore our mounting desperation to touch what the Folk naively touched, to feel what they felt. That desperation drives us in contrary directions: toward a spurning of facsimiles and forgeries because they "tend to be stiff, lifeless, studied, and lacking in the fluidity and spontaneity which characterizes folk art — all art — at its best"; toward a willing suspension of disbelief where the delirious prospect of holding in our hands the genuine article overcomes the likelihood that it is a fake. A fake? What is a fake, in a world where Folk articles seem genuine only when they look used. Imprisoned within Triplex glass, the *Mona Lisa* is safe but "filthy dirty"; were the curators at the Louvre to clean it, would it appear to be a fake? Which is the fake, the ibeji sculpture rubbed smooth by years of devotion to a lost child, or its twin, carved at the same time with the same seriousness but untouched, looking "like new"? The notion of a fake is almost meaningless in African societies, which do not share the Western touristic conceit that old is real. [157]

What of singing the Old songs in the Old way or playing Antique instruments in the Antique manner? Since we are pretty sure we have the notes that earlier composers set down, [158] can we not at least hear as others heard? Paintings, sculptures, woodcarvings obtain a patina that obscures the original as it legitimates it. Mozart's concertos, however, can be heard afresh, simultaneously old, true, and new. "We like to see our pictures of music clean, without layers of nineteenth-century varnish," says Christopher Hogwood, director of the Academy of Ancient Music. [159] Music would seem to solve the riddle of achieving historical authenticity *with* emotional spontaneity.

Exactly, says Will Crutchfield, partisan of the Authentic Music (Original Instrument) movement. Once musicians playing replicas of original instruments learn the performance styles of different eras — timbre, articulation, ornamentation, tempo, dynamics — their historical accuracy affords them a freedom to express themselves through that music, giving rise to "the precise reconstruction of sounds as near as possible to those heard by the composer." [160]

Albert Schweitzer and Wilibald Gurlitt sought to have organs built that could do justice to the organ music of J.S. Bach. Arnold Dolmetsch, born to a French-Swiss organ builder and trained as an instrument maker, attended an ear-opening *concert historique* in 1879 at which he heard the music of Rameau, Handel, Bach, and Scarlatti played on a 1630s organ, a 1679 harpsichord, a 1628 virginal, a 1701 treble viol. Dolmetsch began collecting old viols, lutes, clavichords, and recorders, and materials on how they had been played. He and his family toured Europe at century's turn, playing Elizabethan music on original instruments. Other concert musicians heard his call, notably Wanda Landowska, who brought Bach's music back to the harpsichord.[161]

Dolmetsch's call to historical authenticity arose within the era of the phonograph groove, the perforated player piano roll, sprocketed film, and the punched cards of census taking and industrial tabulation. As a method of performance and as an ideology of listening, Authentic Music complemented these other forms of precise registration and replay. "For the first time... in the history of piano-playing," boasted the Orchestrelle Company of London in 1904 on behalf of the Metrostyle Pianola and its library of piano rolls from Paderewski, Grieg, and Chaminade, "it is possible to fashion one's playing on the actual and authorised interpretations of the virtuosi of to-day." Music instructors debated such an apprenticeship, reading the music and fingering the piano as the roll depressed the keys in the manner of, say, Grieg. But, given that the player piano could be (as composer Conlon Nancarrow has been proving for decades) swifter and surer-fingered than flesh-and-blood, pianists could turn their ambitions from technical virtuosity toward personal drama.[162]

Around 1900, there was drama enough just in hearing a long piece of music repeated. "The zealous concert-goer," wrote a commentator in 1908, "living at a metropolitan center, would hear in a decade perhaps ten performances of Beethoven's Third and Fifth Symphonies, four performances of one of Mozart's last three symphonies, as well as of Schubert's Unfinished and Schumann's First and Second." With the player piano, one could review these and other masterpieces at will. The Aeolian Company of New York showcased its pianola as an encyclopedia: "A waltz by Strauss, a Sousa march, a song, a rag-time hit, a part of Floradora are ever at call, and always fresh, not needing practice. The most gifted pianist the world has ever known has but a small fraction of this repertoire" of eight thousand compositions. The player piano, not the phonograph, aroused expectations of accurate aural replay, for early phonograph cylinders or discs lasted less than four minutes and sounded distant or fuzzy.[163]

Played back on good reproducing pianos, piano rolls presented active ghosts striking or stroking the keys of the piano with the same nuances of their bodily twins. "It is the actual playing of Rachmaninoff, just as if he were personally at the keyboard." puffed the Ampico Company. And with "personality," insisted the designers of the Welte-Mignon (or Vorsetzer). Those who could not afford such wonderful machines heard them in solo concerts in 1918–19 with the Philadelphia Orchestra, the New York Symphony, the San Francisco Symphony; or in movie houses, where piano rolls of mood music and sound effects accompanied reels of silent film; or across the world, from Japan to Joliet, in cafes and corner stores, as coin-operated ancestors of the juke box.[164]

Authentic Music entered our culture of the copy in three-part harmony. Soprano, the reactivating of original intent: how a composer hoped the music would be played. Tenor, the restoring of original experience: how the music was initially played and heard. Bass, the repeating of a performance that would otherwise be lost: how the sound of music may survive the composer and any performer. Like other forms of revivalism, Authentic Music raises questions about the spirits it promises to raise: are they the real thing? where do they come from? Musicians have used their scholarship, their antique (replica) instruments, the halls of castles to put themselves in a direct apostolic line from distant composers and musicians. They have implied that Authentic Music truly recaptures the spirit of a time, a place, an air. In turn they have been accused of soulless performances – "a thinness of sound, a stiffness of rhythm, an avoidance of sentimentality – and a laboriousness of instrumental execution." Never playing a given work twice the same way, wrote the critic Arthur Whiting in 1919, is the pride of a good musician and the delight of his listeners. Piano rolls were the "waxworks of music," though the makers of the Virtuolo "Instinctive" Player Piano claimed that it "lets you throw your very soul into the music."[165]

Glenn Gould, the Canadian pianist, forsook the concert stage in 1964 for the recording studio. As he explained, he was extrapolating a trend. The new concert halls of the 1950s and '60s were more acoustically successful as recording studios than as rooms for collective listening, and the owners of home music "systems" already treated their dens as engineering booths to correct the bass or balance. The majority of the pieces on stereo records themselves consisted of "a collection of tape segments varying in duration upward from one-twentieth of a second," as musicians in studios struggled to perfect a sound, and "it would be impossible for the listener to establish at which point the authority of the performer gave way to that of the producer and the tape editor." Live audiences, wrote Gould, made the classical music played in concert inauthentic for both the listener, whose feelings were moved or muted by those in surrounding seats, and for the musician, whose performance was invariably affected by the "liveness" or "deadness" of the hall (the structure, the coughing people within). Ideally, each listener would, in private, become an electronic collaborator, manipulating dials to achieve a personally enthralling sound from the recorded work of musicians themselves in cahoots with microphones and studio engineers in sealed environs. An owner of piano rolls could adjust the tempo of the music by a switch on the player piano then play along with it, introducing "soul"; an owner of records could adjust volume, balance, treble, and more, speculated Gould, to substantially and individually refine the sound. The replay *should* transcend the original.[166]

Should this seem strange, consider that Authentic Music was lifted out of obscurity by electronics: its repertoire, "with its contrapuntal extravaganzas, its antiphonal balance, its espousal of instruments that chuff and wheeze and speak directly to a microphone – was made for stereo," observed Gould in the 1970s. "It is of course ironic, and a comment on the whole 'authenticity' business," wrote musicologist Nicholas Kenyon in 1988, "that most of the artefacts are in the extremely inauthentic form of recordings without audiences which sound the same every time one plays them." This was the case for the Big Band era as for the baroque, wrote another musicologist: "Nearly every stereo recording purporting to be of a big band is really a multi-microphoned, multi-tracked artificially reverberated collection of individual instrumental lines."[167]

Mechanical players have not replaced human, as the English composer Edward Elgar feared they would, contemplating the player piano in 1907. Instead, musicians have made a pact with their Doppelgängers. In concert, musicians take their chances and make their mistakes, for the gamble of "soul"; in recording studios, miked and Dolbyed and digitized, Doppelgängers do the definitive, replayable work. Which is the more authentic? We are confronted here with serious problems of discernment, for the spirit of live performance is of unrepeatable epiphany, and the spirit of the laser disc, like the spirit of Authentic Music, verges on scientific replication. Performance in front of a "live" audience is about getting right with the moment; performance within a recording studio is about getting the music right once and for all.[168]

Am I confusing very different sorts of authenticity? Isn't the inner authenticity of the Folk a matter quite distinct from the authenticity of an historical reconstruction? Isn't the communal authenticity of a modern performance, whether jazz improvisation on amplified double bass or Early Music on antique instruments, a matter quite distinct from the authenticity of the electronic recording, done straight through in an empty concert hall or pieced together from thousands of perfectly achieved half-seconds? In short, isn't the authenticity of an original a matter wholly distinct from the authenticity of a copy?

No it isn't, not now. The culture of the copy muddies the waters of authenticity. Our recording technologies void most distinctions between the memory of an inimitable voice and its reproducible presence. After all, a cassette tape playback of Ella Fitzgerald's high C can shatter a crystal goblet as well as, and more regularly than, Ella in person. We esteem originals but are electrified by their epigoni. Richard Taruskin, singing the blues in "The Pastness of the Present, and the Presence of the Past," has attacked the exponents of Authentic Music for their charade of rediscovering a past they are, of necessity, inventing, and for that prevarication by which they hide their inventiveness behind historical novenas, making the familiar seem unfamiliar. The truer one is to the music of the past, it seems, the more novel it must sound.[169]

Too true. In our culture of the copy, the medium indemnifies the message and transcends time, as Chester Carlson had hoped to do through spiritualist versions of his medium, xerography. We who can never exactly repeat the past are left to revive and hear ourselves out through devices that descend from music boxes and player pianos. Are we little else but futile reenactments, or is reenactment the little enough that we can be truly about?

VIII. Discernment / Reprise: Unreasonable Facsimiles

> But yet I'll make assurance double sure,
> And take a bond of fate....
>
> — *Macbeth*, IV.i

Striking likenesses have led us down the garden path to unreasonable facsimiles, a world of copies and reenactments difficult to think ourselves through or feel our way around. It would be equally unreasonable to expect that this chapter's reenactment should end at anything more – or less – than an historical mirror, a cultural psyche.

Being done is a comfort only in comedy. I doubt that what we have here is comedy. If it is comedy, it's parodic, and too close for comfort. If it is tragedy, it's romantic, and too close to call. Some may say that the twins, the Doppelgängers, the self-portraits, the Second Nature, the seeing double, the copying, and the reenactments are the best evidence we have of the playfulness of human beings. I would agree, and strongly recommend the virtues of companionship, joyful imposture, irreverent ventriloquism, communion with animals, hide-and-go-seek, the uninhibited spread of art and ideas, the doing of history. This book has never been intended for the pulpit of either/or. It is rather for the congregation of and/also, and it bristles with contradiction.

Among the most pointed of the contradictions is that of the individual, who inheres in these pages as endangered "original growth." There have been times in this book when the individual has stood unimpeached, and other times when the individual has seemed fully compromised. The style of this book is a conscious argument for the value of the individual voice, which should not be a luxury, and for a multitude of voices, which should not be satisfied with echoes. The approach and ambit of this book are conscious arguments for the value of sharing a world with others. That *we* to which I have entrusted much of this book has been the *we* of companionate twins, neither imperial nor (much the same thing) social-scientific. *I* assume responsibility for this book; *we* must assume responsibility for dealing with the dilemmas of celebrity, duplicity, generativity, diversity, virtual reality, fidelity, and authenticity.

Telling true spirit from false has never been simple. Our culture of the copy further discourages discernment, unless it be a kind of doubling back. The more we attempt to tell things apart, the more we end up defending our skills at replication. The more intrepid our assertions of individual presence, the more makeshift seem our identities, the less retrievable our origins. There may come a point of no return.

FIGURE 8.9. *Le Grand métre* (*Great Tape Measure*), by Céjar (Christian Rigal), Paris, 1980. Tape measure roll, .6 × 144 meters, produced on an electrographic machine and unrolled in the main hall of the Louvre in 1982, now in a private collection. Reproduced by permission. Photo by Michel Folco.

FIGURE E.1. 1985 advertisement for high-fidelity stereo speakers. Reproduced by permission of H.H. Scott Company.

Encore

If not for others, how could I be myself?

Once again, I must thank for their hospitality and helpful hints David and Shana Roskies, Anne and Steve Prussing, David and Marjoyre Kunzle, Ivan and Pierrette Keller, Harold and Shelly Boll, Sid and Jackie Blumenthal, and my parents, Harry and Fritzie Schwartz. New to this list are Cristy West, Pat Schmidt, Linda Strauss and Peter John, Jordan Schwartz and György Bacsy, Hy and Tobey Greenspan, and Heidi Piltz Burton and her son Fred.

Once again, I have done the secretarial work myself. The book was composed at an IBM-PC 286 clone and printed out via an HP Deskjet 500. I owe Martin Parks and Berni Claus a great debt for showing me, hard-driven, that my hard drive had not crashed.

Copies of draft chapters were made on a variety of electrographic machines and sent to a cohort of readers: Morris N. Young, Linda Strauss, David Stern, Patricia Schmidt, David Ritchie, Steve Prussing, Robert Mills, Jack Greenstein, Hy and Tobey Greenspan, Laura Greenberg, Janet R. Goff, Stephen D. Cox, John Bermudes, and Trudy Aronson. The final version went to Ramona Naddaff, Jonathan Crary, Meighan Gale, and Ted Byfield, my editors and copyeditors at Zone, in two copies of the typescript and two copies of two floppy disks.

Conversations with my brother Jordan, Michael Schudson, Alice Goldfarb Marquis, Shelly Isenberg, Ann Elwood, Mark Dresser, and Peter Delmonte proved invaluable. I am obliged to Donna Sasso for her shape-shifting and her way through labyrinths, to Nilly Gill for her echoes and mirrors, to Dan Camp for his big pictures and apple pies.

Lydia Ybarra and her staff at UC San Diego, including Nellie Wright, B.J. McClintock, Tammy Deane, and Brad Altman, were efficient and unstintingly friendly trackers of titles. I must also thank Ellen Gartrell, Director, John W. Hartman Center for Sales, Advertising, and Marketing History, Duke University, and the librarians, archivists, and curators at some one hundred institutions who helped me in my pursuit of the twos.

Hillel Schwartz
Encinitas, CA, 1994 and once-over, August 1996

FIGURE N.1. *The Twins*. Etching, 1875, after a painting by Karl Hübner (1814–79).

Notes

The Parallel Universe

Second and subsequent citations within a chapter have been short-titled unless awkwardly distant from the initial reference. Many subtitles have been dropped. The original date of publication is inset in brackets where a later edition or facsimile was used and the argument demands chronological precision. Publishers are listed for books printed within the last forty years, since 1954. Translations are mine unless otherwise indicated. These idiosyncratic abbreviations are used throughout:

AGMG	*Acta Geneticae Medicae et Gemellologiae*
Amer	American
Assoc	Association
Bull	Bulletin
Cal	California
DSB	*Dictionary of Scientific Biography*, ed.-in-chief Charles C. Gillispie (NY: Scribner's, 1970–)
EDSAM	Denis Diderot and Jean Le Rond d'Alembert, eds., *Encylopédie, ou dictionnaire raisonné des sciences, des arts et des métiers* (Stuttgart, Bad Cannstatt: Frommann, 1966 [1751–80])
Ency	Encyclopaedia, Encyclopedia
ER	*Encyclopedia of Religion*, ed.-in-chief Mircea Eliade (NY: Macmillan, 1987)
Eur	European
Inst	Institute, Institutes, Institution
Int	International
J	Journal
L	London
LA	Los Angeles
Lib	Library
Mag	Magazine
Med	Medical; Medicine
NY	New York (City)
OED	J.A. Simpson and E.S.C. Weiner, general eds., *Oxford English Dictionary*, 2nd ed. (Oxford: Clarendon, 1989)
P	Paris
Phil	Philosophy, Philosophical
Proc	Proceedings

q   quotation on [page number]
Q   Quarterly
R   Review
Sci   Science, Scientific
Soc   Society
U   University

Refrain

1. Albert P. Marshall, *The "Real McCoy" of Ypsilanti* (Ypsilanti: Marlan, 1989); Carl W. Mitman, "McCoy, Elijah," *Dictionary of Amer Biography*, ed. Dumas Malone (NY, 1933) VI, 617; Portia P. James, *The Real McCoy; African-American Invention and Innovation, 1619–1930* (Washington, D.C.: Anacosta Museum, 1989) 73.

2. Frederic F. Van de Water, *The Real McCoy* (Garden City, NY, 1931) q vii, q x, q xi, 16. But liquor referred to as "the real McCoy" or "the mac" was usually from Canada: *OED*, IX, 152.

3. *OED*, IX, q152, from a letter in which Stevenson was assuming the identity of one "Thomson" and attributing the identity of one "Johnstone" to his addressee, Charles Baxter, "ye ken – he's the real Mackay, whatever"; Paul R. Beath, "The real McCoy," *Amer Speech* 7 (Feb 1932) 239; Robert Cantwell, *The Real McCoy: The Life and Times of Norman Selby* (Princeton: Auerbach, 1971) 2, 9.

4. Cantwell, *The Real McCoy*, 7–9, 16.

5. *Ibid.*, 9, 12, 16, q24 Runyon. 27, 42, 46–48, 50, q53–54, 55–56, q57, q64; Jack Cuddy, "Rifle inspired Kid McCoy to invent corkscrew punch," *Detroit Free Press* (24 Sept 1939); Sam Greene, "Clinch killed boxing, says 'the Real McCoy,' " *Detroit News* (8 May 1934), attributing the phrase to sportswriter Bill Naughton, differentiating the Kid from another boxer, Pete McCoy.

6. Cantwell, *The Real McCoy*, 61, 69, 75; W.O. Inglis, "Kid M'Coy bigger and stronger than ever and ready for his fight with 'Jim' Corbett," *NY World* (28 Aug 1900) q5, with front-page coverage of the fight (31 Aug 1900).

7. "Corbett runs away: M'Coy fight 'fixed,' " *NY World* (9 Sept 1900) q1; "M'Coy denies charges," *ibid.* (10 Sept 1900) q12.

8. Cantwell, *The Real McCoy*, 73–79; Augustus Thomas, *The Print of My Remembrance* (NY, 1922) 396, 401, 403.

9. Cantwell, *The Real McCoy*, 83, 85, 87, 103, 105, 106, 115. I have also used, as did Cantwell, the clippings on "Selby, Norman" in Locke Collection 2054, Performing Arts Library, NY Public Lib Theatre Collection, Lincoln Center for the Performing Arts, NY. For the quotations, see these clippings: "Kid M'Coy decides not to be detective," *New Jersey Telegraph* (2 Dec 1907); " 'Kid McCoy' gives up attempt to break in to 'high society,' " *ibid.* (25 Feb 1908); G. Bagley, "From the prize ring to the Four Hundred or Kid McCoy butts into South Orange, what?" *The Evening News* (13 June 1907); C.F. Mathison, "Who's who in sport," *The Standard and Vanity Fair* (6 Nov 1908) 8 on the clumsy fight; *NY R* (22[?] June 1912) on posing; *Washington Star* (23 Aug 1912), "exonerated."

10. Clippings from Locke Collection 2054. For quotations, see *Chicago News* (24 June 1913) on "auto bluff"; *Columbus J* (10 June 1917) on marriage; "How to take care of yourself," *Variety* (1 Nov 1912) on his philosophy. On his army work and his age, see Cantwell, *The Real McCoy*, 120–21.

11. "Kid McCoy and Corbett fought their battle twice," *Detroit Free Press* (10 Feb 1933); Daniel G. Streible, Austin, letter to author, 24 Mar 1991 on boxing reenactments; film reviews in *Variety* (1 Mar 1918) – *The House of Glass*, (28 Oct 1921) – *To a Finish*, (4 Aug 1922) – *Oathbound*, and see (22 Nov 1923) – *April Showers*, which had a "crooked fight" scene in which Selby may have participated, unnoted in the credits. D.W. Griffith's *Broken Blossoms* (1919) is now on videocassette (Hollywood Home Theatre, 1981).

12. See Cantwell, *The Real McCoy*, 139–59. I draw other information and all quotations from two series of articles: *NY Times* (13 Nov 1924) 1:6; (9 Dec) 23:6; (12 Dec) 11:1; (13 Dec) q13:3; (17 Dec) q2:7; (20 Dec) q17:7; (27 Dec) 1:7, and *LA Times* (7 Dec 1924) 1; (16 Dec) II, q1; (17 Dec) II,1; (18 Dec) II,1; (19 Dec) II,1; (20 Dec) II, q1, q5; (23 Dec) II,1; (26 Dec) II,6; (27 Dec) II,1; (28 Dec) I,2; (29 Dec) II,1; (30 Dec) II,1. See also "Phonograph played dance on M'Coy raid, man says," *San Diego Union* (13 Dec 1924) 3.

13. Articles in *NY Times* – (18 Dec 1924) q44:4; (23 Dec 1924) 4:3; (30 Dec 1924) 1:6; (21 Feb 1925) 26:2; (17 Mar 1925) 1:5; (11 Apr 1925) 6:1; Cantwell, *The Real McCoy*, 149–50.

14. Cantwell, *The Real McCoy*, 160–63, q163; "Kid M'Coy hailed as hero," *NY Times* (10 July 1934) 3:2; "He's still the Real McCoy, story of heroism reveals," *Detroit News* (13 Feb 1935); "Kid McCoy, with full pardon for murder, may make vaude tour," *Variety* (31 Mar 1937); "Kid McCoy ends his life in hotel room," *Detroit Free Press* (19 Apr 1940); Dale Stafford, "[Night lead McCoy, from AP wire 18 April]," *ibid.* (datestamped 1 May 1940); "Spotlight gone, McCoy finds it in death," *Detroit Times* (19 Apr 1940); "The Kid," *Time* (29 Apr 1940) 42. I thank Ellen Creager of the *Free Press* for providing me with photocopies of (often unpaginated) articles on Selby from the Detroit press.

15. *Variety* (24 Apr 1940) q54; "Chaplin tells how he got his waddle," *NY Times* (20 Feb 1925) q19:7. While Norman Selby was at San Quentin, another Norman Selby (not his son – the Kid had no children by any of his wives) apparently acted with Loretta Young and Douglas Fairbanks, Jr., in the "low comedy" directed by Ted Wilde, *Loose Ankles* (First National, 1930): see *Variety* (26 Feb 1930) review, and the file on *Loose Ankles* in the Margaret Herrick Library, Academy of Motion Picture Arts and Sciences, Beverly Hills.

16. Clipping from Locke Collection, *Columbus J* (10 June 1917), McCoy on his marriages.

17. "The Kid never did like people around him weeping," *Detroit Free Press* (21 Apr 1940); Tom MacMahon, "He licked the world but life finally licked him," *Detroit News* (19 Apr 1940) 41, 43.

18. See esp. William Gaddis, *The Recognitions* (NY: Avon, 1952, 1955) and John Johnston, *Carnival of Repetition: Gaddis's* The Recognitions *and Postmodern Theory* (Philadelphia: U Pennsylvania, 1990); Nigel Dennis, *Cards of Identity* (NY: Vanguard, 1955) a funny novel on fabrications of identity as science and sport; George O. Smith, "Identity," *Astounding Science Fiction* 36 (Nov 1945) 145–78, an equally funny story on duplicating matter, money, and people.

19. Pausanias, *Description of Greece*, trans. W.H.S. Jones (Cambridge, MA: Harvard U, 1979) IV, xxxi.6–9. I recommend here Charles Taylor, *The Ethics of Authenticity* (Cambridge, MA: Harvard U, 1992); John R. Wikse, *About Possession: The Self as Private Property* (U Park: Pennsylvania State U, 1977), from whom I take the *idion* and idiocy. See also Lionel Trilling, *Sincerity and Authenticity* (Cambridge, MA: Harvard U, 1972); Michael

E. Zimmerman, *Eclipse of the Self: The Development of Heidegger's Concept of Authenticity* (Athens: Ohio U, 1981); Theodor W. Adorno, *The Jargon of Authenticity*, trans. K. Tarnowski and F. Will (Evanston: Northwestern U, 1973).

CHAPTER ONE: VANISHING TWINS

1. Arnold Gesell, "Mental and physical correspondence in twins," *Sci Monthly* 14 (1922) 305-31, 415-28, q421; René Zazzo, *Le Paradoxe des jumeaux* (P: Stock, 1984) 19, 24.

2. Zazzo, *Le Paradoxe des jumeaux*, 46ff., transcript of conversation, 16 Oct 1975, in which Tournier confesses to "pillaging" Zazzo's *Les Jumeaux, le couple et la personne* (P: PUF, 1960); Michel Tournier, *Gemini (Les Météores)*, trans. Anne Carter (Garden City, NY: Doubleday, 1981 [1975]) 142, quoted by permission.

3. Salvator Levi, "Ultrasonic assessment of the rate of human multiple pregnancy in the first trimester," *J Clinical Ultrasound* 4 (1976) 3-8, and citing W. Stoeckel's *Lehrbuch der Geburtshilfe* (1945); Katharine D. Wenstrom and Stanley A. Gall, "Incidence, morbidity and mortality, and diagnosis of twin gestations," *Clinics in Perinatology* 15 (Mar 1988) 1-12; Judy W. Hagedorn and Janet W. Kizziar, *Gemini: The Psychology and Phenomena of Twins* (Anderson, SC: Drake House, 1974) 28, citing a U of Louisville study showing that over half of 386 pregnant women did not know until delivery that they were carrying twins; L.K. Csécsei et al., "Pathological consequences of the vanishing twin," *Acta Chirurgica Hungarica* 29 (1988) 173-82; Jens Wessel and Karin Schmidt-Gollwitzer, "Intrauterine death of a single fetus in twin pregnancies," *J Perinatal Med* 16 (1988) 467-76. For the early literature on *foetus papyraceus*, see James E. Kindred, "Twin pregnancies with one twin blighted," *Amer J Obstetrics and Gynecology* 48 (1944) 642-82.

4. Gregg Levoy, "Born rivals," *Psychology Today* (June 1989) 67, and see Helen J. Landy, "The vanishing twin," *AGMG* 31 (1982) 179-94, esp. 180, 187; Jo Jackson and Kurt Benirschke, "The recognition and significance of the vanishing twin," *J Amer Board Family Practice* 2 (Jan-Mar 1989) 58; Kay Cassill, *Twins: Nature's Amazing Mystery* (NY: Atheneum, 1982) 60-64.

5. Eugène Apert, *Les Jumeaux: étude biologique, physiologique et médicale* (P, 1923) 91 on the *vopiscus*; Margaret Atwood, "Kat," *The New Yorker* (5 Mar 1990) 44, quoted with permission. The same magazine has recently published an article on the study of twins which seems to confirm and extend the legend of the vanishing twin: Lawrence Wright, "Double mystery," *The New Yorker* (7 Aug 1995) 45-62, referring (p. 57) to Luigi Gedda's hypothesis that "all left-handed singletons may be survivors of a vanished twin-pair."

6. The incidence of twins in the U.S. is 1-2 percent of live births but yields 11 percent of neonatal deaths, since twins are more likely to present prematurely or with lower birthweights: Kathryn A. Hollenbach and Durton E. Hickok, "Epidemiology and diagnosis of twin gestation," *Clinical Obstetrics and Gynecology* 33 (Mar 1990) 3-9; *Clinics in Perinatology* 15 (Mar 1988) entire issue, esp. Wenstrom and Gall, "Incidence," noting that use of clomiphene during in vitro fertilization may triple the frequency of twin conceptions, while gonadotropins may sextuple it (3). On higher twinning rates with artificially induced ovulation, see R. Derom et al., "Twin pregnancies after medically assisted reproduction," *J Perinatal Med* 19 (1991) 229-33, preprint kindly supplied by authors, Centre for Human Genetics, Catholic U of Leuven. On problems linked with

our skill at detecting the "anomalous" fetus, see J.P. Minogue et al., "Rationale for a standard of care in compromised twin pregnancies," *AGMG* 38 (1989) 184; I.B.M. Van den Veyver et al., "Antenatal fetal death in twin pregnancies: a dangerous condition for the surviving co-twin," *Eur J Obstetrics, Gynecology, and Reproductive Biology* 38 (4 Jan 1991) 69-73; Usha Chitkara, "Selective second-trimester termination of the anomalous fetus in twin pregnancies," *Obstetrics and Gynecology* 73 (1989) 690-94. In 1991, physicians at the Illinois Masonic Medical Center surgically extracted an abnormal fetus three months before a woman gave birth to its healthy twin: "After flawed twin is removed, woman has full-term baby," *NY Times* (21 Apr 1991) 26:1.

7. Between 1774 and 1816, Sweden, with an average age of thirty-one at first maternity, had the highest twinning rate ever calculated for a nation entire – one in every six births: A.W. Eriksson et al., "Secular changes in the rates of multiple maternities in Sweden, 1750-1987," *AGMG* 39 (1989) 111-12, and cf. T. Miura et al., "Twinning in New England in the 17th-19th centuries," *AGMG* 36 (1987) 355-64. On Japan, see Luigi Gedda, *Twins in History and Science*, trans. M. Milani-Comparetti (Springfield, IL: Thomas, 1961) I, 60. Artificial insemination, fertility hormones, and in vitro fertilization improve the chances of monozygotic as well as dizygotic twinning. Most twinning data, based on parturition, ignores spontaneously aborted pairs, stillborns, *foetus papyraceus*, and infanticide. Twinning rates dated from early embryonic stages are likely to be higher – how much higher is answered by the legend of the vanishing twin.

8. Mitchell Creinin and Louis G. Keith, "The Yoruba contribution to our understanding of the twinning process," *J Reproductive Med* 34 (June 1989) 379-87, skeptical of suggested causal links between the Nigerian twinning rate and native species of estrogen-rich yams; Luigi Gedda, "Address to H.H. Pope John Paul II," *AGMG* 39 (1990) 9. See Leon Sirota, "Twins of Yorubaland," *Bull Field Museum Natural History* 38 (July 1967) 4-5, on neighboring traditions. For African customs, see E. Sidney Hartland, "Twins," *Ency of Religion and Ethics*, eds. James Hastings et al. (NY: Scribner's, 1961 [1908-26]) XII, 491-94; Henry A. Carey, "Beliefs and Customs about Twins in Primitive Africa," Ph.D., U Cal, Berkeley, 1925; I. Schapera, "Customs relating to twins in South Africa," *J Royal African Soc* 26 (Jan 1927) 117-37; Aidan Southall, "Twinship and symbolic structure," in *The Interpretation of Ritual*, ed. J.S. La Fontaine (L: Tavistock, 1972) 73-114; Gary Granzberg, "Twin infanticide," *Ethos* 1,4 (1973) 405-12.

9. T.J.H. Chappel, "Yoruba cult of twins in historical perspective," *Africa* 44,3 (1974) 250-65; William B. Fagg et al., *Yoruba: Sculpture of West Africa* (NY: Knopf, 1982) 15-16, q80; Robert P. Armstrong, *The Powers of Presence* (Philadelphia: U Pennsylvania, 1981) 44-45, 73; Robert F. Thompson, *Black Gods and Kings* (Bloomington: Indiana U, 1975) ch. 13. Cf. the agencies used by the Moundag of Chad, surrounded by groups practicing twin infanticide, to transmute the malefic fact of twins into a glorious event: Alfred Adler, "Les Jumeaux sont rois," *L'Homme* 13 (1973) 167-92. On shifts in attitude toward twin infants, see also Jane Belo, "A study of customs pertaining to twins in Bali" [1935] in her *Traditional Balinese Culture* (NY: Columbia U, 1970) 3-56, esp. 30.

10. Marilyn H. Houlberg, "Ibeji images of the Yoruba," *African Arts* 7 (Autumn 1973) 20-23; T.O. Oruene, "The cult of the *ibeji* as reflected in the *oriki ibeji*," *Anthropos* 80,1-3 (1985) 230-37; Val Olayemi, *Orin Ibeji (Songs in Praise of Twins)* (Ibadan: Inst of African Studies, U Ibadan, 1971); Sirota, "Twins of Yorubaland," 6; Fagg, *Yoruba: Sculp-*

ture of West Africa, 16, 80. Cf. the similar twin cult in Mali, where the twinning rate is also high: Pascal J. Imperato, "Bamana and Maninka twin figures," *African Arts* 8 (Sum 1975) 52-60, 83.

11. Fagg, *Yoruba: Sculpture of West Africa*, 35; Houlberg, "Ibeji images," 22, 26; Stephen F. Sprague, "Yoruba photography: how the Yoruba see themselves," *African Arts* 12 (Nov 1978) 52-59, 107.

12. Elizabeth M. Bryan, *The Nature and Nurture of Twins* (L: Baillière Tindall, 1983) ch. 13, advising that stillborn twins be named, photographed, and given a funeral; Joan Woodward, "The bereaved twin," *AGMG* 37 (1988) 173-80; idem, "Only a half: the unique world of the lone twin," *Social Work Today* 21 (5 Oct 1989) 18-19; Jenny Claxton, "Twins: separating the inseparable," *Nursing Times* 85 (5-11 Apr 1989) q34-35. On the consequences of a twin's failure to mourn, see Jacob A. Arlow, "The psychology of twins," *J Amer Psychoanalytic Assoc* 9 (1961) 158-66.

13. For photographs, see esp. Stanley B. Burns, *Sleeping Beauty: Memorial Photography in America* (Altadena: Twelve Trees, 1990) #46; Kathryn McLaughlin Abbe and Frances McLaughlin Gill, *Twins On Twins* (NY: Clarkson N. Potter, 1980). For twin registries, see note 46 below. On the city of twins (not the Twin Cities, St. Paul and Minneapolis, themselves home to national twin research programs), see Sue Marcoux, "Twinsburg, Ohio: Some Kind of Weird Twin Thing," film shown on "Point of View," KCET-TV, LA, 26 June 1991; Abe Frajndlich, "Seeing double," *Life* (Aug 1988) 70-71, the 13th annual Twinsburg Twins Days Festival. For Helen Stoner, see Arthur Conan Doyle, *Complete Sherlock Holmes* (Garden City, NY: 1930) I, 261. Bryan, *Nature and Nurture of Twins*, q63, translates the passage from Achille Geremicca's *I Fantasmi della mia vita*. The epitome of identical twins leading similar lives far apart is the case of Jim Springer and Jim Lewis, on whom see Edwin Chen, "Twins reared apart: a living lab," *NY Times Mag* (9 Dec 1979) q114; for other cases, see Brad Lindeman, *The Twins Who Found Each Other* (NY: Morrow, 1969); Peter Watson, *Twins: An Investigation into the Strange Coincidences in the Lives of Separated Twins* (L: Hutchinson, 1981); Wright, "Double mystery."

14. E.E. Evans-Pritchard, *Nuer Religion* (Oxford: Clarendon, 1956) 128-33; Victor Turner, *The Ritual Process* (Chicago: Aldine, 1969) 44-93.

15. On the fake genealogy business, see Scott E. Meyer, "Mail order family heritage books," *Search: Int J for Researchers of Jewish Genealogy* 10,4 (1990) 12-15; Sutro Library, San Francisco, Fake Genealogies file; "Don't let them take your name in vain," *Changing Times* (Oct 1981) 68, on Beatrice Bayley, Inc.; *Genealogical J* 19, 1-2 (1991) entire issue. On coats of arms, see Diane Dakers, "Heraldry helps families seeking roots," *Victoria Weeklies* insert to *Oak Bay Star (Vancouver Island)* (11 Mar 1992) B10-11. Final quotation in Harvey Stein, text by Ted Wolner, *Parallels: A Look at Twins* (NY: Dutton, 1978) 6.

16. Mary Tew Douglas, *The Lele of the Kasai* (L: Oxford U, 1963) 212, and cf. L. Delaby, "Shamans and mothers of twins," in *Shamanism in Eurasia, Part 2*, ed. Mihály Hoppál (Göttingen: Herodot, 1984) 214-30; C. Pereire and P. Nzete, *Bana Mapasa les Jumeaux* (Yaounde, Cameroun: Cerdotola, 1981) children's book, twins become great healers; Jeanne B. Kozlak, "Identical twins: perception of the effects of twinship," *Humboldt J Social Relations* 5,2 (1978) 105-30, on twins' own beliefs in their ESP; M. Lusson and D. Lusson (the Lusson Twins), *The Beginning or the End* (Virginia Beach, 1975) for twins as psychic prophets; Jo-Ann Scott, "Double trouble twins," *Weekly World News* (2 Jan 1990) 32, and Michele Burgin, "Is it true what they say about twins?" *Ebony* (Dec

1978) 134–35 on psychic bonding; Peter Bakker, "Autonomous languages of twins," *AGMG* 36 (1987) 233–38; Daniel Marks, "Trumpet-tongued against the deep damnation: Jean-Pierre Gorin and his films," *Int Documentary* (Wint 1990) 21–24, on Gorin's *Poto and Cabengo* (1979) about the private language of the Kennedy twins, with whom cf. Marjorie Wallace, *The Silent Twins* (NY: Prentice-Hall, 1986).

17. Bruce Lincoln, "The land of the dead," *History of Religions* 20 (1981) 224–41, q239; René Girard, in *Violence and the Sacred*, trans. Patrick Gregory (Baltimore: Johns Hopkins U, 1977) 56ff, insists that twins are mythopolitically the omens of a sacrificial crisis; one or both must be "exposed" or put to death so as to avoid ensnaring the community in a circle of indiscriminate violence brought on by the fatal collapse of ritual represented by a disruptive physical resemblance.

18. J. Rendel Harris, *Boanerges* (Cambridge, 1913); Donald Ward, "The Indo-European Divine Twins in Germanic Tradition," Ph.D. thesis, U.C. Los Angeles, 1965; idem, *The Divine Twins: An Indo-European Myth in Germanic Tradition* (Berkeley: U Cal, 1968); idem, "The separate functions of the Indo-European divine twins," in *Myth and Law Among the Indo-Europeans*, ed. Jaan Puhvel (Berkeley: U Cal, 1970) 193–202; Maurice Albert, *La Culte de Castor et Pollux en Italie* (P, 1883); Karl Shapiro, "The Twins (March 21, 1942. At Sea)," copyright © 1940, 1987 Karl Shapiro, these and subsequent lines quoted by arrangement with Wieser & Wieser, Inc. 118 East 50th St., New York, NY 10010, all rights reserved. On twin culture heroes in general, see Stith Thompson, *Motif-Index of Folk-Literature* (Bloomington: Indiana U, 1958) A515.1, A910.5, A1273.

19. Jesse B. Carter, "The death of Romulus," *Amer J Archaeology* 13 (1909) 19–29; Pierre Grimal, *Dictionary of Classical Mythology*, trans. A.R. Maxwell-Hyslop (Oxford: Blackwell, 1985) 406–08; R. Schilling, "Romulus l'élu et Rémus le réprouvé," *Revue des études latines* 38 (1960) 182–99; Michael Grant, *Myths of the Greeks and Romans* (Cleveland: World, 1965) 349–57; Dominique Briquel, "Jumeaux à la louve et jumeau à la chèvre, à la jument, à la chienne, à la vache," *Recherches sur les religions de l'Italie antique*, eds. Raymond Bloch et al. (Geneva: Droz, 1976) 73–97; H.H. Scullard, *Festivals and Ceremonies of the Roman Republic* (Ithaca: Cornell, 1981) 65–66, 164; P.M.W. Tennant, "The Lupercalia and the Romulus and Remus legend," *Acta classica (Cape Town)* 31 (1988) 81–93.

20. Raymond Kuntzmann, *Le Symbolisme des jumeaux au Proche-Orient ancien* (P: Beauchesne, 1983) 164–82 on Thomas.

21. For the Zoroastrian polarities, see Ugo Bianchi, "Twins," *ER*, XV, 99–100, 104; Ward, "Separate functions." On the ways by which the polarities dissolve, see Olga M. Davidson, "Dioscurism in Iranian kingship," *Edebiyât*, ser.2, 1 (1987) 103–15.

22. Genesis 38.15–30 delivers up another pair of twins, sons of Judah by daughter-in-law Tamar, and again an important birthright is confuted: Zerah (Zarah) puts out his hand but then draws it back, so first to arrive is Perez, from whose line will come (1 Chr 2.5–15) the House of David. Commentators describe the two *struggling* for primogeniture, but the episode can also be read as expressing Zerah's reluctance to leave the perfect twinship of the womb.

23. Gerson Cohen, "Esau as a symbol in early medieval thought," in his *Studies in the Variety of Rabbinic Cultures* (Philadelphia: Jewish Publication Soc, 1991) 243–69, describing earlier Jewish depictions of Rome as Edom, then Latin Christian identification of Jews with Esau and Jewish attempts to reverse the typology. I thank David Stern for this reference.

24. For Plautus, see Lionel Casson's lively translation: Titus Maccius Plautus, *The Menaechmus Twins* (NY: Norton, 1971 [1963]). For later versions, see esp. Karen A. Newman, "Mistaken Identity and the Structure of Comedy: A Comparative Study of Classical Italian Renaissance and Shakespearean Comedy," Ph.D., U Cal, Berkeley, 1978. Shakespeare himself was father of the twins Judith and Hamnet.

25. George Farquhar, "The Twin Rivals" [1702] in *Complete Works*, ed. Charles Stonehill (NY: Gordian, 1967) 295; A Lady, *The Twin Sisters; or, the Effects of Education* (Dublin, 1792) 79. Gedda, *Twins in History and Science*, 9, finds the first pair of disparate fictive twins in Goldoni's *I Due gemelle veneziani* (1747) and in Goldoni's source, Reynard's *Les Ménechmes, ou les jumeaux* (1705); these are slightly late, but his intuitions are right. Cf. also Jean Perrot, *Mythe et littérature: sous le signe des jumeaux* (P: PUF, 1976). Marc Soriano, *Les Contes de Perrault, culture savante et traditions populaires* (P: Gallimard, 1968) 383ff speculates that the contests between and quests for (long-lost) twins or siblings in the tales of Charles Perrault stem from his life as a twin whose brother had come into the world some hours before him and died in infancy – another influential vanishing twin.

26. Lucy Ellen Guernsey, *The Twin Roses, and How They Were Trained* (NY: Amer Sunday School Union, 1868) 104, 159, 166, 324; Madeline Leslie (= Mrs. H.N. Baker), *The Twin Brothers* (NY, 1843) 3. For lists of German works, see Heinrich Poll, *Zwillinge in Dichtung und Wirklichkeit* (Berlin, 1930) and Helmut L. Karcher, *Wie ein Ei dem Andern: Alles über Zwillinge* (Munich: Piper, 1975); in other languages, Gedda, *Twins in History and Science*, 8-15. Cf. John Gay, with John Kellemu, *Red Dust on the Green Leaves: a Kpelle Twins' Childhood* (Thompson, CT: InterCulture, 1973).

27. One-who-knows-her-well, "Lucy Fitch Perkins: drawing teacher, illustrator, home maker," *School Arts Mag* 14 (1914) 257-67; Lucy Fitch Perkins, *The Cave Twins* (NY, 1916) q8.

28. The Dionne quintuplets, all of whom came from one fertilized egg, had among them a vanished twin, a sextuplet spontaneously aborted in the third month of pregnancy. Among the most provocative science fictions about clones are Elisabeth Mann Borgese, "Twin's Wail" (1959) in *Star Fourteen*, ed. Frederik Pohl (L: Pan, 1966 [1960]) 67-90; Kate Wilhelm, *Where Late the Sweet Birds Sang* (NY: Pocket Books, 1976); John Willett, *Aubade for Gamelon* (NY: Baen, 1984).

29. L.A.J. Quetelet, *A Treatise on Man and the Development of His Faculties*, trans. R. Knox (NY: Burt Franklin, 1968 [1842]) 26, 110; Ludwig Kleinwächter, *Die Lehre von den Zwillingen* (Prague, 1871) 5, 17; Augusto Arcimis et al., "Gemelo," *Diccionario Enciclopedico Hispano-Americano* (Barcelona, 1887) IX, 267-68; Apert, *Jumeaux*, 51, 58; Karl Pearson, *The Life, Letters and Labours of Francis Galton* (Cambridge: Cambridge U, 1914-30) II, 128, infertility of twins. The prime source on maternal age and twinning was J. Matthews Duncan, *Fecundity, Fertility, Sterility and Allied Topics* (Edinburgh, 1866). For declining fertility rates in Western Europe, see David Levine, *Reproducing Families: The Political Economy of English Population History* (Cambridge: Cambridge U, 1987) ch. 4, and a Princeton U Press series, esp. John E. Knodel, *The Decline of Fertility in Germany, 1871-1939* (1974) and Ron J. Lestaeghe, *The Decline of Belgian Fertility, 1800-1970* (1977) 4, summary chart.

30. D.W. Forrest, *Francis Galton: The Life and Work of a Victorian Genius* (NY: Taplinger, 1974) ch. 7, q89 from Francis Galton, *Hereditary Genius*, 2nd ed. (L: Collins, 1962 [1892, 1st ed. 1869]) 56.

31. Forrest, *Francis Galton*, 122-29, q129 from Francis Galton, *English Men of Science*, 2nd ed. (L: Cass, 1970 [1874]) 39.

32. Forrest, *Francis Galton,* 129-32; Francis Galton, "The history of twins, as a criterion of the relative powers of nature and nurture," *Littell's Living Age* 127 (1875) 695-702, q696 – from *Fraser's Mag* 12 (1875) 566-76, revised in *J Anthropological Inst* 5 (1875) 391-406.

33. Augustine of Hippo, *Concerning the City of God Against the Pagans*, trans. Henry Betterson (Harmondsworth: Penguin, 1972) bk. V, ch. 2, 181-85; Peter Brown, *Augustine of Hippo: a Biography* (Berkeley: U Cal, 1967) 148, 177-79, 235, q178 from the *Confessions*, X, xxviii, 39; Derek Parker and Julie Parker, *A History of Astrology* (L: Deutsch, 1983) 79. In rebuttal to the argument that many twins are born hours apart, under shifted skies, Augustine noted that twins must have been conceived simultaneously, under precisely identical skies. So, "if conception has the power to ensure coincidence of destiny [as astrologers claim], then [small differences in time of] birth should not be able to alter it." Modern astrologers perceive significant astral differences every four clock minutes, which is usually enough to distinguish one twin from the next; they define those born under the sun sign Gemini by their two-mindedness – unpredictability, versatility, eagerness for variety.

34. D.J., "Jumeaux, frères, (Physiol.)" *EDSAM*, IX, 57; Apert, *Jumeaux*, 69n, ancient French law designating the later-born twin as the elder since it had been more deeply situated in the womb; Forrest, *Francis Galton*, 101-08; Pearson, *Life of Galton*, II, 128 on Späth, whose paper was published as "Studien über Zwillingen," *Zeitschrift der Wiener Gesellschaft der Ärzte* 15-16 (1860); Gedda, *Twins in History and Science*, 21-24; Francis Galton, *Memories of My Life*, 3rd ed. (L, 1909) 300, on his own experiments with sweet peas; Gedda, "Address," 4. Cf. Gunning S. Bedford, *The Principles and Practice of Obstetrics* (NY, 1861) 431-45 on the general befuddlement about multiple pregnancy in the 1860s.

35. Forrest, *Francis Galton*, 111-13, 132; Galton, "History of twins," 701; Sarah Grand (= Frances E. C. McFall), *The Heavenly Twins* (NY, 1893) 10.

36. Edward L. Thorndike, "Measurement of twins," *Archives of Philosophy, Psychology, and Scientific Methods* 1 (Sept 1905) 1-64, q1, q10; idem, in *A History of Psychology in Autobiography*, ed. Carl Murchison (Worcester, MA, 1930-36) III, 263-70.

37. Stephen Jay Gould, *The Mismeasure of Man* (NY: Norton, 1981) ch. 5.

38. Robert B. Joynson, *The Burt Affair* (L: Routledge & Kegan Paul, 1989) defends Burt against the stiffer charges leveled by L.S. Hearnshaw, *Cyril Burt Psychologist* (Ithaca: Cornell, 1979) esp. 39-40, 229-53. See also Gould, *Mismeasure of Man*, ch. 6, q273 from Cyril Burt, "The inheritance of general intelligence," *Amer Psychologist* 27 (1972) 188, in which, p. 175, Burt details his work with a Galtonian anthropometric survey around 1900. Burt's first published reference to his own twin data, analyzed years after it was collected, appeared in his *The Backward Child* (NY, 1937) 297.

39. *J Heredity* 10 (Dec 1929) 385-432, q387 from David Fairchild, "Twins and their importance as furnishing evidence of the limitations of environment"; Gesell, "Mental and physical correspondence," 309, 421; Zazzo, *Le Paradoxe des jumeaux*, 19; Arnold Gesell and Helen Thompson, "Learning and growth in identical infant twins: an experimental study by the method of co-twin control," *Genetic Psychology Monographs* 6,1 (1929) 1-124. Cf. Jackson A. Smith et al., "Twins who want to be identified as twins," *Diseases of the Nervous System* 29 (1968) 615-18.

40. Pierre Carlet de Chamblain de Marivaux's play, *The Dispute*, appears in *Gallant and Libertine: Eighteenth-Century French Divertissements and Parades*, trans. and ed. Daniel Gerould (NY: Performing Arts J, 1983) 36ff. On wild children, see Harlan Lane, *The Wild Boy of Aveyron* (Cambridge: Harvard U, 1976), amended by Roger Shattuck, *The Forbidden Experiment: The Story of the Wild Boy of Aveyron* (NY: Washington Square, 1980) and by Thierry Gineste and J. Postel, "J.M.G. Itard et l'enfant connu sous le nom de 'Sauvage de l'Aveyron,'" *Psychiatrie de l'enfant* 23 (1980) 251-307. Arnold Gesell himself wrote on the subject: *Wolf Child and Human Child* (NY, 1941), and wild children remain sensational news: Beatrice Dexter, "Two-year-old girl raised by panther," *Weekly World News* (7 Nov 1989) 31. On "controls" in the nineteenth century, see Gerd Gigerenzer et al., *The Empire of Chance* (NY: Cambridge U, 1989) 85-86. "Control" was also the term given to spirit guides or mediums.

41. On the creation of "normal people" and the Average Man, see Ian Hacking, *The Taming of Chance* (NY: Cambridge U, 1990) 1-10, 105-14, 160-69. On the correlation coefficient, see Galton, *Memories of My Life*, 300, 305; Forrest, *Francis Galton*, ch. 14, q197 from Francis Galton, "Co-relations and their measurement, chiefly from anthropometric data," *Proc Royal Soc* 45 (1888) 135; Pearson, *Life of Galton*, IIIA, 50-58. On correlation and factor analysis, see Gould, *Mismeasure of Man*, 239-55, q242; A.D. Lovie and P. Lovie, "Charles Spearman, Cyril Burt, and the origins of factor analysis," *J History Behavioral Science* 29 (1993) 308-21. Spearman too confused the correlative with the causal; see his account in Murchison, ed., *History of Psychology in Autobiography*, I, 299-334.

42. On randomizing, see Stuart H. Hurlbert, "Pseudoreplication and the design of ecological field experiments," *Ecological Monographs* 54 (1984) 187-211, esp. 196-98.

43. Hermann W. Siemens, *Einführung in die allgemeine und spezielle Vererbungspathologie des Menschen*, 2nd ed. (Berlin, 1923) 31, 96, 165-66; Richard D. Rende et al., "Who discovered the Twin Method?" *Behavior Genetics* 20 (Mar 1990) 277-85; Luigi Gedda, *Studio dei gemelli* (Rome, 1951) 70-77; Curtis Merriman, "The intellectual resemblance of twins," *Psychological Monographs* 33 (1924) 21-27, described the method but did not undertake it.

44. Raoul Baudet, "Les Jumeaux," *Annales politiques et littéraires* 86 (6 June 1926) 625; Horatio H. Newman, Frank N. Freeman, and Karl J. Holzinger (statistician), *Twins: A Study of Heredity and Environment* (Chicago: U Chicago, 1937) 133-34, 147. For an earlier study of separated twins with similar timings of illnesses and trains of thought, "almost uncanny," see Paul Popenoe, "Twins reared apart," *J Heredity* 13 (1922) 142-44.

45. Gesell and Thompson, "Learning and growth in identical infant twins," throughout, q5, q8; Josephine R. Hilgard, "The effect of early and delayed practice on memory and motor performances studied by the method of co-twin control," *Genetic Psychology Monographs* 14,6 (1933) 506, summarizing the studies, and see Louise B. Ames, *Arnold Gesell: Themes of His Work* (NY: Human Sciences, 1989) ch. 7.

46. Albert F. Blakeslee and Howard J. Banker, "Identical twins as biological controls in educational and other human problems," *Amer Phil Soc Proc* 69,6 (1930) 379-84; Peter J. Mittler, *The Study of Twins* (Harmondsworth: Penguin, 1971) 72; Mitchell G. Ash, "Psychological twin research under Nazism," paper given at meeting of the Amer Historical Assoc, NY, 28 Dec 1990, to be published within a larger study, "Psychological research under Nazism: modernity, continuity and change," q from Kurt Gottschaldt, "Erbpsychologie der Elementarfunktionen der Begabung," *Handbuch der Erbbiologie des*

Menschen, ed. G. Just, V,1 (Berlin, 1939) 459; Gerald L. Posner and John Ware, *Mengele* (NY: McGraw-Hill, 1986) 3, 11, 29, 35–40; Newman et al., *Twins,* 22, Soviets; Franz J. Kallmann, "Psychogenetic studies of twins," in *Psychology,* ed. Sigmund Koch (NY: McGraw-Hill, 1959) III, 328–62, q340, q348, and cf. Morton M. Hunt, "Doctor Kallmann's 7000 twins," *Saturday Evening Post* (6 Nov 1954) 20–21, 80–82; Gedda, "Address," 4, and Abbe and Gill, *Twins on Twins,* 156 for the 15,000 and other large registries; Zazzo, *Le Paradoxe des jumeaux,* 27–32, 46; James Shields, *Monozygotic Twins Brought Up Apart and Brought Up Together* (L: Oxford U, 1962) 91, 100, 150; Richard J. Rose et al. and Helsinki Department of Public Health, "Shared genes, shared experiences, and similarity of personality: data from 14,288 adult Finnish co-twins," *J Personality Social Psychology* 54 (Jan 1988) 161–71. Two other large-scale projects were reported in 1990: Jack Goldberg et al., "A twin study of the effects of the Vietnam War on post-traumatic stress disorder," *J Amer Med Assoc* 263 (2 March 1990) 1227–32, using 2092 monozygotic twin brothers from the Vietnam Era Twin Registry of 7375 pairs; L.J. Eaves et al., "Religious affiliation in twins and their parents," *Behavior Genetics* 20 (Jan 1990) 1–22, using 3810 twins from the Australian National Twin Registry. Swedish studies present the largest number of cases of twins reared apart; see, for example, N.L. Pedersen et al., "The Swedish adoption twin study of aging: an update," *AGMG* 40 (1991) 7–20.

47. Two exceptions: Helen L. Koch, *Twins and Twin Relations* (Chicago: U Chicago, 1966); Barbara Schave and Janet Ciriello, *Identity and Intimacy in Twins* (NY: Praeger, 1983) – Schave and Ciriello are members of different sets of identical twins.

48. For examples, see – on intelligence: Curtis Merriman, "Intellectual resemblance of twins"; Alex H. Wingfield, "Intelligence of twins and of the inmates of orphanages," *Eugenics R* 22 (Oct 1930) 183–86; Erness B. Brody and Nathan Brody, *Intelligence: Nature, Determinants and Consequences* (NY: Academic, 1976); R. Travis Osborne, *Twins: Black and White* (Athens, GA: Foundation for Human Understanding, 1980). Criminality: Johannes Lange, *Crime as Destiny: A Study of Criminal Twins,* trans. Charlotte Haldane (L, 1931). On sociability: Gordon Claridge et al., *Personality Differences and Biological Variations* (Oxford: Pergamon, 1973) table 2.1, and 128 on sedation. Temperaments: Nathan M. Szajnberg et al., "Affect attunement, attachment, temperament, and zygosity: a twin study," *J Amer Academy Child and Adolescent Psychiatry* 28 (1989) 249–53. Obesity: Albert J. Stunkard et al., "A twin study of human obesity," *J Amer Med Assoc* 256 (4 July 1986) 51–54 with follow-up, "The body-mass index of twins who have been reared apart," *New England J Med* 322 (24 May 1990) 1483–87, and companion piece in same issue, Claude Bouchard et al., "The response to long-term overfeeding in identical twins," 1477–1482. Homosexuality: Elke D. Eckert et al., "Homosexuality in mono-zygotic twins reared apart," *British J Psychiatry* 148 (Apr 1986) 421–25. Depression: Michael Wierzbicki, "Twins' responses to pleasant, unpleasant, and life events," *J Genetic Psychology* 150 (June 1989) 135–45. Suicide: David Lester, "Genetics, twin studies, and suicide," *Suicide & Life-Threatening Behavior* 16 (Sum 1986) 274–85. Emotionality: Auke Tellegen et al. (U Minnesota Twin Study Project), "Personality similarity in twins reared apart and together," *J Personality Social Psychology* 54 (June 1988) 1031–39. Cynicism and much else: Melvin Konner, "Under the Influence," *Omni* (Jan 1990) 62–64, 90. Compulsiveness, submissiveness, pessimism, sexual inhibition, narcissism, passivity, self-expressiveness, and more: Mia Stainsby, "UBC study may reveal extent to which genes determine personality," *Vancouver Sun* (24 Jan 1992) C1, regarding the

work of Kerry Jang, U British Columbia. For a convenient summary, see Susan L. Farber, *Identical Twins Reared Apart: A Reanalysis* (NY: Basic, 1981); Wright, "Double mystery," 45-62.

49. A few of the many: Newman et al., *Twins*, 14; Franz J. Kallmann, *Heredity in Health and Mental Disorder* (NY: Norton, 1953), summarized by Hunt, "Doctor Kallmann's 7000 twins," 81; Carl Ratner, "Do the statistics on identical twins prove that schizophrenia is genetically inherited?" *Int J Social Psychiatry* 28 (Aut 1982) 175-78; Joyce A. Kovelman and Arnold B. Scheibel, "Biological substrates of schizophrenia," *Acta Neurologica Scandinavica* 73 (Jan 1986) 1-32; Richard H. Dworkin et al., "A multidimensional approach to the genetics of schizophrenia," *Amer J Psychiatry* 145 (Sept 1988) 1077-83; Sarnoff A. Mednick and J. Meggin Hollister, eds., *Neural Development and Schizophrenia: Theory and Research* (NY: Plenum, 1995).

50. Mark Bloom, "New theory on the phenomenon of identical twins," *Washington Post* (11 Aug 1992) WH7:1, q from Victor McKusick; Nathaniel D.M. Hirsch, *Twins: Heredity and Environment* (Cambridge, MA, 1930) 7, 20, 23-24. Cf. Hagedorn and Kizziar, *Gemini*, 14. This uncertainty, of course, does not apply to eggs implanted after in vitro fertilization, as for example with the "test-tube" twins recently born to a fifty-nine-year-old woman: "Briton, 59, is oldest on record to give birth to test-tube twins," *LA Times* (27 Dec 1993) A2.

51. Newman et al., *Twins*, 15-16, 35; Cassill, *Twins*, 204-06; N.G. Martin et al., "The power of the classical twin study," *Heredity* 40 (1978) 97-116; Nancy L. Segal, "MZ or DZ? Not even their hairdresser knows for sure," *J Forensic Sciences* 31 (Jan 1986) 10-11; Paul Billings, M.D., Center for Inherited Diseases, Pacific Presbyterian Hospital, San Francisco, interview, 16 April 1991; C. Boklage, "The embryology of human twinning: 'It is well known that...,'" *AGMG* 28 (1989) 118; David T. Lykken et al., "Recruitment bias in twin research," *Behavior Genetics* 17 (July 1987) 343-62; Sandra Scarr, "Environmental bias in twin studies," *Social Biology* 29 (Fall–Wint 1982 [1968]) 221-29, but explaining (228) that despite inaccurate beliefs, parents' behaviors do imply an accurate distinction between monozygotic and dizygotic: the "degree of genetic relatedness is a more important determinant of parental treatment than parents' beliefs that their twins should or should not be similar."

52. Hirsch, *Twins: Heredity and Environment*, 27; C.E. Boklage, "Race, zygosity, and mortality among twins: interaction of myth and method," *AGMG* 36 (1987) 275-88, arguing that same-sex dizygotic prenatal mortality is probably higher than monozygotic prenatal mortality in all populations, and that among black populations, prenatal mortality of dizygotic twins is higher than that of monozygotic twins.

53. For early before-and-after illustrations, see Herbert C. Johnson, "Surgery of cerebral vascular anomalies," in *A History of Neurological Surgery*, ed. Arthur E. Walker (Baltimore, 1951) 258, reproducing from the *Annals of Surgery* a before-and-two-years-after illustration from Benjamin Travers, "A case of aneurism by anastomosis in the orbit, cured by the ligature of the common carotid artery," *Medical-Chirurgical Treatises* 2 (1813) 1-16; Adelaide Hechtlinger, *The Great Patent Medicine Era* (NY: Grosset & Dunlap, n.d.) 72, "The Two Paths: What Will the Boy Become"; "The Grecian Difficulty," *Punch* 18 (1849) 239, from a knot on the left to a maze of knots on the right. On weight-loss before-and-afters, see Hillel Schwartz, *Never Satisfied: A Cultural History of Diets, Fantasies and Fat* (NY: Free Press, 1986) 208-09.

54. R.P. Hall & Co. ad reproduced in *Newsletter* (19 Apr 1963) in Thumbnail Sketches

file, J. Walter Thompson Company Archives, John W. Hartman Center for Sales, Advertising, and Marketing History, Special Collections Library, Duke U, Durham, NC [henceforth, J. Walter Thompson Archives], whence also the Lux ad in the 1932 Ringling, Barnum, Bailey Circus Program (Lux file), and the Double Mint ads in *Amer Mag* (July 1938) and the *Delineator* (Sept 1938), Competitive Ads file, Box 31864, 9:D:6 under Wrigley; Linda Hanrath, Corporate Archivist, Wm. Wrigley Jr. Company, Chicago, IL, letters to the author, 11 April and 31 July, 1990; Otis Shepherd drawings in Abbe and Gill, *Twins on Twins*, 57.

55. Lux ad, *Cleveland Times* (23 Mar 1932) and in Yiddish versions in *NY Jewish Day* (1 and 15 Mar, 1932) from the Lux file, J. Walter Thompson Archives, for which I thank the curator, Ellen Gartrell.

56. Ford ad in *Life* (June 14, 1948), J. Walter Thompson Archives.

57. Toni ads in *Glamour* (16 Mar 1947) 33 and *Ladies' Home J* (Apr 1947) 279, courtesy of Diane F. Carothers, curator, the D'Arcy Collection, Communications Lib, U Illinois, Urbana-Champaign [henceforth, D'Arcy Collection].

58. Stein and Wolner, *Parallels*, 124; Toni ads in *Life* (17 May 1948) 100–101, (25 Apr 1949) 26, (6 Mar 1950) 117, (23 July 1951) 16, and *Ladies' Home J* (May 1949), from the D'Arcy Collection.

59. Lilt ad in *NY Times Mag* (6 Aug 1950), from Competitive Ads file, Box 31815, 8:C:2, J. Walter Thompson Archives; Toni ads in *Life* (17 July 1950) 73, *Life* (14 May 1951) 139, D'Arcy Collection.

60. Karcher, *Wie ein Ei dem Andern*, 17, deodorant; "What's been happening in London," *Company News* (23 May 1962), detergent, and "Pond's International hosts visiting foreign students," *ibid.* (29 Nov 1961), both in J. Walter Thompson Archives; Sharp ad, "Repeat performance," *LA Times Mag* (25 Aug 1990) 22, ad section, fax; Cassill, *Twins*, 137, soup and jeans; "Pepsi-Cola sent cases of its drink – and twins Eileen and Edna Reeke, who will be featured in Pepsi's new advertising stunt," caption to photograph in *PM Newspaper* (8 July 1941) in Picture Collection, NY Public Lib, under "Birth (Human) – Multiple"; cf. Stein and Wolner, *Parallels*, 136, twins in the 1920s sought for hair-coloring ads, on condition that one lose fifteen pounds and the other remain at current weight, presumably to ensure the proper before-and-after effects; Pierre Berton, *The Dionne Years* (Toronto: Seal, 1977) 173–76. The Charnocks, a biracial British couple on the edge of poverty, were upset in 1984 when the notoriety of their twins, one black and one white, *did not* result in television commercials and endorsements: D. Michael Cheers, "Britain's most amazing twins," *Ebony* (Apr 1984) 46. Marilyn Marshall, "The Gaither Quints," *ibid.* (Dec 1985) 36, suggested that black multiple births reap fewer commercial rewards than white multiples.

61. The number of male and female twins born is closer to a 1:1 ratio than the number of male and female singletons born, but there are hints that, as with singletons, neonatal death rates may be slightly higher for males than females. See, for example, John D.H. Doherty, "Perinatal mortality in twins, Australia, 1973–1980: II. Maternal age, lethal congenital malformations and sex," *AGMG* 37 (1988) 321–29.

62. M.B., "Twin lust," *The Shrink Tapes* (N.p.: Southwick Enterprises, 1984) 98–100; Plato, *The Republic and Other Works*, trans. B. Jowett (Garden City, NY: Anchor, 1973) 336–37. On sex between actual twins, see Zazzo, *Le Paradoxe des jumeaux*, 62ff.

63. Frank Clifford, "The Barbi Twins and Me," *LA Times* (4 Sept 1991) E1–2, on Shane and Sia in *Playboy* (Sept 1991), with encore (Jan 1993) 81–91. NBC TV's "Enter-

tainment Tonight," 8 Jan 1993, reported that a Barbi Twins Calendar was the best-selling (pinup) calendar in the world. Cf. Flemming Nielsen (photographer), "The Three Sisters," *Mayfair* 25, 8 (1990) 11-16.

64. Nancy Friday, *My Secret Garden: Women's Sexual Fantasies* (NY: Simon & Schuster, 1973) 158-63, 180-95; Lonnie Barbach, *Pleasures: Women Write Erotica* (NY: Harper & Row, 1985) 274, 289; Judith Rossner, *Attachments* (NY: Simon & Schuster, 1977) 98-99; Rosamond Smith, *Lives of the Twins* (NY: Simon & Schuster, 1987) 45.

65. Toni ad in *Life* (31 Mar 1952) 71, from the D'Arcy Collection; Samson Eitrem, *Die Göttlichen Zwillinge bei den Griechen* (Christiania, 1902) on female dioscuri; Barbara G. Walker, *The Woman's Ency of Myths and Secrets* (San Francisco: Harper & Row, 1983) 1022-23. For the goddess, see Christine Downing, *The Goddess: Mythological Images of the Feminine* (NY: Crossroad, 1981); Miriam R. Dexter, *Whence the Goddesses: A Source Book* (NY: Pergamon, 1990); Tivka Frymer-Kensky, *In the Wake of the Goddesses: Women, Culture, and the Biblical Transformation of Pagan Myth* (NY: Free Press, 1991). One might also suggest, following Carol Gilligan, *In a Different Voice: Psychological Theory and Women's Development* (Cambridge, MA: Harvard U, 1982) 159ff, that the special powers of female twins stem from that fusion of identity and intimacy which is specific to women's psychological development.

66. Roy Wagner, *The Invention of Culture* (Englewood Cliffs: Prentice-Hall, 1975) 60-70; W.F. Haug, *Critique of Commodity Aesthetics: Appearance, Sexuality and Advertising in Capitalist Society*, trans. Robert Bock (Minneapolis: U Minnesota, 1986); David N. Martin, *Romancing the Brand: The Power of Advertising and How To Use It* (NY: Amer Management Assoc., 1989) 2, 5 on cleverness, and 134; Carol Moog, *"Are They Selling Her Lips?" Advertising and Identity* (NY: Morrow, 1990) esp. 118; James C. Wolfe, "It takes a long, long, LONG time to make an idea sink in," *Advertising Age* (24 Sept 1951) on each generation, in Writings and Speeches, Box 38, J. Walter Thompson Archives. Michael Schudson, *Advertising, the Uneasy Persuasion: Its Dubious Impact on American Society* (NY: Basic, 1984), argues against attributing too much power to advertising but concludes (p. 233) with a nod to the oracular: "Advertising picks up some of the things that people hold dear and re-presents them to people as *all* of what they value, assuring them that the sponsor is the patron of common ideals."

67. Catherine P. Hargrave, *A History of Playing Cards* (NY: Dover, 1966) 133, 135 for examples dated 1813-34, and 260, 265, 267, 271, 346, 350 for the routine manufacture of reversible face cards from the 1860s on; John B. Buckstone, *Open House, or, the Twin Sisters* (L, 1833?) 6; Charles H. Smith, *Historical Sketch of the Lives of William Wiggin Smith and Joseph Horton Smith* (Avalon, CA: privately printed, 1941-42) 7; Charles Bartholomew, *Mechanical Toys* (Feltham: Hamlyn, 1979) 73; Abbe and Gill, *Twins on Twins*, 59; J. Robert Davison, "Turning a blind eye: the historian's use of photos," *British Columbia Studies* 52 (Wint 1981-82) 29, plate V; Kemp R. Niver, *Early Motion Pictures*, ed. Bebe Bergsten (Washington, D.C.: Lib of Congress, 1985) 340 on "Twin Brothers."

68. Stefan Kessler, *Die Folie à Deux* (Zurich: Juris, 1970) rehearses the history, as do Alexander Gralnick, "Folie à deux – the psychosis of association, I, II," *Psychiatric Q* 16 (1942) 230-63, 491-520, and Berchmans Rioux, "A review of folie à deux," *ibid.* 37 (1963) 405-28. (Gralnick's and Rioux's personal examples involve twins.) I have also used Charles Lasègue et al., "La Folie à deux [discussion]," *Annales médico-psychologiques*, sér. 5, 11 (1874) 109-14, 253-60; Dr. Maret, "Observation curieuse de folie similaire ou à deux individus," *ibid.* 14 (1875) 46-47; Charles Lasègue and Jules Falret, "La Folie

à deux ou folie communiqué," *ibid.* 18 (1877) 321-55, q324-25, twins on 341-45; E. Marandon de Montyel, "Contribution à l'étude de la folie à deux," *ibid.*, sér. 6, 5 (1881) 28-52; Georg Lehmann, "Zur Casuistik des inducirten Irreseins (Folie à deux)," *Archiv für Psychiatrie* 14 (1883) 145-54 with good bibliography; B. Ball, "De la folie gémellaire ou aliénation mentale chez des jumeaux," *L'Encéphale* 4 (1884) 385-400; D. Hack Tuke, "Folie à deux," *Brain* 10 (Jan 1888) 408-21, esp. 418; Max Schönfeldt, "Über das inducirte Irresein (Folie communiqué)," *Archiv für Psychiatrie* 26 (1894) 202-66; Helene Deutsch, "Folie à deux," *Psychoanalytic Q* 7 (1938) 307-18. For questions asked of twins, Eileen Boxer, Brooklyn, NY, phone interview, 17 Jan 1991, and twin Nina Katz, San Francisco, CA, phone interview, 7 May 1991.

69. Isabel Bolton (= Mary B. Miller), *Under Gemini* (NY: Harcourt Brace Jovanovich, 1966) vii; Abbe and Gill, *Twins on Twins*, 53, the Soyers; Frederick A. Sweet, *Ivan Albright* (Chicago: Art Inst, 1964) 17, 22; Michael Croydon, *Ivan Albright* (NY: Abbeville, 1978) 28, 112-13, plates 22, 38-39; anonymous interview, Laguna Hills, CA, 5 May 1991; Cassill, *Twins*, 129; Elisabeth Kübler-Ross, *On Death and Dying* (NY: Macmillan, 1969); idem, *Death: The Final Stage of Growth* (Englewood Cliffs: Prentice-Hall, 1975); idem, Foreword to Kenneth Ring, *Heading Toward Omega* (NY: Morrow, 1984).

70. Cassill, *Twins*, 132-33; Ann Landers, "Twins," *The Ann Landers Ency* (Garden City, NY: Doubleday, 1978) II, 1236-37, 1239; idem, "Identical twins yearn for lives of their own," *LA Times* (25 June 1991) E14.

71. "Insurance against twins," *Maternity and Child Welfare* 11 (1927) 95-96, citing the *Manchester Guardian*; Amram Scheinfeld, *Twins and Supertwins*, eds. Arthur Falek et al. (Philadelphia: Lippincott, 1967) 75, 111.

72. Benjamin Spock, *Baby and Child Care* (NY, 1946) 456-57. But contrast the Russian view of twins in Anatolii I. Pristavkin, *The Inseparable Twins*, trans. Michael Glenny (L: Picador, 1991).

73. Winifred de Kok's article in *Childhood* (Dec 1949) quoted by Patricia Edge, *Child Care and Management from Neo-Natal Days to Adolescence* (L, 1953) 97; Marjorie R. Leonard, "Twins: the myth and the reality," *Child Study* 30 (1953) 9-10. Cf. Zoot Sims, *I Wish I Were Twins*, sound disc (Beverly Hills: Pablo, 1981).

74. Phyllis Graham, *The Care and Feeding of Twins* (NY: Harper, 1955) 7-8, 148. I thank Kathy Epling for sending me a copy of this book with dust jacket intact.

75. Department of National Health and Welfare, *Up the Years from One to Six* (Ottawa: Queen's Printer, 1955) 42; Dorothy Burlingham, with Arthur T. Barron, "A study of identical twins," *Psychoanalytic Study of the Child* 18 (1963) 367-423, q383, q403, q413. Burlingham is often cited for her *Twins: A Study of Three Pairs of Identical Twins* (NY, 1952).

76. Carol Morse, *Double Trouble* (Garden City, NY: Doubleday, 1964) 25, 40-41, and cf. Charles Jones and Eugene Jones, with Dale Kramer, *Double Trouble: The Autobiography of the Jones Twins* (Boston, 1952). "Doubletrouble" would even serve as headline to a story about the establishment of the first twins clinic in the world, run by pediatrician Elizabeth Bryan and midwife Christina Tom-Johnson, at Queen Charlotte's Hospital, London: P. Holmes, "Double trouble?" *Nursing Times and Nursing Mirror* 84 (15 June, 1988) 16-17. According to Bryan, "Twins in the family," *Midwives Chronicle & Nursing Notes* 103 (Mar 1990) 66-69, the trouble begins at birth, when premature or low-birthweight twins are put into incubators, separated from the mother, whose bonding with the infants is thus handicapped.

77. Pamela P. Novotny, *The Joy of Twins: Having, Raising, and Loving Babies Who Arrive in Groups* (NY: Crown, 1988) vii; Terry Pink Alexander, *Make Room for Twins* (Toronto: Bantam, 1987) esp. 301 on not separating twins who wish to be together; Hillel Schwartz, *Century's End: A Cultural History of the Fin de Siècle from the 990s through the 1990s* (NY: Doubleday, 1990) esp. 210-26, 273-75. The conjunction of images of twins with centurial images and millenarian expectations (or proposals) has been contemplated by Prof. William G. Doty, U Alabama, who presented a paper, "Complementary twin sibs in Native American psychomythology," at the annual fellows meeting of the Society for Values in Higher Education, Colorado Springs, Aug 1989, and by psychologist Howard Teich of San Francisco, in an unpublished paper (1990), "Changing man and changing woman: archetype of the dual/twin hero and heroine," for copies of both of which papers I thank Prof. Doty.

CHAPTER TWO: DOPPELGÄNGERS
1. Kathryn M. Abbe and Frances M. Gill, *Twins On Twins* (NY: Potter, 1980) 68-69; Joel F. Bingham, *The Twin Sisters of Martigny* (Boston, 1899) 67; Karl Miller, *Doubles: Studies in Literary History* (NY: Oxford U, 1985) ch. 20 on the Chaplins, as also Juliet Darling's documentary, "A Pair of One," aired on British television, Channel 4, Spring 1991; David Cronenberg (dir), *Dead Ringers* (Twentieth Century-Fox, 1988), from a novel by Bari Wood and Jack Geasland, *Twins* (NY: New Amer Lib, 1977), from reports in *NY Times* (20 July 1975) 38:4, (21 July) 25:3, (1 Aug) 15:1, (15 Aug) 1:5, (16 Aug) 20:5, (19 Aug) 1:7.
2. G.J. Fisher, "Diploteratology," *Transactions NY State Med Soc* (1866) 223, terms; Helmut L. Karcher, *Wie ein Ei dem Andern. Alles über Zwillinge* (Munich: Piper, 1975) 139, the skeletons; Marija Gimbutas, "Doubleness," *ER*, IV, 423-24.
3. Ottavia Niccoli, " 'Menstruum Quasi Monstruum': monstrous births and menstrual taboo in the sixteenth century," in *Sex and Gender in Historical Perspective*, eds. E. Muir and G. Ruggiero, trans. Margaret A. Gallucci et al. (Baltimore: Johns Hopkins U, 1990) 1-25; Ambroise Paré, *On Monsters and Marvels*, trans. Janis L. Pallister (Chicago: U Chicago, 1982 [1573]) 5, 8-9. On the immediate political significance and medical history of an epidemic of reports of monstrous births during the 1560s, see David Cressy, "De la fiction dans les archives? ou le monstre de 1569," *Annales: é.s.c.* 48 (1993) 1309-29. René Girard, in *Violence and the Sacred*, trans. Patrick Gregory (Baltimore: Johns Hopkins U, 1977) 160, writes more ahistorically: "A fundamental principle, often overlooked, is that the double and the monster are one and the same being."
4. Michel de Montaigne, *The Essays*, trans. Jacob Zeitlin (NY, 1935) bk. II, ch. 30.
5. Jules Berger de Xivrey, *Traditions tératologiques* (P, 1836); Patrick Tort, *L'Ordre et les monstres: le débat sur l'origine des déviations anatomiques au XVIIIe siècle* (P: Le Sycomore, 1980) esp. 24-26, 128 on singularity; Katharine Park and Lorraine J. Daston, "Unnatural conceptions: the study of monsters in sixteenth- and seventeenth-century France and England," *Past & Present* 92 (Aug 1981) 20-54; T[homas] B[edford], *A True and Certaine Relation of a Strange-Birth* (L, 1635) 12n., concorporation; Niccoli, "Menstruum Quasi Monstruum," n.23 on infanticide, n.26 on exhibitions; Paré, *On Monsters*, 9, girls joined at kidneys carted around Italy in 1475, and p. 15 on dissection, as also Jacques Corbin, *Discours sur les jumelles joinctes qui sont nées à Paris* (Lyon, 1605) 7; Fisher, "Diploteratology," esp. 207. For a general review, see Dudley Wilson, *Signs and Portents: Monstrous Births from the Middle Ages to the Age of Enlightenment* (L: Routledge, 1993).

6. *OED*, VI, 156; Robert Bogdan, *Freak Show: Presenting Human Oddities for Amusement and Profit* (Chicago: U Chicago, 1988) 3-6, 25-93; *A Monstrous Birth of Two Female Children joyned together at the Crowne of their heads* (L, 1682) bound with *A Letter from an Eminent Merchant in Ostend, Containing an Account of a Strange and Monstrous Birth* (L, 1682) in a British Lib scrapbook, "Collection of Advertisements," N Tab 2026/25, prefatory insert and #1; Park and Daston, "Unnatural conceptions," 51-54. Leslie Fiedler, *Freaks: Myths and Images of the Second Self* (NY: Simon & Schuster, 1978) 34-36, 197-210, covers some of this ground in a poorly documented if convivial manner.

7. John B. Friedman, *The Monstrous Races in Medieval Art and Thought* (Cambridge, MA: Harvard U, 1981) 179-87; Niccoli, "Menstruum Quasi Monstruum," n.23; Ernest Martin, *Histoire des monstres depuis l'antiquité jusqu'à nos jours* (P, 1880) ch. 9; Kay Cassill, *Twins: Nature's Amazing Mystery* (NY: Athenaeum, 1982) 53-54.

8. The root source is George Buchanan (1506-82), *Rerum Scoticarum Historia*, bk. XIII, ch. 7, in *Opera omnia*, ed. Thomas Ruddiman (Edinburgh, 1715) I, 242b, marginal date 1490, and in idem, *The History of Scotland*, trans. Awnsham Churchill (L, 1690) bk. 13, q4-5. Final quotation, spelling modernized, is from Robert Lindesay of Pitscottie, *The Historie and Cronicles of Scotland*, ed. Aeneas J.G. Mackay (Edinburgh, 1899) I, 234. For a poetic meditation upon the Colloredo twins, see Sharon Olds, "The Twins," *The Gold Cell* (NY: Knopf, 1987) 10-11.

9. Frederick Drimmer, *Very Special People: The Struggles, Loves and Triumphs of Human Oddities* (NY: Bell, 1985) q29-30, Bartholin; Hyder E. Rollins, ed., *The Pack of Autolycus* (Cambridge, MA: Harvard U, 1927) 8-14, q8 from *A Certaine Relation of the Hog-Faced Gentlewoman* (L, 1640), spelling modernized.

10. "Extract of a Letter of William Burnet, Esq;...Leyden, May 9, 1708. N.S.," *Phil Transactions Royal Soc of L* 50 (1757) 315-16, with three other accounts, 310-20; Fisher, "Diploteratology," q225-27 from Escardus, *De sororibus gemellis, cohaerent* (1709).

11. I am relying heavily upon Stephen Jay Gould, "Living with connections," *The Flamingo's Smile* (NY: Norton, 1985) 64-77, q75. Gould, however, has the girls dying after five months; contrast Fisher, "Diploteratology," 270-71, and 31-34 on early deaths. On ambiguity, Tort, *L'Ordre et les monstres*, esp. 24-25. For the scientific context, see Jane M. Oppenheimer, "Some historical relationships between teratology and experimental embryology," *Bull History Med* 42 (1968) 145-59.

12. Arthur W. Towne, "Chang and Eng: Story of the Celebrated Siamese Twins in the Show World, in Medical History, and in Marriage," typescript (final version dated 1943), Box A, pp. 34-35, in Charles W. Towne Collection, Harvard Theatre Collection, Harvard College Library; Irving Wallace and Amy Wallace, assisted by Walter Kempthorne and Elizebethe Kempthorne, *The Two* (NY: Simon & Schuster, 1978) 27-44, and 17 on the names, as also Kay Hunter, *Duet for a Lifetime: The Story of the Original Siamese Twins* (NY: Coward-McCann, 1964) 15; W.S. Bristowe, "Robert Hunter in Siam, 1824-44," *History Today* 24 (Feb 1974) 88-95.

13. Towne, "Chang and Eng," Box B, v, 3-4, and Box B, 56-58; Hunter, *Duet*, 42-43, 49, 52; John C. Warren, *An Account of the Siamese Youths* (Boston, 1829), a printed letter to William Sturgis, 24 Aug 1829, at Massachusetts Historical Soc, Boston, MA; [John W. Hale], *An Historical Account of the Siamese Twin Brothers from Actual Observation* (L, 1829) 1.

14. Archie Robinson, "Chang-Eng's American heritage," *Life* (11 Aug 1952) 79,

descendants claiming that "Part of their professional act had been to...exaggerate their unity of thought and action." On waltzing: "The Siamese Twins, supplementary report," *Lancet* (4 Apr 1874) 493-94. On Hale: J.W. Hale to Charles Harris, 24 Sept, 4 Nov and 14 Nov 1832, in the Papers of Dr. Charles Harris, Box 1 #5, of Thurmond Chatham Papers, P.C. 1139, and Chang-Eng, letter [in first person singular] to [Abel] Coffin, 22 Dec 1831, by the hand of Charles Harris, in Chang and Eng Bunker, Siamese Twins Papers, P.C. 916, all at North Carolina State Archives, Raleigh, NC [henceforth NCSA]; Hale, *Historical Account*, 9-10. On phrenology, O.S. Fowler, *Phrenology Proved, Illustrated, and Applied*, 4th ed. (Philadelphia, 1839) 322-23. Quotation from newspaper poem, "Lines on the Siamese Youths," in Towne, "Chang and Eng," Box A, 22, and see Box B, 6, for *Centinel*.

15. George Buckley Bolton, *On the United Siamese Twins* (L, 1830) 177-80; Hale, *Historical Account*, 12; "The Siamese Twins as told by Judge Jesse Franklin Graves," typescript, pp. 16, 19 on the courtship and bed, in Siamese Twins Papers, NCSA (henceforth Graves, "Siamese Twins"); Wallace and Wallace, *The Two*, 62 for *Evening Post*, 87 for galvanic circuit.

16. Wallace and Wallace, *The Two*, q149 from *La Quotidienne* (Jan 1836), q59 from *Boston Daily Courier* (22 Aug 1829); Towne, "Chang and Eng," Box A, 22, naval surgeon; Gilbert A. A Beckett, *The Siamese Twins* (1834?) in *Cumberland's Minor Theatre* (L, 1830-35) XIV, redone in 1863 as a "Negro burlesque sketch" by Charles White, *Siamese Twins*, in Robert M. DeWitt, *Ethiopian and Comic Drama* (NY, 1874) #38; Prof. Tucker, "Psychological observations on the Siamese Twins, Chang and Eng, made in 1836," *Amer Phil Soc Proc* 2 (1841) 22-28, summarized in J. David Smith, *Psychological Profiles of Conjoined Twins* (NY: Praeger, 1988) 98-101; Edward G.E.L. Bulwer-Lytton, *The Siamese Twins: A Satirical Tale of the Times* (L, 1831) 23, 97, 105; Victor A.G.R. Bulwer-Lytton Lytton, *The Life of Edward Bulwer, First Lord Lytton* (L, 1913) I, 521-26.

17. Coffin *had* booked their passage to England as servants. See Charles Harris to Capt. William Davis, Jr., 11 Apr 1832, Chang-Eng to Davis, 4 July 1832, and Chang-Eng to Mrs. Susan Coffin, 11 July 1832, all in Siamese Twins Papers, NCSA; *A few Particulars Concerning Chang-Eng, the United Siamese Brothers: Published under their own direction* (NY, 1836) 5, 7; John Emory Bryant, Journal No. 1, entry for 22 June 1853, typescript p. 14, on their slaves, in John Emory Bryant Papers, XVIII-C, Manuscript Dept., Duke U Library; Wallace and Wallace, *The Two*, 238 and figure 18.

18. Wallace and Wallace, *The Two*, 130, 228, 274 (rigidified band); J.N. Morehead, *Lives, Adventures, Anecdotes, Amusements, and Domestic Habits of the Siamese Twins* (Raleigh, NC, 1850) 14; Graves, "Siamese Twins" pp. 11-12, 25; Towne, "Chang and Eng," Box A, 140, 146; Robinson, "Chang-Eng's American heritage," 79.

19. Towne, "Chang and Eng," Box A, 146, 148, 151; Wallace and Wallace, *The Two*, 224; A.H. Saxon, *P.T. Barnum: The Legend and the Man* (NY: Columbia U, 1989) 53. Most accounts err in linking Barnum with Chang-Eng from the start of their careers.

20. Towne, "Chang and Eng," Box A, 144, 152-53, 157, 160-61; Nathaniel Hawthorne, *The American Notebooks*, ed. Claude M. Simpson (Columbus: Ohio State U, 1972) 177; Robert P. Harris, "Historical and analogical record of the Siamese Twins," *Amer J Med Sci*, n.s. 68 (1874) 362, 371, 373-74; Eugène Apert, *Les Jumeaux* (P, 1923) 180-81 on separations; "The Siamese Twins," *Lancet* (13 Feb 1869) 228-30; Nannie Bunker's diary, typescript, entries for 22 and 23 Dec 1868, Edinburgh, in Siamese Twins Papers, NCSA; Wallace and Wallace, *The Two*, 282-83.

21. Note in *British Med and Surgical J* n.s. 6 (20 Oct 1870) 260; Towne, "Chang and Eng," 166–69; Graves, "Siamese Twins," 26ff.

22. M., "The Siamese Twins at the College of Physicians," *Philadelphia Med Times* 4 (19 Feb 1874) 324, 326 (statement of Eng's widow), 327; Mr. Brenchley, "The Siamese Twins," *Lancet* (14 Feb 1874) 252; Worth B. Daniels, "The Siamese Twins: Some observations on their life, last illness and autopsy," 1961 typescript, pp. 6–7, MS C78, National Lib of Med; Towne, "Chang and Eng," Box A, 168–72; Wallace and Wallace, *The Two*, 294–301.

23. Alice Gilmer, Mount Airy, NC, to Thomas Slade, 13 Feb 1874, in 1874–1876 folder, William Slade Papers, and Rebecca A. Kelly, Yadkin County, NC, to her aunt Juliet, 14 Feb 1874, in John M. Jarrell Papers, both in Manuscript Dept, Duke U Lib; clipping from *NY Herald* (Jan 1874), quoting Hollingsworth, in Siamese Twins Papers, NCSA.

24. Wallace and Wallace, *The Two*, 300, 307–08; Daniels, "Siamese Twins," q7, from tinsmith, William Augustus Reich, letter of 19 Jan 1874, and q11 for Daniels's own opinion, in MS C78, National Lib of Med; M., "The Siamese Twins at the College of Physicians," q324 from Dr. Harrison Allen.

The two weeks of deliberation about a possible autopsy were not due merely to the siege of the Bunker house. There were widespread fears that dissection made one ineligible for bodily resurrection at the Last Judgment, so working-class crowds in England, for example, often stole the bodies of hanged convicts before they could be claimed for the morgues of medical schools. A full autopsy upon the Siamese Twins would have confirmed their eschatological as well as physiological monstrosity.

25. Uncat. MSS Notebook of correspondence concerning the Siamese Twins, letters of 10 Feb 1874 (casts), 1 Mar 1874 (embalming), 1 Apr 1874 from C.W. and S.D. Bunker, Mount Airy, NC, to Dr. Harrison Allen, in Lib of the College of Physicians of Philadelphia; M., "The Siamese Twins at the College of Physicians," 321–22; "The Siamese Twins," *Lancet* (14 March 1874) 385.

26. For Twain (= Samuel G. Clemens), see his "Personal habits of the Siamese twins," *Sketches New and Old* (NY, 1896) 96–102, originally in the *Saturday Evening Post* (13 July 1869); Paul Fatout, ed., *Mark Twain Speaking* (Iowa City: U Iowa, 1976) 238–39, 276–78, 541–42 on the Twins and temperance. See also Susan Gillman, *Dark Twins: Imposture and Identity in Mark Twain's America* (Chicago: U Chicago, 1989) esp. 58–59; Mark Twain, *Mississippi Writings*, ed. Guy Cardwell (NY: Lib of Amer, 1982) 1083–84, identifying the conjoined twins Giovanni and Giacomo Tocci as the model for *Pudd'nhead Wilson and Those Extraordinary Twins* (1894), in which, again, twins are opposites. Angelo, a teetotaler, contemplating separation from intemperate Luigi, shudders at the thought: "To be separate, and as other men are!... To sleep by himself, eat by himself, walk by himself – how lonely, how unspeakably lonely! No, no, any fate but that." (From Sidney E. Berger's edition [NY: Norton, 1980], p. 136.) On "humanity," see Raymond Williams, *Keywords* (NY: Oxford U, 1985) 121–24. Cf. Marc Shell, *Children of the Earth: Literature, Politics and Nationhood* (NY: Oxford U, 1993) 6–11 on Twain and twins in the context of issues of race and consanguinity. The father of Chang-Eng was Chinese on both sides, their mother half-Chinese, so in Victorian parlance they were in fact more "Chinamen" than Siamese.

27. Herman Melville, *Moby-Dick*, eds. H. Hayford and H. Parker (NY: Norton, 1967 [1851]) 270–71.

28. Fiedler, *Freaks*, 197-99; Lisa Hagberg, "She lets them gawk in the sideshow, but outside she's a bit shy," *Philadelphia Inquirer* (9 June 1980) in clippings file, "Circus Acts: Sideshow Freaks," Theatre Collection, Free Lib, Philadelphia, PA; Alva Johnston, "Sideshow people, III," *The New Yorker* (28 Apr 1934) 90 on fakes, as also Bogdan, *Freak Show*, 8-11. On Millie-Christine see Fisher, "Diploteratology," 227-31; *Biographical Sketch of Millie Christine The Carolina Twin surnamed the Two-Headed Nightingale*... (N.p., 1882?) 4 and throughout; *History and Medical Description of the Two-Headed Girl... Told in "Her Own Peculiar Way" by "One of Them"* (Buffalo, 1869) in the Leonidas Westervelt Circus Collection, N-Y Historical Soc; William C. Daily, Journal, 1851-1861, entry for 21 June 1859, on their voices, in his Papers, Manuscript Dept., Duke U Lib; Leander S. Gash, letter of 2 Feb 1866, in his Papers, P.C. 384, NCSA, printed in Otto H. Olsen and Ellen Z. McGrew, "Prelude to Reconstruction: the correspondence of State Senator Leander Sams Gash, 1866-67, Part I," *North Carolina Historical R* 60 (1983) 61-62, spelling modernized; *Biographical Sketch of Millie Christine The Two-Headed Nightingale* (L, 1871?) 4, q15 from *Liverpool Daily Courier*; Mary Wilson, "The slaves who sang for the Queen," *Sunday Star-News (Wilmington, NC)* (15 Jan 1984) 1E; Michael Mitchell, *Monsters of the Gilded Age* (Toronto: Gage, 1979) 82; Minnie McIver Brown, "Does death come on as a peaceful dream?" *The News and Observer (Raleigh)* (29 Nov 1925) 1, clipping in W.J.L. Millar Papers concerning Millie-Christine, P.C. 266.1, NCSA; Henry King, *Tarheel Tombstones & The Tales They Tell* (Asheboro, NC: Down Home, 1990) 26-27.

29.   Their names came from Wilkie Collins, *The Woman in White* (1859-60), which became the film *The Twin Pawns* (Acme, 1920), where two twins are separated at birth. Chief source here is Daisy and Violet Hilton, scrapbook, Performing Arts Lib, Lincoln Center Theater Collection, NY Public Lib, esp. "as-told-to" articles by Ethelda Bedford, "Private life of the Siamese Twins," in the *NY Journal-American*'s insert, *Amer Weekly* (10, 17, 24 Sept and 1, 8, 15 Oct 1944). I have also used clippings files at the Public Lib of Charlotte and Mecklenburg County, Charlotte, NC, esp. Dot Jackson, "The only bargain we get is our weight for a penny," *Charlotte News* (6 Jan 1969) and Henry Woodhead, "City's Siamese twins buried simply," *ibid.* (9 Jan 1969); Towne, "Chang and Eng," Box B, ch. 15; Helen L. Koch, "Some measurements of a pair of Siamese twins," *J Comparative Psychology* 7 (1927) 313-33; Smith, *Psychological Profiles*, 116; "Chained For Life," *Int Photographer* (1 Sept 1951) 10; Gary Indiana, "Invasion of the geminoids," *Interview* 20 (June 1990) 26; Pastor John R. Sills, Charlotte, NC, letter to author, 29 Apr 1991; Rosemary Lands, Charlotte, NC, interview, 6 Feb 1991.

30.   On 16 Feb 1994, the news wires reported that physicians at Wayne State University had tied off the connection between a pair of twins in utero, saving one and letting the other, conceived without a heart, die off in the womb. On earlier separations, see Apert, *Les Jumeaux*, 180-81; "Xiphopagus, or human doubles," *Sci Amer* 81 (21 Oct 1899) 266. For successful separations since the 1950s, see Karcher, *Wie ein Ei dem Andern*, 155-57; R. Mark Hoyle and Colin C. Thomas, Jr., "Twenty-three-year follow-up of separated ischiopagus tetrapus conjoined twins," *Annals of Surgery* 210 (Nov 1989) 673-79; Wallace and Wallace, *The Two*, 326.

Popular praise: "[The Davies Siamese Twins]" *Illustrated (L)* (16 Jan 1954) 21ff. in the "Birth (Human) – Multiple" file of the Picture Collection, NY Public Lib; Sondra J. Harris, "Twins' separation was a 'symphony' on medical stage," *Asheville (NC) Citizen-Times* (18 Jan 1981) D1; Patricia S. Hansen, as told to Laurie Williams Sowby, "My babies were born Siamese twins," *Redbook* (June 1984) 56; Janet Erickson, "Siamese twins:

double triumph," *Woman's Day* (17 June 1986) 82–86; Marlene Cady, "The pure joy of being alive," *People* (3 July 1989) 64–71.

Ethical issues: "The moral dilemma of Siamese twins," *Newsweek* (22 June 1981) 40, infanticide; Alison Miller et al., "Nursing Lin and Win," *The Canadian Nurse* 82 (Aug 1986) 19–22, on releasing separated twins with prosthetic legs to the care of an impoverished Burmese family; John G. Hubbell, "Why *my* babies?" *Reader's Digest* 131 (Nov 1987) 117–22, grave risks with surgery; George J. Annas, "Siamese twins: killing one to save the other," *Hastings Center Report* 17 (Apr 1987) 27–29 – which is what happened in August 1993 in Philadelphia, where surgeons separated a pair of girls Siamesed at heart and liver. This operation on Amy and Angela Lakeberg has subsequently been the topic of editorials and symposia on biomedical ethics.

Incest and fatality: Ads for the Paul Norman films, *Joined* and *Separated*, in *Leisure Concepts Catalog* (Merrillville, IN, 1990); David Cronenberg (dir), *Dead Ringers* (Twentieth Century–Fox, 1988), script adapted from Wood and Geasland, *Twins*, which stresses their homosexuality.

Fictions: S. Cleveland et al., "Psychological appraisal of conjoined twins," *J Projective Techniques* 28 (1964) 270, quoted in Smith, *Psychological Profiles*, 115; John Barth, "Petition," *Lost in the Funhouse* (NY: Bantam, 1969) 58–72, q61. Contrast Vladimir Nabokov, "Scenes from the life of a double monster," (1950) in *Nabokov's Dozen* (Garden City, NY: Doubleday, 1958) 165–77, and Sergio Jimenez, *Los Siameses que vivan muy juntos y otros historias* (Mexico City: Gaceta, 1984) 59–72, both allowing the companionate. In Judith Rossner's *Attachments* (NY: Simon & Schuster, 1977), the twins are eventually separated.

Some real-life Siamese twins have refused to be separated or are still considered medically inseparable. See Fiedler, *Freaks*, 199, on Mary and Margaret Gibb, as also "Siamese-Twin Gibb girls die at 54," *Philadelphia Inquirer* (1 Jan 1967) in "Circus Acts: Sideshow Freaks" file, Theatre Collection, Free Lib, Philadelphia; Bella Strumbo, "Sisters in a singular world: the lives & times of the only adult Siamese twins still joined at the head," *Washington Post* (27 Aug 1981) B1-7, on Yvonne and Yvette (McCarther) Jones, who died together at the age of forty-three: Burt A. Folkart, "Yvonne, Yvette McCarther: Siamese Twins," *LA Times* (5 Jan 1993) A18:1. Most recently, see Jen M.R. Doman, "One body, two souls," *Life* (Apr 1996) 44ff. on Abigail and Brittany Hensel.

31. René Zazzo, *Le Paradoxe des jumeaux* (P: Stock, 1984) 16 on dominance, and cf. Norman B. Capon, "Twins," *The Child* 17 (May 1927) 226: "When two infants are developing in the uterus their interests must be regarded, in the main, as antagonistic. Almost invariably twins are of different birth-weight, different birth-length and one is quite definitely the stronger baby." For the rest, Arnette Anderson and Beverly Anderson, "Mothers' beginning relationship with twins," *Birth* 14 (June 1987) 94–99, polarizing, with additional evidence in Suzanne Szasz, *The Body Language of Children* (NY: Norton, 1978) 19; M. Robin et al., "Mother-twin interaction during early childhood," *AGMG* 37 (1988) 151–59; Ricardo C. Ainslie et al., "The early developmental context of twinship: some limitations of the equal environments hypothesis," *Amer J Orthopsychiatry* 57 (Jan 1987) 120–24; Jane R. Spillman, "Double exposure – coping with newborn twins at home," *Midwife, Health Visitor & Community Nurse* 23 (Mar 1987) 92, guilt; Marianne Neifert and John Thorpe, "Twins: family adjustment, parenting, and infant feeding in the fourth trimester," *Clinical Obstetrics and Gynecology* 33 (Mar 1990) 102–13, projection; Lawrence Kutner, "The changing attitudes on how best to raise twins," *NY Times* (11 July 1991)

C2, quoting Patricia Maxwell Malmstrom, director, Twin Services; Lannie Steele, "Evil twin masquerades as his brother," *Weekly World News* (13 Feb 1990) 37; Martha Atkins, "My evil twin wants to kill me!" *ibid.* (23 Jan 1990) 27.

32. David Crouch, *The Beaumont Twins* (Cambridge: Cambridge U, 1986) xi, 98.

33. Vincent Canby, "Pseudonym comes to life in a Stephen King tale," *NY Times* (23 Apr 1993) C10, on the film *The Dark Half* (Orion, 1993) directed by George A. Romero, who also directed *Night of the Living Dead* (1968).

34. Robert Musil, *The Man Without Qualities*, trans. E. Wilkins and E. Kaiser (L: Secker & Warburg, 1960 [1932]) III, quotations on 9, 274, 280, 281, 282, 286, 311.

35. Hillel Schwartz, *Century's End: A Cultural History of the Fin de Siècle from the 990s through the 1990s* (NY: Doubleday, 1990) 212; Clifford Hallam, "The Double as incomplete self: toward a definition of Doppelgänger," in *Fearful Symmetry: Doubles and Doubling in Literature and Film*, ed. Eugene J. Crook (Tallahassee: U Presses Florida, 1981) 1–31; Masao Miyoshi, *The Divided Self* (NY: NYU, 1969) q23 from Godwin; Ralph Tymms, *Doubles in Literary Psychology* (Cambridge, 1949).

36. Fyodor Dostoevsky, *The Double: Two Versions*, trans. Evelyn Harden (Ann Arbor: Ardis, 1985 [1846, 1866]) 64, 67, 68, quoted here and below by permission.

37. A.E. Crawley, "Doubles," *Ency of Religion and Ethics*, eds. James Hastings et al. (NY: Charles Scribner's Sons, 1961 [1908–26]) IV, 853–60, summarized and updated by Eric Maple, "Double," *Man, Myth and Magic*, ed. Richard Cavendish (NY: Marshall Cavendish, 1970) II, 672–77; Régis Boyer, *Le Monde du double: le magie chez les anciens Scandinaves* (P: Berg, 1986) 29–54; Claude Lecouteux, "Le double, le cauchemar, la sorcière," *Etudes germaniques* 43 (1988) 395–405; C.J. Wright, "The 'spectre' of science: the study of optical phenomena and the Romantic imagination," *J Warburg & Courtauld Inst* 43 (1980) 186–200; Allienne R. Becker, "[Review of] Aglaja Hildenbrock, *Das andere Ich: Künstlicher Mensch und Doppelgänger in der deutsch- und englisch-sprachigen Literatur*," *German Q* 63 (Wint 1990) 131–33; Centre du Romantisme Anglais, *Le Double dans le romantisme anglo-américain* (Clermont-Ferrand: Faculté des lettres et sciences humaines, 1984) esp. Preface by Christian La Cassagner, and Alain Montandon, "Hamlet ou le fantôme du moi: le double dans le romantisme allemand," 31–56; Paul Coates, *The Double and the Other: Identity as Ideology in Post-Romantic Fiction* (NY: St. Martin's, 1988) 35 on Hoffmann, as also John Herdman, *The Double in Nineteenth-Century Fiction* (Houndmills: Macmillan, 1990) 47.

38. Dostoevsky, *The Double*, 72, 82, 99, 108, 111.

39. Dostoevsky, *The Double*, 130, 132; Edgar Allan Poe, "William Wilson" (1839) in *Selected Poetry and Prose*, ed. T.O. Mabbott (NY, 1951) 131–48, q138. Poe had an older brother named William, and his adoptive father John Allan was also the father of twins born in 1830. See the discussion in Jean Perrot, *Mythe et littérature: sous le signe des jumeaux* (P: PUF, 1976) 166–70.

40. Schwartz, *Century's End*, 210; Dostoevsky, *The Double*, 168. On types of Doubles, see Otto Rank, *The Double: A Psychoanalytic Study*, trans. Harry Tucker, Jr. (Chapel Hill: U North Carolina, 1971 [1925]); John Todd and Kenneth Dewhurst, "The Double: psychopathology and physiology," *J Nervous and Mental Disease* 122 (1955) 47–55; N. Lukianowicz, "Autoscopic phenomena," *Archives of Neurology and Psychiatry* 80 (1958) 199–220.

41. Antonii Pogorel'skii, *The Double, or, My Evenings in Little Russia*, trans. Ruth Sobel (Ann Arbor: Ardis, 1988 [1829]) 13; Dostoevsky, *The Double*, 192.

42. James Ram, *A Treatise on Facts as Subjects of Inquiry*, 2nd Amer ed., revised by John Townshend (NY, 1870) 77; "Doubles," *Chambers's J* 72 (17 Aug 1895) q513; "Doubles," *Spectator (London)* 92 (1904) 688–90; Stanley M. Coleman, "The phantom double," *British J Med Psychology* 14 (1934) 257–60, de Maupassant. For the fin de siècle, see Coates, *The Double and the Other*.

43. John R. Elliott, Jr., "Medieval acting," in *Contexts for Early English Drama*, eds. M.G. Briscoe and J.C. Coldewey (Bloomington: Indiana U, 1989) 238–52, q241 from L. Petit de Julleville, *Les Mystères* (P, 1880) II, 133; Aaron Hill, *The Prompter*, eds. W.W. Appleton and K.A. Burnim (NY: Blom, 1966 [1734–36]) 78 for 13 June 1735; Michael Fried, *Absorption and Theatricality: Painting and Beholder in the Age of Diderot* (Berkeley: U Cal, 1980) 13, "completely caught up," from Abbé Garrigues de Froment, comment on a Chardin painting, and 79.

44. Frederick Brown, *Theater and Revolution: The Culture of the French Stage* (NY: Viking, 1980) ch. 2; George Taylor, " 'The just delineation of the passions': theories of acting in the age of Garrick," in *Essays on the Eighteenth-Century English Stage*, eds. K. Richards and P. Thomson (L: Methuen, 1972) 60–62; Fried, *Absorption and Theatricality*, 82, 208. Cf. Joseph R. Roach, *The Player's Passion: Studies in the Science of Acting* (Newark: U Delaware, 1985).

45. Kirsten G. Holmström, *Monodrama, Attitudes, Tableaux Vivants: Studies on Some Trends of Theatrical Fashion, 1770–1815* (Stockholm: Almqvist and Wiksell, 1967); Martin Meisel, "Wilkie's tableaux vivants," *Master Drawings* (Spr 1973) 55–58; Jack W. McCullough, *Living Pictures on the NY Stage* (Ann Arbor: UMI Research, 1983); James H. Head, *Home Pastimes* (Boston, 1860) 13; Sarah Annie Frost (=Shields), *The Book of Tableaux and Shadow Pantomimes* (NY, 1869) 11–12, 111.

46. Emma C. Rook, *Tableaux, Charades, and Pantomimes* (Freeport, NY: Books for Libraries, 1971 [1889]) 29. Contrast Nina Auerbach, *Private Theatricals: The Lives of the Victorians* (Cambridge, MA: Harvard U, 1990) 10, performance as "grim capitulation to social control," and Richard Sennett, *The Fall of Public Man* (NY: Vintage, 1976). On Delsarte, see Hillel Schwartz, "Torque: the new kinaesthetic of the twentieth century," in *Zone 6: Incorporations*, eds. J. Crary and S. Kwinter (NY: Zone, 1992) 70–127. Descended as much from triumphal floats and royal entries as from biblical woodcuts and religious processions, tableaux vivants were often triply removed from any original (recreations of engravings of etchings of famous paintings).

47. Holmström, *Monodrama*, 111–185, esp. 111 on Goethe, 174–75 on Schlegel and Ida Brun; J.W. von Goethe, *Elective Affinities (Die Wahlverwandtschaften)*, trans. E. Mayer and L. Bogan (Chicago: Regnery, 1963) 185–88 for the satire; Jean-Georges Noverre, *Lettres sur les arts imitateurs en général, et sur la danse en particulier* (P, 1807) I, iv, 146; [Robert Nares], *Remarks on the Nature of Pantomime, or Imitative Dance, Ancient and Modern* (L, 1789) 12; A.H. Saxon, *The Life and Art of Andrew Ducrow* (Hamden: Archon, 1978) q152 from Prince Pückler-Muskau.

48. Saxon, *Andrew Ducrow*, 101–03; Holmström, *Monodrama*, 111, 200–01, 209–12; Brown, *Theater and Revolution*, 41–82, 86–95; Heinrich von Kleist, trans. Matthew Gurewitsch, "Concerning the puppet theatre," (1801) in *Parabola* 6 (Aug 1981) 48–52. Kleist, earlier headed toward a military career, had found drill and drill masters "a living monument to tyranny": Joachim Maass, *Kleist*, trans. Ralph Mannheim (L: Secker & Warburg, 1983 [1957]) q13 and see 227ff on his ideas about acting and puppets, as also Helmut Sembdner, ed., *Kleists Aufsatz "Über das Marionettentheater"* (Berlin: Schmidt, 1967).

49. Brown, *Theater and Revolution*, q120-21 from Jules Janin; Louis Péricaud, *Le Théâtre des Funambules* (P, 1897) 251-55.

50. Péricaud, *Le Théâtre des Funambules*, 18; Paul Hugounet, *Mimes et Pierrots* (P, 1889) 47, 73; Jules Fleury, *Souvenirs et portraits de jeunesse* (Geneva: Slotkine, 1970 [1872]) 64.

51. Bari Rolfe, "Magic century of French mime," *Mime, Mask, and Marionette* 1 (1978) 138-41; Gaspard Deburau and Charles Deburau, *Pantomimes* (P, 1889) prefatory "Etude sur la pantomime" by Paul Hippeau, q xxii-xxiii, and extract from memoirs of Charles Deburau, 257, 275.

52. Robert F. Storey, *Pierrots on the Stage of Desire* (Princeton: Princeton U, 1985) ch. 2 on successors to Deburau; Séverin, le mime, *L'Homme blanc* (P, 1929) 177n; Gordon Craig, "The actor and the über-marionette," (1908) in *Gordon Craig on Movement and Dance*, ed. Arnold Rood (NY: Dance Horizons, 1977) 37-57, q39; Irène Eynat, "Gordon Craig, the über-marionette, and the Dresden Theatre," *Theatre Research Int* 5 (1980) 171-82, on marionettes built for Craig, as also Edward Craig, *Gordon Craig* (NY: Knopf, 1968) 289-92, and see Maurice Maeterlinck, "Un théâtre d'androides," *Annales de la Fondation Maurice Maeterlinck* 23 (1977) 7-33; Thomas Leabhart, *Modern and Post-Modern Mime* (NY: St. Martin's, 1989) ch. 1 on Copeau; Etienne Decroux, *Words on Mime*, trans. Mark Piper (Claremont, CA: *Mime J*, 1985) 8, from a 1947 essay; Jean-Louis Barrault, *Reflections on the Theatre*, trans. Barbara Wall (L, 1951) 79, 121-22. Cf. Herbert Blau, *Take Up the Bodies* (Urbana: U Illinois, 1982).

53. Barrault, *Reflections on the Theatre*, 124, 126-27; Brown, *Theater and Revolution*, 436-37 on Marcel Carné's film of 1943; Schwartz, "Torque," on movement from the solar plexus.

54. Strict necessity for small companies, multiple roles were also the pride of leading players. Virtuoso changes of character, however, often required quick changes of costume so obvious that audiences would clap for the swiftness of the change rather than for the quality of the acting. See "Doubles," *All the Year 'Round* 29 (1 Mar 1973) 372-78.

55. Phyllis Greenacre, "The impostor," *Psychoanalytic Q* 27 (1958) 359-82, q371; Helene Deutsch, "The impostor," *ibid.* 24 (1955) 483-505, "non-ego ego" at 500; Karl Abraham, trans. by Alex Strachey, "The history of an impostor in the light of psychoanalytic knowledge," *ibid.* 4 (1935) 570-87. See also Woody Allen (dir), *Zelig* (Orion/Warner, 1983), central character a human chameleon.

56. *Memoirs of a Social Monster etc.* (L, 1786); *A More Minute and Particular Account* [of Forgeries and Frauds of various kinds, committed by Charles Price] (L, 1786) 11-16, 54, q16. Price was thought the equal of comedian Samuel Foote, who mimicked other actors, and charlatans; see Simon Trefman, *Sam. Foote, Comedian, 1720-1777* (NY: NYU, 1971) 24-25. Price's impostures were aimed at distributing (what else?) forged banknotes.

57. John M. Gutch, *Carabo[o]. Extraordinary Imposture* (Bristol, 1817) with obituary from *Clifton Chronicle* (11 Jan 1865) pasted on flyleaf of the copy at the Beinecke Rare Book Library, Yale U. A recent film directed by Michael Austin, *Princess Caraboo* (1994), would make it seem as if the mystery of the imposture was at last entirely cleared up, which was never the case; nonetheless, the film is notable for its centering of the imposture within a late Georgian environment of self-deception and theatricality.

58. Richard Kingston, *The Life of William Fuller etc.* (L, 1701), with further details

in George A. Campbell, *Imposter at the Bar: William Fuller, 1670-1733* (L: Hodder and Stoughton, 1961).

59. Frederic J. Foley, *The Great Formosan Imposter* (St. Louis: Jesuit Historical Inst, 1968) esp. 62, keeping his name; Harry M. Paull, *Literary Ethics* (Port Washington, NY: Kennikat, 1968 [1929]) 15 on Innes; Rodney Needham, *Exemplars* (Berkeley: U Cal, 1985) 75-116. Susan Stewart, *Crimes of Writing: Problems in the Containment of Representation* (NY: Oxford U, 1991) 23ff takes Psalmanazar from Assyrian kingship to the "commodification of literary discourse which gradually demands an authenticating apparatus" outside the traditional worlds of patronage.

60. U.S. Department of Justice, Federal Advisory Committee on False Identification, *The Criminal Use of False Identification* (Washington, D.C.: GPO, 1976); Alan Hynd, *Professors of Perfidy* (NY: Barnes, 1963) ch. 9.

61. Robert Crichton, *The Great Impostor* (NY: Random House, 1959) q10, q213; Robert Milligan (dir), *The Great Impostor* (UI, 1961); Ray Ruppert, "The 'Great Impostor' pastor in Friday Harbor," *Seattle Times* (7 Jan 1970) A1, A4; " 'The Great Imposter' reportedly a cleric," *NY Times* (8 Jan 1970) 24; "Notes on people," *ibid.* (6 Apr 1978) C2. To my knowledge, no obituary has appeared.

62. Bernard Wasserstein, *The Secret Lives of Trebitsch Lincoln* (New Haven: Yale U, 1988).

63. Pauline Rose Clance, *The Impostor Phenomenon: Overcoming The Fear That Haunts Your Success* (Atlanta: Peachtree, 1985) claims that "Seventy percent of the successful people in [the U.S.] doubt their success is real." Dr. Clance, with Dr. Suzanne Imes, coined the term "impostor phenomenon" in 1974.

64. Greil Marcus, *Dead Elvis* (NY: Doubleday, 1991) 40-41 on Elvis's twin, Jesse Garon, "long rumored to have been kept alive since 1935 for use in an Elvis Resurrection"; Marie Cahill, ed., *I Am Elvis: A Guide to Elvis Impersonators* (NY: Simon & Schuster, 1991) q10 from Clayton Benke-Smith, q12 from Sammy Stone Atchison; [James G. Semple], [*Memoirs of*] *The Northern Impostor*, 6th ed. (L, 1786) title page; Herbert Brean, "Marvin Hewitt Ph(ony) D.," *Life* (12 Apr 1954) 153.

65. On the Tichborne case, see Charles Reade, *Readiana* (NY: AMS, 1970 [1896]) 110-50; Greenacre, "The impostor," 369; G.E. Harris, *A Treatise on the Law of Identification* (Albany, 1892) 417n-418n, on the court's indecision about the identity of the impostor himself, the pseudo-hermaphroditic Arthur Orton of Wapping via Wagga Wagga, even after the imposture was proved. On Martin Guerre, see François Gayot de Pitaval, *Causes célèbres et intéressantes*, ed. François Richer (Amsterdam, 1772) I, 1-42, studied by Natalie Z. Davis, *The Return of Martin Guerre* (Cambridge, MA: Harvard U, 1983), disputed by Robert Finlay, "The refashioning of Martin Guerre," *Amer Historical R* 93 (June 1988) 553-71, response by Davis, 572-603, refashioned by Hollywood as *Sommersby* (1993). On Colvin, see Gerald W. McFarland, *The "Counterfeit" Man: The True Story of the Boorn-Colvin Murder Case* (NY: Pantheon, 1990). On Anastasia, see Peter Kurth, *Anastasia: The Riddle of Anna Anderson* (Boston: Little, Brown, 1983). In each instance the historical record is still cloudy. The court case was *Stevenson v. Harris et al.*, 238 F. 432 (D.C. NY 1917) at 433. Cf. the film *The Great Impersonation* (1921): a lookalike German spy murders an English nobleman and takes over his life.

66. Etienne Ducret, *Le Charlatanisme dévoilé* (P, 1892) 45.

67. Joseph Capgras and J. Reboul-Lachaux, "L'Illusion des 'sosies' dans un délire systématisé chronique," *Bull de la Société Clinique de Médecine Mentale* 11 (1923) 6-16.

68. *Ibid.*, 9–10. On the doubleness of underground worlds, see Wendy Lesser, *The Life Below the Ground: A Study of the Subterranean in Literature and History* (Boston: Faber and Faber, 1987). On the theme of impersonation during World War I, see esp. Jean Cocteau, *The Impostor (Thomas l'imposteur)*, trans. Dorothy Williams (NY: Noonday, 1957 [1923]).

69. J.P. Luauté, "Joseph Capgras and his syndrome," in *The Delusional Misidentification Syndrome*, ed. G.N. Christodoulou (Basel: Karger, 1986) 9–21; Capgras and Reboul-Lachaux, "L'Illusion des 'sosies,'" q16; Jacques Vié, "Les Méconnaissances systématiques," *Annales médico-psychologiques* 102 (1944) 244. Also used: John Todd, "The history of the syndrome of Capgras," in *Historical Aspects of the Neurosciences*, eds. F.C. Rose and W.F. Bynum (NY: Raven, 1980) 117–25; Robert J. Berson, "Capgras' syndrome," *Amer J Psychiatry* 140 (1983) 969–78.

70. G. Halberstadt, "Le Syndrome d'illusion des sosies," *J de psychologie normale et pathologique* 20 (1923) 728–29, on Mme H.; Jacques Vié, "Un trouble de l'identification des personnes: l'illusion des sosies," *Annales médico-psychologiques* 88 (1930) q215.

71. Jacques Vié, "Les Méconnaissances systématiques," *Annales médico-psychologiques* 103 (1944) 10–12.

72. Jean Nohain and François Caradec, *Frégoli, 1867–1936: sa vie et ses secrets* (P: La Jeune Parque, 1968) 22, 23, 66; "He plays fifty parts," *NY Times* (3 May 1896) 10:3; "Fregoli is a wonder," *ibid.* (13 May 1896) 5:7.

73. Nohain and Caradec, *Frégoli*, 81–86.

74. *Ibid.*, 19, 47, 68–69, 78; P. Courbon and G. Fail, "Syndrome 'd'illusion de Frégoli' et schizophrénie," *Annales médico-psychologiques* 85 (1927) 289–90; J.L. Barton and E.S. Barton, "Misidentification syndromes and sexuality," in Christodoulou, *Delusional Misidentification Syndrome*, 105–20. In 1926, just after Fregoli's retirement, German playwright George Kaiser published *Zweimal Oliver*, whose tragic hero, a quick-change artist, ends up in an asylum where he meets Napoleon, Caesar, the Emperor of China – all those, in fact, whom he had impersonated. He becomes the last Czar of Russia. See Brian J. Kenworthy, *George Kaiser* (Oxford: Blackwell, 1957) 156–58. Six years later, just as Hitler and Stalin were revising political identities, Vladimir Nabokov published *Despair* (NY: Putnam, 1966 [1932]), a case of reverse Fregolism in which only the protagonist sees the close physical resemblance between himself and his tramp Double.

75. Jack Finney, *The Body Snatchers* (Boston: Gregg, 1976 [1955]) 10, 19, 31, 38, 134, 153, 157, 187. This is a reprint retaining the original title page, which reads: "The Body Snatchers / by Jack Finney / an original novel, not a reprint." From this novel came the film directed by Don Siegel, *Invasion of the Body Snatchers* (Allied Artists, 1956), discussed in Phil Hardy, *The Ency of Science Fiction Movies* (Minneapolis: Woodbury, 1986) 159, as is (p. 342) the remake by Philip Kaufman (dir), *Invasion of the Body Snatchers* (Solofilm, 1978), in which the original lead, Kevin McCarthy, does a reprise of his role and Siegel plays a cabbie-pod. Cf. John Brunner, *Double, Double* (NY: Ballantine, 1969) – featuring a parasitic shapechanger which, as it feeds, becomes progressively human *and* twins.

76. Robert G. Bankier, "Capgras' syndrome," *Canadian Psychiatric Assoc J* 11 (1966) 426–29, plastic surgery; Joel A. Moskowitz, "Capgras' syndrome in modern dress," *Int J Child Psychotherapy* 1 (1972) 45–64, television; Alvin Goldfarb and Marcella B. Weiner, "The Capgras syndrome as an adaptational maneuver in old age," *Amer J Psychiatry* 134 (1977) 1434–36; Edwin J. Mikkelsen and Thomas G. Gutheil, "Communication and real-

ity in the Capgras syndrome," *Amer J Psychotherapy* 30 (1976) 136-46; Sadamu Kimura, "Review of 106 cases with the syndrome of Capgras," in Christodoulou, *Delusional Misidentification Syndrome*, 121-30; Stephen F. Signer, "Capgras' syndrome," *J Clinical Psychiatry* 48 (Apr 1987) 150.

77. V.S. Naipaul, *The Mimic Men* (NY: Macmillan, 1967) 25, 146, and cf. Homi Bhabha, "Of mimicry and man: the ambivalence of colonial discourse," *October* 31 (Spr 1984) 125-33. For more on "passing," gender, and race, see Chapter VIII.

78. Dostoevsky, *The Double*, 9, 14, 15, 92, 182.

79. Roger Chartier, *The Cultural Uses of Print in Early Modern France*, trans. Lydia G. Cochrane (Princeton: Princeton U, 1987) 76-96; George B. Johnston, ed., *Poems of Ben Jonson* (Cambridge, MA: Harvard U, 1962) 12, 26; "Duplicité," *EDSAM*, V, 169b.

80. "Artificiality," *Chambers's J* 65 (1888) 289-90. On manners and deception, see Karen Halttunen, *Confidence Men and Painted Women* (New Haven: Yale U, 1982); John F. Kasson, *Rudeness and Civility: Manners in Nineteenth-Century Urban America* (NY: Hill & Wang, 1990). The epitome of this kind of doubling appears in Edward E. Hale's satire, *My Double and How He Undid Me* (Boston, 1895 [1862]), in which a minister employs a somewhat uncouth and untutored fellow to stand in for him at tedious civic functions. Furnished with four short, self-effacing stock speeches, the double succeeds until forced by an impatient crowd to make a longer oration, to which his mannerly sentences are inadequate and badly timed.

81. Kay Desmonde, *Dolls and Dolls Houses* (NY: Crescent, 1972) 49-51; Thomas E. Hill, *Hill's Manual of Social and Business Forms*, 183, Unclassified Laws of Etiquette; Georges Vigarello, *Le Corps redressé* (P: Delarge, 1978) on deportment; Kasson, *Rudeness and Civility*, esp. 166-67 on mirrors.

82. T. Edgar Pemberton, ed., *The Life and Writings of Thomas W. Robertson* (L, 1893) 71, 170, q174 from Clement Scott; Kasson, *Rudeness and Civility*, q148 from Henry Adams, *Democracy* (NY, 1952 [1880]) 144; Ellen K. Rothman, *Hands and Hearts: A History of Courtship in America* (NY: Basic, 1984) on indisciplines of the heart.

83. Ian Ousby, *Bloodhounds of Heaven: The Detective in English Fiction from Godwin to Doyle* (Cambridge, MA: Harvard U, 1976); Mrs. K.F. Hill, *The Twin Detectives* (NY, 1888) featuring Bob Brierly as both, in disguise; Kasson, *Rudeness and Civility*, 105-11; Allan Pinkerton, *A Double Life and the Detectives* (NY, 1885) v; John S. Gibson, *Deacon Brodie: Father to Jekyll and Hyde* (Edinburgh: Paul Harris, 1977); R.L. Stevenson, *Strange Case of Dr. Jekyll and Mr. Hyde* (NY, 1909 [1886]) 373-74, 386: F.W.H. Myers, "Letters to R.L. Stevenson," *R L S: The Critical Heritage*, ed. Paul Maixner (L: Routledge & Kegan Paul, 1981) 219.

84. Arthur L. Wigan, *The Duality of the Mind* (N.P.: Joseph E. Bogen, 1985 [1844]) 19, 21, 96; Anne Harrington, *Medicine, Mind, and the Double Brain: A Study in Nineteenth-Century Thought* (Princeton: Princeton U, 1987) ch. 4; Fisher, "Diploteratology," citing *NY J of Med*, 2nd ser., 1 (Nov 1848) 420. After a stage play of 1897, film versions of *Dr. Jekyll and Mr. Hyde* appeared in 1908 (Selig Polyscope), 1909 (*A Modern Dr. Jekyll*, Selig), 1910 (*The Duality of Man*, Wrench), 1910 (*Den Skaebnesv Angre Opfindelse*, Nordisk), 1912 (Thanhouser), 1913 (Imp), 1914 (*Dr. Jekyll and Mr. Hyde Done to a Frazzle*, Crystal-Superba), 1920 (Famous Players), 1920 (Louis Mayer), and so on. Novelistic episode: [Frank] Gelett Burgess, *The White Cat* (Indianapolis, 1907), modeled on George Du Maurier's *Trilby* (1894).

85. Karl Miller, *Doubles* (NY: Oxford U, 1985) ch. 11; Jane M. Gaines, *Contested*

Culture: The Image, The Voice, and the Law (Chapel Hill: U North Carolina, 1991) 52-54, 80-83 on the poses of Wilde, author of the doublesome *The Picture of Dorian Gray* (1891); Gaston Leroux, *The Double Life* (NY, 1909) on Cartouche; "Double," *Ency of Occultism & Parapsychology*, ed. Leslie Shepard (Detroit: Gale, 1978 [1934]) I, 254-59; Edmund Gurney et al., *Phantasms of the Living*, 2 vols. (Gainesville: U Presses Florida, 1970 [1886]); Herbert E. Chase, *Double Life; or, Starr Cross; an Hypnotic Romance* (NY, 1884) 25; Jacob Korg, "The rage of Caliban," *U of Toronto Q* 37 (Oct 1967) 75, ethical convenience; Jules Janet, "L'Hystérie et l'hypnotisme d'après la théorie de la double personnalité," *Revue scientifique* 41 (1888) 621, on hypnotism, as also Morton Prince, "Some of the revelations of hypnotism," *Boston Med and Surgical J* 122 (15 May 1890) 464 and noting the "hidden self," for which see William James, *The Principles of Psychology* (NY, 1890) I, 373-401. For an historical overview, see Ian Hacking, "Double consciousness in Britain 1815-1875," *Dissociation* 4 (1991) 134-46, now part of his larger work, *Rewriting the Soul: Multiple Personality and the Sciences of Memory* (Princeton: Princeton U, 1995).

86. Cf. the prologue "Anna" from the vocal score to Bertolt Brecht and Kurt Weill, *The Seven Deadly Sins of Ordinary People* (*Die Sieben Todsünden*), trans. W.H. Auden and Chester Kallman (EMI/Capitol, 1983 [1933]), in which Anna and her sister are represented at once as a pair of Siamese twins and as disparate halves, one a little mad, the other rational, both together "really one divided being."

87. J.H. van den Berg, *Divided Existence and Complex Society* (Pittsburgh, 1974); Ian Hacking, "The invention of split personalities," in *Human Nature and Natural Knowledge*, eds. Alan Donagan et al. (Dordrecht: D. Reidel, 1986) 63-85, q66, q79 from Théodule Ribot, *Diseases of Memory* (1881); Schwartz, *Century's End*, 212-19; idem, "The three-body problem and the end of the world," in *Zone 4: Fragments for a History of the Human Body, Part 2*, eds. Michel Feher et al. (NY: Zone, 1989) 420-25.

88. R. Osgood Mason, *Telepathy and the Subliminal Self*, 2nd ed. (NY, 1897) 141; Gillman, *Dark Twins*, 45, from Twain's notebooks, Jan 1898.

89. Sigmund Freud, "The 'uncanny,'" (1919) in *The Standard Edition of the Complete Psychological Works*, trans. James Strachey et al. (L, 1955) XVII, 217-56.

90. On the first case, see S.L. Mitchill, "A double consciousness, or a duality of person in the same individual," *Med Repository* n.s. 3 (1816) 185-86, well-studied by Eric T. Carlson, "The history of multiple personality in the United States: Mary Reynolds and her subsequent reputation," *Bull History Med* 58 (1984) 72-82, and see also, for corrections, Michael G. Kenny, *The Passion of Ansel Bourne: Multiple Personality in American Culture* (Washington, D.C.: Smithsonian, 1986) 46-58; Boris Sidis and Simon P. Goodhart, *Multiple Personality: An Experimental Investigation into the Nature of Human Individuality* (NY, 1905) summarizing most nineteenth-century cases; Schwartz, *Century's End*, 216 – numbers of cases and of personalities; Truddi Chase and Robert A. Phillips, Jr., *When Rabbit Howls* (NY: Dutton, 1987) – over ninety personalities; Henry Hawksworth with Ted Schwarz, *The Five of Me* (Chicago: Regnery, 1977) – sociopaths and the Inner Self-Helper; Schwartz, "Three-body problem," n.38, needlework; Catherine G. Fine, "The work of Antoine Despine: the first scientific report on the diagnosis and treatment of a child with multiple personality disorder," *Amer J Clinical Hypnosis* 31 (July 1988) 33-39, and Edwin D. Starbuck, "Double-mindedness," *Ency of Religion and Ethics*, IV, 860-62, adolescents; Vicki Saltman and Robert S. Solomon, "Incest and the multiple personality," *Psychological Reports* 50 (1982) 1127-41, widely cited.

91. Freud, "The 'uncanny,'" 241; Tobin Siebers, *The Mirror of Medusa* (Berkeley: U Cal, 1983) ch. 5, q113 (Freud) from Ernest Jones, *Life and Work of Sigmund Freud* (NY: Basic, 1955) II, 500, and cf. William McGuire, ed., *The Freud–Jung Letters*, trans. R. Mannheim and R.F.C. Hull (Princeton: Princeton U, 1974) 449; Violet Staub de Laszlo, ed., *Basic Writings of C.G. Jung* (NY: Modern Lib, 1959) 314, 362, 305; Herdman, *Double in Nineteenth-Century Fiction*, 157; Mitchell Walker, "The Double: an archetypal configuration," *Spring* (1976) 165-75. For intermediate positions using Kohut's theory of twinship transference, see Jane Simon and Carl Goldberg, "The role of the double in the creative process and psychoanalysis," *J Amer Academy Psychoanalysis* 12 (July 1984) 341-61; F. von Broembsen, "Twinship," *Amer J Psychoanalysis* 48 (1988) 355-65.

To his own Doppelgänger, Arthur Schnitzler, Freud wrote in 1922 on the occasion of the Viennese novelist's sixtieth birthday, confessing that he had been avoiding Schnitzler, "from a kind of reluctance to meet my double" – a man who knows "through intuition – or rather from detailed self-observation – everything that I have discovered by laborious work on other people." See Ernst L. Freud, *The Letters of Sigmund Freud*, trans. Tania and James Stern (NY: Basic, 1960) 339-40.

92. Kathleen V. Wilkes, *Real People* (Oxford: Oxford U, 1988) ch. 4; Schwartz, *Century's End*, 216; Jonathan Fleming, M.D., Sleep Disorders Clinic, U Hospital, U British Columbia, Vancouver, B.C., interview, 4 Nov 1991, on the controversy, as also Paul F. Dell, "Professional skepticism about multiple personality," *J Nervous and Mental Disease* 176 (Sept 1988) 528-31, and David Spiegel, "The treatment accorded those who treat patients of multiple personality disorder," *ibid.*, 535-36; Sarah M. Steinmeyer, "Some hard-learned lessons in milieu management of multiple personality disorder," *Psychiatric Hospital* 22,1 (1991) 1-4, on divisiveness, as also Barbara L. Drew, "MPD: an historical perspective," *Archives Psychiatric Nursing* 2 (Aug 1988) 227-30; Suzanne Lego, "MPD: an interpersonal approach to etiology, treatment, and nursing care," *ibid.* 2 (Aug 1988) 231-35, the strain; Mary Watkins, *Invisible Guests* (Hillside, NJ: Analytic, 1986) q131; Polly Crisp, "Splitting: a survey of the literature," *J Melanie Klein Soc* 5 (June 1987) 89-136, esp. 116-17, link to MPD, and cf. R. Noll, "Multiple personality, dissociation, and C.G. Jung's complex theory," *J Analytical Psychology* 34 (Oct 1989) 353-70; Colin A. Ross, *Multiple Personality Disorder* (NY: Wiley, 1989) q2 on creativity; James F. Masterson, *The Search for the Real Self: Unmasking the Personality Disorders of Our Age* (NY: Free Press, 1990) 25. Contrast H. Merskey, "The production of multiple personality disorder: the manufacture of multiple personalities," *British J Psychiatry* 160 (Mar 1992) 327-40.

93. Jeremy Hawthorn, *Multiple Personality and the Disintegration of Literary Character* (L: Edward Arnold, 1983); Ulf Bartholomae, *Die Doppelpersönlichkeit in Drama der Moderne* (Erlangen-Nürnberg: Friedrich-Alexander-Universität, 1967). For examples, see Rainer Maria Rilke, *The Journal of My Other Self*, trans. John Linton (NY, 1930 [1910]); Michael Richardson's anthology, *DoubleDouble* (Harmondsworth: Penguin, 1987); and works by such fabulists as John Barth, Jorge Luis Borges, Italo Calvino, and Julio Cortázar.

On Reynolds, see Kenny, *Passion of Ansel Bourne*, 58. On Alma Z., see R. Osgood Mason, "Duplex personality," *J Nervous and Mental Disease* 18 (Sept 1893) 593-98. On Fowler, see Morton Prince, *The Dissociation of a Personality*, 2nd ed. (NY, 1908 [Dec 1905]) with follow-up, "Miss Beauchamp: the theory of the psychogenesis of multiple personality," *J Abnormal Psychology* 15 (1920) 67-135; Morton Prince, *Psychotherapy and*

Multiple Personality: Selected Essays, ed. Nathan G. Hale, Jr. (Cambridge, MA: Harvard U, 1975) esp. Hale's introduction, 1–18; Saul Rosenzweig, "Sally Beauchamp's career: a psychoarchaeological key," *Genetic, Social, and General Psychology Monographs* 113 (Feb 1987) 5–60; Adolph Klauber, " 'The Case of Becky' and the real case," *NY Times* (6 Oct 1912) IX, 2:1; *Bachman v. Belasco*, 224 Fed 815 (D.C. NY 1913) and 224 Fed 817 (C.C.A. 2d 1915); "Her Other Self," *Lubin Bull*, release date 26 May 1915, in Siegmund Lubin clippings file, Theater Collection, Lincoln Center Performing Arts Lib, NY Public Lib. On Mansfield, see Claude Rawson, "The mimic art [reviewing Claire Tomalin, *Katherine Mansfield*]," *Times Literary Supplement* (8–14 Jan 1988) q27–28 from Brigid Brophy.

94. Ray Aldridge-Morris, *Multiple Personality: An Exercise in Deception* (Hove: Erlbaum, 1989); Thomas A. Fahey, "The diagnosis of MPD," *British J Psychiatry* 153 (Nov 1988) 597–606 on "borderline personality"; Michael A. Simpson, "MPD," *ibid.* 155 (Oct 1989) 565; Arnold Gesell, "Mental and physical correspondence in twins," *Sci Monthly* 14 (May 1922) q415, Morton Prince on gold mine; Russell C. Packard and Frank Brown, "Multiple headaches in a case of MPD," *Headache* 26 (Feb 1986) 99–102; John Leo, "The 27 faces of 'Charles,' " *Time* (25 Oct 1982) 70, and "His body is host to 27 personalities," *Durham (NC) Morning Herald* (23 Oct 1982); Susan S. Beck and James A. Chu, "The simulation of multiple personalities," *Psychotherapy* 28 (1991) 267–72; Jonathan Fleming, interview, "fascinoma"; Daniel Keyes, *The Minds of Billy Milligan* (Toronto: Bantam, 1981); Ralph B. Allison, "Difficulties diagnosing the multiple personality syndrome in a death penalty case," *Int J Clinical and Experimental Hypnosis* 32 (Apr 1984) 102–17; Martin T. Orne et al., "On the differential diagnosis of multiple personality in the forensic context," *ibid.* 32 (Jan 1984) 118–67, and see Corbett H. Thigpen and Hervey M. Cleckley, "On the incidence of MPD," *ibid.* 32 (1984) 63–66, an attack on the too-frequent diagnosis of MPD – by two men responsible for its reemergence, via *The Three Faces of Eve*, the book (NY: Popular Lib, 1957) and the movie (TCF, 1957); Nicholas Humphrey and Daniel C. Dennett, "Speaking for our selves: an assessment of MPD," *Raritan* 9 (Sum 1989) 68–98, on *folie à deux* and line from *Richard II*. Outside the Atlantic ecumene, MPD appears instead as possession or latah, or in a glamorous Westernized imitation; see G.S.P. Raju Adityanjee and S.K. Khandelwal, "Current status of MPD in India," *Amer J Psychiatry* 146 (Dec 1989) 1607–10.

95. Neal A. Kline, "Multiple personality: the new royal road?" *Amer J Psychiatry* 147 (Apr 1990) 538–39; Catherine G. Fine, "President's message," *ISSMP&D News* (Oct 1991) 2; Jonas Barish, *The Anti-Theatrical Prejudice* (Berkeley: U Cal, 1981); Richard P. Kluft, "The simulation and dissimulation of MPD," *Amer J Clinical Hypnosis* 30 (Oct 1987) 104–18; Philip M. Coons et al., "Multiple personality disorder: a clinical investigation of 50 cases," *J Nervous and Mental Disease* 176 (Sept 1988) 519–27, misdiagnoses; Colin A. Ross and G. Ron Norton, "Suicide and parasuicide in MPD," *Psychiatry* 52 (Aug 1989) 365–71; Colin A. Ross et al., "MPD: an analysis of 236 cases," *Canadian J Psychiatry* 34 (June 1989) 413–18.

96. James A. Chu, "The Critical Issues Task Force report: strategies for evaluating the validity of reports of childhood abuse," *ISSMP&D News* (Dec 1991) 5–7, and idem, "The repetition compulsion revisited: reliving dissociated trauma," *Psychotherapy* 28 (1991) 327–32, parallels to Freud, which however I am taking in a non-Euclidean direction; Larry Wolff, *Postcards from the End of the World: Child Abuse in Freud's Vienna* (NY: Atheneum, 1988), and cf. Jeffrey M. Masson, *The Assault on Truth: Freud's Suppression of the Seduction Theory* (NY: Farrar, Straus and Giroux, 1984); Peggy L. Dawson, "The issue

is – understanding skepticism toward MPD," *Amer J Occupational Therapy* 44 (Nov 1990) 1048-50; Jonathan Fleming, interview, on confirming biographical details; Ross, *Multiple Personality Disorder*, 10, Osiris myth, reinterpreted by Allucquère Rosanne Stone, *The War of Desire and Technology at the Close of the Mechanical Age* (Cambridge, MA: MIT, 1995) ch. 2, meditating upon the court case of an Oshkosh woman, previously diagnosed with MPD, who claimed that a male acquaintance in 1990 had raped her after eliciting one of her most vulnerable multiple personalities, a naive young woman.

97.   Judith Hooper and Dick Teresi, "Mind menagerie," *Omni* 8 (Jan 1986) q104 from Frank Putnam; Saul Rosenzweig, "The identity and idiodynamics of the multiple personality 'Sally Beauchamp': a confirmatory supplement," *Amer Psychologist* 43 (Jan 1988) 45–48, and his "Sally Beauchamp's career." On Eve, see Chris Costner Sizemore and Elen Sain Pittillo, *I'm Eve* (Garden City: Doubleday, 1977) ch. 5; Chris Costner Sizemore, *A Mind of My Own* (NY: Morrow, 1989); Ellen Dean (= Elen Sain Pittillo), transcript of audiotape, 16 July 1973, p. 5, Printed Material folder, Legal and Financial Papers; Louise Edwards, Edgefield, SC, letter of 27 Oct 1975, with response 5 Nov 1975, Correspondence, Jan 1958 – Dec 1975, all in the Christine (Costner) Sizemore Papers, Special Collections Lib, Duke U, used with permission. For Melinda, see Reese Price, "Of multiple personalities and dissociated selves: the fragmentation of the shield," *Transactional Analysis J* 18 (July 1988) 231-77. For Toby, see Robert S. Mayer, *Through a Mind Divided* (NY: Doubleday, 1988).

98.   Sidis and Goodhart, *Multiple Personality*, 57 on continuous history, and cf. 364 on "mental synthesis" of the "dicephalous" person; Wilkes, *Real People*, 121, 129, pressures to unify; Margo Rivera, "Am I a boy or a girl? Multiple personality as a window on gender differences," *Resources for Feminist Research* 17 (June 1988) 41–46, suggesting also that more men might be found to have MPD were they not culturally restrained from talking about themselves as split and were they not physically restrained in jails. For a political parallel, see W. Tschaikovskaja, "Die typologische Struktur des Doppelgängers in der Kunst," *Kunst und Literatur* 30 (Apr 1982) 354–63, arguing that capitalism has used the Doppelgänger to set good against bad, while Marxism uses it as a vehicle for showing (p. 363) the "human being in all its complexity and protean nature."

99.   The mean number of personalities to a case of MPD has risen from 6.3 to 15.7; see Coons et al., "MPD: a clinical investigation of 50 cases," 522; Mary Jo Nissen et al., "Memory and awareness in a patient with MPD," *Brain and Cognition* 8 (Aug 1989) 118; Ross et al., "MPD: an analysis of 236 cases," 413. For the rest of the paragraph, see Edward Shorter, *From Paralysis to Fatigue: A History of Psychosomatic Illness in the Modern Era* (NY: Free Press, 1992); Seymour L. Halleck, "Dissociative phenomena and the question of responsibility," *Int J Clinical and Experimental Hypnosis* 38 (1990) 298–314, a suggestive essay; David Spiegel, "Multiple personality as a post-traumatic stress disorder," *Psychiatric Clinics North Amer* 7,1 (1984) 101-10, updated in B. Bower, "Post-traumatic stress disorder: hypnosis and the divided self," *Sci News* 133 (1988) 197. Contrast P. Flor-Henry et al., "Neurophysiological and neuropsychological study of two cases of multiple personality syndrome...," *Int J Psychophysiology* 10 (Dec 1990) 151–61, organic etiology for MPD. For a contrasting psychological perspective, see Heinz Kohut, *The Restoration of the Self* (NY: Int Universities, 1977) ch. 4 on the bipolar self.

100.   *Brain/Mind Bulletin* 8 (3 Oct 1984) 2, statement by John Beahrs and Brenda O'Regan of the Institute of Noetic Sciences that "Multiples may be *the* most important route to understanding and gaining access to the untapped skills and potentials we all

have"; Betty Edwards, *Drawing on the Right Side of the Brain* (LA: Tarcher, 1979) vii; James Moor, "Split brains and atomic persons," *Phil of Sci* 49 (Mar 1982) 104, replying to the seminal essay by Roland Puccetti, "Brain bisection and personal identity," *British J for the Phil of Sci* 24 (1973) 339-55, and see the entire issue of *J Med and Phil* 2,2 (1977); Robert Silverberg, "In the House of Doubleminds," in his *The Feast of Dionysus* (L: Gollancz, 1976) 155-80; Julian Jaynes, *The Origin of Consciousness in the Breakdown of the Bicameral Mind* (Boston: Houghton Mifflin, 1976).

CHAPTER THREE: SELF-PORTRAITS

1. Hillel Schwartz, *Century's End* (NY: Doubleday, 1990) esp. 166-69, 190-91, 245-46, 281-83 on acceleration; Michael Young, *The Metronomic Society* (Cambridge, MA: Harvard U, 1988); Christopher Lasch, *The Culture of Narcissism* (NY: Warner, 1979); Jay Martin, *Who Am I This Time? Uncovering the Fictive Personality* (NY: Norton, 1988); Guy Debord, *Society of the Spectacle*, trans. Donald Nicholson-Smith (NY: Zone, 1994) esp. pars. 42, 48, 154, 158; Jean Baudrillard, *Simulations*, trans. Paul Foss et al. (NY: Semiotext[e], 1983), and idem, *Selected Writings*, ed. Mark Poster (Stanford: Stanford U, 1988). Much of this is reconsidered by Fredric Jameson, *Postmodernism, or, the Cultural Logic of Late Capitalism* (Durham: Duke U, 1991).

2. Lanny Bell, "Luxor Temple and the cult of the royal *ka*," *J Near Eastern Soc* 44 (1985) 251-94; Peter Kaplony, "Ka," *Lexikon der Ägyptologie*, ed. W. Helck et al. (Wiesbaden: Harrassowitz, 1972-) 175-82; Patricia Springborg, *Royal Persons: Patriarchal Monarchy and the Feminine Principle* (L: Unwin Hyman, 1990) 52-56, 89-109, noting how well the institution of the *ka* fit Egyptian queens as well as kings; Jean-Pierre Vernant, *Mythe et pensée chez les Grecs* (P: La Découverte, 1988) 325-52.

3. W.H. St. John Hope, "On the funeral effigies of the kings and queens of England," *Archaeologia* 60 (1907) 524-27, 541-42; Ernest H. Kantorowicz, *The King's Two Bodies* (Princeton: Princeton U, 1957) 420-25; Frances A. Yates, "French royal funerals in the Renaissance [reviewing Ralph E. Giesey, *The Royal Funeral Ceremony in Renaissance France* (1960)]," *Ideas and Ideals in the North European Renaissance: Collected Essays, III* (L: Routledge and Kegan Paul, 1984) 164-66.

4. Jonathan Z. Smith, *To Take Place: Toward Theory in Ritual* (Chicago: U Chicago, 1987). Contrast Susan Stewart, *On Longing: Narratives of the Miniature, the Gigantic, the Souvenir, the Collection* (Baltimore: Johns Hopkins, 1984). Hans Belting, *Likeness and Presence: A History of the Image Before the Era of Art*, trans. Edmund Jephcott (Chicago: U Chicago, 1994) 409-10, describing "the era of the private image at the end of the Middle Ages," makes much the same set of distinctions between private, portable, timely portraits and public, giant, archaistic portraits as I am making between the miniature and the colossus. On Renaissance portraiture, cf. John Shearman, *Only Connect...Art and the Spectator in the Italian Renaissance* (Princeton: Princeton U, 1992) ch. 3. See also Angelica Dülberg, *Privatporträts: Geschichte und Ikonologie einer Gattung im 15. und 16. Jahrhundert* (Berlin: Mann, 1990) for reproductions of many early modern (and miniature) "private portraits."

5. Marianne Lowe, "Trends in the development of representational play in infants from one to three years," *J Child Psychology and Psychiatry* 16 (1975) 33-47, q45; Mary M. Watkins, *Invisible Guests: The Development of Imaginal Dialogues* (Hillside, NJ: Analytic, 1986).

6. Paolo Squatriti, "Personal appearance and physiognomics in early medieval Italy," *J Medieval History* 14 (Sept 1988) 191-202; William Hood, "Fra Angelico at San Marco,"

in *Christianity and the Renaissance: Image and Religious Imagination in the Quattrocento*, eds. T. Verdon and J. Henderson (Syracuse: Syracuse U, 1990) 108-31; Janet Backhouse, "Illuminated manuscripts and the early development of the portrait miniature," in *Early Tudor England*, ed. Daniel Williams (Wolfeboro: Boydell, 1989) 1-17; Linda Klinger, "Portrait collections and portrait books in the sixteenth century," in *Paolo Giovio: il rinascimento e la memoria* (Como: Società a Villa Gallia, 1985) 181-83; Nicholas Hilliard, *A Treatise concerning the Arte of Limning*, eds. R.K.R. Thornton and T.G.S. Cain (Ashington: Mid-Northumberland Arts, 1981 [1598-1602]); undated ad, late 1700s, in Daniel Lysons, *Collectanea, II: Publick Exhibitions and Places of Amusement*, 140v, a scrapbook in the British Lib, C.103.k.11 (henceforth, Lysons, *Collectanea II*). Cf. Louis Marin, *Portrait of the King*, trans. Martha M. Houle (Minneapolis: U Minnesota, 1988) 121-68 on those miniatures we call "coins of the realm," and Patricia Fumerton, *Cultural Aesthetics: Renaissance Literature and the Practice of Social Ornament* (Chicago: U Chicago, 1991) ch. 3 on the close relationship between bedrooms and miniatures.

7. Alice Van Leer Carrick, *A History of American Silhouettes* (Portland, VT: Tuttle, 1968 [1928]) 4, 11, q51 (King), 126, q140-41 (Edouart), 157-58; Albert Goodwin, "Silhouette, Etienne de," *Ency Britannica* (Chicago, 1965) XX, 653; Rodolphe L. Mégroz, *Profile Art Through the Ages* (NY, 1949) 96; Torben H. Colding, *Aspects of Miniature Painting, Its Origins and Development* (Copenhagen: Munksgaard, 1953) 14-15; Jean Lipman, *Rufus Porter, Yankee Pioneer* (NY: Clarkson N. Potter, 1968) 66.

8. Erasmus, *Ciceronianus* (1528), trans. and ed. A.H.T. Levi, in *Collected Works* (Toronto: U Toronto, 1986) XXVIII, 374. Cf. Richard Bernheimer, *The Nature of Representation: A Phenomenological Inquiry*, ed. H.W. Janson (NY: NYU, 1961) 11, who says, "Unless there is in art a deeper purpose than the mere duplication of reality, it might just as well be abandoned," but links this to "an older attitude which asked for visual objects capable of replacing their prototypes and being identified with them." On this older attitude, see esp. Gilbert Dagron, "Holy images and likenesses," *Dumbarton Oaks Papers* 45 (1991) 23-35; Belting, *Likeness and Presence*.

9. Mary E. Fouratt, "Ruth Henshaw Bascom, itinerant portraitist," in *Itinerancy in New England and New York*, eds. Peter Benes et al. (Concord: Boston U, 1986) 204, as also Joyce Hill, "New England itinerant portraitists," 160, 163; W.T. Stead, *Portraits and Autographs* (L, 1890) 139, 142.

10. Hill, "New England itinerant portraitists," 160 on Brown; Mégroz, *Profile Art*, 93 on Hubard; René Hennequin, *Avant les photographies: les portraits au physionotrace gravés de 1788 à 1830* (Troyes, 1926-27) esp. 5, 5n, 6n, 12 on the Dauphin; Fillmore Norfleet, *Saint-Mémin in Virginia* (Richmond, VA, 1942) 11-33. At the other end of the social scale, Rembrandt Peale sped up the profiling process and charged his fellow Philadelphians two bits: Carrick, *American Silhouettes*, 29-30.

11. Norfleet, *Saint-Mémin in Virginia*, 63-64.

12. Isaac Augustus Wetherby, Account Books, vol. I, entries for 9 July 1839, June (July?) 1840, June 1841, 15 Nov 1841, Oct 1841, Dec 1841, 28 June 1842 (tomb), 6 June 1845, Sept 1846, 11 Dec 1848, Aug 1854, 1855 summary, from photostats at the New-York Historical Soc, NY City; Ross J. Kelbaugh, "Dawn of the Daguerrean era in Baltimore, 1839-1849," *Maryland Historical Mag* 84 (Sum 1989) 101; John Tagg, *The Burden of Representation: Essays in Photographies and Histories* (Amherst: U Massachusetts, 1988) 43; Asa Briggs, *Victorian Things* (L: Batsford, 1988) 130; Anne McCauley, *Industrial Madness: Commercial Photography in Paris, 1848-1871* (New Haven: Yale U, 1994).

13. L.J.M. Daguerre, *An Historical and Descriptive Account of the…Daguerréotype and Diorama* (NY: Kraus, 1969 [1839]) 2; Helmut Gernsheim and Alison Gernsheim, *L.J.M. Daguerre (1787–1851)* (Cleveland: World, 1956) 106–08; Alan Thomas, *Time in a Frame: Photography and the Nineteenth-Century Mind* (NY: Schocken, 1977) 14; Stanley B. Burns, *Sleeping Beauty: Memorial Photography in America* (Altadena: Twelve Trees, 1990) Chronology, esp. 1844 (one of the first books containing a photograph was the *Record of the Death-bed of C.M.W.*); Henry H. Snelling, *The History and Practice of the Art of Photography* (Hastings-on-Hudson: Morgan and Morgan, 1970 [1849]) 24, q41, 57, 64; Betty Miller, ed., *Elizabeth Barrett to Miss Mitford* (L: John Murray, 1954) 208–09, quoted unsourced by Susan Sontag, *On Photography* (NY: Farrar Straus Giroux, 1977) 183.

14. "The future of photography," *Littell's Living Age*, 4th ser., 11 (Dec 1868) 821, originally in *The Imperial R.*

15. Bibliothèque Nationale, *After Daguerre: Masterworks of French Photography (1848–1900)* (NY: Metropolitan Museum of Art, 1981) 29, multi-lens; Reese V. Jenkins, *Images and Enterprise: Technology and the American Photographic Industry, 1839–1925* (Baltimore: Johns Hopkins, 1987); H.J. Moulton, *Houdini's History of Magic in Boston, 1792–1915*, ed. Milbourne Christopher (Glenwood, IL: Meyer, 1983) 57; Michael Mitchell, *Monsters of the Gilded Age: The Photographs of Charles Eisenmann* (Toronto: Gage, 1979) 15.

16. Alan Trachtenberg, *Reading American Photographs* (NY: Hill and Wang, 1989) 31, plate 3; Sontag, *On Photography*, jacket; Burns, *Sleeping Beauty*, #17, #18; Michael Gibbs, "Spiriting in and out," *Perspektief* 34 (Dec 1988) 4–7; Janet Oppenheim, *The Other World: Spiritualism and Psychic Research in England, 1850–1914* (Cambridge: Cambridge U, 1985) 70–71, 351–52; Edward L. Wilson, *Wilson's Cyclopaedic Photography* (NY, 1894) 130; Paul N. Hasluck, *The Book of Photography* (L, 1905) 716, "Doubles" and "Trebles"; M.H. Lockwood, Durham, NC, letter, 21 Feb 1897, Curator's Collection, from the Craven-Pegram Papers, Special Collections Lib, Duke U.

17. Briggs, *Victorian Things*, 122–23; Lewis Carroll, "Hiawatha's Photographing" (1883) in *Complete Illustrated Works*, ed. Edward Guiliano (NY: Avenel, 1982) 250–58; A. Liébert, *La Photographie en Amérique*, 2nd ed. (P, 1874) 167–68; Snelling, *History of the Art of Photography*, 132; Lake Price, *A Manual of Photographic Manipulation*, 2nd ed. (L, 1868) 159; E. Joly, *La Photographie pratique* (P, 1887) 29; Scoville Photographic Series, *The Modern Practice of Retouching Negatives, as Practiced by French, German, English and American Experts*, 8th ed. (NY, 1893, revising 7th ed. by Piquepé) preface, 1–2, 13, 14. A Negafake box is on display at the Museum of Moving Images (L).

18. John Randolph to sister Fanny, letter of 31 Dec 1805, in the Tucker-Coalter Family Papers, Special Collections Library, Duke University; J.P. Ourdan, *The Art of Retouching by Burrows & Colton, revised* (NY: Arno, 1973 [1880]) 11–13; R. Child Bayley, *The Complete Photographer* (NY, 1907) 167; Mitchell, *Monsters of the Gilded Age*, 19–20. Cf. Audrey Linkman, *The Victorians: Photographic Portraits* (NY: Tauris, 1993).

19. Lady Elizabeth Eastlake, "Photography," *Q R* 101 (Apr 1857), cited by Doug Nickel, "The camera and other drawing machines," in *British Photography in the Nineteenth Century*, ed. Mike Weaver (NY: Oxford U, 1989) 1. Cf. Alan Sekula, "The traffic in photographs," in *Modernism and Modernity*, eds. B.H.D. Buchloh et al. (Halifax: College of Art and Design, 1983) 121–54 on capitalism, fetishism, and photography.

20. "Brady's photographs: pictures of the dead at Antietam," *NY Times* (20 Oct 1862) 5; William A. Frassanito, *Gettysburg: A Journey in Time* (NY: Scribner, 1975) 18, 27–28,

30–31, 175, 181, 185, 187–93, using Frederic Ray, "The case of the rearranged corpse," *Civil War Times* 3 (Oct 1961) 19; D. Mark Katz, *Witness to an Era: The Life and Photographs of Alexander Gardner* (NY: Viking, 1991) esp. 68, 122. Roger Fenton's photos of the Crimean War (1854–55) and Felice A. Beato's photos of the Sepoy Mutiny (1857) and Opium Wars (1859) had much the same effect in England as Brady's work in the U.S.: Thomas, *Time in a Frame*, 29–30.

21. *Udderzook v. Commonwealth*, 76 Penn St 340 (1874) at 352–53; Charles C. Moore, *A Treatise on Facts or the Weight and Value of Evidence* (Northport, Long Island, 1908) q705 (*Tome v. Parkersburg Branch Railroad Co.*, 39 Md 36, 95), 707, 1361–63. Cf. Jane M. Gaines, *Contested Culture: The Image, the Voice, the Law* (Chapel Hill: U North Carolina, 1991) ch. 2.

22. Alphonse Bertillon, *La Photographie judiciaire* (P, 1890) 3, 4, q10, 12–13, 20; Suzanne Bertillon, *Vie d'Alphonse Bertillon* (P, 1941) 110, 120; Henry T.F. Rhodes, *Alphonse Bertillon, Father of Scientific Detection* (NY: Abelard-Schuman, 1956) 93–107. Cf. Elwood C. Parry, III, "Thomas Eakins's 'Naked Series' reconsidered," *Amer Art J* 20 (1988) 53–77, similar systems of posing models and criminals.

Some phrenologists, physicians and (later) anthropologists did hope to use photography to classify human types; for most shutterbugs, however, as for detectives and prosecutors, photographs were invaluable to the telling of one face from another. See David A. Hanson, "The beginnings of photographic reproduction in the USA," *History of Photography* 12 (Oct 1988) 364; Tagg, *Burden of Representation*, 5–9, 80–83; Francis Galton, *Memories of My Life*, 3rd ed. (L, 1909) ch. 18.

23. Rhodes, *Alphonse Bertillon*, esp. 28–29, 34–36, 41, 62–63, 73–77, 94, 97–98; Harry Söderman and John J. O'Connell, *Modern Criminal Investigation* (NY, 1940) 40, 43, associating the rise of photographic police files with the end of the branding of criminals (France, 1832; Holland, 1854), and listing 49 false identities pierced by Bertillon's method in 1882, 241 in 1883, 680 in 1892. See also Suzanne Bertillon, *Vie d'Alphonse Bertillon*, 110, 165, and denying that her mother Amélie née Notar, copyist for her father's file of five million profile cards, went mad upon Alphonse's death in 1914.

24. Bertillon, *La Photographie judiciaire*, 8–9, 11; Rodolphe A. Reiss, *La Photographie judiciaire*, dedicated to Bertillon (P, 1903) 9–11, 15–18. On the Shroud, its cloth now dated to 1260–1380 A.D. but the image process still mysterious, see Ian Wilson, *The Evidence of the Shroud* (L: O'Mara, 1986) 4; E.T. Hall, "The Turin Shroud," *Archaeometry* 31,1 (1989) 92–95.

25. Jacques Delarue, "Origines de la carte d'identité," *Histoire* 48 (Sept 1982) 95–99; George Burchett, *Memoirs of a Tattooist*, ed. Peter Leighton (NY: Crown, 1958) 65, 69; Alan B. Govenar, "The changing image of tattooing in American culture," *J of Amer Culture* 5,1 (Spr 1982) 30–37; Suzanne Bertillon, *Vie d'Alphonse Bertillon*, 172; Galton, *Memories*, 250–54; Louise Odes Neaderland, *Life-Sense/License* (NY: Bone Hollow Arts, 1983), and letter to the author, 21 Sept 1992.

26. Jean Nicolas Gannal, *History of Embalming*, trans. R. Harlan (Philadelphia, 1840) 25n, 26–27; Eliab Myers, *The Champion Text-Book on Embalming*, 4th ed. (Springfield, OH, 1900) 223, 234; Clarence G. Strub and L.G. "Darko" Frederick, *The Principles and Practice of Embalming*, 4th ed. (Dallas: Frederick, 1967) 31, 33; Caroline Walker Bynum, *The Resurrection of the Body in Western Christianity, 200–1336* (NY: Columbia U, 1995); Michael Ragon, *The Space of Death* (Charlottesville: U Press Virginia, 1983) 8.

27. Philippe Ariès, *Western Attitudes Toward Death: From the Middle Ages to the*

Present, trans. Patricia M. Ranum (Baltimore: Johns Hopkins U, 1974); Mary Catherine O'Connor, *The Art of Dying Well: The Development of the Ars Moriendi* (NY, 1942); Nancy Lee Beaty, *The Craft of Dying* (New Haven: Yale U, 1970); David Charles Sloane, *The Last Great Necessity: Cemeteries in American History* (Baltimore: Johns Hopkins U, 1991) 120; Myers, *Champion Text-Book* 250-51, 542; Burns, *Sleeping Beauty*, #48, #51, #71, and unpaginated chronology, "Death in America."

28. Sloane, *Last Great Necessity*, 3.

29. Strub and Frederick, *Principles and Practice*, 44; James M. Ball, *The Sack-'em-Up-Men: An Account of the Rise and Fall of the Modern Resurrectionists* (Edingburgh, 1928). Unlikely to rise again – unless impetuous relatives had mistaken coma for death, a common twist in nineteenth-century fiction. Being buried alive was a Poe horror story and a ghost story; embalming insured against both the horror and the haunting.

30. Roland Barthes, *La Chambre claire* (P: Seuil, 1980) 30-31, 128, 145; Burns, *Sleeping Beauty*, q epigraph, #2, 5, 11, 28, 41, 56, 74; Jay Ruby, *Secure the Shadow: Death and Photography in America* (Cambridge, MA: MIT, 1995); Nancy M. West, "Camera fiends: early photography, death, and the supernatural," *Centennial R* 40, 1 (1996) 170-206.

31. Burns, *Sleeping Beauty*, #s 2, 5, 14, 27, 45; E.V. Gillon, Jr., *Victorian Cemetery Art* (NY: Dover, 1972) 4, 12; Sloane, *Last Great Necessity*, 22, 77, 79; Giovanni Grasso and Graziella Pellicci, *Staglieno* (Genoa: Sagep, 1974) 38-40, 56.

32. *Hutchings Cal Mag*, quoted by Burns, *Sleeping Beauty*, unpag. chronology, 1857, and see 1851 for patent of method to embed daguerreotypes in tombstones; Nicholas Penny, *Mourning* (L: Victoria and Albert Museum, 1981) chs. 4-5; John Morley, *Death, Heaven and the Victorians* (Pittsburgh: U Pittsburgh, 1971); David Price, *Magic: A Pictorial History of Conjurors in the Theater* (NY: Cornwall, 1985) 67-69, 75 on black formal dress. The word "lifesize" was itself new to the nineteenth century: *OED*, VIII, 917.

33. Gannal, *History of Embalming*, 19, italics omitted; Robert G. Mayer, *Embalming: History, Theory and Practice* (Norwalk: Appleton and Lange, 1990) esp. 46-47, 53-54 on embalming fluids; Strub and Frederick, *Principles and Practice*, q136.

34. George L. Mosse, *Fallen Soldiers: Reshaping the Memory of the World Wars* (NY: Oxford U, 1990) 81-85; Sloane, *Last Great Necessity*, 143-52, 159-87, 238-39; Eustace Cockrell, "O Death, where is thy sting?" *Fortnight* (June 1955) 27-29; "Cemetery planned for the living," *San Diego Union* (6 Aug 1961) 1:4-8; Forest Lawn Mortuary, *Forest Lawn: History, Religion, Art*, Form #1510-2 (Glendale, 1989).

35. Forest Lawn Mortuary, *Forest Lawn: History, Religion, Art*; Sam Hunter and Don Hawthorne, *George Segal* (NY: Rizzoli, 1984) esp. 35; Christine Lindey, *Superrealist Painting and Sculpture* (L: Orbis, 1980) 130ff; Maurice Blanchot, "Two versions of the imaginary," in his *The Space of Literature*, trans. Ann Smock (Lincoln: U Nebraska, 1982 [1955]) 256-60, q258.

36. Max von Boehn, *Dolls and Puppets*, trans. Josephine Nicoll (NY: Cooper Square, 1966 [1929]) 69-72.

37. Mary Hillier, *History of Wax Dolls* (Cumberland, MD: Hobby House, 1985) 19, 24-25; John Timbs, *Curiosities of London* (Detroit: Singing Tree, 1968 [1867]) 818-20; Boehn, *Dolls and Puppets*, 72, 90, 93-94; David Freedberg, *The Power of Images* (Chicago: U Chicago, 1989) ch. 9, and q199 from Samuel Butler, *Alps and Sanctuaries* (L, 1986 [1881]) 249-51.

38. Boehn, *Dolls and Puppets*, 93-94; Frédéric Dillaye, "Les figures de cire," *J de la*

jeunesse 20 (1882) 151; Hillier, *History of Wax Dolls*, 20–22, 30; Lysons, *Collectanea II*, 139 for Patience Wright; John Timbs, *Curiosities of London* (L, 1871) 350. The young boy was George Smeeton, according to his own manuscript note, p. 40, June 1837, to his *Exhibitions of Mechanical and Other Works of Ingenuity, 1700–1840*, scrapbook in the British Lib, 1269.h.38, as also in Richard D. Altick, *The Shows of London* (Cambridge, MA: Harvard U, 1978) 53, and see Altick's ch. 4 on waxwork and clockwork.

39. Pauline Chapman, *Madame Tussaud's Chamber of Horrors* (L: Constable, 1984) xiii, 2, 5, 10, 12–13, 15, 29, 41, 50; *Madame Tussaud's Guide and Biographies* (L: Madame Tussaud's, 1960) 35; Leonard Cottrell, *Madame Tussaud* (L, 1951) 24–25, q16, 29–30, 89, 92, 95, 97. See also Jean Adhémar, "Les musées de cire en France," *Gazette des Beaux-Arts* 120 (Dec 1978) 203–14.

40. Cottrell, *Madame Tussaud*, 47, 101, q108, 120, 121, 124, 134, 142, and q114 (Nottingham, 24 Sept 1819); Smeeton, *Exhibitions*, 65, Mme Tussaud handbill, Feb 1834, mummy; Chapman, *Madame Tussaud's*, 11, 50; [J. Mead], *London Interiors* (L, 1841) q137. Mme Tussaud initially toured with her husband, who had managed Curtius's salon in London, but François soon returned to France.

41. Mead, *London Interiors*, q138 (my italics); Cottrell, *Madame Tussaud*, q115 ("excellent deception" from a Lincoln newspaper, 1819), 142 on her wax self-portrait.

42. Smeeton, *Exhibitions*, 45 (Dec 1832 handbill for Royal Exhibition of Wax Work), 49 (Mar 1831, Messrs. Ewings' Royal Wax Figures), 55 (1830s, Mons. Robin's wax figures); Cottrell, *Madame Tussaud*, 133; G.B. Bartlett, *Mrs. Jarley's Far-Famed Collection of Waxworks* (NY, 1873) 10, Siamese twins; Dillaye, "Figures de cire," 154, 170–71; Nathaniel Hawthorne, *The American Notebooks*, ed. Claude M. Simpson (Columbus: Ohio State U, 1972) 176–77.

43. Michele Bogart, "Photosculpture," *Art History* 4 (1981) 54–65; Hillier, *History of Wax Dolls*, 50, on Andras; E.J. Pyke, *Biographical Dictionary of Wax Modellers* (Oxford: Clarendon, 1973) listing a multitude of women. For Mrs. Worlidge, see Horace Walpole, *Anecdotes of Painting in England*, ed. Ralph N. Wornum (L, 1862 [1762–80]) II, 718–19. On women's work, see esp. Jeanne Boydston, *Home and Work: Housework, Wages, and the Ideology of Labor in the Early Republic* (NY: Oxford, 1990); Sylvia Walby, *Theorizing Patriarchy* (Oxford: Blackwell, 1990) ch. 8.

44. Norbert Elias, *The Civilizing Process: The Development of Manners*, trans. Edmund Jephcott (NY: Urizen, 1978 [1939]) esp. 129ff; Alain Corbin, *The Foul and the Fragrant*, trans. Miriam L. Kochan et al. (Cambridge, MA: Harvard U, 1986).

45. Ashley Halsey, Jr., "House of illusion," *Saturday Evening Post* (12 Apr 1958) 34, and cf. "Clio's own waxworks: groups for the new Palais de Paris," *Illustrated L News* 219 (15 Dec 1951) 1003; Friedrich von Schiller, "On grace and dignity," (1818) in *The Works*, ed. N.H. Dole (Boston, 1902), quoted by Theodor W. Adorno, *The Jargon of Authenticity*, trans. K. Tarnowski and F. Will (Evanston: Northwestern U, 1973) 164.

46. Movieland Wax Museum, Buena Park, CA, brochures for 1976 and 1984 in the Waxworks clippings file, San Diego Public Lib.

47. Based on my visit, 28 Nov 1990; displays have changed since. For some details, see Cottrell, *Madame Tussaud*, 102, 142 (identifying the "Sleeping Beauty" as Mme de St. Aramanthe).

48. J. Seward Johnson, *Celebrating the Familiar* (NY: Alfred Van der Marck, 1987) 25, 29. On the continuing *trompe l'oeil* of Hanson's sculptures, see, for example, "Medics' job: bring to life artist's creation," AP item, 4 Jan 1991, Fort Lauderdale, FL.

49. Giorgio Vasari, *Lives of the Painters, Sculptors and Architects*, trans. A.B. Hinds (L, 1927 [1547]) II, pt. 2, 100-02.

50. Jonathan Sawday, "The fate of Marsyas: dissecting the Renaissance body," in *Renaissance Bodies*, eds. L. Gent and N. Llewellyn (L: Reaktion, 1990) 111-35; Glenn Harcourt, "Andreas Vesalius and the anatomy of antique sculpture," *Representations* 17 (Wint 1987) 28-61; C.D. O'Malley, *Andreas Vesalius of Brussels 1514-1564* (Berkeley, U Cal, 1964) chs. 7-8.

51. Maria Luisa Azzaroli, "La Specola," in *La Ceroplastica nella scienza e nell'arte* (Firenze: Olschki, 1977) 15-20; Hillier, *History of Wax Dolls*, 20ff; Smeeton, *Exhibitions*, 37, 111, undated clips; Robert M. Isherwood, *Farce and Fantasy: Popular Entertainment in Eighteenth-Century Paris* (NY: Oxford U, 1986) 202, 222; Altick, *Shows of London*, 339-40; Thomas N. Haviland and Lawrence C. Parish, "A brief account of the use of wax models in the study of medicine," *J History Med* 25 (1970) 52-75.

52. Lysons, *Collectanea II*, 133, London display from ad in *Craftsman* (5 Dec 1730); Azzaroli, "La Specola," 19; Smeeton, *Exhibitions*, 37 (transience), 122-23 (Serantoni); Altick, *Shows of London*, 55; Ludmilla Jordanova, "Objects of knowledge," in *The New Museology*, ed. Peter Vergo (L: Reaktion, 1989) 22-40; idem, *Sexual Visions: Images of Gender in Science and Medicine Between the Eighteenth and Twentieth Centuries* (NY: Harvester, 1989) ch. 3, esp. 44. At the end of the nineteenth century, the American physician Robert L. Dickinson would become famous for his construction and use of accurately modeled anatomical mannequins in the training of gynecologists and obstetricians. These were, it appears, the first such models to be used in medical schools. See S. Galishoff, "Dickinson, Robert Latou," *Dictionary of Amer Med Biography*, eds. Martin Kaufmann et al. (Westport, CT: Greenwood, 1984) I, 202-03.

53. Azzaroli, "La Specola," 19; Audrey B. Davis, "Louis Thomas Jérôme Auzoux and the papier mâché anatomical model," in *La Ceroplastica*, 257-72; Gustave Flaubert, *Bouvard and Pécuchet*, trans. T.W. Earp and G.W. Stonier (NY: New Directions, 1954 [1872-80, unfinished]) q76; Gannal, *History of Embalming*, 143-45.

54. Others here might launch into a discussion of surveillance as a modern mode of discipline and dominance. Or into the murkier waters of production and seduction, where the body may be found in a dead-woman's float, bobbing between tides of literary theory and psychoanalysis. Or into the rapids of political economy and fetishism, the body a broken oar in the white waters of commodification, objectification, derealization. Here I hug the shore, with the wax anatomy as a concretion of desire. Cf. esp. Jordanova, *Sexual Visions*; William Pietz, "Fetishism and materialism: the limits of theory in Marx," in *Fetishism as Cultural Discourse* (Ithaca: Cornell U, 1993) 119-51.

55. Wolfram Prinz, "Dal Vero o del modello? Aggiunte e testimonianze sull'uso dei manichini nella pittura del Quattrocento," in *Scritti di storia dell'arte in onore di Ugo Procacci*, eds. M.G. Ciardi Dupre dal Poggetto and Paolo Dal Poggetto (Milan: Electa, 1977) I, 200-08; Boehn, *Dolls and Puppets*, 96-98, figs. 79-80; Emile Michel, "Deux mannequins en bois du XVIe siècle," *Gazette des Beaux Arts*, ser. 3, 32 (1904) 135-39; *OED*, IX, 317; Staatliche Kunsthalle, *Maler und Modell* (Baden-Baden, 28 July - 19 Oct 1969) exhibition catalog, esp. Pietro F. Alberti's *Malerakademie* ca. 1550 (coll. Rijksmuseum, Amsterdam); F.J. Sanchez Canton, "Un maniquí del siglo XVI," *Archivo Español de Arte* 25 (1952) 101-09; E.F. van der Grinten, "Le cachalot et le mannequin," *Nederlands Kunsthistorisch Jaarboek* 13 (1962) 156-79, an invaluable study. Molenaer (ca. 1610-1668)

was a student of Frans Hal, like his wife Judith Leyster, who also painted scenes of tavern gaiety as well as many self-portraits.

56. *OED*, VIII, 736, and IX, 317; van der Grinten, "Le cachalot et le mannequin," 161–62; Charlotte Adams, "Artists' models in NY," *Century Mag* 25 (Feb 1883) 577; Staatliche Kunsthalle, *Maler und Modell*, #107, Trübner's *Atelier-modelle*; William S. Rubin, *Dada, Surrealism, and Their Heritage* (NY: MOMA, 1968) 153, plate 237, Picasso etching.

57. James T. Soby, *Giorgio de Chirico* (NY: MOMA, 1966) 27, 67, 97–101; Isabella Far de Chirico and Domenico Porzio, *Conoscere De Chirico* (Milan: Mondadori, 1979).

58. Tom Calvert, Chris Welman, and Armin Bruderlin of the Human Figure Animation Lab, Simon Fraser U, Burnaby, B.C., interview, 14 May 1991; Thomas W. Calvert, "Towards a computer based language for human movement" (Burnaby, B.C.: Laboratory for Computer and Communications Research, Simon Fraser U, 1985); idem, "The challenge of human figure animation," *Graphics Interface '88* (1988) 203–20; T.W. Calvert et al., "Interacting with complexity in composition and design," (Burnaby, B.C.: Centre for Systems Science, Simon Fraser U, 1989). Feature films that are completely computer animated, such as the Walt Disney Studio/Pixar collaboration on John Lasseter (dir), *Toy Story* (1995), may solve many of the technical problems. On this pathbreaking film, see Brent Schlender, "Steve Jobs' amazing movie adventure," *Fortune* 132 (18 Sept 1995) 155ff.

59. Thecla Schiphorst et al., "Tools for interaction with the creative process of composition," *CHI 90 Proceedings, Assoc for Computing Machinery* (Apr 1990) 167–74; Nancy V. Dalva, "Cunningham computes a new season," and Max Wyman, "Computer program aids dancemakers," in *Dance Mag* (Mar 1991) 12–13.

60. "New England Capitalist," *Harvard Lib Bull* 10 (Spr 1956) 245–53, quoted in Daniel W. Howe, *The Political Culture of the American Whigs* (Chicago: U Chicago, 1979) 96; *Official Descriptive and Illustrated Catalogue of the Great Exhibition* (L, 1851) I, 433.

61. Ian Anstruther, *The Knight and the Umbrella* (L: Bles, 1963) 150; Antonio Averlino [Il Filarete], *Trattato di Architettura*, trans. A.M. Finoli and L. Grassi (Milan: Il Polifilo, 1972 [1464]) II, 676–77 and ft. 3; *OED*, VIII, q736 from *The Art of Painting* (1744); Ethel B. Van der Veer, *The Lay-Figure* (1927) in *The One-Act Theater* (NY, 1936) II, 223–45. Crispijn van de Passe is discussed in van der Grinten, "Le cachalot et le mannequin," 169, 177. His slighting of the lay figure may be put in the context of Dutch Calvinist iconoclasm, sometimes directed against dolls, puppets, and wax effigies: Simon Schama, *The Embarrassment of Riches: An Interpretation of Dutch Culture in the Golden Age* (NY: Knopf, 1987) 184–85.

62. Bruno Schulz, "Tailors' Dummies," in his *The Street of Crocodiles*, trans. Celina Wieniewska (NY: Walker, 1963 [1934]) 40–62, q51, q52, q55; Rubin, *Dada, Surrealism*, 144, plate 215. Schulz (1892–1942) in his own drawings constantly had men bending and scraping to women in fashion-model poses; a sketch, possibly for "Tailor's Dummies," shows a man kneeling to take the measurements of a live nude while the naked torso of a dummy wears a fashionable hat. See Jerzy Ficowski, ed., *Letters and Drawings of Bruno Schulz*, trans. W. Arndt and V. Nelson (NY: Harper & Row, 1988) 23, 66, 76, 103–04, 157.

63. Alan Watts, *In My Own Way* (NY: Pantheon, 1972), quoted in Monica Furlong, *Genuine Fake: A Biography of Alan Watts* (L: Heinemann, 1986) 11. See also Anatole France, *Le Mannequin d'osier* (P, 1897) esp. 124–25.

64. Technics ad, "Made to measure hi-fi," *Time Out (L)* (21–28 Nov 1990) 4–5.

65. On women's self-portraits, see Joyce T. Cohen, comp., *In-Sights: Self-Portraits by Women* (Boston: Godine, 1978); Pascal Bonafoux, *Portraits of the Artist: The Self-Portrait in Painting* (NY: Skira/Rizzoli, 1985) 51, 83, 89, 93-94, 98-99, 102-03, 134.

66. Boehn, *Dolls and Puppets*, 136ff, and suggesting that some of these mannequins may have been lifesize; Carl Fox, *The Doll* (NY: Harrison House, 1988) 34; Lesley Gordon, *Peepshow into Paradise: A History of Children's Toys* (L, 1953) 109.

67. Neil McKendrick, "Commercialization and the economy," in *The Birth of a Consumer Society*, eds. McKendrick et al. (Bloomington: Indiana U, 1982) 43-47; Elias, *Civilizing Process*, 78, 102ff.

68. Léon Riotor, *Le Mannequin* (P, 1900) 28; Diana de Marley, *Worth: Father of Haute Couture*, 2nd ed. (NY: Holmes & Meier, 1990) 23, 103-04. Some of what follows has been surveyed by Emily d'Aulaire and Per Ola d'Aulaire, "Mannequins: our fantasy figures of high fashion," *Smithsonian* 22 (Apr 1991) 66-78.

69. *OED*, VI, q553 from Allan Ramsay, glossary to his 1720 poem, "Rise and Fall of Stocks"; Riotor, *Le Mannequin*, 29-33.

70. For this paragraph and the next, Riotor, *Le Mannequin*, 33, 86-90, 97; Nicole Parrot, *Mannequins*, trans. Sheila de Vallée (L: Academy, 1982) 36, 44-53; Pamela Gramke, "Mannequins: from the beginning," *Visual Merchandising* 111 (May 1980) 41; Barry James Wood, *Show Windows: 75 Years of the Art of Display* (NY: Congdon and Weed, 1982) 7, 14.

71. See Hillel Schwartz, *Never Satisfied: A Cultural History of Diets, Fantasies and Fat* (NY: Free Press, 1986) 159-64; Claudia B. Kidwell and Margaret C. Christman, *Suiting Everyone: The Democratization of Clothing in America* (Washington, D.C.: Smithsonian, 1974), and cf. Bonnita M. Farmer and Lois M. Gotwals, *Concepts of Fit* (NY: Macmillan, 1982) ch. 1, "The Importance of Good Fit." The fashion doll was recreated in post-World War II France, where fabric shortages prevented couturiers from showing full-size samples; restored by the Musée des Arts de la Mode (Paris), 150 of these thirty-inch dolls were shown by the Metropolitan Museum of Art (NY) as "Théâtre de la Mode," 8 Dec 1990 – 14 Apr 1991.

72. [Charles A. Tracy], *Art of Decorating Show Windows and Interiors*, 4th ed. (Chicago, 1909) 28 – Tracy was Baum's successor as editor of *The Merchant's Record and Show Window*, and his manual owed a great deal to Baum; L. Frank Baum, *The Art of Decorating Dry Goods Windows and Interiors* (Chicago, 1900) q intro, 82-87, 149-50; "Prize medal window," *The Show Window* (Jan 1899) 3-4. From here on to the end of this chapter, consider also Kenneth Gross, *The Dream of the Moving Statue* (Ithaca: Cornell U, 1992).

73. *The Rose Lawn Home J* 1 (1 July 1871) 4, in Box 1, L. Frank Baum Correspondence and Papers, Rare Book Room, Columbia U Lib, NY City, as also Russell P. MacFall, "L. Frank Baum – shadow and substance," *Amer Book Collector* 13 (Dec 1962) 9ff, and Roland Baughman, talk before the Zamorano Club, 5 April 1944, p. 14 on the puppets, in folder of "Oz Notes and Bibliography Notebook"; Jack Snow, *Who's Who in Oz* (Chicago: Reilly & Lee, 1954) 269-72; William Leach, "The clown from Syracuse: the life and times of L. Frank Baum" and "A trickster's tale," Introduction and Afterword to *The Wizard of Oz by L. Frank Baum* (Belmont: Wadsworth, 1991) 1-34, 176-82, q8; Frank J. Baum and Russell P. MacFall, *To Please a Child: A Biography of L. Frank Baum, Royal Historian of Oz* (Chicago: Reilly and Lee, 1961).

For the Giant, see Andrew D. White, "The Cardiff Giant: a chapter in the history of human folly – 1869-1870," excerpted from his *Autobiography* (NY, 1905) and appended to a play by Alexander M. Drummond and Robert E. Gard, *The Cardiff Giant* (Ithaca,

1949) 95-115; P.T. Barnum, *Selected Letters*, ed. A.H. Saxon (NY: Columbia U, 1983) 163, letter of 8 Oct 1870; James T. Dunn, *Cardiff Giant Hoax* (Cooperstown, NY: Farmers' Museum [where the Giant now resides], 1948); Alan Hynd, *Professors of Perfidy* (NY: Barnes, 1963) ch. 4, q110.

74. Leach, "Clown from Syracuse," 23-26; Stuart Culver, "What manikins want: *The Wonderful Wizard of Oz* and *The Art of Decorating Dry Goods Windows*," *Representations* 21 (Wint 1988) 97-116, q104; Baum, *Art of Decorating*, 16; Snow, *Who's Who in Oz*, 77, 272, on Glinda, as wise in the books as she is radiant in the 1939 MGM movie; L. Frank Baum, *Ozma of Oz* (Chicago, 1907) q52; Baum and MacFall, *To Please a Child*, q72, Oproar House; Leach, "A trickster's tale," 177, quoting text p. 128.

75. Baum, *Ozma of Oz*, 83, 91 (for which reference I thank Heidi Piltz Burton), and cf. the importance of mirrors in window displays, discussed by Keith Walden, "Speaking modern: language, culture, and hegemony in grocery window displays, 1887-1920," *Canadian Historical R* 70 (Sept 1989) 285-310, at 301; Rachel Bowlby, *Just Looking: Consumer Culture in Dreiser, Gissing, and Zola* (NY: Methuen, 1981) 30-32, 73; Michael Schudson, *Advertising, the Uneasy Persuasion: Its Dubious Impact on American Society* (NY: Basic, 1984) 60ff on advertising and theories of human nature; Nancy C.A. Roeske, "[Review of] *The Evolving Female*," *Amer J Psychiatry* 138 (Jan 1981) 139.

76. Lester Gaba, *The Art of Window Display* (NY, 1952) 7; Tracy, *Art of Decorating Show Windows*, 224; Richard H. Leslie, "Address to convention," *The Show Window* (Aug 1899) 73, and cf. Kenneth Brown, "A merciful wax lady," *ibid.* (Jan 1899) 13; Culver, "What manikins want," 108. In the 1880s, as trimmers began to spice up displays, they sometimes used small automata or hired live models to stand in windows. In Chicago, "a colored lad of ten or twelve years" combined the two genres, drawing crowds who tried to guess whether his jerky repeated movements were those of a living being or a machine. See James H.W. Marriott, *Nearly Three Hundred Ways to Dress Show Windows* (Baltimore, 1889) 12, 55, 184, 192.

77. Ovid, *The Metamorphoses*, trans. Horace Gregory (NY: Viking, 1958) X, 279; Gaba, *Art of Window Display*, 6; Culver, "What manikins want," 109; Leach, "A trickster's tale," 177-79, q179; Tracy, *Art of Decorating Show Windows*, 224. William Leach, "Strategists of display and the production of desire," in *Consuming Visions: Accumulation and Display of Goods in America, 1880-1920*, ed. Simon J. Bronner (NY: Norton, 1989) 99-132, associates the use of the wax (wo)mannequin and electrical displays with Baum's Spiritualism and with the metaphysical importance of light and light rays as agents of transformation at century's end. George Bernard Shaw's *Pygmalion* appeared in 1914.

78. Tracy, *Art of Decorating Show Windows*, 221 on aging, as also E.W. Softley, "The care of wax figures," *The Show Window* (Dec 1899); Pierre Imans, *Les Cires et mannequins d'art* (P, 1927) catalog; Schudson, *Advertising, the Uneasy Persuasion*, 194 on WCTU, as also Wood, *Show Windows*, 15; Carl Percy, *Window Display Advertising* (NY, 1928) 44-51; Gaba, *Art of Window Display*, 6-7; "LIFE goes to a party with…Cynthia," *Life* (13 Dec 1937) 84-87, photos showing nipples; *Young v. Greneker Studios*, 26 NY Supp. 2d, 357-58, my reading more poetic than lawful.

79. Menke Katz, "A manikin," *Atlantic* 207 (June 1961) 70; William Leiss, *The Limits of Satisfaction* (Toronto: U Toronto, 1976) esp. 10, 27, 81.

80. Anna Piotrowska, "Der Mensch im Schaufenster," in *Schaufenster: Die Kulturgeschichte eines Massenmediums* (Stuttgart: Württembergischer Kunstverein, 1974) 176, and 191 for Dalí, and see 285, 294 for paintings by Otto Dix and Otto Griebel turning

people into mannequins; Ekkehard Mai, "Technik, Maschinen, Automaten und der Freiraum der Kunst," *Das Kunstwerk* 33,2 (1980) 4–6; Georges Hugnet, *Surréalistische Schilderkunst Inleidung bij de Internationale Tentoonstelling van het Surrealisme* (Amsterdam: Galerie Robert, 1938) 28 for Victrola; Hal Foster, *Compulsive Beauty* (Cambridge, MA: MIT, 1993) 101–22 on Hans Bellmer's dolls, as also Rosalind E. Krauss, *The Optical Unconscious* (Cambridge, MA: MIT, 1993) 171–76; Hans Bellmer, *Die Puppe* (Berlin: Gerhardt Verlag, 1962). I am grateful to Adam Boxer of the Ubu Gallery (NY), which mounted a show of Bellmer photos and drawings, 14 Sept – 21 Oct 1995, for letting me see some of the materials in his collection. During the 1930s Bellmer had two dolls made, not quite twins, each with many duplicate parts (breasts, legs, arms), then proceeded to photograph these dolls in a series of surreal environments and erotic, dismembered, or monstrous poses.

81. Rubin, *Dada, Surrealism*, 63–64, q154; Galerie Pierre Colle, *Il faut visiter l'exposition surréaliste 7 au 18 juin* (P, 1937). Visitors also encountered Salvador Dalí's *Rainy Taxi*, in the back seat of whose truly wet internal storm sat a womannequin, her hair crawling with snails. Dalí would write of himself as mannequin to a brother who had died in childhood before Dalí was born, and for whom Salvador was named, and in the presence of whom Salvador grew up, "the double and identical twin of the other," living – in his parents' eyes – as the image of the lost child whose photograph hung above him in his bedroom. See *Dalí by Dalí*, trans. Eleanor R. Morse (NY: Abrams, 1970) iii–v, from Dalí's *Secret Life*, 148–53; John Yau, "Celebrated Artist or Artful Celebrity?" *LA Times Book R* (26 Dec 1993) 1, 8, reviewing Meredith Etherington-Smith, *The Persistence of Memory: A Biography of Dalí* (NY: Random House, 1993).

82. Henry Okun, "The Surrealist Object," Ph.D., NYU, 1981 (*Dissertation Abstracts*, 42/02-A, 433); Rubin, *Dada, Surrealism*, 12–13; Parrot, *Mannequins*, 65; "Kunst oder Kaufmann?" debate, 1929, reproduced in *Schaufenster: Die Kulturgeschichte eines Massenmediums*, 234–48; Alice G. Marquis, *Marcel Duchamp: Eros C'est La Vie* (Troy, NY: Whitston, 1981) 155–56, virtues of ready-mades, and 161, Duchamp casually discarding and reproducing them. On Duchamp the *fenêtrier*, see Charles F. Stuckey, "Duchamp's acephalic symbolism," *Art in America* 65 (Jan 1977) 94–99, discussing the erotic and optical aspects of Duchamp's "assisted" womannequin, headless, short-skirted, books in her arms, designed as part of a display, in collaboration with Breton, Matta, and Isabelle Waldman, for the promotion of Breton's essay, *Arcane 17*, in the window (momentarily) of Brentano's bookstore and then of the Gotham Book Mart, NY City, April 1945. Stuckey cites Jean Schuster, "Marcel Duchamp, vite," *Le Surréalisme, même* (Spr 1957) 143–45 on the Bride and the mannequins – at whom balls were thrown in attempts to knock off their heads. Cf. Molly Nesbit, "The language of industry," on ready-mades and mechanical drafting, and Rosalind Krauss, "Where's Poppa," on the Bride, both in *The Definitively Unfinished Marcel Duchamp*, ed. Thierry de Duve (Cambridge, MA: MIT for the Nova Scotia College of Art and Design, 1991) 351–96, 433–78.

83. "The modernistic mannequin," *Vogue* 65 (1 Mar 1925) 56; Guillaume Janneau, "Introduction à l'Exposition des arts décoratifs: considérations sur l'esprit moderne," *Art et décoration*, numéro exceptionnel (May 1925) q174; Clarisse, "La Mode," *Exposition internationale des arts décoratifs et industriels modernes* (P, 1925) 51, 94–95, a review for *L'Art vivant*; Leonard S. Marcus, *The American Store Window* (NY: Watson-Guptill, 1978) q28, Siégel; Parrot, *Mannequins*, 70–77, q74, Vigneau; Imans, *Les Cires et mannequins*, q84, my italics. A good series of photographs of Exposition mannequins appears

in René Herbst, *Devantures, vitrines, installations de magasins à l'Exposition international des arts décoratifs* (P, 1925).

84. Imans, *Les Cires et mannequins*, q4, 84; Robert de Beauplan, "La Féerie des mannequins de cire," *L'Illustration* 165 (7 Mar 1925) 222-23, weights; Parrot, *Mannequins*, 86, 90-96; *Le Pavillon de la ville de Paris. L'Enseignement artistique et professionel* (P, 1925) 128; Marcus, *American Store Window*, 28, 30 on "ready-made daydreams," 36-38. For the French influence upon German mannequins, see *Schaufenster: Die Kulturgeschichte eines Massenmediums*, 47-49, 181.

85. Guy Hartcup, *Camouflage: A History of Concealment and Deception in War* (NY: Scribner's, 1980) 27; Jasper Maskelyne, *Magic: Top Secret* (L, 1949) 20, 51; Henry Dreyfuss, *Designing for People* (NY: Simon & Schuster, 1955) ch. 2; Stuart Ewen, *All Consuming Images: The Politics of Style in Contemporary Culture* (NY: Basic, 1988) 196-99; Marcus, *American Show Window*, 20; Yukio Saito and Toru Ohshima, "Data processing in three-dimensional coordinate measurement of living bodies," *Precision Machinery* 1 (1986) 215-29, degrees of freedom.

86. Maury Wolf, Hollywood, CA, telephone interview, 22 Aug 1991; Wolf & Vine / Greneker, "The dream of a lifetime," faxsheet sent 15 July 1991 by Rex Craig of the Greneker Company, LA; Gramke, "Mannequins: from the beginning," 43; Parrot, *Mannequins*, 164; Mayer, *Embalming*, 54. Filling windows with mannequins was less unusual in Europe than in the U.S.: James H. Picken, *Principles of Window Display* (Chicago, 1927) 254, disapproving.

87. Tracy, *Art of Decorating Show Windows*, 224; G. Felsenthal ad in *The Show Window* (Dec 1899) ad pages, and McGreer & Hicks ad; Christian Bailly, *Automata: The Golden Age 1848-1914* (NY: Harper & Row, 1987) 23, 84ff; Monique Escat, *Musée de l'Automate* (Souillac, 1988) catalog; Wolf interview; "Model on Fifth Avenue," *Life* (12 July 1937) 32-33 on Scovil, as also Guy Talese, "New look in mannequins," *NY Times Mag* (7 Feb 1960) 33; Gramke, "Mannequins: from the beginning," 42-43; Martha Landau, NY, telephone interview, 23 Aug 1991, Greneker; Marcus, *American Show Window*, 38 on Gaba, as also Wood, *Show Windows*, 49; Parrot, *Mannequins*, 139; Herman Frankenthal, *Draping By Frankenthal*, ed. F.F. Purdy (Chicago, 1923).

88. Michael Olmert, "Doubles are cast for leading roles in museum shows," *Smithsonian* 16 (Apr 1985) 167-71, nonwax wax museums; Wolf interview; Gramke, "Mannequins: from the beginning," 43-44; Marcus, *American Show Window*, 44-45; Parrot, *Mannequins*, 114; Jim Buckley, *The Drama of Display* (NY, 1953) 31.

89. Jack Posner, "Mannequins: today and tomorrow," *Visual Merchandising* 111 (May 1980) 48-50; Talk of the Town, "Exciting mannequins," *The New Yorker* 51 (30 June 1975) q25; Michael Southgate, Adel Rootstein Company, NY, telephone interview, 15 Aug 1991; "Twiggy," *Life* (3 Feb 1967) 39; Amelia Anderson, "Designing women," *Ms. Mag* 16 (Oct 1987) q22, Rootstein; Ted Polhemus and Lynn Proctor, "The motionless models," *Design* 439 (July 1985) 36-37; "Greneker Manikins Chronology 1955-1989," faxsheets sent 15 July 1991 by Rex Craig; Parrot, *Mannequins*, 199, 210, 220; d'Aulaire, "Mannequins," 73, 76; Talese, "New look," 33, q36. Marsha Bentley Hale is writing a book on mannequins and hopes to establish a mannequin museum in LA.

90. Eric Lucking, "Mannequins" in *Window Display / Schaufensterkunst*, ed. Walter H. Herdeg (Zurich: Amstutz & Herdeg, 1961) II, 192; Southgate interview, on WOOPies; Picken, *Principles of Window Display*, 256; Evangeline Calvin of Van Calvin Manikin Res-

toration, Portland, OR, interview, 9 Jan 1992; Bruce Weber, "Body shop," *NY Times Mag* 138 (4 Dec 1988) 142; Diana Undercoffer, "Mannequins are forever: refinishing," *Visual Merchandising* 111 (May 1980) 47; George K. Payne, *Creative Display* (NY: National Retail Merchants Assoc, 1965) 7, q11.

91. "LIFE goes to a party with...Cynthia," 86; Gaba, *Art of Window Display*, 11–12, but Gaba resurrected Cynthia in 1952 for a TV comeback which failed, then said he left her "in the attic of a mad scientist in Greenwich Village" (Talese, "New look," 34); Holly Raver, "Mock funeral 'rapes' emotions," *U. (Ball State Daily News)* 4 (Sept 1990) 2, cardiopulmonary mannequin in coffin as if a drunk-driving victim; Joe Novak, "Zombies on parade," *Petersen's Photographic Mag* 8 (Jan 1980) 20, and see Deborah Turbeville, *Wallflower*, eds. Kate Morgan and Marvin Israel (NY: Congreve, 1978); Daniel Mark Epstein, "Mannequins," *Amer Scholar* 50 (1981) 211–12, undead; Howard Nemerov, "To the mannequins," *Poetry* 99 (Nov 1961) 82.

92. Talese, "New look," 34, on Brosnan and Sullivan; Bill Sharpsteen, "Tanya Ragir: mannequin sculptor," *LA* 32 (June 1987) 26; Walter H. Herdeg, ed., *International Window Display*, 2nd ed. (Zurich: Amstutz & Herdeg, 1952) I, 240–41 on Kruse; William B. McDonald, "Cecilia Staples," *Graphis* 5 (1949) 162–67, as also Catherine Sullivan, "Cecilia Staples, designer of window displays," *Amer Artist* (Dec 1950) 52–57; Wood, *Show Windows*, 123, Pratt; "Marisol's mannequins," *Horizon* 5 (Mar 1963) 102–04; Leza Lidow, *Peintures et mannequins* (P: Galerie Carpentier, 1987); Michael Emory, *Windows* (Chicago: Contemporary, 1977) Moore and Pratt quotations opp. fig 36; Polhemus and Proctor, "Motionless models," 36, navel; Harriet Shapiro and Laura S. Healy, "Adel Rootstein knows the fanciest dummies in fashion," *People* 32 (18 Sept 1989) q123–24; Evangeline Calvin interview; Parrot, *Mannequins*, 121 for Colette. Similarly, until at least the 1930s, American women had a leading role in the design of many kinds of dolls, on which see Miriam Formanek-Brunell, *Made to Play House: Dolls and the Commercialization of American Girlhood, 1830–1930* (New Haven: Yale U, 1993).

93. Landau interview; Maria Massey, "Problems of men's wear display," in *Display Manual*, eds. Howard P. Abrahams et al. (NY, 1951) 120; Lucking, Introduction to "Mannequins" (note 90 above); Marcus, *American Store Window*, 90, Currie; Robert Byrne, *Mannequin* (NY: Atheneum, 1988) 15; William E. Jurma, "Media mannequins," *Vital Speeches* 50 (1 Nov 1983) 61–65; E.C. Tubb, *Century of the Manikin* (NY: Daw, 1972) 140, therapy; Sharpsteen, "Tanya Ragir," 26, fists; Michael Gross, "Dummying up," *NY* 21 (13 June 1988) 16–17; Wendy Goodman, "Ralph Pucci ushers in the designer mannequin," *HG (House & Garden)* (Oct 1991) 126; Southgate interview, the mixing of sexes. In a Pucci Fashion Mannequins ad, *Interview* (May 1990) 4–5, nude *man*nequins and *woman*nequins did engage in stylized sexual encounters. See also Carol Moog, *"Are They Selling Her Lips?" Advertising and Identity* (NY: Morrow, 1990) 119, on a Barneys New York 1960s print ad that showed a rather ordinary man standing impassively in a fine suit on a short dais above the caption NO DUMMIES. One dummy, Safe-T-Man, at $119.95, is now sold as a bodyguard.

94. "Dolls," *Littell's Living Age* 99 (Oct–Dec 1868) 286–89; "Dolls: made in America," *Fortune* 14 (Dec 1936) 103–109, 196, 199–200; Barbara Melosh and Christina Simmons, "Exhibiting women's history," in *Presenting the Past*, eds. Susan Porter Benson et al. (Philadelphia: Temple U, 1986) 203–21, on Indiana State Museum's 1984–85 exhibition, "25 Years of Barbie Dolls"; Lisa B. Herskovits, "How Barbie warped me," *Fell Swoop* 16 (1989) 1–6; Aulaire, "Mannequins," 67. A Minneapolis industrial engineer in 1990 cre-

ated a "Happy To Be Me" Doll as alternative to Barbie, who, like womannequins, is unrealistically long of leg and neck: "Move over, Barbie," *NAAFA Newsletter* 21 (Sept–Oct 1990). Barbie is also disproportionately busty, like all Western sex dolls. Indeed, her creator, Ruth Handler, originally modeled Barbie upon a sexy hand-sized German doll intended for men. The doll was a fetishist caricature of Reinhard Beuthien's lubricious comic strip character, Lilli. For sharply different assessments of the fame, fortunes, and figure of Barbie, see M.G. Lord, *Forever Barbie: The Unauthorized Biography of a Real Doll* (NY: Morrow, 1994); Erica Rand, *Barbie's Queer Accessories* (Durham, NC: Duke U, 1995).

95. Southgate interview, on expressions, and cf. George Bennett, *Mannequins* (NY: Knopf, 1977) 25, 29, photos of laughing mannequins, and cf. T.S. Eliot, "The Hollow Men," (1925) in *Selected Poems* (L: Faber & Faber, n.d.) 77.

96. Octave Uzanne, "Les Femmes dociles, visite à l'industriel d'Anvers," preface to Riotor, *Les Mannequins*, xiii–xv.

97. Oskar Kokoschka, *My Life*, trans. David Britt (L: Thames & Hudson, 1974) 115–17; Tate Gallery, *Oskar Kokoschka 1886–1980* (L, 1986) 308–09, plate 41; Hans Peter Bayerdörfer, "Eindringlinge, Marionetten, Automaten. Symbolistische Dramatik und die Anfänge des modernen Theaters," *Jahrbuch der deutschen Schillergesellschaft* 20 (1976) 529–30. I thank Peter Hecht for calling the Kokoschka episode to my attention.

98. Leo Bersani, "Representation and its discontents," *Raritan* 1,1 (1981) 3–17.

99. Tommaso Landolfi, "Gogol's Wife" (1954) in *Gogol's Wife and Other Stories*, trans. Wayland Young (Norfolk, CT: New Directions, 1963); Oreste Macrí, *Tommaso Landolfi* (Firenze: Casa Editrice le Lettere, 1990) 58–59.

100. Schulz, "Tailors' dummies," 49; Uzanne, "Les Femmes dociles," xiv, quote from a speaking doll sold for one hundred louis or more by Mme Van der Mys. In 1968 the Joffrey Ballet premiered Marc Wilde's "The Mannequins," during which five womannequins pursue and castrate the thief of a sixth.

101. D.O.M. Corporation, *Adult Erotica Catalog* (Marina del Rey, CA, 1989) 8, Ms. Wonderful, Aphrodite; Playhouse Products ad in *Hustler* (Dec 1989) 129, Ms. Wonderful; Mailers Security brochure (Hollywood, CA, 1990), SOLID PLEASURE; Doll House ad, *Penthouse* (July 1989) 131, Suzie.

102. D.O.M. Corporation, *Adult Erotica Catalog*, 4; Playhouse Products ad in *Hustler* (Dec 1989) 113; Coast to Coast Distributors, *Price Buster Warehouse Clearance Sale* (Van Nuys, 1991) vagina and star cock; "Sweet Ass" from unsourced clipping; Thomas Laqueur, *Making Sex: Body and Gender from the Greeks to Freud* (Cambridge, MA: Harvard U, 1990); Cynthia Russett, *Sexual Science: The Victorian Construction of Womanhood* (Cambridge, MA: Harvard U, 1989).

103. VCA Mail Order, *Sexy Toys for Sexier Guys and Gals!* (Chatsworth, CA, 1990?) Candy Samples doll; Luis Buñuel (dir), *Ensayo de un Crimen (The Criminal Life of Archibaldo de la Cruz)* (Alianza Cinematografica, 1955); Luis García Berlanga (dir), *Grandeur Nature (Life Size)* (CIC, 1973). See also Alain Robbe-Grillet (dir), *Glissements Progressifs du Plaisir* (Fox/Liva, 1974). On the ultimate inaccessibility of women in pornographic films, see Linda Williams, *Hard Core: Power, Pleasure, and the "Frenzy of the Visible"* (Berkeley: U Cal, 1989).

104. See *Sheldon v. Metro-Goldwyn Pictures Corp.*, 81 F.2d (C.C.A. 1936) 53, on the commonness of the theatrical device of using a womannequin for an escape. On generating revenue, Landau interview; on lifting, Nestor Castro, *Handbook of Window Display*

(NY: Architectural Books, 1954) 77. Quotation is from John Gay's *The Beggar's Opera* (1728).

105. C.T. Onions, ed., *Oxford Universal Dictionary*, 3rd ed. (Oxford, 1955) 1877; Francis Sparshott, "The disappointed art lover," in *The Forger's Art: Forgery and the Philosophy of Art*, ed. Denis Dutton (Berkeley: U Cal, 1983) 246-63, who uses analogies of lovemaking to illuminate problems posed by forgery; I reverse the thrust of his argument. Other arguments will have to be made, elsewhere, about homoerotic sex dolls.

106. Schulz, "Tailors' Dummies," 55.

107. Carlo Collodi, *The Adventures of Pinocchio*, trans. E. Harden, illus. Roberto Innocenti (NY: Knopf, 1988 [1883; English trans., 1944]) 7-9.

108. Concetta D'Angeli, "L'Ideologia 'moderata' di Carlo Lorenzini, detto Collodi," *La Rassegna della letteratura italiana* ser. 7, 86 (1982) 152-77; Nicolas J. Perella, "An essay on Pinocchio," in *The Adventures of Pinocchio by Carlo Collodi*, trans. Perella (Berkeley: U Cal, 1986) 1, 7-9, 13, 34; Italiano Marchetti, *Carlo Collodi*, ed. B.M. Chini (Firenze: Le Monnier, 1967); Elaine De Paul, "'Collodi, Carlo' (Carlo Lorenzini)," *European Authors 1000-1900*, eds. S.J. Kunitz and V. Colby (NY: Wilson, 1967) 184-85; Denis Mack Smith, *Italy: A Modern History* (Ann Arbor: U Michigan, 1959) 123-26, 133-56; Collodi, *Adventures of Pinocchio*, 31, 64.

109. Collodi, *Adventures of Pinocchio*, 12-17; *OED*, IX, 374, and XII, 120-21 (poppet), 854-55 (puppet); Edwin Arnet, foreword to Pierre Gauchat, *Marionettes* (Erlenbach-Zurich, 1949) 5, and see Charles Magnin, *Histoire des marionettes en Europe depuis l'antiquité jusqu'à nos jours* (P, 1852); Charles Nodier, "Les Marionnettes," *Revue de Paris* 2 (Nov 1842) 217-33, q229. Today's English has "marionette" as a string puppet or *fantoccine* and "puppet" as a hand puppet or *burattino*; in the past and in French that distinction was rarely made; Nodier referred to both as "*marionnettes*." I use "puppets" as the larger set of which "marionettes" are part.

110. Mark Morelli, "A letter from Geppetto," *PAH!* (1 May 1991); Willard Gaylin, *Adam and Eve and Pinocchio: On Being and Becoming Human* (NY: Viking, 1990) 127-30, 158; Scott C. Shershow, *Puppets and "Popular" Culture* (Ithaca: Cornell U, 1995) esp. 227ff; Carlo Collodi, *Pinocchio*, trans. Noel Streatfeild, large type edition (NY: Franklin Watts, 1959) "About this Book." Almuth Sellschopp-Rüppel and Michael van Rad, "Pinocchio – a psychosomatic syndrome," *Psychotherapy & Psychosomatics* 28 (1977) 357-60, read Pinocchio as a co-dependent character, unable "to relate inner experiences meaningfully to actions." For his animated cartoon feature, Walt Disney (who never read the book) invented an almost human brother, Figaro, for Pinocchio, exaggerating the co-dependence. See "Pinocchio à la Disney," *Newsweek* (19 Feb 1940) 32-33.

111. Marcus Aurelius, *The Meditations*, trans. George Long (NY, 1937) II.2, III.16, X.38; Paul McPharlin, *The Puppet Theatre in America* (NY, 1949) 33 for Ralph, 47, 48.

112. Do see, however, on the continuing importance of puppet plays to Goethe, to Parisian symbolists, Munich expressionists, Viennese neoromantics, and Danish fabulists: Arnet, Foreword to Gauchat, *Marionettes*, 6; Micheline Legendre, *Marionnettes: art et tradition* (Ottawa: Leméac, 1986) 43-47; Rudolf Drux, *Marionette Mensch: Ein Metaphernkomplex und sein Kontext von Hoffmann bis Büchner* (Munchen: Fink, 1986); Michel Carrouges, *Les Machines célibataires* (P: Chêne, 1976) 16ff; Didier Plassard, *L'Acteur en effigie: figures de l'homme artificiel dans le théâtre des avant-gardes historiques* (Lausanne: L'Age d'Homme, 1992); Bonnie Marranca, "Triptych: Isak Dinesen in three parts," *Performing Arts J* 29,2 (1986) 91-106. Contrast Shershow, *Puppets and "Popular" Culture*.

113. Frank Proschan, "Puppet voices and interlocutors: language in folk puppetry," *J Amer Folklore* 94 (1981) 527-37; Magnin, *Histoire des marionettes*, 41-42.

114. Jacques de Vaucanson, *An Account of the Mechanism of an Automaton, or Image Playing on the German-Flute*, trans. J.T. Desaguliers (L, 1742) 9 for echo, 11, 19, 22-23 for contrivance; Jean D'Alembert, "Androide," *EDSAM*, I, 451 for comment; Pierre-François Guyot Desfontaines, *Observations sur les écrits modernes* 12 (1738) Lettre CLXXX, 337-42, q338, q340 (at II, 361-63 of reprint [Geneva: Slatkine, 1967]); Linda Strauss, "Automata: A Study in the Interface of Science, Technology, and Popular Culture, 1730-1885," Ph.D., U Cal, San Diego, 1987, 10-31; D.M. Fryer and J.C. Marshall, "Motives of Jacques de Vaucanson," *Technology and Culture* 20 (1979) 257-69; Joannes Baptiste De la Chapelle, *Le Ventriloque ou l'engastrimythe* (L, 1772) 17-19; *Account of the Performance of Different Ventriloquists* (Edinburgh, 1828) rept. from *Edinburgh J of Science* 9 (1828) 252-59. Vaucanson's directions for achieving a musical echo are nearly identical to those given by the *Ency Britannica* (Cambridge, 1911) XXVII, 1012, for ventriloquism: "the breath is allowed to escape very slowly, the tones being muffled by narrowing the glottis and the mouth opened as little as possible, while the tongue is retracted and only its tip moves."

115. [Antonio Blitz], *Everybody a Ventriloquist: A History of Ventriloquism* (Philadelphia, 1856) 4-9.

116. Strauss, "Automata," 117-25, q120; Alfred Chapuis and Edouard Gélis, *Le Monde des automates* (Geneva: Slatkine, 1984 [1928]) II, ch. 22, esp. 208; Karl G. Windisch, *Inanimate Reason; or, a Circumstantial Account of that astonishing Piece of Mechanism, M. de Kempelen's Chess-Player* (L, 1784) 47, von Kempelen's speaking machine.

117. Philip Thicknesse, *The Speaking Figure, and the Automaton Chess-Player, Exposed and Detected* (L, 1784) 4-5, 16; Isherwood, *Farce and Fantasy*, 47, boy in dummy; *Account of the Performance*, 255-56, Fitz-James.

118. Strauss, "Automata," 122-24; D'Alembert, "Androide," I, 451, and see Dugald Stewart, *Observations on Ventriloquism* (1828) in *Collected Works*, ed. William Hamilton (Edinburgh, 1854) IV, 126n on D'Alembert's own facility at vocal mimicry; H.J. Moulton, *Houdini's History of Magic in Boston 1792-1915*, ed. Milbourne Christopher (Glenwood: Meyerbooks, 1983) 8-9; Nicholas Marie Alexandre, *Memoirs and Anecdotes of Monsieur Alexandre* (L, 1822); E.T.A. Hoffmann, "Automata" (1814) in *Best Tales of Hoffmann*, ed. E.F. Bleiler, trans. Alexander Ewing (NY: Dover, 1967) 71-103, q79. On false automata, I draw from an interview with John Gaughan, historian, collector, and restorer of automata, LA, 4 June 1991. See also John Gaughan and Jim Steinmeyer, *The Mystery of Psycho* (LA: Gaughan, 1987).

119. George W. Kirbye, *Autobiography* (Milford, NH, 1860?) 18, ventriloquist, equilibrist, and India-rubber man.

120. Isherwood, *Farce and Fantasy*, 198; Jean Prasteau, *Les Automates* (P: Gründ, 1968) 12; Saxon, *P.T. Barnum*, 70; Phineas T. Barnum, *Selected Letters*, ed. A.H. Saxon (NY: Columbia U, 1983) 35; Chapuis and Gélis, *Le Monde des automates*, II, 208; Blitz, *Everybody a Ventriloquist*, 15; "The late Signor Blitz," *NY Times* (30 Jan 1877) 3:6, obit from the *Philadelphia Ledger*; George W. Kirbye, *Origin and History of Ventriloquism* (Philadelphia, 1861) 35; Moulton, *Houdini's History of Magic*, 33, 66, 68, 72, 73, 104, 113; John Nevil Maskelyne, "Automata," *Leisure Hour* 28 (1879) 28, 268; *OED*, IV, 1117; Antonio Blitz, *Fifty Years in the Magic Circle* (San Francisco, 1871) 114-15, 117.

121. Moulton, *Houdini's History of Magic*, 104, citing *Boston Post* (11 Jan 1889); *NY*

Times (29-30 Jan 1877) 3:6; Price, *Magic*, 49; L. Frank Baum, *The New Wizard of Oz* (Indianapolis, 1903) 147-50; Henry Cockton, *Life and Adventures of Valentine Vox the Ventriloquist* (NY, 1904); Cullen Murphy, "Hey, let me outta here!" *Atlantic* 264 (Aug 1989) 67.

122. Murphy, "Hey, let me outta here!" 62, 64, 66, q67 from ventriloquist John Arvites; Darryl Hutton, *Modern Ventriloquism* (L: Kaye & Ward, 1974) q24. Absent its conscience, as in Richard Attenborough (dir), *Magic* (Twentieth Century-Fox, 1978), the dummy may contract with evil.

123. Julian Jaynes, *The Origin of Consciousness in the Breakdown of the Bicameral Mind* (Boston: Houghton Mifflin, 1976) 79, 97, 99, 104, 107, 119, 174, 202, 317-38.

124. Rick Marschall, *The History of Television* (NY: Gallery, 1986) 214.

125. The very first successful American sound-on-film motion picture, *The Jazz Singer* (1927), became subject to an incredible confusion of dubbings in its sequels, *The Jolson Story* (1946) and *Jolson Sings Again* (1949): Otis L. Guernsey, Jr., "Ghosts in the reel," *Saturday Review* 38 (30 Apr 1955) 27-28; Michael Rogin, "'Democracy and burnt cork': the end of blackface, the beginning of civil rights," *Representations* 46 (Spr 1994) 1-34, esp. 10ff, putting *The Jazz Singer* and its sequels in the context of the visual dubbing and redoubling of blackface. On dubbing when silent film stars' voices failed to meet the demands of talkies, see Stanley Donen (dir), *Singin' in the Rain* (MGM, 1952). On Italian dubbing: William Tuohy, "Film dubbing – in Rome, it's the big word," *LA Times* (17 Jan 1975) 1, 20; Hank Kaufman, "Nobody dubs it better," *Attenzione* (May 1984) 35-38; Daniela Bisogni, "Rubadub of Dante's lingo on the track," *Variety* (2 May 1990) 178; Catherine Ventura, "Get the last word – see Roma and dub," *ibid.* (3 Dec 1990) 56, noting however that the 1976 Cannes Film Festival prize for best actress was awarded jointly to Dominique Sanda and to Ada Serra Zanetti, the woman who dubbed her voice in *Ereditaria Ferramonti*. On Indian dubbing, above all for singing: Pico Iyer, *Video Night in Katmandu* (NY: Knopf, 1988) 248, 257. On the disengagement of dubbers: Paul Gardner, "A few become dubbing bums," *NY Times* (24 July 1966) qD4; Kenneth Harvey, "Actor on dubbing," *NY Times* (30 Oct 1966) D2; "Labials and fricatives," *The New Yorker* (9 Mar 1968) 33. For debates over dubbing, see Jack P. Gabriel and Stanley Kauffmann, "To dub, or not to dub – two views," *Theatre Arts* 45 (Oct 1961) 20-21, 68-69, 74-76, and "Dubbing" files, Margaret Herrick Lib, Academy of Motion Picture Arts and Sciences, Beverly Hills.

126. "Milli Vanilli didn't sing its pop hits," *NY Times* (16 Nov 1990) C20, with follow-ups (19 Nov) A18 and (20 Nov) C15; Carefree Sugarless Gum, "How long will the flavor last? 'Til these guys sing for themselves," TV commercial aired June 1991. On political puppetry, Sidney Blumenthal, *The Permanent Campaign*, rev. ed. (NY: Touchstone, 1982); "Biden's debate finale: an echo from abroad," *NY Times* (12 Sept 1987) 1:4, with follow-up (16 Sept) q1:5 and (17 Sept) 1:4, editorial 34:1; Mickey Kaus et al., "Biden's belly flop," *Newsweek* (28 Sept 1987) 23-24.

127. Robert M. Adams, *Bad Mouth: Fugitive Papers on the Dark Side* (Berkeley: U Cal, 1977) 21-42, q29. Used in therapy (for speech disorders) and in criminal investigations (to elicit details of abuse from children), puppets and dummies become instead confidantes or surrogates, with ventriloquism a means to expressing that which would otherwise be repressed. Here the voice is not thrown but found. Cf. Hutton, *Modern Ventriloquism*, ch. 10.

128. Otto V. Mayr, *Authority, Liberty & Automatic Machinery in Early Modern Europe*

(Baltimore: Johns Hopkins, 1986). Cf. G.I. Belov, "Automaton," *Great Soviet Ency*, 3rd ed. (NY: Macmillan, 1976) I, 504. Vaucanson himself designed punched cards for looms, a metal-cutting lathe, and processes for making endless chain and fine mesh.

129. John Randolph, Jr., Philadelphia, letter to Fanny Tucker, 23 March 1794, in the Tucker-Coalter Family Papers, Special Collections Library, Duke U; Moulton, *Houdini's History of Magic*, 2.

130. Michael Wallace, "Mickey Mouse history: portraying the past at Disney World," in *History Museums in the United States*, eds. W. Leon and R. Rosenzweig (Urbana: U Illinois, 1989) 164; Robert de Roos, "The magic worlds of Walt Disney," *National Geographic* (Aug 1963) 204, 207 on Lincoln; Maskelyne, "Automata," 156, on Koppen's Componium "improvising"; Smeeton, *Exhibitions*, 244 (*Galignani's Messenger* [Jan 1836 or 1838], violinist); Raymond Bernard (dir), *Le Joueur d'Echecs* (1930), a silent film with mime Charles Dullin, redone in 1939 as a talkie, both revolving upon Catherine the Great's cheating, for which see also "Automata," *Chambers's J* 13 (1876) 88; George Allen, "The history of the automaton chessplayer in America," in *The Book of the First American Chess Congress*, ed. Daniel W. Fiske (NY, 1859) 424-25, 431n on Napoleon; Joseph E. Arrington, "John Maelzel, master showman of automata and panoramas," *Pennsylvania Mag of History and Biography* 84,1 (1960) 56-92; Johann Nepomuk Maelzel, *Maelzel's Exhibition, Masonic Hall…May 17, 1834* (Philadelphia, 1834), [false] automaton chessplayer rectifying "miss-moves."

131. Thicknesse, *The Speaking Figure, and the Automaton Chess-Player*, 11 for child, q16; "Automate joueur d'échecs," *Magasin pittoresque* 2 (1834) 155, a dwarf, as also, still, Mildred Jailer, "Automata: 'toys' for adults," *Antiques and Collecting Hobbies* 94 (Oct 1989) 74; R. Shelton Mackenzie, ed., *Memoirs of Robert-Houdin, Ambassador, Author, and Conjuror*, trans. Lascelles Wraxall (L, 1860) 118-22, amputee; Henry Howe, *Memoirs of the Most Eminent American Mechanics* (NY, 1847) 460-69; interview with John Gaughan, who has reconstructed the Kempelen-Maelzel chess player; Nelly Weeton (later Mrs. Stock), *Miss Weeton's Journal of a Governess*, ed. Edward Hall (Newton Abbot: David and Charles, 1969) II, 124-25, letter of 27 July 1814 — these were Haddock's Androides, seen in New York City in 1820: Moulton, *Houdini's History of Magic*, 12.

132. Richmond Lattimore, trans., *The Iliad of Homer* (Chicago: Phoenix, 1961) bk. XVIII, lines 417ff; James D. Ellsworth, "Automata and women in early Greek poetry," in *Apollo Agonistes*, comp. M.E. Grenander (Albany: SUNY, 1979) I, 6-14; Strauss, "Automata," 42-44; John Passarow, Albany, NY, letter to Samuel Curtis on women in audience, 20 Aug 1829, in Johann Nepomuk Maelzel Papers, Misc. Mss. M, Amer Antiquarian Soc, Worcester, MA; Christine Woesler De Panafieu, "Automata – a masculine utopia," in *Nineteen Eighty-Four: Science Between Utopia and Dystopia*, eds. E. Mendelsohn and H. Nowotny (Dordrecht: Reidel, 1984) 127-45; William Hosea Ballou, *Automatic Wife: A Novel of the New Code of Honor* (NY, 1891) q278. Cf. Claude Pujade-Renaud, *La Ventriloque* (P: Des Femmes, 1978) on ventriloquism and women. On another implicit theme, men as creators of life apart from women, see Chapter VIII.

133. Auguste, comte de Villiers de l'Isle-Adam, *Tomorrow's Eve (Eve futur)*, trans. Robert M. Adams (Urbana: U Illinois, 1982 [1886]) intro., q43, q61, q67.

134. Strauss, "Automata," ch. 2; J.D. Bruce, "Human automata in classical tradition and mediaeval romance," *Modern Philology* 10 (Apr 1913) 511-26; Stuart Piggott, "Background to a broadcast," in his *Ruins in a Landscape* (Edinburgh: Edinburgh U, 1976) 77-99; Harry M. Geduld and Robald Goestman, eds., *Robots, Robots* (Boston: NY Graphic

Soc, 1978) 114, 116; "Electric man," *Sci Amer* 73 (24 Aug 1895) 120 – and recently, "Her eyes see all, her face reveals nothing: Anne Droid is the shoplifter's nemesis," *People Weekly* (23 Oct 1989) 97; Jean-Claude Beaune, *Le Vagabond et la machine: essai sur l'automatisme ambulatoire, médecine, technique et société, 1880–1910* (Seyssel: Champ Vallon, 1983); Baum, *Ozma of Oz*, 55–56, and see also his *Tik-Tok of Oz* (Chicago, 1914); Karel Čapek, *R.U.R.* (1920), trans. Paul Selver, in *The Arbor House Treasury of Science Fiction Masterpieces*, comp. R. Silverberg and M.H. Greenberg (NY: Arbor House, 1983) 96–143.

135. E.E. Free, "Our new electric supermen," *World Today* 54 (July 1929) 129; Olaf Stapledon, *Last and First Men and Star Maker* (NY: Dover, 1968 [1931]) 157–65 and ch. 11; Hubert Sarrazin, "Bernanos's vision of France: against the robots," *Chesterton R* 15–16 (Nov 1989 – Feb 1990) 529–46, q535 from Bernanos, *La France contre les robots* (1946).

136. Jean-Claude Beaune, *L'Automate et ses mobiles* (P: Flammarion, 1980) 11, 13, 17; CSE Microelectronics Group, *Microelectronics: Capitalist Technology and the Working Class* (L: CSE, 1980) ch. 7 on robots; Phil Berger, *The State-of-the-Art Robot Catalog* (NY: Dodd & Mead, 1984) 97–142; Gilbert Simondon, *Du mode d'existence des objets techniques* (P: Aubier-Montaigne, 1969) 9–11, 46–49; Ib Johansen, "The monster and the automaton: variations on the grotesque and the sublime in science fiction," *The Dolphin (Aarhus)* 17 (1989) 101–21 on *Blade Runner*.

137. Walter Benjamin, "Unpacking my library" (1931), "The work of art in the age of mechanical reproduction" (1936), and "Theses on the philosophy of history" (1940) in *Illuminations*, ed. Hannah Arendt, trans. Harry Zohn (NY: Schocken, 1969) 217–264, quotes and paraphrases on 67, 221, 223, 253, and see Arendt on the hunchback, 6–7, and collecting, 45, quoting Benjamin's 1930 essay, "Lob der Puppe" (Praise for the doll). See also Walter Benjamin, "Not for Sale," in his *One-Way Street and Other Writings*, trans. E. Jephcott and K. Shorter (L: New Left Books, 1979) 87–88 for his most explicit comments on puppets and automata. For apt analyses of Benjamin, see esp. Ian Balfour, "Reversal, quotation (Benjamin's history)," *MLN* 106 (Apr 1991) 622–47; Natalie Heinich, "L'Aura de Walter Benjamin," *Actes de la recherche en sciences sociales* 49 (1983) 107–09; Jeffrey Mehlman, *Walter Benjamin for Children: An Essay on His Radio Years* (Chicago: U Chicago, 1993) esp. 59ff on his reading the *Tales of Hoffman* in secret as a child.

CHAPTER FOUR: SECOND NATURE

1. Ulisse Aldrovandi, *Ornithologiae* (Bonon, 1646 [published posthumously]) I, bk. 11, 323a; Dominique G. Homberger, *The Lingual Apparatus of the African Grey Parrot* (Washington, D.C.: Ornithologists' Union, 1986); Jane Stern and Michael Stern, "Parrots," *The New Yorker* 66 (30 July 1990) 56.

2. Hastings William Sackville Russell, 12th Duke of Bedford, *Parrots and Parrot-like Birds in Aviculture* (L, 1929) q56; John Phillips, *Dear Parrot: Pertaining to the Care, Nurture, and Befriending of Man's Oldest Pet* (L: Dent, 1979) 50, on Bedford; "Parrots and their treatment," *All the Year 'Round* 43 (1879) 521, jugglery; Marriott, *Parrot-Keeper's Guide* (L, 1876) 35, on loosing the tongue, which was of no physiological use; John Sparks and Tony Soper, *Parrots: A Natural History* (NY: Facts on File, 1990) 97, hymn; Grover M. Allen, *Birds and Their Attributes* (Boston, 1925) 224, warning system. New reports suggest that parrots in the wild may engage in some mimicry: J. Lee Kavanau, *Lovebirds, Cockatiels, Budgerigars: Behavior and Evolution* (LA: Science Software Systems, 1987) 269–75.

3. Brian Reade, *An Essay on Edward Lear's Illustrations of the Family of Psittacidae or Parrots* (L: Pion, 1978); C.E. Jackson, *Bird Illustrators* (L: Witherby, 1975) 13, 16, 32-35; Susan Hyman, *Edward Lear's Birds* (NY: Morrow, 1980) esp. 18, q26.

4. Steven Feld, *Sound and Sentiment: Birds, Weeping, Poetics, and Song in Kaluli Expression*, 2nd ed. (Philadelphia: U Pennsylvania, 1982) 218.

5. Sparks and Soper, *Parrots*, 97; Stern and Stern, "Parrots," 59; Joyce B. Flueckiger, "Land of wealth, land of famine: the suā nāc (parrot dance) of Central India," *J Amer Folklore* 100 (1987) 39-57.

6. Claude Lévi-Strauss, *Tristes tropiques*, trans. John and Doreen Weightman (NY: Atheneum, 1974) 234; G. Charbonnier, *Conversations with Claude Lévi-Strauss*, trans. idem (L: Cape, 1969) 149.

7. Julian Barnes, *Flaubert's Parrot* (NY: Knopf, 1985) 17, précis and trans. of Gustave Flaubert, "Un coeur simple" (1877), *Trois contes* (P, 1910) 3-74, q64; Martin Bidney, "Parrots, pictures, rays, perfumes: epiphanies in George Sand and Flaubert," *Studies in Short Fiction* 22 (Spr 1985) 209-17.

8. Ziya'u'd-din Nakhshabi, *Tales of a Parrot*, trans. Muhammed A. Simsar (Cleveland: The Museum of Art, 1978) q12, q14. Originally a Sanskrit tale, the *Tuti-Nama* was rewritten in Arabic for a fourteenth-century Indo-Islamic audience.

9. Lucien Lévy-Bruhl, *Les Fonctions mentales dans les sociétés inférieures*, 6th ed. (P, 1922 [1910]) 77; Karl von den Steinen, *Unter den Naturvölkern Zentral-Brasiliens* (NY: Johnson, 1968 [1894]) ch. 17, esp. 456, 463, 476, 511-13, and pl. XXVII; Theodorus P. van Baaren, "Are the Bororo parrots or are we?" in *Liber Amicorum: Studies in Honour of Prof. Dr. C.J. Bleeker*, eds. G. Widengren et al. (Leiden: Brill, 1969) 8-13; Lev S. Vygotsky, *Thought and Language* (Cambridge, MA: MIT, 1962) 72.

10. Giovanni Boccaccio, *Genealogie Deorum Gentilium Libri*, ed. Vincenzo Romano (Bari, 1951) I, 206 (= bk. IV, ch. 49), claiming to draw upon the Latin of Theodontius, which may have been a hoax: Charles B. Osgood, *Boccaccio on Poetry* (NY, 1930) 190.

11. Joseph M. Forshaw, *Parrots of the World* (Neptune, NJ: TFH, 1977) 33; Sparks and Soper, *Parrots*, 98-100; Gerhard Herrlinger, *Totenklage um Tiere in der antiken Dichtung* (Stuttgart, 1930) 47-53, 81-91, 131-34; Guy Lee, trans., *Ovid's Amores* (NY: Viking, 1968) 74-79, Amores 2.6. During the Renaissance, this elegy was reversed, so that a man is at first upset by a parrot's call for his and its dead mistress, then finds the parrot a companion in memorial. See Jan Ziolkowski, "Tito Vespasiano Strozzi's 'Ad psyttacum': a Renaissance Latin poet parrots the past," *Harvard Lib Bull* 35 (Spr 1987) 139-49, poem from Strozzi's *Eroticon* (1514) bk. 6, poem 11 (written ca. 1463).

12. J. Christopher Crocker, "My brother the parrot," in *The Social Use of Metaphor*, eds. J.D. Sapir and J.C. Crocker (Philadelphia: U Pennsylvania, 1977) 164-92.

13. Herbert Friedmann, *A Bestiary for Saint Jerome: Animal Symbolism in European Religious Art* (Washington, D.C.: Smithsonian, 1980) 116, 118, 280-81.

14. Terence Turner, "'We are parrots,' 'twins are birds': play of tropes as operational structure," in *Beyond Metaphor*, ed. James W. Fernandez (Stanford: Stanford U, 1991) 121-58. For a critical review of the earlier literature, see Jonathan Z. Smith, "I am a parrot (red)," *History of Religions* 11 (1972) 391-413.

15. Thomas E. Vesce, trans., *The Knight of the Parrot* (NY: Garland, 1986) 5; Gerard J. Brault, "Papegai," *Early Blazon* (Oxford: Clarendon, 1972) 254; Beryl Rowland, *Birds with Human Souls: A Guide to Bird Symbolism* (Knoxville: U Tennessee, 1978) 120-23.

16. W.H. Hudson, "A talk about parrots," *Saturday R* 91 (1901) 765-66. Cf. Frank

Loveland, "Of mauli, macaws and other things: what it means to be among the Rama Indians of Eastern Nicaragua," *Latin Amer and Indian Literatures J* 1 (1985) 137–47.

17. Sparks and Soper, *Parrots*, 102; James W. Fernandez, "Revitalized words from 'The Parrot's Egg' and 'The Bull that Crashes in the Kraal': African cult sermons," in *Essays on the Verbal and Visual Arts*, ed. June Helm (Seattle: Amer Ethnological Soc, 1967) 47; Joan B. Lloyd, *African Animals in Renaissance Literature and Art* (Oxford: Clarendon, 1971) 27, 47; "Perroquet," *Grand dictionnaire universel du XIXᵉ siècle* (P, 1869) XII, 656 for Creed; Andrew Malcolm, ed., *Two Early Renaissance Bird Poems* (Washington, D.C.: Folger Lib, 1984) esp. 77, *The Birds Devotions*.

18. John Skelton, "Speke, Parrot" (ca. 1522), *Complete English Poems*, ed. John Scattergood (New Haven: Yale U, 1983) 230–46, q lines 1, 13, 112, 213–16, spelling modernized; F.W. Brownlow, "The Boke Compiled by Maister Skelton, Poet Laureate, Called Speake Parrot," *English Literary Renaissance* 1 (1971) 14, philosopher's stone. Is it making too much of Parrot to note that Thomas More, who had a dozen parrots flying free inside his house, succeeded Wolsey as Lord Chancellor?

19. Pauline M. Watts, "Prophecy and discovery: on the spiritual origins of Christopher Columbus's 'Enterprise of the Indies,'" *Amer Historical R* 90 (1985) 73–102; Paolo Emilio Taviani, *Columbus: The Great Adventure*, trans. L.F. Farina and M.A. Beckwith (NY: Orion, 1991, [1985, 1985]) 91–94; Oliver Dunn and James E. Kelley, Jr., eds. and trans., *The Diario of Christopher Columbus's First Voyage to America 1492–1493, Abstracted by Fray Bartolomé de las Casas* (Norman: U of Oklahoma, 1988) 32–33, 44–45, 52–55, a bilingual edition whose English I have compared with Robert H. Fuson, trans., *The Log of Christopher Columbus* (Camden, ME: Int Marine, 1987). On the birds as shearwaters (a kind of puffin), see Sparks and Soper, *Parrots*, 103–04.

20. Milton Rugoff, *The Travels of Marco Polo* (NY: New Amer Lib, 1961) 260, and noting, p. xi, that Colombo read Polo carefully; Taviani, *Columbus*, esp. 104–05, 146; Dunn and Kelley, *Diario of Christopher Columbus*, 64–65, 138–39, 212–13, 224–25; Fuson, *Log of Christopher Columbus*, 105.

21. Gerald Sider, "When parrots learn to talk, and why they can't: domination, deception, and self-deception in Indian-White relations," *Comparative Studies in Society and History* 29 (1987) 3–23, and contrast Antonio T. Gaspar and Eduardo A. Vallejo, "Lessons from the Canaries: the first contact between Europeans and Canarians, c. 1312–1477," *Antiquity* 66 (1992) 120–29; Taviani, *Columbus*, 101–02, 103–06, 124, 141, 163, 248–49; Dunn and Kelley, *Diario of Christopher Columbus*, 64–69, 72–75, 94–95; Fuson, *Log of Christopher Columbus*, 76–80, 86, hammocks; Wilma George, "Sources and background to discoveries of new animals in the sixteenth and seventeenth century," *History of Sci* 40 (June 1980) 79–81; Sparks and Soper, *Parrots*, 104, 107, 111; Jan Balis, *Merveilleux plumages: dix siècles de livres d'oiseaux* (Bruxelles: Bibliothèque Royale, 1969) 28; Hugh Honour, *The New Golden Land: European Images of America from the Discoveries to the Present Time* (NY: Pantheon, 1975) figs. 7, 9(b), 18, 46(a), 77, 80, 92, 105, pls. VI, XVI, XXI.

22. Dunn and Kelley, *Diario of Christopher Columbus*, 104–05; Taviani, *Columbus*, 104, 182; A.E. Decoteau, *Handbook of Macaws* (Neptune, NJ: TFH, 1982) 47–48; Sparks and Soper, *Parrots*, 148–49; Alfred W. Crosby, *The Columbian Exchange: Biological and Cultural Consequences of 1492* (Westport, CT: Greenwood, 1972); James C. Simmons, "Macaw madness," *National Wildlife* 20 (June–July 1982) 6, Zapotec. Cf. Stephen Greenblatt, *Marvelous Possessions: The Wonder of the New World* (Chicago: U Chicago, 1991) 90,

105–06, suggesting that Colombo (mis)took the gift of parrots as a sign of the vulnerability of the indigenes, like their bright scars.

23. Douglas Botting, *Humboldt and the Cosmos* (NY: Harper & Row, 1973) 65, 76; L. Kellner, *Alexander von Humboldt* (L: Oxford, 1963) 34, 44; Alexander von Humboldt, *Memoiren* (Leipzig, 1860) 234, entry for 31 May 1800; Gustave Flaubert, *Correspondance: Supplément (1872 – Juin 1877)*, eds. René Dumesnil et al. (P, 1954) 28 July 1876, trans. by Barnes, *Flaubert's Parrot*, 184, and see *Correspondance (1873–1876)* (P, 1930) #1595 to niece Caroline (whom Flaubert called "mon Loulou") and #1599.

24. Petra Deimer, *Parrots*, trans. Robert and Rita Kimber (NY: Barron's, 1983) 8, giving 326 species; Stern and Stern, "Parrots," 55, 70, giving 332 species; Sparks and Soper, *Parrots*, 13, giving 333 species, pp. 21–23 on fossil record, p. 23 on proximity to other orders, p. 108 on Conrad Gessner's *Historia Animalum* with its 14 species; Forshaw, *Parrots of the World*, 18–19; Don Stap, *A Parrot without a Name: The Search for the Last Unknown Birds on Earth* (NY: Knopf, 1990) 216, 221. For a history of taxonomies, see Alfred Newton, "Parrot," *Ency Britannica*, 11th ed. (L, 1910–11) XX, q864, and Nicholas Aylward Vigors, "A reply to some observations in the *Dictionnaire des sciences naturelles* upon the newly characterized groups of the Psittacidae," *Zoological J* 3 (1828) 91–123, disagreeing that the genus *Psittacus* is "so *natural*" it should not be subdivided.

25. E. Trouessart, "Perroquet," *La Grande encyclopédie* (P, 1886–1902) XXVI, 436, head of class; Ronald Pearson, *The Avian Brain* (L: Academic, 1972) 594; Lauren J. Harris, "Footedness in parrots," *Canadian J Psychology* 43 (Sept 1989) 369–96; Deimer, *Parrots*, 17, "true love"; Peter Scheitlin, *Versuch einer vollständigen Thierseelenkunde* (Stuttgart, 1840) II, 21–22, 360–61; Nancy Price, *Bright Pinions* (Oxford, 1952) 22, Duchess of Richmond; Joseph Taylor, *Ornithologia Curioso* (L, 1807) 206–07, Jennings; J.J. Sprenger, "A bird among birds" (1887), reprinted in *Audubon* 89 (Mar 1987), S10–12.

26. "Buy pretty Polly!" *Chambers's J* 35 (1861) q163 (phoenix, old man); Sparks and Soper, *Parrots*, 212 on age spans; Cessa Feyerabend, "Personality and training," in *Parrots Exclusively*, eds. K. Plath and M. Davis (Fond du Lac, WI: All-Pets, 1955) 44; Harold T. Wilkins, "Everyman and his parrot," *English R* 50 (Apr 1930) q476, from Stevenson's *Treasure Island* (1881–82); François Levaillant, *Histoire naturelle des perroquets* (P, 1804–05) I, 6, epilepsy; Hyman, *Edward Lear's Birds*, 12; Barnes, *Flaubert's Parrot*, 56–57; John Hampden, *Seventy-One Parrots: Folk-Tales of Ancient Egypt and Mongolia* (L: Deutsch, 1972) 99–103, playing dead, as also T. Bainbridge Fletcher and C.M. Inglis, *Birds of an Indian Garden* (Calcutta, 1936) 156; Larousse, "Perroquet," XII, 655 for derivations; *OED*, XI, 191; Philippe Bonnefis, "Exposition d'un perroquet," *Revue des sciences humaines* 181 (1981) 72, 75, psittacosis and Flaubert's story, written three years before the discovery of what is known today as "ornithosis," since it is actually transmitted by many different birds.

27. William Thomas Greene, *Parrots in Captivity* (L, 1884–87) II, 47 (scream); Alexander Theroux, "I sing the parrot!" *Reader's Digest (Canadian ed.)* 122 (May 1983) 104, sounds; Mr. Symes, *Just Arriv'd from Italy, the Artificial Aviary* (L, 1754) playbill; Weeks Museum, *Final Sale: A Catalogue* (L, 1834) 7, #70; Robert de Roos, "The magic worlds of Walt Disney," *National Geographic* (Aug 1963) 202 on the Tiki Room; Christian Bailly, *Automata: The Golden Age 1848–1914* (NY: Harper & Row, 1987) 50, nightingale.

28. John Locke, *An Essay Concerning Human Understanding* (Chicago: Regnery, 1956 [1690]) 141 = bk. 3, ch. 2, par. 7; *The Parrot: Addressed to Young Gentlemen* (Salisbury, 1785?) songsheet; Georges Louis Leclerc, Comte de Buffon, *Histoire naturelle des oiseaux*,

ed. C.S. Sonnini (P, 1803 [written before 1788]) XXVIII, 91 – his descriptions and plates drawn often from deteriorated stuffed specimens or engravings, says Levaillant, *Histoire naturelle des perroquets*, I, 47, 65; *The Teaching Parrot* (Philadelphia, 1809); Gerald Lee Gutek, *Joseph Neef: The Americanization of Pestalozzianism* (U: U of Alabama, 1978) q54, Maclure, 19 Sept 1826, from Arthur Bestor, ed., *Education and Reform at New Harmony* (Indianapolis, 1948) 368; "Pretty Poll," *Leisure Hour* 12 (1863) 550; Carol Leigh, Betty Comden and Adolph Green, lyrics to Moose Charlap's *Peter Pan* (NY: RCA Victor, 1954).

29. Greene, *Parrots in Captivity*, II, xi, 42-43; Karl Russ, *The Speaking Parrots*, trans. Leonora Schultze (L, 1884) 41-42, 45.

30. James P. Porter, "Intelligence and imitation in birds," *Amer J Psychology* 21 (Jan 1910) q3 from Royce; Darold A. Treffert, *Extraordinary People: Understanding "Idiot Savants"* (NY: Harper & Row, 1989) esp. chs. 1 and 4; Robin W. Doughty, *The Mockingbird* (Austin: U Texas, 1980) esp. 46; "Sur les oiseaux imitateurs: le moqueur," *Magasin pittoresque* 2 (1834) 319-20; James Jennings, *Ornithologia, or, The Birds: A Poem* (L, 1828) 374n.; David S. Carter, "Complex Avian Song Repertoire: Songs of the Mockingbird," Ph.D., U Cal, Riverside, 1981, mystified; Sparks and Soper, *Parrots*, 203-04 on Sparkie; Toby (an African gray), Washington, D.C., interview at home of Richard Restak, 6 Jan 1991; A. Nicaise, "Intelligence of parrots," *Sci Amer* 66 (25 June 1892) 402 on volition; Padma Sudhi, *Virtues of Parrot-learning*, q5, but contrast Rabindranath Tagore, *The Parrot's Training* (Calcutta, 1918) 3-7.

31. Larousse, "Perroquet," 657a, sense of justice; Irene M. Pepperberg, "Cognition in the African Grey parrot," *Animal Learning & Behavior* 11 (1983) 179-85; idem, "Social modelling theory," *The Auk* 102 (Oct 1985) 854-65; idem, "Interspecies communication: a tool for assessing conceptual abilities in the African Grey parrot," in *Cognition, Language, and Consciousness*, eds. G. Greenberg and E. Tobach (Hillsdale, NJ: Erlbaum, 1987) 31-56; idem, "Numerical competence in an African grey parrot," *J Comparative Psychology* 108 (Mar 1994) 36-44; idem, "Vocal learning in grey parrots: effects of social interaction, reference, and context," *Auk* 111 (Apr 1994) 300-13; Irene M. Pepperberg et al., "Mirror use by African grey parrots," *J Comparative Psychology* 109 (June 1995) 182-95; Elizabeth Vitton, "Smart Alex!" *3-2-1 Contact* (Mar 1992) 8-11, for which reference I thank Frederick L. Burton. Some suspect that Pepperberg or her assistants may be unknowingly cueing Alex; precautions have been taken against this, but skeptics should note that human discourse also depends on subtle visual and social cues: Philip N. Hineline, "Can verbal be nonsocial? Can nonsocial be verbal?" in *Psychological Aspects of Language*, eds. P.N. Chase and L.J. Parrott (Springfield, IL: Thomas, 1986) 123-27. Insisting that "Animals in the wild are not automatons," Pepperberg argues that social interaction drives the learning of bird repertoires in general, but she will not go so far as to call Alex's speech "language." Quoted by Douglas Starr, "This bird has a way with words," *National Wildlife* 26 (Feb-Mar 1988) 34-36, and see Stern and Stern, "Parrots," 57.

32. Theroux, "I sing the parrot!" 104; Nossiat Peseschkian, *Oriental Stories as Tools in Psychotherapy: The Merchant and the Parrot* (Berlin: Springer, 1986) epigraph, and cf. Marjorie Wallace, *The Silent Twins* (NY: Prentice-Hall, 1986) 36; Earl Schneider, ed., *Know Your Parrot* (NY: Pet Lib, 1970?) 18, violence; Paul Bowles, "All parrots speak," in *Their Heads Are Green and Their Hands Are Blue* (NY: Ecco, 1984) q155; Ezekiel Leavitt, *The Parrot Gods* (Boston: Talmud Society, 1921) 15; Vicki León, *Parrots, Macaws & Cockatoos* (San Luis Obispo, CA: Blake, 1991?) 11, "huddle species"; Parrot Jungle and Gar-

dens, Information Kit (Miami, 1989); Weldon Kees, "Obituary," in *A Book of Animal Poems*, ed. W. Cole (NY: Viking, 1973) 25; Charles Henri Valentin Alkan (1813–1888), *Funeral March on the Death of a Parrot*, for four-part chorus with mixed voices, ed. Raymond Lewenthal (NY: Schirmer, 1972) – a hoax?; Dick King-Smith, *Harry's Mad* (NY: Crown, 1984) – ten-year-old inherits parrot in which resides the spirit of his great uncle; Robin Skelton, *The Parrot Who Could, and Other Stories* (Victoria, BC: Sono Nis, 1987) 119–24, man inherits parrot who speaks and does macrame like his uncle.

33. Mary E. Wilkins, "The Parrot," *Harper's New Monthly Mag* 101 (1900) 603–04; Hudson, "A talk about parrots," 765, glad mad; Wilfrid Gibson, "The Parrot," *Oxford Book of Modern Verse*, ed. W.B. Yeats (NY: Oxford U, 1936) 174, cursing; Eliza Haywood, *The Parrot. With a Compendium of the Times* (L, 1746) #1, A4v–A5, A7, #2; Richard Restak, Washington, D.C., interview, 6 Jan 1991.

34. Nurse Lovechild, *Tommy Thumb's Song Book* (NY, 1946 [1744]) 12–13; *The Adventures of Old Dame Trudge and Her Parrot* (Philadelphia, 1811); Mary Elliott, *Confidential Memoirs: Or, Adventures of a Parrot, a Greyhound, a Cat, and a Monkey* (L, 1821) q4, 16, 22; Bonnefis, "Exposition d'un perroquet," 61, 65–66; Barnes, *Flaubert's Parrot*, 172, translation of Flaubert's dream of 1845.

35. Allen, "Pretty Poll," q46; Buffon, *Histoire naturelle des oiseaux*, XXVII, 21–22; "Parrots," *Chambers's J* 53 (1876) 745. Cf. Konrad Lorenz, *Studies in Animal and Human Behaviour*, trans. Robert Martin (L: Methuen, 1970) I, 89: "It is remarkable that in interpreting the psychological characteristics of the large parrots one is continually confronted with difficulties similar to those otherwise encountered only in the higher animals."

36. Young, *Life of Vertebrates*, 452, 454; William C. McDermott, *The Ape in Antiquity* (Baltimore, 1938); H.W. Janson, *Apes and Ape Lore in the Middle Ages and the Renaissance* (L, 1952); Albertus Magnus, *Man and the Beasts: De animalibus (Books 22–26)*, trans. James J. Scanlan (Binghamton, NY: SUNY, 1987) 174–75 (bk. 22.136); Margaret M. Hallissy, "The she-ape in Chaucer's Parson's Tale," *Essays in Literature* 9 (Spr 1982) 127–32; *OED*, I, 543, Antichrist as ape of our Lord (1561), devil as God's ape (1607); Joyce E. Salisbury, *The Beast Within: Animals in the Middle Ages* (NY: Routledge, 1994) 139–46, apes and monkeys as hybrids, neither animal nor human.

37. John G. Burke, "The wild man's pedigree," in *The Wild Man Within*, eds. E. Dudley and M.E. Novak (Pittsburgh: U Pittsburgh, 1972) 266–68, as also Eberhard Bahr, "Papageno: the unenlightened wild man in 18th-century Germany," 249–57, and Geoffrey Symcox, "The wild man's return: the enclosed vision of Rousseau's *Discourses*," 223–47; Edward Tyson, *Orang-Outang sive Homo Sylvestris: Or, the Anatomy of a Pygmie Compared with that of a Monkey, an Ape, and a Man* (L, 1699) Epistle Dedicatory, Preface, 55; Robert Wokler, "Tyson and Buffon on the orang-utan," *Studies on Voltaire and the Eighteenth Century* 155 (1976) 2301–19, q2308 from Diderot's *Suite du Rêve d'Alembert*, ii.90.

38. Arthur O. Lovejoy, *The Great Chain of Being* (Cambridge, MA: Harvard U, 1936) 234–36; Robert Wokler, "Perfectible apes in decadent cultures: Rousseau's anthropology revisited," *Daedalus* 107 (Sum 1978) 107–35; Ingrid Roscoe, "Mimic without mind – singerie in northern Europe," *Apollo* 114 (Aug 1981) 96–103, 99 for Watteau's *Monkey Painter*, as also M. Gauthier, *Watteau* (NY: Yoseloff, 1960) pls. III, X (*The Monkey Sculptor*); Lucinda Lambton, *Beastly Buildings* (L: Cape, 1985) 9–10, 52; Honour, *New Golden Land*, 103, plate XVI; Jean Prasteau, *Les Automates* (P: Gründ, 1968) 50–51, 114; Daniel

Lysons, *Collectanea, II: Publick Exhibitions*, 5, 26, British Library scrapbook, the earlier chimp reported in *L Mag* (Sept 1738) 465, and cf. *OED*, III, 123. Cf. George S. Rousseau, "Madame Chimpanzee," in his *Enlightenment Crossings* (NY: Manchester, 1991) 198-209.

39. Harriet Ritvo, *The Animal Estate: The English and Other Creatures in the Victorian Age* (Cambridge, MA: Harvard U, 1987) 30-41; William Irvine, *Apes, Angels, and Victorians* (NY: Time, 1955) 169-74; Walter Scott, *Count Robert of Paris and the Surgeon's Daughter* (L, 1901), see W. Hatherell's frontispiece to *Count Robert*, "Hereward rescues Bertha," and 296-300, orangutan threatening to carry off the heroine. For Frederick Engels, see his *Dialectics of Nature*, trans. and ed. Clemens Dutt (NY, 1940 [written 1872-82]) ch. 9, q283-84, and cf. A.R. Luria and L.S. Vygotsky, *Ape, Primitive Man, and Child*, trans. Evelyn Rossiter (NY: Harvester, 1992) ch. 1 on apes, by Luria, refining Engels with material from the experiments of Pavlov and Wolfgang Köhler. On the walking stick image, see Wokler, "Tyson and Buffon," 2301-03.

40. Arthur Keith, "[Review of Marcellin Boule's] *Les Hommes fossiles*," *Nature* 107 (12 May 1921) 324; Caroline Grigson, "Missing links in the Piltdown fraud," *New Scientist* 125 (13 Jan 1990) 55-58. A recent antievolutionary treatise hopes to resurrect at least part of the Piltdown man: Michael A. Cremo and Richard L. Thompson, *Forbidden Archeology: The Hidden History of the Human Race* (San Diego: Bhaktivedanta Institute, 1993) esp. 501-26.

41. George J. Romanes, *Animal Intelligence*, 3rd ed. (L, 1883 [1881-82]) xi, 7, 267-70, 477, 495, 497, q269. Cf. Edward Fry, "Imitation as a factor in human progress," *Littell's Living Age* 181 (1889) 728-39. Mockingbirds may also imitate, for sheer joy, the songs of other birds; we do not know.

42. Richard Lynch Garner, *Gorillas & Chimpanzees* (L, 1896) 20, 64, 95.

43. Lysons, *Collectanea*, 15, on 1785 "Child of the Sun"; Etienne Ducret, *Le Charlatanisme dévoilé* (P, 1892) 160-63; "Narcisse" pictorial, *The Theatre* 6 (1906) 137; Franz Kafka, "Ein Bericht für eine Akademie," in *Sämtliche Erzählungen*, ed. Paul Raabe (Frankfurt: Fischer, 1970) 147-55; *OED*, IX, 1006, "monkey-suit"; Keith Thomas, *Man and the Natural World: Changing Attitudes in England, 1500-1800* (L: Allen Lane, 1983) ch. 4; Ritvo, *Animal Estate*, Part I; "Animal reverence," *Littell's Living Age* 99 (Dec 1868) 810-13; Nicolas Pike, "The chacma or South African baboon," *Sci Amer* 65 (12 Dec 1891) 371-72.

44. David Murray, *Museums, Their History and Their Use* (Glasgow, 1904) I, 50-55, 63, 113, 196, 203-04; S. Peter Dance, *Animal Fakes & Frauds* (Maidenhead: Sampson Low, 1976) 77-80; Mark Jones et al., *Fake? The Art of Deception* (Berkeley: U Cal, 1990) 85; Jean Nicolas Gannal, *History of Embalming*, trans. R. Harlan (Philadelphia, 1840) 215; Christopher Stoate, *Taxidermy* (L: Sportsman's, 1987) 1-8, q1 from Peter Kalm, *Account of a Visit to England*; Montagu Browne, *Practical Taxidermy*, 2nd ed. (L, 1884) 10-13. For a detailed account, see Paul L. Farber, "The development of taxidermy and the history of ornithology," *Isis* 68 (1977) 550-66.

45. Edward Hall, ed., *Miss Weeton's Journal of a Governess* (Newton Abbot: David & Charles, 1969) I, 107; Handasyde Buchanan, *Nature into Art* (NY: Mayflower, 1979) 79, 82; Jean Anker, *Bird Books and Bird Art* (The Hague: Junk, 1979); Levaillant, *Histoire naturelle des perroquets*, I, 108, and II, 23; S. Peter Dance, *The Art of Natural History* (L: Country Life, 1978) 98-99 on Audubon, as also Robert H. Welker, *Birds and Men: American Birds in Science, Art, Literature, and Conservation, 1800-1900* (NY: Atheneum, 1966) 82, 86 fig. 22, and Ann S. Blum, *Picturing Nature: American Nineteenth-Century Zoological Illustration* (Princeton: Princeton U, 1993) 34 and ch. 3; Walsall Museum and Art

Gallery, *Birds in Art: The R.S.P.B. Centenary Exhibition* (Walsall: The Museum, 1989) 8-9; Paul L. Farber, *The Emergence of Ornithology as a Scientific Discipline, 1760–1850* (Dordrecht: Reidel, 1982) 105–06; Gary Kulik, "Designing the past: history-museum exhibitions from Peale to the present," in *History Museums in the United States: A Critical Assessment*, eds. W. Leon and R. Rosenzweig (Urbana: U Illinois, 1989) 5.

46. Browne, *Practical Taxidermy*, 14, q15; Norman Moore, "Waterton, Charles," *Dictionary of National Biography*, XX, 906–08; Charles Waterton, *Wanderings in South America... with original instructions for the perfect preservation of birds and [sic] for cabinets of natural history*, ed. L. Harrison Matthews (L: Oxford U, 1973 [lacking frontispiece of 1825 edition]) 79–80, 171–72, 180, 197, and 5th ed. (1852) q254, whether possible.

47. Stoate, *Taxidermy*, 10–11; Browne, *Practical Taxidermy*, q15–16; Karl P. Schmidt and Austin L. Rand, "Taxidermy," *Ency Britannica* (Chicago: Benton, 1965) XXI, 849–52, including 1883 caricatures of the worst sort of taxidermy. Cf. Franklin H. North, "The taxidermic art," *Century Illustrated Monthly Mag* 26 (1883) 230–39, an American taxidermist unimpressed by the German school ("cheap and inaccurate") and opposed to the mounting of specimens on moss or twigs (because of insects); he did admire the late Frères Verreaux of Paris, from whom "you could order a stuffed elephant, giraffe, or Bengal tiger, as you would a flitch of bacon from your butcher or a boiled lobster from the fishmonger."

48. Stoate, *Taxidermy*, 13–15; Bailly, *Automata*, 43–44 et passim; Ralph H. Lutts, *The Nature Fakers: Wildlife, Science, and Sentiment* (Golden, CO: Fulcrum, 1990) 26; Welker, *Birds and Men*, figs. 35–40, birds in hats, 1883–98. Cf. Blum, *Picturing Nature*, 310, on scientific schematization of zoological illustrations.

49. Frank M. Chapman, *Autobiography of a Bird Lover* (NY, 1933) 23, 29–30, 47–48, 69–70; John Rowley [Chief, Taxidermy Dept., American Museum of Natural History], *The Art of Taxidermy* (NY, 1907) 196, 199n on foliage.

50. Chapman, *Autobiography*, 78–80, 163–67. See Robert W. Shufeldt, *Scientific Taxidermy for Museums* (Washington, D.C., 1892) for Italian, English, and American antecedents to Chapman's work. An even broader and more astute account is provided by Karen E. Wonders, "Bird taxidermy and the origin of the habitat diorama," in *Nonverbal Communication in Science Prior to 1900*, ed. R.G. Mazzolini (Florence: Olschki, 1993) 414–47. Wonders shows how changes in nineteenth-century biology, which became increasingly concerned with evolution through time and across land masses, eventually opened up museum display to the illusionistic spaces of "scientific" dioramas and panoramas. Although primarily a North American (and South Kensington, London) phenomenon, museum habitats also began to appear in Swedish museums during the 1890s.

51. Donna Haraway, *Primate Visions: Gender, Race, and Nature in the World of Modern Science* (NY: Routledge, 1989) ch. 3; Hillel Schwartz, *Century's End* (NY: Doubleday, 1990) 182, 340 n.260 on degeneration and exhaustion; Rowley, *Art of Taxidermy*, 196–99. Closely related to "habitats" were displays of "primitive" families imported with their trappings and huts to form "native villages" at late-nineteenth-century expositions: Paul Greenhalgh, *Ephemeral Vistas: The Expositions Universelles, Great Exhibitions, and World Fairs, 1851–1939* (Manchester: Manchester U, 1988) ch. 4.

52. Rowley, *Art of Taxidermy*, 122; Carl E. Akeley and Mary L. Jobe Akeley, *Adventures in the African Jungle* (NY: Dodd, Mead, 1954) q173, 175–77; Haraway, *Primate Visions*, esp. 36–37; Wilfred H. Osgood [Curator of Zoology, Field Museum], introduc-

tion to *The Work of Carl E. Akeley in the Field Museum of Natural History* (Chicago, 1927) 2. On taxidermic problems with large animals, see Harold J. Shepstone, "Mounting big animals," *World's Work* 5 (1905) 623-31, who notes the expertise of Prof. W.T. Hornaday, then of the Bronx Park Zoo. Hornaday was one of several men who may well have preceded Akeley in the creation of animal groups, on which see a great early partisan of such groups – Shufeldt himself, *Scientific Taxidermy*, 407-28.

53. *Work of Carl E. Akeley*, "Old Man of Mikeno – Mountain Gorilla"; Akeley and Akeley, *Adventures*, 3-4, 6, 181-85; Haraway, *Primate Visions*, 31-35, 47, q31. Mt. Mikena was in what was then the Belgian Congo. Wonders, "Bird taxidermy," argues against Haraway that the Akeley hunting ethos was quite distinct from the central historical motives for creating bird dioramas, and that the diorama is not inherently masculinist.

54. Akeley and Akeley, *Adventures*, 95; Stoate, *Taxidermy*, 23-25; David Colley, "Bringing back the days when dinosaurs stalked the earth," *Nation's Business* 78 (June 1990) 16 on animated replicas for museums. Cf. John Simpkins, *Techniques of Biological Preparation* (Glasgow: Blackie, 1974).

55. Edward L. Thorndike, *Animal Intelligence: Experimental Studies* (NY, 1965 [1911]), experiments on cebus monkeys proving that they "associate" rather than reason; Dorothy L. Cheney and Robert M. Seyfarth, *How Monkeys See the World: Inside the Mind of Another Species* (Chicago: U Chicago, 1990), esp. good on distinctions between monkey and ape capacities, and on lying; Gordon Gallup et al., "A mirror for the mind of man, or will the chimpanzee create an identity crisis for *Homo sapiens*?" *J Human Evolution* 6 (1977) 303-14; Stephen Horigan, *Nature and Culture in Western Discourses* (L: Routledge, 1988) 94, metaphor; Young, *Life of Vertebrates*, 485; Adrian J. Desmond, *The Ape's Reflexion* (L: Bloud & Briggs, 1979) 14; Nicholas L. Tilney, "Renal transplantation between identical twins," *World J Surgery* 10 (June 1986) 381-88, a good review; Lawrence K. Altman, "Liver transplant passes a key test; biopsy finds no sign that man's body is rejecting organ from a baboon," *NY Times* (11 July 1992) 8.

56. Jane Goodall, *Through a Window: My Thirty Years with the Chimpanzees of Gombe* (Boston: Houghton Mifflin, 1990) q207; Malcolm Gladwell, "Common monkey may supplant rarer species in AIDS research," *Washington Post* (12 June 1992) A8:1. See also Haraway, *Primate Visions*, throughout.

57. Hélène Toussaint, *Gustave Courbet 1819-1877* (L: Arts Council of Great Britain, 1978) 39, 41, 168; Petra ten-Doesschate Chu, ed. and trans., *Letters of Gustave Courbet* (Chicago: U Chicago, 1992) 185, 279-92, 673 on F.286; E. de Jongh, "Erotica in Vogelperspectief," *Simiolus* 3 (1969) 22-74, 51 on Pieter de Hooch's seventeenth-century *Paar bij Papegaaienkooi*, where a couple stands by a cage whose door the man has unlatched and a parrot drinks from a cup held by the woman; Nanette Salomon, "Courbet's *Woman with a Parrot* and the problem of realism," in *Tribute to Lotte Brand Philip*, eds. William W. Clark et al. (NY: Abaris, 1985) 144-53; Charles Sterling and Margaretta Salinger, *French Paintings* (NY: Metropolitan Museum of Art, 1966) II, 124-27; Henri d'Ideville, *Gustave Courbet* (P, 1878) 64. Courbet's painting was contested by Edouard Manet, who did his own *Woman with a Parrot* in 1866, this woman fully vertical and gowned neck to toe, polar opposite of Manet's *Olympia* of 1863, which may have inspired Courbet's *Woman with a Parrot*. See Mona Hadler, "Manet's *Woman with a Parrot* in 1866," *Metropolitan Museum J* 7 (1973) 115-27.

58. Chu, *Letters*, 217; Hadler, "Manet's *Woman with a Parrot*," esp. 118-19; Elaine Shefer, "Deverell, Rossetti, Siddal, and 'The Bird in the Cage,'" *Art Bull* 47 (Sept 1985)

q437–48 from *Temple Bar* (1861) 58; Joseph M. Flora, "Woman with Parrot in *The Ox-Bow Incident*," *Amer Notes & Queries* 17 (Jan 1979) 74–76; Bonnefis, "Exposition d'un perroquet," 63, parrot as *"moins image du sexe que sexe de l'image*." Cf. Never Saw A Bird Blush, "Undressing [in front of parrot] ruffles a few feathers," letter to Ann Landers in *San Diego Union Tribune* (24 Aug 1992).

59. Werner Lantermann, *The New Parrot Handbook*, trans. Rita Kimber and Robert Kimber (Woodbury, NY: Barron's, 1986) 8; Tennessee Williams, *A Perfect Analysis Given by a Parrot* (NY: Dramatists Play Service, 1958) 11; Madeleine Boyd, ed., *The Memoirs of Jacques Casanova* (NY, 1929 [completed by 1797]) 370–72, parrot as lover's revenge; Beatrice Dexter, "Blabbermouth parrot testifies at divorce trial," *Weekly World News* (13 Feb 1990) 2; Stevie Smith, "Who Killed Lawless Lean?" in *Treasury of English Poetry*, eds. M. Caldwell and W. Kendrick (NY: Doubleday, 1984); Erle Stanley Gardner, *The Case of the Perjured Parrot* (NY, 1939).

60. Raymond Rosenthal, trans., *Aretino's Dialogues* (NY: Ballantine, 1971 [written 1534–38]) 1–3; David Hamilton, *The Monkey Gland Affair* (L: Chatto & Windus, 1986); Young, *Life of Vertebrates*, 463, noting that menstrual cycles have not been demonstrated for New World monkeys; Jeanne Altmann, *Baboon Mothers and Infants* (Cambridge, MA: Harvard U, 1980) 6, dual careers; Ernest R. Curtius, *European Literature and the Latin Middle Ages*, trans. Willard R. Trask (NY: Harper & Row, 1963) 539; Albertus Magnus, *Man and the Beasts*, 175; Janson, *Apes and Ape Lore*, 30–34, 109; Eric Partridge, *Dictionary of the Underworld* (NY: Bonanza, 1961) 323, "have a Chinaman (or monkey) on one's back," and 446–47. Londa Schiebinger observes, in *Nature's Body: Gender in the Making of Modern Science* (Boston: Beacon, 1993) ch. 3, that later eighteenth-century studies of primates looked precisely to primary and secondary sexual attributes in order to preserve a distinction between humans and all other animals elevated by Linnaeus in 1758 to the same zoological "first rank." Characteristics of gender as well as of sexual behavior were therefore historically and philosophically critical to the illustration and taxonomy of apes, orangutans, monkeys, and baboons.

61. Goodall, *Through a Window*, 77–78; Altmann, *Baboon Mothers and Infants*, esp. 187–89; Susan Sperling, "Baboons with briefcases: feminism, functionalism, and sociobiology in the evolution of primate gender," *Signs* 17 (Aut 1991) 1–27. Cf. Karen Ericksen Paige and Jeffery M. Paige, *The Politics of Reproductive Ritual* (Berkeley: U Cal, 1981).

62. Sperling, "Baboons with briefcases," q4, q11; Haraway, *Primate Visions*, and see also her *Simians, Cyborgs, and Women: The Re-invention of Nature* (NY: Routledge, 1991); Emily Hahn, *Eve and the Apes* (NY: Weidenfeld & Nicolson, 1988). Cf. the novel by John Collier, *His Monkey Wife or, Married to a Chimp* (L: Rupert Hart Davis, 1957). As to the extreme obliteration of borders, read Scotty Paul, "Real-life Dr. Frankenstein breeding man-apes," *Weekly World News* (19 Dec 1989) 33. On Japanese primate studies and handling of anthropomorphism, see Chapter VIII.

63. Clara M. Harlow, ed., *From Learning to Love: The Selected Papers of Harry F. Harlow* (NY: Praeger, 1986) xx, and see the 1966 paper reprinted on pp. 281–94, "Maternal behavior of rhesus monkeys deprived of mothering and peer associations in infancy." Haraway, *Primate Visions*, devotes ch. 9 to "Harry Harlow and the Technology of Love."

64. Hahn, *Eve and the Apes*, 66–68 for Lintz.

65. Justin Leiber, *Can Animals and Machines Be Persons?* (Indianapolis: Hackett, 1985) 14–16, 71.

66. Robert M. Young, "Animal soul," *Ency of Phil*, ed.-in-chief Paul Edwards (NY:

Macmillan, 1967) I, 122-27; Plotinus, *The Six Enneads*, trans. S. MacKenna and B.S. Page (Chicago, 1952) 1st Ennead, I.11, and 4th Ennead, III.6; Edward P. Evans, *The Criminal Prosecution and Capital Punishment of Animals* (L, 1906) esp. Appendix F, prosecutions to 1906(!); Esther Cohen, "Law, folklore, and animal lore," *Past & Present* 110 (Feb 1986) 6-37 – but severely doubted by William Chester Jordan, reviewing her *The Crossroads of Justice: Law and Culture in Late Medieval France* (Leiden: Brill, 1992) in the *Amer Historical R* 98 (Oct 1993) 1227; Tom Regan and Peter Singer, eds., *Animal Rights and Human Obligations* (Englewood Cliffs, NJ: Prentice-Hall, 1976) excerpting Aquinas, *Summa contra gentiles*, bk. III, pt. II, ch. 92; Thomas, *Man and the Natural World*, q19.

67. Andreas-Holger Maehle and Ulrich Tröhler, "Animal experimentation from antiquity to the end of the eighteenth century," in *Vivisection in Historical Perspective*, ed. Nicolaas A. Rupke (L: Croom Helm, 1987) 14-47, q15 for Galen; Anita Guerrini, "The ethics of animal experimentation in seventeenth-century England," *J History Ideas* 50 (July-Sept 1989) 391-407, q401-02, Hooke and Evelyn.

68. Hillel Schwartz, *Knaves, Fools, Madmen, and that Subtile Effluvium* (Gainesville: U Presses Florida, 1978) 31-41, q21 from *British Apollo* 1 (16-18 June 1708); Pierre Bayle, "Rorarius, Hieronymus," in his *Historical and Critical Dictionary: Selections*, eds. and trans. R.H. Popkin and C. Brush (Indianapolis: Bobbs-Merrill, 1965 [1697-1702]) 213-54, on the precariousness. Cf. Kathleen Wellman, *La Mettrie: Medicine, Philosophy, and Enlightenment* (Durham: Duke U, 1992) esp. 172, 177, though criticized by Aram Vartanian in his review in the *Amer Historical R* 98 (Oct 1993) 1237-38.

69. Nikolaus Mani, "Jean Riolan II (1580-1657) and medical research," *Bull History Med* 42 (1968) 121-44; Donald Greene, "Latitudinarianism and sensibility: the genealogy of the 'man of feeling' reconsidered," *Modern Philology* 75 (1977) 159-83; D.P. Walker, *The Decline of Hell: Seventeenth-Century Discussions of Eternal Torment* (Chicago: U Chicago, 1964); Lloyd G. Stevenson, "Religious elements in the background of the British anti-vivisection movement," *Yale J Biology and Med* 29 (1956) 125-57; Harcourt Brown, "Jean Denis and the transfusion of blood, 1667-1668," *Isis* 39 (1948) 15-29; Thomas, *Man and the Natural World*, 116-125, 137-42; Gresset, *Ver-Vert: or, the Nunnery Parrot*, trans. anon. (L, 1759) last lines.

70. Stephen Walker, *Animal Thought* (L: Routledge & Kegan Paul, 1983) 20-29; Aram Vartanian, "Diderot's rhetoric of paradox, or, the conscious automaton observed," *Eighteenth-Century Studies* 14 (1981) 390-91; Andreas-Holger Maehle, "Literary responses to animal experimentation in seventeenth- and eighteenth-century Britain," *Med History* 34 (1990) 27-51, q42 Samuel Johnson, from his *Idler* 17 (5 Aug 1758); Immanuel Kant, "Duties to animals," from his *Lectures on Ethics*, excerpted in Regan and Singer, *Animal Rights and Human Obligations*, 122. For an early advocate of the moral standing of animals, see Kerry S. Walters, "The 'peaceable disposition' of animals: William Bartram on the moral sensibility of brute creation," *Pennsylvania History* 56 (July 1989) 157-76.

71. Arthur Schopenhauer, "A critique of Kant," from his *On the Basis of Morality*, excerpted in Regan and Singer, *Animal Rights*, 124-28; Stevenson, "Religious elements," 126-27; James Turner, *Reckoning with the Beast: Animals, Pain and Humanity in the Victorian Mind* (Baltimore: Johns Hopkins U, 1980); Maurice Agulhon, "Le Sang des bêtes: le problème de la protection des animaux en France au XIXe siècle," *Romantisme* 11,31 (1981) 81-109; Ritvo, *Animal Estate*, ch. 3.

72. George T. Angell, *Autobiographical Sketches and Personal Recollections* (Boston, 1892?) 1, 13, q26-27.

73. Ritvo, *Animal Estate*, 157-63, q163, Cobbe; Turner, *Reckoning with the Beast*, 86-91; Hebbel H. Hoff et al., trans., *The Cahier Rouge of Claude Bernard* (Cambridge, MA: Schenkman, 1967 [written 1857-60]); Agulhon, "Le sang des bêtes," 100; James L. Nelson, "Symbol and sensibility," *Anthrozoös* 3,2 (1990) 86-88, discussing an essay by Cora Diamond, "Experimenting on animals: a problem in ethics" (1981). See also Bennett J. Cohen and Franklin M. Loew, "Laboratory animal medicine: historical perspectives," in *Laboratory Animal Medicine*, eds. J.G. Fox et al. (NY: Academic, 1984) 1-17, veterinarians and animal experimentation.

74. Andrew Rowan, *Of Mice, Models, and Men* (Albany: SUNY, 1984) 109, Ferrier; Mary T. Phillips and Jeri A. Sechzer, *Animal Research and Ethical Conflict: An Analysis of the Scientific Literature, 1966-1986* (NY: Springer, 1989) q8-9 from Bernard; Harlow, *From Learning to Love*, q xxii; Tom Regan, "The case for animal rights," in *In Defence of Animals*, ed. Peter Singer (Oxford: Basil Blackwell, 1985) 22, and see Part III, "The Activists and Their Strategies"; Scott LaFee, "We, the apes," *San Diego Union Tribune* (26 Jan 1994) E1, E4, on the call for a "Bill of Rights" for primates, as espoused in *The Great Ape Project*; "Buy pretty Polly!" *Chambers's J* 35 (1861) q164.

75. Roderick F. Nash, *The Rights of Nature: A History of Environmental Ethics* (Madison: U Wisconsin, 1989) 50-57; Lutts, *The Nature Fakers*; Heini Hediger, *The Psychology and Behaviour of Animals in Zoos and Circuses*, trans. Geoffrey Sircom (NY: Dover, 1968 [1955]) 8-11; Global Awareness in Action, "Some facts about the environment," factsheet (Anse St.-Jean, Quebec, 1988) and Earth Concert brochure, p. 4, "The planetary ecological clock."

76. "Out and about," *Washington Post* (15 Dec 1989) D3; Alex Pacheco with Anna Francione, "The Silver Spring monkeys," in Singer, ed., *In Defence of Animals*, 135-47; *International Primate Protection League v. Institute for Behavioral Research, Inc.*, 799 F. 2d 934 (4th Cir 1986), all of this followed up recently by Caroline Fraser, "The raid at Silver Spring," *The New Yorker* (19 Apr 1993) 66-84; Susan Sperling, *Animal Liberators: Research and Morality* (Berkeley: U Cal, 1988), critical of the movement, as is Katie McCabe, "Beyond cruelty," *The Washingtonian* 25 (Feb 1990); Mary Zeiss Stange, "Logic gets a skinning when 'faux' replaces fox," *LA Times* (20 Dec 1989) B7, esp. on slogan, "Real people wear fake fur"; "Animal research: ups and downs," *Sci News* (17 March 1990) 174; Frederick K. Goodwin, in *Public Affairs* 3 (1989) 2355-56, quoted in Patrick H. Cleveland, "Animal rights and public perceptions: a dangerous combination," paper distributed as "an open letter to the research community," Med School campus, U Cal, San Diego, 1991.

77. Donald R. Griffin, *Animal Thinking* (Cambridge, MA: Harvard U, 1984), reviewing behaviorist theories and discussing, p. 191, dolphins imitating a diver; Bernard Rollin, "Animal consciousness and scientific change," *New Ideas in Psychology* 4 (1986) 141-44; Herbert Lansdell, "Laboratory animals need only humane treatment," *Int J Neuroscience* 42,3/4 (1988) 170, obligations (part of larger debate over proofs of altruism among animals); Michael A. Fox, *The Case for Animal Experimentation* (Berkeley: U Cal, 1984) esp. 27-28, 45, pleasure and self-awareness; Robert J. White, "A defense of vivisection," in Regan and Singer, *Animal Rights and Human Obligations*, 163-69, q165; Rowan, *Of Mice, Models, and Men*, 65-66, and, on rhesus monkeys, Alice Steinbach, "Whose life is more important: an animal's or a child's?" *Glamour* (Jan 1990) 169; S.L. Washburn, "Human behavior and the behavior of other animals," *Amer Psychologist* 33 (1978) 405-18; Don Bannister, "The fallacy of animal experimentation in psychology," in *Animals in Research*, ed. David Sperlinger (Chichester: Wiley, 1981) 307-17; Roger E. Ulrich, "Animal research:

a psychological ritual," *The Animals' Agenda* 11 (May 1991) 40-44; Office of Technology Assessment, *Alternatives to Animal Use in Research, Testing, and Education* (Washington, D.C.: GPO, 1986) 8, dose tests; Emery M. Roe, "Nonsense, fate, and policy analysis: the case of animal rights and experimentation," *Agriculture and Human Values* 6,4 (1989) 21-29.

78. Willard Gaylin, *Adam and Eve and Pinocchio: On Being and Becoming Human* (NY: Viking, 1990) 12-13; Anthony J. Mastromarino and Stephen P. Tomasovic, "Animal research," *Cancer Bull* 42,4 (1990) 210 – and see entire issue; D.M. Stark et al., "The future development of alternatives to whole animal lab testing," *The Contribution of Lab Animal Science to the Welfare of Men and Animals* (Stuttgart: Fischer, 1985) 301-03; Office of Technology Assessment, *Alternatives to Animal Use*, ch. 6; Steinbach, "Whose life is more important?" 170-71; Peter Singer, critique of *Use of Laboratory Animals in Biomedical and Behavioral Research* (National Academy, 1988), in "Unkind to animals," *NY R of Books* (2 Feb 1989) 36-37; Bannister, "Fallacy of animal experimentation," 316, cooperative experiments; Kathleen V. Wilkes, *Real People: Personal Identity Without Thought Experiments* (Oxford: Oxford U, 1988) 25. Cf. David Hubel, "Interview," *Omni* (Feb 1990) 110, on the inadequacy of computer simulation as compared to live animal subjects. Hubel, a neuroscientist, bases his findings about the human visual cortex on invasive experiments with rats, cats, and monkeys.

79. Clarence R. Carpenter, "Rhesus monkeys (Macaca Mulatta) for American laboratories," *Science* 92 (1946) 284-86; Goodall, *Through a Window*, ch. 19; Donald D. Jackson, "Pursued in the wild for the pet trade, parrots are perched on a risky limb," *Smithsonian* 16 (April 1985) 59, 62, 64-65; Sparks and Soper, *Parrots*, 158; Int Council for Bird Preservation, Parrot Working Group, *Conservation of New World Parrots*, ed. Roger F. Pasquier (St. Lucia: ICBP, 1980) 21. See also Miroslav Holub, "Experimental Animals," trans. Daniel Simko, in *Contemporary East European Poetry*, ed. Emery George (Ann Arbor: Ardis, 1983) 219-20.

80. "Speaking of pictures...chimpanzees love to have their pictures taken," *Life* (16 Mar 1942) 10-11.

CHAPTER FIVE: SEEING DOUBLE

1. Nelson C. White, *Abbott H. Thayer* (Peterborough, NH, 1951) 78, 109.

2. Sharon E. Kingsland, "Abbott Thayer and the protective coloration debate," *J History Biology* 11 (Fall 1978) 223-44; Susan Hobbs, "Nature into art: the landscapes of Abbott Handerson Thayer," *Amer Art J* 14 (Sum 1982) 4-55; Frank M. Chapman, *Autobiography of a Bird Lover* (NY, 1933) 78-80; William S. Rusk, "Thayer, Abbott Handerson," *Dictionary of Amer Biography* (NY, 1936) IX, 399-401; Abbott H. Thayer to Charles L. Freer, letter of 21 Aug 1901, microfilm roll 77 in the Archives of American Art, NY, NY. Debate continues over the evolutionary value of mimicry; neither Poulton's (and Henry W. Bates's) theory of the tasty mimicking the disgusting nor Johann F. Müller's theory of mimicry among unpalatable species has been entirely disproven. See the symposium on "Mimicry and the Evolutionary Process," supplement to *Amer Naturalist* 131 (June 1988). The degree of mimetic resemblance among butterflies, reaching "a level of perfection far beyond its effect on the general viability of the species," would in fact lead to major reconsiderations of the processes of natural selection, on which see Sharon E. Kingsland, *Modeling Nature: Episodes in the History of Population Ecology* (Chicago: U Chicago, 1985) q120 and throughout.

3. Hobbs, "Nature into art," 37; Abbott H. Thayer, caption to peacock frontispiece and his Appendix B (p. 246 for macaw) to his son Gerald H. Thayer's *Concealing-Coloration in the Animal Kingdom* (NY, 1909).

4. White, *Abbott H. Thayer*, 132-34; Barry Faulkner, *Sketches from an Artist's Life* (Dublin, NH: Bauhan, 1973) 18-19; Kingsland, "Abbott Thayer," 241-42; Thayer, *Concealing-Coloration*, 14 for the Law; E.B. Poulton, "[Review of] Thayer, *Concealing-Coloration*," *Nature* 107 (12 May 1921) 338-40; Lida Rose McCabe, "Camouflage – war's handmaid," *Art World* 3 (Jan 1918) 314; "Abbott H. Thayer, noted painter, dies," *NY Times* (30 May 1921) 9.

5. William Morton Wheeler, "Impostors among animals," *Century* 40 (1901) q369, Drummond.

6. Pliny the Elder, *Natural History*, trans. Horace Rackham (Cambridge, MA, 1942) II, 543 (= bk. VII, xii, "Exempla similitudinum"); Roger Caillois, *The Mask of Medusa*, trans. George Ordish (NY: Potter, 1964) 43-52; Jurgis Baltrusaitis, *Aberrations*, trans. Richard Miller (Cambridge, MA: MIT, 1989) 59-87; Michel Foucault, *The Order of Things*, trans. anon. (NY: Vintage, 1970) 17-30; John F. Michell, *Simulacra: Faces and Figures in Nature* (L: Thames and Hudson, 1979) 47, 50, q104 for Lear, q9 for Strindberg.

7. Denis F. Owen, *Camouflage and Mimicry* (Chicago: U Chicago, 1982) 26 on the potoo, a South American bird resembling a scrap of wood; Caillois, *Mask of Medusa*, 16-17. For metaphor, see the issue on "Metaphor and analogy," *Communication & Cognition* 22,1 (1989). On anthropomorphism, which is today enjoying something of a scientific revival, see Natalie Angier, "Flouting tradition, scientists embrace an ancient taboo," *NY Times* (9 Aug 1994) B5; Theodore X. Barber, *The Human Nature of Birds* (NY: St. Martin's, 1993). One must also make a nod here toward Owen Barfield, *Saving the Appearances* (L: Faber & Faber, 1957) 142-43 on the need to perform "acts of figuration" consciously.

8. Henry Drummond, *Lowell Lectures on the Ascent of Man*, 3rd ed. (NY, 1894) 17.

9. Chapman, *Autobiography*, 78-80; William J. Mackey, Jr., *American Bird Decoys* (NY: Dutton, 1965) 12-13; Bob Ridges, *The Decoy Duck* (L: Dragon's World, 1988) 15-17; George Reiger, *Floaters and Stick-ups* (Boston: Godine, 1986) 3, 7, 24-25, 31, 41, 43, q50 from Joel Barber's *Wild Fowl Decoys*; Jeff Waingrow, *American Wildfowl Decoys* (NY: Dutton, 1985) 84; W.H. Auden, "The Decoys" (1932) in his *Collected Shorter Poems, 1930-1944* (L, 1950) 134, "seeming kindness."

10. Ridges, *Decoy Duck*, 21; Reiger, *Floaters and Stick-ups*, 14-15, 158; Mackey, *American Bird Decoys*, 209ff on mass-produced decoys; Waingrow, *American Wildfowl Decoys*, 8-14, 24, 88, 100. Since the Migratory Bird Act of 1918, which banned the shooting of shorebirds, American decoys have migrated from marsh to front lawns and thence, scooting around pink flamingos, to the shelves of collectors, who have paid as much as $74,000 for detailed "antique" carvings – of species of birds never hunted. Environmental historian Jennifer Price is presently writing on the "natural history" of the plastic pink flamingo, designed in 1957 by Don Featherstone (!) of Union Products.

11. For an overview, see Marie-Louise d'Otrange Mastai, *Illusion in Art: Trompe L'oeil, a History of Pictorial Illusionism* (NY: Abaris, 1975). Details: Thomas D. Kaufmann, *The Mastery of Nature: Aspects of Art, Science, and Humanism in the Renaissance* (Princeton: Princeton U, 1993) 36-46; Marie-Christine Gloton, *Trompe-l'oeil et décor plafonnant dans les églises romaines de l'âge baroque* (Rome: Edizioni di Storia e Letteratura, 1965).

12. Mastai, *Illusion in Art*, 160-64 on Gysbrechts, et passim; Alberto Veca, *Inganno*

& *realtà: trompe l'oeil in Europa XVI–XVIII sec.* (Bergamo: Galleria Lorenzelli, 1980); Columbus Museum of Art, *More Than Meets the Eye: The Art of Trompe L'oeil* (Columbus, OH: The Museum, 1985) esp. fig. 74; Miriam Milman, *Trompe-l'oeil Painting* (Geneva: Skira, 1982). For early modern Protestants, Catholic religious images, like the Roman teachings on transubstantiation, might be taken as nothing other than *vanitas* and trompe l'oeil or, as Martin Bucer would say, "decoy birds" leading people away from true piety; see Carlos M.N. Eire, *War Against the Idols: The Reformation of Worship from Erasmus to Calvin* (Cambridge: Cambridge U, 1986) q92. An enduring undercurrent of iconoclasm may inform the scorn for illusionism among more modern commentators. On Thayer's scorn for the "photographic school," see Hobbs, "Nature into art," 37. Cf. Jean Baudrillard's scorn for trompe l'oeil as "objects in a *second state*," in "The trompe l'oeil," in *Calligram: Essays in the New Art History from France*, ed. Norman Bryson (Cambridge: Cambridge U, 1988) 53–62, q56.

13. Pliny the Elder, *Natural History*, 308–11 (= bk. XXXV); Mastai, *Illusion in Art*, 298–99, plates 83, 109, 196 for parrots, and 49, 51, 56, plates 13–14, 68–69, 298, 374 for flies. See also Charles C. Nahl's *Lady with a Parrot* (1850), in *Reality and Deception* (LA: U Southern Cal, 1974) 47, and back cover reproduction of *Homage to a Parrot* (c. 1870) by De Scott Evans.

14. "Flesh-colour," *All the Year 'Round* 45 (10 Jan 1880) 160–64; Maggie Angeloglou, *A History of Make-up* (NY: Macmillan, 1970) 99–118; Richard Corson, *Fashions in Makeup* (NY: Universe, 1972) 361–92.

15. Alfred Frankenstein, *After the Hunt: William Harnett and Other American Still Life Painters 1870–1900*, rev. ed. (Berkeley: U Cal, 1969) 82–83, q55; idem, "Entirely with the brush and with the naked eye," *Illusionism & Trompe L'oeil* (San Francisco: Cal Palace of the Legion of Honor, 1949) 25ff; Mastai, *Illusion in Art*, ch. 8; Murray T. Bloom, *Money of Their Own: Great Counterfeiters* (NY: Scribners, 1957) 36–47, 135, q39 from Daniel T. Ames, q45 from Silas Packard; "Counterfeiting as a profession," *Banker's Mag (NY)* 34 (1879) 378–81 on counterfeit ringmaster Frederick Biebusch, who shook off fifty arrests during his profitable career; Sigmund Krausz, "Ancient and modern counterfeiters," *New England Mag* n.s. 32 (1905) 52–56. Jacques Derrida, *Given Time: I. Counterfeit Money*, trans. Peggy Kamuf (Chicago: U Chicago, 1992) 96, suggests that counterfeit money in any context is a machine for provoking events, as it certainly is in the case of contemporary money artist J.S.G. Boggs, "Art under arrest," *Art & Antiques* (Oct 1987) 99–104, 126–27. Cf. the literary analysis by Walter Benn Michaels, *The Gold Standard and the Logic of Naturalism* (Berkeley: U Cal, 1987) 165ff.

16. Frankenstein, *After the Hunt*, 115–17, q116. For context, see also Edward J. Nygren, "The almighty dollar: money as a theme in American painting," *Winterthur Portfolio* 23 (1988) 129–50.

17. L. Placide Canonge, "A painter's freak," *L'Abeille de la Nouvelle-Orléans* (30 May 1886), trans. by Mastai, *Illusion in Art*, 302; Frankenstein, *After the Hunt*, 99–114, q116.

18. Judith S. Neaman, "The mystery of the Ghent bird and the invention of spectacles," *Viator* 24 (1993) 189–214, amending Edward Rosen, "The invention of eyeglasses," *J History Med* 11 (1956) 13–46, 183–218; Dora Jane Hamblin, "What a spectacle! Eyeglasses, and how they evolved," *Smithsonian* 13 (Mar 1983) 100–10; Jean-Claude Margolin, "Des lunettes et des hommes ou la satire des mal-voyants au XVIᵉ siècle," *Annales: é.s.c.* 30 (1975) 375–93; Giuliana Biavati, "Gli occhiali: una storia attraverso l'ottica delle ambivalenze iconografiche," in Museo Civico di Storia Naturale Giacomo Doria, *La Lente:*

storia, scienza, curiosità attraverso la collezione Fritz Rathschüler (Genoa: ECIG, 1988) 11-31; Wolf Winkler, ed., A Spectacle of Spectacles, trans. Dorothy Jaeschke (Leipzig: Carl-Zeiss-Stiftung, 1988) esp. Claus Baumann's essay, "Eyeglasses and art"; Michael Rhodes, "A pair of fifteenth-century spectacle frames from the City of London," Antiquaries J 62 (1982) 57-73; Vincent Ilardi, "Renaissance Florence: the optical capital of the world," J European Economic History 22 (1993) 507-41, esp. on the widespread sale of concave lenses; John Dreyfus, "The invention of spectacles and the advent of printing," The Library, 6th ser., 10,2 (1988) 93-106; George C. Boon, "Potters, oculists and eye-troubles," Britannia 14 (1983) 1-12, prevalence of eye problems and popularity of Saint Lucia.

19. Margolin, "Des lunettes et des hommes," 388, 393; Richard Corson, Fashions in Eyeglasses (L: Peter Owen, 1967) 37, quoting Georg Bartisch; R. Child Bayley, The Complete Photographer, 2nd ed. (NY, 1907) q3 from Roger Bacon's Perspectiva. On the tactile versus the visual in the shaping of artistic style, see E.H. Gombrich, Art and Illusion: A Study in the Psychology of Pictorial Representation, 2nd ed. (Princeton: Princeton U, 1961) 18-19, summarizing the theories of Alois Riegl.

20. I. Bernard Cohen, Revolution in Science (Cambridge, MA: Belknap, 1985) esp. 83-84, 147-52, 500-05; Steven Shapin and Simon Shaffer, Leviathan and the Air-pump (Princeton: Princeton U, 1985) esp. ch. 6; Simon Schaffer, "Glass works: Newton's prisms and the uses of experiment," in The Uses of Experiment, eds. David Gooding et al. (NY: Cambridge U, 1989) 67-104; Vasco Ronchi, The Nature of Light: An Historical Survey, trans. V. Barocas (Cambridge, MA: Harvard U, 1970), disputed by David C. Lindberg and Nicholas H. Steneck, "The sense of vision and the origins of modern science," in Science, Medicine, and Society in the Renaissance, ed. Allen G. Debus (NY: Science History, 1972) I, 29-45, rebutted by Ronchi, "Two thousand years of conflict between 'reason' and 'sense,'" Atti della Fondazione Giorgio Ronchi 30 (1975) 525-55, assessed by Vincent Ilardi, "Eyeglasses and concave lenses in fifteenth-century Florence and Milan," Renaissance Q 29 (1976) 341-60; Antonio Ferraz, "'Lux' et 'lumen' aux XVIe et XVIIe siècles," Proc XIVth Int Congress on the History of Sci (Tokyo, 1975) IV, 245-48; David C. Lindberg, Theories of Vision from Al-Kindi to Kepler (Chicago: U Chicago, 1976) esp. 122-35, and cf. Paul-Marie Maurin, trans. Rosalind Greenstein, "On the visual perception hypotheses of Hobbes, Gibson and Ronchi," Leonardo 8 (1975) 301-05.

21. Francis Bacon, "Of the dignity and advancement of learning," in his Works (L, 1850-74) IV, 403; Stillman Drake, introduction and notes to his translation of Discoveries and Opinions of Galileo (NY: Doubleday, 1957); Hillel Schwartz, "Sun and salt, 1500-1770," Diogenes 117 (Spr 1982) 26-41; Barbara J. Shapiro, Probability and Certainty in Seventeenth-Century England (Princeton: Princeton U, 1983) 20-23 and throughout. Replication in science is discussed in more detail in Chapter VII.

22. Peter Laslett, "The history of aging and the aged," in his Family Life and Illicit Love in Earlier Generations (Cambridge: Cambridge U, 1977) 174-213; James H. Cassedy, American Medicine and Statistical Thinking 1800-1860 (Cambridge, MA: Harvard U, 1984) q39-40 from 1828; W.A. Evans, Dr. Evans' How to Keep Well (NY, 1922) ch. 11; A.W. Calhoun, "Effects of student life upon the eyesight," U.S. Bureau of Education Circulars of Information, No. 6 (Washington, D.C., 1881) 12-13; George M. Beard, A Practical Treatise on Nervous Exhaustion, ed. A.D. Rockwell, 5th ed. (NY, 1905) 40-43.

23. Gerald L'E. Turner, "Spectacles over 700 years," in Winkler, Spectacle of Spectacles, 11-12; Adolf Zander, The Ophthalmoscope, trans. R.B. Carter (L, 1864); Stanley J. Reiser, Medicine and the Reign of Technology (Cambridge, MA: Harvard U, 1978) 47-49;

"Ocular astigmatism: a historical sketch," *The Optician* 144 (7 Dec 1962) 549-53; James E. Lebensohn, "Notes to 'Astigmatism,'" *Survey of Ophthalmology* 7 (1962) 177-83; James P.C. Southall, *Introduction to Physiological Optics* (L, 1937) 144-54.

24. One can see the history of the clasps, brackets, and frames for eyeglasses at Pierre Marly's Musée des Lunettes et des Lorgnettes de Jadis, Paris, or read Pierre R. Marly, *Les Lunettes* (P: Hachette/Massin, 1980) and idem, *Spectacles & Spyglasses*, texts by Jean-Claude Margolin and Paul Biérent, trans. Barry Tulett (N.p.: Hoëbeke, 1988) esp. 22 on seeing double. Speculation: Were gothic tales of Doppelgängers, seen often out of the corners of eyes, artefacts of freak reflections off misfitted glasses? Were the crossed eyes of readers peering through shifty lenses, or the dizzinesses of embroiderers, nostrils clamped shut by tight spectacles, as conducive to seeing double as the intemperance of eighteenth-century drinkers of distilled spirits?

25. Turner, "Spectacles over 700 years," 13; Patrick Robertson, *The Book of Firsts* (NY: Bramhall House, 1974) 313, relying in part upon Corson, *Fashions in Eyeglasses*, 69-70; Philip Conisbee, *Chardin* (Lewisburg: Bucknell U, 1985) frontispiece, fig. 6, fig. 218 – Chardin's self-portrait in eyeglasses so striking that in 1867 Philippe Rousseau would copy the portrait into his painting, *Chardin et ses modèles*; Margolin, "Des lunettes et des hommes," 375 for Goethe; Baumann, "Eyeglasses and art," 30, 39, 48; Asa Briggs, "'The Philosophy of the Eye': spectacles, cameras, and the new vision," in his *Victorian Things* (Chicago: U Chicago, 1988) q105, Horne, from *Fraser's Mag* (Dec 1876).

26. For microscopes, see Catherine Wilson, *The Invisible World: Early Modern Philosophy and the Invention of the Microscope* (Princeton: Princeton U, 1995) esp. 181 on the tendency of early modern investigators to favor the microscope over the telescope as a truth-telling device, 215-27 on the Ronchi hypothesis and the ambiguity of microscopic images. Cf. Marian Fournier, *The Fabric of Life: Microscopy in the Seventeenth Century* (Baltimore: Johns Hopkins U, 1995). For specifics in this paragraph, see J. van Zuylen, "On the microscope of Antoni van Leeuwenhoek," *Janus* 68 (1981) 159-98; Brian Bracegirdle, "The performance of seventeenth- and eighteenth-century microscopes," *Med History* 22 (1978) 187-95; Bruno Zanobio, "L'immagine filamentoso-reticolare nell'anatomia microscopia del XVII al XIX secolo," *Physis* 2 (1960) 299-317; Ian Hacking, "Do we see through a microscope?" *Pacific Phil Q* 62 (Oct 1981) 305-22; Gerald L'E. Turner, *Essays on the History of the Microscope* (Oxford: Senecio, 1980) esp. 44-45, 161, 166-75. On preconceptions, Ann S. Blum, *Picturing Nature: American Nineteenth-Century Zoological Illustration* (Princeton: Princeton U, 1993) q313, and see her entire ch. 7. For medical doubts about the value of microscopic evidence, dispelled after the success of diphtheria antitoxin in the 1890s, see John Harley Warner, *The Therapeutic Perspective: Medical Practice, Knowledge, and Identity in America, 1820-1885* (Cambridge, MA: Harvard U, 1986) 277-83.

27. J. Marion Sims, *The Story of My Life*, ed. H. Marion-Sims (NY, 1894) 121-25, 234, and see his *Clinical Notes on Uterine Surgery* (NY, 1873 [1866]) 14-20; Elisabeth Bennion, *Antique Medical Instruments* (Berkeley: U Cal, 1979) 131 and pl. 22, on a tubular speculum with mirrored interior designed in 1855 by the English physician William Ferguson; Ornella Moscucci, *The Science of Women: Gynecology and Gender in England, 1800-1929* (NY: Cambridge U, 1990) 112-26, a less simple-minded account of the speculum, which was used in England after 1866 (and passage of the Contagious Diseases Acts) for the forcible examination of prostitutes, coming thus to be a clear metonym for rape. On X-rays, see Nancy Knight, "'The New Light': x rays and medical futurism," in *Imagining Tomorrow*, ed. Joseph J. Corn (Cambridge, MA: Harvard U, 1986) 10-34.

See also "The Roentgen ray and second sight," *J Amer Med Assoc* 26 (May 1896) 1065, reporting a suggestion that those gifted with "second sight" might be able to see through opaque media because they registered the passage of X-rays.

28. Mastai, *Illusion in Art*, pls. 268 (French School, *The Deception*, eighteenth century) and 285 (Laurent Dabos, *Peace Treaty between France and Spain*, after 1801), color pls. 19 (De Scott Evans, *Homage to a Parrot*) and 22 (trade card); Millman, *Trompe-l'oeil Painting*, 61 (L.L. Boilly, *Self-Portrait with Broken Glass*, c. 1805-10), and cf. Keith Walden, "Speaking modern: language, culture, and hegemony in grocery window displays, 1887–1920," *Canadian Historical R* 70 (Sept 1989) 297, a smashed window simulated in 1899. On hallucinations, see Paul Schiller, "Experiments on imagination, after-images, and hallucinations," *Amer J Psychiatry* 13 (1933) 597-611; Louis Lewin, *Phantastica: Narcotic and Stimulating Drugs, Their Use and Abuse* (NY: Dutton, 1931 [1886]) 103; Edward H. Clarke, *Visions: A Study of False Sight (Pseudopia)* (Boston, 1878) 184 for cannabis story; V. Kandinsky, "Zur Lehre von den Hallucinationen," *Archiv für Psychiatrie und Nervenkrankheiten* 11 (1881) 453-64, quoted in and trans. by Ronald K. Siegel and Murray E. Jarvik, "Drug-induced hallucinations in animals and man," in *Hallucinations: Behavior, Experience and Theory*, eds. Siegel and Louis J. West (NY: Wiley, 1975) 109-10. For the Lewin reference and much else, I am indebted to a thoughtful letter, 16 June 1990, from Michael R. Aldrich of the Fitz Hugh Ludlow Memorial Lib (San Francisco) on the history of experiences of "doubling" under the influence of hallucinogens.

29. Abbott H. Thayer, "Introduction" to Gerald H. Thayer, *Concealing-Coloration*, 3, 7; Michael Schudson, *Discovering the News: A Social History of American Newspapers* (NY: Basic, 1978) 95-105; Aline Ripert and Claude Frère, *La Carte postale: son histoire, sa fonction sociale* (Lyon: Presses Universitaires de Lyon, 1983) esp. 63-64.

30. Alan Delgado, *Victorian Entertainment* (NY: Amer Heritage, 1971) 77-79; Hugo Münsterberg, *The Film: A Psychological Study* (NY: Dover, 1970 [1916]) 14-15; Noel Harris, "A subversive form," in John L. Fell et al., *Before Hollywood: Turn-of-the-Century American Film* (NY: AFA, 1986) 48-49 on deception, which I take contrariwise; Charles Musser, *The Emergence of Cinema* (NY: Scribner, 1991) 19; Drummond, *Lowell Lectures*, 105. Siegmund Lubin, one of the earliest American movie makers and distributors, began as an optician and patented spectacles "with hooks": Joseph P. Eckhardt with Linda Kowall, *Peddler of Dreams: Siegmund Lubin and the Creation of the Motion Picture Industry, 1896-1916* (Philadelphia: National Museum of Amer Jewish History, 1984) 1.

31. On sexual congress in the early cinema, see Linda Wilson, *Hard Core: Power, Pleasure, and the "Frenzy of the Visible"* (Berkeley: U Cal, 1989) chs. 2-3, esp. 60-72. On psychophysiology, see Edwin G. Boring, *Sensation and Perception in the History of Experimental Psychology* (NY, 1942) 233-45; S.P. Thompson, "Optical illusions of motion," *Brain* 3 (1880) 289-98, reprinted in *Visual Perception: The Nineteenth Century*, ed. William N. Dember (NY: Wiley, 1964) 84; J.O. Robinson, *The Psychology of Visual Illusion* (L: Hutchinson, 1972); R.L. Gregory, *The Intelligent Eye* (NY: McGraw-Hill, 1970). See also the valuable study by Jonathan Crary, *Techniques of the Observer: On Vision and Modernity in the Nineteenth Century* (Cambridge, MA: MIT, 1990) for the effects of theories of vision and of experiences with new visual devices upon the theory and practice of art.

32. Boring, *Sensation and Perception*, 246-56; Hermann Ludwig von Helmholtz, "Unconscious conclusions," *Helmholtz's Treatise on Physiological Optics*, trans. from 3rd German ed. "by several hands," ed. J.P.C. Southall (Rochester, NY, 1924-25 [1909-11]), III, 2-6, 11-13, repted in Dember, ed., *Visual Perceptions*, 163-71; Roy R. Behrens, *Art*

& *Camouflage: Concealment and Deception in Nature, Art, and War* (Cedar Falls: *North Amer R*, 1981) 67–69. See also Rudolf Arnheim, *New Essays on the Psychology of Art* (Berkeley: U Cal, 1986) esp. pt. II.

33. Poulton, "[Review of] *Concealing-coloration*," note 4 above. Thayer applied his gestaltist sensibility to works of art, which should never be altered "by so much as a pin-point," for "*every particle*" of a painting or sculpture was crucial to its effect: "It is the very mark of a masterpiece that every part of it is a masterpiece." It was Thayer's insistence upon Nature as a masterpiece, that is, upon the functionalism of *all* naturally occurring animal colors and patterns, that led scientists to part ways with him. See Abbott H. Thayer, overleaf to peacock frontispiece, in Thayer, *Concealing-Coloration*; Poulton, "Thayer," 597; A.H. Thayer, "'Restoration': the doom of pictures and sculpture," *Int Studio* 70 (Mar 1920) xiii–xvii; Blum, *Picturing Nature*, 336–43.

34. John Keegan, *The Face of Battle* (NY: Viking, 1976) 204–84; J.J. Lhermitte, *Les Hallucinations clinique et physiopathologique* (P, 1951) 136, typhus; Henri Hecaen and J. de Ajuriaguerra, *Méconnaissances et hallucinations corporelles* (P, 1952) 317, sleeplessness, anxiety, and Doubles. By 1909 typhus had been reproduced in monkeys and shown to be transmitted by body lice, but no effective medicine existed until 1943.

35. Keegan, *Face of Battle*, 231ff; Eric J. Leed, *No Man's Land: Combat & Identity in World War I* (Cambridge: Cambridge U, 1979) 99, and ch. 5 on war neurosis; Elmer F. Southard, *Shell-Shock and Other Neuropsychiatric Problems* (NY: Arno, 1973 [1919]) 310–11, 316, q420.

36. Southard, *Shell-Shock*, 311, 439, 457, 658–62; Lewis R. Yealland, *Hysterical Disorders of Warfare* (L, 1918) 237–48; Robert David Ritchie, "One History of 'Shellshock,'" Ph.D., U Cal, San Diego, 1986.

37. Maurice G. Debonnet, "Camouflage and the use of paint in warfare," typescript, 1918, p. 2, in Archives of the Hoover Inst on War, Revolution, and Peace, Stanford, CA; Poulton, "[Review of] *Concealing-Coloration*," 338, citing the *Penny Cyclopaedia* of 1836; Behrens, *Art & Camouflage*, 9; J. Bowyer Bell (pseud.), *Cheating: Deception in War & Magic, Games & Sports, Sex & Religion, Business & Con Games, Politics & Espionage, Art & Science* (NY: St. Martin's, 1982) 49.

38. Guy Hartcup, *Camouflage: A History of Concealment and Deception in War* (NY: Scribner's, 1980) q12–13 from Major-Gen. J.F.C. Fuller, *Conduct of War* (1962) 140; Debonnet, "Camouflage," 3; C.H.R. Chesney and J. Huddlestone, *The Art of Camouflage* (NY, 1943) 62–63; J. André Smith, "Notes on camouflage," *Architectural Record* 42 (Nov 1917) 469–77; W. Kolossovsky, "Camouflage in the Russian army," *Military Engineer* 16 (Mar–Apr 1924) 117.

39. Alon Bement, "Camouflage," *Teachers' College Record* 18 (Nov 1917) 458–59; Chesney and Huddlestone, *Art of Camouflage*, 66–67, 94; William G. Fischer et al., "History of remote sensing," in *Manual of Remote Sensing*, ed.-in-chief Robert G. Reeves (Falls Church, VA: Amer Soc of Photogrammetry, 1975) I, 27–30, 32; Matthew Luckiesh, *Visual Illusions* (NY, 1922) 219–21; Lee Kennett, *The First Air War, 1914–1918* (NY: Free Press, 1991) esp. 37.

40. Solomon J. Solomon, *Strategic Camouflage* (L, 1920) v–vii, q1; Eric J. Leed, *No Man's Land: Combat and Identity in World War I* (Cambridge: Cambridge U, 1979) 103; Debonnet, "Camouflage," 4; Olga S. Phillips, *Solomon J. Solomon (1860–1927)* (L, 1933) 139, 179–82, 188, q175; McCabe, "Camouflage – war's handmaid," 314; Chesney and Huddlestone, *Art of Camouflage*, 45, 68; Charles W. Glover, *Civil Defense* (L, 1941) q558;

Greville Rickard, "Progress of camouflage in the U.S. Army during World War I," pamphlet, Bibliography folder, Edward M. Farmer Papers, Archives of the Hoover Inst.

41. Leed, *No Man's Land*, 103, 134-37; Sarah Griffiths, "War painting: a no-man's land between history and reportage," *Leeds Arts Calendar* 78 (1976) 24-32; Elizabeth L. Kahn, *The Neglected Majority: "Les Camoufleurs," Art History, and World War I* (Landham, MD: U Presses of Amer, 1984) 56-77, 93-95, 127, 137.

42. Gertrude Stein, *Picasso* (1959 [1938]) 11, quoted by Stephen Kern, *The Culture of Time and Space 1880-1918* (Cambridge: Harvard U, 1983) 288, and see his ch. 11 on "The Cubist War"; Debonnet, "Camouflage," 4; Hartcup, *Camouflage*, 17; Homer Saint-Gaudens, "Camouflage reminiscences," *Military Engineer* 25 (May-June 1933) 248; Chesney and Huddlestone, *Art of Camouflage*, 70, on "the miraculous" at the camouflage factory in Amiens; McCabe, "Camouflage — war's handmaid," 313-15; Kahn, *Neglected Majority*, q37, Scévola. On the numbers, Bement, "Camouflage," 462: one of every two hundred men in the French army was supposedly engaged in camouflage work. Gombrich, *Art and Illusion*, 281, observes that Cubism essentially opposed illusionism.

43. Raymond H. Fredette, *The Sky on Fire: The First Battle of Britain 1917-1918* (NY: Holt, Rinehard, Winston, 1966) 5, 11, 79, pls. between pp. 102-03, 231, and q20-21; Brian Robertson, *Aircraft Camouflage and Markings 1907-1954*, ed. D.A. Russell (Marlow, Bucks.: Harleyford, 1956) 9-11, 47, 60; Kolossovsky, "Camouflage in the Russian army," 116. For a German perspective, see Peter Fritzsche, *A Nation of Fliers: German Aviation and the Popular Imagination* (Cambridge, MA: Harvard U, 1992) esp. ch. 2 on the war ace and 173-84 on the geopolitical (aerial) eye.

44. Anthony Ordway, "Painted ships," *Ken* 2 (20 Oct 1938) 58; Charles Bittinger, "Naval camouflage," *U.S. Naval Inst Proc* 66 (Oct 1940) 1394-98; David Williams, *Liners in Battledress* (St. Catharines, Ont.: Vanwell, 1989) 28; Luckiesh, *Visual Illusions* 222-23; Debonnet, "Camouflage," 3, 5; Kingsland, "Abbott Thayer and the protective coloration debate," 241.

45. Ordway, "Painted ships," 58-89; Debonnet, "Camouflage," 5; Kingsland, "Abbott Thayer and the protective coloration debate," 242; Williams, *Liners in Battledress*, 37-41, 57-62, 73-74, 80; Luckiesh, *Visual Illusions*, 219, on hocus-pocus; Bement, "Camouflage," 461; Hartcup, *Camouflage*, 9; Hugh B. Cott, "Camouflage in nature and in war," *Royal Engineers J* 52 (Dec 1938) 501-17; Behrens, *Art & Camouflage*, 45.

46. Williams, *Liners in Battledress*, 76-78; Howard S. Bennion, "Discussion" of Aymar Embury, II, "Reminiscences of a camouflage officer," *Military Engineer* 19 (May-June 1927) 238-39; Faulkner, *Sketches*, 94; Nemo, "The 'camouflage' soldier," *Spectator* 118 (23 June 1917) 696-97; Le Corbusier, *L'Art décoratif d'aujourd'hui* (P, 1925) iii. On Freud I take my lead from Behrens, *Art & Camouflage*, 53; Sigmund Freud, *Civilization and Its Discontents*, trans. and ed. James Strachey (NY: Norton, 1961 [1929-31]) 90.

47. Ernst L. Freud, ed., *The Letters of Sigmund Freud*, trans. Tania Stern and James Stern (NY: Basic, 1960) 336, letter of 20 Dec 1921; Sigmund Freud, *The Future of an Illusion*, trans. and ed. James Strachey (NY: Norton, 1961 [1927]); Donald Prater, *A Ringing Glass: The Life of Rainer Maria Rilke* (Oxford: Clarendon, 1986) q384; Rainer Maria Rilke, *Briefe aus Muzot 1921 bis 1926*, eds. R. Sieber-Rilke and C. Sieber (Leipzig, 1936) 335-36, trans. by O.B. Hardison, Jr., *Disappearing Through the Skylight* (NY: Viking, 1989) 132.

48. Daniel Starch, *Principles of Advertising* (NY, 1923) 447-48; Robert D. Friedel, *Pioneer Plastic: The Making and Selling of Celluloid* (Madison: U Wisconsin, 1983) esp. 12-13, 29-31, 88-89.

49. John Jewkes et al., *The Sources of Invention*, 2nd ed. (NY: Norton, 1969) 233-34; Aaron J. Ihde, "Baekeland, Leo Hendrik," *Dictionary of Amer Biography* (NY: Scribner's, 1973) Supp. III, 25-27; Bakelite ad, "Helping the Family Keep Well," *Fortune* (Apr 1936) 211.

50. *OED*, III, 992, dating "costume jewelry" to 1933; Agatha Christie, *A Murder Is Announced* (L, 1950) 60; Riccardo Nobili, *The Gentle Art of Faking* (L, 1922) 18ff; Vivienne Becker, *Fabulous Fakes: The History of Fantasy and Fashion Jewellery* (L: Grafton, 1988) 2-3, 5, 11-16; Lord Twining, *A History of the Crown Jewels of Europe* (L: Batsford, 1960) 160-63, 275; "Doublets," *EDSAM*, V, 81; Petra von Trott zu Solz, "Stras: Simili-Diamantschmuck des 18. Jahrhunderts," *Waffen- und Kostümkunde* 28,2 (1986) 130-44. Stras (= Joseph Strasser, from Vienna) may have stolen techniques already known to English jewelers.

51. Lillian Baker, *One Hundred Years of Collectible Jewelry, 1850-1950* (Paducah, KY: Collector, 1978) 129-33, 4-8, 118, 141; Becker, *Fabulous Fakes*, 16, 29, 32-39, 47, 51, 67, 71-74.

52. Jody Shields, *All That Glitters* (NY: Rizzoli, 1987) 18-22, 19 for Marshall Field 1925 catalog and for *Vogue*; Becker, *Fabulous Fakes*, 8, 76, 82-83, 95-104, 119, 146-47; "Production of large artificial diamonds," *Sci Amer* 77 (18 Sept 1897) 183; Baker, *One Hundred Years*, 140, 82-83; *OED*, V, 378. See also the many films of the 1920s whose plots centered upon the production of artificial diamonds, beginning with Léonce Perret (dir), *L'Empire du diamant* (Pathé, 1920).

53. Becker, *Fabulous Fakes*, 127-28, 140-41, 146-47; Burlington Fine Arts Club, *Catalogue of a Collection of Counterfeits, Imitations and Copies of Works of Art* (L, 1924) #191-92; "Junk jewelry: a flashy fad for simple styles," *Life* (31 Jan 1938) 34; Shields, *All That Glitters*, 18.

54. Gordon M. Kline, "Plastics," *Ency Americana* (NY: Americana, 1962) XXII, 221r-223; "Plastics," *Fortune* 13 (Mar 1936) 69-75, 143; Eduard Farber, "Baekeland, Leo Hendrik," *DSB* (NY: Scribner's, 1970) I, 385; J.H. DuBois, *Plastics* (Chicago, 1943) iii. Seymour S. Schwartz, LA, letter to author, 12 Dec 1992, notes that acrylic aircraft canopies were "indeed shatterable" – DuBois's enthusiasm got the better of him. See also Seymour S. Schwartz and Sidney H. Goodman, *Plastics Materials and Processes* (NY: Van Nostrand Reinhold, 1982) esp. Table 1.1.

55. Anne Hollander, *Seeing Through Clothes* (NY: Avon, 1978) 340-44; Jewkes et al., *Sources of Invention*, 245-48, 275-77.

56. On Busby Berkeley, see Williams, *Hard Core* 159, citing Lucy Fischer, *Shot/Countershot: Film Tradition and Women's Cinema* (Princeton: Princeton U, 1989) 74. On Hayward, see Frank S. Nugent, "[Review of] *Man in the Iron Mask*," *NY Times* (14 July 1939) 11:1. On double stage roles, see "Doubles," *All the Year 'Round* 29 (1 Mar 1873) 372-78. Perhaps the climax of singleton-as-twin films was *The Dark Mirror* (1946). When Olivia de Havilland turns out to be her murderous identical twin, the audience feels as flummoxed as the police detective.

57. On twin stage performers, see *The Bystander* (22 May 1929) 425; Kathryn M. Abbe and Frances M. Gill, *Twins on Twins* (NY: Clarkson N. Potter, 1980) 72-73, 92-93. On the most revealing of the twin films, *A Modern Cain*, see *American Film Institute Catalog of Motion Pictures Produced in the United States* (Berkeley, U Cal, 1988) F2.3663. The reference to the Fox Theatre Company's "Seeing Double idea," *The Last Word* 4 (18 June 1930) I owe to a chance encounter with Greg Bell. "Seeing Double" was linked

to contests for the most talented, most perfectly alike twins, and tied in commercially with the Golddust (kitchen cleanser) Twins.

58. Moviemaking itself was a camouflage screen behind which producer-director Alexander Korda could spy for the British while scouting locations for spy thrillers like *The Scarlet Pimpernel* (1935). See Richard Brooks, "U.K.'s Korda Was World War II Spy," *NY Observer* (25 Nov 1991), clipping provided by Mark Helprin.

59. "Doubles," *All the Year 'Round*, 376–77.

60. Cliff Lyons, as told to William F. French, "Double's troubles," *Saturday Evening Post* (25 July 1936) 16; Florabel Muir, "They risk their necks for you," *ibid.* (15 Sept 1945) 26; Elizabeth Wilson, "Hollywood hardpans," *Liberty* (20 Oct 1945) 30; "Danger for a living," *Newsweek* (13 Aug 1956) 94.

61. This and the next two paragraphs are based on an assortment of sometimes poorly sourced clippings, "Stand-ins" file, Margaret Herrick Library, Academy of Motion Picture Arts and Sciences, Beverly Hills, CA – including: Dan Thomas, "Pay cuts raise hopes of picture stand-in," *Post Record* (31 Jan 1935); "Records prove that stand-ins seldom reach stardom," *LA Herald* (9 May 1936); *Citizen* (1 Apr 1938); *LA Herald* (9 Dec 1939); *LA Examiner* (13 Mar 1944); Lowell E. Redelings, "Man behind the scenes," *Hollywood Citizen-News* (10 Feb 1947); John Scott, "Screen star's stand-in has thankless job: chances of becoming noted in own right practically nil," *LA Times* (10 Feb 1955); Trish Huether, "Scarlett O'Hara's double now Santa Anan," *The Santa Ana Register* (4 Oct 1973); *People* (18 June 1990) 103. See also Penny Stallings, *Flesh and Fantasy* (NY; St. Martin's, 1978) 199–207, 280–86.

62. Liza Wilson, "A matter of status," *LA Herald Examiner Cal Weekly* (17 May 1964) q8–9, Lamarr, and noting, on the identification of stand-in with star, that Irene Crosby died within two weeks of the woman for whom she stood in, Marilyn Monroe. On *It Happened in Hollywood*, see "Doubles for movie stars get their own chance for a movie," *Life* (18 Oct 1937) 78, 80. As the Jewish barber in *The Great Dictator* (1940), Chaplin himself doubled for Adolf Hitler, who, according to a satirist in *Punch* (7 Feb 1940), "easily bored by the polite functions that not even dictators can wholly avoid," had used a ceremonial stand-in since his rise to power.

63. CBS TV's *Entertainment Tonight*, 22 Feb 1993, reported on the attempts of women who serve as body doubles in nude scenes in mainline films to get their names in the credits; at the moment they, like other stand-ins, remain anonymous. See also Brian de Palma (dir), *Body Double* (Columbia, 1984), which mixes the motifs of voyeurism, vampirism, stand-ins, and deception.

64. Hugo Münsterberg, *The Film: A Psychological Study* (NY: Dover, 1970 [1916]) 100; idem, *On the Witness Stand* (NY, 1908) 17, 43, 108, 167; Matthew Hale, *Human Science and Social Order: Hugo Munsterberg and the Origins of Applied Psychology* (Philadelphia: Temple U, 1980) 111–21. Münsterberg's gallery of devices would inspire the creation of the polygraph machine, or "lie detector."

65. Peter Hain, *Mistaken Identity: The Wrong Face of the Law* (L: Quartet, 1976) 131–32 on line-ups, q165 from *Committee of Inquiry into the Case of Adolf Beck* (1904); Eric R. Watson, *Adolf Beck (1877–1904)* (Edinburgh, 1924); Clifford Sully, *Mistaken Identity* (L, 1925) esp. 7 on the "false evidence given in good faith" at line-ups; Elizabeth F. Loftus, *Eyewitness Testimony* (Cambridge, MA: Harvard U, 1979) 1–2 on Sacco-Vanzetti. In July 1993, a case of possibly mistaken identity by even more witnesses was decided by the Supreme Court of Israel in favor of the defendant, John Demjanjuk. For the back-

ground, see Willem A. Wagenaar, *Identifying Ivan: A Case Study in Legal Psychology* (Cambridge, MA: Harvard U, 1988).

66. Asa S. Herzog and A.J. Erickson, *Camera, Take the Stand!* (NY, 1940) 4, 5, q7; briefing, 15 Dec 1936, in Creative Organization Staff Meetings files, Box 7, folder 2, pp. 4, 6, q9, J. Walter Thompson Company Archives, John W. Hartman Center for Sales, Advertising, and Marketing History, Special Collections Lib, Duke U, Durham, NC, as also ad in *Saturday Evening Post* (19 June 1937) from Eastman Kodak Consumer files, Box 7.

67. Kodak ads: *Literary Digest* (10 May 1930) 53; *The New Yorker* (7 July 1930) and (23 May 1930); *Life* (18 Apr 1930); *National Geographic* (Aug 1939), clips of each in Eastman Kodak Consumer Account files, Box 1 and Box 9, J. Walter Thompson Company Archives, preceding note. Ad for Kodak Retina in *The New Yorker* (16 Mar 1935) 71.

68. Walter D. Binger and Hilton H. Railey, *What the Citizen Should Know About Civilian Defense* (NY, 1942) 79; "Camouflage," *Architectural Forum* 76 (Jan 1942 – "Civilian Defense Reference Number") 14–18; Fischer et al., "History of remote sensing," 35–40; Robert P. Breckenridge, *Modern Camouflage*, 3rd ed. (NY, 1942) 19; idem, "War paint," *Saturday Evening Post* (1 May 1943) 26; R. Myerscough-Walker, "The camoufleur and his craft. 2. Methods," *The Builder* 157 (22 Sept 1939) 457; Ralph R. Root, *Camouflage with Planting* (Chicago, 1942) 54; *Science in War*, 2nd ed. (L, Nov 1940) q42.

69. Seymour Reit (a pseudonym: See More Right?), *Masquerade: The Amazing Camouflage Deceptions of World War II* (NY: Hawthorn, 1978) 14, 108ff; "Camouflage," *Architectural Forum*, 20. MIT researchers thought to do for Boston what the Germans did for Hamburg, but eventually abandoned the project. See the VisLab papers in Special Collections, Scripps Institute of Oceanography, La Jolla, CA.

70. Charles G. Cruickshank, *Deception in World War II* (Oxford: OUP, 1979) q6, 7, 9, 196, 217; Jane Goodman, *Edward Seago: The Other Side of the Canvas* (L: Colliers, 1978) 176, teaching with ventriloquism; Geoffrey Barkas and Natalie Barkas, *The Camouflage Story from Aintree to Alamein* (L, 1952) 126; Edwin P. Hoyt, *The Invasion Before Normandy: The Secret Battle of Slapton Sands* (NY: Stein & Day, 1985) 74, 78; Reit, *Masquerade*, 24–27, 33.

71. Breckenridge, "War paint," 26; Reit, *Masquerade*, 183–90. Before World War II, in 1937, Japanese bombers had themselves been deceived by Chinese battleships of bamboo and painted paper: *Recent Overseas Camouflage including Air Force Combat Notes from the Far East*, Camouflage Memo 101 (Fort Belvoir, VA, 30 Sept 1942), in Edward M. Farmer Papers, Archives of the Hoover Inst.

72. Reit, *Masquerade*, 88; Harper Goff, "Camouflage in America is more than a science," *Architect and Engineer* 152 (Jan 1943) 26–31, 36; Hoyt, *Invasion Before Normandy*, 74; Robertson, *Aircraft Camouflage*, 137–38; Williams, *Liners in Battledress*, 110, 117; Rosamond Gilder, "You bet your life: report on a camouflage show," *Theatre Arts* (Sept 1944) 521–27 for song, also in Behrens, *Art & Camouflage*, 64.

73. William M. Spierer, "U.S. Army camouflage. What it demands from the artist who wants to be a camoufleur," *Art News* 41 (1–14 Nov 1942) 9–13; "Jane Berlandina: stage entrance," *ibid.*, 27; Homer Saint-Gaudens, "Concealment needs," *Military Engineer* 34 (Jan 1942) 4–7; Reit, *Masquerade*, 77.

74. "Jane Berlandina," 27; "Camouflage," *Architectural Forum*, q5; Louis Philippe ad, "Only an Expert...," *The New Yorker* (2 Mar 1935) 43; Lawrence Corwin, "Tangled web," contribution to undated forum held by the *Architectural Record*, in course folder, Edward M. Farmer Papers, Archives of the Hoover Inst.

75. John Gaughan and Jim Steinmeyer, *The Mystery of Psycho* (LA: John Gaughan & Associates, 1987); David Fisher, *The War Magician* (NY: Coward-McCann, 1983) q13, q23, *et passim*; Bell, *Cheating*, 239-61; Jasper Maskelyne, *Magic – Top Secret* (L, 1949) q15.

76. Tet Schlemmer, ed., *The Letters and Diaries of Oskar Schlemmer*, trans. Krishna Winston (Middletown, CT: Wesleyan U, 1972) 381-82, and cf. Behrens, *Art & Camouflage*, 58-59; Werner Haftmann, *Painting in the Twentieth Century*, trans. Janet Seligman (NY: Praeger, 1965) I, 235-41 and II, pls. 756-62, esp. 758, *Group of Fourteen in Imaginary Architecture* (1930).

77. Sibyl Moholy-Nagy, *Moholy-Nagy: Experiment in Totality* (NY: Harper, 1950) *passim*, q42, q116, q150. It is instructive in this context to read Terry Castle, "Phantasmagoria: spectral technology and the metaphorics of modern reverie," *Critical Inquiry* 15 (Aut 1988) 26-61.

78. Robert F. Sumrall, "Ship camouflage (World War II)," *U.S. Naval Inst Proc* 99,2 (1973) 67-81; Behrens, *Art & Camouflage*, 61-62, quotation on Gorky from Julien Levy in W.C. Seitz, *Arshile Gorky* (NY: MOMA, 1972) 8.

79. Schlemmer, *Letters and Diaries*, 389; W. Jackson Rushing, "Ritual and myth: Native American culture and abstract expressionism," in *The Spiritual in Art: Abstract Painting 1890-1985*, eds. M. Tuchman and J. Freeman (NY: Abbeville, 1986) 273-95, q291 from Jackson Pollock, "My painting," *Possibilities* 1 (Wint 1947-48) 78; Haftmann, *Painting in the Twentieth Century*, I, 348; Harold Rosenberg, *The Anxious Object* (NY: Mentor, 1966) ch. 3; most recently, insistent upon the horizontality and *effacement* of Pollock's work, Rosalind E. Krauss, *The Optical Unconscious* (Cambridge, MA: MIT, 1993) ch. 6, esp. 289. Cf. Michaels, *The Gold Standard*, 162ff on the relationship between flatness, surface, and trompe l'oeil.

80. Fischer, *The War Magician*, 57; Benjamin H.D. Buchloh, "The primary colors for the second time," *October* 37 (Summer 1980) 48-50 on Klein; Henry A. Gardner, "Protective Concealment Paints," Circular No. 634 (National Paint, Varnish and Lacquer Assoc, 1941?), in Paints and Materials Folder, Edward M. Farmer Papers, Hoover Inst Archives; Robertson, *Aircraft Camouflage*, 153-54; Williams, *Liners in Battledress*, 110-12; Sumrall, "Ship camouflage," 67-81; Donald Kuspit, "Concerning the spiritual in contemporary art," in Tuchman and Freeman, eds., *The Spiritual in Art*, 313-25 on Reinhardt, Rothko, Beuys and "silent" painting.

81. Diana Agrest, "Architecture of mirror / mirror of architecture," *Oppositions* 26 (Spr 1984) 118-33, and see Mildred Hall and Edward Hall, *The Fourth Dimension in Architecture.... Eero Saarinen's Administrative Center for Deere & Company, Moline, Illinois* (Santa Fe, NM: Sunstone, 1975). On seasonality, see Konrad F. Wittman, "The camouflage dilemma," *Pencil Points* 23 (Jan 1942) 14.

82. Andy Warhol, *The Philosophy of Andy Warhol (From A to B and Back Again)* (NY: Harcourt Brace Jovanovich, 1975) 21, 69; Ultra Violet (= Isabelle Collin Dufresne), *Famous for 15 Minutes: My Years with Andy Warhol* (San Diego: Harcourt Brace Jovanovich, 1988) 6, 16, 39, 43-45, 97; Victor Bockris, *The Life and Death of Andy Warhol* (NY: Bantam, 1989); Carter Ratcliff, "The work of Roy Lichtenstein in the age of Walter Benjamin's and Jean Baudrillard's popularity," *Art in America* 77 (Feb 1989) 110-23; Barbara Haskell, curator, *Claes Oldenburg: Object into Monument* (Pasadena: Pasadena Art Museum, 1972) – and note how many of the drawings are aerial or telescopic views; Barbara Rose, "Decoys and doubles: Jasper Johns and the modernist mind," *Arts Mag* 50 (May 1976) 68-73; William Gass, "Johns," *NY R of Books* (2 Feb 1989) 22-27; Eugene Schwartz,

Breakthrough Advertising (Englewood Cliffs, NJ: Prentice-Hall, 1966) 186. On Charlie McCarthy, see Candice Bergen, *Knock Wood* (NY: Simon & Schuster, 1984) 45, 77; Stallings, *Flesh and Fantasy*, 282. On the Campbell Soup Company, I thank Paul N. Mulcahy, President, CSC Advertising, Inc., letter to Gabriel E. Danch in response to my questions, 9 July 1991.

83. Kurt Vonnegut, *Bluebeard* (NY: Delacorte, 1987) throughout, q211, q281, q294.

84. Loftus, *Eyewitness Testimony*, ix (foreword by John Kaplan), 35; David G. Berger, *They All Look Alike* (San Francisco: R and E, 1975); Marly, *Spectacles & Spyglasses*, 15; Linda Seidel with Irene Copeland, *The Art of Corrective Makeup: How To Camouflage Unattractive Scars and Blemishes* (Garden City, NY: Doubleday, 1984); "Illusionary Dressing Techniques Video," *Spectrum (Minneapolis)* 1 (1991) 8, ad; Kern, *Culture of Space and Time*, 288. Contrast Michel Foucault, *Discipline and Punish: The Birth of the Prison*, trans. Alan Sheridan (NY: Pantheon, 1977) on nineteenth-century surveillance as a cultural offensive.

85. Aaron S. Hecht, ed., *Optics and Images in Law Enforcement II* (Bellingham: International Society for Optical Engineering, 1982) 11, 27; Jon Zonderman, *Beyond the Crime Lab: The New Science of Investigation* (NY: Wiley, 1990) ch. 5 on debate over DNA typing.

86. Charles Jencks, "Trompe l'oeil counterfeit," *Studio Int* 190 (Sept–Oct 1975) 109-14; Tim Plant, *Painted Illusions: A Creative Guide to Painting Murals and Trompe L'oeil Effects* (Topsfield, MA: Salem, 1988); Karen Tsujimoto and Susan F. Yeh, *Images of America: Precisionist Painting and Modern Photography* (Seattle: U Washington, for San Francisco Museum of Modern Art, 1982); Sally Boothe-Meredith, "Introduction" to *Real, Really Real, Super Real: Directions in Contemporary American Realism* (San Antonio: The Museum, 1981); Christine Lindey, *Superrealist Painting and Sculpture* (L: Orbis, 1980) 7-9, 20-21; Gerrit Henry, "The real thing," *Art Int* 16 (Sum 1972) rept. in *Super Realism: A Critical Anthology*, ed. Gregory Battcock (NY: Dutton, 1975) 3-20.

87. Interviews with Rebecca Davenport (who hoped originally to be an abstract expressionist), Idelle Weber, Janet Fish in *Real, Really Real, Super Real*, 43, 58, 72; Donald J. Brewer, "Introduction" to *The Reality of Illusion* (Quaker Hill, CT: Amer Art R, 1979) 8-21; Alan B. Govenar, "The changing image of tattooing in American culture," *J Amer Culture* 5 (Spr 1982) 35-37. See also Louis K. Meisel, *Richard Estes: The Complete Paintings, 1966-1985* (NY: Abrams, 1986) esp. 11 on the cleanliness of Estes's city streets and his difficulties painting garbage. Another prominent photorealist, Chuck Close, also made the transition from action painting and abstract expressionism: Lisa Lyons and Robert Storr, *Chuck Close* (NY: Rizzoli, 1987) 14.

88. Ivan C. Karp, O.K. Harris Galleries, NY, personal interview, 23 Oct 1990, on status of realist paintings; Katrine Ames, "The art of double exposure," *Newsweek* (29 June 1987) 68; Joseph Jacobs, "The Starn Twins," *Splash* (Nov–Dec 1987); Richard B. Woodward, "It's art, but is it photography?" *NY Times Mag* (9 Oct 1988) 28-29; idem, "Doug and Mike Starn: at Stux," *Artnews* (Oct 1990) 183-84; Andy Grundberg and Robert Rosenblum, *Mike and Doug Starn* (NY: Abrams, 1990). I have also used a clippings file on the Starns at the Int Center of Photography, NY. On the Garcías, see Antonio Palomino de Castro y Velasco, *An Account of the Lives and Works of the Most Eminent Spanish Painters* (L, 1739) 58.

89. Yrjö Edelmann, *Artificial Landscape with Birds IV* (1978), Michelangelo Pistoletto, *The Parrot* (1976) and Ron Rizk, *Small Russian Package* (1978) in *The Reality of Illusion*, pls. 17, 59 and 65; Daniel C. Noel, *Approaching Earth: A Search for the Mythic*

Significance of the Space Age (Amity, NY: Amity House, 1986) esp. ch. 10 on aerial archaeology, meditating upon Leo Deuel, *Flights into Yesterday* (NY: St. Martin's, 1969), and paraphrasing (p. 56) astronaut William Anders, Earth as a fragile ornament, cited by Gyorgy Kepes, "Art and ecological consciousness," in *Arts of the Environment*, ed. Kepes (NY: Braziller, 1972) 10.

CHAPTER SIX: DITTO

1. Nelson C. White, *Abbott H. Thayer* (Peterborough, NH, 1951) 89; Abbott H. Thayer to Charles L. Freer, letters of 15 and 30 Aug 1901, microfilm roll 77 in the Archives of American Art, NY, discussed also in Susan Hobbs, "Nature into art: the landscapes of Abbott Henderson Thayer," *Amer Art J* 14 (Sum 1982) 42.

2. László Moholy-Nagy, *The New Vision and Abstract of an Artist* (NY, 1947) 79-80.

3. Cheryl Bernstein (= Gregory Battcock), "The fake as more," in *Idea Art*, ed. Battcock (NY: Dutton, 1973) 41-45, q42, stimulated by Jorge Luis Borges, "Pierre Menard, Author of the *Quixote*," in his *Labyrinths*, trans. D.A. Yates and J.E. Irby (NY: New Directions, 1962) 36-44.

4. Jaroslav Pelikan, *The Emergence of the Catholic Tradition (100–600)* (Chicago: U Chicago, 1971) 191-256, q194-95, q201; Timothy Ware, *The Orthodox Church* (Harmondsworth, UK: Penguin, 1967) 28-32. On the West, see Karl F. Morrison, *The Mimetic Tradition of Reform in the West* (Princeton: Princeton U, 1982) ch. 6; Charles E. Trinkaus, *In Our Image and Likeness: Humanity and Divinity in Italian Humanist Thought*, 2 vols. (Chicago: U Chicago, 1970). Cf. Erich Auerbach, *Mimesis: The Representation of Reality in Western Literature*, trans. Willard Trask (Garden City, NY: Doubleday, 1957).

5. Jane E. Merdinger, "Africa vs. Rome: Ecclesiastical Politics in the Era of St. Augustine," Ph.D., Yale U, 1985, q136; B.R. Rees, *Pelagius: A Reluctant Heretic* (Woodbridge: Boydell, 1988); Pelikan, *Emergence of the Catholic Tradition*, 308-18.

6. Miranda Marvin, "Copying in Roman sculpture," in Center for Advanced Studies in the Visual Arts, *Retaining the Original: Multiple Originals, Copies, and Reproductions* (Hanover, NH: U Press New England, 1989) 29-45; Brunilde S. Ridgway, *Roman Copies of Greek Sculpture: The Problem of the Originals* (Ann Arbor: U Michigan, 1984), copying was mostly paraphrase; H.C. Teitler, *Notarii and Exceptores: An Inquiry Into the Role and Significance of Shorthand Writers in the Imperial and Ecclesiastical Bureaucracy of the Roman Empire* (Amsterdam: Gieben, 1985) 1-14; Serge Lancel, *Actes de la Conférence de Carthage en 411* (P: Cerf, 1972) I, 66-73, 342-46, 390-91. The term "Catholic" here is a bit deceptive; at the time, both sides claimed to be "catholic," that is, to be acting on behalf of the entire (Christian) world.

7. Teitler, *Notarii*; Henri Leclercq, "Notaire," *Dictionnaire d'archéologie chrétienne et de liturgie*, ed. Fernard Cabrol (P, 1936) XII, 1623-40. Roman notaries had also transcribed the last words of Christian martyrs. These they sold dearly to the Western Church, which shaped the *Acts of the Martyrs* so that the notaries themselves seem to notarize the suffering. For this reason, and because canon law was not fixed, the early Church esteemed its own notaries, using them as administrators, sending them as emissaries to councils, elevating them to bishoprics.

8. See Mario Amelotti and Giorgio Costamagna, *Alle origini del notariato italiano* (Rome: Consiglio Nazionale del Notariato, 1975) and cf. Emile Tyan, *Le Notariat et le régime de la preuve par écrit dans la pratique du droit musulman* (Beirut, 1945?).

9. *Le Notariat: histoire, art, actualité* (P: Chambre interdépartementale des notaires, 1979) 5.

10. Carlo M. Cipolla, *Before the Industrial Revolution* (NY: Norton, 1976) 81–82; Christopher R. Cheney, *Notaries Public in England in the Thirteenth and Fourteenth Centuries* (Oxford: Clarendon, 1972); *Le Notariat*, 20–21; Jean-Paul Poisson, *Notaires et société* (P: Economica, 1985); R.A. Houston, *Scottish Literacy and the Scottish Identity* (Cambridge: Cambridge U, 1985) 196–200; J.-L. Laffont, ed., *Notaires, notariat, et société sous l'ancien régime* (Toulouse: Presses Universitaires du Mirail, 1990); L.W. Abbott, *Law Reporting in England, 1485–1585* (L: U London, 1973). See also Carlo Ginzburg, *The Cheese and the Worms*, trans. John Tedeschi and Anne Tedeschi (Harmondsworth, UK: Penguin, 1982) ix, notarial role as recorders to the Inquisition, helping to shape the figure of the heretic and of the witch.

11. Francis W. Steer, ed., *The Scriveners' Company Common Paper, 1357–1628* (L: L Record Soc, 1968) xxi for Grantham; Joseph J. Duggan, "Performance and transmission: aural and ocular reception in the twelfth- and thirteenth-century vernacular literature of France," *Romance Philology* 43 (Aug 1989) 49–58, 55 on "internal dictation"; Christopher De Hamel, *Scribes and Illuminators* (Buffalo: U Toronto, 1992) esp. 43 on women as copyists; Marc Drogin, *Anathema! Medieval Scribes and the History of Book Curses* (Totowa, NJ: Allanheld, Osmun, 1983) 15, q18 from Florencio's colophon. In scriptoria, different portions of a text were assigned simultaneously to several scribes; it was therefore rare for one scribe to copy a complete Bible. It was not rare for a scribe to become so familiar with a text that he copied out what he was *expecting* to find: William Macbain, "Scribal memory and its relevance to manuscript tradition," *Manuscripta* 26 (1982) 8.

12. Gerald Donaldson, *Books – Their History, Art, Power, Glory, Infamy and Suffering* (NY: Van Nostrand Reinhold, 1981) 14; Concetta Luna, "I Tempi di copia di due scribi del XIV secolo," *Scriptorium* 43 (1989) 111–19; Carla Bozzolo and Ezio Ornato, *Pour une histoire du livre manuscrit au moyen âge* (P: CNRS, 1983) 46–48; Jean Destrez, *La Pecia dans les manuscrits universitaires du XIIIe et du XIVe siècle* (P, 1935); Graham Pollard, "The *pecia* system in the medieval universities," in *Medieval Scribes, Manuscripts and Libraries*, eds. M.B. Parkes and A.G. Watson (L: Scolar, 1978) 145–61; L.E. Boyle, "Peciae, apopeciae, and a Toronto MS. of the *Sententia Libri Ethicorum* of Aquinas," in *The Role of the Book in Medieval Culture*, ed. Peter Ganz (Turnhout: Brepols, 1986) 75–77. In Islam, texts were first published orally, recited from memory in a mosque to copyists who took dictation. Transcripts in turn were certified through public recitations before the author. Copyists then could prepare fair copies to sell in markets: Johannes Pedersen, *The Arabic Book*, trans. Geoffrey French (Princeton: Princeton U, 1984) 24–31, 43–51.

13. István Hajnal, *L'Enseignement de l'écriture aux universités médiévales*, 2nd ed. (Budapest: Académie des Sciences de Hongrie, 1959); M.B. Parkes, *Scribes, Scripts and Readers* (L: Hambledon, 1991) ch. 2, "Tachygraphy in the Middle Ages," describes the influence of rapid writing (under the duress of taking lecture or sermon notes) on the development of new, personal letter forms and abbreviations in the thirteenth century; tachygraphy was among a series of changes in modes of thought and design that made a late medieval handwritten book differ (p. 66) "more from its early medieval predecessors than it does from a printed book of our own day." For Erasmus, see A.S. Osley, ed. and trans., *Scribes and Sources* (L: Faber and Faber, 1980) q35.

14. Jonathan Goldberg, *Writing Matter: From the Hands of the English Renaissance*

(Stanford: Stanford U, 1990) ch. 3; Stephen Greenblatt, *Renaissance Self-Fashioning* (Chicago: U Chicago, 1980) ch. 2; Albert Kapr, *The Art of Lettering: The History, Anatomy, and Aesthetics of the Roman Letter Forms*, trans. Ida Kimber (Munich: Saur, 1983) esp. 86, 96, 150–52; Richard W. Clement, "Italian 16th-century writing books and the scribal reality in Verona," *Visible Language* 20 (1986) 393–412. See also Baldessare Castiglione, *The Book of the Courtier*, trans. Charles S. Singleton (Garden City, NY: Anchor, 1959 [1527]) 43ff, and the Preface, the book printed because many divergent manuscript copies were in circulation. On the general transition from a "memorial" to a "documentary" culture, see M.T. Clanchy, *From Memory to Written Record: England, 1066–1307* (Cambridge, MA: Harvard U, 1979), occasionally reversed by Mary J. Carruthers, *The Book of Memory: A Study of Memory in Medieval Culture* (Cambridge: Cambridge U, 1990).

15. Garth S. Jowett, "Extended images," in *Contact: Human Communication and Its History*, ed. Raymond Williams (NY: Thames & Hudson, 1981) 186; Ernst P. Goldschmidt, *Medieval Texts and Their First Appearance in Print* (L, 1943) 90; Philip J. Weimerskirch, "The earliest catalogs locating manuscripts in more than one library," in *Supplementum Festivum: Studies in Honor of Paul Oskar Kristeller* (NY: SUNY, 1987) 55–64; Elizabeth L. Eisenstein, *The Printing Press as an Agent of Change* (Cambridge: Cambridge U, 1979) I, 45–47, on difficulties of estimating the volume of manuscript copying; Donaldson, *Books – Their History, Art, Power*, 24, 35. Cf. Henri-Jean Martin with Bruno Delmas, *Histoire et pouvoirs de l'écrit* (P: Perrin, 1988) 217–18, 228, for lower estimates on incunabula but higher estimates on print runs.

16. Donaldson, *Books – Their History, Art, Power*, 48–49; Drogin, *Anathema!*, 99; Eisenstein, *Printing Press as an Agent of Change*, I, 113–26. In book-printing a "signature" is a set of pages printed together on a larger sheet, so laid out that it can be folded to yield a section of a book of the size required – quarto, two folds producing four leaves and eight pages; octavo, four folds producing eight leaves and sixteen pages, and so on.

17. Johannes Trithemius, *In Praise of Scribes*, ed. Klaus Arnold, trans. Roland Behrendt (Lawrence, KS: Coronado, 1974 [1494]) 35, 61, 63, 65, 67; Eisenstein, *Printing Press as an Agent of Change*, I, 50–51; Klaus Arnold, *Johannes Trithemius (1462–1516)*, 2nd ed. (Würzburg: Schöningh, 1991) 62–68.

18. Trithemius, *In Praise of Scribes*, 10, 14, 21; Verner W. Clapp, "The story of permanent/durable book-paper, 1115–1970," *Restaurator*, supp. 3 (1972) 4; Alan D. Crown, "Studies in Samaritan scribal practices and manuscript history," *Bull John Rylands Lib* 65 (1983) 72–94, 66 (1983) 97–123, esp. 108, and 67 (1984) 349–84; David Carlson, "The writings and manuscript collections of the Elizabethan alchemist, antiquary, and herald Francis Thynne," *Huntington Lib Q* 52 (Spr 1989) 203–72, esp. 205; Paul F. Grendler, *Schooling in Renaissance Italy* (Baltimore: Johns Hopkins U, 1989) 323–28, penmanship pedagogy.

19. Philip Kerr, ed., *The Penguin Book of Lies* (NY: Viking, 1990) 252–53; Trithemius, *In Praise of Scribes*, 9–10.

20. B.M. Metzger, "Literary forgeries and canonical pseudepigrapha," in his *New Testament Studies* (Leiden: Brill, 1980) 1–22; James E.G. Tetzel, *Latin Textual Criticism in Antiquity* (NY: Ayer, 1981) 17; Thomas F. Tout, "Mediaeval forgers and forgeries," in *The Collected Papers* (Manchester, 1934) 117–44; Giles Constable, "Forgery and plagiarism in the Middle Ages," *Archiv für Diplomatik, Schriftgeschichte, Siegel- und Wappenkunde* 29 (1983) 1–41, 11 for Juliana; Elizabeth A.R. Brown, "*Falsitas pia sive reprehensibilis*. Medi-

eval forgers and their intentions," in *Fälschungen im Mittelalter*, ed. Horst Fuhrmann (Hanover: Hahnsche, 1988) I, 101–20, arguing against Constable that medieval thinkers considered all forms of forgery reprehensible; Nicole Hermann-Mascard, *Les Reliques des saints* (P: Klincksieck, 1975) 107–40, esp. 137–38.

21. See Anthony Grafton, *Forgers and Critics: Creativity and Duplicity in Western Scholarship* (Princeton: Princeton U, 1990) and my essay review, "Appropriationism," *J of Unconventional History* 2 (Spr 1991) 82–91. For a systematic (modern) classification of forgeries, see Umberto Eco, "Tipologia della falsificazione," in *Fälschungen im Mittelalter*, I, 69–82.

22. Lewis Rappaport, "Fakes and facsimiles," *Amer Archivist* 42 (Jan 1979) 19, irreproducible signatures; Nigel Ramsay, "Forgery and the rise of the London Scriveners' Company," in *Fakes and Frauds* (Winchester: St. Paul's Bibliographies, 1989) 99–108; David Cressy, *Literacy and the Social Order: Reading and Writing in Tudor and Stuart England* (Cambridge: Cambridge U, 1980) 25, 57–58; Joseph E. Fields, "The history of autograph collecting," in *Autographs and Manuscripts*, ed. Edmund Berkeley, Jr. (NY: Scribner's, 1978) 43; Alan N.L. Munby, *The Cult of the Autograph Letter in England* (L: U London, 1962) 10–11, q3 from Ralph Thoresby (1715), 48 for Turner's *Guide... Towards the Verification of Manuscripts, by Reference to Engraved Facsimiles of Hand-writing*. The valuing of autographs arose, of course, in the context of the valuing of individual authorship and "signature" pieces; it was further enhanced by the late-eighteenth-century idea that the most personal of letters had public and lasting value. See Peggy Kamuf, *Signature Pieces: On the Institution of Authorship* (Ithaca: Cornell U, 1988); Dena Goodman, "Epistolary property: Michel de Servan and the plight of letters on the eve of the French Revolution," in *Early Modern Conceptions of Property*, eds. J. Brewer and S. Staves (L: Routledge, 1995) 323–38.

23. Platt R. Spencer, *Spencerian Key to Practical Penmanship* (NY, 1875) 134–35, and cf. Emile Javal, *Physiologie de la lecture et de l'écriture* (P, 1905) 241; Ray Nash, *American Penmanship 1800–1850* (Worcester, MA: Amer Antiquarian Soc, 1969); Rappaport, "Fakes and facsimiles." The "military precision" of nineteenth-century penmanship instruction may have been due to the production (1830) of steel nibs for pens, whose sharpness led to a cramped hand that had to be controlled by exact rules: Kapr, *Art of Lettering*, 186. See Michael Fried, *Realism, Writing, Disfiguration* (Chicago: U Chicago, 1987) on conjunctions between late-nineteenth-century handwriting, art, surgery, character, and literature.

24. Etienne Charavay, *Faux autographes: affaire Vrain-Lucas* (P, 1870); "Pascal forgeries in the French Academy," *Penn Monthly Mag* 1 (1870) 151–58, 191–200; Charles Whibley, "Literary forgers," *Cornhill Mag* 85 (1902) 628–36, q635.

25. Alexander Howland Smith, Scrapbook of clippings, most from the *Edinburgh Evening Dispatch*, Forgeries (Box) in Rare Book and Manuscripts Dept., NY Public Lib.

26. Maxwell Whiteman, *Forgers & Fools: The Strange Career of "Baron" Weisberg* (NY: Typophiles, 1986).

27. Hilary Jenkinson, "The teaching and practice of handwriting in England," *History* 11 (1926–27) 215, secretaries; David S. Landes, *The Unbound Prometheus: Technological Change and Industrial Development in Western Europe from 1750 to the Present* (Cambridge: Cambridge U, 1969) q41 (rapid, regular); Louis, chevalier de Jaucourt, "Ecriture (art méch.)," *EDSAM*, V, 371–72; Charles Perregaux and F.-Louis Perrot, *Les Jaquet-Droz et Leschot* (Neuchâtel, 1916) 104, q108.

28. Linda M. Strauss, "Automata: A Study in the Interface of Science, Technology, and Popular Culture, 1730-1885," Ph.D., U Cal, San Diego, 1987, pp. 125-27; Jenkinson, "Handwriting in England," 215-18; Philip Hofer, introduction to George Bickham, *Universal Penman* (NY: Dover, 1954 [1743]) on the round hand; Roger Chartier, *The Cultural Uses of Print in Early Modern France*, trans. Lydia G. Cochrane (Princeton: Princeton U, 1987) 143, notaries; Javal, *Physiologie de la lecture et de l'écriture*, ch. 4 on evolution of stenography, as also Thomas A. Reed, *A Chapter in the Early History of Phonography* (L, 1887), and Henry Pitman, *Hints on Lecturing: and Notes on the History of Shorthand* (L, 1879) 26-28.

29. Laetitia Yeandle, "The evolution of handwriting in the English-speaking colonies of America," *Amer Archivist* 43 (1980) 306; Silvio A. Bedini, *Thomas Jefferson and His Copying Machine* (Charlottesville: U Press Virginia, 1984) xi, 1-2, and 89 for letter from Jefferson, 19 Aug 1804.

30. Paul L. Rose, "Jacomo Contarini (1536-1595)," *Physis* 18 (1976) 125; "Pantographe," *EDSAM*, XI, 827; James P. Muirhead, *Life of James Watt* (Alburgh, Norfolk: Archival Facsimiles, 1987 [1858]) q273; Bedini, *Thomas Jefferson and His Copying Machine*, 31, 34, 38-49, q81 for 15 June 1804 ad from the *Federal Gazette* (triumph), q152.

31. Julian P. Boyd, ed., *The Papers of Thomas Jefferson* (Princeton: Princeton U, 1950-) VII, 575; Muirhead, *Life of James Watt*, 273; W.B. Proudfoot, *The Origin of Stencil Duplicating* (L: Hutchinson, 1972) 21; Abraham Rees, "Copying of letters, and other writings," *The Cyclopaedia* (L, 1819) IX, prefatory pages.

32. Eric Robinson and Douglas McKie, eds., *Partners in Science: Letters of James Watt and Joseph Black* (Cambridge, MA: Harvard U, 1970) q88 from letter of 29 Mar 1780, and 95-98 on inks; Dorothy M. Schullian, "Early print transfer," *J History Med* 7 (Wint 1952) 86-88, quotation is her paraphrase (?) from Pierre Borel's *Historiarum et observationum medico-physicarum centuriae IV* (P, 1656) LXXVI, 339-40, referring to a similar Italian invention and then to the grand claims of Samuel Hartlib, on whom see Charles Webster, *The Great Instauration: Science, Medicine and Reform, 1626-1660* (NY: Holmes & Meier, 1975) esp. 164, 219 for double-writing devices; Rees, *Cyclopaedia*, IX, on Franklin. During the eighteenth century, Bank of England notes were printed on only one side, so counterfeiters could indeed have used the copying press, if only its images had been crisper.

33. Bedini, *Thomas Jefferson and His Copying Machine*, 11, 19, 22, q18 from Rev. Manasseh Cutler on the speed of a copying press owned by Franklin, q27 for notice from 14 Apr 1798 issue of *Federal Gazette*; Boyd, *Papers of Thomas Jefferson*, VIII, 462, to Madison, response at IX, 333, and see XVI, 288n., for State Department; Franz H. Mautner and Henry Hatfield, trans. and eds., *The Lichtenberg Reader* (Boston: Beacon, 1959) q14 for Boswell.

34. R. Shelton Mackenzie, ed., *Memoirs of Robert-Houdin, Ambassador, Author, and Conjuror*, trans. Lascelles Wraxall (L, 1860) 149-54; Linda Strauss, "Reflections in a mechanical mirror: automata as doubles," in *Research in Science and Technology Studies, Volume 10*, ed. Shirley Gorenstein, forthcoming. Many nineteenth-century automaton writers, like magician John Nevil Maskelyne's famous Zoë, were false automata, covert pantographs with a backstage human accomplice writing or drawing at one end of the device.

35. Art polygraphy: Joseph Booth, *An Address to the Public, On the Polygraphic Art* (L, 1787?); British Library scrapbook by Daniel Lysons, *Collectanea*, 170 from "Polygraphic Exhibition," *Gazetteer* (15 May 1789). Lithography and chromolithography: Peter

Marzio, *The Democratic Art: An Exhibition on the History of Chromolithography in America, 1840–1900* (Fort Worth: Amon Carter Museum of Western Art, 1979–80). Stereotyping: Boyd, *Papers of Thomas Jefferson*, X, 322–23; Gaskell, *New Introduction to Bibliography*, 201–05. Photography as copying: Robert Hunt, *A Manual of Photography*, 4th ed. (L, 1854) 21, on calotyping. On nineteenth-century type-facsimiles or "period" printing, see A.W. Pollard et al., " 'Facsimile' reprints of old books," *Library*, ser. 4, 6 (Mar 1926) 307–11.

36. Bedini, *Thomas Jefferson and His Copying Machine*, q60 from Latrobe, 22 Feb 1804, q99 for ad from *Poulson's Amer Daily Advertiser* (6 Dec 1804) female hand; Cindy S. Aron, *Ladies and Gentlemen of the Civil Service: Middle-Class Workers in Victorian America* (NY: Oxford U, 1987) 72–74; Mary Elizabeth Adams, "Women in the Modern Office: Female Clerical Workers, 1900–1930," Ph.D., U Cal, Berkeley, 1989, pp. 64ff; Margery W. Davies, *Woman's Place Is at the Typewriter: Office Work and Office Workers, 1870–1930* (Philadelphia: Temple U, 1982) 13, 29 *et passim*; Sharon H. Strom, *Beyond the Typewriter: Gender, Class, and the Origins of Modern American Office Work, 1900–1930* (Urbana: U Illinois, 1992) 177, and cf. Gregory Anderson, *Victorian Clerks* (Manchester, UK: Manchester U, 1976).

37. Robert E. MacKay, "Managing the Clerks: Office Management from the 1870s through the Great Depression," Ph.D., Boston U, 1985, pp. 15–17, 29–30 on franchising business schools. Cf. Charles L. Vaughn, *Franchising: Its Nature, Scope, Advantages, and Development* (Lexington, MA: Heath, 1974) ch. 1. Contrast Thomas S. Dicke, *Franchising in America…1840–1980* (Chapel Hill: U North Carolina, 1992) on "business-format franchising," a development Dicke reserves to the twentieth century, while Harold Brown, *Franchising, Realities and Remedies*, 2nd ed. (NY: Law J, 1977) 1, finds it in the licensing of beer gardens in the 1870s.

On printers, see Edith Abbott, *Women in Industry* (NY, 1910) 254–57; Ava Baron, "The masculinization of production: the gendering of work and skill in U.S. newspaper printing, 1850–1920," in *Gendered Domains: Rethinking Public and Private in Women's History*, eds. D.O. Helly and S.M. Reverby (Ithaca: Cornell U, 1992) 277–88, showing that when publishers did seek women as linotypists for their "nicety of touch," men exaggerated the physical strain and dirtiness of the job, for which they would be thought more suited.

38. On women as art copyists, see Paul Duro, "The 'demoiselles à copier' in the Second Empire," *Woman's Art J* 7 (Spr–Sum 1986) 1–7, q1 from Léon Lagrange; Kathleen D. McCarthy, *Women's Culture: American Philanthropy and Art, 1830–1930* (Chicago: U Chicago, 1991) 16, 18, 92, 102, 106; Carol H. MacKay, "Hawthorne, Sophia, and Hilda as copyists: duplication and transformation in *The Marble Faun*," *Browning Inst Studies* 12 (1984) 93–120, q95. The devaluing of the mechanicalness of copying underlies James Joyce's story, "Counterparts" in the *Dubliners* (1914).

39. Cynthia E. Russett, *Sexual Science: The Victorian Construction of Womanhood* (Cambridge, MA: Harvard U, 1989) q50, q54.

40. Dee Garrison, *Apostles of Culture: The Public Librarian and American Society, 1876–1920* (NY: Free Press, 1979) q88 (Hill), 182, 188–90 (copying and penmanship), q227 (monotony).

41. Adams, "Women in the Modern Office," q15 for male stenographer, from *Good Words* (1864) 318, and q86 for "device," from *J of Commercial Education* 26,3 (1905) 153; Reed, *Early History of Phonography*, 50–51; Davies, *Woman's Place Is at the Type-*

writer, 29-33, 52, 64, 71, 90; William H. Leffingwell, ed., *Office Appliance Manual* (n.p., 1926) for photos of women, almost exclusively, at office machines; Hans Speier, *German White-Collar Workers and the Rise of Hitler* (New Haven: Yale U, 1986 [written 1933]) 28-29, on male clerks refusing to learn "women's" skills of typing and shorthand; North American Phonograph Company, *Edison Phonograph*, [7]; MacKay, "Managing the Clerks," 135, for Ida C. Murray, "How I pleased a difficult employer," *Ladies' Home J* 23 (Oct 1906) 70, and see Andrea Stevens, "Life as a machine," *NY Times* (14 Oct 1990) H26 on Sophia Treadwell's 1928 play about a young woman stenographer, *Machinal*. Helen B. Thompson, *The Mental Traits of Sex* (Chicago, 1905) found that women did excel men in forming new motor coordination, but she argued that superior manual dexterity and capacious memory were not intrinsic; such qualities were as socially produced as women's resort to "the more reproductive mental processes," given "the absence of a sufficient social spur toward originality and inventiveness."

42. G.T.W. Patrick, "The psychology of woman," *Popular Sci Monthly* 47 (1895) 209-25, reprinted in *The Psychology of Women: Selected Readings*, ed. Juanita H. Williams (NY: Norton, 1979) q7, and cf. Stephanie A. Shields, "Functionalism, Darwinism, and the psychology of women," 12-34; Michael Adler, *The Writing Machine* (L: Allen & Unwin, 1973) 42 on speeds – a stenotypist could do 120 wpm, claimed *The Typist's R* 1 (Oct 1903) 15; Alfred D. Chandler, *The Visible Hand: The Managerial Revolution in American Business* (Cambridge, MA: Belknap, 1977); Strom, *Beyond the Typewriter*, 19, 26; Davies, *Woman's Place Is at the Typewriter*, 90-91.

43. Thermo-Fax ad, "White Copies on a 'Thermo-Fax' Copying Machine?" *Time* (24 Aug 1962) 79; James River Graphics ad, "Tecnifax diazo film," *Reprographics* 19 (May-June 1981) back cover. On cleanliness, see an ad for Fels-Naptha (bleaching out ink stains from a woman's blouse after she cleans a typewriter or changes its ribbon) in Alan Delgado, *The Enormous File: A Social History of the Office* (L: John Murray, 1979) 43-44. On images of the homemaker, see Christine Frederick, *The New Housekeeping* (Garden City, NY: 1914); Susan Strasser, *Never Done: A History of American Housework* (NY: Pantheon, 1982). Cf. Linda Kerber, "Separate spheres, female worlds, woman's place: the rhetoric of women's history," *J Amer History* 75 (June 1988) 9-39.

44. Henry Petroski, *The Pencil* (NY: Knopf, 1989) 86ff on handling carbon papers; Proudfoot, *Origin of Stencil Duplicating*, 24-34, q34. See Bedini, *Thomas Jefferson and His Copying Machine*, 155-56 on the stylograph (1806), which used paper blacked on both sides – "It is not pleasant in its use, and I think will not take the place of the Polygraph," wrote Jefferson, who also noted (p. 164) that "the smell of [copying press] paper is so fetid, that one could not stay in a room where there was much of it." Carbon paper was still being made by hand in the 1890s: Delgado, *Enormous File*, 79. On varieties of carbon papers, some of which, interleaved, could yield 15-25 typed copies at a time, see William H. Leffingwell and Edwin M. Robinson, *Textbook of Office Management*, 3rd ed. (NY, 1950) 154-59, 292. The F.S. Webster Company claimed that one sheet of its Multi Kopy Carbon Paper could make one hundred copies "that actually rival the original in clearness." Ad, *Literary Digest* 47 (11 Oct 1913) 648.

45. Proudfoot, *Origin of Stencil Duplicating*, esp. 29-31, 34, 57, 81-92; "Autographic printing," *All the Year 'Round* n.s. 25 (1880) 160-63; A.B. Dick ad, "Writing by Mimeograph," *Century Mag* 72 (1906) 83. The cultural analogy in Bram Stoker's *Dracula* (1896) between blood and ink, the bite mark and the typed impression, vampirism and copying, is analyzed by Friedrich Kittler in *Discourse Networks 1800/1900*, trans. Michael Metteer

with Chris Cullens (Stanford: Stanford U, 1990) 353ff, who also notes (pp. 359–61) the attraction of Kafka to Felice Bauer, a woman typist and stenographer who told him that she *enjoyed* copying. Kittler suggests (p. 199) that the typewriter's "desexualization" of the act of writing allowed women professional access to both typing and writing; insofar as typewriters (women and machines) were clean and sexless, their writing could be no threat.

46. Thomas J. Schlereth, *Cultural History and Material Culture* (Ann Arbor: U Michigan, 1990) 156; Adler, *Writing Machine*, 58, and Henri Dupont and L.-F. Canet, *Les Machines à écrire* (P, 1901) 15, typewriters with keys laid out piano-style; Javal, *Physiologie de la lecture et de l'écriture*, 162, speeds at century's turn, much lower than the 170 wpm (roughly 850 characters per minute) achieved on a manual machine in 1918 by Margaret Owen: *1988 Guiness Book of World Records* (Toronto: Bantam, 1988) 480–82. A recent study accepts temporary speeds of 1800 notes per minute on the piano and 1020 characters per minute on electronic typewriters: David E. Rumelhart and Donald E. Norman, *Simulating a Skilled Typist*, CHIP Report 102 (La Jolla: Center for Human Information Processing, 1981) 2–3, 6. On literary consequences of typing, see Edward W. Bok, "Authors and the typewriter," *The Author* 2 (1890) 40; Leffingwell and Robinson, *Textbook of Office Management*, 154–59, 174; Sue Walker, "How typewriters changed correspondence," *Visible Language* 18 (Spr 1984) 102–17. On "ditto," used in English since 1625, see *OED*, IV, 880–81.

47. James Moran, *Printing Presses: History and Development* (Berkeley: U Cal, 1973) ch. 11; MacKay, "Managing the Clerks," 52–59; *The Typist's R* 1 (Oct 1903) 9, Gem paper clips; Michael Schudson, *Discovering the News: A Social History of American Newspapers* (NY: Basic, 1978) esp. ch. 3; Reginald Pound and Geoffrey Harmsworth, *Northcliff* (NY: Praeger, 1959) 264–67; Lucy C. Bull, "Being a typewriter," *Atlantic Monthly* (Dec 1895) 822; Kurt Gabriel, Büromuseum der Stadt Mühlheim an der Ruhr, personal tour, 8 Nov 1990, copying capacity of early typewriters.

48. On the new benzene-soaked tracing papers of the mid-nineteenth century, see James H. Andrew, "The copying of engineering drawings and documents," *Transactions Newcomen Soc of the History of Engineering and Technology* 53 (1982) 2. On the lie detector, see Eloise Keeler, *The Lie Detector Man: The Career and Cases of Leonarde Keeler* (Boston: Telshare, 1984).

49. Charles Bartholomew, *Mechanical Toys* (Feltham: Hamlyn, 1979) 29–31, 78–79, 89–100, 127; Blair Whitton, *Toys* (NY: Knopf, 1984) 106–115; Louis H. Hertz, *Messrs. Ives of Bridgeport: The Saga of America's Greatest Toymakers* (Wethersfield, 1950) 52, 56, 76; Barry James, "Sprockets of progress: Myrdal's Meccano," *Int Herald Tribune* (6 Nov 1990); Egerton Swartout, "The use of large scale models in architecture," *Architecture* 24 (1911) 130–33; Frederic C. Hirons, "The use of scale models," *Pencil Points* 1 (Nov 1920) 4–7; [Harvey L. Page], "Model making by architects," *Amer Architect* 118,2 (1920) 749–50; Berthold Audsley, "Miniatures and their value in architectural practice," *The Brickbuilder* 23 (Sept 1914) q213. See also Daniel Calhoun, *The Intelligence of a People* (Princeton: Princeton U, 1973) 235–55 on modeling in shipbuilding, as also Thomas Wright, "Scale models, similitude and dimensions: aspects of mid-nineteenth-century engineering science," *Annals of Science* 49 (May 1992) 233–54.

50. Francis Wharton, *A Commentary on the Law of Evidence in Civil Issues* (Philadelphia, 1877) I, 87, sec. 72, letterpress copies; Dupont and Canet, *Les Machines à écrire*, 34, on an 1896 Pennsylvania decision that typewritten documents had the same valid-

ity as handwritten, and that the word "writing" could apply to letters created at/by a machine; *The Typist's R* 1 (Oct 1903) 17 and (March 1904) 159, courtroom use of type-written copies; Leffingwell, *Office Appliance Manual*, 208-10, 389-90; Maygene Daniels, "The ingenious pen: American writing implements from the eighteenth century to the twentieth," *Amer Archivist* 43,3 (1980) 312-24; H. Keith Thompson, "The autopen and the Signa-signer," in *Autographs and Manuscripts*, ed. Edmund Berkeley, Jr. (NY: Scrib-ner's, 1978) 100-06; Schlereth, *Cultural History and Material Culture*, 156 on Marx. I have considered the cautions about ideological traps in Susan M. Reverby and Dorothy O. Helly, "Converging on history," in *Gendered Domains: Rethinking Public and Private in Women's History*, eds. Reverby and Helly (Ithaca: Cornell, 1992) 1-24.

51. Sarah Eisenstein, *Give Us Bread But Give Us Roses: Working Women's Consciousness in the United States, 1890 to the First World War* (L: Routledge & Kegan Paul, 1983) ch. 4, esp. 73-80; Adams, "Women in the Modern Office," 108-113; Paul Attewell, "The clerk de-skilled: a study in false nostalgia," *J Historial Sociology* 2 (Dec 1989) 357-88; Samuel Cohn, *The Process of Occupational Sex-Typing: The Feminization of Clerical Labor in Great Britain* (Philadelphia: Temple U, 1985) ch. 3, esp. 83-89; Strom, *Beyond the Typewriter*, 3-8; Lisa M. Fine, *The Souls of the Skyscraper: Female Clerical Workers in Chicago, 1870-1930* (Philadelphia: Temple U, 1990) esp. 85-90; Leffingwell, *Office Appliance Man-ual*, throughout; *The Typist's R* 1 (Oct 1903) 22 on personality of each typewriter; Paul L. Kirk, *Crime Investigation* (NY, 1953) 467; Bull, "Being a typewriter," 824-27 on idio-syncratic stenography; William B. Todd, "The White House transcripts," *Papers of the Bibliographical Soc of Amer* 68 (1974) 267-95, discerning 15 different stenotypists pro-ducing 700 artful contrivances, 2300 silent deletions.

52. OK, OK, a photocopy of a photocopy, or a photo of a photo, reenacts the orig-inal process; see below on copy art. On the halftone image, halfway between reenactment and appropriation, see Neil Harris, "Iconography and intellectual history: the half-tone effect," *Cultural Excursions* (Chicago: U Chicago, 1990) 304-17, relying upon Estelle Jussim, *Visual Communication and the Graphic Arts: Photographic Technologies in the Nine-teenth Century* (NY: Bowker, 1974). Unlike earlier methods of illustration, the halftone screen, a constellation of dots, was fully type-compatible. Illustrators began to draw *for* photoreproduction.

53. On photograms, see Anna Atkins, *Sun Gardens: Victorian Photograms*, text by Larry Schaaf (NY: Aperture, 1985). On blueprinting, Channing Whitaker, "Apparatus for printing by the blue process," *J Assoc of Engineering Soc* 1 (1882) 349-60; Andrew, "Copying of engineering drawings," 7-10; Molly Nesbit, "Ready-made originals: the Duchamp model," *October* 37 (Summer 1986) 55-59. Cf. Gilles Deleuze, trans. Rosalind Krauss, "Plato and the simulacrum," *October* 27 (Wint 1983) 45-56.

54. Chester F. Carlson, "Some notes for a talk on the history of electrostatic record-ing and xerography," 1 Nov 1963, in Box 80, Papers of Chester F. Carlson, Rare Book and Manuscripts Dept., NY Public Lib (henceforth, Carlson Papers). Carlson was using Carl Brinitzer, *A Reasonable Rebel: Georg Christoph Lichtenberg*, trans. Bernard Smith (NY: Macmillan, 1960). See also Olexa M. Bilaniuk, "Lichtenberg, Georg Christoph," *DSB*, VIII, 320-22; Franz H. Mautner and F. Miller, "Remarks on G.C. Lichtenberg, humanist-scientist," *Isis* 43 (1952) 223-24. For quotation, Joseph P. Stern, *Lichtenberg: A Doctrine of Scattered Occasions* (Bloomington: Indiana U, 1959) 42. For a history of research lead-ing to xerography, see J. Mort, *The Anatomy of Xerography: Its Invention and Evolution* (Jefferson, NC: McFarland, 1989).

55. Rainer Baasner, *Georg Christoph Lichtenberg (1742-99)* (Darmstadt: Wissenschaft-liche Buchgesellschaft, 1992) 13-15, 165-66; Horst Gravenkamp, *Geschichte eines elenden Körpers: Lichtenberg als Patient* (Göttingen: Wallstein, 1989); Stern, *Lichtenberg*, 4-5, 39 ("scorn"), 88-89, 90 ("he jumps"), 285-86 ("whole man"); Brinitzer, *Reasonable Rebel*, 16, 17 ("body"), 111-12, 113 ("mind"), 114-16; Franz H. Mautner and Henry Hatfield, trans. and eds., *The Lichtenberg Reader* (Boston: Beacon, 1959) 9-11, 23 ("totality"), 27; Franz H. Mautner, *Lichtenberg: Geschichte seines Geistes* (Berlin: de Gruyter, 1968) 174-98. On physiognomy, see John Liggett, *The Human Face* (NY: Stein and Day, 1974) 180-205; Johannes Saltzwedel, *Das Gesicht der Welt: Physiognomisches Denken in der Goethezeit* (Munich: Fink, 1993).

56. Stephen Perkins, "He who rode a tiger: Chester Carlson (1906-1968)," *Factsheet Five* 30 (1988) 61-63; Alfred Dinsdale, "Chester F. Carlson: inventor of xerography," *Photographic Science and Engineering* 7,1 (1963) q2-3 from Carlson; John H. Dessauer, with Oscar Schisgall, *My Years with Xerox* (Garden City, NY: Doubleday, 1971) 21-22; Carlson Diary 1928-29, entries for 14 Apr (overwritten 3 Nov) 1928, 8 July (= 21 April) 1929, and 13 Sept 1929, Box 74, Carlson Papers; *The Typist's R* 1 (Dec 1903) 62, "crabbed form of the scribe." For German work during the 1920s on photoelectric effects and pure alkali halides, see Jürgen Teichmann, "Pohl, Robert Wichard," *DSB*, XVIII, 715-18.

57. Carlson Diary 1928-29, entries for 4 Feb (= 17 Apr), 15 Feb (= 9 May), 26 Feb (= 11 May), 27 Feb (= 28 May), 14 Apr (= 3 Nov) 1928, for 17 Jan (= 26 Mar), 15 Sept, 26 Sept 1929, and for 24-25 Oct 1929 (= 7 Jan 1930), Box 74, Carlson Papers, as also Chester Carlson, "Early xerography experiments," *Haloid-O-Scope* (March 1954) 1, Box 80; Xerox Corporation, *The Story of Xerography* (Stamford: Xerox, [1978]) 3. Clough's lines appear in A.L.P. Norrington, ed., *Poems of Arthur Hugh Clough* (L: Oxford U, 1968) 90. On Carlson's career during the Depression, see James E. Brittain, "Carlson, Chester Floyd," *Dictionary of Amer Biography* (NY: Amer Council of Learned Soc, 1988) Supp. VIII, 70-72, based in part upon a 1965 interview, typescript at the Center for the History of Electrical Engineering, Rutgers, NJ.

58. Dessauer, *My Years with Xerox*, 85, on change in Carlson ca. 1953. For inventions, Diary 1932, Box 74, Carlson Papers. For the rest, letter to William E. Cox (1 May 1961), Box 65; letter to Karlis Osis (25 Oct 1963), Box 66, which also contains ASPR correspondence and notice of 1962 funding of Osis, who would co-author *At the Hour of Death* (NY: Avon, 1977).

59. For article by T.D. Duane and Thomas Behrendt, *Science* (15 Oct 1965) 367, clippings file, Box 68, Carlson Papers. For the rest, letters to Francis Green (18 Apr 1960) and to Jose M. Feola (23 Oct 1967), Box 65; to U of Pittsburgh Comptroller (6 June 1964), Box 66. H.S. Burr's *Blueprint for Immortality: The Electric Pattern of Life* (L: Spearman, 1972) made blatant an electrodynamic philosophy implicit in the book Carlson probably saw, *The Nature of Man and the Meaning of Existence* (Springfield, IL: Thomas, 1962). R.A. McConnell later disavowed his biophysical studies supported by Carlson: *Parapsychology in Retrospect: My Search for the Unicorn* (Pittsburgh: Biological Sci Dept., U Pittsburgh, 1987).

60. Mautner, *Lichtenberg*, 85-88; Mautner and Hatfield, *Lichtenberg Reader*, 3; Brinitzer, *Reasonable Rebel*, 57; Stern, *Lichtenberg*, 72, Photorin, q126 ("gain"), 230-33; Sigmund Freud, *Jugendbriefe an Eduard Silberstein*, ed. Walter Boehlich (Frankfurt: Fischer, 1989) 85; idem, "Why war?" (1932) in *Collected Papers*, trans. and ed. James

Strachey (NY: Basic, 1959) V, 281; idem, *Jokes and Their Relation to the Unconscious* (1905) in *Standard Edition of the Complete Psychological Works*, eds. and trans. James Strachey et al. (L: Hogarth, 1953-74) VIII, 34, 59-60, 66-86, 91-93.

61. Chester F. Carlson, "Early history of xerography," talk delivered 9 Mar 1961 to the Xerox Research Dept., Box 80, and "Development of electrophotography," in Writings file, Box 80, Carlson Papers; Dinsdale, "Chester F. Carlson," 3; Sol M. Linowitz, *The Making of a Public Man* (Boston: Little, Brown, 1985) 49-50, 65, and observing (p. 72) that very early in the development of xerography, the directors of Haloid were "already making speeches about the use of xerography as a means of communication with beings on other planets."

62. Dessauer, *My Years with Xerox*, xii, 4-7, 14, 43-44; Xerox Corporation, "The story of xerography," 7; *The Story of Rectigraph: The Photocopying Machine For Every Purpose* (Rochester, 1936) in Photostat File, Box 13, Records of the Joint Committee [of the Social Science Research Council, Amer Lib Assoc, Amer Council of Learned Soc, the Amer Documentation Inst] on Materials for Research, Manuscript Division, Lib of Congress, Washington, D.C., henceforth the Joint Committee Records.

63. Daniel M. Costigan, *Fax: The Principles and Practice of Facsimile Communication* (Philadelphia: Chilton, 1971) 1-6; Carolyn H. Sung, *Archives and Manuscripts: Reprography* (Chicago: Soc of Amer Archivists, 1982) 7-11, early use of microfilm and photostat machines; "Present state of photographic copying on micro film," 22 July 1936 memorandum, Box 63, Joint Committee Records; B. Botte, "Les Débuts de l'emploi du microfilm pour l'étude des manuscrits," *Studia codicologica*, eds. K. Treu et al. (Berlin: Akademie, 1977) 109-11, some six thousand boxes of microfilm of the manuscripts of Johannes Scotus Erigena (and associated authors) accumulated, 1928-38, by Belgian medievalists; A.B. Dick ad, "New Worlds To Conquer," *Vogue Decoration* (1930), from "Duplicating Machines" file, Picture Collection, NY Public Lib.

64. In Joint Committee Records: Robert C. Binkley, "Micro-copying as an international problem for the American National Committee on Intellectual Cooperation," 1937 memorandum in Copyright General Correspondence file, Box 57; "Present state of photographic copying on micro film," p. 2 of 22 July 1936 memorandum, Box 63; Electro Copyist brochures, *A New Simplified Method of Photo-copying* and *Now ANYONE can make Fast TRUE COPIES of Important Documents and Papers* (Syracuse, 1936) and Lumastat brochure (NY, 1934?) 2, in Reflection Copying File, Box 13; Spencer C. Duty, untitled report on reflection copying (ca. 1941), Non-commercial Methods of Reproduction file, Box 14, wherein also the Hectographing file for the Speedograph Junior, for Ditto, Inc., *Copies: Their Place in Business* (Chicago, 1935) 2-3, and for Standard Mailing Machines Company, *Facts About School Executives' Biggest Problem of Today* (Cleveland, 1935?). On Peter Force, see Sung, *Archives and Manuscripts*, 7. On the Gestetner apparatus, Proudfoot, *Origin of Stencil Duplicating*, 57, 65ff, 111. On the Roto machine, Volker Wiebels, ed., *Kontor-Träume* (Büromuseum: Mühlheim, 1988?) 13.

65. Ditto, Inc., *Copies*, 4, 25, 27, 29, 31, in Hectographing file, Box 14, and Binkley, "Micro-copying" memorandum, 1937, Copyright General Correspondence file, Box 57, both in Joint Committee Records (much of which consists of carbon copies).

66. "Present state of photographic copying on micro film," page 2 of 22 July 1936 memorandum, Box 63, Joint Committee Records; Concetta Luna, "I Tempi di copia di due scribi del XIV secolo," *Scriptorium* 43 (1989) 118; Adams, "Women in the Modern Office," 140; Lumastat brochure (NY, 1934?), Reflection Copying File, Box 13, Joint

Committee Records; Edmund S. Morgan, Center Conway, NH, handwritten (!) letter to author, 1 Oct 1991.

67. Ad found in 1953-54 [Haloid Company] Diary, Box 74, Carlson Papers. In Maastricht in 1990, one photocopying business called itself "Kopie Kopie," a Dutch idiom for "ain't I smart?" In our culture of the copy, the act may be father to the wish.

68. Chester F. Carlson, "Some notes for a talk on the history of electrostatic recording and xerography," 1 Nov 1963, Box 80, Carlson Papers; Peter C. Wensberg, *Land's Polaroid* (Boston: Houghton Mifflin, 1987). esp. 84, Land's explanation of the relationship between his polarizing technology and the one-step dry photographic process; Mark Olshaker, *The Instant Image: Edwin Land and the Polaroid Experience* (NY: Stein and Day, 1978) 32-33, 37-38 on vectography.

69. Haloid Company Press Release, 22 Oct 1948, p. 3, in Scrapbooks, vol. I, Carlson Papers; Wensberg, *Land's Polaroid*, 17, observing that at the very first public presentation "the distinction between verbs was being discussed": Polaroid pictures were not *made* but *taken*; Olshaker, *Instant Image*, 56-57, Land on taking and making, from an article in *Photographic J*.

Also on 22 October 1948, *Gone with the Wind* was ultrafaxed by RCA and Kodak in two minutes, but the uprush in facsimile transmission began only in the 1980s: T.R. Kennedy, Jr., "Novel copied, sent by air in two minutes," *NY Times* (22 Oct 1948) 27; Waldo Abbot, *Handbook of Broadcasting: The Fundamentals of AM, FM, FAX, and TV*, 3rd ed. (NY, 1950) 38-42, but just four lines (p. 124) in the 4th ed. (1957); Udayan Gupta, "Fax machine craze," *Wall Street J* (29 Aug 1989) B1. The word "fax" and the use of a compact Desk-Fax by Western Union date to 1948: *OED*, V, 777; Daniel M. Costigan, *Fax: The Principles and Practice of Facsimile Communication* (Philadelphia: Chilton, 1971) 7, 9.

Also in 1948, IBM introduced its first commercial electronic computer that multiplied and divided. Earlier, Thomas Watson had been asked to fund xerographic research but had turned Carlson down: Thomas Watson, Jr., with Peter Petre, *Father, Son & Co.: My Life at IBM and Beyond* (NY: Bantam, 1990) 199, 218.

70. Chester Carlson, "Development of electrophotography," p. 2, in Writings file, Box 80, Carlson Papers; Wensberg, *Land's Polaroid*, esp. 34, q92, 149, 180.

71. Articles in *Democrat-Chronicle (Rochester)* (23 Oct 1948) and *Newsweek* (1 Nov 1948) 50-51, in Scrapbook, vol. 1, Carlson Papers; Eastman Kodak Verifax ad, "Over my dead body – it's our last copy!" *Time* (17 Aug 1957) 83; Minnesota Mining and Mfg. ad, "Now! 4-second copies *made the All-Electric way*," *Time* (6 Aug 1956) 73; Haloid Xerox ad, "Makes copies on ordinary paper," *Business Week* (25 Feb 1961) 128.

72. Dessauer, *My Years with Xerox*, 44, 63-65, 70, 81; Xerox Corp., *Story of Xerography*, 7-8; Linowitz, *Making of a Public Man*, 68, 74, 104, 109; James G. Hodgson, *Xerography in Reproductive Processes for Libraries* (Fort Collins, 1953) 7, in Technical Papers file, Box 34, and Carlson Diary 1953-54, entry for 29 March 1953, Box 74, Carlson Papers; Mort, *Anatomy of Xerography*, 50-53; Amer Lib Assoc, Copying Methods Section, *Library Uses of Rapid Copiers* (Berkeley: U Cal Lib Photographic Service, 1958). The silver diffusion process, a German discovery, was first observed in 1938, as Carlson was experimenting in Astoria.

73. Xerox ad, "This was the beginning...," *Fortune* (Oct 1961) 188-89; Dessauer, *My Years with Xerox*, 145-46. At least one artist did find a use for outmoded carbon papers: Larry Rivers, with Carol Brightman, *Drawings and Digressions* (NY: Clarkson N.

Potter, 1979) ch. 13, esp. his *Rainbow Rembrandt* (1977), a retracing of Rembrandt's (?) *The Polish Rider.*

74. Dessauer, *My Years with Xerox*, xv, 146, 172, 177; Louise Weinberg, "The photo-copying revolution and the copyright crisis," *The Public Interest* 38 (Wint 1975) 100; Richard E. Hanson, *The Manager's Guide to Copying and Duplicating* (NY: McGraw-Hill, 1980) 3; William J. Spencer, "The paperless office," *IEEE Spectrum* (Nov 1990) 125, quoting Coopers and Lybrand, *Information and Image Management* (1987); Patrick Firpo et al., *Copyart* (NY: Marek, 1978) 13 for $8 billion worldwide revenues.

75. Hanson, *Manager's Guide*, 5-6; Bedini, *Thomas Jefferson and His Copying Machine*, q122; Elizabeth Waddell, "Blame the typewriter," *Harper's Weekly* (1 Apr 1916) 347; A.B. Dick ad, "New Worlds To Conquer"; Louise Odes Neaderland, "Introduction," *ISCAgraphics January 13 to February 13, 1989* (Sarnia, Ont.: Public Lib and Art Gallery, 1989) on the leaking of the Pentagon Papers – of which only fifteen copies were secretly in circulation before Daniel Ellsberg photocopied them: Editors of the *NY Times*, *The Pentagon Papers* (NY: Bantam, 1971) xxii; Xerox ad, "Introducing the Xerox 9400. Will miracles never cease?" *Fortune* (17 Nov 1980) 73; Michael Parks, "Soviets free the dreaded photocopier," *LA Times* (5 Oct 1989) 8:1.

76. Mark Chrysler, "Canon: more than just cameras," *IEEE Spectrum* (Nov 1990) 113-16; Linowitz, *Making of a Public Man*, 101; Louise Odes Neaderland, "Introduction," *ISCAgraphics: The Traveling Exhibition of the International Society of Copier Artists* (Sarasota: The Gallery at the Ringling School of Art and Design, [1989, no © symbol]) for quota-tion paraphrased from McLuhan – which I leave unsourced in the spirit of the art; William Larson, "Copier art: the precedents," *Print R* 20 (1985) 5-12; Julie O'Connor, "The art of copying," *Huguenot and Highland Herald* (9 Nov 1989); Louise Odes Neader-land, NY, NY, interview, 20 Oct 1990; Pati Hill, *Letters to Jill: A Catalogue and Some Notes on Copying* (NY: Kornblee, [1979]) 22.

77. Stewart Home, ed., *Plagiarism: Art as Commodity and Strategies for Its Negation* (L: Aporia, 1987–no © symbol) ch. 13 on mail art, as also John Held, Jr., "Eighties mail art networking," *Factsheet Five* 34 (1990) 80-83; Monique Brunet-Weinmann, "The work of art in the age of its electrophotographic reproduction," in Georg Mühleck and Monique Brunet-Weinmann, *Medium: Photocopy – Canadian and German Copygraphy* (Montreal: Transatlantic, 1988), 79 on Olbrich, 99 on *101 Dalmatians*, for which see Frank Thomas and Ollie Johnston, *Disney Animation: The Illusion of Life* (NY: Abbeville, 1983) 281-82, 329-30, and a review by Dugald Stermer in *Communication Arts* (Dec 1983) 198; Chris-tian Rigal, "Le Musée international de l'électrographie," *Réproduire* 103 (1990).

78. Brunet-Weinmann, "The work of art in the age of its electrophotographic repro-duction," 19, 25; Walter Benjamin, "The work of art in the age of mechanical reproduc-tion," (1936) in *Illuminations*, ed. Hannah Arendt, trans. Harry Zohn (NY: Schocken, 1985) 217-52, q223, with quotations on collecting from "Unpacking my library" (1931), *ibid.*, 61; Walter Benjamin, "A small history of photography," in *One-Way Street and Other Writings*, trans. E. Jephcott and K. Shorter (L: New Left Books, 1979) esp. 250. Janice Woo, "An ambiguity of function: xerographic artists books," *ISCA Q* 7 (Sum 1989) puts xerography within the frame of Benjamin's arguments more usefully than Jean Baudrillard, *Xerox and Infinity*, trans. anon. (L: Agitac, 1988). See also Michael Diers, "Kunst und reproduktion: der Hamburger Faksimile-Streit," *Idea, Jahrbuch der Hamburger Kunsthalle* 5 (1986) 124-37, discussing Benjamin's work in the context of Erwin Panofsky's 1930 essay, "Original und Faksimilereproduktion," reproduced in *ibid.*, 111-23.

79. Hannah Arendt, Introduction, *Illuminations*, 6-7, and *ibid.*, q255 from "Theses," and contrast Julian Roberts, *Walter Benjamin* (L: Macmillan, 1982) 197, 218; Gershom Scholem, *Walter Benjamin: The Story of a Friendship*, trans. Harry Zohn (Philadelphia: Jewish Publication Soc, 1981) 4, on the myopia. Jeffrey Mehlman, *Walter Benjamin for Children: An Essay on His Radio Years* (Chicago: U Chicago, 1993), notes that many of Benjamin's radio scripts concerned magic, imposture, and forgery; one script, "Das dämonische Berlin," detailed his secretive childhood reading of Hoffman's *Tales*, forbidden by his parents, and another script, "Rastelli erzählt," concerned a juggler who plays with a single ball inside of which are tucked a dwarf and steel springs, clear precedents to the *buckliger Zwerg* inside the racheted automaton of history. See also John McCole, *Walter Benjamin and the Antinomies of Tradition* (Ithaca: Cornell U, 1993) on Benjamin's attitudes to history.

80. Benjamin, "Theses," 255; Mort, *Anatomy of Xerography*, 50ff; Roberts, *Benjamin*, 51, 160-61; Walter Benjamin, "Lichtenberg: Ein Querschnitt," in *Gesammelte Schriften*, ed. Tillman Rexroth (Frankfurt: Suhrkamp, 1973) IV, pt. 2, 696-710; Kittler, *Discourse Networks 1800/1900*, 101, archive; Stern, *Lichtenberg*, q111; Rainer Nägele, *Theater, Theory, Speculation: Walter Benjamin and the Scenes of Modernity* (Baltimore: Johns Hopkins U, 1991) 104-07 on physiognomy, as also Benjamin's "Unpacking my library," 60, and "A small history of photography," q255; Scholem, *Walter Benjamin*, 8.

81. Hans Friederici, comp., *Lichtenbergs Werke in einem Band* (Berlin: Aufbau, 1982) 9, 83-85; Scholem, *Walter Benjamin*, 9; Benjamin, "Theses," 263. I have also benefitted from seeing the text of a talk given by J. Hillis Miller, "The Work of Cultural Criticism in the Age of Digital Reproduction" (1991), kindly provided Prof. Miller.

82. Brinitzer, *Reasonable Rebel*; Chester Carlson, Diary 1958-59, in Box 74, Carlson Papers; Benjamin, "The work of art in the age of mechanical reproduction," 251, n.21; Ben Belitt, "Xerox," *The New Yorker* (3 Mar 1973) 42 ("double our witness"). I suspect that there are also connections here to yet another "little hunchback," the technological wizard and socialist visionary Charles Steinmetz, on whom see Ronald R. Kline, *Steinmetz: Engineer and Socialist* (Baltimore: Johns Hopkins U, 1992), and John S. Staudemaier's review thereof, in *Amer Historical R* 98 (Dec 1993) 1693.

83. Mühleck and Brunet-Weinmann, *Medium: photocopy*, 105, 118; Wolfgang Ziemer-Chrobatzek, *Spielerei Autogenese* (Cologne: Offene Galerie, 1987), and interview, Cologne, 8 Nov 1990; Céjar (= Rigal), "The Great Tape Measure," *High Performance* 22 (1983) 34; Mautner and Hatfield, *Lichtenberg Reader*, q3; Christian Rigal, "Copy art," *Beaux Arts Mag* 11 (Mar 1984) 43 on Jakobois performance, Musée d'Art Moderne de la Ville de Paris, 1981, and Secter's 1977 film, *Blow Dry*; Joseph Kadar, "Electro-image art" and "In place of a curriculum vitae," publicity sheets (P, 1990?).

84. Jean-François Robic, "Auto-interview," *Lola-Fish* 10 (1990), photocopies as entropic and the photocopier as melancholic, copy kindly provided by Bruno Pommey; Thomas Kempf, "Within the scope of the technical ensemble: some fundamental digressions on 'copy art,'" *European Photography* 7 (Oct-Dec 1986) q37. For the Philosopher's Stone, see Eirenaeus Philalethes, *L'Entrée ouverte au palais fermé du roi*, trans. Maxime Préaud (P: Denoël, 1970 [1645]) ch. 3 on multiplication, ch. 4 on projection. On women and copy art, see Brunet-Weinmann, "The work of art in the age of its electrophotographic reproduction," 39; Marilyn McCray, *Electroworks* (Rochester, NY: Eastman House, 1979) q7 from Pati Hill, 8 on color copier, 75-76 on Connie Fox; Joanna Scott, "You can't judge a book by its cover," *Afterimage* (Jan 1988) 4-5, on the Shulmans; Chris-

tian Rigal, *L'Artiste et la photocopie* (P: Galerie Trans/Form, 1981), Maciel and Torey.

85. Roy Proctor, "1708 provides a showcase for photocopier art," *Richmond News Leader* (14 Apr 1990), photocopy kindly provided by Louise Odes Neaderland; Hill, *Letters to Jill*, 117-19. On the history of the value given to originality, see esp. Roland Mortier, *L'Originalité: une nouvelle catégorie esthétique au siècle des lumières* (Geneva: Droz, 1982).

86. Sidney Lumet (dir), *The Verdict* (Twentieth Century-Fox, 1992), screenplay by David Mamet.

87. Dallas D. Irvine to Robert C. Binkley, 16 Aug 1934, in Copyright 5.7c file, Box 57, Joint Committee Records.

88. On precedents to copyright, see Lyman R. Patterson, *Copyright in Historical Perspective* (Nashville: Vanderbilt U, 1968); Cyril B. Johnson, *Elizabethan Book-Pirates* (Cambridge: Harvard U, 1934); John How, *Some Thoughts on the Present State of Printing and Bookselling* (L, 1709). For the Englishman, see "Copyright in China," *Academy and Literature* 65 (1903) 215. Cf. William P. Alford, *To Steal a Book Is an Elegant Offense: Intellectual Property Law in Chinese Civilization* (Stanford: Stanford U, 1995) 19-20, arguing that, for the Chinese, the past was so indispensable that common access to it overrode concerns for private or state ownership of texts.

89. Catharine Macaulay, *A Modest Plea for the Property of Copyright* (Bath, 1774) 13-14, and see Mark Rose, "The author as proprietor: *Donaldson v. Becket* and the genealogy of modern authorship," *Representations* 23 (Sum 1988) 51-85; Laura J. Rosenthal, "(Re)writing Lear: literary property and dramatic authorship," in *Early Modern Conceptions of Property*, eds. Brewer and Staves, 323-38. For European attitudes, see Edouard Calmels, *De la propriété et de la contre-façon des oeuvres de l'intelligence* (P, 1856) esp. 41; Claude Colombet, *Propriété littéraire et artistique*, 2nd ed. (P: Dalloz, 1980) 3-7. On differences between American and European approaches, I have benefitted from an interview with Evgueni Guerassimov, Legal Officer, Copyright Division, UNESCO, Paris, 30 Oct 1990. On Bali and China, and international copyrights, Edward W. Ploman and L. Clark Hamilton, *Copyright: Intellectual Property in the Information Age* (L: Routledge & Kegan Paul, 1980) 4-5, 140-47; World International Property Organization, *Committee of Governmental Experts on the Evaluation and Synthesis of Principles on Various Categories of Works* (Geneva: UNESCO, 1988) pink pages. For final quotation, Barbara Ringer, *The Demonology of Copyright* (NY: Bowker, 1974) 6. See also Irving L. Horowitz, "The protection and dissemination of intellectual property," *Book Research Q* 2 (Sum 1986) 6, and entire issue.

90. Augustine Birrell, "[Review of] Ch. Lyon-Caen and Paul Delalain, *Lois français et étrangères sur la propriété littéraire et artistique* and of *A Bill to Consolidate and amend the law relating to Copyright...March 4, 1898*," *Edinburgh R* 191 (Jan 1900) 141. Consider also the first underleaf to a book in 75 copies by the Critical Art Ensemble, *Texthypertext* (n.p., 1989): "This / work cannot / be plagiarized. / The way it is written / prevents it. A unique qualification / of the text makes copyright violation / impossible." But the fifth underleaf (a gag?) quotes Guy Debord: "Plagiarism / is necessary. Progress implies it." And on the twelfth overleaf: "No rights reserved."

91. I.A. Gringol'ts, "Copyright," *Great Soviet Ency*, trans. of 3rd Russian ed. (NY: Macmillan, 1976) I, 597-98; Critical Arts Ensemble, "Hypertext," *Real Life* 20 (1990) 22; Bernard Edelman, *Ownership of the Image: Elements for a Marxist Theory of Law*, trans. Elizabeth Kingdom (L: Routledge & Kegan Paul, 1979); Ronald W. Bettig, "Critical perspectives on the history and philosophy of copyright," *Critical Studies in Mass Com-*

munications 9 (June 1992) 131-55; Ken Gofton, "Copyright and developing countries," in *Copyright: Legalized Piracy?*, ed. N.N. Gidwani (Bombay: Indian Committee for Cultural Freedom, 1968) 16-20.

On the U.S., see James C. Ginsburg, "A tale of two copyrights: literary property in Revolutionary France and America," in *Publishing and Readership in Revolutionary France and America*, ed. C. Armbruster (Westport, CT: Greenwood, 1993) 95-116; James J. Barnes, *Authors, Publishers and Politicians: The Quest for an Anglo-American Copyright Agreement, 1815-1854* (Columbus: Ohio State U, 1974); Frederick Saunders, "The Early History of the International Copyright Movement in America," unpub. mss. (1888), Lit. (case 42), Rare Books and Manuscripts Dept., NY Pub Lib; Edward Eggleston, "The blessings of copyright piracy," *Century Mag* 1 (1881-82) 942-45, noting acerbically that reprints of English books in the U.S. were cheaper than books by American authors; Ralph Oman, Register of Copyrights, "Statement to Subcommittee on Intellectual Property, House Judiciary Committee," 10 Apr 1991, pp. 23-30.

92. Emile Zola, "Literary property," *Bookman (NY)* 3 (July 1896) 412, 416, and cf. Archibald Alison, "The copyright question," *Blackwood's Edinburgh Mag* 51 (1842) 117.

93. *Williams & Wilkins Co. v. U.S.*, 487 F.2d 1345 (Ct. Claims 1973); "The Congress of Authors," *Dial* 15 (16 July 1893) 28-29; Drogin, *Anathema!*; Elizabeth Armstrong, *Before Copyright: The French Book-Privilege System, 1498-1526* (NY: Cambridge U, 1990) 5; George H. Putnam, *Books and Their Makers During the Middle Ages* (NY: Hilary House, 1962 [1896-97]) II, 344-70 on privileges.

94. A.V. Barry to Donald Gilchrist, 13 July 1935, in Copyright 5.7c file, Box 57, Joint Committee Records. Cf. Stanley M. Besen and Sheila Nataraj Kirby, *Private Copying, Appropriability, and Optimal Copying Royalties* (Santa Monica: RAND, 1987).

95. See esp. Stephen Breyer, "The uneasy case for copyright: a study of copyright in books, photocopies, and computer programs," *Harvard Law R* 84 (1970) 281-351, and cf. *Transcript of the National Commission on New Technological Uses of Copyrighted Works Meeting Number 17* (Washington, D.C.: Lib of Congress, 1977) esp. 99-A-D on databases, now affected by the ruling in *Feist Pubs v. Rural Telephone Co.*, 111 U.S. 1282 (1991) on the issue of whether facts are ever "original." For more recent, provocative essays, see Lewis Flacks, "The evolution of copyright," *Book Research Q* 2 (Sum 1986) 14-20; David A.D. Hunter, "Protecting the 'look and feel' of computer software in the U.S. and Australia," *Santa Clara Computer and High-Tech Law J* 7 (1991) 95-155; Donald S. Chisum, "The patentability of algorithms," with response by Allan Newell, "The models are broken, the models are broken," *U Pittsburgh Law R* 47 (1986) 959-1035; Donald L. Wenskay, "Intellectual property protection for neural networks," *Neural Networks* 3 (1990) 229-36; Ithiel de Sola Pool, *Technological Boundaries: On Telecommunications in a Global Age* (Cambridge, MA: Harvard U, 1990) 252-57; Frederick Turner, "The universal solvent," *Performing Arts J* 35/36 (1990) 75-98. I have also drawn from interviews with Kevin A. Cahill of Kolodny & Pressman, San Diego, 2 Sept 1991, and with Larry Abel, president, Amer Soc of Music Copyists, NY, NY, 25 Oct 1990. See Xerox Corp., *Team Xerox: A World of Innovation At Your Fingertips* (NY: Xerox, 1988) 9 for Xerox 5090 Duplicator. On the nature of © as symbol, my words have been contaminated by Jacques Derrida, "Du droit à la littérature," lecture, U Cal, San Diego, 20 Oct 1978.

96. U.S. National Commission on New Technological Uses of Copyrighted Works, *Final Report* (Washington, DC: Lib of Congress, 1979) 37 for Hersey. On the copying of computer programs, see esp. *Lasercomb America, Inc. v. Holliday Steel Rule Die*, 911

F.2d 970 (4th Cir., 1990). See, most recently, U.S. Department of Commerce, *Intellectual Property and the National Information Infrastructure: The Report of the Working Group on Intellectual Property Rights* (Washington, D.C.: Information Infrastructure Task Force, 1995).

97.   On acceptance of the "cybernetic metaphor," see an eloquent essay by Bill Nichols, "The work of culture in the age of cybernetic systems," *The Screen (L)* 29 (Wint 1988) 22-46.

98.   Eleanor Heartney, "Appropriation and the loss of authenticity," *New Art Examiner* (Mar 1985) 26-30; Thomas Lawson, text to *A Fatal Attraction: Art and the Media* (Chicago: Renaissance Soc, U Chicago, 1982). On quotation, see Jacques Derrida, "Limited Inc. a b c…," *Glyph* 2 (1977) 162-254, in which – toying with © – Derrida quotes nearly in full but with paragraphs out of order, an essay by J.D. Searle to which he is responding; Arthur Danto, "Artworks and real things," *Theoria* 39 (1973) 2-17. On fair use, see Pierre N. Leval, "Fair use or foul," *J Copyright Soc U.S.A.* 36 (Apr 1989); M. Les Benedict, " 'Fair Use' of unpublished sources," *Perspectives* 28 (Apr 1990) 1. On images, I draw from interviews with art dealer Ivan C. Karp, O.K. Harris Galleries, NY, NY, 23 Oct 1990; attorney Martin Bressler, Visual Artists and Galleries Assoc, NY, NY, 17 Jan 1991; attorney Steven Strauss, Cardiff, CA, 8 June 1991. I have also benefitted from talks with art historian David Kunzle on Disney control of the Donald Duck image, for which cf. John S. Lawrence, "The administration of copyrighted imagery: Walt Disney Production," in *Fair Use and Free Inquiry: Copyright Law and the New Media*, eds. J.S. Lawrence and B. Timberg (Norwood, NJ: Ablex, 1980) 43-60, 157-67. On Warhol, see Rob Fenner, "Fair warning?" *Art & Antiques* 5 (Dec 1988) q27 from Ronald Sosinski, and discussion (Apr 1989) 16-17; Paul Taylor, "Rauschenberg recalls Warhol as the pioneer," *NY Times* (18 Jan 1991) A30; Gay Morris, "Artists' use of photographs," *Artnews* (Jan 1981), rept. in John H. Merryman and Albert E. Elsen, eds., *Law, Ethics, and the Visual Arts*, 2nd ed. (Philadelphia: U Pennsylvania, 1987) I, q200-201 from Rivers, whose *Homage to Picasso* can be found in Sam Hunter, *Larry Rivers* (NY: Rizzoli, 1989) pl. 324.

99.   Don Cameron, text to *Art and Its Double: El Arte Y Su Doble* (Madrid: Fundación Caja de Pensiones, 1987) 24 for Salle, as also "Art & the law II: David Salle sued," *Art in America* (Sept 1984) 248; Susan Krane and Phyllis Rosenzweig, *Sherrie Levine: Art at the Edge* (Atlanta: High Museum, 1988); Gerard Marzorati, "Art in the (re)making," *Artnews* 85 (May 1986) 90-99, Levine protesting against her work being "boxed in" as an attack on the inauthenticity of bourgeois expression, saying it was also meant to be "fun"; William Morrow, "Pastiche, bricolage and appropriation: post-modernism and the infringement of copyright," *Art Monthly: Australian and Int* 15 (Oct 1988) 26-28; Elisabeth Sussman, "The last picture show," in *Endgame: Reference and Simulation in Recent Painting and Sculpture* (Cambridge, MA: MIT / Inst Contemporary Art, 1986) 61, and see therein, Thomas Crow, "The return of Hank Herron," 11-27; Paula Marincola, *Image Scavengers: Photography* (Philadelphia: U Pennsylvania / Inst Contemporary Art, 1983) 24, Levine on the "plagiarist"; Klaus Ottmann, ed., *Sturtevant 1987* (NY: Stux Gallery, 1987); Dan Cameron, "A salon history of appropriation with Leo Castelli and Elaine Sturtevant," *Flash Art* (Nov-Dec 1988) 76-77, q77.

100.   Morrow, "Pastiche, bricolage and appropriation," 27; Jeanne Siegel, "After Sherrie Levine [interview]," *Arts Mag* 59 (June 1985) 141. Mike Bidlo, who not only re-painted works of Jackson Pollock but reenacted infamous scenes in the life of Pollock and of Warhol, wrote that his work was "a vehicle for empowerment and demys-

tification. But most importantly it changes my relationship with its subject. It is my personal exorcism." See his letter to the editor, "Bidlo on appropriation," *New Art Examiner* (June 1985) 3. Levine did an "After Bidlo." See also Kate Linker, "On Richard Prince's photographs," *Richard Prince* (Villeurbanne: Le Nouveau Musée, 1983) 4, Prince rephotographing commercial advertisements to expose the degree to which "our reality has been invaded by fiction...a reality in which the roles of both creator and copyist have been replaced by the more complex one of the arranger who...'manages' the production of imagery."

101. See, for example, Nelson Goodman, *Languages of Art* (Indianapolis: Bobbs-Merrill, 1968), the controversy followed in Trudi Jacobson, "The aesthetic dimensions of forgeries and copies in art: an annotated biblography," *Bull of Bibliography* 44 (Sept 1988) 197–202; Denis Dutton, ed., *The Forger's Art: Forgery and the Philosophy of Art* (Berkeley: U Cal, 1983); Center for Advanced Studies in the Visual Arts, *Symposium Papers VII. Retaining the Original: Multiple Originals, Copies, and Reproductions* (Hanover, NH: U Press of New England, 1989). On debates over (il)legitimate Rembrandts, see Josua Bruyn et al., *A Corpus of Rembrandt Paintings*, trans. D. Cook-Radmore (The Hague: Nijhoff, 1982-); Ben P.J. Broos, *Impact of a Genius: Rembrandt, His Pupils and Followers in the Seventeenth Century* (Amsterdam: Waterman, 1983) 35–59; Svetlana Alpers, *Rembrandt's Enterprise* (Chicago: U Chicago, 1988) esp. 60ff; Anthony Bailey, "A young man on horseback," *The New Yorker* (5 Mar 1990) 45–77; Gary Schwartz, "The Rembrandt Research Project and the Question of Authorship," Regents' Lecture, William Andrews Clark Library, UCLA, 18 May 1990, with commentary by Hillel Schwartz; Gary Schwartz, "Rembrandt research after the age of connoisseurship," *Annals of Scholarship* 10, 3–4 (1993) 313–36.

102. For overviews, see Susan Lambert, *The Image Multiplied: Five Centuries of Printed Reproductions of Paintings and Drawings* (L: Trefoil, 1987); William M. Ivins, Jr., *Prints and Visual Communication* (Cambridge, MA: MIT, 1969 [1953]). For particulars, Andrew Ladis and Carolyn Wood, eds., *The Craft of Art: Originality and Industry in the Italian Renaissance and Baroque Workshop* (Athens, GA: U Georgia, 1995) esp. essays by Bruce Cole and Malcolm Campbell; Otto Kurz, "Early art forgeries; from the Renaissance to the eighteenth century," *J Royal Soc of Arts* 121 (Jan 1973) 74–90; Riccardo Nobili, *The Gentle Art of Faking* (L, 1922); Caroline Karpinski, "The print in thrall to its original: a historiographic perspective," and Beverly L. Brown, "Replication and the art of Veronese," in *Retaining the Original*, 101–24, as also Jeffrey M. Muller, "Measures of authenticity: the detection of copies in the early literature of connoisseurship," 141–49; Jonathan Richardson, "The connoisseur" (1719) in *The Works* (L, 1792) q146; Mansfield K. Talley, Jr., "Connoisseurship and the methodology of the Rembrandt Research Project," *Int J of Museum Management and Curatorship* 8 (June 1989) 175–214, invaluable; Charles Hope, "The real Leonardo," *NY R of Books* (17 Aug 1989) 16–18. For an intriguing case study, see Mark Rogerson, *The Dalí Scandal* (L: Gollancz, 1987) – estimating a half million faked Dalí prints on the market, and discussing Dalí's signing in 1974 of 17,500 blank sheets of paper as promissory notes to fulfilling a contract for a deck of tarot cards to be lithographically reproduced.

103. Martha Woodmansee, "The genius and the copyright: economic and legal conditions of the emergence of the 'author,'" *Eighteenth-Century Studies* 17 (1984) 425–48, but contrast Deborah N. Losse, "From *auctor* to *auteur*: authorization and appropriation in the Renaissance," *Medievalia et Humanistica* 16 (1988) 157–63; Giorgio Tonelli, "Genius from the Renaissance to 1770," and Rudolf Wittkower, "Genius: individual-

ism in art and artists," *Dictionary of the History of Ideas*, ed.-in-chief Philip P. Wiener (NY: Scribner's, 1973) II, 293–312; A.T. Carter, "Curiosities of copyright law," *Law Q R* 4 (1888) 176, "great picture"; Philip H. Nicklin, "[Review of] *Remarks on Literary Property* (1838)," *North Amer R* 48 (1839) 259, "own creation," a sentiment earlier expressed by François A.A. Pluquet, *Lettres à un ami sur les affaires actuelles de la libraire* (P, 1778) Letter I, 6. On the betrayal of copywork, I am paraphrasing Pierre Larousse, "Copie," *Grand dictionnaire universel du XIXe siècle* (P, 1869) V, 68. Abbott Thayer, defending the pristine integrity of masterpieces, argued that art restorers themselves took great paintings – paintings that "soared too high for the complete control of their author" – and turned them into "the dead ground-plans of the miracles they were." A.H. Thayer, " 'Restoration': the doom of pictures and sculpture," *Int Studio* 70 (Mar 1920) xiii–xvii.

104. Edwin Bale, "Artistic copyright," *J Soc of Arts* 48 (1899) 293–305; Gilbert E. Samuel, "Copyright in works of fine art, I and II," *Mag of Art* 15 (1892) 375–78, 403–07, q375; *West v. Francis*, 5 Barn & Ald 743 (KB 1822) for Bailey; William H. White and T. Mellard Reade, "Architects' copyright," *Amer Architect and Building News* 38 (1892) 45–47. Cf. Peter H. Karlen, "Worldmaking: property rights in aesthetic creations," *J Aesthetics and Art Criticism* 45 (Wint 1986) 183–92.

On the tricky problem of photography and copyright, see Edouard Copper, *L'Art et la loi* (P, 1903) 40–44; Edelman, *Ownership of the Image*, reexamined by Jane M. Gaines, *Contested Culture: The Image, the Voice, and the Law* (Chapel Hill: U of North Carolina, 1991) 1–83; Barnett Hollander, *International Law of Art* (L: Bowes & Bowes, 1959) 75–76, case of *Turner v. Robinson* (1859); "Getting the big picture," *Time* (26 Sept 1977) 82–83; Polaroid Corporation, *The Polaroid Museum Replica Collection* (Cambridge, MA: Polaroid, 1991?).

105. See Bruce Robertson, "Joseph Goupy [ca. 1689-1769] and the art of the copy," *Bull [Cleveland] Museum of Art* 75 (1988) 355–75, on the influence of a painter of gouache copies and exact-scale copies of Old Masters to replace originals sold off by impoverished owners. On the history of art as copying, see Egbert Haverkamp-Begemann, with Carolyn Logan, *Creative Copies: Interpretive Drawings from Michelangelo to Picasso* (L: Sotheby's, 1988) esp. 16–21, as also Adam Gopnick. "St. Peter's feet and Rembrandt's fountain," *The New Yorker* (4 July 1988) 61–65; Theodore Reff, "Degas's copies of older art," *Burlington Mag* 105 (1963) 241–51; Charles Chetham, *The Role of Vincent van Gogh's Copies in the Development of His Art* (NY: Garland, 1976); Jean-Auguste Dominique Ingres, *Ecrits sur l'art* (P, 1947) 24, 80; Rosalind E. Krauss, "You Irreplaceable You," in *Retaining the Original*, 151–59 – Ingres also had his paintings engraved for multiple prints. On the tradition of self-copying, see also Alexandre Ananoff, "Les Répliques de François Boucher," *L'Oeil* 374 (Sept 1986) 66–71; James Orrock, *Repeats and Plagiarisms in Art, 1888* (L, 1889) 4–6. For twentieth-century examples, see Gérard Bertrand, "Le Tableau d'après le tableau," *Revue d'esthétique* 27 (Jan–Mar 1974) 57–76; Carlo L. Ragghianti, "Il caso de Chirico," *Critica d'arte* 44 (Jan-June 1979) 3–54, listing, for example, twenty-two repetitions of *Trovatore*.

106. Otto Kurz, *Fakes* (NY: Dover, 1967) 253, ceramics; Victor I. Carlson, introduction to *The Inspired Copy: Artists Look at Art* (Baltimore: Museum of Art, 1975); Peter Shee, *Painter, Who continues copying Pictures of Value...* (Dublin, 1765) handbill in British Library with handwritten notation; David A. Hanson, "The beginnings of photographic reproduction in the U.S.A.," *History of Photography* 12 (Oct–Dec 1988) 357–76;

▲, "Photo-engravings: their place as reproductions," *Athenaeum (L)* 3126 (2 Apr 1887) 412; Foreign Plastic Art Company, *Catalog of Plaster Casts* (Boston, 1904); Joshua Reynolds, *Discourses on Art*, ed. R.R. Wark (San Marino, CA: Huntington Lib, 1959) VI, 96 – who also connived in the secret substitution of copies of paintings by Poussin and Rubens so that the originals could be stolen out of Italy: "Sir Joshua Reynolds helped to pirate Old Masters," *NY Times* (1 Feb 1914) V,1; Jean Paul Friedrich Richter, *Levana; or, The Doctrine of Education* [with autobiography], trans. A.H. (L, 1876 [1811, autobiography ca. 1818]) 22, 57 for marionettes. On art pedagogy, see Clive Ashwin, *Drawing and Education in German-Speaking Europe, 1800–1900* (Ann Arbor: UMI, 1981); Richard D. Palmer, "A History of the Concept of Imitation in American Art Education," Ph.D., Pennsylvania State U, 1978 (DA 39/04, p. 2005–A); Richard Shiff, "Representation, copying, and the technique of originality," *New Literary Age* 15,2 (1984) 331–63; Anthony Dyson, "Originality and originals, copies and reproductions: reflections on a primary school project," *J Art and Design Education* 3,2 (1984) 181–90; Paul Duncum, "To copy or not to copy: a review," *Studies in Art Education* 29 (Sum 1988) 202–10.

107. Brigitte Delluc and Gilles Delluc, "Lascaux II: a faithful copy," *Antiquity* 58 (Nov 1984) 194–96, and for a tourist's view, Nicholas Delbanco, *Running In Place: Scenes from the South of France* (NY: Atlantic Monthly, 1989) 9–12; Ralph Rugoff, "House of mirrors: the Nixon Library reflects a distorted image – or none at all," *LA Weekly* (19–25 Oct 1990) 45.

108. I rely here upon interviews at the J. Paul Getty Museum, Malibu, CA, 30 May 1991, with Robert Keefe (frames), Elisabeth Mention (painting restoration), and Brian Considine (decorative arts), and upon an interview with Frank D. Preusser, Associate Director, Programs, Getty Conservation Inst, Marina del Rey, CA, 31 May 1991. See also Stephen E. Weil, *Rethinking the Museum and Other Meditations* (Washington, DC: Smithsonian Inst, 1990) 161–66 on "Legal aspects of the display of imitations." On El Greco, see Kathryn C. Johnson, "Fakes, forgeries, and other deceptions," in *Fakes and Forgeries* (Minneapolis: Inst of Arts, 1973) unpag. The Pushkin Gallery in Moscow is also a Museum of Copies.

109. See David Murray, *Museums, Their History and Their Use*, 3 vols. (Glasgow, 1904); Germain Bazin, *The Museum Age*, trans. Jane van Nuis Cahill (NY: Universe, 1967); Oliver Impey and Arthur MacGregor, eds., *The Origins of Museums: The Cabinet of Curiosities in Sixteenth and Seventeenth-Century Europe* (Oxford: Clarendon, 1985); Göran Schildt, "The idea of the museum" and E.H. Gombrich, "The museum: past, present and future," both in *The Idea of the Museum*, ed. Lars Aagaard-Mogensen (Lewiston, ME: Mellen, 1988) 85–126.

110. John W. Bradley, *A Dictionary of Miniaturists, Illuminators, Calligraphers, and Copyists* (L, 1887) I,112; Gary Schwartz, "Art within Art: *Kunstkamer* Painting and Its Meanings," Leventritt Lecture, Harvard U, April 1990, typescript kindly provided by the author; Karl Schütz, "David Teniers der Jungere als Kopist im Dienst Erzherzog Leopold Wilhelms," in *Original – Kopie – Replik – Paraphrase*, ed. Heribert Hutter (Vienna: Akademie der Bildenden Kunste in Wien, 1980) 21–33; Frances A. Yates, *The Art of Memory* (Chicago: U Chicago, 1966); Thomas D. Kaufmann, *The Mastery of Nature: Aspects of Art, Science, and Humanism in the Renaissance* (Princeton: Princeton U, 1993) 177ff; Horst Bredekamp, *The Lure of Antiquity and the Cult of the Machine: The Kunstkamer and the Evolution of Nature, Art and Technology*, trans. Allison Brown (Princeton: Wiener, 1995); Eilean Hooper-Greenhill, *Museums and the Shaping of Knowledge* (L: Routledge,

1992) 91-104, 112ff, and esp. fig. 23, Johann Bretschneider's *The Imperial Gallery in Prague* (1714), a German painting incorporating 140 other paintings.

111. Antonio Palomino de Castro y Velasco, *An Account of the Lives and Works of the Most Eminent Spanish Painters, Sculptors, and Architects* (L, 1739) 76, his examples, and Franciscus Junius the Younger, *The Painting of the Ancients* (L, 1638) 348, both quoted by Talley, "Connoisseurship," 177.

112. Anthony Radcliffe, "Replicas, copies, and counterfeits of early Italian bronzes," *Apollo* n.s. 124 (Sept 1986) 183-87; John M. Montias, "Art dealers in the seventeenth-century Netherlands," *Simiolus* 18 (1988) 244-56, up to 18 percent copies in a dealer's inventory, and see, on growing fears in the 1600s of being duped into buying a copy as if an original, Catherine M. Goguel, "Taste and trade: the retouched drawings in the Everard Jabach collection at the Louvre," *Burlington Mag* 130 (Nov 1988) 829; Francis Haskell and Penny Haskell, *Taste and the Antique: The Lure of Classical Sculpture 1500-1900* (New Haven: Yale U, 1981) 31-36; David Robbins, *The Camera Believes Everything / Die Kamera Glaubt Alles*, trans. Thomas Braun (Stuttgart: Schwarz, 1988) 25; Paul Duro, "*Un livre ouvert à l'instruction*: study museums in Paris in the nineteenth century," *Oxford Art J* 10,1 (1987) 44-58; Ingres, *Ecrits sur l'art*, 24. Known forgeries were also collected for the study galleries: Kurz, "Early art forgeries," 88-89.

113. Benjamin R. Andrews, *Museums of Education, Their History of Use* (NY, 1909) 8, first such opened in Ontario with samples of U.S. "school models" that Canadian manufacturers might duplicate; Albert Boime, "Le Musée des copies," *Gazette des Beaux-Arts* 64 (1964) 237-47; Pierre Vaisse, "Charles Blanc und das 'Musée des Copies,'" *Zeitschrift für Kunstgeschichte* 39,1 (1976) 54-66; Roger Benjamin, "Recovering authors: the modern copy, copy exhibitions, and Matisse," *Art History* 12 (June 1988) 176-201, q179 from the French Academy's *Dictionnaire*.

114. Trevor Fawcett, "On reproduction," *Art Lib J* 7 (Spr 1982) 9-16; idem, "Graphic versus photographic in the nineteenth-century reproduction," *Art History* 9 (June 1986) 185-212, q192, "imperishable"; Ingres, *Ecrits sur l'art*, 24, the Titian; Axelle de Gaigneron, "Le Temps des copies," *Connaissance des arts* 368 (Oct 1982) 92-93; H. Wilson, "Modern processes of reproduction," *Art J* 32 (1880) q270. See also J.C. Robinson, "On spurious works of art," *Nineteenth Century* 30 (Nov 1891) 694-95, the Louvre's directors not admitting as a forgery a Donatello bust until they compared a *photo* of the bust with a *photo* of the model hired by the forger, Giovani Bastianini.

115. I am here indebted to Benjamin, "Recovering authors," q180 from Mirbeau. Benjamin notes earlier gallery shows (by, for example, Odilon Redon) in which copies had been shown, but they had never been the focus, although Bernard Rackham's introduction to Burlington Fine Arts Club, *Catalogue of a Collection of Counterfeits, Imitations and Copies of Works of Art* (L, 1924) 19, notes that part of the 1908 Spring Exhibition of the Whitechapel Art Gallery was devoted to copies (and fakes and reproductions were exhibited in Copenhagen in 1915 and Philadelphia in 1916). Bazin, *The Museum Age*, 261, notes a proposal made by Franklin W. Smith in 1900 that a walled city be built in Washington, D.C., made up of pastiches of the great buildings of the world and filled with copies of renowned masterpieces. On collage, see Eddie Wolfram, *History of Collage* (L: Studio Vista, 1975); Arni R. Haraldsson, "Tracing collage, montage and appropriation," in *Transference* (Banff: Walter Phillips Gallery, 1987) 7-12; Donald Kuspit, "Collage: the organizing principle of art in the age of the relativity of art," in his *The New Subjectivism* (Ann Arbor: UMI, 1988) 503-20. Cf. a history of poetic copying

as fabulated by Harold Bloom, *The Anxiety of Influence* (NY: Oxford U, 1973).

116. Anne-Marie Stein, as told to George Carpozi, Jr., *Three Picassos Before Breakfast: Memoirs of an Art Forger's Wife* (NY: Hawthorne, 1973) 11, and seconded by Tom Keating, *The Fake's Progress* (L: Hutchinson, 1977) 82, 84–85; C. Carr, "The shock of the old," *Village Voice* (30 Oct 1984) 103–04, Bidlo; Friderike Klauner, "Kopie und Geschmack," in Hutter, ed., *Original-Kopie-Replik-Paraphrase*, 6–17, a study of copying permits, 1870–1979, in German art museums; G. Schack, ed., *Horst Janssen: Die Kopie* (Hamburg: Christians, 1977) – Janssen (p. 9) in his apologia quotes none other than Lichtenberg ("Ist Genialität etwas anderes als Wiederfinden?"); Uli Bohnen, ed., *Hommage-demontage* (Cologne: Wienand, 1988) 7 on Japanese copyists, as also Bo Gunnarsson, "Yoshihro / Liljefors," in *Kopior, Förfalskningar, Parafraser, Plageat, Pastischer, Repliker, Original, Reproduktioner* (Gothenburg: Göteborgs Konstmuseum, 1988) 38–39, copies by Yoshihro Shimoda; Bradford Art Galleries and Museum, *New Life for Old Masters: Paintings by Barrington Bramley* (Bradford: the Museum, 1982) q2–3; Hope B. Werness, "Han van Meegeren fecit," in Dutton, *Forger's Art*, 1–57. In the 1980s an Italian firm sponsored an exhibition entitled "The Museum of Museums," with one hundred reproduced masterpieces from Giotto to Warhol, "the perfection of which rivals the world's great forgeries." See William Olander, *Fake: A Meditation on Authenticity* (NY: New Museum of Contemporary Art, 1987) 42.

117. On multiple originals, see Toni del Rienzo, "Multiple authenticity," *Art and Artists* 9 (July 1974) 22–27; Arts Council of Great Britain, *3 → ∞: New Multiple Art* (L: Whitechapel Art Gallery, 1971); Karl Graak, "Original – Reproduktion – Original-reproduktion," *Artis* 31 (Nov 1979) 16–18. On True Fakes Ltd., see William H. Honan, "Art world trying to cope in age of the fake," *NY Times* (3 Sept 1991) B1. For the Galerie Daniel Delamare, I rely upon an interview with Daniel Delamare and Danielle van Santen, Paris, 30 Oct 1990; Danielle van Santen, *Les Grands maîtres restitués*, 1990 press-kit, q10; CBS TV, *Sixty Minutes* segment on art copyists, rerun 7 July 1991. Cf. M. Pabst Battin, "Exact replication in the visual arts," *J Aesthetics and Art Criticism* 38 (Wint 1979) 153–58 on the Société des Arts, Lettres, et Techniques in Paris, selling copies of Rembrandt and Monet.

118. On copying techniques and the art copying industry, see, for example, Ursel Berger, "Ein 'Rodin' per Post? Zu neuen Entwicklungen auf der Reproductionsmarkt," *Die Weltkunst* 58 (15 May 1988) 1542–45; [John F. Povey], "First word," *African Arts* 20 (Aug 1987) 1; Alice Goldfarb Marquis, "Mall-to-mall art: is it 'schlock' or what?" unpublished paper presented at the 1993 Conference of the Popular Culture Association. For Japan, see Chapter VIII, Reprise VI.

119. Henry Kamm, "Dauntless restorer, 6 years at task, is rescuing Leonardo's 'Last Supper,'" *NY Times* (20 Mar 1983) 6; Preusser interview; Mahasti Afshar, Getty Conservation Inst, Marina del Rey, personal interview, 24 May 1991.

120. Hal Foster, *Recodings: Art, Spectacle, Cultural Politics* (Port Townsend, WA: Bay, 1985) 6ff. on Barthes, Baudrillard, and the "fetishism of the signifier." Cf. Colin Thompson, "Why do you need to see the original painting anyway?" *Visual Resources* 2 (Fall 1981/Spr 1982) 21–36, on the preference of sixth-formers for bright color slides than for drabber originals.

121. Fawcett, "Graphic versus photographic," 193; Kenneth Hudson, *Museums of Influence* (Cambridge: Cambridge U, 1987) 49; Terry Trucco, "The shopping boom at your local museum," *Artnews* 76 (Oct 1977) 56–60; Povey, "First word," 6; Neil Harris,

"Museums, merchandising, and popular taste," in his *Cultural Excursions* (Chicago: U Chicago, 1990) 56-81; Terry Davies, "Plagiarism and wood firing," *Ceramics Monthly* 37 (Dec 1989) 22, 61, on problems posed by reproductions of Japanese ceramics; William Hunt, "Museums, profits and reproductions," *Ceramics Monthly* 34 (April 1986) 25-27; Roberta Stothart, Director, Museum Shops, Armand Hammer Museum of Art, LA, interview, 26 May 1991. When the Met was founded in 1870, it was assumed that its European collection would be primarily copies, of which over two thousand had been made by 1904, at which time the financier J.P. Morgan forcefully insisted that the Met become a museum of originals.

122. C. Arthur Pearson ad, found stuck into a copy of *Cornhill Mag* 85 (1902); Honan, "Art world trying to cope," B2 on Ethan Allen; "Bamboozled," *House Beautiful* (May 1989) 13-15; Kittinger Company *A Library of Eighteenth-Century English and American Designs* (Buffalo, 1976), quoted in *The Eye of the Beholder: Fakes, Replicas, and Alterations in American Art*, ed. Gerald W.R. Ward (New Haven: Yale U Art Gallery, 1977) 15; Adele Earnest, "Reproductions as big business," *Horizon* 21 (Nov-Dec 1978) q54-55, Rockefeller.

123. George Kubler, *The Shape of Time: Remarks on the History of Things* (New Haven: Yale U, 1963) 39.

124. Louis Peters, trans. Donald Tuckwiller, "Only appearances aren't deceptive – Sturtevant, Bidlo and Co.: copyright and iconoclastic controversy," in Bohnen, ed., *Hommage-Demontage*, 63 for rumor; Selma Holo, "Color reproductions will dull the Barnes Collection," *LA Times* (17 June 1991) F3; John M. Taylor et al., "Applications of a laser scanner to the recording and replication of museum objects," in *ICOM Committee for Conservation: 8th Triennial Meeting, Sydney, Australia, 6-11 September,1987* (preprint) I, 93-97; Albert Elsen and John Merryman, "Art replicas: a question of ethics," *Artnews* 78 (Feb 1979) 61, and cf. Assoc of Art Museum Directors, Ethics and Standards Committee, "Guidelines for reproductions of works of art," *Professional Practices in Art Museums* (Savannah: AAMD, 1971) App. B; *Carol Barnhart Inc. v. Economy Cover Corp.*, 773 F.2d 411 (2d Cir. 1985), assessed by Shira Perlmutter, "Conceptual separability and copyright in the designs of useful articles," *J Copyright Soc U.S.A.* 37 (Apr 1990) 339-81 at 360; Revell ad, "A Los Angeles man...," *Communication Arts* (Dec 1983) 12. On the recent sophistication of (miniature) models, see also Alison Theaker, "A model profession," *British J of Photography* 134 (27 Mar 1987) 362-64; Hugh Aldersey-Williams, "Perfect fakes," *Industrial Design* 34 (Nov-Dec 1987) 56-61.

125. Peter Lowe, Asst. Director, ICC Counterfeiting Intelligence Bureau (CIB), Barking, Essex, interview, 26 Nov 1990, and CIB Factsheet; Musée de la Contrefaçon, Paris, visited Oct 1990; Arthur C. Danto, *The Transfiguration of the Commonplace* (Cambridge, MA: Harvard U, 1981) 8. Cf. Jonathan S. Jennings, "Trademark counterfeiting: an unpunished crime," *J of Criminal Law and Criminology* 80 (Fall 1989) 805-41. On counterfeit and comedy, see Hugh Kenner, *The Counterfeiters* (Garden City, NY: Anchor, 1973). On labeling and high art, see David Phillips, *Don't Trust the Label: An Exhibition of Fakes, Imitations, and the Real Thing* (Manchester: Arts Council, 1986-87), catalog sponsored by the Association of British Foods. I have also benefitted from a conversation with Margaret K. Morrell, International Anticounterfeiting Coalition, Washington, D.C., phone interview, 15 Aug 1991, noting the widespread sale of counterfeit *costume* jewelry.

126. Jonathan Fenby, *Piracy and the Public: Forgery, Theft and Exploitation* (L: Muller,

1983) q51 from lawyer Patrick Brunet, for Vuitton. On motifs of degeneration and regeneration, copying and copyists, see esp. Cynthia Ozick's story, "Puttermesser paired," *The New Yorker* (8 Oct 1990) 40–75.

127. Symposium on the machine, *Studio Potter* 15 (Dec 1986) 2–23, q19 (Kames), q22 (Higgins); Hunt, "Museums, profits and reproductions," 25; Avrum Stroll, "Linguistic clusters and the problem of universals," *Dialectica* 27 (1973) 219–59.

CHAPTER SEVEN: ONCE MORE, WITH FEELING

1. H.G. Wells, *Little Wars* (Boston, 1913) 41, q43, 50–52, 55, q152–53, q154, q157.

2. Hans Delbruck, *History of the Art of War*, trans. Walter J. Renfroe, Jr. (Westport, CT: Greenwood, 1975–85) IV, 157–59; Frank Tallett, *War and Society in Early Modern Europe, 1495–1715* (L: Routledge, 1992) 24–28; William H. McNeill, *The Pursuit of Power: Technology, Armed Force, and Society since A.D. 1000* (Chicago: U Chicago, 1982) 125–35. Maurice's cousins, Count William Louis and John of the House of Nassau, were also instrumental in developing drill; all three were inspired by newly printed Greek and Roman treatises on the art of war.

3. McNeill, *Pursuit of Power*, 125–35, 154; Tallett, *War and Society*, 26–28; Manuel De Landa, *War in the Age of Intelligent Machines* (NY: Zone, 1991) 64ff on "entrainment"; Georges Vigarello, *Le Corps redressé: histoire d'un pouvoir pédagogique* (P: Delarge, 1978) on alignment and military carriage.

4. Francis J. McHugh, *Fundamentals of War Gaming*, 3rd ed. (Newport, RI: Naval War College, 1966) ch. 2; Andrew Wilson, *The Bomb and the Computer: Wargaming from Ancient Chinese Mapboard to Atomic Computer* (NY: Delacorte, 1968) 2–6; Sidney H. Giffin, *The Crisis Game* (Garden City, NY: Doubleday, 1965) using John P. Young, *A Survey of Historical Developments in War Games* (Staff Paper 98, Operations Research Office, Johns Hopkins U, 1960); J.G.J. Venturinus, *Beschreibung und Regeln eines neuen Krieges Spiels* (Schleswig, 1798), summarized in Douglas C. MacCaskill, "Wargaming," *Marine Corps Gazette* 57,10 (1973) 19–21; Peter R. Perla, *The Art of Wargaming* (Annapolis: Naval Inst, 1990) 23, von Reisswitz, as also Theodore E. Sterne, "War games: what they are and how they evolved," *Army* 16 (Mar 1966) 45.

5. On luck, competition, and vertigo, see Roger Caillois, *Man, Play, and Games*, trans. Meyer Barash (NY: Free Press, 1961).

6. MacCaskill, "Wargaming," 21, the 1866 campaign; Charles A.L. Totten, *Strategos* (NY, 1880) I, Epigraph, quoting Baron A.H. Jomini on Napoleon; Sterne, "War games," 46 on Clerk; Michael Balfour and Julian Frisby, *Helmuth von Moltke* (L: Macmillan, 1972) 2–5 on his ancestor; Eberhard Kessel, *Moltke* (Stuttgart: Koehler, 1957) 52, 61–62; Gunther E. Rothenburg, "Moltke, Schlieffen, and the doctrine of strategic deployment," in *Makers of Modern Strategy*, ed. Peter Paret (Princeton: Princeton U, 1986) q296.

7. Balfour and Frisby, *Helmuth von Moltke*, 2; Rothenburg, "Moltke, Schlieffen," 296–313; Sterne, "War games," 45; Capt. Charles W. Raymond, "The war game," *Field Glass* 1 (Oct 1879) 183n.; Giffin, *Crisis Game*, 37–39 on Germany; John Prados, *Pentagon Games: Wargames and the American Military* (NY: Harper & Row, 1987) 4, D-Day. On claims that the wargamed Schlieffen plan made World War I inevitable, see Charles S. Maier, "Wargames: 1914–1919," *J of Interdisciplinary History* 18 (Spr 1988) 832, arguing that "*repetition* [was] the crucial destabilizing variable," not the plan but "iterative crises." Note that the German *Kriegsspiel* has one *s* in English usage.

8. Henry H. Spenser Wilkinson, *Thirty-Five Years 1874–1909* (L, 1933) 2–25, q6.

Asked (p. 33) to comment on current wars for the *Manchester Guardian*, Wilkinson found that technologies of copying forced him to be a prophet. Since he relied heavily upon maps, "My problem was how to reproduce in the paper such portions of the map as would adequately illustrate the operations.... [The] only means we had of producing a map was to have it copied by a wood engraver, and from his block to produce a metal casting which could be inserted in the page of type. The production of this metal block took a whole week from the day on which the map to be copied was handed to the draughtsman or the engraver. I had therefore to foresee by at least a week the probable site of any engagement."

9. Rothenburg, "Moltke, Schlieffen," 299, fear of deadlocks; John Ellis, *A Social History of the Machine Gun* (NY: Pantheon, 1975) q25 from salespitch for the Union Repeating Gun; Totten, *Strategos*, I, ix, Automaton Regiment; Stephen Vincent Benet, "John Brown's Body" (1927) in *Selected Works* (NY, 1942) I, 82.

10. Raymond, "The war game," *Field Glass* 1 (June 1879) 101–02, (Aug 1879) 142–44, and (Oct 1879) 183–84, q183; Sterne, "The war game," 46 on Gettysburg map.

11. William R. Livermore, *The American Kriegsspiel* (Boston, 1882 [1879]) paraphernalia; Totten, *Strategos*, I, 2 and epigraph for quotation from *Studies in Troop-Leading* by von Verdy du Vernois, 84n on casualties, 94 on the God of Wars. On flinching, Wilson, *The Bomb and the Computer*, 12.

12. Capt. P.H. Colomb, "Broadside fire, and a naval war game," *Field Glass* 1 (Dec 1879) 224. The war statistics are for both soldiers and civilians.

13. John B. Hattendorf, "Technology and strategy: a study in the professional training of the U.S. Navy, 1900–1916," *Naval War College R* 24,3 (1971) 25–48, q44 Little, q42 Norris; William McCarty Little, letter to William Livermore, 4 Dec 1891, p. 3, on kriegspiel as music, in Box 1, f.5, Correspondence, MS Coll. 13, Naval Historical Collection, Naval War College, Newport, RI; Francis J. McHugh, "Gaming at the Naval War College," *U.S. Naval Inst Proc* 90,3 (1964) 48–55.

14. Hattendorf, "Technology and strategy," q36 from lecturer, Commandant Vogelsang. On Jane, who published in his *Annual* the silhouettes of each nation's ships that they might be more readily identified on the horizon, see Barry J. Carter, *Naval War Games: World War I and World War II* (NY: Arco, 1975) 36; Perla, *Art of Wargaming*, 37; *Who Was Who, 1916–1928* (L: Adam & Charles Black, 1967) 551. On the 1912 Fort Andrews, see Records of the Chiefs of Arms, Coast Artillery War Instruction, Fort Andrews, MA, 1913–18, Document Files 1–3, 35, 46, 120, and 280 in Record Group 177, National Archives, Washington, DC.

15. McHugh, "Gaming at the Naval War College," q51. Cf. Tim Travers, *The Killing Ground: The British Army, the Western Front and the Emergence of Modern Warfare, 1900–1918* (L: Allen & Unwin, 1987) 43–51, prewar debate on whether more drill or individual initiative was needed to overcome the firepower of modern war.

16. Giffin, *Crisis Game*, 27, 59–60; Hattendorf, "Technology and strategy," 43; Wilson, *The Bomb and the Computer*, 17; William McCarty Little, letter to Livermore, 4 Dec 1891, as above, n.13; idem, *The Strategic Naval War Game or Chart Maneuver* (Newport, RI, 1912), offprint from *U.S. Naval Institute Proc* 38,4 (1912) q1219–20; Margaret H. Hazen, Potomac, MD, letter, 19 May 1992, on fire drills, and see photo of "Fire Drill by the Ushers of Proctor's 125th Street Theatre," in *The Theatre* 4 (1904) 166; Jacques Vié, "Les Méconnaissances systématiques," *Annales médico-psychologiques* 102 (1944) 248; Perla, *Art of Wargaming*, xii, foreword by Adm. Thomas B. Hayward on gaming against

Japan, 45 on the Japanese (who credited wargames with their 1905 success in Mongolia and wargamed all campaigns of World War II); Thomas B. Buell, "Admiral Raymond A. Spruance and the Naval War College: Part I – preparing for World War II," *Naval War College R* 23,7 (1971) 30-51; Office of the Chief of Infantry, General Correspondence 1921-42, "Third Army Maneuvers, May 5-25, 1940," document 353/6190, Box 17, Record Group 177, Records of the Chiefs of Arms, National Archives; Jean R. Moenk, *A History of Large-Scale Army Maneuvers in the U.S., 1935-1964* (Fort Monroe, VA: U.S. Continental Army Command, 1969) 1-47, q32.

17. G. Patrick Murray, "The Louisiana maneuvers," *Louisiana History* 13,2 (1972) 117-38; Richard M. Ketchum, "Warming up on the side lines for World War II," *Smithsonian* 22 (Sept 1991) 88-103; Moenk, *Large-Scale Army Maneuvers*, 10, 47ff; Dwight D. Eisenhower, *At Ease* (Garden City, NY: Doubleday, 1967) q243-44, bridge anecdote.

18. Moenk, *Large-Scale Army Maneuvers*, q118, 162, 196-98, 209-12, 287, 312; Prados, *Pentagon Games*, 5-6, 12ff; Donald Mackenzie, "From Kwajalein to Armageddon? Testing and the social construction of missile accuracy," in *The Uses of Experiment*, eds. David Gooding et al. (NY: Cambridge U, 1989) 409-35; Jacques Derrida, trans. C. Porter and P. Lewis, "No apocalypse not now," *Diacritics* 14 (Sum 1984) 30. Apocalyptic Cold War films tied wargaming to nuclear war: Sidney Lumet (dir), *Fail Safe* (Paramount, 1964) 111 min.; Stanley Kubrick (dir), *Dr. Strangelove, or How I Learned to Stop Worrying and Love the Bomb* (Columbia, 1964) 94 min.; Joseph Sargent (dir), *The Forbin Project* (Universal, 1969) 100 min. – Western and Soviet defenses given over to wargaming computers who unite toward world domination; Peter Watkins (dir), *The War Game* (BBC – but banned by British television as "too realistic," 1966) 50 min. Cf. Arthur Kopit, *End of the World: A Play* (NY: Hill and Wang, 1984) 57ff, wargamers Jim and Pete saying that the only way to get players to "go nuclear" has been to convince them that nuclear weapons are entirely defensive and, "you have to posit here that events are moving rapidly. A short time frame is crucial to this scenario."

19. Theodore E. Sterne, "Wargames: validity and interpretation," *Army* (Apr 1966) 64-68; Wilson, *The Bomb and the Computer*, 24-25; McHugh, "Gaming at the Naval War College," 52 for Nimitz, whose claim must be reconsidered in light of Edward S. Miller, *War Plan Orange: The U.S. Strategy to Defeat Japan, 1897-1945* (Annapolis: Naval Inst, 1991), reviewed by Stephen Pelz in *Amer Historical R* 98 (Feb 1993) 272-73.

20. Thomas B. Allen, *War Games* (NY: McGraw-Hill, 1987) 10, critics, as also Wilson, *The Bomb and the Computer*, 210; Philip Caputo, *A Rumor of War* (NY: Holt, Rinehart, and Winston, 1978) 100, 255, 297, quoted in Don Gifford, *The Farther Shore* (NY: Atlantic, 1990) 40; Thomas B. Allen, "War games and world realities," *Sea Power* 28 (Apr 1985) 76-78, Hormuz. See also William Spanos, *Repetitions: The Postmodern Occasion in Literature and Culture* (Baton Rouge: Louisiana State U, 1987) 43: an American rescue squad in Florida in 1970 rehearsed attacks upon a full-scale replica of a Viet Cong POW camp which, it turned out, held no prisoners.

21. Thomas B. Allen, "Simulation: 'It's the Real Thing,'" *Sea Power* 28 (Dec 1985) 12 on sonar trainers, 16 on Honeywell Helmet-Mounted System; Prados, *Pentagon Games*, 15, NORAD; John Badham (dir), *War Games* (MGM/UA/Sherwood, 1983); Barnaby, *Automated Battlefield*, 107.

22. Walter V. Robinson, "So far, this war's heroes aren't human," *Boston Globe* (30 Jan 1991) 3; John Scott, "I saw the news today oh boy: television and the Gulf War," *Canadian Art* 8 (Spr 1991) 15-16; Greg Johnson, "A 'war-torn' town will be built at Camp

Pendleton to train marines," *LA Times* (29 Oct 1991) D15, senior project architect saying, "I drew heavily upon my experience of watching World War II movies late at night." For a brief critique of the 363 U.S. wargames being played as of 1984, see Josh Martin, "Fighting WW III with quarters," *Washington Monthly* 16,9 (1984) 48–51: "Many officers already prefer the war-games, because the wars are clean and fought according to plan." On the gendered discourse behind wargaming, see Carol Cohn, "Wars, wimps, and women: gender and thinking war," in *Gendering War Talk*, eds. M. Cooke and A. Wollacott (Princeton: Princeton U, 1993) 227–48.

23. The Micro-Prose *F-19 Simulation Game* (1988) was demonstrated for me by Max Blumenthal when he was thirteen; Harry N. Roehl, comp., *Player Piano Treasury*, 2nd ed. (Vestal, NY: Vestal, 1973) 125; San Diego Aero-Space Museum, permanent exhibit of Link Trainer; David Noble, *Forces of Production: A Social History of Industrial Automation* (NY: Knopf, 1984) 107–111; Danny Cohen, Information Sciences Inst, U Southern Cal, Marina Del Rey, CA, interview, 24 May 1991, on sweating to death. See also Manuel De Landa, "Real-time," *Millennium Film J* 20/21 (Fall–Wint 1989) 66–76. A prototype for flight simulators may have been a Kansas City show of 1905 during which the audience boarded a narrow theater set up like a passenger car and watched a screen on which was projected a film of a train trip while the seats rocked and the room echoed with the clatter of tracks: Charles Musser, *The Emergence of Cinema* (NY: Scribner, 1991) 429–30. On the popularity of video game simulations, see Craig Kubey, *The Winners' Book of Video Games* (NY: Warner, 1982) esp. xi–xiv.

24. *Kriegsspielzeug: Ist das noch Spielzug?*, 2nd ed. (Berlin: Frölich & Kaufmann, 1982 [1979]). Cf. novelist Luise Rinser's *Kriegsspielzeug: Tagebuch 1972–1978* (Frankfurt: Fischer, 1978), 51, disturbed by the idea of neutron bombs – wargamers' ideal weapons, since they would eliminate opposing forces but not territory or factories (that is, the gameboard).

25. Michael Sorkin, "Faking it," in *Watching Television*, ed. Todd Gitlin (NY: Pantheon, 1986) 162–82, q164; Richard Middleton, "Paint killers," *Encounter* 73 (Nov 1989) q34–35; *Paint Check* 1 (Sept 1989).

26. Perla, *Pentagon Games*, 7, business simulation games inspired since 1957 by wargames, and see the run since 1972 of *Simulation & Gaming*, esp. 21 (1990) 96–98, Jeffrey Chin's review of MORALS, a game from the Sociology Laboratory, Belmont, CA. Cf. artist Jenny Holzer's "Green Table" (permanent installation, Muir Campus, U Cal, San Diego, 1993), incised with sententia such as "The beginning of the war will be secret."

27. Richard Rosen, *Not Available in Any Store* (NY: Pantheon, 1990) 12–13, Venus 360b; Charles Grant, *The War Game* (L: Adam & Charles Black, 1971) q10.

28. Donald F. Featherstone, *War Games Through the Ages 3000 B.C. to 1500 A.D.*, 2 vols. (L: Stanley Paul, 1972–74) I, 9, and idem, *Wargaming, Ancient & Medieval* (Newton Abbott: David & Charles, 1975) 9, q11.

29. Or insurance nuclear but civilian: after the disaster at Three Mile Island, the U.S. Nuclear Regulatory Commission mandated exact-replica interactive simulators of reactor control rooms to train personnel in order to discern patterns of alarms during long shifts of "99 per cent boredom and 1 per cent sheer terror." David Crouse, Principal Engineer, Esscor, Inc., Solana Beach, CA, interview, 21 Nov 1991. The threat of nuclear meltdown was presented in the style of a wargame by James Bridges (dir), *The China Syndrome* (IPC, 1979), released weeks before the accident at Three Mile Island. On the "conceivable," see Herman Kahn, *Thinking About the Unthinkable* (NY: Avon, 1962).

30. Joseph Morschauser III, *How To Play War Games in Miniature* (NY: Walker, 1962) q14; Historical Simulations, Inc., White Plains, NY, brochure (1990); idem, ad in *Omni* (Mar 1990) 72-73.

31. Kenneth M. Colby, *Artificial Paranoia: A Computer Simulation of Paranoid Processes* (NY: Pergamon, 1975), on PARRY, discussed by Daniel C. Dennett, "Can machines think?" in Raymond Kurzweil's *The Age of Intelligent Machines* (Cambridge, MA: MIT, 1990) 54-56; Leonora Ritter, "Russrev – the creation of a historical simulation," *History Microcomputer R* 5 (1989) 29 – claiming that a *weakness* in the program drives players to become "more extreme and absolute," but noting that the computer is instructed to secretly track players who run the simulation in circles and to assassinate them on their sixth entry. Final quotations are from Electronic Arts Distribution's 1989 leaflet for Bullfrog's computer simulation game, "Populous."

32. Benjamin Disraeli, in attendance, wrote about the procession in his novel, *Endymion* (NY, 1880) 266-68, as did another guest, Mrs. Daniel Webster, in her journals: Catherine Le Roy Webster, *Mr. Webster and I*, eds. C.M. Fuess and I. Washburn (NY, 1942) 110-12. The rest is from Ian Anstruther, *The Knight and the Umbrella* (L: Bles, 1963) q78.

33. Anstruther, *The Knight and the Umbrella*, q14.

34. *Ibid*, App. I, historical list of tournaments; Rollin G. Osterweis, *Romanticism and Nationalism in the Old South* (New Haven, 1949) 3-5, 130, 169; T.J. Jackson Lears, *No Place of Grace: Antimodernism and the Transformation of American Culture, 1880–1920* (NY: Pantheon, 1981) esp. 117-24; John J. MacAloon, *This Great Symbol: Pierre de Coubertin and the Origins of the Modern Olympic Games* (Chicago: U Chicago, 1981) q5 from Pierre Coubertin, the *Rénovateur* of the Olympic Games, and q14 paraphrasing Jesse R. Pitts, "Change in bourgeois France," in Stanley Hoffmann et al., *In Search of France* (NY: Harper, 1965) 235-304; Charles Darwin, *The Origin of Species* (Garden City, NY: Doubleday, 1958 [1859, 1860]) 74; George Santayana, *The Life of Reason* (NY, 1917 [1905]) I, 284.

35. Karen Halttunen, "From parlor to living room: domestic space, interior decoration, and the culture of personality," in *Consuming Visions: Accumulation and Display of Goods in America 1880–1920*, ed. Simon J. Bronner (NY: Norton, 1989) 157-190.

36. Daniel J. Sherman, *Worthy Monuments: Art Museums and the Politics of Culture in Nineteenth-Century France* (Cambridge, MA: Harvard U, 1991) q213 on "necropolis," from a French curator in 1903. See Joel J. Orosz, *Curators and Culture: The Museum Movement in America, 1740–1870* (Tuscaloosa: U Alabama, 1990) 129-30 on Cincinnati's "Dorfeuille's Hell," 220-31 on Barnum's American Museum, and 238-57 on the polemical recasting of museum history during the early 1900s; Simon J. Bronner, "Object lessons: the work of ethnological museums and collections," in Bronner, ed., *Consuming Visions*, 217-54, as also William Leach, "Strategists of display and the production of desire," 99-132.

37. Gösta Berg, "Hazelius, Artur," *Svenskt Biografiskt Lexikon*, XVIII, 359-64; Jay Anderson, *Time Machines: The World of Living History* (Nashville: Amer Assoc for State and Local History, 1984) 17ff; John Timbs, *Curiosities of London* (Detroit: Singing Tree, 1968 [1867]) 597; Germain Bazin, *The Museum Age*, trans. Jane van Nuis Cahill (NY: Universe, 1967) 236ff. Cf. Richard Schechner, *Between Theater & Anthropology* (Philadelphia: U Pennsylvania, 1985) esp. 79-91.

38. Lawrence R. Borne, *Dude Ranching: A Complete History* (Albuquerque: U New Mexico, 1983) 7, 11, 14, 19; Anderson, *Time Machines*, 24-25; Jacqueline Calder, "Cherry

Hill: evolution of a colonial revival home, 1882–1955" in *Creating a Dignified Past*, ed. Geoffrey L. Rossano (Savage, MD: Rowman & Littlefield, 1991) 30–31, as also Douglas Kendall, "Tea in Yorktown parlor: Wallace Nutting's legacy at the Joseph Webb house," 97, 107; Karal Ann Marling, *George Washington Slept Here: Colonial Revivals and American Culture, 1876–1986* (Cambridge, MA: Harvard U, 1988) q74, Theodore F. Randolph, president of the Washington Association, speaking 5 July 1875 at the Henry A. Ford House; Mark Seltzer, *Bodies and Machines* (NY: Routledge, 1992) q153, Sen. George G. Vest defending in the *Congressional Record* (1 Mar 1883) a Yellowstone National Park.

39. George Gilbert Scott, *A Plea for the Faithful Restoration of Our Ancient Churches* (L, 1850) 27n., 126; E.E. Viollet-le-Duc, *On Restoration*, trans. Bucknall (L, 1875 [1863]) 9, 26; Michel Parent, "Invention, théorie et équivoque de la restauration," *Monuments historiques* 112 (1980) 2–9. Cf. William J. Murtagh, *Keeping Time: The History and Theory of Preservation in America* (Pittstown, NJ: Main Street, 1988).

40. Stefano Gizzi, "Evoluzione dei concetti di conservazione, di musealizzazione e di restauro in epoca tardo-antica e medievale," *Museologia* 10 (July–Dec 1981) 28–45; Madeline H. Caviness, " 'De convenientia et cohaerentia antiqui et novi operis': medieval conservation, restoration, pastiche and forgery," in *Intuition und Kunstwissenschaft: Festschrift für Hanns Swarzenski* (Berlin: Gebr. Mann, 1973) 205–21, q206, Abbot Suger on his twelfth-century restoration of St. Denis, whose eighth-century nave was repaired.

41. Washington Irving, *Letters of Jonathan Oldstyle, Gent.*, eds. B.I. Granger and M. Hertzog (Boston: Twayne, 1977) q17 from the *Morning Chronicle* (11 Dec 1802); Allardyce Nicoll, *The Garrick Stage, Theatres and Audience in the Eighteenth Century* (Athens: U Georgia, 1980) 162–68, q168; James R. Planché, *Recollections and Reflections* (NY: Da Capo, 1978 [written 1870–72]) q36–37.

42. Planché, *Recollections*, q38; A.M. Nagler, *A Source Book in Theatrical History* (NY, 1952) 480–81, Kean; Seymour Lucas, "The art of dressing an historical play," *Mag of Art* 17 (1894) q280.

43. Eric Breitbart, "The painted mirror: historical re-creation from the panorama to the docudrama," in *Presenting the Past*, eds. Susan Porter Benson et al. (Philadelphia, Temple, 1986) 105–06; T. Edgar Pemberton, ed., *The Life and Writings of Thomas W. Robertson* (L, 1893) q179, 206; Maynard Savin, *Thomas William Robertson: His Plays and Stagecraft* (Providence, RI, 1950) 17, q56.

44. I am strongly indebted here to David Glassberg, *American Historical Pageantry: The Use of Tradition in the Early Twentieth Century* (Chapel Hill: U North Carolina, 1990), esp. 89, 159ff, 208–11. See also Michael Kammen, *Mystic Chords of Memory: The Transformation of Tradition in American Culture* (NY: Knopf, 1991) on the Party of Memory, ascendant after 1870, making history the core of American civic religion (p. 12).

45. *Ibid.*, 16–19, 27, 101, 132, 136, and 55, where Glassberg notes that pageant fireworks compensated for municipal crackdowns on dangerous private fireworks; in this sense, too, the pageant was like a field maneuver with safely executed explosions.

46. *Ibid.*, 178–79, 237, 257, 265, 267, 269; Kammen, *Mystic Chords of Memory*, ch. 4, "The Civil War Remembered – but Unreconciled." On *America*, I am using also KPBS-TV, San Diego, "D.W. Griffith, Father of Film," aired 24 Mar 1993. Critics said that the dull story got "in the way of brilliant flashes of American history," such as the Battle of Bunker Hill – which was recreated not from documents but from a famous painting by Howard Pyle.

47. John Bodnar, *Remaking America: Public Memory, Commemoration, and Patriotism*

in the Twentieth Century (Princeton: Princeton U, 1992) 129, 133, 172–73; Glassberg, *American Historical Pageantry*, 270ff on Ogburn.

48. Charles B. Hosmer, Jr., *Presence of the Past: A History of the Preservation Movement in the United States Before Williamsburg* (NY: Putnam's, 1965) q11–12 from foreword by Walter Muir Whitehall, quoting William Sumner Appleton, founder in 1910 of the Society for the Preservation of New England Antiquities. See also James M. Lindgren, *Preserving Historic New England: Preservation, Progressivism, and the Remaking of Memory* (Oxford: Oxford U, 1995).

49. Murtagh, *Keeping Time*, 26; Emma Lazarus, "In the Jewish Synagogue in Newport," in *Eyewitnesses to American Jewish History*, eds. A. Eisenberg and H.G. Goodman (NY: UAHC, 1976) I, 74–77, q76–77; Hosmer, *Presence of the Past*, 13.

50. Hosmer, *Presence of the Past*, 33, 214, q215–16 from George F. Dow (my italics); Glassberg, *American Historical Pageantry*, 143; Anderson, *Time Machines*, 27–30; Kammen, *Mystic Chords of Memory*, 358–70 and ch. 17. "Period rooms," regarded as a U.S. specialty, were further exalted in 1924 when the Metropolitan Museum opened its American Wing (its historic interiors stripped from houses not yet designated for preservation), but the Swiss National Museum in Zurich had sixty-two period rooms in 1898.

51. Anderson, *Time Machines*, q31, 41; Warren Leon and Margaret Piatt, "Living-history museums," in *History Museums in the United States*, eds. W. Leon and R. Rosenzweig (Urbana: U Illinois, 1989) 64–97; Else Mogensen, "A living museum," in *The Idea of the Museum*, ed. Lars Aagaard-Mogensen (Lewiston, ME: Mellen, 1988) q23.

52. Richard Dawkins, *The Selfish Gene* (NY: Oxford U, 1976) 206–14; Patricia C. Albers and William R. James, "Travel photography," *Annals of Tourism Research* 15 (1988) 134–58, postcards; Joseph Cornet, "African art and authenticity," *African Arts* 9 (Oct 1975) 52–55, airport exotica and folk art; Lawrence D. Loeb, "Creating antiques for fun and profit: encounters between Iranian Jewish merchants and touring co-religionists," *Hosts and Guests: The Anthropology of Tourism*, ed. Valerie L. Smith (Philadelphia: U Pennsylvania, 1989) 185–92. For a fine critique of the dangers of "folklore" *and* a defense of its potential as a weapon against repression, see Sabra J. Webber, *Romancing the Real: Folklore and Ethnographic Representation in North Africa* (Philadelphia: U Pennsylvania, 1991).

53. Jafar Jafari et al., "A sociological study of tourism as a factor of change," *Annals of Tourism Research* 17 (1990) q469; Keith Hollinshed, "Cultural tourism," *ibid.*, 292–94; Dean MacCannell, *The Tourist: A New Theory of the Leisure Class* (NY: Schocken, 1976) esp. ch. 5 on "Staged Authenticity"; Nicholas Lemann, "Fake masks," *The Atlantic* 260 (Nov 1987) 24–38, African masks carved to look as if they had been used in tribal rituals, so as to be more saleable; "Fakes, fakers, and fakery: [a symposium on] authenticity in African art," *African Arts* 9 (Apr 1976) 20–31, esp. 21, noting that signs of wear may indicate forgery, since forgers habitually age and scar their artifacts; Travcoa, *1991 Orient China*, brochure (Newport Beach, CA, 1991) q2, q79. On the need for changelessness, see Richard Lowenthal, "The timeless past," in *Memory and American History*, ed. David Thelen (Bloomington: Indiana U, 1989) 134–51.

54. Charles B. Hosmer, Jr., *Preservation Comes of Age: From Williamsburg to the National Trust, 1926–1949* (Charlottesville: U Virginia, 1981) 57; Williamsburg Reproductions ad, *House Beautiful* (Nov 1958) 13; Gerald W.R. Ward, ed., *The Eye of the Beholder: Fakes, Replicas, and Alterations in American Art* (New Haven: Yale U Art Gallery, 1977) 74; Murtagh, *Keeping Time*, q87; Michael Olmert, "The new no-frills Wil-

liamsburg," *Historic Preservation* 37 (Oct 1985) 27-33, q27. In 1775 the population of Williamsburg was 52 percent African-American.

55. Rossano, ed., *Creating a Dignified Past*, q116, discussion; Stefan Muthesius, "Why do we buy old furniture? Aspects of the authentic antique in Britain, 1870-1910," *Art History* 11 (June 1988) 231-54; Brian Considine, Curator, Decorative Arts, J. Paul Getty Museum, Malibu, CA, interview, 30 May 1991, on upholstery; Henry Merritt, *Pictures and Dirt Separated in the Works of Old Masters* (L, 1854) 1-4; J.C. Robinson, "On spurious works of art," *Nineteenth Century* 30 (Nov 1891) 687 on Old Masters, 698 on wormholes; Seymour Howard, *Bartolomeo Cavaceppi, Eighteenth-Century Restorer* (NY: Garland, 1982); Arnold Nesselrath, "The Venus Belvedere: an episode in restoration," *J Warburg & Courtauld Inst* 50 (1987) 205-14; M.H. Spielmann, "Art forgeries and counterfeits," *Mag of Art* 27 (1902-03) 503ff. On wallpaper, I am indebted to a letter of 13 Aug 1991 from Robert M. Kelly, editor of *Wallpaper Reproduction News* (whose issues of Aug 1990 and Aug 1991 I use here), and to Edward L. Kallop, Jr., "Wallpaper conservation – puzzling priorities," *J Amer Inst for Conservation* 20 (1981) 53-57, q56. Since nineteenth-century wallpapers were often trompe-l'oeils of curtains, lattices, or columns, restoring such wallpaper is triply problematic; see Odile Nouvel, *Wallpapers of France, 1800-1850*, trans. Margaret Timmes (NY: Rizzoli, 1981).

56. Pierre Nora, trans. Marc Roudebush, "Between memory and history: les *lieux de mémoire*," *Representations* 26 (Spr 1989) 7-25, q17; Stephen E. Weil, *Rethinking the Museum* (Washington, D.C.: Smithsonian, 1990) 11, 28. Cf. David Lowenthal, *The Past Is a Foreign Country* (Cambridge: Cambridge U, 1985).

57. Hillel Schwartz, *Century's End* (NY: Doubleday, 1990) esp. 166-69, 245-46, 271, 281; David E. Nye, *Electrifying America* (Cambridge: MIT, 1992) 128, Coney Island; "'Encore fiends' hissed at the opera house," unsourced clip, 11 Feb 1901, from "Curtain Calls" file, Billy Rose Theatre Collection, Performing Arts Research Center at Lincoln Center, NY Public Lib; Alison Kelly, "Mrs. Coade's stone," *Connoisseur* 197 (Jan 1978) 14-25; Christopher Sells, "Géricault, Dedieux-Dorcy et la pierre artificielle," *Bull de la société de l'histoire de l'art français* (1985) 207-15; Theodore H.H. Prudon, "Simulating stone, 1860-1940," *Art Bull* 21,3-4 (1989) 79-91; Jean Baudrillard, *Simulations*, trans. Paul Foss et al. (NY: Semiotext[e], 1983) 88 on stucco as "a representative substance, a mirror of all the others."

58. Suzanne Fleischman, *The Future in Thought and Language* (Cambridge: Cambridge U, 1982) 129, 140-44; Schechner, *Between Theater & Anthropology*, 81-91, q81, q84; Isabel O'Neil Studio Workshop, NY, NY, brochure, July 1991. On faux work see also *Historic Preservation* 43 (Jan/Feb 1991) 21, 48-51, 64-65, 69-70. On the critical position that all historical work is necessarily invention and storytelling, see the neat essay by Albert Rabil, Jr., "Can the jackals be kept at bay? And is that a scary question?" *Soundings* 76 (Sum-Fall 1993), an issue devoted to the question(s).

59. On conservation, see Hanna Jedrzejewska, *Ethics in Conservation* (Stockholm: Kungl. Konsthögskolan, 1976) 9; Robert M. Kelly, "Conservation materials in the installation of reproduction wallpapers," *Wallpaper Reproduction News* 2 (Aug 1991) q3. On the spread of a theory of recycling, see esp. Shirley Lord, "Beauty's new nature," *Vogue* (Oct 1990) 394-98. On the Sequel: Marilyn E. Hicken, *Sequels*, 8th ed. (L: Assoc of Asst Librarians, 1986), preface; James L. Limbacher, *Haven't I Seen You Somewhere Before?* (Ann Arbor: Pierian, 1979); Jeremy G. Butler, "Toward a Theory of Cinematic Style: The Remake," Ph.D., Northwestern U, 1982.

Humphrey Bogart in *Casablanca* (1942) actually said, "Play it, Sam." Our culture of the copy insists upon the "again" – especially in the United States, writes Umberto Eco, where "for historical information to be absorbed, it has to assume the aspect of a re-incarnation." See the 1975 title essay in his *Travels in Hyperreality*, trans. William Weaver (San Diego: Harcourt Brace Jovanovich, 1986) q6.

60. Bodnar, *Remaking America*, 213-14, and cf. David G. Chandler, "Military peres-troika," *History Today* 39 (Nov 1989) 3-4 on the vogue for historical reenactments of battles; Alan C. Miller, "Veterans find peace in Vietnam," *LA Times* (5 July 1990) A1. On therapy, the quotation (by permission) is from Rebecca and David Grudermeyer, clini-cal psychologists, Del Mar, CA, and cf. the works of Alice Miller. It would follow that psychohistorians these days should be particularly attentive to repetition compulsions and "traumatic relivings"; see, above all, Rudolph Binion, *Soundings: Psychohistorical and Psycholiterary* (NY: Psychohistory, 1981).

61. Garry Thomson, *The Museum Environment* (L: Butterworths, 1978) esp. 13, 14, 135, 215, 241, and pl. 10.

62. Elaine Greene, "The quintessence of authenticity," *House & Garden* 154 (Nov 1982) q106, on Margaret Schiffer's restoration of a 1730 house; Kathleen D. McCarthy, *Women's Culture: American Philanthropy and Art, 1830-1930* (Chicago: U Chicago, 1991) q245.

63. See Frederick W. Conner, " 'To dream with one eye open': the wit, wisdom, and present standing of George Santayana," *Soundings* 74 (Spr-Sum 1991) 159-78.

64. John McCormick, *George Santayana: A Biography* (NY: Knopf, 1987) 5, 173, 446-47, q277 from Santayana's *The Realm of Essence* (1927); Conner, " 'To dream with one eye open,' " 166 from statement by Santayana for *Twentieth-Century Authors*, ed. Stanley Kunitz (NY, 1942) 1231. Cf. Louis O. Mink, "On the writing and rewriting of history," *Historical Understanding*, eds. Brian Fay et al. (Ithaca: Cornell, 1987) 89-105.

65. Conner, " 'To dream with one eye open,' " q164, aesthete; Angus Kerr-Lawson, "Toward one Santayana," *Transactions of the Charles S. Peirce Soc* 27 (Wint 1991) 1-25, q5 on Germans from Santayana's *Soliloquies in England* (1922); McCormick, *Santayana*, 173, q447 from Santayana's 1929 essay on Oswald Spengler. For an example of the use of Santayana's epigram to urge action from two opposite positions, contrast Robert A. Pastor, *Condemned to Repetition: The U.S. and Nicaragua* (Princeton: Princeton U, 1987) 7, and former U.S. Education Secretary William J. Bennett: "Our students will not rec-ognize the urgency in Nicaragua if they cannot recognize the history that is threatening to repeat itself," introduction to Benson et al., *Presenting the Past*, xv.

66. Conner, " 'To dream with one eye open,' " q161 from Santayana's *Character and Opinion in the United States* (1920); Kerr-Lawson, "Toward one Santayana," 21 on "disin-toxication"; George Santayana, *The Life of Reason, I: Reason in Common Sense*, (NY, 1917 [1905]) q284-88.

67. Lawrence J. Peter, *Peter's Quotations* (NY: Morrow, 1977) q248, Darrow, un-sourced; Ray Ginger, *Six Days or Forever? Tennessee v. John Thomas Scopes* (L: Oxford U, 1958) ch. 3 on Darrow; John Grierson, "Flaherty's poetic *Moana*," *NY Sun* (8 Feb 1926), in Lewis Jacobs, ed., *The Documentary Tradition: From Nanook to Woodstock* (NY: Hop-kinson and Blake, 1971) 25-26.

68. Grierson, "Flaherty's poetic *Moana*," 25-26; idem, "Directors of the Thirties," in *Film: An Anthology*, ed. Daniel Talbot (Berkeley: U Cal, 1959) q128-29.

69. Paul Rotha, "Some principles of documentary," in Talbot, *Film*, 235-37; Lewis

Jacobs, "Precursors and prototypes," in his *Documentary Tradition*, 7-9, as also Ricciotto Canudo, "Another view of *Nanook*," 20; Richard M. Barsam, *Nonfiction Film* (NY: Dutton, 1973) 132-33.

70. Barsam, *Nonfiction Film*, 1133, Flaherty, as also Larry Gross et al., "Introduction," *Image Ethics*, ed. Gross (NY: Oxford U, 1988) 21; Sergei Eisenstein, *Film Form and The Film Sense*, trans. and ed. Jan Leyda (NY: Meridian, 1957) q7 from *The Film Sense* (1942). On the many movies and newsreels made by American trade unionists, communists, and socialists between 1907 and 1929, see Steven J. Ross, "Struggles for the screen: workers, radicals, and the political uses of silent film," *Amer Historical R* 96 (Apr 1991) 333-67.

71. I am indebted here to a fine essay by Margaret B. Blackman, " 'Copying people': Northwest Coast native response to early photography," *British Columbia Studies* 52 (Wint 1981-82) 86-112. See also Caspar W. Weinberger, Jr., "Curtis, Edward S.," *Dictionary of Amer Biography*, Supp. V, 148-49; Ira Jacknis, "Franz Boas and photography," *Studies in Visual Communication* 10 (Wint 1984) 2-60. On the word "documentary," see *OED*, IV, 917.

72. Alan Thomas, *The Expanding Eye: Photography and the Nineteenth-Century Mind* (L: Schocken, 1977) 138-44; Terry Tafoya, "Dancing with Dash-Kayahi: the mask of the cannibal woman," *Parabola* 6 (Aug 1981) 6-11; Maren Stange, *Symbols of Ideal Life: Social Documentary Photography in America, 1890-1950* (NY: Cambridge U, 1989) 10, q19, 20; Blackman, " 'Copying people,' " 110.

73. *Film in National Life* (L, 1932) viii, a British government report quoted in *OED*, IV, 917; Linda Williams, *Hard Core: Power, Pleasure, and the "Frenzy of the Visible"* (Berkeley: U Cal, 1989) 39-52 on the eroticism in Muybridge and in Fred Ott's sneeze.

74. Fred Balshofer and Arthur Miller, with Bebe Bergsten, *One Reel a Week* (Berkeley: U Cal, 1967) 9-10; Charles Musser, *High-Class Moving Pictures: Lyman H. Brown and the Forgotten Era of Traveling Exhibition, 1880-1920* (Princeton: Princeton U, 1991) 53, early film subjects; Brooks McNamara, "Scene design and the early film," in John L. Fell et al., *Before Hollywood: Turn-of-the-Century American Film* (NY: AFA, 1986) 51-56; clipping from *Dramatic Mirror* (27 Dec 1911) in Box 1, Scrapbooks, Dec 1911 - Sept 1916, Lubin Manufacturing Co., Theatre Collection, Free Lib, Philadelphia; KPBS-TV, "D.W. Griffith." Cf. Jay Leyda, *Dianying/Electric Shadows: An Account of Films and the Film Audience in China* (Cambridge: MIT, 1972) 22-23.

75. Charles Musser, *The Emergence of Cinema* (NY: Scribner, 1991) 244, q256-57; Albert E. Smith, with Phil A. Koury, *Two Reels and a Crank* (Garden City, NY, 1952) 66-67, Manila; Leyda, *Dianying*, 4-6. Despite the motto of the *NY Sun*, "If you see it in the *Sun*, it's so," American reporters frequently colluded in the creation and perpetuation of faked news, fraudulent interviews, and false photographs: William Salisbury, *The Career of a Journalist*, 2nd ed. (NY, 1908) 58, 61, 94, 102, 119, 127, 136, 168, 177-78. Film "news" also heated up the controversy over what part of (fictionalized) "news" was copyrightable, on which see Sidney J. Low, "Newspaper copyright," *National R* 19 (1892) 648-66.

76. Neil Harris, "A subversive medium," in Fell et al., *Before Hollywood*, 47-48; Gordon Hendricks, *The Kinetoscope* (NY: Beginnings of the Amer Film, 1966) 75, 79, 92, q102, 103-09, 166, 168.

77. Dan Streible, Austin, TX, letters to author, 24 Mar and 16 June, 1991, and idem, "A history of the boxing film, 1894-1915: social control and social reform in the

Progressive Era," *Film History* 3,3 (1989) 235-58; Joseph P. Eckhardt, Montgomery County Community College, Blue Bell, PA, letter to author, 5 Mar 1991, quoting a Lubin ad in the *NY Clipper* (3 Mar 1900) 24; idem, with Linda Kowall, *Peddler of Dreams: Siegmund Lubin and the Creation of the Motion Picture Industry, 1896–1916* (Philadelphia: National Museum of Amer Jewish History, 1984) 5; Lubin ad, "Fitzsimmons–Jeffries Fight," *NY Clipper* (19 Aug 1899) 502; Balshofer and Miller, *One Reel a Week*, q9. On the Corbett-McCoy fight, see "Corbett runs away: M'Coy fight 'fixed,'" *NY World* (9 Sept 1900) 1; "M'Coy denies charges," *NY World* (10 Sept 1900) q12; and an unsourced newsclip (21 Mar 1923) in the Lubin File, Theatre Collection, Free Lib, Philadelphia, which I overlooked but was kindly provided by Prof. Eckhardt.

78. Eckhardt and Kowall, *Peddler of Dreams*, q15; Francis A. Collins, *The Camera Man* (NY, 1916) 4, 15-16; KPBS-TV, "D.W. Griffith," on *The Battle of the Somme*. Some still photographs of the misery in the trenches did circulate: D.L. LeMahieu, *A Culture for Democracy: Mass Communication and the Cultivated Mind in Britain between the Wars* (Oxford: Clarendon, 1988) 77.

79. Donald B. Smith, *Long Lance: The True Story of an Impostor* (Toronto: Macmillan, 1982) q191; *Binns v. Vitagraph Co of America*, 210 NY 51 (1913) q56; Nye, *Electrifying America*, 21, radio; Colin Bingham, comp., *Men and Affairs: A Modern Miscellany* (NY: Funk & Wagnalls, 1967) q147, Santayana misquotation. Cf. Natalie Zemon Davis, "'Any resemblance to persons living or dead': film and the challenge of authenticity," *Yale R* 76 (1987) 457-82.

80. Smith, *Long Lance*, throughout, q147 from Paul Radin. Long Lance, it should be noted, was born into a region where Native American identities were themselves confused and at issue; see Gerald M. Sider, *Lumbee Indian Histories: Race, Ethnicity, and Indian Identity in the Southern United States* (Cambridge: Cambridge U, 1993).

81. Dziga Vertov, "A film-show in a village" (1920), trans. Masha Enzensberger, quoted by Thomas Waugh, "Why documentary filmmakers keep trying to change the world, *or* why people changing the world keep making documentaries," in *"Show Us Life": Toward a History and Aesthetics of the Committed Documentary*, ed. Waugh (Metuchen: Scarecrow, 1984) xii, as also Bert Hogenkamp, "Workers' newsreels in Germany, the Netherlands, and Japan during the Twenties and Thirties," and Russell Campbell, "Radical documentary in the United States, 1930-1942," 47-88; Robert T. Elson, "De Rochemont's *The March of Time*," in Jacobs, *Documentary Tradition*, 104-11; Barsam, *Nonfiction Film*, 72, and ch. 5.

82. Edward W. Said, "On repetition," in *The Literature of Fact*, ed. Angus Fletcher (NY: Columbia U, 1976) q152, Kierkegaard; Søren Kierkegaard, *Repetition: An Essay in Experimental Psychology*, trans. Walter Lowrie (Princeton, 1941 [1843]) q5-6; Daniel Boorstin, *The Image, or What Happened to the American Dream* (NY: Atheneum, 1962) 37 on iridescence; James P. Wood, *Advertising and the Soul's Belly: Repetition and Memory in Advertising* (Athens, GA: U Georgia, 1961) ch. 2 for historical survey, and see Henry Foster Adams, *Advertising and Its Mental Laws* (NY, 1926) 218, citing a bit incorrectly the (Hermann) Ebbinghaus Law that the "amount learned varies directly with the number of repetitions"; William Stott, *Documentary Expression and Thirties America*, new ed. (Chicago: U Chicago, 1986) 40-41n for testimonials, 56, 130 for *Life* etc., 138 for the jobless.

83. Stott, *Documentary Expression*, 132, 155 on participant observers, q269, Evans; James Curtis, *Mind's Eye, Mind's Truth: FSA Photography Reconsidered* (Philadelphia:

Temple U, 1989) q24 (Curtis about Evans), 36 on Evans, q49 for Lange, 49–53, 67, 71–76 on Rothstein; *LA Times* (18 Nov 1978) 1, cited in Gross et al., "Introduction," *Image Ethics*, 13–14; Arthur Rothstein, "Setting the record straight," *Camera* 35,22 (Apr 1978) 50–51.

84. Boorstin, *The Image*, ch. 1 on "pseudo-events"; Karal Ann Marling and John Wetenhall, *Iwo Jima: Monuments, Memories, and the American Hero* (Cambridge, MA: Harvard U, 1991) 6, 43, 47ff; Breitbart, "The painted mirror," 110; Gary B. Mills and Elizabeth S. Mills, "Roots and the new 'faction,'" *Virginia Mag of History and Biography* 89 (1981) 3–26, and cf. Richard N. Current, *Arguing with Historians: Essays on the Historical and the Unhistorical* (Middletown, CT: Wesleyan U, 1987) 155–56; Kammen, *Mystic Chords of Memory*, 641–45. An estimated 130 million people watched the *Roots* miniseries on its first go-round.

85. Daniel Cerone, "Made-for-TV heroes," *LA Times* (3 Oct 1991) F1, qF9; Joel Katz, "From archive to archiveology," *Cinematograph* 4 (1991) 96–103; Peter Davis, "South Africa's media war: from the student's revolt to *Mapantsula*," *Int Documentary* (Wint 1990) 10–15, q11; *Cineaste* 19 (Wint 1992), entire issue devoted to Stone's *JFK*; Stanley Yates, Curator, American Archives of the Factual Film, Ames, Iowa, letter to author, 12 June 1990.

86. "Biased Afghan coverage at CBS," *Extra! A Publication of FAIR (Fairness & Accuracy In Reporting)* 3 (Oct 1989) 1, 11; Jay Sharbutt, "Film maker focuses from Afghan trenches," *LA Times* (29 July 1987) Cal. Sect., 1, 9; Janet Wilson, "The Afghan affair," *NY Post* (27 Sept 1989) 5, with follow-ups (28 Sept) 2–3, (29 Sept) 7, (30 Sept) 3, and see also Trip Gabriel, "The cliffhangers," *Outside* (Oct 1985) 86 on Hoover; "Spy tape verdict: ABC blew it," *Washington Journalism R* 11 (15 Sept 1989) 15. Andrew Goodwin, in "News, lies, and videotape," *East Bay Express* (1 Sept 1989) 9, has asked rhetorically, "Are we really supposed to believe that the use of actors renders the news any more 'staged' than it already is?" Quoted by Walter T. Anderson, *Reality Isn't What It Used to Be* (NY: Harper & Row, 1990) 128–29.

87. Waterford ad, "Once in a lifetime...," *Bon Appetit* (Oct 1992) 101; Breitbart, "The painted mirror," q110, David Wolper. Cf. David W. Rintels, "In defense of the television 'docudrama,'" *NY Times* (22 Apr 1979) II:1. On docudrama as an historian's educational tool, see Robert B. Toplin, "Inside *Lincoln and the War Within*," *AHA Perspectives* (Dec 1991) 1, 16–17, 20–21. On instant replays as "in fact, one of the more important developments in human history" and in political campaigning, see Tony Schwartz, *Media: The Second God* (NY: Random House, 1981) q26.

88. When, after six years of trial, the National Football League decided in 1992 to end the official videotape-reviewing of problematic calls, the decision came in response to the game delays these reviews caused; no one denied the truth-telling virtues of the instant replay, which continues to be used ad nauseam by commentators who show us again almost every play. See Amram Ducovny, "Play it again, Don, Giff, O.J.: instant replay is more than a TV technique – it's a way of life," *Boston Mag* 76 (Nov 1984) q122. Jack McCallum, in "Don't play it again," *Sports Illustrated* (7 Sept 1987) 130, argued that it was ludicrous to want replays to correct game "injustices"; babies dying in poverty, innocent men sent to jail, these were injustices, but a mistaken clipping penalty? As a sport, what was vital to football was rhythm, not righteousness: "Imperfect owners own teams, imperfect coaches coach them, imperfect players play on them, and imperfect spectators spectate at them. So imperfect officials can sure as hell officiate them."

On the wedding, Dennis P. Slattery, "An Orwellian wedding," *Newsweek* (13 Nov 1989) 10.

89.   Ved Mehta, *The Photographs of Chachaji: The Making of a Documentary Film* (NY: Oxford U, 1980) q14, 81, 136, q144, 150, q172, q231, q237.

90.   McCormick, *George Santayana*, q173.

91.   Curtis, *Mind's Eye, Mind's Truth*, 67, q47 from Aphorism CXXIX, Book One, of Francis Bacon's *Novum Organum* (1620), from a translation differing slightly from that which I am using for the first part of the sentence, by James Spedding et al., *The Works*, VIII (Boston, 1863), reprinted in Francis Bacon, *The New Organon and Related Writings*, ed. Fulton H. Anderson (Indianapolis: Bobbs-Merrill, 1960) 119. The original Latin has "...*sine superstitione aut impostura....*"

92.   Bacon, *The New Organon*, bk. I, aphorism CXVIII, and bk. II, aphorism XLI, and (in same volume) *Preparative Toward a Natural and Experimental History*, sec. IX. On Bacon's influence, see Charles Webster, *The Great Instauration: Science, Medicine and Reform, 1626-1660* (NY: Holmes & Meier, 1975). Cf. W.H. Donahue, "Kepler's fabricated figures: covering up the mess in the *New Astronomy*," *J for the History of Astronomy* 19 (Nov 1988) 217-37.

93.   Barbara J. Shapiro, *Probability and Certainty in Seventeenth-Century England* (Princeton: Princeton U, 1983) 66-69 *et passim*; Jacqueline Feldman et al., eds., *Moyenne, milieu, centre* (P: Ecole des Hautes Etudes en Sciences Sociales, 1991), esp. essays by Michel Armatte, Eric Brian, and Gérard Lagneau, q127 from E. Cheysson.

94.   Benjamin Matalon, "Le Traitement de la variabilité en psychologie," in *ibid.*, 289-96; Karl Pearson, "The laws of chance, in relation to thought and conduct" (1892), rept. in *Biometrika* 32 (Oct 1941) 89-100.

95.   Harry Gold, Nathaniel T. Kwit, and Harold Otto, "The xanthines (theobromine and aminophylline) in the treatment of cardiac pain," *J Amer Med Assoc* 108 (26 June 1937) 2173-79, reporting on five years of experiments; Hillel Schwartz, "Putting the question: pain, truth, and treason," *Threepenny R* (Sum 1986) 4-6; Elaine T. Scarry, *The Body in Pain* (NY: Oxford U, 1985) 27-59; Ernst L. Freud, *Letters of Sigmund Freud*, trans. Tania Stern and James Stern (NY: Basic, 1960) Letter to Wilhelm Knöpfmacher, 6 Aug 1878; Max Schur, *Freud: Living and Dying* (NY: Int U, 1972); Jeffrey M. Masson, trans. and ed., *The Complete Letters of Sigmund Freud to Wilhelm Fliess 1887-1904* (Cambridge, MA: Belknap, 1985) q85; Kenneth Levin, *Freud's Early Psychology of the Neuroses* (Pittsburgh: U Pittsburgh, 1978) ch. 5; Sharon Romm, *The Unwelcome Intruder: Freud's Struggle with Cancer* (NY: Praeger, 1983) q33, q71, q139. On "nociceptors" and early neurological studies, see Karl M. Dallenbach, "Pain: history and present status," *Amer J Psychology* 52 (1939) 331-47. For a good review to 1984, see William D. Willis, *The Pain System* (Basel: Karger, 1985).

96.   O.H. Perry Pepper, "A note on the placebo," *Amer J Pharmacy* 117 (1945) 409-12; Louis Lasagna, "Placebos," *Sci Amer* 193 (1955) 68-71, esp. concerning experiments on the effectiveness of pain-relief by placebos; Berton Roueché, "Placebo," *The New Yorker* (15 Oct 1960) 85-103; *OED*, XI, 942; George B. Mychaliska, "The Placebo Effect: Historical, Sociological, and Philosophical Perspectives," M.S. thesis, U Cal, Berkeley, 1989; Andrew A. Lipscomb et al., eds., *Writings of Thomas Jefferson* (Washington, D.C., 1905) XI, 245-46, letter of 21 June 1807 to Dr. Casper Wistar.

97.   H. Beecher, "The powerful placebo," *J Amer Med Assoc* 152 (1955) 1602; S. Wolf, "Pharmacology of the placebo," *Pharmaceutical R* 11 (1959) 689; Jerry E. Bishop, "Pla-

cebos are harmless, but they work...," *Wall Street J* (25 Aug 1977) 1, 21; Robert J. Connelly, "Nursing responsibility for the placebo effect," *J Med and Phil* 16 (1991) 327; Jon D. Levine et al., "The mechanism of placebo analgesia," *Lancet* 2 (1978) 654-57; Michael Jospe, *The Placebo Effect in Healing* (Lexington, MA: Heath, 1978) 43, 89-90; Sissela Bok, "The ethics of giving placebos," *Sci Amer* 231 (Nov 1974) 17-23, q18; Howard Brody, "The lie that heals: the ethics of giving placebos," *Annals Internal Med* 97,1 (1982) 112-18.

98. Arthur K. Shapiro, "A contribution to a history of the placebo effect," *Behavioral Sci* 5 (1960) 109-35, epigraph; Herbert Reid, "The politics of time," *The Human Context* 4 (1972) 476, the focus of political scientists and economists upon replicability; Murray A. Straus and Joel I. Nelson, *Sociological Analysis: An Empirical Approach through Replication* (NY: Harper & Row, 1968) q1. Cf. Constance Holden, "Ethics in social science research," *Science* 206 (2 Nov 1979) 537-38, 540 on the degree to which much social psychological research relies on "some degree of deception."

99. Steven Shapin and Simon Schaffer, *Leviathan and the Air-pump* (Princeton: Princeton U, 1985) ch. 6; H.M. Collins, "The seven sexes:...the replication of experiments in physics," *Sociology* 9 (1975) 205-24; idem, *Changing Order: Replication and Induction in Scientific Practice* (L: Sage, 1985), neatly condensed in idem, "The meaning of experiment: replication and pleasurableness," in *Dismantling Truth: Reality in the Post-Modern World*, eds. H. Lawson and L. Appignanesi (NY: St. Martin's, 1989) 82-92, and hilariously disputed by Malcolm Ashmore, "The life and opinions of a replication claim," in *Knowledge and Reflexivity*, ed. Steve Woolgar (L: Sage, 1988) 126ff; David R. Hershey, "Fraud, sloppiness, and mistakes in horticultural science," *Hortscience* 24 (Aug 1989) 540; Lawrence Busch, "Irony, tragedy, and temporality in agricultural systems, or, how values and systems are related," *Agriculture and Human Values* 6,4 (1989) q5; Straus and Nelson, *Sociological Analysis*, q2. For a revealing exchange on methodology, see Wallace Kantor, " 'Pseudo-effects' in experimental physics," *Social Studies of Sci* 8 (Aug 1978) 355-58, reply by George Magyar, 358-59. On pain as "the ultimate of individual experience," see David Bakan, *Disease, Pain and Sacrifice* (Chicago: U Chicago, 1968) q62.

100. Ashmore, "Life and opinions," q126, letter from Collins, March 1983; Neil Friedman, *The Social Nature of Psychological Research: The Psychological Experiment as a Social Interaction* (NY: Basic, 1967) q148-49 and epigraph to Part I. For a critique of the scientific paradigm, see Stanley Aronowitz, *Science As Power: Discourse and Ideology in Modern Society* (Minneapolis: U Minnesota, 1988) esp. 145.

101. David Goodstein and Suzanne Hadley, "Scientific Integrity and Fraud," Second Whitehill Symposium on Biomedical Ethics, UC San Diego, 17 Oct 1991, on the fuzziness of reproducibility in the biosciences, pitfalls of relying upon replication, and reluctance of the National Institutes of Health (NIH) to fund replicative work; P.B. Medawar, "Is the scientific paper fraudulent?" *Saturday R* (1 Aug 1964) 42-43, arguing that scientists publicly misrepresent their methods, confirmed by G. Nigel Gilbert and Michael Mulkay, *Opening Pandora's Box: A Sociological Analysis of Scientists' Discourse* (Cambridge: Cambridge U, 1984) q52 on replication, and throughout. On N-rays, see R. Blondlot, *"N" Rays*, trans. J. Garcin (NY, 1905) q82-83; "The question of the N Rays," *Atheneum* 4804 (1906) 141-42; O. Lummer, "M. Blondlot's *n*-ray experiments," *Nature* 69 (18 Feb 1904) 378-80; Jean Rostand, *Error and Deception in Science*, trans. A.J. Pomerans (L: Hutchinson, 1960) 11-29.

102. F. David Peat, *Cold Fusion: The Making of a Scientific Controversy* (Chicago: Con-

temporary, 1989); John R. Huizenga, *Cold Fusion: The Scientific Fiasco of the Century* (Rochester, NY: U Rochester, 1992) 30 on early confirmations, including (p. 153) support by Edward Teller, who explained the fusion as the result of a neutral particle he conceived and called the "Meshugatron."

103. Peat, *Cold Fusion* 106 on Lewis; Robert P. Crease and N.P. Samios, "Cold fusion confusion," *NY Times Mag* (24 Sept 1989) 34–38, q35; David H. Freedman, "Fission in fusion camp," *Discover* (Dec 1989) 32–42; H.S. Bosch et al., "Electrochemical cold fusion trials at IPP Garching," *J Fusion Energy* 9 (June 1990) 165–86, and see entire issue; Joel Brind, "Cold fission," *Sci News* 137 (17 Mar 1990) 163. For one explanation of the physical problem of reproducing cold fusion, see Peter H. Handel, "Intermittency, irreproducibility, and the main physical effects in cold fusion," *Fusion Technology* 18 (Nov 1990) 512–17. Cf. Allan Franklin, *The Neglect of Experiment* (NY: Cambridge U, 1986) ch. 2. Huizenga, *Cold Fusion*, 32, notes that Pons and Fleischmann had problems with their baseline control experiment from the start.

104. Hillel Schwartz, *Century's End* (NY: Doubleday, 1990) 279, 283, on energy and fatigue in the fin de siècle; Crease and Samios, "Cold fusion confusion," q38 from Fleischmann; Editorial, "Nuclear fusion: the power source of tomorrow?" *Computer & Technology Guide* (June 1989) 11.

105. Jean-Pierre Briand and Michel Froment, "La fusion 'froide' dix-huit mois après," *La Recherche* 21 (Oct 1990) 1282–84; J.O'M. Bockris, "Letter on cold fusion," *Science* 249 (3 Aug 1990) 463; Robert Pool, "Cold fusion: only the grin remains," *Science* (9 Nov 1990) 754–55, q754; I. Amato, "Cold fusion saga," *Sci News* 137 (16 June 1990) 374, tritium a contaminant. On forgery, William J. Broad and Nicholas Wade, *Betrayers of the Truth* (NY: Simon & Schuster, 1982) ch. 4. On fudging, Alexander Kohn, *False Prophets: Fraud and Error in Science and Medicine* (Oxford: Blackwell, 1987) 37ff; Adil E. Shamoo and Zoltan Annau, "Data audit – historical perspective," *Accountability in Research* 1,2 (1990) 87–95. On fraud, Robert L. Engler et al., "Misrepresentation and responsibility in medical research," *New England J Med* 317 (1987) 1383–89, on Robert A. Slutsky, M.D., accused of producing twelve fraudulent papers and forty-eight questionable papers (with seventy-seven valid papers) in seven years, or one dubious paper every forty-three days – some of which affected strategies of critical care; Morton Hunt, "A fraud that shook the world of science," *NY Times Mag* (1 Nov 1981) 42–75, on Vijay R. Soman, M.D. On pathological science, see Denis L. Rousseau, "Case studies in pathological science," *Amer Scientist* 80 (Jan–Feb 1992) 54–63, the term itself originated by Irving Langmuir.

106. David H. Freedman, "A Japanese claim generates new heat," *Science* 256 (24 Apr 1992) 438; Andy Coghlan, "Test-tube fusion lives on in exile," *New Scientist* (5 Sept 1992) 8; L.C. Case, "The reality of 'cold fusion,'" *Fusion Technology* 20 (Dec 1991) 478–80; Y. Arata and Yue-Chang Zhang, "Reproducible cold fusion reaction using a complex cathode," *Fusion Technology* 22 (Sept 1992) 287–95; Andy Wright, "Clawing back respectability for cold fusion?" *Electronics World* 99 (Oct 1993) 869–71; Goldie Blumenstyk, "U. of Utah finds a buyer for rights to cold fusion," *Chronicle of Higher Education* 40 (15 Dec 1993) A28; Edmund Storms, "Warming up to cold fusion," *Technology R* (May–June 1994) 19–29; Mary Marcus, "The resurrection of cold fusion," *USA Today Mag* (Sept 1994) 55–57; Huizenga, *Cold Fusion*, "fiasco."

107. Patricia Woolf, "Fraud in science: how much, how serious?" *Hastings Center Report* 11 (Oct 1981) 9–14, q10 from Philip Handler, president, National Academy of

Sciences; Gilbert and Muklkay, *Opening Pandora's Box*, ch. 5, critical of the scientific faith in a "Truth Will Out Device," or "TWOD"; Eugene Garfield and Alfred Welljams-Dorof, "The impact of fraudulent research on the scientific literature. The Stephen E. Breuning case," *J Amer Med Assoc* 163 (9 Mar 1990) 1424-26, discounting the impact of a researcher whose invented data was the basis for the prescription of stimulants to hyperactive and retarded children during the 1980s, on which see Constance Holden, "NIMH finds a case of 'serious misconduct,'" *Science* 235 (27 Mar 1987) 1566-67.

108. Augustus De Morgan, "Scientific hoaxes," *Macmillan's* 1 (1859-60) q220; Collins, *Changing Order*, 54-56; Diane B. Paul, "The nine lives of discredited data: old textbooks never die – they just get paraphrased," *The Sciences* 27 (May–June 1987) 326-30; William J. Broad, "Would-be academician pirates papers," *Science* 208 (1980) 1440; Engler et al., "Misrepresentation," q1385; Collins, *Changing Order*, 55; Broad and Wade, *Betrayers of Truth*, q77; David J. Miller and Michael Hensen, eds., *Research Fraud in the Behavioral and Biomedical Sciences* (NY: Wiley, 1992). On the myth, see Patricia K. Woolf, "Deception in scientific research," *Project on Scientific Fraud and Misconduct, Report on Workshop Number One* (Washington, D.C.: AAAS, 1988) I, 61-62.

109. Nathaniel Hawthorne, "Near Oxford," *Our Old Home* (1863), in the *Centenary Edition of the Works of Nathaniel Hawthorne*, eds. Fredson Bowers et al. (Columbus: Ohio State U, 1970) V, 183-84.

110. Edwin H. Miller, *Salem Is My Dwelling Place: A Life of Nathaniel Hawthorne* (Iowa City: U Iowa, 1991) 338, q406; Nathaniel Hawthorne, *The Letters, 1853-1856*, eds. Thomas Woodson et al. (Columbus, OH: Ohio State U, 1987) 537; Graham Reed, *The Psychology of Anomalous Experience* (Buffalo: Prometheus, 1988) 106-07, frequency of déjà vu; Susan Jimison, "I died in Ohio 76 years ago...& was born again in 1948 – to live another life!" *Weekly World News* (6 Mar 1990) 24-25; Henry F. Osborn, "Illusions of memory," *North Amer R* 138 (1884) q476; Roger Penrose, *The Emperor's New Mind* (Oxford: Oxford U, 1989) 439-48 – although Penrose never discusses "déjà vu" and argues finally that the mind's time is nonlinear; Sandra Blakeslee, "The brain may 'see' what eyes cannot," *NY Times* (16 Jan 1991) C1, covert awareness; W.H. Burnham, "Memory, historically and experimentally considered," *Amer J Psychology* 2 (1889) 441-42; *Omni* (June 1990) 80, cartoon by "Heath." See Vernon M. Neppe, *The Psychology of Déjà Vu: Have I Been Here Before?* (Johannesburg: Witwatersrand U, 1983) for a good review of the literature. This decade, the déjà vu has become the central gimmick of several interesting movies, including Harold Ramis (dir), *Groundhog Day* (Columbia TriStar, 1993), and Jack Sholden (dir), *12:01* (which I saw as a rerun on Fox TV, July 1993) concerning a "time bounce" causing a repetition of April 27th – my birthday.

111. E. Boirac, "Correspondance," *Revue philosophique* 1 (1876) 430-31; Burnham, "Memory," q433.

112. F.-L. Arnaud, "Un Cas d'illusion du 'déjà vu' ou de fausse mémoire," *Annales médico-psychologiques* (May–June 1896), assessed by Pierre Janet, "A propos du 'déjà vu,'" *J de psychologie, normale et pathologique* 2 (1905) 289-307, at 293 *et passim*, for this paragraph and the next. Janet's hypotheses were in part confirmed by Heymans; see H.N. Sno and D. Draaisma, "An early Dutch study of déjà vu experiences," *Psychological Med* 23 (Feb 1993) 17-26.

113. Henri Bergson, "Le Souvenir du présent et la fausse reconnaissance," *Revue philosophique* 66 (1908) 561-93, and cf. Gilles Deleuze, *Bergsonism*, trans. H. Tomlinson and B. Habberjam (NY: Zone, 1988 [1966]) ch. 3, "Memory as Virtual Coexistence." In

support of this position is the fact that most déjà vu experiences, unlike Hawthorne's, are of rather humdrum situations.

114. Dale Boesky, "The reversal of déjà raconté," *J Amer Psychoanalytic Assoc* 17 (1969) 1114-41 on Freud's positions; Sigmund Freud, *The Psychopathology of Everyday Life* (1901), in *The Standard Edition of the Complete Psychological Works*, trans. and eds. James Strachey et al. (L: Hogarth, 1955-64) VI, 266; idem, "Fausse reconnaissance (déjà raconté) in psychoanalytic treatment" (1914) in *ibid.*, XIII, 201-10, q207; idem, "The 'uncanny'" (1919), *ibid.*, XVIII, q245, 247-48; idem, "A disturbance of memory on the Acropolis" (1936), in *ibid.*, XXII, 239-50, q245; Harry Slochower, "Freud's déjà vu on the Acropolis: a symbolic relic of 'mater nuda,'" *Psychoanalytic Q* 39 (1970) 90-102; Jacques Lacan, *The Four Fundamental Concepts of Psycho-Analysis*, ed. J.-A. Miller, trans. Alan Sheridan (NY: Norton, 1978) 48-55 on repetition. G.E. Berrios, "Déjà vu in France during the nineteenth century: a conceptual history," *Comprehensive Psychiatry* 36 (Mar–Apr 1995) 123-29, argues that the predominance of psychological and "parapsychological" interpretations of déjà vu, in company with a narrowly associationist idea of memory, set back research on the topic for many years. For a more recent neurological assessment of the experience of déjà vu, see J. Bancaud et al., "Anatomical origin of déjà vu and vivid 'memories' in human temporal lobe epilepsy," *Brain* 117 (Feb 1994) 71-90, trying – and failing – to localize the experience in one part of the brain, possibly the superior temporal gyrus of the lateral temporal neocortex.

115. Jay A. Sigler, *Double Jeopardy* (Ithaca: Cornell, 1969); David G. Savage, "Limit on 'double jeopardy' to get high court hearing," *LA Times* (28 April 1992) A16; Sigmund Freud, "Remembering, repeating and working-through (further recommendations on the technique of psycho-analysis II)," in *Standard Edition*, XII, 146-56; Gilles Deleuze, *Différence et répétition* (P: PUF, 1968) 30, on psychiatric transference, where that repetition which constitutes illness and loss becomes health and redemption. Cf. Avital Ronell, *The Telephone Book* (Lincoln: U Nebraska, 1989) 430 *et passim* on Heideggerian views of technology and repetition. See also H. Banister and O.L. Zangwill, "Experimentally induced visual paramnesias," *British J Psychology* 32 (1941a-42a) 30-51.

116. Ulric Neisser, "John Dean's memory," in *Memory Observed*, ed. Neisser (San Francisco: Freeman, 1982) 158, repisodes; Wilder Penfield, "The permanent record of the stream of consciousness," in *Readings in Physiological Psychology*, ed. Thomas K. Landauer (NY: McGraw-Hill, 1967) 352-73; Eli Marcovitz, "The meaning of déjà vu," *Psychoanalytic Q* 21 (1952) 481-89, second chance; Jacob Arlow, "The structure of the déjà vu experience," *J Amer Psychoanalytic Assoc* 7 (1959) 628 on reassuring distortions. Cf. the uses of movie flashbacks: Maureen Turim, *Flashbacks in Film* (L: Routledge, 1989).

117. Burnham, "Memory," 440, epileptics and déjà vu; Owsei Temkin, *The Falling Sickness: A History of Epilepsy*, 2nd ed. (Baltimore: Johns Hopkins U, 1971) 154-61.

118. From the start of studies in the 1800s (and through to the 1950s) the incidence of stuttering among "primitives" was thought to be practically nil. When found among Native Americans and Central Africans, stuttering was then correlated to the degree of contact with "civilization." See Oliver Bloodstein, *A Handbook on Stuttering* (Chicago: National Easter Seal Soc, 1975) 92-96; Denyse Rockey, *Speech Disorder in Nineteenth-Century Britain: A History of Stuttering* (L: Croom Helm, 1980) 25-28; George H. Shames, "Stuttering: an RFP for a cultural perspective," *J Fluency Disorders* 14 (1989) 67-77. On earlier images of stutterers (as "barbarians"), see Ynez V. O'Neill, *Speech and Speech Disorders in Western Thought Before 1600* (Westport: Greenwood, 1980).

119. Andrew J. Lees, *Tics and Related Disorders* (Edinburgh: Churchill Livingstone, 1985) q1, 2, 7, q15, 20–21; Edward Warren, "Remarks on stammering," *Amer J Med Sci* 21 (1837) 75–99, rept. in *J Communication Disorders* 10 (1977) 159–79, q163 on convulsive motions; Elizabeth Loftus and Katherine Ketcham, *Witness for the Defense* (NY: St. Martin's, 1991) ch. 10, stuttering associated with nervousness, guilt; Kelly D. Hall and Ehud Yairi, "Fundamental frequency, jitter, and shimmer in preschoolers who stutter," *J Speech and Hearing Research* 35 (Oct 1992) 1002–08; Howard I. Kaplan et al., *Comprehensive Textbook of Psychiatry*, 3rd ed. (Baltimore: Williams & Wilkins, 1980) I, q1014, devices.

120. For the therapies, see Lees, *Tics and Related Disorders*, 7ff; A. Guillaume, "Bégaiement ou psellisme," *Dictionnaire encyclopédique des sciences médicales* (P, 1868) VIII, 695–755; James M. Rymer, *The Unspeakable; Or, The Life and Adventures of a Stammerer* (L,1855) throughout; J.G. McKendrick, "Stammering," *Ency Britannica*, 9th ed. (Edinburgh, 1875) XXII, 447–48; Eugene F. Hahn, *Stuttering: Significant Theories and Therapies*, 2nd ed. prepared by Elise S. Hahn (Stanford: Stanford U, 1956); Mark Onslow, "Choosing a treatment procedure for early stuttering," *J Speech and Hearing Research* 35 (Oct 1992) 983–93. For genetic/neurological explanations, see William H. Perkins et al., "A theory of neuropsycholinguistic function in stuttering," *Speech and Hearing Research* 34 (Aug 1991) 734–52; Roger J. Ingham, "Stuttering," *Human Communication and Its Disorders*, ed. Harris Winitz (Norwood: Ablex, 1990) esp. 45; John P. Brady, "The pharmacology of stuttering," *Amer J Psychiatry* 148 (Oct 1991) 1309–16, noting that stuttering is very susceptible to the placebo effect – but does this account for the success of injections of botulinum toxin into the vocal chords of stutterers by Mitchell F. Brin at Columbia U, reported by Thomas H. Maugh, III, "Drug treatment attacks mechanisms that cause stuttering, neurologist says," *LA Times* (8 May 1992) A12? Cf. Oliver Sacks, "Tics," *NY R of Books* 34 (29 Jan 1987) 37–41, blending psychiatry and neurology.

121. Lees, *Tics and Related Disorders*, 170, telegraphy; G.B. Pfeffer, "The history of carpal tunnel syndrome," *J Hand Surgery, British Vol* 13 (Feb 1988) 28–34; George S. Phalen, "The carpal-tunnel syndrome: seventeen years' experience in diagnosis and treatment of six hundred fifty-four cases," *J Bone and Joint Surgery* 48 (1966) 211–28; Centers for Disease Control, "Occupational disease surveillance: carpal tunnel syndrome," *J Amer Med Assoc* 162 (18 Aug 1989) 886; Robert J. Spinner et al., "The many faces of carpal tunnel syndrome," *Mayo Clinic Proc* 64 (July 1989) 829–36; J.C. Stevens et al., "Carpal tunnel syndrome in Rochester, Minnesota," *Neurology* 38 (Jan 1988) 134–38, incidence; M.C. de Krom et al., "Carpal tunnel syndrome: prevalence in the general population," *J Clinical Epidemiology* 45 (Apr 1992) 373–76.

122. Arthur K. Shapiro et al., *Gilles de la Tourette Syndrome*, 2nd ed. (NY: Raven, 1988) esp. 5ff on exaggeration of echolalia and coprolalia, which they believe is due to nosological error; Y. Lebrun et al. "On echolalia, echo-answer, and contamination," *Acta neurologica belgica* 71 (1971) 301–08.

123. Rymer, *The Unspeakable*, q20; Guillaume, "Bégaiement," 707, 712–13 on the surgery, from which at least eighty-five stutterers died; David E. Comings, *Tourette Syndrome and Human Behavior* (Duarte: Hope, 1990) 17, on the ability of some to imitate *animal* sounds perfectly; Charles Van Riper, *The Nature of Stuttering*, 2nd ed. (Englewood Cliffs, NJ: Prentice-Hall, 1982) 202; H. Meige and E. Feindel, *Tics and Their Treatment* [*Les confessions d'un ticqueur*], ed. and trans. by S.A.K. Wilson (NY, 1907 [1902]), quoted in Sacks, "Tics," 38.

124. Elinor O. Keenan, "Making it last: repetition in children's discourse," in *Child Discourse*, eds. S. Ervin-Tripp and C. Mitchell-Kernan (NY: Academic, 1977) 125–38; Steve Bonner, "Redundancy in natural languages," *Verbatim* 17 (Wint 1991) 1–3; Deborah Tannen, "Repetition in conversation," *Language* 63 (Sept 1987) 574–605; John R. Pierce, *Symbols, Signals and Noise: The Nature and Process of Communication* (NY: Harper & Row, 1961) 163; John C. Burnham, *Bad Habits* (NY: NYU, 1993) ch. 8, swearing in American history; Paul Fussell, *Wartime: Understanding and Behavior in the Second World War* (NY: Oxford, 1989) 79–95, 263–67; Bruce F. Kawin, *Telling It Again and Again: Repetition in Literature and Film* (Ithaca: Cornell, 1973); Greil Marcus, *Lipstick Traces: A Secret History of the Twentieth Century* (Cambridge, MA: Harvard U, 1989) 435, explicitly linking punk, coprolalia, and Tourette Syndrome; Bruce Bower, "The ticcing link," *Sci News* 138 (21 July 1990) 42–44; Comings, *Tourette Syndrome*, i.

125. Donald J. Cohen et al., *Tourette's Syndrome and Tic Disorders* (NY: Wiley, 1988) q9; Sacks, "Tics," q38, from Meige and Feindel. Recent studies indicate that Tourette Syndrome is likely to be classed along a spectrum of choreas caused by an immune-system response to streptococcal bacterial infection and a consequent antibody "biological mimicry" affecting healthy neurotransmitter cells in the basal ganglia of the brain. Tourette's and later psychologists' insistence upon the clear distinction of his psychopathological "syndrome" from other choreas had, even in his own time, a weak medical rationale, but such insistence was compatible with a culture of the copy in which one's attention is drawn to the dramatically, remorselessly repetitive as a disorder emblematic of the culture itself, whether a sign of "being stuck" or of going into inevitable decline. As a result, those who suffer from the disorder which Tourette knew so little about at first-hand have labored under the curse of the stereotype of the ticqueur as someone whose life is the epitome of copying gone crazy. See Howard I. Kushner, "Medical fictions: the case of the cursing marquise and the (re)construction of Gilles de la Tourette's syndrome," *Bull History of Med* 69 (1995) 224–54; Howard I. Kushner and Louise S. Kiessling, "The controversy over the classification of Gilles de la Tourette's syndrome, 1800–1995," *Perspectives in Biology and Med* 39 (Wint 1996), which Prof. Kushner has kindly shown me in preprint.

126. John Hollander, *The Figure of Echo: A Mode of Illusion in Milton and After* (Berkeley: U Cal, 1981) q10 for Bacon, 11.

127. James Boswell, "On quotations," *L Mag* (June 1779), in *Boswell's Column*, ed. Margery Bailey (L, 1951) q124, q127; James L. Rolleston, "The politics of quotation: Walter Benjamin's Arcades project," *PMLA* 104 (Jan 1989) 13–27; Ian Balfour, "Reversal, quotation (Benjamin's history)," *MLN* 106 (1991) 622–47; John McCole, *Walter Benjamin and the Antinomies of Tradition* (Ithaca: Cornell U, 1993) ch. 1. Benjamin's favorite nineteenth-century Frenchman, Gustave Flaubert, himself postulated a novel entirely of quotations. In his unfinished *Bouvard et Pécuchet*, whose protagonists are always recopying local items of news, he and they express "the pleasure there is in the material act of recopying." See Michel Schneider, *Voleurs de mots* (P: Gallimard, 1985) q27.

128. J. Hillis Miller, *Fiction and Repetition: Seven English Novels* (Cambridge, MA: Harvard U, 1982) 6, summarizing Deleuze, *Differérence et répétition*, on mimetic or platonic repetition (true by correspondence to that which it copies) and on Nietzschean (ungrounded) repetition. Here would be the spot to consider camp, cliché, and kitsch, disorders of repetition ostensibly under our control, but I won't. Do see Susan Sontag, "Notes on 'camp,'" *Against Interpretation* (NY: Delata, 1966) 275–92; Sidney Blumenthal,

"Reaganism and the neokitsch aesthetic," in *The Reagan Legacy*, eds. Blumenthal and Thomas Byrne Edsall (NY: Random House, 1988) 251-94.

129. On painting-by-number, born in 1952, see "These fads have built a billion-dollar business," *Business Week* (28 Nov 1953) 84-85; Jerome Ellison, "Anyone can paint a picture," *Saturday Evening Post* (19 Dec 1953) 22-23; Arthur Guptill, "Those ubiquitous numbered painting sets," *Amer Artist* 17 (Dec 1953) 58-61; William Gaddis, *The Recognitions* (NY, 1952, 1955) q601; CBS Evening News, 9 May 1992, reporting that one collection of completed paintings-by-number is presently valued at one million dollars.

On lipsynching, see esp. Richard Conniff, "In Wisconsin: lip sync live, on stage tonight," *Time* (14 Dec 1987) 10 – winner a man in camouflage attire making robotic movements and stuttering "nuh-nuh-nuh-nineteen" to a monologue about being nineteen in Vietnam.

On direct quotation, see Pierre-Louis Vaillancourt, "Rhétorique et éthique de la citation," *Renaissance and Reformation* n.s. 62 (1982) 103-21; *Oxford Dictionary of Quotations*, 355, from the *Essais*, III, xii; Pierre Coste, ed., *Essais de Michel Seigneur de Montaigne* (L, 1745) I, vi; Richard L. Regosin, "Sources and resources: the 'pretexts' of originality in Montaigne's *Essais*," *Substance* 21 (1978) 103-15; Christine M. Brousseau-Beuerman, "La 'Copie' de Montaigne: étude sur les citations dans les *Essais*," Ph.D., Harvard U, 1986.

130. Barry Sandrew, President of Animation, American Film Technologies, San Diego, CA, interview, 19 Sept 1991, whose company, which has a near-monopoly on colorizing films, consults (when possible) the original designers on what the tones should be. Cf. Elise K. Bader, "A film of a different color: copyright and the colorization of black and white films," *Copyright Law Symposium (ASCAP)* 36 (1989) 138, 145 – asking what claims to copyright colorizing affords, given the decision of the Library of Congress in 1987 to accept on a class basis claims to copyright in computer color-encoded versions of black-and-white films, and see Register of Copyrights, *Technological Alterations to Motion Pictures and Other Audiovisual Works* (Washington, D.C.: U.S. Copyright Office, 1989) x, 5, 7, 11, 57-59, as also Craig A. Wagner, "Motion picture colorization, authenticity, and the elusive moral right," *NYU Law R* 64 (June 1989) 628-725. See Bernard Beck, "Inglorious color," *Society* 24 (May–June 1987) 4-12, on interpretation, as also Arthur Asa Berger, "Film technology's latest Frankenstein," 12-13, and, per contra, Michael Schudson, "Colorization and authenticity," 18-19, the Scarlatti analogy. For Matisse and reframing, see Sam Roberts, "For Woody Allen, a new audience on Capitol Hill," *NY Times* (14 May 1987) B1, and cf. Gerald Mast, "Film study and the copyright law," *Fair Use and Free Inquiry*, 83-105, arguing that once the Director's Guild surrendered control of the shape of the frame for films being reprocessed for TV, Satan was loose and colorizing useful, since TV does poorly with deep blacks and glaring whites. For the corpse, Roland Barthes, *La Chambre claire: note sur la photographie* (P: Seuil, 1980) 127-28.

131. Linda Williams, *Hard Core: Power, Pleasure, and the "Frenzy of the Visible"* (Berkeley: U Cal, 1989) esp. 59-60 on primitivism; *Oldies but Hornies* (Amateur Sex Productions, 1990); Andrea Simakis, "Telephone love," *Village Voice* (17 July 1990) 35; George N. Gordon, *Erotic Communications* (NY: Hastings House, 1980) esp. 248-49 on *Sometimes Sweet Susan*, which Gordon lauds for its sex scenes, "clearly authentic without conventional tokens of good faith"; Lisa Gubernick, "A shady past, a questionable future," *Forbes* (17 Sept 1990) 165-67, on laser discs, whose masters can supposedly last many

centuries, even longer than a porno star's erection: C.H. Roads, "Archivist's view of the desiderata for long term image permanence," *J Photographic Sci* 36 (1988) 118-19.

132. Bailey, *Boswell's Column*, 128; Laurence Sterne, *The Life and Opinions of Tristram Shandy, Gentleman*, ed. James A. Work (NY: 1940) 350-51 (= V,iii); Bernard Beugnot, "Un Aspect textuel de la réception critique: le citation," *Oeuvres et critiques* 1,2 (1976) 5-19; idem, "Dialogue, entretien et citation à l'époque classique," *Canadian R of Comparative Literature* 3 (Wint 1976) 39-50; Antoine Compagnon, *La Seconde main: ou, le travail de la citation* (P: Seuil, 1973) esp. 40, 246 on quotation marks.

133. Herbert Paul, "The decay of classical quotation," *Nineteenth Century* 39 (Apr 1896) 636-46, q644, Macaulay; Paolo Bellezza, "La Citazione e gli Anglosassoni," *Studi di filologia moderna (Catania)* 1,3-4 (1908) 247-77; Thomas Mann, *Reflections of a Nonpolitical Man*, trans. Walter D. Morris (NY: Ungar, 1983 [1919]) q2-3, merged with the translation by Joseph P. Stern, *Lichtenberg: A Doctrine of Scattered Occasions* (Bloomington: Indiana U, 1959) q144. Cf. the attitudes of Mann's contemporaries, assessed by Gerhard R. Kaiser, *Proust, Musil, Joyce: Zum Verhältnis von Literatur und Gesellschaft am Paradigma des Zitats* (Frankfurt: Athenäum, 1972).

134. Louise A. Jackson et al., "Teacher, Johnny copied!" *Education Digest* 53 (Feb 1988) 39-41; Doris R. Dant, "Plagiarism in high school," *English J* 75 (Feb 1986) 81-85; Joyce A. Carroll, "Plagiarism: the unfun game," *ibid.* 71 (Sept 1982) 92-95, citing as the source for "paraplage" Michael T. O'Neill (*ABCA Bull*, 1980); Linda Greenhouse, "As libel case opens, a debate on what is truth," *NY Times* (15 Jan 1991) A16, suit alleging malicious misquotation by reporter Janet Malcolm, who on 3 June 1993 was found guilty by a San Francisco District Court jury of having fabricated two defamatory quotations which her lawyers had defended as acts of "compression"; American Historical Association, "Revised Statement on Plagiarism and Related Misuses of the Work of Other Authors," *AHA Perspectives* (Nov 1993) 16 on dangers of paraphrase; Paul Rudnick and Kurt Andersen, "The irony epidemic," *San Francisco Chronicle* (21 Mar 1989) B3, on "air quotes," cited by Anderson, *Reality Isn't What It Used to Be*, 147; Paul F. Boller, Jr., *Quotesmanship: The Use and Abuse of Quotation for Polemical and Other Purposes* (Dallas: SMU, 1967); Paul F. Boller, Jr. and John George, *They Never Said It: A Book of Fake Quotes, Misquotes and Misleading Attributions* (NY: Oxford U, 1989); Patricia Mayes, "Quotation in spoken English," *Studies in Language* 14 (1990) 325-63; Mikhail Bakhtin [authorship disputed], *Le Marxisme et la philosophie du langage*, trans. Marina Yaguello (P: Minuit, 1977) 161-93; Madeleine Frédéric, *La Répétition: étude linguistique et rhétorique* (Tubingen: Niemeyer, 1985); Hermann W.G. Peter, *Wahrheit und Kunst: Geschichtschreibung und Plagiat im klassischen Altertum* (Hildesheim: Olms, 1965 [1911]) 433; Richard Hurd, *A Letter to Mr. Mason* (NY: Garland, 1970 [1757]) q44.

135. Harry M. Paull, *Literary Ethics* (Port Washington: Kennikat, 1968 [1929]) 62-65, q62 from the printer John Dunton, q65 for Saintsbury; [Anonymous], "Johnson's *Rasselas*," *Bibliographer* 3 (May 1883) 172-75, q172; Boorstin, *The Image*, 132-38; Paul C. Rodgers, Jr., "Alexander Bain and the rise of the organic paragraph," *Q J of Speech* 51 (1965) 399-408; Robert M. Gray et al., "Image compression and tree-structured vector quantization," in *Image and Text Compression*, ed. James A. Storer (Boston: Kluwer, 1992) 7-9 — my "et al." here being one of the lossiest and most biased of compressions: the name listed first in joint authorships is usually senior and male, the names dropped and lost more often younger and, given the restricted access of women to academic-scientific seniority, female.

136. Gertrude Himmelfarb, "Where have all the footnotes gone?" *NY Times Book R* (16 June 1991) 1, 24; David H. Fischer, "The braided narrative," in *The Literature of Fact*, ed. Angus Fletcher (NY: Columbia U, 1976) 113-31, defending the substantive footnote as the means whereby the historian's equivalent of a scientific experiment may be repeated and results replicated; John Onians, editorial response to a letter from Michael Fried, in *Art History* 11 (June 1988) 155-57, q155, "anything fresh"; Robert K. Merton, "The Matthew Effect in science, II: cumulative advantage and the symbolism of intellectual property," *Isis* 79 (Dec 1988) 606-23, reasserting his indebtedness to Harriet Zuckerman; Stephen Greenblatt, "Capitalist culture and the circulatory system," in *The Aims of Representation*, ed. Murray Krieger (NY: Columbia, 1987) 257-73, esp. 264, "the capitalist aesthetic demands acknowledgments"; Jon Weiner, "The footnote fetish," *Dissent* 21 (1974), rpt. in *Telos* 31 (1977) 172-77 – on citations, not footnotes, and on political bias in citation indexing; "The dynamic dozen: top ranked U.S. universities in the biological sciences, 1981-91," *Science Watch* (Jan 1993), digested in *Brandeis R* 12 (Spr 1993) 4; Blaise Cronin, *The Citation Process: The Role and Significance of Citations in Scientific Communication* (L: Taylor Graham, 1984).

In this endnote I am rewarding my alma mater; honoring a mentor, David Hackett Fischer; placing myself in the estimable company of *Isis*; hitching my wagon to Greenblatt; deflecting criticism onto Himmelfarb (who blames the decline of the footnote upon Rousseau, who in his *Second Discourse, On Inequality* [1755], relegated his notes to the end, where "Those who have the courage to begin again will be able to amuse themselves the second time in beating the bushes"); disclaiming responsibility for Wiener's accusations of bias; proving my fairhandedness by respectful reference to the extreme position of Onians; and demonstrating my erudition. As a modern scholar, of course, I wish still to be credited with originality, although this endnote about footnotes itself has forebears, notably in the satire by Peter Riess, *Towards a Theory of the Footnote* (Berlin: de Gruyter, 1983), who lists among the forms of the footnote the precautionary, amnesial ("what is added should have occurred to the author before"), and narcissistic.

137. You Poh Seng, "Historical survey of the development of sampling theory and practice," *J Royal Statistical Soc*, ser. A, 114 (1951) 214-32, reviewing the work of the Norwegian statistician A.N. Kiaer, the first to use a considered sampling method, in 1894; Alain Desrosières, "The part in relation to the whole: how to generalise? The prehistory of representative sampling," in *The Social Survey in Historical Perspective, 1880-1940*, eds. Martin Bulmer et al. (NY: Cambridge, 1991) 217-45; Frederick F. Stephan, "History of the uses of modern sampling procedures," *J Amer Statistical Assoc* 43 (1948) 12-39; Herbert W. Armstrong, "How do we know the answers?" *The Plain Truth* (June 1979) q1.

138. Desrosières, "The part in relation to the whole," q231; Morris J. Slonim, *Sampling* (NY: Simon & Schuster, 1960) q2. Cf. Isaac Asimov, "Franchise," in his *Earth Is Room Enough* (Garden City, NY: Doubleday, 1957) 58-73. That sampling was congruent with digesting was the discovery of the *Literary Digest*, whose publishers had been polling successfully since 1916 – until FDR in 1936 attracted an overplus of lower-income voters who wreaked havoc with their election survey. The publishers had sent out millions of ballots to addresses sampled from telephone directories, but in 1936 telephones were nonrandomly distributed; the richer you were, the more likely you would have a telephone and be voting for Wendell Wilkie.

139. Leo Steinberg, "The glorious company" (of horse thieves), introduction to Jean Lipman and Richard Marshall, *Art About Art* (NY: Dutton, 1978) q25. Contrast Stefan Morawski, "The basic functions of quotation," in *Sign, Language, Culture,* eds. A.J. Greimas et al. (The Hague: Mouton, 1970) 690-705, esp. 704: "Quotations accumulate in art when the boundaries between it and other forms of social conscious[ness] become muddied."

140. For an overview, see William J. Mitchell, *The Reconfigured Eye: Visual Truth in the Post-Photographic Era* (Cambridge, MA: MIT, 1992). For the specifics, see Paul Haeberli, "Paint by numbers," *Computer Graphics* 24 (Aug 1990) 207-14; Scitex Corporation, *You are about to unfold the next chapter...* (Herzlia, Israel, and Bedford, MA, 1988?) brochure for Colorfill System; Sandrew interview; Allan Ripp, "Whose picture is it anyway?" *Amer Photographer* 18 (June 1987) 74, 77; Robert X. Cringely (pseud.), "Star tech – Hollywood goes digital," *Forbes ASAP* (7 Dec 1992) 48; Bennett Daviss, "Picture perfect," *Discover* (July 1990) 54-55; Fred Ritchin, *In Our Own Image...How Computer Technology is Changing Our View of the World* (NY: Aperture, 1990) q23, Blank.

141. Scitex Corporation, *Scitex Response Systems* (Herzlia, Israel, and Bedford, MA, 1989?) 4; Dick Donovan, "Scientists take wraps off mummy's face," *Weekly World News* (27 Feb 1990) 33, quoting Robert B. Pickering, curator of anthropology, Children's Museum, Indianapolis, on the results of computerized tomography scans of a sixth-century-B.C. mummy; "Ad of the month," *TV Guide* (18 Apr 1992) 4; Michael O'Connor, "Life in the machine," *Photo/Design* (Dec 1984) quoting Mark Hughes, Art Director, Doyle Dane Bernbach; Robert Atkins, "Making faces," *Contemporanea* 24 (Jan 1991) 54-57, on the "aging machine" of artist Nancy Burson, for which see her book of photographs, with Richard Carling and David Kramlich, *Composites: Computer Generated Portraits* (NY: Morrow, 1986); Donald R. Katz, "Why pictures lie," *Esquire* (June 1990) 93-95; Ritchin, *In Our Own Image,* 21; Timothy Binkley, "Camera fantasia: computed visions of virtual reality," *Millennium Film J* 20/21 (Fall-Wint 1989) 22ff on the escalating "deniability" of the image, and cf. Daniel Sheridan, "The trouble with Harry," *Columbia Journalism R* 28 (Jan-Feb 1990) 4-6, on video reporting and electronic editing without any actual reportorial presence.

142. Arthur Wertheim, *Radio Comedy* (NY: Oxford U, 1979) 95, 170; Dick Hobson, "The Hollywood Sphinx and his laff box," in *Television,* ed. Barry G. Cole (NY: Free Press, 1970) 194-200, q197-98 from Arthur Julian, q200 from Cooper.

143. Molly McGraw, "Sound sampling protection and infringement in today's music industry," *High Tech Law J* 4 (1989) 147-69, q150-51; Frank Zappa, "Digital sampling and the guitar," *Guitar Player* 17 (Dec 1983) 110; Alan Di Perna, "Technology transfigures pop with one keystroke," *Rolling Stone* (14 June 1990) 108-09; Kyle Gann, "Noises of fate," *Village Voice* (24 July 1990) q92, Stein; John Oswald, "Ethics and the wonderful new world of sampling," *Canadian Composer* 232 (July-Aug 1988) 18-23, q22.

144. Peter Blaumer, "Free samples," *NY* 19 (20 Oct 1986) q32, Sammy Merendino; Jeffrey Ressner, "Sampling amok?" *Rolling Stone* (14 June 1990) q103 for Mike D., Parker, Hassell. See also Tamara J. Byram, "Digital sound sampling and a federal right of publicity: is it live, or is it Macintosh?" *Computer Law J* 10 (1990) 365-92. I have also benefitted from a discussion with Nelson Bloodrocket and Reg of the Mudguards, London, 26 Nov 1990, on the "dodgy ground" of sampling.

145. Thomas C. Moglovkin, "Original digital: no more free samples," *Southern Cal Law R* 64 (Nov 1990) 135-74; J.D. Considine, "Larcenous art?" *Rolling Stone* (14 June

1990) 107–08; Handelman, "Is it live or…," 16; Ressner, "Sampling amok?" q103, Sill. On reiterable novelty, one must take note also of the waves of "pattern-pulse" repetitive-chord music (popularized by composer Philip Glass) which preceded by a decade the first waves of digital sampling. See Dennis K.M. Kam, "Repetition and the Drift Toward Constant Focus in the Pattern-Pulse Works of Terry Riley and Steve Reich," Ph.D., U Ill at Urbana-Champaign, 1974, a dissertation whose second part is a somewhat derivative score entitled "Ditto Varianti."

146. On the emergence of plagiarism as a "crime," see Walter L. Bullock, "The precept of plagiarism in the Cinquecento," *Modern Philology* 25 (Feb 1928) 293–312; Harold O. White, *Plagiarism and Imitation during the English Renaissance* (Cambridge, MA, 1935); Françoise Kaye, *Charron et Montaigne: du plagiat à l'originalité* (Ottawa: U Ottawa, 1982); Erich Welslau, *Imitation und Plagiat in der französischen Literatur von der Renaissance bis zur Revolution* (Berlin: Schauble, 1976); Thomas Mallon, *Stolen Words: Forays into the Origins and Ravages of Plagiarism* (NY: Ticknor and Fields, 1989) ch. 1. On accusations, see Charles Nodier, *Questions de littérature légale. Du plagiat…* (P, 1812) 10 on the Stoic, Chrysippus, condemned for taking all of Euripides's *Medea*, and also 7n, Macrobius documenting Virgil's thefts; R.W. Scheller, *A Survey of Medieval Model Books* (Haarlem: Bohn, 1963) 34–35. For Dumas, see Henry H. Breen, *Modern English Literature, Its Blemishes and Defects* (L, 1857) 218. Final quotation from Brander Matthews, *Pen and Ink* (Freeport: Books for Libraries, 1971 [1888]) 35–36.

147. On Bishop William Warburton, see his *An Enquiry into the Nature and Origin of Literary Property* (L, 1762); Miles (pseud.), "Imitation and plagiarism," *Congregational Mag* 6 (1823) 245–47. On Coleridge, see Peter Shaw, "Plagiary," *Amer Scholar* 51 (Sum 1982) 333–36 for Coleridge; Mallon, *Stolen Words*, 26–37, q31 on ventriloquism from Coleridge's *Biographia literaria*; Norman Fruman, *Coleridge: The Damaged Archangel* (NY: Braziller, 1971); J.W. Calcraft, "Plagiarism and accidental imitation," *Dublin U Mag* 73 (1869) 120, Coleridge saying that "Plagiarists are always suspicious of being stolen from." On Poe, see Shaw (above), 332–33; Robert Regan, "Hawthorne's 'plagiary'; Poe's duplicity," *Nineteenth-Century Fiction* 25,3 (1970) 281–98; Edgar Allan Poe, "William Wilson," in *Selected Poetry and Prose*, ed. T.O. Mabbott (NY, 1951) 131–48, q138; and recall René Magritte's *La Reproduction interdite*, in which a black-haired man in a suit looks at a mantelpiece mirror in which he sees his own back, and we see, on the mantel, a copy of Poe's *Adventures of Gordon Pym*.

I wonder whether Pierre Bayle, whose *Dictionnaire historique et critique* (1697, 4th ed. 1730) was the first reference book to make a point of noting the plagiarisms by (in)famous authors (see entries for Alstedius, André, Ephore, Musurus, Nihusius, Strigelius, Villareal), was also, like the partridge, one who hatched the eggs laid by other birds (for metaphor, see under Duaren). Cf. the exposures in Johann Burkhard Mencke's *The Charlatanry of the Learned*, trans. F.E. Litz, ed. H.L. Mencken (NY, 1937 [1715, 5th ed. 1747]), who himself wrote (pp. 49–50), "I do not deny that in my argument I have borrowed the thoughts of Erasmus, Agrippa, Naudaeus, Lilienthal and others, but I have added much of my own." Destined to be entered into any new edition of Mencke's work is the Abbé Jacques Paul Migne, who published on average a book every ten days for thirty years and who was, as R. Howard Bloch writes, *God's Plagiarist: Being an Account of the Fabulous Industry and Irregular Commerce of Abbé Migne* (Chicago: U Chicago, 1994).

148. For theory on this, see Gérard Genette, *Palimpsestes: la littérature au second degré* (P: Seuil, 1982); Michel Schneider, *Voleurs de mots: essai sur le plagiat, la psychoanalyse,*

et la pensée (P: Gallimard, 1985); Patricia L. Skarda, "Vampirism and plagiarism: Byron's influence and Polidori's practice," *Studies in Romanticism* 20 (Sum 1989) 249-69.

149. Nicholas Pastore, "On plagiarism: Buffon, Condillac, Porterfield, Schopenhauer," *J History Behavioral Sciences* 9,4 (1973) 378-92; S.L. Zabell, "Buffon, Price, and Laplace: scientific attribution in the eighteenth century," *Archive for the History of Exact Sciences* 39 (1988) 173-81; Robert S. Kahan et al., "Plagiarism in the 'first' American book about photography," *Papers Bibliographical Soc Amer* 67,3 (1973) 283-304; R.M. Sargent, "Plagiarism," *Congregational Q* 9 (1867) 367-73, sermons; Gregg Easterbrook, "The sincerest flattery," *Newsweek* (29 July 1991) 45-46; Robert Burchfield, "Dictionaries new and old: who plagiarises whom, why and when?" *Encounter* 63,3 (1984) 10-19, with reply by Laurence Urdang, " 'To plagiarise, or to purloin, or to borrow...'?" *ibid.* 63,5 (1984) 71-73, whose argument leans upon that of Voltaire in *A Philosophical Dictionary*, trans. E.R. Dumont (NY, 1932) II, 295; Mallon, *Stolen Words*, 100, Oregon. I have found the pages of a university library book bracketed in pencil with the clear intent of lifting paragraphs bodily into a paper; the book: Arthur Herzog's *The B.S. Factor: The Theory and Technique of Faking It in America* (1973).

150. W.H. Davenport Adams, "Imitators and plagiarists, I," *Gentleman's Mag* n.s. 48 (1892) 510 for number, attributed to "Dr. Hooke," and cf. Spider Robinson's title story in *Melancholy Elephants* (NY: Penguin, 1984); Susan Gillman, *Dark Twins: Imposture and Identity in Mark Twain's America* (Chicago: U Chicago, 1989) q32-33 from Twain's *Letters*, II, 731; Theodate L. Smith, "Paramnesia in daily life," *Amer J Psychology* 24 (1913) 52 for Keller.

151. On recipes, see Alan Davidson, "The natural history of British cookery books," *Amer Scholar* 52,1 (1982-83) 98-106; Mary Cole, *The Lady's Complete Guide; or, Cookery in All Its Branches* (L, 1788) 1; William Bayer and Paula Wolfert, "A delicious little cookbook scandal," *NY* 10 (12 Dec 1977) 67ff; Richard Sax, "The case of the purloined recipes," *Cuisine* 13 (Feb 1984) 106-10 – noting that, "Like chemical formulations, recipes are considered to be in the public domain. Only the wording of a recipe is protected under the copyright law." On King, see Peter Waldman, "To their dismay, King scholars find a troubling pattern," *Wall Street J* (9 Nov 1990) A1, A4; Paul Dean, "The paper chase," *LA Times* (11 Dec 1990) E1, E10; "Becoming Martin Luther King, Jr. – plagiarism and originality: a round table," *J Amer History* 78 (June 1991) 11-123, q17 from Harold De Wolf, q106 from Horton, the latter cited by John Higham, "Habits of the cloth and standards of the Academy," 106-10. Did Alex Haley belong to the same rhetorical tradition? See Herb Boyd, "Plagiarism and the Roots suits," *First World* 2 (Dec 1979) 31-34.

152. B.D., " 'Second storey work' or inspiration?" *Spectator (L)* 139 (24 Sept 1927) 456-57; K.R. St. Onge, *The Melancholy Anatomy of Plagiarism* (Lanham: U Presses of Amer, 1988) q15, "multiple verbal personality," and ch. 10 on Biden; Loompanics Unlimited, *1990 Main Catalog* (Port Townsend, WA, 1990) 31-40 on new IDs; June Noble and William Noble, *Steal This Plot: A Writer's Guide to Story Structure and Plagiarism* (Middleboro, VT: Eriksson, 1985) and see the thick clippings file on "Plagiarism" at the Herrick Library of the Academy of Motion Pictures, Beverly Hills, CA; Jorge Contreras et al., "NEC v. INTEL: Breaking new ground in the law of copyright," *Harvard J of Law and Technology* 3 (Spr 1990) 209-22 on reverse engineering, as also J.H. Reichman, "Goldstein on copyright law: a realist's approach to a technological age," *Stanford Law R* 43 (Apr 1991) 943-81 at 974; Walter Shapiro, "Biden's familiar quotations," *Time* (28 Sept 1987) 17.

153. Karen Eliot, "Plagiarism as negation in culture," in *Plagiarism: Art as Commodity and Strategies for Its Negation*, ed. Stewart Home (L: Aporia, 1987) 5; Ed Baxter, "A footnote to the Festival of Plagiarism," *Variant* 5 (Sum-Aut 1988) 26-30; Louise Imogen Guiney, "A little treatise on plagiarisms," *Lippincott's Mag* 41 (1888) 786-92, q790, Mr. Tupper being Martin Forquahr Tupper, a popular moralizing poet, author of *Proverbial Philosophy* (1837-38); Monty Cantsin (pseud.) et al., *Smile* 11 (1989) 3 for Jorn, and entire issue, critical of the aestheticism of the Situationist International; Stuart Cosgrove, "In praise of plagiarism," *New Statesman & Society* 2 (1 Sept 1989) 38; Critical Arts Ensemble, "Hypertext," *Real Life* 20 (1990) 21-28, plagiarism as a revolutionary act.

154. D. Hollis, "In defence of plagiarism," *Spectator (L)* 139 (20 Aug 1927) q277; Robert DeMaria et al., *Originality and Attribution* (Poughkeepsie: Vassar, 1988?) q1; Mark Bloch, *The Last Word: Art Strike, Word Strike, Plagiarism and Originality* (NY: Panman, 1990) q28 and throughout for a critique of the 1989 Festival of Plagiarism in Glasgow; Mallon, *Stolen Words*, 146-93 on historian Jayme A. Sokolow; Carol Felsenthal, "Plagiarism: what you don't know could hurt you," *Seventeen* (May 1985) 178, 199-200; Michael Moffatt, *Coming of Age in New Jersey: College in American Culture* (New Brunswick: Rutgers, 1989) q297.

155. Ralph D. Mawdsley, *Legal Aspects of Plagiarism* (Topeka: National Organization on Legal Problems in Education, 1985) on difficulty of prosecution; Neil Hertz, "Teacher and plagiarist," *Harper's Mag* 273 (Nov 1986) 24-28, on the many plagiarists who escape prosecution from teachers unsure of their own originality; Morris Freedman, "Plagiarism among professors or students should not be excused or treated gingerly," *Chronicle of Higher Education* (10 Feb 1988) A48; Avi Adnavourin, "Academic assassination and a three-university plagiarism cover-up: the case of Robert M. Frumkin," *Phil and Social Action* 14 (Jan-Mar 1988) 15-19, the sad fate of a whistleblower; "Case III: Plagiarism," *AHA Perspectives* (Sept 1990) 6. On scientific plagiarism, see Mark S. Davis, "The Perceived Seriousness and Incidence of Ethical Misconduct in Academic Science," Ph.D., Ohio State U, 1989; Morton Hunt, "Did the penalty fit the crime?" *NY Times Mag* 138 (14 May 1989) 36, 69. On Sterne, see Mallon, *Stolen Words*, 21, using W.B.C. Watkins, *Perilous Balance: The Tragic Genius of Swift, Johnson, and Sterne* (Princeton, 1939). On the metaphor of addiction, see Eve K. Sedgwick, "Epidemics of the will," in *Zone 6: Incorporations*, eds. J. Crary and S. Kwinter (NY: Zone, 1992) 582-95.

156. Adams, "Imitators and plagiarists, II," 619-20 on Eccles, as also Paull, *Literary Ethics*, 14-15; Otto Kurz, "Early art forgeries: from the Renaissance to the eighteenth century," *J of the Royal Soc of Arts* 121 (Jan 1973) 87 on Bourdon. I am excluding those forgers who counterfeit current negotiable instruments.

157. I borrow the metaphor of the ricochet from Susan Stewart, *Crimes of Writing* (NY: Oxford U, 1991) 132. Cf. Ian Mackenzie, "Gadamer's hermeneutic and the uses of forgery," *J of Aesthetics and Art Criticism* 45 (Fall 1986) 41-48. On inventive forgers, see esp. W.H. Davenport Adams, "Literary frauds, follies, and mystifications," *Gentleman's Mag* n.s. 45 (1890) 238-54; Carolyn Springer, "History, fantasy, and fraud – the status of historical representation in Sciascia's *Il Consiglio d'Egitto*," *Italia* 66 (Sum 1989) 176-85. On stamps, see Lowell Ragatz, ed., *Fournier Album of Philatelic Forgeries* (Worthington, OH: Janet van den Berg, 1970 [1928]) preface; Jean de Sperati, *La Philatelie sans experts* (P, 1946), memoirs of another stamp forger who deceived all the experts. For Dossena, see Frank Arnau (=Heinrich Schmitt), *Three Thousand Years of Deception in Art and Antiques*, trans. J. Maxwell Brownjohn (L: Cape, 1961) 211-25, q223; David

Sox, *Unmasking the Forger: The Dossena Deception* (L: Unwin Hyman, 1987), blaming unscrupulous dealers for turning Dossena's recreation(s) into forgeries by misattributing them.

158. Robert Harris, *Selling Hitler:... The Faking of the Hitler "Diaries"* (NY: Pantheon, 1986), and cf. Ian Hayward, *Faking It: Art and the Politics of Forgery* (Brighton, Sussex: Harvester, 1987) 2-5 on the irony of faking diaries which, had they been genuine – notes Alan Bullock – would still have been untrustworthy, given Hitler's habit of lying. On the Mormon and other forgeries by Mark Hofmann, see Linda Sillitoe and Allen D. Roberts, *Salamander: The Story of the Mormon Forgery Murders* (Salt Lake City: Signature, 1988). On Hofmann's *The Freeman's Oath*, see James N. Gilreath, ed., *The Judgment of Experts* (Charlottesville: U Presses of Virginia, 1990); Marcus A. McCorison, "The routine handling of forgeries in research libraries: or, can dishonesty ever be routine?" in *Forged Documents*, ed. Pat Bozeman (New Castle: Oak Knoll, 1990). On Mrugalla, see John Dornberg, "Truth or consequences," *Artnews* 87 (Oct 1988) 17-18. On Utrillo, see Gilbert Bagnani, "On fakes and forgeries," *The Phoenix* 14 (1960) q229. On the map, see T.A. Cahill, et al., "The Vinland map, revisited: new compositional evidence on its inks and parchment," *Analytical Chemistry* 59,6 (1987) 829-33; Laurence C. Witten, II, "Vinland's saga recalled," *Yale U Lib Gazette* 64 (Oct 1989) 11-37. I have benefitted here from an interview with Jennifer S. Larson, Owner, Yerba Buena Books, San Francisco, 12 Apr 1991, who tells me that many Hofmann forgeries, still at large, would be unsuspected had not Hofmann boasted about them while in prison.

159. Emily Lawless, "A note on the ethics of literary forgery," *Nineteenth Century* 41 (1897) 84-95, q90; Alessandro Marabottini, "Falsificazioni e disconoscimenti nell'arte contemporanea," *I Problemi di Ulisse* 12 (1973) 156-69 on art in series and industrial production; Anthony Grafton, *Forgers and Critics: Creativity and Duplicity in Western Scholarship* (Princeton: Princeton U, 1990); Mark Jones, ed., *Fake? The Art of Deception* (Berkeley: U Cal, 1990) fig. 49 on chastity belts, for which some evidence does exist, it seems, from fourteenth-century Italy.

160. Curator Sandy Nairne, at symposium, 23-24 Jan 1987, *2D/3D: "Where Do We Go From Here?"* (Newcastle-upon-Tyne Polytechnic, UK, 1988) q4; Grafton, *Forgers and Critics*; Francis Sparshott, "The disappointed art lover," in *The Forger's Art: Forgery and the Philosophy of Art*, ed. Denis Dutton (Berkeley: U Cal, 1983) 246-63, comparing forgery to loveless sex and to a dirty joke; NOVA, "The Fine Art of Faking It," aired on PBS TV, 18 Dec 1991. Eric Hebborn, a forger of more than a thousand Old Master drawings, sold his work only (and therefore ethically, said he) to those who made their name and livelihoods from claims to be able to tell copy from original, fake from genuine. Eric Hebborn, *Drawn to Trouble: The Forging of an Artist* (Edinburgh: Mainstream, 1991) 211-12. See also Lord Kenneth Clark's defense in "Forgeries," *History Today* 29,11 (1979) 724-33, and the attack upon pomposity by Orson Welles (dir), *F for Fake* (Astrosphere/ Saco/Janus, 1973), discussed in terms of film history by Gilles Deleuze, *Cinéma 2: l'image-temps* (P: Minuit, 1985) 191.

161. Cleone Knox (=Magdalen King-Hall), *Diary of a Young Lady of Fashion in 1764-65*, ed. Alexander Blacker Kerr, Introduction by Frank Delaney (L: Folio Soc, 1982 [1925]) q14-15, q16.

162. See the fine book by Wolf Lepenies, *Melancholy and Society*, trans. J. Gaines and D. Jones (Cambridge, MA: Harvard U, 1992). I am also using Madeleine Bouchez, *L'Ennui, de Sénèque à Moravia* (P: Bordas, 1973); Reinhard C. Kuhn, *The Demon of*

Noontide: Ennui in Western Literature (Princeton: Princeton U, 1976) 1-50.

163. Peter Berger, "Some general observations on the problem of work" and Eli Chinoy, "Manning the machines – the assembly-line worker," both in *The Human Shape of Work*, ed. Berger (South Bend, IN: Gateway, 1964) 212-20, 57-65; Lepenies, *Melancholy and Society*, q71, Offenbach; Stanley Wyatt and J.M. Langdon, *Fatigue and Boredom in Repetitive Work* (L, 1937), source for the theory behind Muzak, on which see Jerri A. Husch, "Music of the Workplace: A Study of MUZAK Culture," Ph.D., U Mass, 1984.

164. CBC Six O'Clock News, 28 Jan 1992, sound bite from Roberta Bonder; *OED*, V, 271, "fiend Ennui"; Piero Camporesi, *The Fear of Hell: Images of Damnation and Salvation in Early Modern Europe*, trans. Lucinda Byatt (Cambridge, MA: Polity, 1991); Nova Pharmaceuticals ad, *J of Clinical Psychiatry* 52 (June 1991) opp. 282. Jean-Paul Sartre's *No Exit (Huis Clos)* (1944) begins with Garcin's comment on the drawing room, furnished in a style for which he never cared: "To tell the truth, I had quite a habit of living among furniture that I didn't relish, and in false positions.... Bogus in bogus, so to speak." (Translation by Gilbert Stuart [NY, 1949] 3.)

165. George Steiner, "The great ennui," *In Bluebeard's Castle* (New Haven: Yale U, 1971) 1-26, and cf. Wayne C. Booth, "The discovery of boredom," *The Vocation of a Teacher* (Chicago: U Chicago, 1988) 282-83; Guy Sagnes, *L'Ennui dans la littérature française de Flaubert à Laforgue, 1848-1884* (P: Colin, 1969) q15 from Jules Barbey d'Aurevilly, 1867; Emile Tardieu, *L'Ennui: étude psychologique* (P, 1903) q1-2; Orrin E. Klapp, *Overload and Boredom: Essays on the Quality of Life in the Information Society* (NY: Greenwood, 1986) 30 on "placebo" institutions "which produce artificial pleasures and thrills to compensate for lack of such in real life," and throughout; Woodburn Heron, "The pathology of boredom," *Sci Amer* 196 (Jan 1957) 52-56 on sensory deprivation; Norman D. Sundberg et al., "Boredom in young adults: gender and cultural comparisons," *J Cross-Cultural Psychology* 22 (June 1991) 209-23.

166. Kuhn, *Demon of Noontide*, q11 from Gide, q146 from Mme Du Deffand; Robin Damrad-Frye and James D. Laird, "The experience of boredom: the role of the self-perception of attention," *J of Personality and Social Psychology* 57 (Aug 1984) 315-20.

167. *OED*, III, 917; "Copy-cats," *Spectator (L)* 108 (23 Mar 1912) 468-69. On copycatting as a twentieth-century cultural phenomenon and *idée fixe*, see Damon Runyon, "Larcenous ladies," *Short Takes* (NY, 1946) 407-08; Margaret Engel, "Copycat goods: are you buying dangerous fakes?" *Glamour* 83 (Mar 1985) 246; Andrew N. Meltzoff, "Imitation of televised models by infants," *Child Development* 59 (1988) 1221-29 (two-week-old infants copying the gestures they see on television); Sharon Lerner, in cooperation with the Children's TV Workshop's "Sesame Street," *Big Bird's Copycat Day* (NY: Random House, 1984) and contrast Kathleen and Donald Herson, *The Copycat* (Boston: Atheneum, 1989) also for preschoolers; David Dressler, "Case of the copycat criminal," *NY Times Mag* (10 Dec 1961) 42; Neal Karlen with Michael Reese, "A copycat assault?" *Newsweek* (22 Oct 1984) 38, after a docudrama; Martin Scorsese (dir), *Taxi Driver* (Columbia, 1976), whose copycat vigilante was then copycatted by a man who pursued Jodie Foster, an actress in the movie; "Copycat killers on the prowl," *Time* (7 July 1986) 41, wondering whether multiple murders with the same "M.O." were copycat murders; John P. Murray, "Television and violence: implications of the Surgeon General's research programme," in *Children and Television*, ed. Ray Brown (Beverly Hills: Sage, 1976) 285-96; Patricia M. Greenfield, *Mind and Media: The Effects of Television, Video Games,*

and Computers (Cambridge, MA: Harvard U, 1984) 50; Hugh Pentecost (pseud.), *The Copycat Killers* (Boston: G.K. Hall, 1983) 7-8.

168. J.-B. Cazauvieilh, *Du Suicide, de l'aliénation mentale et des crimes contre les personnes* (P, 1840) 49; Amariah Brigham, "Statistics of suicides in the United States," *Amer J of Insanity* 1 (Jan 1845) 234, quoted in Howard I. Kushner, *Self-Destruction in the Promised Land: A Psychocultural Biology of American Suicide* (New Brunswick, NJ: Rutgers, 1989) 44-45; A.J.F. Brierre de Boismont, *Du suicide et de la folie suicide*, 2nd ed. (P, 1865) 234.

169. Kushner, *Self-Destruction in the Promised Land*, ch. 4 on statistics, as also Olive Anderson, *Suicide in Victorian and Edwardian England* (Oxford: Clarendon, 1987) Part I; Kevin McCoy, "Sparks over exorcism," *NY Daily News* (6 Mar 1990) 5, Ozzy Osbourne; David P. Phillips, "Natural experiments on the effects of mass media violence on fatal aggression," *Advances in Experimental Social Psychology* 19 (1986) 207-50; Larry Martz et al., "The copycat suicides: two death pacts kill six troubled teenagers, triggering fears of a new national epidemic," *Newsweek* (23 Mar 1987) 28-29.

170. Vladimir Jankelevitch, *L'Aventure, l'ennui, le sérieux* (P: Aubier, 1963) 113ff on Schopenhauer; Greil Marcus, *Lipstick Traces* (Cambridge, MA: Harvard U, 1989) 80, punk; Patricia M. Spacks, "The necessity of boredom," *Virginia Q R* 65 (Fall 1989) 581-99, q590 on materialism from "a Buddhist" otherwise unidentified, the rest from Spacks herself; Saul Bellow, *Humboldt's Gift* (NY: Viking, 1975) 201, 203; Lepenies, *Melancholy and Society*, q197.

171. Brigitte Jordan and Nancy Fuller, *Birth in Four Cultures* (Montreal: Eden, 1980) q16; *Sony Corp. of America et al. v. Universal City Studios, Inc.*, 464 U.S. 417-500 (1984) at 421, 445; Deborah S. Zwick, "Photography as a tool toward increased self-awareness of the aging self," *Art Psychotherapy* 5 (1978) 135-41.

CHAPTER EIGHT: DISCERNMENT

1. Jean de La Fontaine, "Les Amours de Psyche et de Cupidon," *Oeuvres complètes*, ed. Louis Moland (P, 1876) VI, 3-194, discussed by Julien Eymard, *Le Thème du miroir dans la poésie française (1540-1815)* (Lille: Université de Toulouse-Le-Mirail, 1975) 180ff, and 7 for riddle, next paragraph. On mirrors as both vanity and verity, illusion and disillusion, themes I must neglect, see Jürgen Baltrusaitas, *Le Miroir: essai sur une légende scientifique* (P: Elmayan, 1978); James Fernandez, "Reflections on looking into mirrors," *Semiotica* 30 (1980) 27-39; Jenijoy La Belle, *Herself Beheld: The Literature of the Looking Glass* (Ithaca: Cornell U, 1988).

2. Henry James, "The Real Thing" (1892) in *The Complete Tales*, ed. Leon Edel (Philadelphia: Lippincott, 1963) VIII, 229-58, and cf. Miles Orvell, *The Real Thing: Imitation and Authenticity in American Culture, 1880-1940* (Chapel Hill: U North Carolina, 1989) 122-23. On Anyone, see Peter Sloterdijk, "Anyone, or: the most real subject of modern diffuse cynicism," in his *Critique of Cynical Reason*, trans. Michael Eldred (Minneapolis: U Minnesota, 1987) 195-210, 195 for Anyone as a lay figure. I am also using Kenelm Burridge, *Someone, No One: An Essay on Individuality* (Princeton: Princeton U, 1979).

3. Oscar Wilde, "London models," *English Illustrated Mag* 6 (Jan 1889) q313, q315; Muriel Segal, *Painted Ladies: Models of the Great Artists* (NY: Stein & Day, 1972) 134-35 on Simonetta; Frances Borzello, *The Artist's Model* (L: Junction, 1982) 5; *Maler und Modell* (Baden-Baden: Staatliche Kunsthalle, 1969); France Borel, *The Seduction of Venus: Art-*

ists and Models, trans. Jean-Marie Clarke (NY: Skira/Rizzoli, 1990) 96, Hébuterne, and throughout. See also Karen L. Kleinfelder, *The Artist, His Model, Her Image, His Gaze: Picasso's Pursuit of the Model* (Chicago: U Chicago, 1993).

4. Keith Christiansen, "Caravaggio and *L'Esempio davanti del naturale*," *Art Bull* 68 (Sept 1986) 421-45; James H. Rubin, "Academic life-drawing in eighteenth-century France," *Eighteenth-Century French Life-Drawing* (Princeton: Art Museum, 1977) 15-42; Borzello, *Artist's Model*, 16-27; John Milner, *The Studios of Paris* (New Haven: Yale U, 1988) 13-17; E. McSherry Fowble, "Without a blush: the movement toward acceptance of the nude as an art form in America, 1800-1825," *Winterthur Portfolio* 9 (1974) 113.

5. Deborah Cherry, *Painting Women: Victorian Women Artists* (L: Routledge, 1993) ch. 3; Segal, *Painted Ladies*, 153 on Langtree; Lois W. Banner, *American Beauty* (NY: Knopf, 1983) 255-65, beauty contests and the status of models; Borzello, *Artist's Model*, 27-29, 33, 51-53, 60, 62, 93; "Ballad of the professional model," *Punch* (27 Jan 1894) 41; Albert D. Vandam, "About models (apropos of Trilby)," *Saturday R* 80 (1895) 649.

6. Charlotte Adams, "Artists' models in New York," *Century* 25 (Feb 1883) 569-77; Vance Thompson, "Women who pose," *Idler* 22 (1902-03) 526-35; George Holme, "Artists' models," *Munsey's Mag* 10 (1893-94) q528 on Margot; Lois Cantwell, *Modeling* (NY: Watts, 1986) 17, on "real-people" models. On the modernist inclination to prefer amateur or nonprofessional models to professional models in twentieth-century painting, see Elizabeth Hollander, "Artists' models in 19th-century America," *Annals of Scholarship* 10, 3-4 (1993) 300-01.

7. *OED*, I, 787, no date earlier than 1905 for the use of *au naturel* to mean "undressed"; Harriett Shepard and Lenore Meyer, *Posing for the Camera* (NY: Hastings House, 1960) q11; A. Van B. Berg, "Art in photography and photographic models," *Cosmopolitan* 21 (1896) q22; Ruth Tolman, World Modeling Assoc, phone interview, 16 Aug 1991, esp. on the insistence, now, that "the motion is the pose"; Burt A. Folkart, "Cleo Dorman: artists' model for thousands," *LA Times* (10 Aug 1990) A30. Cindy Sherman, posing as a celebrated film actress or model for her own photos, has played and preyed upon these relationships; see esp. the catalog to her *Déjà Vu 25 octobre – 13 novembre 1982* (Dijon, 1982).

8. On vanishing names, see esp. Adrian Room, *A Dictionary of Pseudonyms and Their Origins* (Jefferson, NC: McFarland, 1989).

9. Dare I use *real* without inverted commas? Then again, a magazine about celebrities and "very interesting" folk started up in 1988 under the title *Real People*. But contrast a defense of anonymity as that toward which art most aspires: E.M. Forster, "Anonymity: an inquiry," *Atlantic Monthly* 136 (1925) 588-95. On pseudonymity and masks, see Gerhart Söhn, *Literaten hinter Masken: Eine Betrachtung über das Pseudonym in der Literatur* (Berlin: Haude & Spener, 1974), esp. 90ff on use of pseudonyms by women.

10. Borel, *Seduction of Venus*, 76, 149ff on Delacroix; Katharine Pyle, "Some types of artists' models," *Cosmopolitan* 21 (1896) 21, hiked fees; James Lord, *A Giacometti Portrait*, rev. ed. (NY: Farrar Straus Giroux, 1980) q10. See also René Magritte's *The Attempt of the Impossible* (1928), a painting of a painter painting out of thin air a model standing across from him, her left arm incomplete.

11. Samuel D. Warren and Louis D. Brandeis, "The Right to Privacy," *Harvard Law R* 4 (1890) 193-220, at 195, 205, 211, 214; J. Thomas McCarthy, *The Rights of Publicity and Privacy* (Deerfield, IL: Clark Boardman Callaghan, 1990, updated 4/1993) release #7, 1-11-1-13.

12. *Roberson v. Rochester Folding-Box Co. and Franklin Mills Co.*, 65 NY Supp. 1109 (1900) at 1109.

13. *Roberson v. Rochester Folding Box Co. et al.*, 64 App. Div. 30 (NY Sup Ct, 1901) at 31, 36; Peter L. Felcher and Edward L. Rubin, "Privacy, publicity, and the portrayal of real people by the media," *Yale Law J* 88 (July 1979) 1578 n8 on Cooley.

14. *Abigail M. Roberson, an Infant, by Margaret E. Bell, her Guardian, ad litem, Respondent, v. The Rochester Folding Box Co. et al., Appellants*, 171 NY 538 (1902) at 545 for absurdity, at 544 for implication, at 554 for line of demarcation.

15. Editorial, "An actionable right of privacy?" *Yale Law J* 12 (1902–03) 34–38, q37, q38. As Warren and Brandeis were writing, Anglo-American courts were starting to concede the innocence of those who, for the sake of privacy or commercial pseudonymity, executed instruments under an assumed name: T.W. Brown, "Forgery of fictitious names," *Amer Law R* 30 (1896) 505–06, 511. See also Samuel Spring, *Risks and Rights in Publishing, Television, Radio, Motion Pictures, Advertising and the Theater*, 2nd ed. (NY: Norton, 1956) 14, suggesting that the New York statute ensured the growth of commercial modeling as a profession.

16. "Parker taken to task by an indignant woman," *NY Times* (27 July 1904) 1:5.

17. *Pavesich v. New England Life Insurance Co.*, 122 Ga. 190 (1905) at 213–14, quoting *Roberson v. Rochester Folding Box Co. et al.*, 171 N.Y. 538 (1902) at 563 for Gray.

18. *Ibid.*, 220.

19. *Ibid.*, at 213–14, discussed by McCarthy, *Rights of Privacy and Publicity*, 1–17. Cf. Edouard Sauvel, *De la propriété artistique en photographie, spécialement en matière de portraits* (P, 1897) on the distinction in French law between the purchase of a painted portrait, in which the purchaser is entitled to reproduce it at will, and the purchase of a print of a photographic portrait, in which the photographer owns the rights to reproduction of the negative while sitters control the rights to publication and distribution.

20. See, for a concise history, McCarthy, *Rights of Publicity and Privacy*, who notes that the right of privacy has no standing in English law but has since the 1790s had unquestioned standing, as a moral right, in French law. His ch. 6 surveys the international standing of a right of publicity. I will follow the course of U.S. law, whose ox-bows are most revealing.

21. *Chaplin v. Amador et al.*, 269 P. 544 (Ct. App. 1928). Did the lawyers at IBM appreciate the irony when they began to use (by permission) a Chaplin lookalike to promote their copiers and personal computers in the 1970s and '80s? See Jane Caputi, "On remembering and forgetting – Charlie Chaplin, IBM, and 1984," *J of Popular Film and Television* 14 (Sum 1986) 76–79.

22. *Woody Allen v. National Video*, 610 F Supp 612 (1985) – the defense claiming (at 618) that the ad depicted a Woody Allen fan "so dedicated that he has adopted his appearance and mannerisms, who is able to live out his fantasy by receiving star treatment at National Video"; the court would have none of this fantasy. See also William R. Greer, "The double life of a look-alike," *NY Times* (18 Jan 1984) qC16 from Boroff. Cf. Randy Eder, "When imitation is not the sincerest form of flattery: the search for a standard for performers' rights," *J Copyright Soc USA* 37 (Apr 1990) 407–37. Jane Gaines, "Dead ringer: Jacqueline Onassis and the look-alike," first in *South Atlantic Q* 88 (Spr 1989) 461–86, revised in her *Contested Culture: The Image, the Voice, and the Law* (Chapel Hill: U North Carolina, 1991) ch. 3, discusses the problem of (p. 85) "two different legal subjects who assert proprietorship over the same photographic likeness, on the basis

that they are both entitled to 'authorize' the use of their own images," a problem posed by *Onassis v. Christian Dior NY, Inc.*, 472 NYS.2d. 254 (S.Ct. N.Y.Co. 1983).

23. *Ed Sullivan v. Ed Sullivan Radio & T.V.*, 145 NY Supp 2d 114 (1955) at 116, appealed and reversed, 152 NY Supp 2d 227 (1956). Ironically, Ed Sullivan the television host was the surviving singleton of twins, claims Kay Cassill, *Twins: Nature's Amazing Mystery* (NY: Atheneum, 1982) 129. I first heard about the Sullivan case (but not about the twins) during a discussion with Martin Bressler and Robert Panzer, respectively counsel and executive director for the Visual Artists and Galleries Association, NY City, 17 Jan 1991. That discussion has become the springboard for this section, though our opinions diverge.

24. See esp. "Speaking of pictures...these look-alikes win watches," *Life* (17 Jan 1938) 2-4, an early contest won by Mrs. Oscar Nelson as aviatrix Amelia Earhart, who had vanished over the Pacific the year before – as if the judges hoped to bring Earhart back to *Life* via this twin; John Mendelssohn and Denise Zweben, "Did anyone ever say you look just like...?" *LA Mag* (Nov 1980) 94-102. For Ron Smith, see a clipping from the *LA Herald Examiner* (7 Oct 1978) in the "Actors & Actresses: Look-a-likes" file, Margaret Herrick Lib, Academy of Motion Picture Arts and Sciences, Beverly Hills, where I also found Marie Moneysmith, "The (mirror) image of success," *The Hollywood Reporter 53rd Annual* (Nov 1983) q110 on getting wrapped up. The lookalike mania, which began ca. 1977 in the U.S., had reached the former Soviet Union by 1990: "A stageful of impostors," *Soviet Life* (June 1991) 62 – among the winners a Raisa Gorbachev, whose real counterpart was in the audience. The redoubling has gone so far that NBC TV's *Hard Copy*, 6 Aug 1991, profiling a brothel that had offered look-alikes of Jean Harlow, Clara Bow, Mae West et al., and which in its heyday attracted the likes of Jackie Gleason and Humphrey Bogart, reenacted a scene at the brothel using hired celebrity lookalikes for the women and the men.

25. Stuart Goldman, "In Vegas, dead legends live on and on," *LA Times* (18 Dec 1983) Calendar Sect., 4. As of 1987, over one hundred American women (and how many men?) had livelihoods impersonating Marilyn Monroe: Bob Greene, "Some like it hot," *Esquire* (Oct 1987) 59-62. After all, said one of them, she and Marilyn were both Geminis: Patricia W. Biederman, "Movie look-alikes keep a family busy," *LA Times* (23 Nov 1984) CCII, 1-2.

26. Gaines, *Contested Culture*, 175, discussing *Lugosi v. Universal Pictures, Inc.*, 25 Cal.3d 813, and see all of her ch. 6. Of course, Lugosi's Dracula was already descended, through many previous versions, from the 1897 book by Bram Stoker.

27. *Schuyler v. Curtis*, 15 N.Y. Supp 787 (1892) at 788; *Schuyler v. Curtis*, 147 N.Y. 434 (1895) at 445.

28. *Schuyler v. Curtis et al.*, 19 N.Y. Supp 264 (1892) at 265; *Schuyler v. Curtis et al.*, 147 N.Y. 434 (1895) at 447, reversal. Justice Gray had dissented here too (at 453-55). Since "the jurisdiction of equity is not made to depend upon the existence of corporeal property," Gray believed that the mantle of the "sacred right of privacy...should cover not only the person of the individual, but every personal interest which he possesses and is entitled to regard as private."

29. Spring, *Risks and Rights*, 21, Kentucky case; McCarthy, *Rights of Publicity and Privacy*, q2-7 from Justice Potter Stewart in *Rosenblatt v. Baer*, 383 US 75 (1966) at 92, and see 1-40-44; Gaines, *Contested Culture*, 176ff; California Civil Code, par. 990, "Deceased personality."

30. S.J. Stoljar, *Groups and Entities* (Canberra: Australian National U, 1973) q5, and throughout for a critique of the notion of legal personality; David P. Derham, "Theories of legal personality," in *Legal Personality and Political Pluralism*, ed. L.C. Webb (Melbourne: Melbourne U, 1958) 5-13; Morton J. Horowitz, *The Transformation of American Law, 1870-1960* (NY: Oxford U, 1992) 100-07, debates over corporate personhood.

31. Erving Goffman, *The Presentation of Self in Everyday Life* (Garden City, NY: Doubleday, 1959); John Rowan, *Subpersonalities: The People Inside Us* (L: Routledge, 1990); Mark Poster, *Critical Theory and Poststructuralism* (Ithaca: Cornell, 1989) 53ff on the decentered self; Elinor and Joe Selame, *The Company Image: Building Your Identity* (NY: Wiley, 1988) and cf. *Spectrum*, trade journal from Personal Image Merchandising, Minneapolis; Gary K. Wolf, *Who Censored Roger Rabbit?* (NY: St. Martin's, 1981) q17 –a novel predicated on the use of cartoon stand-ins for all indignities suffered by cartoon stars, who can create Doppelgängers at will, and cf. David B. Feldman, "Finding a home for fictional characters," *Cal Law R* 78 (May 1990) 687-720. On holography, read Paul Pietsch, *Shufflebrain* (Boston: Houghton Mifflin, 1981), hologramic neurology, and see Brigitte Burgmer's *Pribram auf der Suche nach dem Engram* in *Lichte-Blicke* (Frankfurt: Deutsches Filmmuseum, 1984) 164; Marion J. Francoz, "Holography: a new kind of perception," *New Orleans R* 8 (Wint 1981) 55-58; Peter Zee, trans. Deborah Fahrend, "Dieter Jung: the authenticity of the image," *Holosphere* 13 (Fall 1985) 16-18; Philippe Boissonnet, trans. M. Grand and R. Lafleur, "Holography and the imaginary double," *Leonardo* 22,3/4 (1989) 375-78. (I thank Ron Erickson of the Museum of Holography, NY City, for his help.) On narcissism, see esp. Christopher Lasch, *The Culture of Narcissism* (NY: Norton, 1979), put into context by Eugene T. Gendlin, "A philosophical critique of narcissism," in *Pathologies of the Modern Self*, ed. David M. Levin (NY: NYU, 1987) 270-303, and by C. Fred Alford, *Narcissism: Socrates, the Frankfurt School, and Psychoanalytic Theory* (New Haven: Yale U, 1988). See Tobin Siebers, *The Mirror of Medusa* (Berkeley: U Cal, 1983) on the mythic nexus between narcissism and celebrity.

32. Bill Watterson, *Scientific Progress Goes "Boink"* (Kansas City: Andrews and McMeel, 1991), 55-61, a collection of his "Calvin and Hobbes" syndicated comic strips.

33. Philip Kerr, ed., *The Penguin Book of Lies* (NY: Viking, 1990) 3; Pamela S. Zurer, "Workshop airs research ethics and monitoring of scientific misconduct," *Chemical & Engineering News* 65 (5 Oct 1987) q44, Patricia K. Woolf; Paul H. Weaver, *News and the Culture of Lying* (NY: Free Press, 1993).

34. See Perez Zagorin, *Ways of Lying: Dissimulation, Persecution, and Conformity in Early Modern Europe* (Cambridge, MA: Harvard U, 1990).

35. Johann P. Sommerville, "The 'New Art of Lying': equivocation, mental reservation, and casuistry," in *Conscience and Casuistry in Early Modern Europe*, ed. Edmund Leites (NY: Cambridge U, 1988) 159-84, q160.

36. Sommerville, "The 'New Art of Lying,'" 176-79, the title in quotes referring to a tract of 1624 by Henry Mason, who attacked the practice; Lowell Gallagher, *Medusa's Gaze: Casuistry and Conscience in the Renaissance* (Stanford: Stanford U, 1991) q4, 6-7, 263-64, and throughout, an invaluable work.

37. John Arbuthnot, *Proposals for printing a very curious discourse . . . intitled, Pseudologia Politike, or A Treatise of the Art of Political Lying: with an abstract of the first volume of the said treatise* (L, 1712) but also attributed to Jonathan Swift (as by Kerr, *Penguin Book of Lies*, 151-55) q13-14, q17-18, q19; Robert M. Adams, *Bad Mouth* (Berkeley: U Cal, 1977) q60.

38. Hector Gavin, *Feigned and Fictitious Diseases, Chiefly of Soldiers and Seamen* (L,

1843) ii (quoting F.E. Foderé's *Traité de médecine légale* [Paris, 1813] II, 452), vii, 10, 13-14, 15, 36, 51, 54.

39. Sir John Collie, *Malingering and Feigned Illness*, 2nd ed. (L, 1917 [1913]) vii, qxi, 1, 3, q4, 191-92; A.B. Jones and L.J. Llewellyn, *Malingering, or the Simulation of Disease* (Philadelphia, 1917) 80, quoted in Philip J. Resnick, "Malingered psychosis," in *Clinical Assessment of Malingering and Deception*, ed. Richard Rogers (NY: Guilford, 1988) q44.

40. Lewis R. Yealland, *Hysterical Disorders of Warfare* (L, 1918) ch. 9, q244; Elmer F. Southard, *Shell-Shock and Other Neuropsychiatric Problems* (NY: Arno, 1973 [1919]) esp. 311, 439, 446, q657, 661-62; Collie, *Malingering*, 9, use of faradic current. Cf. Robert David Ritchie, "One History of 'Shellshock,'" Ph.D., U Cal, San Diego, 1986. For Yossarian, see Joseph Heller, *Catch-22* (NY: Dell, 1961).

41. See Jason Brandt, "Malingered amnesia," in Rogers, *Clinical Assessment*, 65-83; James L. Cavanaugh and Richard Rogers, eds., "Malingering and deception," special issue of *Behavioral Sciences & the Law* 2 (Wint 1984); Erin D. Bigler, "Neuropsychology and malingering," *J Consulting and Clinical Psychology* 58 (Apr 1990) 244-48, with reply by David Faust and Thomas J. Guilmete, 248-50, on inability of psychologists to detect malingerers; Ellen Rothchild, "Fictitious twins, factitious illness," *Psychiatry: Interpersonal and Biological Processes* 57,4 (1994) 326-47; Stanley Rabinowitz et al., "Malingering in the clinical setting," *Psychological Reports* 67 (Dec 1990) 1315-18, personality disorder.

42. Guy Durandin, *Les Fondements du mensonge* (P: Flammarion, 1972) on lying as central to our humanity; H.G. Wells, *Love and Mr. Lewisham* (L, 1924 [1899]) ch. 23, q205.

43. Sissela Bok, *Lying: Moral Choice in Public and Private Life* (NY: Pantheon, 1978) q244 and throughout; *OED*, VIII, q900 from *Gentleman's Mag* 11 (1741) 647, and cf. "Mensonge," *EDSAM* X, 336-37; Wells, *Love and Mr. Lewisham*, q209. Timothy J. Cooney, speechwriter for several presidential candidates but uncredentialed as a philosopher, submitted a manuscript to Random House in 1983 together with a forged letter of endorsement from a notable philosopher. Cooney's book, accepted by Random House but, after the forgery was revealed, published by a smaller press, was entitled *Telling Right from Wrong: What Is Moral, What Is Immoral, and What Is Neither One Nor the Other*. See Paul Kurtz, "Publisher's Note" to Timothy J. Cooney, *Telling Right from Wrong* (Buffalo: Prometheus, 1985); Ari Posner, "The culture of plagiarism," *The New Republic* (18 Apr 1988) 19-24, on the blurbs Cooney invented for his bookjacket.

44. Richard Asher, "Munchausen's Syndrome," *Lancet* 1 (1951) 339-41.

45. Herzl R. Spiro, "Chronic factitious illness," *Archives of General Psychiatry* 18 (1968) 569-79, q569; Donald A. Swanson, "The Munchausen Syndrome," *Amer J Psychotherapy* 35 (1981) 436-43; Peter Reich and Lila A. Gottfried, "Factitious disorders in a teaching hospital," *Annals Internal Med* 99 (1983) 240-47. More men than women have been diagnosed with Munchausen's, perhaps because male physicians dismiss women with factitious complaints as "crocks," while men who assume sick roles have been privileged with a syndrome. However, in a newly defined Munchausen Syndrome by Proxy, a parent, usually a mother, is found to be making a child sick, using the child's constant or baffling illnesses to draw attention to herself as a concerned, devoted, caring martyr.

46. Allen J. Cunien, "Psychiatric and medical syndromes associated with deception," in Rogers, ed., *Clinical Assessment*, 21-25; Ellen L. Toth and Andrea Baggaley, "Coexistence of Munchausen Syndrome and Multiple Personality Disorder," *Psychiatry* 54 (May 1991) 176-83.

47. Hilary Klein, "Couvade syndrome: male counterpart to pregnancy," *Int J of Psychiatry in Med* 21 (1991) 57-69; Patrice Laplante, "The couvade syndrome," *Canadian Family Physician* 37 (July 1991) 1633-36, 1660; Jack Heinowitz, *Pregnant Fathers: How Fathers Can Enjoy and Share the Experiences of Pregnancy and Childbirth* (Englewood Cliffs, NJ: Prentice-Hall, 1982); Jodi Duckett, "Empathy belly lets dad endure pregnancy," *LA Times* (18 May 1990) E8; Roberta Sandberg, Cardiff, CA, interview, 18 Feb 1993.

48. Nor Hall, "Broodmale: a psychological essay on men in childbirth," introduction to Warren R. Dawson, *The Custom of Couvade* (Dallas: Spring, 1989 [1929]); Karen E. Paige and Jeffery M. Paige, *The Politics of Reproductive Ritual* (Berkeley: U Cal, 1981) 40-41, 189-208; Rita M. Gross, "Couvade," *ER*, IV, 132-33; Robert Munroe et al., "The couvade: a psychological analysis," *Ethos* 1 (1973) 30-74; Gwen J. Broude, "Rethinking the couvade," *Amer Anthropologist* 90 (1988) 902-11, with response by Robert L. Munroe and Ruth H. Munroe, *ibid.*, 91 (1989) 730-38; Alan Dundes, "Couvade in Genesis," in *Studies in Aggadah and Jewish Folklore*, eds. I. Ben-Ami and J. Dan (Jerusalem: Magnes, 1983) 35-53.

49. *The People, ex. rel Bush and Higby, v. Collins*, 7 Johnson 548 (1811), 4 NY Reports; *Padgett v. Lawrence*, 10 Paige 170 (1843) q176-77, 4 NY Chancery Reports. Cf. *Fleet v. Youngs*, 11 Wendell 523 (1833), 11 NY Common Law Reports, Court of Errors, on Samuel Youngs, Jr. Second.

50. Alice R. Rossi, "Naming of children in middle-class families," *Amer Sociological R* 30 (1965) q504n.

51. Louis Perouas et al., *Léonard, Marie, Jean, et les autres: les prénoms en Limousin depuis un millénaire* (P: CNRS, 1984) 12, 22, 33-34, 49, 121; Anne Lefebvre-Teillard, *Le Nom: droit et histoire* (P: PUF, 1990) esp. 102-14; Arlette Lebigne, "Le Nom de famille, cet inconnu," *L'Histoire* 138 (Nov 1990) 84-87. Renaissance scholars, desiring to credit individual achievement, began researches that culminated in Johannes Moller's *Homonymoscopia* (1697), one same-name differentiated from the next across a thousand pages: Archer Taylor and Fredric J. Mosher, *The Bibliographical History of Anonyma and Pseudonyma* (Chicago, 1951) 4n, 12n.

52. Catherine Cameron, *The Name Givers* (Englewood Cliffs, NJ: Prentice-Hall, 1983) 28-29, q31; *OED*, VIII, 314, "Junior," and XIV, 825, "Second," and 972, "Senior." A suffixed II refers back to a patrilineal uncle or grandfather and should not be confused, as often it is in our culture of the copy, with Jr. Etiquette requires that one's signature change at each death. Depending on one's attachment to a Jr. or III, "This could feel like a whole identity change," as Richard L. Zweigenhaft et al. suggest in "The psychological impact of names," *J Social Psychology* 110 (1980) 203-10, when "junior" implies something less than the "real thing," while numerals imply a link in a valuable chain.

53. Robert Crichton, *The Great Impostor* (NY: Random House, 1959); *OED*, XVI, 270, "spittin' image" (1901) < "spit an' image" (1895) < "very spit of," as in "the very spit of your father" (1836); Richard Lasky, *Evaluation of Criminal Responsibility in Multiple Personality and Related Dissociative Disorders* (Springfield: Thomas, 1982) 87-88.

54. Marc Shell, *Children of the Earth: Literature, Politics and Nationhood* (NY: Oxford, 1993) on the problem of consanguinity; Alex Shoumatoff, *The Mountain of Names: A History of the Human Family* (NY: Simon & Schuster, 1985) q244 on genetics; Rex Taylor, "John Doe, Jr.: a study of his distribution in space, time, and the social structure," *Social Forces* 53 (1974) 11-21, and cf. Andrew Billingsley, *Climbing Jacob's Ladder: The Enduring Legacy of African-American Families* (NY: Simon and Schuster, 1992). Cameron, *The*

Name Givers, 35, says that abused children and boys in detention homes more often bear a father's name than do other children.

55. *Davis v. Davis*, Tenn Cir. Ct Blount Cy, No. E 14496, (Sept 21, 1989), abstracted in 15 Family Law Reporter 1551; Lee May, "Estranged wife awarded custody of frozen embryos," *LA Times* (22 Sept 1989) 1, 19; Janice G. Raymond, "Of ice and men: the big chill over women's reproductive rights," *Issues in Reproductive and Genetic Engineering* 3,1 (1990) 45–50. Most IVF programs implant embryos (called "preembryos" in Britain) consisting of no more than eight cells.

56. Raymond, "Of ice and men," 46–47; James Lieber, "The case of the frozen embryo," *Saturday Evening Post* 261 (Oct 1989) 50–53. It was also men – ten men and one woman – who made the *Ethical Considerations of the New Reproductive Technologies* for the American Fertility Society in 1986 (Birmingham, AL: AFS, 1986), and who decided that (p. 5S) "the interests and values supporting the right to reproduce by sexual intercourse apply equally to noncoital activities involving the extracorporeal preembryo." That phrase, "extracorporeal preembryo," is modern jargon for the first stage of couvade. On the degree to which the medical establishment has been insensitive to the tribulations of women undergoing the IVF procedure, see esp. Renate Klein, *The Exploitation of Desire: Women's Experiences with In Vitro Fertilisation* (Geelong, Victoria: Women's Studies Summer Institute / Deakin U, 1989).

57. László András Magyar, "History of artificial insemination," *Therapia Hungarica* 39,3 (1991) 151–53, calling attention also to the demonological myth of incubi stealing the nocturnal emissions of men to secretly introduce semen into the wombs of women; John Stoltenberg, *Refusing To Be a Man: Essays on Sex and Justice* (Portland, OR: Breitenbush, 1989) 91–100, q96; J. Marion Sims, *Clinical Notes on Uterine Surgery* (NY, 1873 [1866]) 364–69, 375; G.J. Barker-Benfield, *The Horrors of the Half-Known Life: Male Attitudes Toward Women and Sexuality in Nineteenth-Century America* (NY: Harper, 1976) 110, the sons. Sims noted that George Harley, M.D., of London had previously tried injections of semen into the uterine cavity, without result. His failures, like those of Sims, were probably due to bad timing: nineteenth-century doctors thought that women were most fertile in the first week after their period, and scheduled injections accordingly.

58. T.M. McIntosh, "Artificial impregnation," *Medical World* 27 (1909) 197; A.D. Hard, "Artificial impregnation," *ibid.*, 163; N.J. Hamilton, "Artificial impregnation," *ibid.*, 253. On French successes, including a twin pregnancy, see André Girault, *Etude sur la génération artificielle dans l'espèce humaine* (P, 1869), cited in Matthew D. Mann, ed., *A System of Gynecology by American Authors* (Philadelphia, 1887) I, 475–76; Derek Jones, "Artificial procreation, societal reconceptions: legal insight from France," *Amer J Comparative Law* 36 (Sum 1988) 525–45.

Often cited here is a secondhand account about the English physician John Hunter, who sometime in the late eighteenth century advised a husband with a defective urethra to insert into his wife's vagina semen taken up with a syringe, wherefrom a baby was born. See Everard Home, "An account of the dissection of an hermaphrodite dog," *Phil Trans Royal Soc of L* 18,2 (1799) 162, dating the pregnancy-by-syringe to the years before Lazaro Spallanzani had done his studies of animal reproduction. The date is vague, chauvinist, and dubious, since Spallanzani published his first studies in 1768, when Hunter was not likely to have been consulted in such a case.

59. Hard, "Artificial impregnation," 163–64; C.H. Newth, "Contracted pelves – arti-

ficial impregnation," *Medical World* 27 (1909) 197; Hard, "Artificial impregnation," rebuttal, *ibid.*, q306, my italics.

60. Peter Singer and Deane Wells, *The Reproduction Revolution: New Ways of Making Babies* (Oxford: Oxford U, 1984) 72, numbers. Robert H. Blank, *Regulating Reproduction* (NY: Columbia U, 1990) 25, estimates that a half million children in the U.S. had been born through artificial insemination by 1989.

61. Singer and Wells, *Reproduction Revolution*, ch. 1, a good account of the development of IVF; Peter Gwynne et al., "All about that baby," *Newsweek* 92 (7 Aug 1978) 67ff on the Browns.

62. Carol Delaney, "The meaning of paternity and the Virgin Birth debate," *Man*, n.s. 21 (1986) 494–513; Blank, *Regulating Reproduction*, 30, the four thousand; Mary Anne Warren, "IVF and women's interests: an analysis of feminist concerns," *Bioethics* 2,1 (1988) 37–57, putting IVF in the context of hysterectomies and the male biomedical establishment's control of research on women's infertility, for which see also Adele E. Clarke, "Controversy and the development of reproductive sciences," *Social Problems* 37 (Feb 1990) 18–39; Downie, *Babymaking*, 84; May, "Estranged wife," 19. On the French background, see Catherine Labrusse-Riou, "Should there be governmental guidelines in bioethics? The French approach," *Boston College Int and Comparative Law R* 12 (Wint 1989) 89–101. For an English perspective, see Mary Warnock, *A Question of Life: The Warnock Report on Human Fertilisation and Embryology* (Oxford: Blackwell, 1984–85) 56.

63. *Davis v. Davis*, Tenn Ct. App., No. 180 (Sept. 13, 1990) in 59 USLW 2205, and affirmed in Tenn Sup. Ct., No. 34 (June 1, 1992) as reported in 60 USLW 2770; "Divorced couple is awarded joint custody of seven embryos," *NY Times* (14 Sept 1990) A20; "Tennessee case may guide others in embryo matters," *ibid.* (7 June 1992) E2; Ronald Smothers, "Man is given embryos after a custody case," *ibid.* (14 June 1993) A11; Raymond, "Of ice and men," 48 on phallic and fetal rights; "Preborn children or blastocysts?" *NY Times* (11 Aug 1989) qA26, rape. Contrast a French case of posthumous insemination, *Parpalaix v. CECOS*, in which the sperm from a late husband was thawed to impregnate his devoted widow: Jones, "Artificial procreation," 525ff; Edouard Bone, "From biotechnology to bioethics: the shock of the future," *Bull pro mundi vita* 101 (185) 14.

64. Some donated embryos come not from IVF but from "intrauterine transfer": an egg that has been fertilized either by artificial insemination within the womb or by standard intercourse is then removed and implanted in a second woman, who will carry the genetically unrelated child as her own. Whether by IVF or by transfer, women bearing these embryos were called "gestational surrogates," of which there had been some eighty worldwide by the time that Anna Johnson's case came before the court. On the numbers, see Susan Tifft, "It's all in the (parental) genes," *Time* (5 Nov 1990) 77 – the parentheses around "parental" only further confusing the parent/theses.

65. Margaret Atwood, *The Handmaid's Tale* (Boston: Houghton Mifflin, 1986); Volker Schlondorff (dir), *The Handmaid's Tale* (Cinecom, 1991). In this context, it is notable that Crispina Calvert and Anna Johnson worked as nurses at the same Orange County hospital.

66. Hillel Schwartz, *The French Prophets: The History of a Millenarian Group in Eighteenth-Century England* (Berkeley: U Cal, 1980) 212–14; Wendy E. Chmielewski et al., *Women in Spiritual and Communitarian Societies in the United States* (Syracuse: Syracuse U, 1993) on Shaker women, esp. essays by Rosemary D. Gooden, Priscilla J. Brewer, and by Karen K. Nickless and Pamela J. Nickless. Was Ann Lee's prophetic stance a reac-

tion to industrialization, a process that threatened to conflate childbearing with mechanical operations and economic production? See Henri Desroche, *The American Shakers From Neo-Christianity to Presocialism*, ed. and trans. John K. Savacool (Amherst: U Mass, 1971) 39; Andrea Henderson, "Doll-machines and butcher-shop meat: models of childbirth in the early stages of industrial capitalism," *Genders* 12 (Wint 1991) 100-19.

67.   Caroline W. Bynum, *Holy Feast and Holy Fast: The Religious Significance of Food to Medieval Women* (Berkeley: U Cal, 1987) 154, 157, 203-04, 257; James K. Hopkins, *A Woman to Deliver Her People: Joanna Southcott and English Millenarianism in an Era of Revolution* (Austin: U Texas, 1982) 199–210, q200, q202, q203, q269–70 n.71.

68.   George D. Bivin and M. Pauline Klinger, *Pseudocyesis* (Bloomington, IL, 1937) In and throughout: Robert N. Rutherford, "Pseudocyesis," *New England J Med* 224 (1941) 639–44; Lewis M. Cohen, "A current perspective of pseudocyesis," *Amer J Psychiatry* 139 (Sept 1982) 1140–44; Chantal J. Whelan and Donna E. Stewart, "Pseudocyesis – a review and report of six cases," *Int J Psychiatry in Medicine* 20,1 (1990) 97–108; Mary A. Brady et al., "Circadian, ultradian, and episodic gonadotropin and prolactin secretion in human pseudocyesis," *Acta Endocrinologica* 124 (May 1991) 501–19; Rhoda S. Frenkel, "The early abortion of a pseudocyesis," *Psychoanalytic Study of the Child* 46 (1991) 237–54, who downplays the analytic recourse to "penis envy" (the fetus as a penis), preferring to speak of separation anxieties and a young woman's desire for symbiosis with her mother. In some cases, pseudocyesis may be a defense against the memory of molestation. That damaging inversion of male couvade in which a man pretends to be able to impregnate a prepubertal girl becomes the traumatic inversion of female couvade in which a woman years later registers the consequences of the violation as a pregnancy. See Marybeth K. Hendricks-Matthews and Douglas M. Hoy, "Pseudocyesis in an adolescent incest survivor," *J Family Practice* 36 (Jan 1993) 97, 101–03, with statistics on the extent of misdiagnosis.

69.   Sims, *Clinical Notes*, 34–35, false quickening in middle-aged women with "a tendency to *embonpoint*"; Samuel Hochman, "Mental and psychological factors in obesity," *Med Record* 148 (1938) 108–11; George H. Reeve, "Psychological factors in obesity," *Amer J Orthopsychiatry* 12 (1942) 674–70; Israel Bram, "Psychosomatic obesity, with comments on 924 cases," *Med Record* 157 (1944) 673–76; Hillel Schwartz, "The three-body problem and the end of the world," in *Zone 4: Fragments for a History of the Human Body, Part 2*, eds. Michel Feher et al. (NY: Zone, 1989) 406–65. On rare occasions men do exhibit false pregnancy: Michael S. Shutty, Jr., and Robert A. Leadbetter, "Recurrent pseudocyesis in a male patient...," *Psychosomatic Med* 55 (Mar–Apr 1993) 146–48.

70.   Lori B. Andrews, *Between Strangers: Surrogate Mothers, Expectant Fathers, and Brave New Babies* (NY: Harper & Row, 1989) 267, Baby M case, as also Carmel Shalev, *Birth Power: The Case for Surrogacy* (New Haven: Yale U, 1989) 1–4; *Anna Johnson et al. v. Mark Calvert et al.*, 19 Cal Reporter, 2d (1993) 494–519, at 499; Richard C. Paddock and Rene Lynch, "Surrogate has no rights to child, court says," *LA Times* (21 May 1993) A1, A27–28; "Surrogate gives birth to boy, custody fight," *LA Times* (20 Sept 1990) A35, renaming child after lawyer.

71.   *Johnson v. Calvert*, Kennard at 516; Rita Arditti, "Reproductive engineering and the social control of women," *Radical America* 19.6 (1985) 9–26, 12 on the misnomer, as also Christine Ewing, "[Critique of the] Draft report on surrogacy issued by the Australian National Bioethics Consultative Committee," *Issues in Reproductive and Genetic Engineering* 3,2 (1990) 144; Barbara K. Rothman, *Recreating Motherhood: Ideology and*

Technology in a Patriarchal Society (NY: Norton, 1989) esp. 40-45, q45. Consider also the stridency of George J. Annas's attack on surrogacy in contrast to the more tempered analyses of surrogacy by Bonnie Steinbock and Ruth Macklin in *Surrogate Motherhood: Politics and Privacy*, ed. Larry Gostin (Bloomington: Indiana U, 1988). Cf. Katha Pollitt, "When is a mother not a mother?" *The Nation* (31 Dec 1990) 844: "We don't need any more disposable relationships in the world of children."

72. Shulamith Firestone, *The Dialectics of Sex: The Case for Feminist Revolution* (NY: Morrow, 1970) q233; Annette Baran and Reuben Pannor, *Lethal Secrets: The Shocking Consequences and Unsolved Problems of Artificial Insemination* (NY: Warner, 1989) q163; Downie, *Babymaking*, 333-37, on male pregnancy; Gena Corea, "The reproductive brothel," in *Man-Made Women*, eds. Corea and Renate Klein (L: Hutchinson, 1985) 38-51. Cf. the doubts and bitterness of Elizabeth Kane, *Birth Mother: The Story of America's First Legal Surrogate Mother* (San Diego: Harcourt Brace Jovanovich, 1988) 275, 278; Kim Cotton, with Denise Winn, *Baby Cotton: For Love and Money* (L: Dorling Kindersley, 1985). For a happier and forthright couvade, see Maggie Kirkman and Linda Kirkman, *My Sister's Child: A Story of Full Surrogate Motherhood Between Two Sisters Using in Vitro Fertilisation* (Harmondsworth, UK: Penguin, 1988) esp. 3, 8, 308-09. On twins, see "Briton, 59, is oldest on record to give birth to test-tube twins," *LA Times* (27 Dec 1993), and Jane Mohr, as told to Elaine Fein, "Love multiplied by three," *Redbook* (Aug 1989) 100-01, two pairs of twins born twenty-one months apart from the same set of withdrawn eggs; in the first pair, one twin died in utero and the other was delivered prematurely: vanishing twins *and* Doppelgängers.

73. Rosalind P. Petchesky, "Fetal images: the power of visual culture in the politics of reproduction," *Feminist Studies* 13 (1987) 263-92, q287, and see also pp. 275-77 on the way in which ultrasonograms visually detach the fetus from the mother and make it seem far more active and (male *or* female) masculine. On stewardship, Irene Diamond, "Babies, heroic experts, and a poisoned earth," in *Reweaving the World: The Emergence of Ecofeminism*, eds. Diamond and Gloria Orenstein (San Francisco: Sierra Club, 1990?) 201-10. On the terms, James Kirkup, "To My Children Unknown, Produced by Artificial Insemination," *White Shadows Black Shadows* (L: Dent, 1970) 32-34; Robyn Rowland, "Response to the draft report of the National Bioethics Consultative Committee, *Surrogacy*," *Issues in Reproductive and Genetic Engineering* 3,2 (1990) 147. Cf. Lynda Birke et al., *Tomorrow's Child: Reproductive Technologies in the '90s* (L: Virago, 1990), seeking to bring the technologies "more in tune with women's needs" (p. 58). As of January 1, 1996, there were nearly 200 citations in the Medline database on research into parthenogenesis, including discoveries of those biochemical factors responsible for *preventing* mammalian cell division in the absence of fertilization by sperm.

74. William D. Marbach et al., "Building the bionic man," *Newsweek* (12 July 1982) q79 from William Dobelle, M.D., and cf. "Replaceable you," *Life* (Feb 1989) 56. On prosthetics and modern culture, an issue I cannot follow here, see Peter Sloterdijk, "Artificial limbs: funtionalist cynicisms II. On the spirit of technology," in his *Critique of Cynical Reason*, 443-59; Mark Seltzer, *Bodies and Machines* (NY: Routledge, 1992) 152-58. For an argument defending IVF as a procedure no less costworthy than breast augmentation or hair transplants, see Singer and Wells, *The Reproduction Revolution*, 65. On autobiography, see esp. Paul J. Eakin, *Fictions in Autobiography: Studies in the Art of Self-Invention* (Princeton: Princeton U, 1985); Michelle E. Lentzner, "My life, my story, right? Fashioning life story rights in the motion picture industry," *Hastings Communica-*

tion/Entertainment Law J 12 (Sum 1990) 627–64 on the legal detachability of one's life story from one's ongoing life.

75. On brain death, see the symposium with Lori Andrews, William May, Andrew Kimbrell, and Jack Hitt, in "Sacred or for sale?" *Harper's* 281 (Oct 1990) 55. On body parts and organ transplants, see, for starters, Russell Scott, *The Body As Property* (NY: Viking, 1981); Stuart J. Younger et al., "Psychosocial and ethical implications of organ retrieval," *New England J Med* 313 (1 Aug 1985) 321–23; Helen B. Holmes, reviewing the "Conference Report: people as products: the ethical, legal, and social issues in reproductive technologies and other procedures involving the commercialization of body parts and tissues, Boston, 6–7 Nov 1989," *Issues in Reproductive and Genetic Engineering* 3,2 (1990) 179–80; Center for Biomedical Ethics, U Minnesota, *The Use of Human Fetal Tissue* (Minneapolis: CBE, 1990).

76. Glen C. Graber and David C. Thomasma, debate, "Should abnormal fetuses be brought to term for the sole purpose of providing infant transplant organs?" in *Biomedical Ethics Reviews 1989*, eds. J.M. Humber and R.F. Almeder (Clifton, NJ: Humana, 1990) 5–54.

77. Dermalogica Institute and Research Center ad, "Permanent Cosmetic Make-up," *Attention Nurses (Glendale, CA)* (Mar 1993) 16; "Sam Butcher Micro Pigment Implanting Clinic," *Cal Women* (July 1993) q15. Permanent make-up is also used in cases of disfigurement from cleft lip, vitiligo, and burns, and in cases where a disabled woman cannot physically manage her own make-up.

78. John Liggett, *The Human Face* (NY: Stein and Day, 1974) 124–27; Blair O. Rogers, "The development of aesthetic plastic surgery," *Aesthetic Plastic Surgery* 1 (1976) 3–24; Rhoda Truax, *The Doctors Warren of Boston* (Boston: Houghton Mifflin, 1968) 199–201; Sandor Gilman, *The Jew's Body* (NY: Routledge, 1991) 183–88.

79. Gilman, *The Jew's Body*, 183–88, 191; E. Vaubel, "German pioneers and teachers of plastic and reconstructive surgery," *Annals of Plastic Surgery* 26 (Jan 1991) 16, on "Lewin"; Liggett, *Human Face*, 197; Rogers, "Development of aesthetic plastic surgery," 9.

80. Charles Conrad Miller, *Cosmetic Surgery: The Correction of Featural Imperfections* (Philadelphia, 1924 [1907]) q57; Rogers, "Development of aesthetic plastic surgery"; A. Suzanne Noël, *La Chirurgie esthétique* (P, 1926) 5, 10–11, 15, 17–18; J.P. Lalardrie and R. Mouly, "History of mammaplasty," *Aesthetic Plastic Surgery* 22, (1978) 167–76; Frederick M. Grazer and Jerome R. Klingbeil, *Body Image: A Surgical Perspective* (St. Louis: Mosby, 1980) 63–74; Max Thorek, "Possibilities in the reconstruction of the human form," *NY Med J* 116 (1922) 572–75.

81. Miller, *Cosmetic Surgery*, v, 256; Mary Louise Roberts, "Samson and Delilah revisited: the politics of women's fashions in 1920s France," *Amer Historical R* 98 (June 1993) 657–84, q671 from Dr. Fouveau de Courmelles.

82. T. Jeamson, *Artificial Embellishments* (Oxford, 1665) sig A4.

83. Pamela Barber, Encinitas, CA, interview, 15 Aug 1991; John M. Goin and Marcia K. Goin, *Changing the Body: Psychological Effects of Plastic Surgery* (Baltimore: Williams and Wilkins, 1981) q145, and 28 for "environmentalist" protests against facelifts as removing the lines of pain and experience which dignify faces; Paule Paillet and André Gaté, *Changer de corps* (P: Inter, 1980) throughout, esp. on alibis; Karl Menninger, "Polysurgery and polysurgery addiction," *Psychoanalytic Q* 3 (1934) 177, 187; "On the cutting edge," *People* (27 Jan 1992) q68 from Cybill Shepherd; Edwin A. Weinstein, "Patterns of reduplication in organic brain disease," *Handbook of Clinical Neurology* (Amsterdam: North

Holland, 1969) III, ch. 14. See also Wolfgang Mühlbauer, "Plastic surgery on identical twins," *Annals of Plastic Surgery* 26 (Jan 1991) 30-39 – to make twins more identical, at their request.

84. "Fire of the vanities," *Omni* (June 1990) 37, laser facelifts at a "Skin Institute" in Rancho Mirage (!), CA; CosmetiCare ad, *Orange Coast* (Dec 1993) 170, and see Jeannette DeWyze, "Body revisionists," *San Diego Reader* (24 Nov 1993) 22ff; Donald Robinson, "The truth about cosmetic surgery," *Reader's Digest* 138 (Feb 1991) 75-82, statistics; Diana Dull and Candace West, "Accounting for cosmetic surgery: the accomplishment of gender," *Social Problems* 38 (Feb 1991) 54-70, 54 for statistics, q56, and cf. the results of a survey on cosmetic surgery in *Glamour* 89 (Mar 1991) 177; Patricia Morrisroe, "Forever young: plastic surgery on the fast track," *NY Mag* 19 (9 June 1986) 43-50, men, as also Diane Sustendal, "Youth lifts," *Harper's Bazaar* 124 (Mar 1991) 88; David A. Hyman, "Aesthetics and ethics: the implications of cosmetic surgery," *Perspectives in Biology and Medicine* 33 (Wint 1990) 192, gift certificates. Dr. Hyman complained that since patients are the arbiters of the success of these operations, cosmetic surgery undermines the physician's authority and imposes (horrors!) a consumer model on doctor–patient relations. This was hardly so for breast implants, about which women were not told – or physicians disregarded – the health risks. See Lalardrie and Mouly, "History of mammaplasty," 171-73; Morrisroe, "Forever young," 48-49; "Breast implants," *Chatelaine* (Aug 1991) 14; Kim Painter, "Emotions flood implant hearings," *USA Today* (20 Feb 1992) 3A – emotions especially high because 20 percent of implants are done after breast removals and may be tied psychologically to full recovery from cancer.

85. John Frankenheimer (dir), *Seconds* (Paramount, 1966), starring Rock Hudson, recently revealed to have been leading a double life as a female heartthrob on the silver screen and as a gay man at home; M. Sharon Webb, "Disfigurement: personal, psychosocial and ethical aspects," *J Med Humanities and Bioethics* 8,2 (1987) 110-19, q111; Dull and West, "Accounting for cosmetic surgery." Consider Harry Benjamin, *The Transsexual Phenomenon* (NY: Julian, 1966) 55: "To a people that accept false teeth and spectacles, plastic surgery and artificial limbs, [the sex change operation] ought not to appear unreasonable."

86. Randolph Trumbach, "London's sodomites: homosexual behavior and Western culture in the eighteenth century," *J Social History* 11 (1977) 1-33; idem, "The birth of the queen: sodomy and the emergence of gender equality in modern culture, 1670-1750," in *Hidden from History*, eds. Martin B. Duberman et al. (NY: New Amer Lib, 1989) 129-40; Terry Castle, "The culture of travesty: sexuality and masquerade in eighteenth-century England," in *Sexual Underworlds of the Enlightenment*, eds. G.S. Rousseau and Roy Porter (Manchester: Manchester U, 1987) 156-80, q175 from Christopher Pitt, "On the Masquerades," *Poems and Translations* (L, 1727) lines 51-52; Vern L. Bullough and Bonnie Bullough, *Cross Dressing, Sex, and Gender* (Philadelphia: U Pennsylvania, 1993) q119 from Edward Ward, *Secret History of Clubs* (L, 1709) 290 on couvade, as also Peter Ackroyd, *Dressing Up, Transvestism, and Drag: The History of an Obsession* (L: Thames & Hudson, 1979) 60; Gary Kates, "D'Eon returns to France: gesture and power in 1777," in *Body Guards: The Cultural Politics of Gender Ambiguity*, eds. J. Epstein and K. Straub (NY: Routledge, 1991) 80-111; Ann R. Jones and Peter Stallybrass, "Fetishizing gender: constructing the hermaphrodite in Renaissance Europe," *ibid.*, 80-111.

87. Castle, "Culture of travesty," q158, q175; Thomas Laqueur, *Making Sex: Body*

and *Gender from the Greeks to Freud* (Cambridge, MA: Harvard, 1992), on which see the critical review by Angus McLaren, *Amer Historical R* 98 (June 1993) 832–33; Michel Foucault, *The History of Sexuality. I. An Introduction*, trans. Robert Hurley (NY: Pantheon, 1978) on repression and the science of sexuality; Jones and Stallybrass, "Fetishizing gender," *Body Guards*, 80–111; Marjorie Garber, *Vested Interests: Cross-Dressing and Cultural Anxiety* (NY: Routledge, 1992) 11, possibility.

88. Garber, *Vested Interests*, q369; Jan Morris, *Conundrum* (NY: Harcourt Brace Jovanovich, 1974) 3, "I was three or four years old when I realized that I had been born into the wrong body, and should really be a girl." On category disputes and crossovers *within* the transsexual community, see Anne Bolin, "Transcending and transgendering: male-to-female transsexuals, dichotomy and diversity," in *Third Sex, Third Gender: Beyond Sexual Dimorphism in Culture and History*, ed. Gilbert Herdt (NY: Zone, 1994) 447–85, who argues that the opposition of cross-dresser to transsexual is no longer apt, if ever it was an actuality.

89. Harry Benjamin, "Introduction" to *Transsexualism and Sex Reassignment*, eds. R. Green and J. Money (Baltimore: Johns Hopkins, 1969) 6n, birth certificate, as also Gilbert Oakley, *Man into Woman* (L: Walton, 1964) 17; C.N. Armstrong and T. Walton, "Transsexuals and the law," *New Law J* (5 Oct 1990) 1384, 1389–90; Thomas Kando, *Sex Change: The Achievement of Gender Identity Among Feminized Transsexuals* (Springfield, IL: Thomas, 1973) q111. On the transvestite endorsement of male–female stereotypes as opposed to the relative freedom of transsexuals, see Deborah H. Feinbloom, *Transvestites and Transsexuals: Mixed Views* (NY: Delacorte, 1976) esp. 247–49; Annie Woodhouse, *Fantastic Women: Sex, Gender and Transvestism* (Houndmills: Macmillan, 1989) xv, 81, 138–39, 144; Shapiro, "Transsexualism: reflections on the persistence of gender and the mutability of sex," in Epstein and Straub, eds., *Body Guards*, 248–79. But this may be stereotyping those who cross-dress. Consider the gender-bending roles of male and female impersonators: Sara Maitland, *Vesta Tilley* (L: Virago, 1986) 9, 31–32, and throughout; Roger Baker, *Drag: A History of Female Impersonation on Stage* (L: Triton, 1968); Erika Munk, "The rites of women," *Performing Arts J* 29 (1986) 35–42. See also San Francisco Lesbian and Gay History Project, " 'She even chewed tobacco': a pictorial narrative of passing women in America," in Duberman et al., eds., *Hidden from History*, 183–94; Anne Herrman, " 'Passing' women, performing men," *The Female Body: Figures, Styles, Speculations*, ed. Laurence Goldstein (Ann Arbor: U Michigan, 1991) 178–89.

90. Nariette P. Allen, *Transformations: Crossdressers and Those Who Love Them* (NY: Dutton, 1989) on pregnancy; Society for the Second Self, *Chi-Delta-Mu: What Is It? Whom Is It For? What Are Its Goals?*, introductory brochure (Tulare, 1989?); Sandy Stone, "The *Empire* strikes back: a post-transsexual manifesto," in Epstein and Straub, eds., *Body Guards*, 280–304, esp. 285–87 on Kreutz, and assessing Janice Raymond, *The Transsexual Empire: The Making of the She-Male* (Boston: Beacon, 1979) who argues that M→F transsexual surgeries are another way for men to coopt and dominate women; Lili Elbe (= Einar Wegener, pseud. for Andreas Sparre), *Man into Woman*, ed. Niels Hoyer (pseud for E.L.H. Jacobsen), trans. H.J. Stenning (L, 1933) q244, q268, q273, q286, the last surgery an ovarian transplant. Terence Rafferty, "Realness," *The New Yorker* (25 Mar 1991), 72–74, reviewing a film documentary on drag competitions, *Paris Is Burning* by Jennie Livingston, noted that the newer generation of cross-dressers tends to implants and sex changes, departing from the "humor of drag classicism" – a further indication of the deep appeal of couvade.

91. Elbe, *Man into Woman*, 20; Martha H. Field, *Surrogate Motherhood* (Cambridge, MA: Harvard U, 1988) 1–2 on Denise Thrane, who changed her mind and got custody of the ensuing child after Mr. and Mrs. Noyes decided not to pursue a case weakened by the fact of the transsexual surgery; Bullough and Bullough, *Cross Dressing*, 318–22 on physiological explanations, as also Robert A. Butler, "New light on the causes of crossdressing," in *Chi-Delta-Mu* brochure. Contrast Gilbert Herdt, "Mistaken gender: s-alpha reductase hermaphroditism and biological reductionism in sexual identity reconsidered," *Amer Anthropologist* 92 (1990) 433–46. See also Terry FitzSimons, "Gender dysphoria," *The Ear (Irvine, CA)* 9 (Spr 1992) 32–47, a wonderful essay, citing for technical support Ray Blanchard et al., "Heterosexual and homosexual gender dysphoria," *Archives of Sexual Behavior* (Apr 1987) 138–52. Final quotation from Feinbloom, *Transvestites and Transsexuals*, 7.

92. Leslie M. Lothstein, *Female-to-Male Transsexualism* (Boston: Routledge & Kegan Paul, 1983) esp. 20–23 for the history; Bullough and Bullough, *Cross Dressing*, 255–56; Garber, *Vested Interests*, 67, 102; Shapiro, "Transsexualism," 269–70; Joan Riviere, "Womanliness as a masquerade" (1929) in *Formations of Fantasy*, eds. Victor Burgin et al. (L: Methuen, 1986) 35–44, with assessment by Stephen Heath, "Joan Riviere and the masquerade," 45–61.

93. Margaret O. Hyde and Lawrence E. Hyde, *Cloning and the New Genetics* (Hillside, NJ: Enslow, 1984) on the history of attempts at cloning; Singer and Wells, *The Reproduction Revolution*, 150–66; John Brunner, *Double, Double* (NY: Ballantine, 1969); Paul Billings, M.D., Center for Inherited Diseases, Pacific Presbyterian Medical Center, San Francisco, interview, 16 Apr 1991; Robert G. McKinnell, *Cloning: A Biologist Reports* (Minneapolis: U Minnesota, 1979) q102 and throughout. Cf. Katharine Lowry, "The designer babies are growing up," *LA Times Mag* (1 Nov 1987) 7–12ff, on results of the eugenic experiment of the Repository for Germinal Choice, Escondido, CA, which freezes the sperm only of those who have won Nobel Prizes or are of high IQs. The first thing a donor-inseminated mother of one "designer baby" wanted to show the reporter was how much her daughter looked like her husband.

94. Ohio Willow Wood Company, brochure on *Carbon Copy System III* (Mount Sterling, OH, 1991); Richard Golob and Eric Brus, eds., *The Almanac of Science and Technology* (Boston: Harcourt Brace Jovanovich, 1990) q87–89, and see 91 on the "reverse transcriptase" enzyme, and cDNA, copies of DNA complementary to the RNA of the enzyme; Bruce Alberts and Rolf Sternglanz, "Recent excitement in the DNA replication problem," *Nature* 269 (20 Oct 1977) q655–56, fidelity. There *is* a (partial) alternative to DNA theory: the cytoplasmic theory of inheritance, which is nonchromosomal, non-Mendelian, and non-nuclear; see Jan Sapp, *Beyond the Gene: Cytoplasmic Inheritance and the Struggle for Authority in Genetics* (NY: Oxford U, 1987).

95. For cloning fictions, see esp. Ursula K. Le Guin, "Nine Lives," (1974) in *Biofutures*, ed. Pamela Sargent (NY: Vintage, 1976) 97–132, q132, with an epigraph from an essay by biologist James D. Watson (he of the DNA double helix), "Moving toward the clonal man," *The Atlantic* (May 1971). Cf. Kate Wilhelm, *Where Late the Sweet Birds Sang* (NY: Harper & Row, 1976), and the very funny novel by Richard Cowper, *Clone* (Garden City, NY: Doubleday, 1972), asking on the book flap, "Can four clones, saintlike, with perfect eidetic memories and rather plain features, find happiness in the brutish world of 2072?"

96. See Ruth F. Chadwick, "Cloning," *Phil* 57 (1982) 201–09 for a short, cogent analy-

sis of objections to cloning, and Francisco J. Ayala, "Between Utopia and Hades," *San Jose Studies* 4 (Nov 1978) 9–22, for a lyrical condemnation. On genetic engineering, see Rollin D. Hotchkiss, "Portents for a genetic engineering," *J of Heredity* 56 (1965) 197–202, q201; Jeremy Rifkin, *Algeny* (NY: Viking, 1983), con; the President's Commission for the Study of Ethical Problems in Medicine and Biomedical and Behavioral Research, *Splicing Life: The Social and Ethical Issues of Genetic Engineering with Human Beings* (Washington, D.C.: GPO, 1982), pro. On problems with genetic counseling and prophetic acuity, see esp. Marlene Huggins et al., "Ethical and legal dilemmas arising during predictive testing for adult-onset disease: the experience of Huntington disease," *Amer J Human Genetics* (1990) 4–12. I have also benefitted here from interviews with Nachama L. Wilker, Executive Director, Council for Responsible Genetics, Boston, 29 Jan 1991, and with Dr. Paul Billings, note 93 above.

97. Alexander Pope, "On gardens," *The Guardian* 173 (1713) in Paul Hammond, ed., *Selected Prose of Alexander Pope* (Cambridge: Cambridge U, 1987) 59–61; Miles Hadfield, *Topiary and Ornamental Hedges: Their History and Cultivation* (L: Black, 1971) 11, 41, q21 from Joshuah Sylvester's translation of the verse from Guillaume de Salluste du Bartas, *La Première semaine ou la Création* (ca. 1590); Barbara Gallup and Deborah Reich, *The Complete Book of Topiary* (NY: Workman, 1987) 18, 247, q252 from John Parkinson, *Paradisi in sole, paradisus terrestris* (1629).

98. Timothy Nourse, *Campania foelix* (L, 1700), 322, cited and discussed in S. Lang, "The genesis of the English landscape garden," *The Picturesque Garden and Its Influence Outside the British Isles*, ed. Nikolaus Pevsner (Washington, D.C., 1974) 8; Gallup and Reich, *Complete Book of Topiary*, 19, 23, 27, q13 from T. James, *The Carthusian: A Miscellany in Prose and Verse* (1839).

99. Herman Melville, "The Paradise of Bachelors and The Tartarus of Maids" (1855) in *Pierre… [&] Uncollected Prose*, ed. Harrison Hayford (NY: Lib of Amer, 1984) 1266–78; Judith A. McGaw, *Most Wonderful Machine: Mechanization and Social Change in Berkshire Paper Making, 1801–1885* (Princeton: Princeton U, 1987) ch. 10; "Artificial flower trade of London and Paris," *Every Saturday* 14 (1873) 315–19; Mary Van Kleeck, *Artificial Flower Makers* (NY, 1913) – 10,000 American women and children employed in making artificial flowers by 1910, much of this as cottage (that is, tenement) industry; W.H. Rideing, "Flora in a garret," *Appleton's Mag* 20 (Aug 1878) 97–103, q97, q100.

100. Edward D. Andrews and Faith Andrews, *Work and Worship: The Economic Order of the Shakers* (Greenwich, CT: NY Graphic Soc, 1974) 53–61.

101. I am heavily indebted here to the fine book by Jack R. Kloppenburg, Jr., *First the Seed: The Political Economy of Plant Biotechnology, 1492–2000* (NY: Cambridge U, 1988) 52, 55–56.

102. *Ibid.*, 61, q68 from W.A. Orton.

103. *Ibid.*, 64, 80, q88 from a 1936 agricultural yearbook, 110, 117–19, 162–63.

104. *Ibid.*, q132, 133, 244–45, 273; Frederick H. Buttel and Jill Belsky, "Biotechnology, plant breeding, and intellectual property," *Sci, Technology, & Human Values* 12 (Wint 1987) 31–49; Biotechnica Agriculture, Inc., *The Future in Corn*, brochure (Overland Park, KS, 1990), and Biotechnica International, Inc., *Innovative Applications of Genetic Engineering* presskit (Cambridge, MA, and Overland Park, KS, 1990–91); Keith Redenbaugh, "Application of artificial seed to tropical crops," *HortSci* 25,3 (1990) 251–56. Cf. Lawrence Busch et al., *Plants, Power and Profit* (Oxford: Blackwell, 1991).

105. Michael Hansen et al., "Plant breeding and biotechnology," *Biosci* 36 (Jan 1986)

29–39; Kloppenburg, *First the Seed*, 245–46, 271; Edward Yoxen, *The Gene Business* (NY: Oxford U, 1983) 142–45; Jeffrey Burkhardt, "Agribusiness ethics: specifying the terms of the contract," *J Business Ethics* 5 (1986) 333–45; Lawrence Busch et al., "Culture and care: ethical and policy dimensions of germ-plasm conservation," in *Biotic Diversity and Germplasm Preservation: Global Imperatives*, eds. I. Knutson and A.K. Stoner (Norwell, MA: Kluwer, 1989) 43–62, q48 from Martin Heidegger, *The Question Concerning Technology and Other Essays* (NY: Harper & Row, 1977) 17; Lawrence Busch, "Irony, tragedy, and temporality in agricultural systems," *Agriculture and Human Values* 6,4 (1989) 4–11, q7. Cf. Michael Pollan (sic!), *Second Nature: A Gardener's Education* (NY: Atlantic, 1991).

106. D. Pimentel et al., "Benefits and risks of genetic engineering in agriculture," *Biosci* 39 (Oct 1989) 606–14; Busch et al., "Culture and care," 51; Hansen et al., "Plant breeding and biotechnology," 30; Jeffrey Burkhardt, "The morality behind sustainability," *J Agricultural Ethics* 2 (1989) 113–28.

107. In the Matter of the Application of Malcolm E. Bergy, John H. Coats, and Vedpal S. Malik, 563 F.2d 1031 (1977), at 1034, 1038, 1039; Sheldon Krimsky, *Biotechnics and Society: The Rise of Industrial Genetics* (NY: Praeger, 1991) 47, prior patents involving single-celled organisms; *Diamond v. Chakrabarty*, 447 U.S. 303 (1980) q311, Commissioner of Patents in 1889, from *Ex parte Latimer*, 1889 Dec. Com. Pat. 123.

108. *Diamond v. Chakrabarty*, 447 U.S. 303 (1980). Four justices dissented, on the grounds that the history of legislation showed that Congress had been unfailingly anxious to keep bacteria, fungi, and multicellular animals out of reach of patent law.

109. Krimsky, *Biotechnics and Society*, 47–49. According to one reading of the 1976 revision of U.S. copyright law, all genetically engineered "works" after 1978 were protected by copyright, that is, from a "plagiarism" of the organism. Looking forward, Irving Kayton in 1982 suggested that "the best of all possible worlds" would be available to the author/inventor of genetic works, if "copyright protection can inhere in his specific DNA compilation simultaneously with patent protection that encompasses the idea which that DNA sequence and its legal equivalents represent": see his "Copyright in living genetically engineered works," *George Washington Law R* 50 (1982) 191–218, q194, q216.

110. Elizabeth Corcoran, "A tiny mouse came forth," *Sci Amer* 260 (Feb 1989) 73; Steve Olson, *Shaping the Future: Biology and Human Values* (Washington, D.C.: National Research Council, 1989) 86, primates and rodents, 90–94 for bacteria; R. Ian Freshney, *Culture of Animal Cells* (NY: Liss, 1987); Richard D. Palmiter and Ralph L. Brinster, "Transgenic mice," *Cell* 41 (1985) q343; Office of Technology Assessment, *Patenting Life*, New Developments in Biotechnology, 5 (Washington, D.C.: GPO, 1989) 9, q14. On breeding, see Harriet Ritvo, *The Animal Estate: The English and Other Creatures in the Victorian Age* (Cambridge, MA: Harvard U, 1987) Part I. On the explicit creation of "neutroids" and breeding of chimps as surrogate human children, see the prophetic tale by Walter M. Miller, Jr., "Conditionally human" (1952) in *The Best of Walter M. Miller, Jr.* (NY: Pocket Books, 1980) 207–65.

111. Editorial, "What price Mighty Mouse?" *New Republic* (23 May 1988) 6 on Quigg; Marla Cone, "The mouse wars turn furious," *LA Times* (9 May 1993) A1, A18–19, qA18 from Daniel Kevles.

112. David Dickson, "Europe says no to animal patents," *Science* (7 July 1989) 25; Kathleen Hart, "Making mythical monsters," *The Progressive* 54 (Mar 1990) 22; Donna Haraway, "When Man™ Is on the Menu," in *Zone 6: Incorporations*, eds. J. Crary and S.

Kwinter (NY: Zone, 1992) 38–43, reproducing a DuPont ad for the OncoMouse™, which Haraway discusses as a cyborg, and cf. Paul Rabinow, "Artificiality and enlightenment: from sociobiology to biosociality," *ibid.*, 234–52.

113. Marcia Barinaga, "A muted victory for the biotech industry," *Science* 249 (20 July 1990) q239; Julia S. Bach, ed., *Biomedical Ethics: Opposing Viewpoints* (St. Paul, MN: Greenhaven, 1987) 74; Cone, "Mouse wars," A19 on DNX. Tumored human spleen cells provide superb hybridomas, "immortal" cell lines whose cancerous cells, incessantly dividing, keep the line going, and whose genetic machinery is geared to producing various marketable antibodies. After Dr. David Golde of UCLA removed a leukemic spleen from John Moore in 1976, he used Moore's tissue to establish a cell line for the manufacture of an immune-system booster of considerable medical and economic value. Moore sued for a piece of the action. The California Supreme Court ruled in 1990 that "a patient does not own his own tissues once removed from his body, or have rights to profit from products researchers derive from those tissues."

114. Alan M. Turing, "Computing machinery and intelligence," *Mind* 59 (Oct 1950) 433–60.

115. Andrew Hodges, *Alan Turing: the Enigma* (NY: Simon and Schuster, 1983) ch. 8, q469, and see "A shot in the dark," *Health* (Jan–Feb 1993) 22 for the resurgence of female hormone treatment for male sex offenders. For the history of cybernetic theory, see Vernon Pratt, *Thinking Machines: The Evolution of Artificial Intelligence* (Oxford: Blackwell, 1987); Keith Gunderson, "Cybernetics," *Ency of Phil*, ed.-in-chief Paul Edwards (NY: Free Press, 1967) II, 280–84. Consider also Linda Gordon, "On 'difference,'" *Genders* 10 (Spr 1991) 91–111.

116. Babylonian Talmud, Sanhedrin 65b, and see Emily Bilski with Moshe Idel and Elfi Ledig, *Golem! Danger, Deliverance and Art* (NY: Jewish Museum, 1988) 10–35, historical overview; Karel Čapek, *R.U.R. and the Insect Play*, trans. P. Selver (L: Oxford U, 1961 [1923]); Al Bertino, retired animator for WED (Disney) Enterprises, Van Nuys, CA, interview, 3 June 1991; Hubert L. Dreyfus and Stuart E. Dreyfus, *Mind over Machine: The Power of Human Intuition and Expertise in the Era of the Computer* (NY: Free Press, 1986), and contrast Hans Moravec, *Mind Children: The Future of Robot and Human Intelligence* (Cambridge: Harvard U, 1988), anticipating an Independence Day.

117. Turing, "Computing machinery and intelligence," 434.

118. H.M. Collins, *Artificial Experts: Social Knowledge and Intelligent Machines* (Cambridge, MA: MIT, 1990) q6, q215, and see esp. ch. 13 – but Collins thinks that Turing assumed that the interrogator would easily tell the man from the woman, wherefore a machine could succeed in the man's place, for to pretend to be a man pretending to be a woman was easier (in the 1950s) than pretending to be a man "acting authentically," since the man's pretenses would be limited (very limited, in the 1950s) by the stereotypes men had of women. I think that Turing saw the telling of male from female as problematic, therefore most suitable prelude to a paradigmatic test of our ability to tell human from machine. On the related issue of giving social ("expert") knowledge to computers, see Marianne LaFrance, "Stories knowledge engineers tell about expert systems," *Social Science Computer Review* 8 (Spr 1990) 13–23.

119. Mark Halpern, "Turing's test and the ideology of artificial intelligence," *Artificial Intelligence R* 1,2 (1987) 79–94, q88, which should be put in the historical context provided by Judith V. Grabiner, "Artificial intelligence: debates about its use and abuse," *Historia mathematica* 11,4 (1984) 471–80. Cf. David H. Adams, "Self-organisation

and living systems: is DNA an artificial intelligence?" *Medical Hypotheses* 29 (Aug 1989) 223-29.

120. Turing, "Computing machinery and intelligence," q442, q448, q445 for Jefferson, discussed by Hodges, *Alan Turing*, 404-06. On self-consciousness, thought, and logic, see Douglas Hofstadter, *Gödel, Escher, Bach* (NY: Basic, 1979); Peter Caws, "Subjectivity in the machine," *J for the Theory of Social Behavior* 18 (1988) 291-308. On the (sexist) kitchen, General Electric ad in *Smithsonian* (Apr 1985) 68-69. On children and computers, see Sherry Turkle, *The Second Self: Computers and the Human Spirit* (NY: Simon & Schuster, 1984); idem, "Romantic reaction: paradoxical responses to computer presence," in *The Boundaries of Humanity: Humans, Animals, Machines*, eds. J.J. Sheehan and M. Sosna (Berkeley: U Cal, 1991) 224-52.

121. Turing, "Computing machinery and intelligence," q448, q449. J. David Bolter, *Turing's Man: Western Culture in the Computer Age* (Chapel Hill: U North Carolina, 1984) 229, accuses Turing of being "insensitive to the historical and intellectual context of his work." Turing was apolitical in his approach to mathematical and biological problems, as observes Hodges, *Alan Turing*, ch. 8, but he was not insensitive to their context.

122. For warnings, see Dreyfus and Dreyfus, *Mind over Machine*, q xiv; J. David Bolter, "Artificial intelligence," *Daedalus* 113,3 (1984) 1-18. For AI models, see Patrick K. Simpson, *Artificial Neural Systems* (NY: Pergamon, 1990) esp. 136-45, a history; J.R. Doyle, "Supervised learning in N-tuple neural networks," *Int J of Man–Machine Studies* 33 (July 1990) 21-40, q35 from Igor Aleksander; Michael A. Arbib, *The Metaphorical Brain 2: Neural Networks and Beyond* (NY: Wiley, 1989); Warren S. McCulloch, *Embodiments of Mind* (Cambridge, MA: MIT, 1965) q194, ethical circuitry. On "artificial life" programs, see Christopher G. Langton, ed., *Artificial Life* (Redwood City, CA: Addison-Wesley, 1989) esp. title essay by Langton and P. Hogeweg's "MIRROR beyond MIRROR, puddles of life"; Mike Edelhart, "The cradle of artificial life," *PC Computing* 4 (Feb 1991) 152-54. These programs rely on the theory of cellular automata adumbrated by John von Neumann, a lightning-fast calculator and prodigious mnemonist in his Hungarian youth, a cyberneticist and militarist in his American majority, who pushed for the development of the H-bomb and hypothesized a universal self-replicating machine before dying in 1957 from the self-replicating cancer cells in his bones, result of exposure to radiation at the Bikini atomic tests. Von Neumann's work ultimately referred back to the "Turing machine" of 1936. See William Poundstone, *The Recursive Universe: Cosmic Complexity and the Limits of Scientific Knowledge* (NY: Morrow, 1985) 177; Kendall Preston, Jr., and Michael J.B. Duff, *Modern Cellular Automata* (NY: Plenum, 1984).

123. Roger C. Schank, "Where's the AI?" *AI Mag* 12 (Wint 1991) 38-49, upping the ante; Ronald D. Schwartz, "Artificial intelligence as a sociological phenomenon," *Canadian J of Sociology* 14 (Spr 1989) 179-202; Michael Heim, *Electric Language: A Philosophical Study of Word Processing* (New Haven: Yale U, 1987); Georges Canguilhem, trans. M. Cohen and R. Cherry, "Machine and organism," in Crary and Kwinter, eds., *Incorporations*, 44-69, as also Didier Deleule, trans. Randall Cherry, "The living machine: psychology as organology," 203-33; Lance J. Hoffman, ed., *Rogue Programs: Viruses, Worms, and Trojan Horses* (Florence, KY: Van Nostrand Reinhold, 1990), good on the history, as also Tom Forester and Penny Morrison, *Computer Ethics* (Oxford: Blackwell, 1990); Inman Harvey et al., "Issues in evolutionary robotics," in *From Animals to Animats 2*, eds. Jean-Arcady Meyer et al. (Cambridge, MA: MIT, 1993) 364-73, as also Federico Cecconi and Domenico Parisi, "Neural networks with motivational units," 346-55, and

Gregory M. Werner and Michael G. Dyer, "Evolution of herding behavior in artificial animals," 393-99; Raymond Kurzweil, comp., *The Age of Intelligent Machines* (Cambridge, MA: MIT, 1990) esp. 465-83, a chronology that begins with dinosaurs roaming the earth and ends (in 2020-2070) with a computer passing the Turing test. Cf. Geoff Simons, *Are Computers Alive? Evolution and New Life Forms* (Brighton: Harvester, 1982) and idem, *The Biology of Computer Life: Survival, Emotion, and Free Will* (Sussex: Harvester, 1985).

124. J. David Bolter, "Artificial intelligence," *Daedalus* 113,3 (1984) 1-18, q11; Grant H. Kester, "Out of sight is out of mind: the imaginary space of postindustrial culture," *Social Text* 35 (1993) 72-92, on virtual reality and social conscience.

125. On the connection of the visual arts to virtual reality, see Myron W. Krueger, *Artificial Reality II* (Reading, MA: Addison-Wesley, 1991); J.T., "The fake and the functional," *Artnews* (Oct 1990) 34; Timothy Binkley, "Camera fantasia: computed visions of virtual reality," *Millennium Film J* 20/21 (Fall-Wint 1989) 6-43.

126. For a flashy account of the historical development of VR, see Howard Rheingold, *Virtual Reality* (NY: Summit, 1991). On the experience of VR, see Steven Levy, "Brave new world," *Rolling Stone* (14 June 1990) 92-100; Doug Stewart, "Through the looking glass into an artificial world – via computer," *Smithsonian* 21 (Jan 1991) 37-45; A.J.S. Rayl, "The new, improved reality," *LA Times Mag* (21 July 1991) 16-20, 30. For meditations upon the cultural significance of VR systems, see Allucquère Rosanne Stone, *The War of Desire and Technology at the Close of the Mechanical Age* (Cambridge, MA: MIT, 1995); Grant H. Kester, "Out of sight is out of mind: the imaginary space of postindustrial culture," *Social Text* 35 (1993) 72-92; James Wolcott, "Sweaty palms," *The New Yorker* (17 May 1993) 102-05; Michael Heim, "The metaphysics of virtual reality," in *Virtual Reality: Theory, Practice, and Promise*, eds. S.K. Helsel and J.P. Roth (Westport: Meckler, 1991) 27-34. For parables about VR and cyberspace, see the ABC TV miniseries produced by Oliver Stone, "Wild Palms," aired 16-18 May 1993; William Gibson, *Count Zero* (NY: Ace, 1986).

127. Rayl, "New, improved reality," q19, Lanier; Stanislaw Lem, trans. Michael Kandel, "In Hot Pursuit of Happiness," *View from Another Shore*, ed. Franz Rottensteiner (NY: Jove, 1978) 21-68; Daniel Herskowitz, "Cyborgs and philosophers: an interview with Michael Heim," *The New Indicator (UC San Diego)* 18 (Apr 1993) 5, 12; Donna Haraway, *Simians, Cyborgs, and Women: The Reinvention of Nature* (L: Free Assoc, 1991); Jack Imes, Jr., *Special Visual Effects* (NY: Van Nostrand Reinhold, 1984) 7. See Jerome C. Glenn, *Future Mind: Artificial Intelligence: The Mystical and the Technological in the Twenty-First Century* (Washington, D.C.: Acropolis, 1989) for a rather full embrace of the cyborg.

128. Helge Kragh, *Dirac: A Scientific Biography* (NY: Cambridge U, 1990) 88-92, 95-103, q92, q95; Robert L. Forward and Joel Davis, *Mirror Matter: Pioneering Antimatter Physics* (NY: Wiley, 1988) 23.

129. Kragh, *Dirac*, 111; Forward and Davis, *Mirror Matter*, 7, 28, 37, q40, 41-43, 51, 151; H. Poth, "On the production and investigation of atomic antimatter," *Comments on Atomic and Molecular Physics* 22,4 (1989) 211-15; Jerry E. Bishop, "Researchers collect 'bottle' of antimatter," *Wall Street J* (2 Mar 1989) B1, B5, positrons captured in magnetic field; Malcolm W. Browne, "Physicists strive to create atoms of antihydrogen from antimatter," *NY Times* (15 Nov 1994) B7; *OED*, I, 515, dating "anti-matter" to 1953. See Nick Herbert, *Quantum Reality* (Garden City: Anchor, 1987) 172-75 for physicists' theories of parallel universes.

130. See the *Antisense Research R* (1991-) for molecular genetic work on the strand of DNA that is *not* transcribed.

131. James Trefil, *The Dark Side of the Universe* (NY: Anchor, 1988) q94; Shawna Vogel, "Strange matter," *Discover* (Nov 1989) 63-66.

132. Ryusaku Tsunoda et al., comps., *Sources of Japanese Tradition* (NY: Columbia U, 1964) I, 1-132, 11 on Nippon; Harry D. Harootunian, "The functions of China in Tokugawa thought," and Samuel C. Chu, "China's attitudes toward Japan at the time of the Sino-Japanese War," both in *The Chinese and the Japanese*, ed. Akira Iriye (Princeton: Princeton U, 1980) 9-36, 74-95. On the sensitivities of the Chinese to copies true and false, see esp. Wen Fong, "The problem of forgeries in Chinese painting," *Artibus Asiae* 25 (1962) 95-119.

133. Shigemi Inaga, "La Réinterpretation de la perspective linéaire au Japon 1740-1830 et son retour en France 1860-1910," *Actes de la recherche en sciences sociales* 49 (Sept 1983) 29-45.

134. F.G. Notehelfer, ed., *Japan Through American Eyes: The Journal of Francis Hall, Kanagawa and Yokohama, 1859-1866* (Princeton: Princeton U, 1992) 42, q68, q69, q81, 84, 112, 127, 142, q218; Jacqueline Pigeot, "Le Japon aux prises avec l'autre," *Critique* 30 (Feb 1974) 174-88, reviewing Hirakawa Sukehiro, *Wakon yōsai no keifu* (Tokyo: Kawade shobō, 1971); Barbican Art Gallery, *Karakuri Ningyo: An Exhibition of Ancient Festival Robots from Japan* (L: Barbican, 1985); A.H. Saxon, ed., *Selected Letters of P.T. Barnum* (NY: Columbia U, 1983) 80.

135. Tsunoda, *Sources of Japanese Tradition*, 14-15; Benjamin Goldberg, *The Mirror and Man* (Charlottesville, VA: U Press of Virginia, 1985) ch. 4; Charles A. Pomeroy, *Traditional Crafts of Japan* (NY: Weatherhill, 1967) 12-13, 20-21; Masao Watanabe, *The Japanese and Western Science*, trans. Otto T. Benfey (Philadelphia: U Pennsylvania, 1990) ch. 2.

136. George Burchett, *Memoirs of a Tattooist*, ed. P. Leighton (NY: Crown, 1958) 48-51.

137. Siegfried Wichmann, *Japonisme: The Japanese Influence on Western Art in the Nineteenth and Twentieth Centuries*, trans. Mary Whitall et al. (NY: Harmony, 1981); Elizabeth Bisland, ed., *The Japanese Letters of Lafcadio Hearn* (Boston, 1910) q17, q18. See also Robert A. Rosenstone, *Mirror in the Shrine: American Encounters with Meiji Japan* (Cambridge, MA: Harvard U, 1988) on Japan as a mirror *for* Americans, esp. 1; Neil Harris, "All the world a melting pot? Japan at American fairs, 1876-1904," in *Mutual Images: Essays in American-Japanese Relations*, ed. Akira Iriye (Cambridge, MA: Harvard U, 1975) 24-54; Cynthia A. Brandimarte, "Japanese novelty stores," *Winterthur Portfolio* 26 (Spr 1991) 1-26, esp. p. 22, Western ladies in kimonos.

138. Bisland, *Japanese Letters of Lafcadio Hearn*, q269, q10; Carl Dawson, *Lafcadio Hearn and the Vision of Japan* (Baltimore: Johns Hopkins U, 1992) esp. 21, 61-62, 87-106, q16 from a letter to Ernest Fenollosa, 13 Apr 1890. Cf. Edward Said, *Orientalism* (NY: Random House, 1978) on the "Orient" as a place in which Europeans sought their origins; Marilyn Ivy, *Discourses of the Vanishing: Modernity, Phantasm, Japan* (Chicago: U Chicago, 1995) on Japan always appearing to vanish before Western eyes.

139. Bisland, *Japanese Letters of Lafcadio Hearn*, q317, q10; Watanabe, *The Japanese and Western Science*, 8, 12; Notehelfer, *Japan Through American Eyes*, 4; James R. Bartholomew, *The Formation of Science in Japan* (New Haven: Yale U, 1989) q76; Gabriel Tarde, *Les Lois de l'imitation*, 3rd ed. (P, 1900 [1895]) xvi.

140. E. Sydney Crawcour, "Industrialization and technological change, 1885-1920," in *Cambridge History of Japan*, ed. Peter Duus (NY: Cambridge U, 1988) VI, 403-04, 420; Shunsuke Kamei, "The sacred land of liberty: images of America in nineteenth-century Japan," in Iriye, ed., *Mutual Images*, 55-72; Bartholomew, *Formation of Science in Japan*, 5, 66, 166, 182, 191; Pigeot, "Le Japon aux prises avec l'autre," 179-82; Yokoyama Toshio, *Japan in the Victorian Mind: A Study of Stereotyped Images of a Nation, 1850-80* (Houndmills, UK: Macmillan, 1987) q175 from Algernon B. Mitford's *The Attaché at Peking* (L, 1900). Earlier, Mitford had been disgusted at the sight of Japanese soldiers in ill-fitting European uniforms – "disfiguring into the semblance of apes men who really used to look well in their own national dress" (p. 107).

141. Galen M. Fisher, *Creative Forces in Japan* (West Medford, MA, 1923) q8-9; Miriam Beard, *Realism in Romantic Japan* (NY, 1930) q89.

142. Francis J. McHugh, "Gaming at the Naval War college," *U.S. Naval Inst Proc* 90,3 (1964) 52; John W. Dower, *War Without Mercy: Race and Power in the Pacific War* (NY: Pantheon, 1986) 182-88, Japanese as apes, monkeys, and missing links; Anthony R.E. Rhodes, *Propaganda: The Art of Persuasion in World War II* (NY: Chelsea House, 1984) II, 260; Don Hultzman, "Battery-operated toys," in *Collecting Toys No. 5*, ed. Richard O'Brien (Florence, AL: Books Amer, 1990) 203ff. Consider also Nathan Glazer, "From Ruth Benedict to Herman Kahn: the postwar Japanese image in the American mind," in Iriye, ed., *Mutual Images*, 138-68, Japan seen as a land of paradoxes, the Japanese as unstable but capable of a robotlike discipline and patient craftmanship.

143. *OED*, III, 123; Pigeot, "Le Japon aux prises avec l'autre," 182, Richet; Pamela Asquith, "Anthropomorphism and the Japanese and Western traditions in primatology," in *Primate Ontogeny, Cognition, and Behavior*, eds. J.G. Else and P.C. Lee (NY: Academic, 1986) 61-72; Peter Kharoche, trans., *Once the Buddha Was a Monkey: Arya Sura's Jatakamala* (Chicago: U Chicago, 1989) esp. #24; Tru'o'ng Chinh, *The Real and the Fake Monkey, Adapted by Zhang Cheng from the Classical Chinese Novel,* The Journey to the West, *by Wu Chengen of the Ming Dynasty* (Beijing: Zhaohua, 1983); Mark Jones et al., ed., *Fake? The Art of Deception* (Berkeley: U Cal, 1990) 115, Sosen; Emiko Ohnuki-Tierney, "The monkey as self in Japanese culture," *Culture Through Time*, ed. Ohnuki-Tierney (Stanford: Stanford U, 1990) 163-73, q171; idem, *The Monkey as Mirror: Symbolic Transformations in Japanese History and Ritual* (Princeton: Princeton U, 1987) esp. ch. 2.

144. Ohnuki, *The Monkey as Mirror*, 63, 66, 119; Densaburo Miyadi, "Social life of Japanese monkeys," *Science in Japan*, ed. Arthur H. Livermore (Washington, D.C.: AAAS, 1965) 315-34; Asquith, "Anthropomorphism," 63-64; Kinji Imanishi et al., *Japanese Monkeys*, ed. Stuart A. Altmann (Atlanta: Emory U / Altmann, 1965) q38, q47, 119.

145. Akio Morita, with Edwin M. Reingold and Mitsuko Shimomura, *Made in Japan: Akio Morita and Sony* (NY: Dutton, 1986) 57ff; Ian Buruma, *Behind the Mask* (NY: Pantheon, 1984) 67-68, q70. See also the earnest if incompletely successful effort made by Merry White, in her *The Material Child: Coming of Age in Japan and America* (NY: Free Press, 1993), to avoid identifying the Japanese and American youth cultures as dark twins of each other.

146. Mark Gayn, *Japan Diary* (Rutland: Tuttle, 1981) describes, the Japanese resistance to the American Occupation directives; William Chapman, *Inventing Japan: The Making of a Postwar Civilization* (NY: Prentice-Hall, 1991) insists on the novelty of much of what the Japanese themselves came up with after 1945, rebutting the myth (to which Gayn contributed) that Japan managed to maintain its old ways under new guises; Bruce

Cumings, "Archaeology, descent, emergence: Japan in British/American hegemony, 1900-1950," in *Japan in the World*, eds. Masao Miyoshi and H.D. Harootunian (Durham: Duke U, 1993) 79-111 puts both views into larger context. On plastic surgery, see James Kirkup, *Japan Behind the Fan* (L: Dent, 1970) 90. On business, John G. Roberts, *Mitsui: Three Centuries of Japanese Business*, 2nd ed. (NY: Weatherhill, 1989); Kunio Yoshihara, *The Rise of Ersatz Capitalism in South-East Asia* (Singapore: Oxford U, 1988); James Risen, "Carbon copies," *LA Times (San Diego ed.)* (22 Jan 1990) D1-D2.

147. Kirkup, *Japan Behind the Fan*, 71; Edwin O. Reischauer, *The Japanese* (Cambridge, MA: Belknap, 1977) q146, q203, 225-27; Robert C. Christopher, *The Japanese Mind: The Goliath Explained* (NY: Simon & Schuster, 1983) 33 on business secrets (most of which, says Christopher, the Japanese got from Americans); Dennis S. Karjala, "Copyright protection of computer software in the U.S. and Japan, Part I," *European Intellectual Property R* 13 (June-July 1991) 195-202, 231-37, as also W.R. Swinyard et al., "The morality of software piracy – a cross-cultural analysis," *J Business Ethics* 9 (Aug 1990) 655-64; Myron W. Krueger, *Artificial Reality II* (Reading, MA: Addison-Wesley, 1991) 77, disassembling toys; "Who are the copy cats now?" *The Economist* 311 (20 May 1989) q91; Taizo Yakushiji, *The Dynamics of Techno-Industrial Emulation* (Berkeley: Berkeley Roundtable on the Int Economy, U Cal, 1985) q132 – for confirmation of which, see Brooke Hindle, *Emulation and Invention* (NY: NYU, 1981); Darwin H. Stapleton, *The Transfer of Early Industrial Technologies to America*, Memoirs, 177 (Philadelphia: Amer Phil Soc, 1987). Cf. Joseph J. Tobin, "Domesticating the West," in *Re-Made in Japan: Everyday Life and Consumer Taste in a Changing Society* (New Haven: Yale, 1992) 1-41, Japan now "the most important Other...ally, competitor, and secret sharer" (p. 36).

148. Boye De Mente, *Made In Japan* (Lincolnwood: Passport, 1987) q ix for *Time* (1 Aug 1983), q15; Donald Richie, *The Inland Sea* (NY: Weatherhill, 1978 [1971]) 31; Frederik L. Schodt, "In the land of robots," *Business Month* (Nov 1988) 67-75; George Haggerty (dir), "Robotopia," Knowledge Network Equinox Series, aired on KNO-TV, Vancouver, B.C., 9 Feb 1992; A.J.S. Rayl, "The new, improved reality," *LA Times Mag* (21 July 1991) 30.

Mounting Western concern for the plight of the subordinated Japanese woman is, I suspect, a concomitant of anxiety over a reversal of power relations, where Japan:West:: male:female. In this context, it is notable that Americans, long in awe of the skill of Kabuki male actors playing women's parts, are now fascinated – as are the Japanese – by theatrical women who impersonate men, on which see Karin Faber, "Takarazuka – a success story," *Japan Illustrated* 14 (Wint 1976) 10-17; Buruma, *Behind the Mask*, ch. 7. For a tempered assessment of women in Japanese society, see Sumiko Iwao, *The Japanese Woman: Traditional Image and Changing Reality* (NY: Free Press, 1993).

149. Hidetoshi Katō, "America as seen by Japanese travelers," in Iriye, ed., *Mutual Images*, 197, q198.

150. Gorō Fukuoka and Taku Komai, *Studies on Japanese Twins*, in Komai, ed., *Contributions to the Genetics of the Japanese Race, II* (Kyoto, 1937) esp. 1, 35; Noboru Nakamura (dir), *Twin Sisters of Kyoto* (Shochika, 1963); Masako Tanimura et al., "Child abuse of one of a pair of twins in Japan," *Lancet* 336 (24 Nov 1990) 1298-99; "Twins and abuse," *NY Times* (27 Nov 1990) C8; Leslie Helm, "In Japan, scorn for America," *LA Times* (25 Oct 1991) A1, A14-15. Here see Jonathan Rauch, *The Outnation: A Search for the Soul of Japan* (Boston: Harvard Business School, 1992) 3-4: "We have been mystified by Japan for at least a century, but at no time has our mystification run deeper or mattered more."

151. Stephen Perkins, "He who rode a tiger: Chester Carlson (1906-1968)," *Factsheet Five* 30 (1988) 61-63; *Filmfacts* 11 (1968-69) 365-66, reproducing the reviews of this Charles Crichton film, distributed in Britain in 1966.

152. Saul Linowitz, *The Making of a Public Man* (Boston: Little, Brown, 1985) q65.

153. Leonard Krishtalka, "Missing links," *Carnegie Mag* 59 (July-Aug 1989) 11, 42-43, Himalayan fossils; Jeffrey K. Yelton, with reply by D.J. Blakeslee, "A comment on John Rowzée Peyton and the mound builders: the elevation of a nineteenth-century fraud to a twentieth-century myth," *Amer Antiquity* 54 (Jan 1989) 161-65; John F. Mills and John M. Mansfield, *The Genuine Article: The Making and Unmasking of Fakes and Forgeries* (L: BBC, 1979) 20, trade in shrunken heads fabricated by the Jivaro from the skins of apes; Francis W. Kelsey, "Archaeological forgeries at Wyman, Michigan," *Nation* 54 (28 Jan 1892) q71 from Morris Jastrow; Theodore C. Blegen, *The Kensington Rune Stone: New Light on an Old Riddle* (St. Paul: Minnesota Historical Soc, 1968); H. Norman Evans, "The mystery of Glozel and a short history of faked antiquities," *World Today* 51 (Mar 1928) 415-26, to which contrast Nicole Torchet, *L'Affaire de Glozel* (P: Copernic, 1978), no hoax; Armin W. Geertz, "Book of the Hopi: the Hopi's Book?" *Anthropos* 78 (1983) 547-56, with a longer essay in *Authentizität und Betrug in der Ethnologie*, ed. Hans Peter Duerr (Frankfurt: Suhrkamp, 1987) 153-80 – and see all of this invaluable anthology, as well as Patricia C. Albers and William R. James, "Historical fiction as ideology: the case of Hanta Yo," *Radical History R* 25 (1981) 149-61; Richard de Mille, *Castaneda's Journey: The Power and the Allegory* (Santa Barbara: Capra, 1976), ambivalent, and cf. Rodney Needham, *Exemplars* (Berkeley: U Cal, 1985) 196-207, skeptical; John Nance, *The Gentle Tasaday: A Stone Age People in the Philippine Rain Forest*, new ed. (Boston: Godine, 1988 [1975]) still favorable, but contrast Jean-Paul Dumont "Quels Tasaday? De la découverte et de l'invention d'autrui," *L'Homme* 27 (July-Sept 1987) 27-42, and Judith Moses, "Still debating Tasaday data," *Science News* (28 Apr 1990) 259.

154. Edward Sapir, "Culture, genuine and spurious" (1924) in his *Selected Writings*, ed. David G. Mandelbaum (Berkeley: U Cal, 1963) q314-15, q316. Cf. the discussions in James R. Dow and Hannjost Lixfeld, eds. and trans., *German Volkskunde: A Decade of Theoretical Confrontation, Debate, and Reorientation (1967-1977)* (Bloomington: Indiana U, 1986).

155. Richard Dorson, "Fakelore" in his *American Folklore and the Historian* (Chicago: U Chicago, 1971) 3-14; Christine M. Havelock, "The archaic as survival versus the archaic as a new style," *Amer J of Archaeology* 69 (Oct 1965) 331-40; Charles Mitchell, "Archaeology and romance in Renaissance Italy," *Italian Renaissance Studies*, ed. E.F. Jacob (NY: Barnes and Noble, 1960) 455-83, q470 from Cyriac of Ancona; James Macpherson, *Fragments of Ancient Poetry (1760)*, introduction by John J. Dunn (LA: William Andrews Clark Memorial Lib, 1966) q23; Fiona J. Stafford, *The Sublime Savage* (Edinburgh: Edinburgh U, 1988) esp. 128; Dave Harker, *Fakesong: The Manufacture of British 'Folksong' 1700 to the Present Day* (Milton Keynes, UK: Open U, 1985) 3, q70 from Hogg's mother, and throughout; Timothy H. Evans, "Folklore as utopia: English medievalists and the ideology of revivalism," *Western Folklore* 47 (Oct 1988) 245-68, but contrast the eloquent rebuttal by Hermann Bausinger, "Toward a critique of folklorism criticism," in *German Volkskunde*, 113ff.

156. Harker, *Fakesong*, q110 from Frances James Child, whose eight volumes of English and Scottish popular ballads (1857-58) remain a major source for folksingers. On "tradition," see J.G.A. Pocock, "[Review of] Shelley Burtt, *Virtue Transformed*,"

Amer Historical R 98 (June 1993) 869-70, as also Eric Hobsbawm and Terence Ranger, eds., *The Invention of Tradition* (NY: Cambridge U, 1983). On memory and plagiarism, see Daniel Barrett, "Freedom of memory *v.* copying at law: the American premiere of *Caste*," *Theatre Research International* 8 (1983) 43-52; "Copy before publication," *Amer Law R* 3 (1866-67) 450-57, q454 from *Crowe v. Aiken*, 2 Biss. 208, Circuit Court, Southern District of Illinois, 31 Dec 1869, with commentary on the impossibility of verbatim memorization of a play seen once; Arthur G. Sedgwick, "International copyright by judicial decision," *Atlantic M* 43 (1879) 225-27; Thomas Henry Huxley, "Prof. Huxley before the English Copyright Commission," *Popular Sci M* 14 (1878-79) 171, 180, sermons and lectures. On neurology, see Susan Allport, *Explorers of the Black Box: The Search for the Cellular Basis of Memory* (NY: Norton, 1986). On therapeutic recollection, see, for example, Eugene E. Levitt, "A reversal of hypnotically 'refreshed' testimony," *Int J of Clinical and Experimental Hypnosis* 38 (1990) 6-9; Elizabeth Loftus, *Witness for the Defense* (NY: St. Martin's, 1991). On photographic memory, see John Buchan, *The Thirty-Nine Steps and the Power-house* (Edinburgh: Blackwood, 1958 [1915]) 95, and put in the context of mnemonic systems by Robert Alan Hrees, "An Edited History of Mnemonics from Antiquity to 1985," Ph.D., Indiana U, 1986, esp. I, 75-76, and ch. 33; Jean-Paul Sartre, *Imagination: A Psychological Critique*, trans. Forrest Williams (Ann Arbor: U Michigan, 1962 [1936]) q120 from Alain, *Système des beaux arts* (P, 1926) 22, "puerile."

157. Museum of Folk Art, NY, *April Fool: Folk Art Fakes and Forgeries 1-30 April 1988*, ed. Samuel Pennington (Waldoboro: Maine Antique Digest, 1988) q3 from Frank J. Miele; Ginger Danto, "*Mona Lisa*: What becomes a legend most," *Artnews* 88 (Sum 1989) 148-51, q151 from Pierre Rosenberg, chief curator, Dept. of Paintings, the Louvre; "Fakes, fakers, and fakery: authenticity in African art," symposium, *African Arts* 9 (Apr 1976) 20-31, 22 for Herbert M. Cole on the ibeji issue, and contributions by Thomas K. Seligman and M.D. McLeod; Guy de Plaen, "Authenticity, an uncertain concept," *The Museum* 41 (1989) 127-28. Cf. Deirdre Evans-Pritchard, "The Portal Case: authenticity, tourism, traditions, and the law," *J Amer Folklore* 100 (1987) 287-96, on Navajo makers of jewelry and silver, protected from Anglo- and Hispanic-American competition and copies by the Museum of New Mexico, although it was originally (ca. 1870) a Mexican who showed the Navajo how to do silversmithing.

158. Pretty sure, but see Leo Treitler, "Oral, written and literate process in the transmission of medieval music," *Speculum* 56 (July 1981) 471-91; Russell Stinson, *The Bach Manuscripts of Johan Peter Kellner and His Circle* (Durham, NC: Duke U, 1990) 56-57, 130, inaccuracies; Barry S. Brook, "Piracy and panacea: on the dissemination of music in the eighteenth century," *Proc Royal Musical Assoc* 102 (1975-76) 13-36, misattributions; Cliff Eisen, "Problems of authenticity among Mozart's early symphonies," *Music & Letters* 70 (Nov 1989) 505-16 – and noting, p. 511, that Mozart's father often copied out his son's symphonies, "for we do not wish to give it out to be copied as it would be stolen" (letter of 15 April 1770).

159. Michael Walsh, "Letting Mozart be Mozart: authenticity is the original-instrument movement's goal," *Time* (5 Sept 1983) q58.

160. Will Crutchfield, "Fashion, conviction, and performing style in an age of revivals," in *Authenticity and Modern Music: A Symposium*, ed. Nicholas Kenyon (Oxford: Oxford U, 1988) q25.

161. Howard M. Brown, "Pedantry or liberation? A sketch of the historical perfor-

mance movement," in Kenyon, ed., *Authenticity and Early Music*, 35, 38; Margaret Campbell, *Dolmetsch: The Man and His Work* (L: Hamilton, 1975) 9.

162. Orchestrelle Company ad, *The Athenaeum* (29 Oct 1904) q601; F.J. Allen, "Piano-players and player-pianos," *Literary Digest* 47 (20 Sept 1913) 468–69, following up G.H. Bryan, "Piano-players, human and mechanical," *ibid.* 46 (21 June 1913) 1376, and C.W.C. Wheatley, "Discriminating player-pianos," *ibid.* 47 (12 July 1913) 52, from a debate in *Nature*; Arthur Whiting, "The mechanical player," *Yale R* 8 (1919) 828–35. On the tempi and complexity of Nancarrow's compositions, see Conlon Nancarrow, *Selected Studies for Player Piano*, ed. Peter Garland, with interview (Berkeley: Soundings, 1977); Philip Carlsen, *The Player-Piano Music of Conlon Nancarrow* (Brooklyn: ISAM, 1988). A five-minute piece may take Nancarrow a year to punch on a piano roll and may be "not even remotely playable by human hands": Charles Amirkhanian's liner notes to Conlon Nancarrow, *Complete Studies for Player Piano, Volume 1* (Berkeley: Arch Records S1768, 1977).

163. Leo Rich Lewis, "Music-education and 'automatics,'" *Atlantic M* 101 (Mar 1908) q387; Harry N. Roehl, comp., *Player Piano Treasury*, 2nd ed. (Vestal, NY: Vestal, 1973) q7, Aeolian; Arthur W.J.G. Ord-Hume, *Player Piano: The History of the Mechanical Piano and How to Repair It* (L: Allen & Unwin, 1970) 35–36.

164. Craig H. Roell, *The Piano in America, 1890–1940* (Chapel Hill: U North Carolina, 1989) 39–55, q43, Ampico; Larry Givens, *Re-enacting the Artist: A Story of the Ampico Reproducing Piano* (Vestal, NY: Vestal, 1970) q77, Ampico on Rachmaninoff; Werner König, "The 'Welte-Mignon' reproducing piano and its place in musical history," in Heinrich Weiss-Stauffacher, *The Marvelous World of Music Machines*, trans. James Underwood (Tokyo: Kodansha, 1976) App. I, 195, 201; Ord-Hume, *Player Piano*, 40, Japan. Between 1915 and 1927, public "tone tests" of Edison phonograph discs vis-à-vis live singers were conducted across America, sometimes in the dark, proving that audiences could not tell the singer's voice on the disc from the same singer's voice in person; indeed, when the lights came up, the live singer would have left the stage, vanished twin to the phonograph playing merrily on. See Walter L. Welch, "Preservation and restoration of authenticity in sound recordings – to standards," *Lib Trends* 30 (Fall 1981) 298–300.

165. Peter Le Huray, *Authenticity in Performance: Eighteenth-Century Case Studies* (Cambridge: Cambridge U, 1990) 3 *et passim* on intent; Raymond Leppard, *Authenticity in Music* (L: Faber, 1988) esp. 34 on historical context; Charles Rosen, "The shock of the old," *NY R of Books* (19 July 1990) 46–52, on the ultimate soullessness of much Authentic Music; Samuel Lipman, "Cutting Beethoven down to size," *Commentary* 89 (Feb 1990) q54; Brown, "Pedantry or liberation?" 28; Whiting, "The mechanical player," q834–35; Rohel, *Player Piano Treasury*, q38.

166. Tim Page, ed., *The Glenn Gould Reader* (NY: Knopf, 1985) q337, q339 and throughout.

167. Page, *Glenn Gould Reader*, q335; Editor's "Introduction," Kenyon, ed., *Authenticity and Early Music*, q4; David Ranada, "Mikes and authenticity," *Musical America* 108 (Nov 1988) 96. On the popularity, see Joel Cohen and Herb Snitzer, *Reprise: The Extraordinary Revival of Early Music* (Boston: Little, Brown, 1985); "Rhapsody in ultramarine: how far can authentic music go?" *The Economist* (22 July 1989) 79.

168. Arthur Ord-Hume, *Pianola: The History of the Self-playing Piano* (L: Allen & Unwin, 1984) q2, Elgar; Laurence Dreyfus, "Early Music defended against its devotees: a

theory of historical performance in the twentieth century," *Musical Q* 64 (1983) 297–322 on the scientism, objectivism, and "motoric rhythms" of Early Music, and how these may be overcome.

169. Richard Taruskin, "The pastness of the present, and the presence of the past," in Kenyon, ed., *Authenticity and Early Music*, 137–207; idem, "Resisting the Ninth," *Nineteenth Century Music* 12 (Spr 1989) 241–56. Cf. Charles Rosen's well-tempered discussion of Taruskin in "The shock of the old."

FIGURE N.2. An early Before-and-After illustration. Successful eye surgery on a pulsating exophthalmus, performed by Benjamin Travers in 1809, from the *Annals of Surgery*. From Arthur E. Walker, ed., *A History of Neurological Surgery* (Baltimore: Williams & Wilkins, 1951).

Index

Unless the topic of a paragraph, the following have been omitted from this index: nations, governmental units, corporations and businesses, placenames, titles of books, artworks, films, and songs, as well as some personal names mentioned only once and in passing. (Here too, doubling and repetition assure that the original and individual are recognized and retrieved.) Names mentioned as couplets have been retained under a single heading.

Colomb, Philip, 264
Colombo (Columbus), Cristoforo, 147–48, 152
Colonial Williamsburg, 276, 278
colonialism, 77–78
colossus, colossi, 90, 93, 94, 100, 137, 140, 324
Coltrane, John, 310
Colvin, Russell, 72
Comings, David E., 303
compression: data, 308; historical, 279; time, 262–63, 266, 308
compulsiveness, 36, 302–03
computers: animation, 110; antiques, 279; children and, 361; as copying machines, 238, 245; imaging, 43; information processing, 245; Japanese, 254; metaphors, 245–46; mine, 383; rights of, 360–62; as social prosthesis, 360; software piracy and copyright, 245, 370; thinking, 357, 360–61
con(fidence) men, 71–72. *See also* impersonation; imposture
Confucianism, 180
connoisseurs, 212, 248, 249, 251, 255
consanguinity, 24, 401 n.26
conservation, theories of, 252, 280. *See also* ecology
consumption, mass, 112, 116, 118, 124–25, 127
Cooney, Timothy J., 513 n.43
Cooper, Jackie, 310
Copeau, Jacques, 69
copiers, instant, 19
copies: as actors and subjects, 235; antiqued, 251; authentic, 214; better than originals, 237; of events, 258–319; fair and foul, 217–18; hand, 249; of the natural world, 174–209; necessary, 232; of our own productions, 210–57; of ourselves, as Doppelgängers, Doubles, and conjoined twins, 48–87; of ourselves, among parrots and monkeys, 142–73; of ourselves, as twins, 18–47; of ourselves, in various media, 88–141; sustaining the fabric of life, 233; typewritten, 227–28
copy art, 67, 98, 230, 239–40
Copy, Intact, as root metaphor, 214
copycats, 319, 370; Copycat machine, 237
copying: as appropriation, 228–30, 234–35; of art, 151, 211, 225, 246–57, 306, 315, 325; as assimilation, 246; defined, 238; documents, 225, 233; ENTIRETIES, 223–41; an eschatological program, 240; hand, 233–34, 315; hand, accuracy of, 215–18; hand, speed of, 215–17, 235; machine, speed of, 226, 234, 237, 245; machines, 220, 226, 315, 370; as making or taking, 236, 247; of manners, 12; of manuscripts, 210, 213–18; music, 245; piecemeal, 244; as reinvention, 252; as reenactment, 228–29, 234–35; simultaneity of, 223–25; s/t/r/o/k/e/-/b/y/-/s/t/r/o/k/e, 223–41; transcendent, 232–33, 370; transformative, 215; virtues of, 211; volume of, 237
copying press, 222–24
copyists: art, 225, 249, 252, 325; Japanese as, 368, 370; monastic, 215–17; women as, 224–29, 417 n.23
copyLeft, 244
copyright: in algorithms, 245; Anglo-American law and, 243; in art, 242, 247–49; in boxing matches, 286; China and, 243; in computer software, 245; continental law and, 243; in drawings, 248; in engravings, 248; history of, 243–45; in lithographs, 248; in news, 489 n.75; Marxism and, 244; in photographs, 246–47
copyright symbol, 242, 245
Corbett, Jim, 12–13, 285–86
Corday, Charlotte, 102
Corot, Jean Baptiste Camille, 253
corpses, 98, 100–01
correctness, 104, 109–10, 114, 118, 126–28, 140
cosmetics: automaton and, 321; camouflage and, 188, 201; "corrective," 207; make-up artists, 196; painting and, 180; permanent, 345, 350; in pornography, 306; rejuvenating, 279–80; toxicity tests, 171; women and, 350. *See also* retouching, photographic; surgery, cosmetic
costumes, historical, 272–74, 276, 279, 280, 284
Cott, Hugh, 191
Council of Nicaea, 212–13
counterfeit money, 180–81, 223, 404 n.56
counterfeits: century of, 20; perfect, 207; in world trade, 256
counter-intelligence, 362. *See also* espionage
countershading, 175–76, 191
Courbet, Gustave, 164
Courtney, Pete, 285
couvade, 337–51, 362
Craig, Gordon, 69

This edition designed by Bruce Mau
with Chris Rowat
Type composed by Archie at Archetype
Printed and bound Smythe-sewn by Maple-Vail